Risk Finance and Asset Pricing

Founded in 1807, John Wiley & Sons is the oldest independent publishing company in the United States. With offices in North America, Europe, Australia and Asia, Wiley is globally committed to developing and marketing print and electronic products and services for our customers' professional and personal knowledge and understanding.

The Wiley Finance series contains books written specifically for finance and investment professionals as well as sophisticated individual investors and their financial advisors. Book topics range from portfolio management to e-commerce, risk management, financial engineering, valuation and financial instrument analysis, as well as much more.

For a list of available titles, please visit our Web site at www.WileyFinance.com.

Risk Finance and Asset Pricing

Value, Measurements, and Markets

CHARLES S. TAPIERO

John Wiley & Sons, Inc.

Published by John Wiley & Sons, Inc., Hoboken, New Jersey.
Published simultaneously in Canada.

For general information on our other products and services or for technical support, please contact our Customer Care Department within the United States at (800) 762-2974, outside the United States at (317) 572-3993 or fax (317) 572-4002.

Wiley also publishes its books in a variety of electronic formats. Some content that appears in print may not be available in electronic books. For more information about Wiley products, visit our web site at www.wiley.com.

Library of Congress Cataloging-in-Publication Data:

Tapiero, Charles S.
  Risk finance and asset pricing : value, measurements, and markets / Charles S. Tapiero.
    p. cm. — (Wiley finance ; 563)
  Includes index.
  ISBN 978-0-470-54946-9 (cloth); 978-0-470-89237-4 (ebk); 978-0-470-89238-1 (ebk)
  1. Financial engineering. 2. Financial risk management. 3. Finance—Mathematical models. 4. Investments—Mathematical models. I. Title.
  HG176.7.T37 2010
  658.15′5—dc22
                                                                              2010015106

Printed in the United States of America

10 9 8 7 6 5 4 3 2 1

To Carole, Oscar, Bettina, Scarlett, Laura-Julia,
Talya, and not least, Arielle

Contents

Introduction   **XV**
   Who This Book Is For   xvi
   How This Book Is Structured   xvii
   What's on the Companion Web Site   xix

CHAPTER 1
Risk, Finance, Corporate Management, and Society   **1**
   Overview   1
   Risks Everywhere—A Consequence of Uncertainty   1
   Risk and Finance: Basic Concepts   4
     Finance and Risks   6
   Financial Instruments   7
     Securities or Stocks   7
   Example: An IBM Day-Trades Record   7
     Bonds   9
     Portfolios   10
   Example: Constructing a Portfolio   11
     Derivatives and Options   12
     Real and Financial Assets   15
     Financial Markets   16
   Option Contracts   16
   Problem 1.1: Options and Their Prices   17
     Options and Specific Needs   18
   Example: Options and The Price of Equity   19
   Example: Management Stock Options   19
   Options and Trading in Specialized Markets   20
     Trading the CO_2 Index   20
     Trading on Commodities (Metal, Gold, Silver, Corn, Oil) 20
     Trading the Weather and Insurance   21
     Securitization, Mortgage-Backed Securities, and Credit Derivatives 21
   Real-Life Crises and Finance   22
     The ARS Crisis   22
     The Banking–Money System Crisis   23
   The 2008 Meltdown and Financial Theory   24
   Finance and Ethics   27
     Crime and Punishment   29
   Summary   30

CHAPTER 2

Applied Finance   **35**

Overview   35
  Finance and Practice   35
    Risk Finance and Insurance   35
    Infrastructure Finance   36
    Finance, the Environment, and Exchange-Traded Funds Indexes   37
    Finance and Your Pension   38
    Contract Pricing and Franchises   39
    Catastrophic Risks, Insurance and Finance   40
    The Price of Safety   41
    The Price of Inventories   42
    Pricing Reliability and Warranties   42
    The Price of Quality Claims   43
  Financial Risk Pricing: A Historical Perspective   44
  Essentials of Financial Risk Management   47
    Comprehensive Financial Risk Management   49
  Technology and Complexity   49
    Retailing and Finance   51
    Finance, Cyber Risks, and Terrorism   52
    IT and Madoff   52
    Virtual Markets   52
    Virtual Products   52
    Virtual Markets Participants   53
    Virtual Economic Universes   53
  Market Making and Pricing Practice   53
    Market Makers, Market Liquidity, and Bid-Ask Spreads   55
    Alternative Market Structures   56
  Summary   57

CHAPTER 3

Risk Measurement and Volatility   **63**

Overview   63
  Risk, Volatility, and Measurement   63
  Moments and Measures of Volatility   66
    Expectations, Volatility, Skewness, Kurtosis, and the Range   67
Example: IBM Returns Statistics   69
Example: Moments and the CAPM   70
Problem 3.1: Calculating the Beta of a Security   72
  Modeling Rates of Return   72
  Models of Rate of Returns   73
  Statistical Estimations   77
    Least Squares Estimation   77
    Maximum Likelihood   79
    ARCH and GARCH Estimators   80
Example: The AR(1)-ARCH(1) Model   81

Example: A GARCH (1,1) Model   83
  High-Low Estimators of Volatility   83
  Extreme Measures, Volume, and Intraday Prices   84
    Statistical Orders, Volume, and Prices   85
Problem 3.2: The Probability of the Range   87
  Intraday Prices and Extreme Distributions   87
  Data Transformation   88
Example: Taylor Series   89
  Value at Risk and Risk Exposure   90
  VaR and Its Application   92
Example: VaR and Shortfall   94
Example: VaR, Normal ROR, and Portfolio Design   95
  The Estimation of Gains and Losses   97
  Summary   99

CHAPTER 4
Risk Finance Modeling and Dependence   **109**
Overview   109
  Introduction   109
    Dependence and Probability Models   111
  Statistical Dependence   111
    Dependence and Quantitative Statistical Probability Models   113
    Many Sources of Normal Risk: Aggregation and Risk Factors
    Reduction   114
Example: Risk Factors Aggregation   115
Example: Principal Component Analysis (PCA)   116
Example: A Bivariate Data Matrix and PCA   117
Example: A Market Index and PCA   119
  Dependence and Copulas   120
Example: The Gumbel Copula, the Highs and the Lows   123
Example: Copulas and Conditional Dependence   124
Example: Copulas and the Conditional Distribution   125
  Financial Modeling and Intertemporal Models   126
    Time, Memory, and Causal Dependence   127
    Quantitative Time and Change   129
    Persistence and Short-term Memory   130
  The R/S Index   133
  Summary   135

CHAPTER 5
Risk, Value, and Financial Prices   **141**
Overview   141
  Value and Price   141
  Utility, Risk, and Money   143
    Utility's Normative Principles: A Historical Perspective   144
    Prelude to Utility and Expected Utility   145
  Lotteries and Utility Functions   147

Example: The Utility of a Lottery   148
    Quadratic Utility and Portfolio Pricing   149
    Utility and an Insurance Exchange   150
Example: The Power Utility Function   151
Example: Valuation and the Pricing of Cash Flows   152
Example: Risk and the Financial Meltdown   153
Utility Rational Foundations   155
    The Risk Premium   155
    Utility and Its Behavioral Derivatives   156
Examples: Specific Utility Functions   159
    The Price and the Utility of Consumption   161
Example: Kernel Pricing and the Exponential Utility Function   164
Example: The Pricing Kernel and the CAPM   165
Example: Kernel Pricing and the HARA Utility Function   166
    The Price and Demand for Insurance   167
    Summary   170

CHAPTER 6
Applied Utility Finance   177
Overview   177
    Risk and the Utility of Time   177
        Expected Utility and the Time Utility Price of Money   177
        Risk, Safety, and Reliability   178
    Asset Allocation and Investments   180
Example: A Two-Securities Problem   182
Example: A Two-Stocks Portfolio   184
Problem 6.1: The Efficiency Frontier   185
Problem 6.2: A Two-Securities Portfolio   187
    Conditional Kernel Pricing and the Price of Infrastructure Investments   188
    Conditional Kernel Pricing and the Pricing of Inventories   191
    Agency and Utility   193
Example: A Linear Risk-Sharing Rule   194
    Information Asymmetry: Moral Hazard and Adverse Selection   195
    Adverse Selection   196
    The Moral Hazard Problem   197
    Signaling and Screening   199
    Summary   200

CHAPTER 7
Derivative Finance and Complete Markets   205
Overview   205
    The Arrow-Debreu Fundamental Approach to Asset Pricing   206
Example: Generalization to n States   210
Example: Binomial Option Pricing   212
Problem 7.1: The Implied Risk-Neutral Probability   213
Example: The Price of a Call Option   213

Example: A Generalization to Multiple Periods 215
Problem 7.2: Options and Their Prices 218
  Put-Call Parity 218
Problem 7.3: Proving the Put-Call Parity 219
Example: Put-Call Parity and Dividend Payments 219
Problem 7.4: Options Put-Call Parity 220
  The Price Deflator and the Pricing Martingale 220
  Pricing and Complete Markets 222
    Risk-Neutral Pricing and Market Completeness 224
  Options Galore 226
    Packaged and Binary Options 227
Example: Look-Back Options 227
Example: Asian Options 227
Example: Exchange Options 228
Example: Chooser Options 228
Example: Barrier and Other Options 228
Example: Passport Options 229
  Options and Their Real Uses 229
  Fixed-Income Problems 231
Example: Pricing a Forward 231
Example: Pricing a Fixed-Rate Bond 232
  Pricing a Term Structure of Interest Rates 232
Example: The Term Structure of Interest Rates 234
Problem 7.5: Annuities and Obligations 235
  Options Trading, Speculation, and Risk Management 235
    Option Trading Strategies 237
Problem 7.6: Portfolio Strategies 240
  Summary 245
  Appendix A: Martingales 246
    Essentials of Martingales 246
    The Change of Measures and Martingales 248
Example: Change of Measure in a Binomial Model 249
Example: A Two-Stage Random Walk and the Radon Nikodym
    Derivative 251
  Appendix B: Formal Notations, Key Terms,
  and Definitions 253

CHAPTER 8
Options Applied **259**
Overview 259
  Option Applications 259
    Risk-Free Portfolios and Immunization 260
    Selling Short 261
    Future Prices 262
Problem 8.1: Pricing a Multiperiod Forward 264
  Pricing and New Insurance Business 264

Example: Options Implied Insurance Pricing   266
   Option Pricing in a Trinomial Random Walk   267
   Pricing and Spread Options   269
   Self-Financing Strategy   270
  Random Volatility and Options Pricing   271
  Real Assets and Real Options   273
   The Option to Acquire the License for a New Technology   275
  The Black-Scholes Vanilla Option   276
   The Binomial Process as a Discrete Time Approximation   277
   The Black-Scholes Model Option Price and Portfolio Replication 278
   Risk-Neutral Pricing and the Pricing Martingale   281
  The Greeks and Their Applications   284
  Summary   287

CHAPTER 9
Credit Scoring and the Price of Credit Risk   **291**
Overview   291
  Credit and Money   291
Credit and Credit Risk   **294**
  Pricing Credit Risk: Principles   296
  Credit Scoring and Granting   299
   What Is an Individual Credit Score?   299
   Bonds Rating or Scoring Business Enterprises   300
   Scoring/Rating Financial Enterprises and Financial Products 301
  Credit Scoring: Real Approaches   304
   The Statistical Estimation of Default   305
Example: A Separatrix   **310**
Example: The Separatrix and Bayesian Probabilities   **311**
  Probability Default Models   312
Example: A Bivariate Dependent Default Distribution   **314**
Example: A Portfolio of Default Loans   **315**
Example: A Portfolio of Dependent Default Loans   **316**
Problem 9.1: The Joint Bernoulli Default Distribution   **317**
  Credit Granting   317
Example: Credit Granting and Creditor's Risks   **319**
Example: A Bayesian Default Model   **322**
Example: A Financial Approach   **323**
Example: An Approximate Solution   **326**
Problem 9.2: The Rate of Return of Loans   **327**
  The Reduced Form (Financial) Model   327
Example: Calculating the Spread of a Default Bond   **328**
Example: The Loan Model Again   **329**
Example: Pricing Default Bonds   **330**
Example: Pricing Default Bonds and the Hazard Rate   **331**
  Examples   332
Example: The Bank Interest Rate on a House Loan   **333**

Example: Buy Insurance to Protect the Portfolio from Loan
   Defaults   333
Problem 9.3: Use the Portfolio as an Underlying and Buy or Sell
   Derivatives on This Underlying   334
Problem 9.4: Lending Rates of Return   334
   Credit Risk and Collateral Pricing   334
Example: Hedge Funds Rates of Return   337
Example: Equity-Linked Life Insurance   338
Example: Default and the Price of Homes   339
Example: A Bank's Profit from a Loan   341
   Risk Management and Leverage   342
   Summary   344

CHAPTER 10
Multi-Name and Structured Credit Risk Portfolios   **353**
Overview   353
   Introduction   353
   Credit Default Swaps   357
Example: Total Return Swaps   359
   Pricing Credit Default Swaps—The Implied Market Approach   359
Example: The CDS Price Spread   360
   Example: An OTC (Swap) Contract under Risk-Neutral
   Pricing and Collateral Prices   362
Example: Pricing a Project Launch   364
   Credit Derivatives: A Historical Perspective   368
   Credit Derivatives: Historical Modeling   369
   Credit Derivatives and Product Innovation   372
CDO Example: Collateralized Mortgage Obligations (CMOs)   376
Example: The CDO and SPV   377
   Modeling Credit Derivatives   379
   CDO: Quantitative Models   380
Example: A CDO with Numbers   380
Example: A CDO of Zero Coupon Bonds   382
Example: A CDO of Default Coupon-Paying bonds   385
Example: A CDO of Rated Bonds   387
Examples: Default Models for Bonds   391
   CDO Models and Price Applications   395
Example: The KMV Loss Model   396
   CDOs of Baskets of Various Assets   397
   Credit Risk versus Insurance   398
   Summary   399

CHAPTER 11
Engineered Implied Volatility and Implied Risk-Neutral Distributions   **407**
Overview   407
   Introduction   407
   The Implied Volatility   409

Example: The Implied Volatility in a Lognormal Process   410
    The Dupire Model   411
   The Implied Risk-Neutral Distribution   412
Example: An Implied Binomial Distribution   413
Example: Calculating the Implied Risk-Neutral Probability   414
   Implied Distributions: Parametric Models   417
Example: The Generalized Beta of the Second Kind   418
   The A-parametric Approach and the Black-Scholes Model   420
Example: The Shimko Technique   421
   The Implied Risk Neutral Distribution and Entropy   423
Examples and Applications   426
   Risk Attitude, Implied Risk-Neutral Distribution and Entropy 431
   Summary   432
   Appendix: The Implied Volatility—The Dupire Model   433

Acknowledgments   439

About the Author   441

Index   443

Introduction

At both theoretical and practical levels, finance theory has made extraordinary intellectual strides while contributing immensely to economic development. At the same time it has enriched the many financial engineers able to innovate and trade in financial products that create greater liquidity, predict and price assets, manage financial risks, and contribute to the growth of financial markets.

Today, risk finance and engineering is confronted with immense challenges and opportunities. They include:

- Bridging theory and practice following the important contributions made these past decades by Kenneth Arrow and Gerard Debreu's fundamental theory of asset pricing and its many uses to better comprehend the working of financial markets and price assets and their derivatives.
- Reconciling the doubts raised by assumptions of fundamental finance and opportunities to profit by the initiated who can appreciate the pro and cons of these theories.

The motivation for this book arose in the course of my lectures in the Department of Finance and Risk Engineering at the New York University (NYU) Polytechnic Institute following the financial meltdown of 2008–2009. This was a year when risks and all their financial manifestations struck at the heart of financial citadels and world economies. No firm was too big to fail, and risks hitherto conceived of theoretically, ignored, or only dreamed of have revealed their potency. This was also a year when extreme events have come into their own: ex ante ignored, but factual and painful ex post for all those who ignored the unlikely. The whole world was hurting: Unemployment, deflation of assets, and times of reckoning with greed, regulation, constraints, and finiteness of resources have become the underlying tune of financial discourse. Both persons and institutions have questioned the validity of financial models and their practical implications. On the academic front, challenging questions have been raised against the fundamental and complete markets dogma of finance, claiming that models can default and that incomplete markets are far more prevalent than theoretical finance would have us believe.

The financial meltdown of 2008–2009 has also ignited a far greater concern for the underlying purposes of finance, not only as a means to get rich but to confront the risks that beset us—whether predictable or not. These include population growth, environmental challenges, globalization of finance, infrastructure, wellness, and so on. These are real problems of common and personal importance. Financial transparency is called for to be part of the answer. The intent of this book is to provide an accessible formulation of theoretical financial constructs embedded in a broad variety of real and useful problems.

The crisis of 2008–2009 has revealed that risks borne by those uninitiated in the complexity of financial products and markets can be very costly. It has also become apparent that corporations and financial firms, traditionally managing real resources, have gradually shifted their economic activity by turning to financial manipulations, acting as intermediaries, with losses assumed by uninformed investors. These firms have capitalized on leverage and short-term returns while strapping healthy corporations with a debt they may not be able to bear. Governmental institutions have not been spared either. They, too, have turned to financial markets to seek the funds needed for investments in infrastructure or to meet their financing needs. Pandora's financial box has been opened, and finance—for all the good and the risks it deals with and manages—has at the same time the potential to cause great damage if not understood.

Further, there is an increased awareness that financial systems are changing. For example, the traditional role of banks to provide liquidity to borrowers and business firms may have been jeopardized in their pursuit of (short-term) profits. These financial institutions have become marketers of financial products and intermediaries to ever-growing financial markets, rather than filling the role of providers of liquidity which underlies their charter granted by society and its governments. In the pursuit of profits, new financial institutions and previously nonfinancial firms have emerged and converged in new enterprises that both offer financial services and manage their own economic interests. These firms, such as insurance companies, provide liquidity and are transforming the financial system. In these processes, financial engineers remain the means to provide financial products and help decide how and where to invest and how to manage risks. The insurance-finance convergence has also afforded a means to assure buyers and sellers and thus contribute to the liquidity needed. The creation of a global insurance exchange in New York to cover complex risks, modeled after Lloyd's of London, is just such an example. Finally, the recent financial crisis has revealed that liquidity matters very much and the future may be unpredictable. Non-transparency, complexity and ambiguity have combined with greed to induce "Management's Risks" as being able to derail financial sustainability and produce financial models that are not efficient. These revelations have increased our awareness that financial expectations can and do falter. This renewed awareness may alter the financial regulatory environment, financial markets, financial attitudes and by extension the future challenges of financial risk engineering. In such an environment, we may be confronted with new problems and new opportunities to provide the solutions needed by financial, corporate firms and individuals.

WHO THIS BOOK IS FOR

This book is intended for both beginning and practicing financial engineers and seeks to engender an appreciation for and understanding of pricing of real financial problems. Throughout my classes I have become aware that many concepts transparent to mathematically savvy students are not understood by others. Inversely, many students with an extensive mathematics background fail to understand that financial engineering is not about mathematics but about complex relationships between buyers and sellers acting in financial markets, imputing values and prices to just about everything that can be traded. To better appreciate what financial engineering is, can do, and its limitations, it is necessary to have a strong footing in principles of economics and finance, data and statistical analysis, personal utility, and their behavioral manifestations in financial markets and financial modeling. In particular, financial modeling provides a means to interpret implied values and prices such as options, credit derivatives, and so on.

In this sense, financial engineering is both real and virtual. Its usefulness is fueled by the needs of financial parties and by its potential contributions to investors, speculators, and society at large. The perspectives of this book, unlike many important books in financial engineering and mathematics, are thus: to bridge theory and practice; to study financial engineering as a means and not only as an end to make money; and to emphasize a real finance that can provide the support needed to meet both individual and collective needs. At the same time, the book emphasizes an intuitive and comprehensive approach to the foundations of risk finance and its many applications to asset pricing, real financial problems, and financial risk management. In such a frame of mind, the book's theoretical frameworks for expected utility, the Arrow-Debreu foundations of fundamental finance, and basic statistical manipulations of data and financial modeling, are shown to be useful, relevant, and complementary.

HOW THIS BOOK IS STRUCTURED

Theoretical concepts and theories applied mindlessly can have dire consequences. Thus, understanding the underlying rationales that financial engineers use in financial modeling, optimization, and decision making is important. By the same token, financial engineers cannot be the canary in the coal mine and ought to recognize that there is an inherent social and ethical responsibility that need not contradict the pursuit of wealth and money. There are as many opportunities to profit by contributing to economic sustainability—via investment in needed infrastructures, preventing booms and busts, reducing social inequities, pointing to market potential defaults and failures, and so on—as there are opportunities to profit from the design of complex and marketable financial products that provide greater and needed financial liquidity, and from seeking arbitrage opportunities and better forecasting financial market prices.

The many applications treated in this book, drawn from a variety of financial, engineering, and business professions, include insurance, pricing corporate loans and managing their risks, pricing safety and reliability, pricing franchises, operations risks, environmental quality and its control, infrastructure pricing, pricing water, pricing the insurance of rare events and uncommon risks, and more. These applications are used to establish a motivation and a background for a greater appreciation of finance and its risk engineering. Throughout the book, simplifications are made to focus greater attention on the problem-solving rationality financial engineers use. The required quantitative level needed for the book is kept at a consistent and introductory level. Some sections, however, require a slightly more advanced mathematical background; these are marked with an asterisk (*) in the table of contents and offer an added motivation to ambitious students. Additional extensions to each of the book chapters and problems solved are relegated to a web site companion, www.charlestapiero.com. This web site introduces as well in far greater detail facets of continuous-time finance that this book has sought to avoid as a price for simplicity.

The book is structured as follows. Chapters 1 and 2 provide an introduction to the business of finance, risk, and their many applications. Issues such as ethics and finance are discussed.

Chapters 3 and 4 are an introduction to risk measurement and to various statistical approaches to doing it. These chapters use data to measure risk and to estimate financial trends, financial volatility, and the many terms that make up the essential content of basic financial applications. These two chapters introduce the student to the need to confront the measurement, the *quantification* of finance, and to perform basic analyses using financial data. Chapter 4 is of a more advanced nature, however, and emphasizes the problems of dependence including statistical dependence, complexity, contagious risks, latent risks, and black swan risks. The rationale for introducing these complex issues prior to a thorough study of financial and economic constructs used by financial engineers is to point out the true complexity of quant finance, which cannot always be explained by available theories. Allowing students to grapple with complicated issues sooner rather than later offers a challenge that is similar to the concerns and the manner in which we proceed to financial risk management.

Chapters 5 and 6 introduce the concept of utility and financial risk management. Many theories applied in financial economics are applications of or interpreted in terms of utility concepts. These include risk aversion, portfolio selection, certain equivalents in financial valuation, the capital asset pricing model (CAPM), kernel pricing, insurance, and utility-based risk management. These applications are still profusely used (explicitly or implicitly) in many practical problems. The presumption that financial engineering is essentially concerned with options pricing is, I believe, misguided. These chapters will show through applications that underlying financial theory there are almost always three issues to reckon with: the rationality of the parties to a financial transaction, their private and common information, and the market price. In many cases, any two would imply the other. In other words, any model in fundamental finance implies in fact an underlying rationality—which when violated leads to model defaults.

Chapter 7 outlines the Arrow-Debreu framework in discrete states and time for assets and derivatives (options) pricing. An intuitive introduction to martingales and their importance for asset pricing is included in the appendix to Chapter 7. Chapter 8 provides a review of financial markets and optional portfolios used to manage and trade risks. These two chapters present the basic concept of fundamental finance. The theory is discussed, criticized, and applied to many examples. To keep this introduction tractable (without losing its essential implications and applications) simple binomial, multinomial, and discrete state models are used. Extensions to continuous-time finance are considered briefly, and specific problems are posted on the book web site, www.charlestapiero.com. Applications to a variety of problems including derivatives pricing, default bonds, pricing insurance contracts, stochastic volatility models, multiple sources of risks models, and a plethora of problems commonly treated in practice and in advanced texts are also presented simply to explain the rationale that the Arrow-Debreu financial framework uses to solve such problems. Throughout these chapters, issues and instruments of current interest, such as the financial meltdown of 2008, volatility and chaos, globalization, outsourcing, and so on, are used to explain these important facets of financial practice and the limits of the current theoretical models of finance.

Chapters 9, 10, and 11 can be seen as a whole that can be delivered as one course on credit risk. Chapters 9 and 10 deal with credit risk and scoring, multi-name credit risk, and credit derivatives. Several approaches to pricing credit risk are outlined. Following the credit crisis, a greater awareness has developed that these risks ought to be better regulated. Chapter 10 focuses on multi-name credit risk portfolios and structured financial products such as collateralized debt obligation (CDO), collateralized mortgage obligation (CMO), and collateralized loan obligation (CLO). Finally, Chapter 11 addresses the important and practical problems in calculating an implied volatility and an implied risk-neutral distribution. Three approaches are emphasized: parametric, a-parametric, and a utility-rationality–based approach.

Chapters also include:

- *Examples and problems.* These highlight both some of the techniques used in asset pricing and their very broad applications.
- *"Test Yourself."* Most chapters end with a series of questions to test your newfound knowledge.

WHAT'S ON THE COMPANION WEB SITE

At www.wiley.com/go/tapiero (password: risk) you will find a number of additional resources for this book, including:

- Additional examples, errata, and updates to the book.
- Links to the author's other publications.
- Recommended reading.
- Information about the author's classes at the New York University Polytechnic Institute.

The Instructor's site includes answers to the problems and "Test Yourself" material found in the book, as well as PowerPoint slides and other materials for classroom use.

CHAPTER 1

Risk, Finance, Corporate Management, and Society

OVERVIEW

Financial engineering is a profession that bridges theoretical finance and financial practice. It spans the many occupations prevalent in financial services. This chapter provides a nonquantitative introduction to financial management and risk engineering. Terms such as *risk, uncertainty, securities, bonds, derivatives, options,* and the like are defined and their applications to a broad number of financial concerns outlined. Terms such as *trading, investing, speculating, credit, leverage, environmental finance, securitization,* and others are defined and applications considered. Real-life financial problems, including safety, reliability, claims, insurance, your pension, and so forth, are highlighted to emphasize the relevance of financial analysis and management to everyday life. Finally, outstanding financial issues, a growing concern for financial ethics, and regulation are also discussed. This chapter may be covered singly or together with the next chapter in one or two lectures with students reading and commenting on the issues the chapter raises.

RISKS EVERYWHERE—A CONSEQUENCE OF UNCERTAINTY

Uncertainty is part of our lives. Its presence underlies our attitudes, our search for information, and the efforts we expend to mitigate and manage its positive and adverse consequences. To do so, we seek definitions, measurements, and the quantification of uncertainty in order to analyze the risks, protect ourselves from the losses uncertainty may lead to, and profit from the opportunities it can provide. In theory and in practice, uncertainty is latent in everything we do. It remains a shadow that never departs, always challenging, for better or for worse.

Risk may be specific or have broad connotations to various persons or groups. For some, it is a threat; for others it is an opportunity to be sought and to revel in. In all cases, risk results from uncertain events and their consequences: whether positive or negative; whether direct or indirect; whether they are accounted for or not; whether of external origin or internally induced; whether predictable or not; and whether of concern to individuals, firms, or the society at large. Uncertain events may be due to failures of persons or machines, a misjudgment by investors or speculators, accidental hazards, or macroeconomic and environmental factors over which we have partial or no control. To mitigate or profit from risk (also known as *risk management*), preventive means, controls, insurance, hedging, trades in optional markets, and other actions are taken *ex ante* (before the fact) and *ex post* (after the fact, seeking to recover from adverse consequences). These activities broadly summarize the function of financial and risk management.

Risk mitigation is common to many professions, each of which has an approach and uses techniques based on the needs and the accrued experience specific to that profession and acquired over long periods of time. For example, a machine operator maintains a machine to prevent failure or nonconforming operations. Careful diet and exercise, medicines, and planned visits to a doctor for a checkup are used preventively to maintain one's health and avoid disease. By the same token, an airplane has numerous built-in fail-safe mechanisms to counter predictable (albeit extremely rare) potential components or system failures.

Risk finance is focused in particular on money: how to invest it and manage it; how to price assets, contracts, options, and so on; and how to use it for the many real ends for which individuals and corporate, social, or other entities may need it. Pricing assets and the risks of mispricing are particularly important. When an asset is priced properly it allows an efficient exchange between the many parties that consume and supply such an asset. When it is mispriced, exchanges may be severely curtailed, contributing to a lack of liquidity. Financial pricing of an asset allows one to unlock the values embedded in the asset, whether real or virtual values, and render such an asset tradable.

For example, to price a corporate firm engaged in a real economic activity (such as producing cars, making movies, selling a service, performing high-tech or medical research and development, etc.), its value is unlocked by trading current and future returns and risks in units called *securities* or shares of *stock*. A security then translates the firm value into money by letting a buyer and a seller exchange money in a financial market for the right to own part of the firm's future monetary potential. Such an exchange defines, then, both the price of the security and the monetary value that buyers and sellers of the security ascribe to the firm being traded. Real firms and assets and their prospects are thus *securitized* and exchanged in denominated price contracts (in this case, a unit of stock ascribing to its owner some rights over the firm). Predicting the price of a security can be quite complex, however, based on all available real and financial data, future predictions regarding the economic environment, competitive forces, technology, management, and other factors that contribute to enhancing or decreasing the value of firms and their price. A common belief is that such prices cannot be predicted with absolute certainty but may be guessed at best by using the information we can assemble, interpret, and understand, based on insights and an understanding of the market mechanism.

To meet the many challenges of finance and its application in real life, financial institutions and financial markets have defined and commercialized standard financial instruments that are traded, including, among many others, securities, insurance contracts, bonds, options, credit contracts, and the like. In addition, a plethora of financial institutions—banks, insurance firms, brokers, credit providers, and so forth—have conspired to provide the means for investors, speculators, firms, and persons to improve their financial well-being while managing the risks of financial transactions. In other words, investors willing to assume more risks will do so, and those who seek to assume less risk will do so as well.

This is possible, of course, if markets are liquid. In some cases, a price results from contractual negotiations between specific parties. These contracts assume many forms, such as insurance contracts, over-the-counter (OTC) trades, and so on. In other cases, prices are set arbitrarily to a price level or allowed to fluctuate between two specific levels (for example, in some countries the prices of certain commodities are set by political decisions while in others they are set by exchanges and allowed to fluctuate between upper and lower limits). When markets are not liquid, we can expect firms and persons to cling to their money, each uncertain of the market price. In these conditions, a lack of business and a lack of needed funds to function may cause firms to falter. For this reason, financial institutions seek to provide liquidity for businesses to remain active, both for their own good and for the public good. The potential for financial institutions to make money in such processes is both immense and varied.

For example, insurance firms set a price that insured parties pay, while at the same time seeking a market price for the risks they aggregate in portfolios. They do so both to profit from a spread between insurance cost and the portfolio price and to maintain the capacity to meet claims when they occur. To mitigate insurance risks, insurers can also buy and sell these risks to other parties (to reinsurers who share payments if claims are made, in return for a portion of the premium paid by the insured) or use securitization—that is, selling standardized revenues and their associated claims in an insurance portfolio to financial markets. The same approach is used by mortgage lenders that *aggregate* mortgage contracts into a portfolio, which is sold through intermediaries to financial markets (as is discussed in Chapters 9 and 10). By the same token, a municipality seeking to build a subway by issuing a debt obligation will float a proposal to be priced by buyers (the banks) or financial intermediaries seeking to finance such a transaction through financial markets. Throughout, financial engineering contributes by financial innovations that unlock value that can be traded and priced viably and sustainably by an exchange of buyers and sellers.

On the environmental front, financial markets are assuming a growing responsibility to price and allocate, economically and efficiently, environmental risks. In particular, in the matter of global warming, standardized units of carbon dioxide emission rights are traded. Current beliefs are that carbon emissions would be better controlled by money equivalents and thus would contribute to global and sustainable emission levels (at the same time, carbon taxes may be used to raise additional taxes for needed government revenues). Discussions at the World Economic Forum in Davos, Switzerland, and the U.S. policy of 2009 have emphasized the need to use financial markets for greater environmental and social (economic) efficiency. For some, the concern about global warming has become an opportunity to profit. For example, for countries or firms owning rights that they do not use, it becomes a bounty they never had (which of course leads detractors of such a scheme to assert that carbon trades contribute only to an important transfer of financial resources from developed to undeveloped countries). Nonetheless, there are a growing number of financial markets specializing in such trades, such as the Chicago Climate Exchange and Amsterdam markets. Research and applications are needed, however, to develop this potential further and to understand the mechanism for the market making of environmentally friendly products, priced sustainably. Our concern is to define these problems and use finance to manage the risks and the opportunities they imply.

Globalization and financial technology have also provided an extraordinary boost to global finance and financial markets and at the same time have contributed to appreciable investment opportunities and risks. However, whether globalization contributes to an increase in risk dependence and risk contagion (see Chapters 4 and 10) across financial markets remains an issue that has no simple or clear-cut answer. Networking, the density of human settlements and their consequences (both good and bad), and other factors have contributed to a far greater awareness that risks are dependent and have many sources. Further, identity thefts, cyber-crimes, virtual enterprises that operate globally, and the breakdown of traditionally secured pension funds and the like are colluding to highlight that risk is no longer an abstract financial issue but a real one—felt by each one of us, wherever we may be. In a global world, risks are global, and risks are thus assumed, exchanged, shared, traded, valued, and priced globally. They are also implied in corporate strategies, whether financial or not. In such an environment, finance and the risk business are necessarily far greater than ever before.

There are many risks that are not easily defined in monetary terms, however, and cannot be exchanged to produce an agreed-on price. For example, rare events (with an extremely small probability of occurring) and catastrophic risks are notoriously difficult to price as only very few financial parties may have the capacity to bear the implied risks. Such risks are a financial engineering challenge—to better manage, define, value, and price these risks, either uniquely or approximately, and unlock the value or financial consequences embedded in them.

RISK AND FINANCE: BASIC CONCEPTS

Risk and finance are defined by a complex set of factors, each determining the others. It has been claimed that a risk with no financial consequence is not a risk. This statement, of course, cannot be true since one's accidental death might not have any financial consequence. For our purposes here, risk and finance are defined implicitly and explicitly by factors that have an underlying financial value. Monetizing this value is a financial engineering challenge. Seven essential factors are used to define the value and price of risk:

1. Events and their probabilities (whether common or rare).
2. Predictability and timing of these events and their recurrence.
3. Uncertain financial consequences (whether adverse or beneficial).
4. Individuals' tolerance for risk bearing, implied in their preferences.
5. Individuals' information and ability to measure and to assess risks.
6. Risk sharing and exchange (contractual or not).
7. Market pricing, arising from the interaction of many buyers and sellers in a fair and efficient manner with common and shared information.

The first two factors, events and their probabilities and their predictability and timing, need not have financial relevance if they have no financial consequence. An individual's rationality and personal information expressing a latent preference for uncertain outcomes (see Chapters 5 and 6) are relevant to personal finance but might or might not be relevant to financial markets pricing. Finally, risk sharing and exchange as well as financial markets pricing imply the value of a trade, product, or rights conferred by an exchange, reached at an agreed-on price. Each of these factors underlies the concerns of investors, traders, speculators, and financial engineers. For example, the value of an asset or returns derived from an asset held by an investor will depend on the returns or the obligations of the asset and the timing of those returns—whether uncertain or not. The market price of an asset, however, is defined by the buyers and the sellers trading in this asset. When a price is not set by a market, it may be defined by a contractual agreement between a buyer and a seller or by a collective entity (such as by a government that regulates prices, or by a private agreement between an insured and an insurer).

An individual's rationality (or that of a corporate entity) expresses the subjective predisposition of an investor to bear risks and to choose and pay for an investment as a function of its risk/reward characteristics. These factors, combined with macroeconomic effects (such as interest rates, employment statistics, etc.) contribute to a pricing of all valuable assets, with prices based on the attitudes of all parties to a trade.

Risk may be more or less accepted or abhorred by individuals and firms. History offers examples where risk is accepted and even sought out: Egyptians knew of the floods of the river Nile, but knew also that floods would irrigate their agricultural fields near the banks of the river. Thus, Egyptian farmers intentionally settled next to the river with the prospect of growing abundant crops. It was impossible to predict the *amount* of the flooding from year to year, but over many centuries the ancient Egyptians were able to anticipate *when* the flooding would occur (it occurs at about the same time every year). By the same token, many hedge funds nurture their funds with risky bets in expectation of extremely large returns. Individual investors, corporations, and societies relate differently to the risks they assess, assume, or are willing to bear. *Risk behavior*, as well as the *attitudes* it implies, is therefore a fundamental concept (expanded on further in Chapters 5 and 6). It characterizes the degree to which an investor accepts *probabilities* of adverse consequences. Similarly, it underlies the investor's need to hedge and tailor the risks assumed to a tolerable level, where the risk and its rewards are balanced (in the investor's view and interest, of course).

Risk events, their timing, and their consequences have both direct and indirect effects. The former are usually well defined and accounted for, while the latter are harder to assess and might be neglected. It is therefore useful to categorize risks to better appreciate their origins and their consequences. For brevity, we can summarize the categories of risk as follows:

- *External-hazard risks* (such as weather risks, macroeconomic risks to a firm, or risks over which we have little or no control).
- *Endogenous risks* (such as some operational risks arising from human, organizational, mechanical, or process dysfunctions; *endogenous* indicates that these risks are inherent to the process in place).
- *Strategic or counterparty risks* (originating in exchanges between multiple parties, each with different agendas and risk attitudes; for example, counterparty and contractual risks, information and power asymmetries are such risks and are considered in Chapters 9 and 10).

■ *Risk externalities* or risks with consequences and origins that are disparate (e.g., when risk consequences are not assumed by the perpetrator—as is sometimes the case in environmental pollution). These risks can have both an adverse and a positive consequence.

Examples of strategic and risk externalities abound. The pollution perpetrated by a chemical firm spilling its wastes in nature is a risk externality. By the same token, a large bank that assumes exuberant risks in the pursuit of short-term profits and huge bonuses because it believes that it is too big to fail is another form of a polluter that puts at risk the financial system. When the parties to business or financial transactions have different objectives, whether these are conflicting or not, a counterparty or strategic risk arises. Similar risks recur in contractual risk exchanges or risk sharing between parties that have different objectives and use their information to take advantage of contract clauses. In this vein, OTC contracts as well as insurance contracts may have a strategic risk (more on this in Chapters 9 and 10).

The definition and measurement of these risks is difficult, however, compounded by the use of risk as a panacea for the many ills, real, potential, or imaginary, that individuals and corporate firms face (either internally or externally). In an era of globalization, some of these risks may become intractable and therefore nontransparent. For example, securitization (the process by which many risks are compounded, confounded, marketed, and traded as a package—in whole or in parts) in global financial markets and transferring risk from one entity to another (from investors, debtors, etc.) through multiple intermediaries have contributed to increased disparities between real and perceived risks. Risks have thus become less transparent, less specific, and more complex. As a result, many financial risks are ill understood, poorly measured, and may potentially contribute to an incentive to assume ever-greater risks (referred to by Robert Shiller as *irrational exuberance*). The measurement of risk is therefore both important and challenging and is addressed in greater detail in Chapters 3 and 4.

Finance and Risks

Financial institutions are motivated by five essential purposes:

1. Provide liquidity (the intent of bank charters and therefore their legal responsibility).
2. Price and manage financial risks—whether these risks are or are not predictable.
3. Allocate wealth to financial and other assets to meet investors' objectives. To do so, finance seeks to define and explain investors' risk attitudes, meet their risk/reward expectations, and prevent or counteract the effects of risk, regulation, and taxes.
4. Provide a decision framework to guide and justify individuals' and firms' financial decisions.
5. Innovate and design financial instruments that meet the needs of investors, individuals, firms, and society for profit, risk bearing, and liquidity.

Financial economic theory, based on specific assumptions of rational behavior, has provided a strong anchor to financial modeling and decision making to support these needs. The *efficient market hypothesis* (EMH), which claims that under specific assumptions financial markets are rational, is such an example. While the EMH is a powerful and useful theoretical framework, it is also violated in practice, leading to some competing theories—albeit none as general as the EMH. Behavioral finance (BH) in particular seeks to integrate human and behavioral processes into financial decision-making processes. Financial practice, in contrast, seeks the best it can do for financial principals, intermediaries, or agents in a given situation. It is not constrained by theory but by its financial performance, with the stance that its proof is in its results.

FINANCIAL INSTRUMENTS

Financial instruments are varied, including essentially securities, bonds, options, and portfolios on these assets, as well as a large variety of agreements for credit risk and credit derivatives. These instruments and their variants are used for specific financial purposes.

Securities or Stocks

Factories, retail firms, banks, film companies, soft-drink bottlers, utilities, and so on are economic entities transforming assets, production, and services into returns. Stocks are obligations to share in the equity of a firm, and they give the owner of the equity the right to vote for governing board members and to share in the firm's residual profits. These rights confer a value, priced by the security market price. Financial markets have, then, an important role in *liquefying* (or securitizing) the firm's real functions into a financial product that is bought and sold and shared with investors. The ownership of securities publicly traded is thus a common ownership of obligations and returns derived from these stocks.

In 1938, John Burr Williams postulated that the value of *any* financial asset (a stock) equals the present value of all of its future cash flows. For example, if a firm provides its shareholders a periodic cash distribution—the stock dividend—then the stock price equals the present value of these planned disbursements by the firm. The price of a stock and its prediction includes many more considerations, however, expressing the firm's current and future macroeconomic environment, its management, the firm's returns and growth, investors' motives summarized by their risk attitudes and the information they possess, and so forth. In this sense, a stock price expresses more than just current and expected cash flows. The manner in which we calculate the price of securities is critically important, complex, and useful, and is the topic of several chapters where different approaches are used—both subjective estimation using utility-based approaches and by financial market EMH-based theories.

EXAMPLE: AN IBM DAY-TRADES RECORD

Consider the IBM security price recorded daily as shown in Table 1.1. Such information is available daily in the great majority of financial markets and for all products traded. *Open* defines the day's opening price; *high*, *low*, and *close* prices define the

TABLE 1.1   IBM Stock Price over Five Years

Date	Open	High	Low	Close	Volume	Adj Close
01/02/2003	78.8	80.57	78.19	80.57	7,864,500	74.38
01/03/2003	80.7	81.65	80.21	81.65	5,962,300	75.38
01/06/2003	81.9	84.8	81.81	83.59	7,921,300	77.17
01/07/2003	83.95	86.18	83.75	86	11,906,900	79.39
01/08/2003	85.55	85.69	84.07	84.19	9,508,800	77.72
01/09/2003	84.75	87.02	84.75	87	10,711,600	80.32
01/10/2003	85.85	88.04	85.7	87.68	9,955,400	80.94
01/13/2003	88.31	88.95	87.35	87.51	10,499,000	80.79
01/14/2003	87.23	88.59	87.22	88.58	7,569,100	81.78
...	...	...	...	...	...	...
...	...	...	...	...	...	...
12/18/2008	85.77	86.64	82.96	84	8,029,500	83.11
12/19/2008	85.22	85.22	82.97	83.52	13,098,600	82.64
12/22/2008	83.27	83.45	80.32	81.99	7,083,300	81.12
12/23/2008	82.35	82.81	80.13	80.6	6,374,400	79.75
12/24/2008	80.55	81.22	79.92	80.52	2,415,200	79.67
12/26/2008	80.93	81.8	80.55	81.33	3,101,300	80.47
12/29/2008	81.72	81.72	79.68	81.25	6,062,600	80.39
12/30/2008	81.83	83.64	81.52	83.55	5,774,400	82.67
12/31/2008	83.5	85	83.5	84.16	6,667,700	83.27

prices statistics for that day; *volume* denotes the number of trades effected during that day. Such data may be used to predict trends in IBM's stock price, although predicting IBM's price from one day to the next may be tricky. The study of a historical stock price can provide ex post a technically acceptable explanation of price movements. An ex ante prediction of prices is much more difficult. However, Chapter 3 provides a number of statistical approaches to characterize security price processes, asking questions such as whether a security price change is due to macroeconomic factors, statements by corporate leaders or leading analysts, a perceived future profit potential for the security, or other factors. These questions are, of course, difficult to analyze quantitatively, but numerous attempts to do so are made nonetheless.

Pricing a firm's security based only on its daily price record might not reflect the true value of the firm. Macroeconomic factors (such as the gross national product, interest rates, exchanges rates, etc.) as well as industry- and firm-specific factors (such as the industry market structure, technology, management, regulation, government support, etc.) are also important. Some firms are cost-driven, augmenting their profits by increasing their costs (for example, public transportation, health care, etc.), while others are value-driven, based on consumers' ability to pay the value they extract by buying a product or service (in particular, luxury and consumer-branded goods). In general, both costs and values interact in a push-pull process that causes certain firms to have prospective profits or losses (and thereby to have a greater or a lesser value). Prices set in financial markets are then derived from firms' cost and value push-pull processes with a large number of financial parties (including investors, speculators, pension funds, insurance firms, etc.) expressing their needs and choices by buying and selling firms' securities. In this sense, a financial price, unlike a product market price, is a value imputed to a firm's security by the exchange of financial parties.

Bonds

A bond is an obligation that pays a defined amount of money (a coupon paid periodically and/or its nominal price at the bond maturity) at a given future date T—the bond maturity. Unlike securities, bond payments are assumed to be risk-free, are able to meet their future commitments, and are predictable. Such certainty is based on the belief of a trusting bondholder that the bond issuer will meet all its obligations.

When corporate firms issue bonds (or raise their debt), they expect that in the future they will be able to repay this debt or at least be able to refinance it. When they can do so abundantly, they do not default and are able to meet their financing needs. In such an environment, debt increases and firms become more leveraged. However, when there is no liquidity and firms are unable to repay or renew their debt (either from cash flow or access to credit), such firms default. For this reason, bonds and credit contracts are two instruments, each entailing specific obligations. While bonds have been used for a long time and traded in extremely large quantities (far more than securities), credit products (such as credit default swaps [CDSs], credit derivatives [CDs], etc.) have only recently come into their own as independent financial products based on portfolios of various assets such as mortgage-backed securities (MBSs) and, generally, collateralized debt obligations (CDOs). These products are considered in Chapter 10.

Let's take the example of a risk-free, zero-coupon traded bond defined by a $1 nominal price, paid at a future (maturity) time T. The price of such a bond at a given time t is $B_f(t, T)$. This price expresses the time preference of money in a given market at time t for the *sure payment of* $1, T - t$ periods hence. We can write the bond price as a function $R_f(t, T)$ which is called the *going risk-free rate* paid as a return for a debt of $1 to be reimbursed for sure in $T - t$ periods. The functional form $R_f(t, T)$ is also called the *term structure of interest rates* and varies over time, reflecting various economic conditions. The price of a risk-free zero-coupon bond is then given by:

$$B_f(t, T) = \left(\frac{1}{1 + R_f(t, T)} \right)^{T-t}$$

or

$$R_f(t, T) = \left[B_f(t, T) \right]^{-\frac{1}{T-t}} - 1 \tag{1.1}$$

In practice, bonds rates are often defined in terms of a summarizing and single rate which we call the *yield*. A growth in this yield will imply a growth in the discount rate, and vice versa. Say that the market price for a zero-coupon bond with one year to maturity is currently quoted at $0.90. Its discount rate would be 11.11 percent, or:

$$B(0, 1) = 0.90 = \frac{1}{1 + R_f(0, 1)}$$

Or

$$R_f(0, 1) = \frac{1.}{0.90} - 1 = 0.1111 \tag{1.2}$$

A bond that matures in two years and has a price of \$0.80 can be calculated in two ways. First, note that:

$$B(0, 2) = 0.80 = \left(\frac{1}{1 + R_f(0, 2)}\right)^2 \text{ or } R_f(0, 2) = \frac{1}{\sqrt{0.80}} - 1 \text{ and } R_f(0, 2) = 0.118034 \tag{1.3}$$

where $R_f(0, 2)$ is the yearly interest rate applied for a two-year bond. By the same token, since the bond has a guaranteed payment, its price can be calculated as follows:

$$B(0, 2) = 0.80 = \left(\frac{1}{1 + R_f(0, 1)}\right)\left(\frac{1}{1 + R_f(1, 2)}\right) \text{ or }$$

$$0.80 = \left(\frac{1}{1 + 0.1111}\right)\left(\frac{1}{1 + R_f(1, 2)}\right) \tag{1.4}$$

where $R_f(1, 2)$ is the next-year interest rate to be applied for one year. Such a rate is called the *forward* rate and is equal to:

$$R_f(1, 2) = \left(\frac{1}{0.80\,(1.1111)}\right) - 1 = 0.125$$

This simple example indicates that the market expects growth in the interest rate in the following year.

Bonds may be used for many purposes. Governments sell bonds to finance their budgets, wars, or specific projects. Firms sell bonds to augment their working capital by leveraging with bond issues. Bondholders, unlike security holders, have no claim on the firm except the bond covenant that specifies the conditions and the explicit exchange terms of the bond.

Portfolios

When an investor or a firm owns several assets, consisting of securities, bonds, derivatives, real assets (such as real estate), cash, and so forth, the holdings define a *portfolio*. For example, assume an investor owns n shares of a security whose price and dividend at time t are S_t and d_t and the coupon bond whose price is $B_c(t, T)$ paying C_t at time t. The portfolio price defines then a wealth state at time t, denoted by W_t:

$$W_t = n\,(S_t + d_t) + C_t + B_c(t, T)$$

Portfolios can of course be far more complex, consisting of many securities held in various proportions, changing over time when trading in these assets. It may consist also of other financial instruments such as options, whose values are realized at some future date (although these values can have a current price), and other assets of various liquidities (such as real estate holdings). Financial engineers use such portfolios for many purposes. For example, a portfolio may be constructed to meet an investor's financial needs. Portfolios are also used to replicate an unknown asset price but whose financial characteristics are identical to the known portfolio price. If prices are unique, the known price would necessarily be equal to the unknown one (such a procedure is used repeatedly in Chapters 7, 8, 9, and 10 to price options and other assets).

EXAMPLE: CONSTRUCTING A PORTFOLIO

Let a person's wealth be $100,000 to be invested in one of three portfolios consisting of holdings in the Google security, currently priced at $300, and Treasury bills (TB) (riskless bonds) priced at $100. These portfolios are given by:

Portfolio 1	Portfolio 2	Portfolio 3
50% Google, 50% TB	60% Google, 40% TB	40% Google, 60% TB
Number of shares 166.66	Number of shares 200	Number of shares 133.33
Number of TB 500	Number of TB 400	Number of TB 600

Assume that the investor believes that Google's security will either increase by 15 percent or by 10 percent or decrease by 5 percent or by 20 percent, and let the risk-free rate for Treasury bills (TB) be 6 percent. What are the future portfolio prices?

Consider portfolio 1. The initial price of the portfolio is:

$$W = 166.66(300) + 500(100) = 100,000$$

If the stock price increases, the portfolio price is:

$$166.66[300(1.15)] + [500(100)](1.06) = 107,497.70$$

If the stock price decreases by 10 percent, the portfolio price would then be:

$$166.66[300(0.90)] + [500(100)](1.06) = 97,998.20$$

How would the first portfolio compare to portfolios 2 and 3? Each allocation has different outcomes depending on the future performance of the Google security, over which the investor has no control. The choice of an allocation by an investor is thus a bet based on the investor's predictions (derived from the information he has) and his risk attitude, as considered in Chapter 5.

A *self-financing portfolio* is defined as a portfolio with investments and returns made only by the portfolio returns. In other words, the price of such a portfolio is given by the market prices of its components (securities and bonds) changing over time. In such portfolios, profits are reinvested and losses absorbed without changing the portfolio composition. This process is used repeatedly (see Chapter 8) to price assets and optional products using a portfolio that replicates the asset we seek to price. For example, the combination of securities and a bond might be used to replicate the price of a derivative if one is able to demonstrate that the price of the portfolio and its returns will coincide at all times and at all their future states.

Derivatives and Options

A derivative is an asset whose price is derived from some feature of an underlying asset (such as a security price, defined by financial markets) that trades the rights these derivatives confer. Options are particular derivatives that are now traded in many financial markets and in extraordinarily large volumes. They are used both for risk hedging and for speculating, singly or in a combined manner to create desired risk profiles, assuming or selling selected parts of an underlying asset or their combination. Options are defined in a standard manner, each defined by its specific characteristics. Essential and profusely traded derivatives include futures and forward contracts, call and put options—whether European or American—as well as exotic options such as hybrids and credit derivatives (these options are defined in the next section). Options are traded on many products, indexes, securities, and portfolios such as commodities, metals, securities, market indexes, currencies, the weather, carbon emissions, and so on.

In practice, options and derivatives can be used creatively to deal with a broad set of managerial and financial purposes. These span hedging, risk management, incentives for employees (serving often the dual purpose of an incentive to perform and a substitute for cash outlays in the form of salaries), and constructing financial remuneration packages. Options are also used to manage commodity trades, foreign exchange transactions, interest risk (in bonds, mortgage transactions, etc.), and to price real assets and options on these real assets—real options. Their use includes simple buy-sell decisions, as stated earlier, as well as complex trading strategies over multiple products, multiple markets, and multiple periods of time. In this sense, derivatives provide an opportunity to trade future financial outcomes here and now. Pricing these assets, theoretically and practically, is therefore extremely important.

Over-the-Counter Options   Unlike some other options, over-the-counter (OTC) options are not traded in financial markets but are used to fit specific contractual needs. For example, swaps between banks and intermediaries or between insurers and reinsurers, trades in credit portfolios, and credit derivatives are such products (see in particular Chapters 9 and 10). Consider an airline company that contracts the acquisition of (or the option to acquire) a new-technology airplane at some future time. The contract may involve a stream or a lump-sum payment to the contractor (Boeing or Airbus) in exchange for the delivery of the plane at a specified time. Since payments are often made prior to the delivery of the plane, a number of clauses are added in the contract to manage the risks sustained by each of the parties if any of the parties were to deviate from the terms of the contract (for example, late deliveries, technological obsolescence, etc.). Similarly, a manufacturer can enter into binding bilateral agreements with a supplier by which agreed-on (contracted) exchange terms are used to meet the needs of both parties. This can involve future contractual prices, delivery rates at specific times (to reduce inventory holding costs), and a set of clauses intended to protect each party against possible failures by the other in fulfilling the terms of the contract.

Throughout these cases, the advantage resulting from negotiating a contract is to reduce, for one or both parties, the uncertainty concerning future exchanges and their costs. In this manner, the manufacturer will be eager to secure long-term sources of supply and their timely availability while the investor, the buyer of the options, would avoid too large a loss implied by the acquisition of a risky asset, currency, or commodity.

Since for each contract there is one (or many) buyer(s) and one (or many) seller(s), the price of the contract can be interpreted as the outcome of a negotiation process where both parties are induced to enter into a contractual agreement. For example, the buyer and the seller of an option can be conceived of as parties involved in a strategic two-person game, the benefits of which for each are derived from the risk and rewards transferred from one party to the other. Some risks may be strategic, implied by the parties' preferences and the information each possesses. Note that given the information available to each of the parties, the utility of entering into a contractual agreement to both parties is always positive ex ante; otherwise there would not be any contractual agreement (unless such a contract were imposed on one of the parties!). When the number of buyers and sellers of such contracts becomes extremely large, transactions become impersonal and it is the market price that defines the value of the contract. Strategic behaviors tend to break down, the larger the group and the closer the price is to that of a market price.

On Incentive Options and Taxes   Individual executives and employees in high-tech firms are often paid with options instead of cash. These options are used by firms as a mean to secure employees' commitment to the firm's bottom line and to delay cash outlays. These also help to delay the costs of compensation on the company's current balance sheet. Executives, too, profit from such a payment—often accounted for as a bonus, retention, or hiring incentive—due to the tax advantages it may confer. How and how much an executive can be taxed on future payments is an important question that has plagued lawyers, tax accountants, and tax authorities in general. The many billions of dollars that banks pay yearly in the form of stock options to their executives and employees is a testament to their attractiveness and to their tax advantages. This practice is not limited to financial institutions, however. A firm's ability to offer an attractive total compensation package, including a deferred compensation plan, is also a valuable recruiting tool for both for-profit and nonprofit organizations. While for-profit organizations have generally greater flexibility in offering deferred compensation plans to employees, there are limits on tax-exempt organizations. There are potential alternatives for deferral of compensation, however, including private stock option plans, split-dollar life insurance plans, and severance plans (see the American Institute of Certified Public Accountants [AICPA], July 2001).

For the recipient of stock options there are important tax ramifications. Generally there is no tax imposed upon the receipt of a nonqualified (common) stock option, the general guideline being that if there is no ascertainable value for the option at the time it is granted, then there is no tax liability to be paid until the option is exercised. At the option's exercise, common options are subject to federal income tax withholding by the employer, and employees may actually have to pay money to the employer to facilitate withholding. At the time of exercise a number of alternatives are usually given to the option's holder:

- Cashing out at the time of exercise—exercising the option and having the stock sold simultaneously to pay the option price and taxes.
- Holding on when there is good reason to believe that the price of the stock may go up substantially.

Participating in like-kind exchanges. This allows for a pyramid or exchange of stock to defer tax, where the executive exercising the option delivers the shares purchased in exchange for a renewed option grant on the employer's shares (see the American Law Institute, http://ali.org/ for more details).

For example, consider incentive stock options (ISOs). These are statutory arrangements to avoid the recognition of a taxable gain on the option after it is exercised. To avoid this recognition, the stock has to be kept for at least one year after exercise. Then when the income is recognized, it can be characterized as capital gains income as opposed to an ordinary income (which has a much higher tax rate). To qualify as ISOs, the following requirements must be met:

- The exercise price must be equal to what the fair market value of the stock was on the date it was granted.
- ISOs cannot be granted to any person who owns more than 10 percent of the voting power of all classes of stock.
- ISOs may only be granted to employees. Once the employment relationship terminates, by reason other than death, the employee only has 90 days to exercise the ISOs, after which they lose their tax-qualified status.
- The number of ISOs granted annually is limited to $100,000 worth of stock priced at the underlying fair market value at the time of the grant.
- ISOs cannot be transferred to any person or entity other than at death by will, laws of descent, or beneficiary designation. If stock acquired in an ISO is transferred within one year of the exercise, then income has to be recognized on such disqualifying disposition (see the American Law Institute for further details).

Options of various sorts are granted by various parties and usually have well-defined properties with specific tax implications that require careful valuation and financial planning. For example, for *common* options, when they have an ascertainable fair market value by reason of being listed on a published exchange (the option must be listed, not just the stock), the tax on such returns may equal the personal income tax. In some unusual arrangements, the right to exercise such an option is conditioned on additional services such as competition covenants of the employee. In these situations, no income is recognized until such time as the option has an ascertainable fair market value and the employee is no longer subject to substantial risk of forfeiture with respect to the arrangement.

The tax differences may thus be important. If the option is considered as ordinary income it can be taxed as high as 40 percent, whether the option holder sells his stock shares or not. If shares are not sold at the time the options are exercised, any additional increase in the share price from then until the time shares are sold is treated as a long-term capital gain, and therefore taxed at a lower rate.

Buying Long and Selling Short The decision of prospective investors and speculators to buy (a *long* contract) and to short-sell (i.e., to borrow an asset or security now in order to resell it later, without the investor necessarily owning it) is not only based on their risk profiles. Perceived and estimated expected changes in stock prices, in risk, in interest rates, and in related economic and financial markets, as well as the private information of investor-speculators, are essential ingredients applied to solve the basic questions of what to do, when, and where by these investors-speculators.

Real and Financial Assets

A real asset, although worth money, is not a financial instrument traded in financial markets (as it is in the case of a security, a bond, or a derivative), but an asset whose owner may keep it or sell it at a going price. An apartment, a bridge, and a power station are examples of real assets. Real assets have value derived from the returns they provide, the rights they confer to their owners or imply, their appreciation (actual or expected), as well as their holding and maintenance costs. Real assets are not generally liquid (i.e., it takes time to sell them—try to sell an apartment you own!). Real assets can be liquefied, however, by pulling together similar assets into a portfolio and selling shares in such a portfolio. This is possible, of course, only if there are buyers and sellers who trade in these shares.

This process has assumed an increased importance in finance. It has also contributed significantly to the management and the growth of credit (see Chapter 9). At the same time it has been labeled as one of the culprits in the financial meltdown of 2008. For example, pulling together mortgage payments into portfolios and securitizing these portfolios (called mortgage-backed securities, or MBSs), buying and selling their various returns and obligations (in case of default), has made it possible to increase the volume of mortgages sold by banks.

At the same time, this practice has contributed to a massive shift of risk, owned traditionally by mortgage-granting banks, to abstract investors who buy and sell cash flows without being fully aware of the intricate risks these securitized mortgage contracts imply. In this case, mispricing, excess zeal in granting mortgages by bankers, as well as macroeconomic shifts (such as substantial increases in interest rates) can induce a market meltdown, as was the case in 2008. For example, say that a bank provides a mortgage of $900,000 for a house whose current price is $1,000,000 and which serves as collateral for the mortgage. If house prices keep increasing faster than the mortgage-holder debt, then of course there can be no default from the bank's viewpoint. However, if the house depreciates suddenly by 20 percent, the mortgage holder will be strongly tempted to default and let the bank face the loss of value of the house. Securitization is nevertheless an extremely popular technique (and likely to remain an essential financial tool in the future) applied to a broad set of products, including for example insurance contracts, debts of various sorts, credit derivatives, and so forth.

Financial Markets

Financial assets are traded in financial markets. These markets operate all over the world, some of them specializing in trading specific financial products (securities, bonds, options, commodities, carbon, currencies, metals, etc.). These markets may be differentiated by:

- The type of financial asset being traded.
- The location of the financial market (including its currency and local trade regulation).
- The process for price setting or market making in the financial market.
- The technology used for trading.
- The financial regulation in effect.

For example, the Montreal Stock Exchange focuses on options trading, while at the exchanges in New York, Chicago, Tel Aviv, Paris, London, Hong Kong, Shanghai, Frankfurt, and other large metropolises an extremely large number of financial products and their derivatives are traded; these products are also compiled into indexes that characterize the evolution of prices and are used as well to market derivatives on such prices. The Dow Jones of New York in particular has indexes including the Industrial Average (DJIA), DJ Transportation, the DJ Utilities Average, and the DJ 65 Average. Standard and Poor's (S&P) also publishes and trades on its index, the S&P 500. Other indexes include the New York Stock Exchange (NYSE) Composite Index, the NASDAQ composite index, the AMEX Market Value Index, the Russell 2000 Stock Index, the Wilshire 5000 Equity Index, and the like. By the same token, the Chicago Board of Exchange (CBOE) is a very active financial market trading in commodities and options as well as other securities. In some cases, certain securities are traded in multiple markets at the same time, providing opportunities for trading on the same security in different time regions.

Overall, the quality of a financial market is defined in terms of its liquidity, size, transaction costs, transparency, and regulation. A public firm's decision to list its security in one market or another is therefore a strategic decision, which may affect the price of the firm and its access to the capital it requires for its development.

OPTION CONTRACTS

Although most people believe that derivatives are a recent innovation, they date as far back as twelfth-century practices by Flemish traders. The first futures and options contracts resembling current option types were in fact implemented in the seventeenth century in Amsterdam, which was at that time the financial capital of the Western world, and in the rice market of Osaka. Practice in derivatives has expanded into global financial markets following developments in financial and economic theory that have made it possible to price such contracts (see Chapters 7 and 8). A number of such options are defined next.

A *call (long)* option is an option contract that gives the holder the right but not the obligation to buy a specified amount of the commodity, stock, or foreign currency (the *underlying asset*) for a premium on or before the exercise date. A *call (short)* option is an obligation to meet the terms of this contract.

Put options give the holder the right to sell at a specified price—called the *strike price*—on (or before, for an American option) a specific expiration date. The short side of such a contract carries an obligation to meet the terms of this contract.

For example, a long call consists in paying $3 now to have the right to buy in three months an IBM share at the strike price of $52. If the price in three months turns out to be $59, then at the exercise date of the option, the buyer (long) of the call option would collect $59 less $52, or $7. If the price turns out to be below $52, the holder of the option collects nothing.

PROBLEM 1.1: OPTIONS AND THEIR PRICES

The data in Tables 1.2 and 1.3 summarize the record of options on IBM traded in a financial market. This data can be collected from Yahoo Finance, the *Wall Street Journal*, the *Financial Times*, and the many other financial services that publish such data daily. This data set provides all option prices of IBM that expired Friday, March 20, 2009. Buyers and sellers of options use such information for various purposes. Note in particular:

- The *bid* price—the price that a buyer of the option is willing to pay.
- The *ask* price—the price that a seller of the option is willing to accept.
- The *last* (current) and its change from the price at which a trade transaction has previously been made.
- The *volume*—the number of options traded.

These prices also indicate traders' beliefs regarding the future price of IBM security prices. If the price of the call option increases, this means that the most traders expect the IBM price to increase.

The *spread* at any given time is the difference between the ask and bid prices. It is used by market makers, whose essential function is to create liquidity (i.e., meeting as much as possible all requests for trades). Changing prices from instant to instant reflect both the spread and the inequalities between the bid and the ask sides, as well as changing expectations regarding IBM's future price.

Use the following questions to review your understanding of the data summarized in Tables 1.2 and 1.3:

- What do the IBM options indicators IBMFL.X, IBMFO.X, and the like, mean? Why are there so many such indicators?
- What are the prices of the call and put options? (Select a few.) Why do they differ?
- What is a bid and what is an ask price for some of these options?
- What is the spread, and what does a spread mean for a trader?
- What does the volume traded in options represent?

TABLE 1.2 Call Options (expire at close, Friday, June 19, 2009)

Strike	Symbol	Last	Change	Bid	Ask	Volume	Open Interest
60	IBMFL.X	45.35	0	47.4	48.1	1	1
75	IBMFO.X	31.3	0	32.4	33.1	23	33
80	IBMFP.X	26.4	0	27.4	27.8	5	35
85	IBMFQ.X	22	1	22.5	22.7	11	231
90	IBMFR.X	17.4	0.4	17.5	17.7	52	1,016
95	IBMFS.X	13	0.2	12.6	12.8	98	1,773
100	IBMFT.X	8.1	0.5	7.7	7.9	298	4,172
105	IBMFA.X	3.5	0	3.4	3.6	3,810	15,764
110	IBMFB.X	0.8	0.1	0.75	0.85	2,451	12,248
115	IBMFC.X	0.1	0	0.05	0.1	283	7,707
120	IBMFD.X	0.03	0.02	N/A	0.05	14	1,881
125	IBMFE.X	0.05	0	N/A	0.05	4	407
130	IBMFF.X	0.02	0	N/A	0.05	10	10
140	IBMFH.X	0.05	0	N/A	0.05	0	117

Source: Yahoo! Finance.

- Using this data set, can you see a relationship between the spread of specific options and the volume traded in such options?
- What is the strike of an option?
- What is the option price? What is the option price change?

Options and Specific Needs

Other options, some of which are not traded, are used to fit specific needs. For example, exotic options such as Bermudan options are used to provide the right to

TABLE 1.3 Put Options (expire at close Friday, June 19, 2009)

Strike	Symbol	Last	Change	Bid	Ask	Volume	Open Interest
60	IBMRL.X	0.05	0	N/A	0.05	10	310
65	IBMRM.X	0.05	0	N/A	0.05	10	15
70	IBMRN.X	0.02	0	N/A	0.05	10	607
75	IBMRO.X	0.05	0	N/A	0.05	50	981
80	IBMRP.X	0.03	0	N/A	0.05	2	1,721
85	IBMRQ.X	0.04	0.01	N/A	0.05	9	1,739
90	IBMRR.X	0.04	0.01	N/A	0.05	44	6,288
95	IBMRS.X	0.06	0.04	0.05	0.15	146	9,461
100	IBMRT.X	0.24	0.11	0.2	0.25	1,177	9,351
105	IBMRA.X	0.9	0.3	0.9	0.95	3,431	9,891
110	IBMRB.X	3.19	0.41	3.2	3.3	977	3,496
115	IBMRC.X	7.4	0.1	7.4	7.6	225	897
120	IBMRD.X	12.2	0.4	12.3	12.5	21	365
125	IBMRE.X	17.3	0	16.9	17.5	4	6
140	IBMRH.X	38.6	0	31.9	32.6	6	10

Source: Yahoo! Finance.

exercise the option at several specific dates during the option lifetime, while Asiatic options define an exercise price for the option as an average of the value attained over a certain time interval. Of course, each option, defined by its specific characteristics, is priced accordingly. In Chapters 8 and 9, options are dealt with in greater detail. Options on bonds as well as options on credit risk portfolios (credit derivatives) are priced in Chapters 9 and 10.

Option prices are defined by the bets exercised by buyers and sellers of options. The prices express option buyers' and sellers' beliefs regarding future market prices of the assets that underlie the options. As a result, these future prices (implied in current option prices) can be used for hedging or for speculating based on beliefs regarding the future prices that option prices reveal (see Chapter 11). Option uses are thus versatile. Some uses include:

- Buying and selling options to hedge a downside risk and to speculate.
- Estimating an underlying asset volatility.
- Motivating management and employees.
- Delaying a tax payment.
- Raising money for investments.

The use of options requires a competent understanding of options theory, financial markets, and financial engineering. Applications are considered next.

EXAMPLE: OPTIONS AND THE PRICE OF EQUITY

The equity value of stockholders is defined by the claims they have on the residual value of the firm—the value remaining once the firm has met its obligations to its debtors, the bondholders. For example, if a firm defaults on its interest payments for a loan, bondholders can force the firm into bankruptcy to recover the loan. A stockholder, a junior claimant in this case, has nothing left to claim. Hence, a bondholder has the right to sell the company at a given threshold or, equivalently, the bondholder holds a put on the value of the firm that the stockholder must hold short. Hence, a stock can be viewed as a claim or option on the value of the firm that is shared with bondholders.

EXAMPLE: MANAGEMENT STOCK OPTIONS

Stock options are granted to managers and consist of options to buy the firm's stock at a given future date and at a given (often very advantageous) price. These rights are granted to align executives' and employees' welfare with that of the shareholders. The rationale for such compensation is to skew executive's income to be heavily dependent on an upward movement of the firm's stock price. As a result, it is believed that executives will be more likely to pursue an aggressive policy leading to a stock price rise, as executives' payoff is a convex increasing function of the stock price. Shareholders will benefit from such a rise but they assume a risk due to the call (stock) option's limited liability granted to the executives. In practice, however, some executives' options payouts occur regardless of the firm's stock performance!

For this reason, stock options remain a much discussed and criticized means of payment to executives.

OPTIONS AND TRADING IN SPECIALIZED MARKETS

Options are traded for many purposes and in many markets. In this section we consider some specific examples such as trading carbon emissions; trading commodities such as metals, gold, silver, corn, oil, or orange juice; trading the weather, which consists in buyers and sellers of weather contracts betting on future temperatures; and so on. A brief introduction to securitization and its uses in marketing MBSs and CDOs (expanded in detail in Chapters 9 and 10) is included as well. Of course, these represent only a very small sample of the many financial products traded in specialized financial markets.

Trading the CO_2 Index

Following the ratification of the Kyoto Protocol agreement on carbon dioxide emission standards, European Union officials created a market for trading pollution credits. They claimed it to be a cost-conscious way to save the planet from global warming. "The results of CO_2 (pollution) trading using a number of optional contracts has not always delivered a cleaner environment however" (*International Herald Tribune*, July 24, 2006, page 10). "I do not suppose the environment has noticed the European emissions trading scheme," said William Blyth, director of Oxford Energy Associates in Oxford, England. The utilities that use CO_2 trading as well as traders and some hedge funds have done very well, though. Further, CO_2 emission contracts have on the whole been very volatile and perhaps irrelevant to improving the quality of the environment and global warming. The *International Herald Tribune* article just cited states further that Open Europe—a policy group that assesses EU laws—claims further that the $44 billion a year market is "an environmental and economic failure." To put it mildly, the jury is still out regarding the efficiency of financial markets for CO_2 emissions.

The U.S. entrance into carbon trading in 2009 introduced further confusion regarding the usefulness of such instruments to manage the quality of the environment. There are numerous explanations for this state of affairs. It is a commonly known fact that the EU was largely tolerant in its distribution of emission standards, signaling a preference for economic activity over environmental stewardship. At the same time, an increase in oil and gas prices in 2005 and 2006 has favored the production of energy by burning coal (which has a direct impact on the price of emission standards). Further, the codependence of energy prices and emission standards combined with governments' intents have induced an appreciable volatility in this market, which was noted by hedge funds and traders who have largely profited from such trades. The future of carbon trading, while presumed to be important in the future, is only at its beginnings today.

Trading on Commodities (Metal, Gold, Silver, Corn, Oil)

Commodity markets originated in the trading of agricultural products in the nineteenth century (cattle, hogs, corn, and wheat were widely traded at that time in the

United States with standard instruments). The need to manage the risks of price fluctuation, driven mostly by variations in supply and demand, has led to the expansion of commodities trades and to the inclusion of other commodities such as gold and silver, soybeans, and energy products (such as crude oil, natural gas, electricity, etc.). There are today 48 major commodity exchanges worldwide that trade more than 96 commodities. The high volatility and high return in this market has recently attracted a wave of new investments to what was previously considered a specialist market. New entrants including hedge funds, financial institutions, and speculators are some of the many parties involved in trading in such markets. In addition, a broad number of instruments are used including forwards, futures, and options of all sorts.

Tradable commodities include:

- *Precious metals*: gold, silver, platinum.
- *Other metals*: nickel, aluminum, copper.
- *Agro-based commodities*: wheat, corn, cotton, oils, oilseeds.
- *Soft commodities*: coffee, cocoa, sugar.
- *Livestock*: live cattle, pork bellies, and so on.
- *Energy*: crude oil, natural gas, gasoline, and so on.

Statistical time series broadly and openly available indicate the extent and the importance as well as the volatility of commodities markets.

Trading the Weather and Insurance

Trading the weather, which is traded on the Chicago Mercantile Exchange (CME), is done by buyers and sellers to hedge their energy- and climate-related costs. Insurance firms use such trades to better manage the risks of their climate-related claims. Typically, weather trade contracts consist in a payout based on certain weather conditions being met over a finite time period. For example, a ski resort could hedge against the risk that less than three inches of snow will fall in February (which would reduce the resort's income). Farmers, theme parks, and gas and power companies are the more important users of weather derivative products.

The first weather derivative contract consisted in a deal for purchasing electric power, in which the price was conditional on the weather of a specific place at a specific time. The CME currently trades weather derivative contracts for 18 cities in the United States, 9 in Europe, 6 in Canada, and 2 in Japan. Heating degree day (HDD) and cooling degree day (CDD) are the underlying quantitative indexes used to measure weather conditions and related to energy consumption—the basis for the most common type of weather derivative.

Securitization, Mortgage-Backed Securities, and Credit Derivatives

Ever since the 1930s, S&Ls have been profiting from a favorable regulation (Regulation Q), which gave them a competitive edge over commercial banks in this financial activity. However, the rise of interest rates in the 1970s made it possible for commercial banks to attract investors by providing better terms than S&Ls. This led to the demise of S&L banks as a preferential means for savings. The mortgage crisis that followed had dramatic consequences on the S&L sector as well as on many savers, which led to the creation in 1968 of the Government National Mortgage Association (GNMA), called Ginnie Mae; the Federal National Mortgage Association (FNMA), known as Fannie Mae; and finally in 1970 the Federal Home Loan Mortgage Corporation (FHLMC), also called Freddie Mac. These institutions, by securing S&L obligations, have made it possible for S&Ls to repackage their liabilities at attractive rates.

The recent 2008 financial meltdown has emphasized that overleveraging and oversecuritization without risk controls can lead to the demise of financial corporate entities, even as large as Freddie Mac and Fannie Mae. Conditions imposed on capital guarantees on such firms—such as a maximal capital assets ratio to loan, or capital to value of the underlying asset—have made it possible to build portfolios of liabilities backed by assets that were subsequently securitized. In this manner, S&Ls were able to reduce their credit (mortgage) risks and reduce their capital requirements, allowing them to augment their loans to home buyers and make more money. In the 1980s these arrangements evolved into what we currently call mortgage-backed securities (MBSs). This has grown since then into an extraordinarily large and active market, in the trillions of dollars. In the United States more than 75 percent of mortgages are in fact securitized. Similar problems arose in England and France as well as in other countries, with the same remedy applied. Thus, MBSs and their derivatives have become an important part of financial trades.

Subsequent to the creation of MBSs, other categories of debt have also been securitized, with new products permanently introduced in financial markets. These instruments have provided loans to home buyers at generous terms and have at the same time generated large fees for the lending institutions. For some, the financial debacle of 2008 is due essentially to the uncontrolled proliferation of these contracts. Chapters 9 and 10 consider such contracts at length.

REAL-LIFE CRISES AND FINANCE

The ARS Crisis

Auction-rated securities (ARSs) are financial instruments renegotiated at regular intervals of time (a week, a month) through an auction of buyers and sellers (holders of the securities) to determine the contracted rates of return that such securities will pay. The intent of such securities is to provide liquidity to the buyers and sellers even though these are usually securities secured by terms spanning long periods of time. For example, to reduce the high cost of municipal bonds, municipalities have used ARSs to reduce their borrowing costs. They do so by pegging the security to a short-term spot interest rate (since the interest payment is determined each time the auction is taken). This seems to be a win-win for buyers and sellers, but important problems can arise. In mid-February 2008, sellers overwhelmed potential buyers, causing widespread auction failures for the first time:

> *The magnitude of the liquidity crunch that developed as a result of auction failures was not expected given that the market has operated smoothly for almost 25 years. Despite the relatively strong credit quality of the underlying*

collateral, the pronounced imbalance of sellers to buyers has overwhelmed all other considerations.
    —CITI Smith Barney, "Fixed Income Securities," February 29, 2008

Problems thus arose owing to the lack of liquidity, not because of a rise in default risk. This has created many other problems (through diffusion-contagion and market dependencies, introduced in Chapter 4).

The Banking–Money System Crisis

The credit and liquidity crisis of 2008–2009 was extremely harmful, threatening the future of financial institutions and the banking system constructed so laboriously over many years. This system is based on the fiduciary trust granted to banks by depositors and governments to oversee the supply of money and to be in a position to redeem depositors' claims. For some, this trust was violated, leading to a near breakdown of our financial system and to the dire credit liquidity crisis of 2009. The subsequent Troubled Asset Relief Program (TARP) support to banks, a massive influx of government funds into financial markets to stimulate some liquidity and credit, has only been a short-run measure, with the fracture of finance as its essential long-run concern.

Such problems are not a new phenomenon, however. James Macdonald (*Financial Times*, March 7, 2009, p. 13) recalled a similar story, from 1719 to 1720 in France, involving the king's default on his finances (a notorious recurring problem). Its effects, like today, were a high followed by a dramatic low and loss of confidence. It started with a public debt of 100 percent of the national income in 1714 and was subjected to forced reductions of principal and interest. Confidence collapsed; government paper sold for discounts of up to 75 percent and the economy was in recession (as was the case in 2008). To face these problems, a Scot, John Law, suggested that debt be exchanged for shares in the Compagnie des Indes (a French corporation for the Americas, called also the Mississippi Company [MC], which owned all rights for economic exchanges between France and the Americas). He proposed that the government issue a new series of bonds on the company, paying 3 percent in exchange for its old debts, which had paid 4 to 5 percent. In this manner, service charges of the debt would be reduced.

However, the MC was an empty shell at that time, generating no profits. To stimulate activity in these worthless shares, John Law introduced *securitization* and activated it in as many trades as possible in shares of the MC. These trades led to the historic MC bubble. John Law's plan succeeded, and the French debt was sold, which seemed far more profitable but was based on a credit-driven bubble due to the MC which, in the end, had to default. This default created an economic problem, and it took a great many years for France to recover from it. The dramatic default resulted in losses and a loss of liquidity, as this was the case recently. It was at this time that the term *millionaire* was coined. Law used such a term to describe his investors at the top of the bubble, although he died penniless and a fugitive a few years after being arguably the most powerful man in the world!

The effects of a breakdown in liquidity and a fractured finance are in fact very important and a key source of collateral risk to other sectors, including the real economic sector, with GDP growth rates and consumer spending affected. In such an environment, a financial crisis has been nurtured by financial markets and by the fear factor (measured by the VIX index, a volatility index). This has resulted in the threat of deflation, a lack of trust in financial institutions, and consumers keeping their money rather than consuming or investing. These factors were understood by central bankers who sought to reduce interest rates to stimulate spending and provide greater liquidity (by tax repayments to consumers, by augmenting central banks' lending to financial institutions, etc.). For example, the European Central Bank, citing "tensions in the euro money market," injected more than $130 billion in August 9, 2009, in the type of emergency operation that had not been conducted since the aftermath of the September 2001 terrorist attacks.

The *Wall Street Journal* (March 8–9, 2008, p. B14), for example, laid some of the blame for the losses of some banks on extremely poor financial risk man-agement due to amateurish management blunders, and on the greed of bankers who appropriated the majority of corporate profits while acting only as interme-diaries in the process of real wealth creation. The big losers did not have effective firmwide systems for collecting data about their risks. They allowed business heads too much leeway in setting and enforcing risk limits, and didn't work to break down bureaucratic barriers that kept bad news from flowing upward. This resulted in busi-nesses focusing on immediate profits and ignoring consequences. At best, techniques based on static value at risk (VaR) models (see Chapter 3) and external ratings (see Chapter 9) were used to direct their actions, rather than a deeper understand-ing of credit risk derivatives. As a result, even when the dimensions of the crisis were revealed, it was too late to do anything about it. Errors were thus made, not only due to quants' analyses and the existence of derivatives that had made it all possible, but essentially due to greed, a lack of appropriate regulation to mitigate the misdeeds of financial markets, ignoring and misusing the basic elements of risk management.

THE 2008 MELTDOWN AND FINANCIAL THEORY

The meltdown of Lehman Brothers and AIG, the Wall Street liquidity crisis of 2008, and their extraordinary subsequent fallouts are probably the most significant and catastrophic financial events since the Wall Street Crash of 1929. While many expla-nations and reasons are yet unfolding, it is mostly agreed that financial markets and some financial processes were functioning under economic and financial assumptions that could not be sustained. This raised challenging theoretical problems to reconcile the financial and economic dogma (or the efficient market hypothesis, developed further in subsequent chapters) with financial practice. While some critics may have overreacted against the theory of finance, there remain some concerns. Ten of these concerns are as follows:

1. *Equilibrium.* The stable economic equilibrium implied in financial pricing and analysis has turned out to be fool's gold. The assumptions used in financial theory based on stable financial markets equilibrium may have been overly restrictive. The question is, are financial markets defined by a stable equilibrium, or is a dynamic equilibrium process with cyclical booms and busts more appropriate?

Answers to such a question will necessarily pit the conventional financial dogma against theories that have yet to be developed.

2. *Future implications.* The credit and liquidity crisis characterizing the financial meltdown of 2008–2009 has important implications to the future of finance. What are the theoretical and practical implications? How does liquidity affect the pricing process? The financial meltdown has revealed that economically viable assets became almost worthless due to a lack of liquidity! Two types of liquidity articulated by the Basel Committee on Bank Supervision are the *funding liquidity risk* of a firm unable to meet its obligations, and *market liquidity risk*, denoting the risk that a firm cannot offset a position or eliminate a position at the market price because of inadequate market depth or market disruption (Golub and Crum 2010). Liquidity, in particular, rather than being a firm-specific problem has been shown to be a common risk that can ignite default contagions and dislocation of financial market prices.

3. *Finance and complexity.* Ashby's second law of cybernetics essentially states that complexity can be managed only if regulators and controllers are more astute than the managers and processes they seek to manage (Ashby 1964). This in turn stimulates increased innovation and greater complexity and thereby contributes to a vicious cycle of complexity growth. The end result: Either financial managers or their regulators are overwhelmed. While simplicity and transparency would clearly be helpful rules for financial risk management in a complex world, one may argue for the opposite case. On the one hand, there is an apparent need for more regulation to protect investors and restore fiduciary trust in the banking system. On the other hand, financial managers have always found the means to circumvent financial regulation. This is particularly the case in a financial multipolar system, with financial centers and capitals competing with each other to attract capital. In addition, when markets are functioning well, asset prices (due to arbitrage) tend toward their intrinsic value. However, arbitrage depends on the presence of expert investors who actually know what the intrinsic value is. When markets falter, either experts do not know the intrinsic value or, even if they know, their positions may entail extremely large losses due to contagious behavior and a breakdown in financial market liquidity. For this reason, in complex markets, when the intrinsic price is very difficult to determine, there will actually be few experts trading, and thus the market will be dramatically reduced (see also Chapter 10).

4. *Financial intermediation.* Many financial institutions have become marketers while owning all the know-how and information regarding financial products and markets. This has created situations where all counterparty risks (moral hazard and adverse selection, introduced in Chapter 6) are held by consumers/investors while these same institutions hang on to all the profits. These have led to a large collection of corrupt practices, legalized insider trading, and the extraordinary heist that financial institutions were able to embark on with no threat of punitive action. These situations may in the future require a careful restructuring of financial products and their regulation to ensure they are *ethically green*. While greed can hardly be constrained willingly, greed prevention may be embedded in the manners in which financial products and transactions are made and managed. For example, if financial transactions can be made transparent and all parties involved in such transactions maintain a stake in them,

financial responsibility may be maintained across the financial supply chain that bridges the gap between those needing money for some productive ends and investors—the suppliers of funds.

5. *Integrated financial risk management.* Industrial enterprises have in these past decades undergone a revolution in the manner in which they manage quality, moving from controls to prevention and on to incentive-based prevention and robust design. Equivalently, such a revolution is being felt and needed in banking and other financial institutions seeking to unwind the complexity of financial products and financial markets while adopting an integrated view of financial risk management processes focused on the multiple and dependent risks financial institutions face (see Chapter 4).

6. *Globalization and finance's multipolarity.* Globalization in financial markets, unlike industrial globalization, cannot be managed or controlled by edicts, even if they are made by the strongest nation on earth. Money flows where it is most prized. A policy that does not recognize this fact is likely to fail. Further, the growth of global economies has led in parallel to the growth of financial markets and their numbers. As each has its own systems, cultural values, and regulation, this growth may result in competitive financial markets that are difficult to regulate.

7. *Complex financial products and insurance finance.* Complex financial and securitized products such as CDOs, and the like, are indeed intricate and cannot be treated routinely like securities of specific industrial enterprises (see Chapter 10). Further, the central role of insurance in marketing (i.e., to augment financial liquidity) has revealed that insurance finance has become an essential part of the market-making process. In a financial world where both buyers and sellers seek a flight from risk, without insurance, buyers and sellers of such products would be reluctant to assume the liquidity, market, and counterparty risks that such products carry. By the same token, rating of financial firms and products is both partial (and therefore misleading) and too slow in responding to major and sudden shifts in the economic environment of firms. In other words, there is an acute information and claim risk to raters' pronouncements in time of crisis.

8. *Intervention in financial markets.* The belief that markets are self-stabilizing has also turned out to be fool's gold. Rather, a new neo-financial Keynesian belief and practice has set in, calling for an active role of a national policy in managing as well as regulating financial markets and institutions. Issues such as *too big to fail* (Taleb and Tapiero 2010); the moral hazard implication of rescuing failed financial firms, and so forth, remain both an economic and a political problem. Restoring trust in the banking system and financial markets has, however, been the focus of the United States' and other nations' policies.

9. *Financial measurement.* Variability-like measurements (such as returns' standard deviations and their quantile value at risk effects, outlined in Chapter 3) have been found useless when struck by *black swans*, those rare and unpredictable events that nevertheless recur (Taleb 2007a, 2007b). As a result, financial risk management based on such measurements has proved to be insufficient, calling for an alternative approach embedded in processes, seeking to be in tune and integrated in the financial trading and speculation process without necessarily stifling the creativity and profitability of risk taking.

10. *Management's risk and moral hazard.* Last but not least, the economic and liberal financial theories that have contributed immensely to the economic and social welfare of modern societies are now challenged to compensate for the growth of biased financial intermediation, economic and financial behavior out of equilibrium, and off-equilibrium financial transactions and processes that have a negative social value (for example, contributing to social inequalities, hijacking of corporate profits by the few at the expense of the many, etc.). The persistent and extraordinary profits that financial institutions have made and the bonuses taken by lead bankers and traders in both good and bad times may have evoked social concerns whose effects on financial markets can yet trigger unpredictable reactions.

The credit crisis of 2008 has thus forced financial parties and institutions to rethink the current state of financial theories and their practice as well as realign financial risk management with the *reality* of finance and not its implied prices and processes only. In particular, behavioral finance, based on an observed rationality of decision makers and a return to expected utility with calibrated models consistent with the EMH, is providing preliminary approaches to reconcile real facts with the theoretical constructs of finance.

FINANCE AND ETHICS

> *Ethical considerations can only legitimately appear when the truth has been ascertained: they can and should appear determining our feeling towards the truth, and our manner of ordering our lives in view of the truth, but not as themselves dictating what the truth is to be.*
> —Bertrand Russel

Economic and financial decisions are about rational choices, often derived from values, culture, and politics. For example, is more (money) always better? Are the proper objectives of firms to maximize their profits and stock prices? If the attainment of self-satisfaction is socially condoned in our culture, then how can one question those entrepreneurs who do improve their lot? Is the credo of more money for executives at any cost ethical? By the same token, is wholly or partly fraudulent risk transfer to other investors ethical? Answer to these and related questions are not obvious, for ethical values (in their mild form) are often the product of our personal values, our tolerance, our social acceptance, and our inability to measure, audit, and control financial processes and their consequences. Financial risk consequences that are not assumed by their perpetrators are risk externalities. Voluntary compliance to prevent such risks and/or assume responsibility for them underlies ethical behavior, while risk perpetrators profiting from opportunities while consequences are assumed by other parties is unethical. For these reasons, in order to compel perpetrators to assume their responsibilities and compensate for their behavior, financial regulation is needed.

Do issues of partial information, insider trading, risk taking, and market power by some imply behavior that is not ethical? If speculators and profit takers assume the risks of their actions, there is no reason to claim that their profits were not ethical. Without such speculators, willing to assume risks, no market can be efficient. However, if financial managers assume extraordinary risks but not, at the same time, their consequences, then there is a strong case to believe that this is unethical behavior. When such managers are celebrated as financial heroes because of the size of their returns, it may reflect the values of a society that celebrates winners who take all, whether ethical or not.

For example, the *New York Times* (December 29, 2009, Front Page) relates that a mortgage-based security called Abacus, launched when the real estate market became unglued, was created to make money for Goldman Sachs in case the market were to turn sour. Goldman, in selling Abacus shares to its clients, made millions while its clients lost billions on securities they believed were solid investments (according to former Goldman employees with direct knowledge of the deal, who asked not to be identified because they have confidentiality agreements with the firm). Are such behaviors, engaged in by other financial firms, ethical? Are they legal? These are questions that financial managers are confronted with daily on trading floors and in managing other people's money. They underlie fundamental questions regarding what is and what is not ethical behavior. If financial and economic choices are measured in terms of one's own interests only (as some economic theories support), irrespective of their consequences for others, would such pursuits be ethical or not?

These questions highlight many of the issues we deal with when evaluating financial institutions and their executives' pay. For example, are the extraordinary profits realized by Goldman Sachs ethical? Is the pursuit of profits combining self- and conflicting interest justified by such an august institution? Of course, these are relative matters: Goldman Sachs may turn out to be a hero for some and a villain to others, based on their assessment that no risk assumed by such large financial institutions can (or ought to) provide such returns. Insider trading is strongly regulated with penalties designed to impede those who have the opportunity to profit when they ought not to profit. Thus, in this context, unethical behavior would be clearly defined by the laws that regulate financial transactions. Such laws also ought to reflect responsibility for intended or unintended consequences. For example, does a polluter at sea assume responsibility for his actions? And if not, what are the laws of the sea that can be drafted and applied to such an unethical attitude by polluters so that they stop the acts whose consequences they do not assume responsibility for?

But these ethical and nonethical behaviors imply far more. They are complicated further by the growth of multinational and global corporate firms that have no national authority to respond to, or no accounting standards (and at times no values) to comply with. Some attempts are being made to mitigate this state of affairs by promoting international collaboration in regulating financial and other enterprises. For example, the International Federation of Accountants (IFAC) sought to set global accounting standards and recognizes the conceptual impossibility of creating one set of standards for a diverse world. Alternative standards might be discussed; ethics education, assurance, and a convergence of cross-boundary standards and regulation might be helpful in resolving the problems of accounting. However, in multicultural and complex global markets and firms, these problems are likely to remain daunting.

Of course, more courageous whistle-blowing by both corporate employees and the media would be helpful. This would point to excesses, facilitate better predictions, and open the way for an educated analysis of firms' or analysts' deviant behaviors. These occurrences of whistle-blowing are likely to remain outliers rather than the norm and might even produce a plethora of false-alarm whistle-blowers with their own specific agendas. For example, while intense attention is given to manipulations of derivatives accounting, making it possible for some transactions to be opaque (and, as a result, direct huge profits to executives at the expense of shareholders and firms), these same derivatives ethically and properly used contribute hugely to financial risk management, economic efficiency, and financing for solutions to many of the outstanding social challenges of our day.

Crime and Punishment

Ken Lay and Jeffrey Skilling (Enron), Martha Stewart (Living Omnimedia), Bernard Ebbers (WorldCom), Dennis Kozlowski (Tyco), Richard Scrushy (HealthSouth), Frank Quattrone (Credit Suisse First Boston), Fannie Mae (the government-sponsored mortgage company), Bernie Madoff (the huge Ponzi scheme), and so many others are outstanding cases that have garnered media attention in 2000–2008. Such attention often turns into frenzy, seeking to remind corporate executives that crime does not pay. These are difficult lessons, however, for in finance, *crime* is often ill defined and the punishment is often a reflection of a financial ethic that is subject to the tunes of the times.

For example, when does personal information become an insider trading advantage? Inversely, would an investor, a hedge fund trader, or a market specialist trade on stock information he alone possessed, or only on common knowledge? Are arbitrageurs' decisions based on a strategy or on an appreciation, acquired by various means, that there are opportunities to profit from or due to mispricing and partial information? If financial markets are efficient, then there can be no profits without risk. In this case, why would a risk-averse investor invest in these efficient markets? If your tax rate (federal, state, and city) is 50 percent of your profits and risk-free (banking) rates are 1 percent with an inflation rate of 3 percent, what can you do legally with your investments? There is very little one can do unless one assumes financial risks. The assumption of financial risk by investors is therefore inherent to all financial activities.

These are limits that ethics and finance must confront, however, in order to establish a proper code of behavior—defined by a number of laws and regulations—that can be sustained by businesses and productive firms. Since the Enron verdict, which found Chairman Kenneth Lay and CEO Jeff Skilling guilty of wrongdoing, both the media and concerned readers have expressed widely differing views. Some claim that tolerance of unethical practices has led to excesses that financial markets, investors, and businesses cannot sustain. Some of the issues raised reveal an extraordinary complexity. Are accounting rules doing what they are assumed to do? Can accounting firms maintain their clients while at the same time not meeting their demands? Are accounting scandals imposing too big a burden on businesses that have to conform to new regulations? Can excessive controls impose costs on firms that would render them noncompetitive compared to foreign and unregulated firms? Are such firms likely to migrate to some markets and countries that are not subject to such regulation? A lesson learned from Enron demise has been that many of the machinations that allowed the company to book false profits, create cash flow out of thin air and hide billions of dollars of debt were at least arguably legal—hence they'd done nothing wrong. As often as not, Enron stretched accounting rules, contorted them, twisted them to its own obvious end, but didn't actually break them. And many of the things Enron did that were illegal were extremely difficult to explain, because they had to do with arcane accounting rules.

In fact, most businesses do behave in an ethical manner, conforming to the law and to codes of ethical behavior. The reaffirmation of an ethical code of finance is the essential message that U.S. courts sent to corporations across America: that the line between properly acquired profits and improperly acquired profits can be thin!

The punishments to be met by those who would not comply are both lessons and a warning. Bernard Ebbers was found guilty of an $11 billion fraud that led the company to bankruptcy; he was sentenced to 25 years in prison. Dennis Kozlowski was convicted of looting Tyco of $150 million and was sentenced to 8.5 to 25 years—and not allowed out on bail. Martha Stewart was found guilty of lying to federal investigators looking into her sale of ImClone stock in December 2001. She spent five months in prisons, while her financial loss following her conviction was immeasurably larger than the few dollars profit she had accrued via insider trading. Richard Scrushy was accused of being involved in a $2.7 billion accounting fraud (although a federal jury in 2005 found the former chief executive not guilty on all charges). Frank Quattrone, battling charges of obstruction of justice, was exonerated. Fannie Mae, which had repeatedly overstated its profits, has been fined $400 million and has agreed to a list of restrictions and reforms. Fannie Mae's main regulator found that the company had overstated its profits consistently between 1998 and 2004 so that its bosses qualified for bigger bonuses: Of the $92 million paid to Franklin Raines, the then chief executive, $52 million was linked to profit targets. To accomplish this, it used political influence and applied shoddy controls and accounting practices In 2009, Bernie Madoff, the ex-president of NASDAQ, the swindler of the century, with a $65 billion Ponzi scheme, who has swindled so many individuals and firms—financial and others, with incalculable damage—is now in jail for the rest of his life. These punishments are forerunners of an increased intolerance of excesses that seeks to convey a louder and clearer message: that *ethics in finance does matter*.

SUMMARY

Risk can be found everywhere. It is omnipresent whenever we invest in securities or manage any resources, financial or otherwise. Risk is affected by the behavior of both traders and investors who interact in a financial market, leading to the establishment of the prices at which commodities, securities, and other risk-bearing assets are traded. Ethical and moral behavior is needed for market efficiency to be sustainable, and it has important effects on the risks we all (rather than a select few) assume and the price at which assets can or ought to be traded. The field of risk finance seeks to price these risks and at the same time to manage their adverse effects.

In this chapter, we considered some basic financial instruments (stocks, bonds, derivatives, real assets, and portfolios) that are needed to carry out financial investment and hedging and to price financial and real assets. In addition, a number of outstanding problems have been defined to motivate exploration and pinpoint some of the special problems this book seeks to focus on.

TEST YOURSELF

1.1　Evaluating risk:
　　a. Why is it important to price risk?
　　b. Why is it important for a CFO to manage risk?
　　c. Name five types of risk you have encountered in your life.
　　d. Name five risks a chief financial officer might be confronted with.
　　e. What are financial managers assumed to do?
　　f. Name three financial intermediaries, define what they do, and explain how they intermediate and between whom.

1.2　What are securities, bonds, and options? How do they differ?

1.3　What are call and put options? How do they differ?

1.4　Why do we need to *value* assets? Why do we need to price a financial asset, and why it is important? How do valuation and pricing differ?

1.5　What are risk sharing and risk pooling, and how do they differ? How do insurance firms use risk pooling, and how do they share risks with insureds and with reinsurance firms?

1.6　What is a hedge fund, and how does it differ from an investment bank?

1.7　What are currency exchange rates?

1.8　What does a security price stand for?

1.9　What are the differences and the similarities between the insurance, businesses and investment and banking?

1.10　What is a rare event, and how does it differ from a normal event? Why are rare events so important in risk management?

1.11　What are environmental risks? How do they differ from a personal risk? How do environmental risks differ from and how are they similar to financial risks?

1.12　What are the effects of genetic testing on individuals relative to insurance? What are the implications of personalized DNA profiles on health insurance?

1.13　All the following institutions are involved in the risk business. Explain how they are similar and how they differ:
　　a. Insurance firms.
　　b. Pension funds.
　　c. Banks.
　　d. Equity funds.
　　e. Brokerage houses.
　　f. Mortgage banks.
　　g. Savings and loan banks.
　　h. Hedge funds.
　　i. Investment-hedge funds.
　　j. Lloyd's of London.
　　k. Reinsurers.

1.14 What are the problems in pricing risk events that are rare but have catastrophic consequences?

1.15 What are the problems in managing asset risks that are (1) very, (2) somewhat, and (3) mildly correlated?

REFERENCES

American Institute of Certified Public Accountants. 2001. [AICPA], July 21.
Arrow, K. J. 1951. Alternative approaches to the theory of choice in risk-taking situations. *Econometrica*, October.
———. 1965. *Aspects of the theory of risk-bearing*. Helsinki: Yrjo Jahnssonin Säätiö.
———. 1971. *Essays in the theory of risk bearing*. Chicago: Markham.
———. 1982. Risk perception in psychology and in economics. *Economics Inquiry* (January): 1–9.
Ashby, W. R. 1964. *An introduction to cybernetics*. London: University Paperbacks.
Bachelier, L. 1900. *Théorie de la spéculation*. Paris: Thèse de Mathématique.
Basel Committee on Bank Supervision. 2008. http://www.bis.org/bcbs/.
Bernoulli, D. 1954. Exposition of a new theory on the measurement of risk. *Econometrica*, January.
Black, F., and M. Scholes. 1973. The pricing of options and corporate liabilities. *Journal of Political Economy* 81:637–659.
Borch, K. H. 1968. *The economics of uncertainty*. Princeton, NJ: Princeton University Press.
Bouchaud, J. P., and M. Potters. 1997. *Théorie des risques financiers*. Eyrolles, Saclay, France.
Carr, M., and S. Kishan. 2006. EU pollution plan turns into "playground." *International Herald Tribune*. July 24, p. 10.
CITI Smith Barney. 2008. "Fixed Income Securities," February 29.
Cootner, P. H. 1964. *The random character of stock prices*. Cambridge, MA: MIT Press.
Cramer, H. 1955. *Collective risk theory*. Jubilee volume. Skandia Insurance Company, Stockholm, Sweden.
Duffie, D. 1988. *Security markets: Stochastic models*. New York: Academic Press.
Duffie, D. 1992. *Dynamic asset pricing theory*. Princeton, NJ: Princeton University Press.
———. 1965. The behavior of stock market prices. *Journal of Business* 38:34–105.
———. 1970. Efficient capital markets: A review of theory and empirical work. *Journal of Finance* 25 (2):383–417.
Federal Bureau of Investigation (FBI). 2006. Mortgage Fraud Report. www.fbi.gov/publications/fraud/mortgage_fraud06.htm#6.
———. 2007. Mortgage Fraud Report. www.fbi.gov/publications/fraud/mortgage_fraud07.htm#6.
———. 2008. Year in Review. www.fbi.gov/publications/fraud/mortgage_fraud08.htm#6.
Financial Times. 2009. By James Macdonald, March 7, 13.
Golub, B., and C. C. Crum. 2010. Risk management lessons worth remembering from the credit crisis of 2007–2009. Working paper, Blackrock, January 9.
Hull, J. 1993. *Options, futures and other derivatives securities*. 2nd ed. Englewood Cliffs, NJ: Prentice Hall.
Ingersoll, J. E. Jr. 1987. *Theory of financial decision making*. Totowa, NJ: Rowman and Littlefield.
Jarrow, R. A. 1988. *Finance theory*. Englewood Cliffs, NJ: Prentice Hall.
Jaynes, E. T. 1957a. Information theory and statistical mechanics. *Physical Review* 106:620.
———. 1957b. Information theory and statistical mechanics II. *Physical Review* 108:171.

Lowenstein, R. 2000. *When genius failed: The rise and fall of Long Term Capital Management.* New York: Random House.

Lucas, R. E. 1978. Asset prices in an exchange economy. *Econometrica* 46:1429–1445.

Markowitz, Harry M. 1959. *Portfolio selection: Efficient diversification of investments.* New York: John Wiley & Sons.

Merton, R. C. 1990. *Continuous time finance.* Cambridge, MA: Blackwell.

Modigliani, F., and M. Miller. 1958. The cost of capital and the theory of investment. *American Economic Review.*

Morgenson, G. 2009. Banks bundled debt, bet against it and won. *New York Times* [Business/Financial Desk], December 29.

Muth, J. 1961. Rational expectations and the theory of price movements. *Econometrica* 29:315–335.

Peter, Edgar E. 1995. *Chaos and order in capital markets.* New York: John Wiley & Sons.

Pliska, S. 1986. A stochastic calculus model of continuous trading: Optimal portfolios. *Mathematics of Operations Research* 11:371–382.

Raiffa, H., and R. Schlaiffer. 1961. *Applied statistical decision theory.* Boston: Harvard University, Division of Research, Graduate School of Business.

Samuelson, Paul A. 1963. Risk and uncertainty: A fallacy of large numbers. *Scientia* 98:108–163.

Sargent, T. J. 1979. *Macroeconomic theory.* New York: Academic Press.

Sharpe, W. F. 1964. Capital asset prices: A theory of market equilibrium under risk. *Journal of Finance* 19:425–442.

Taleb, N. 2007a. *The black swan: The impact of the highly improbable.* New York: Random House.

———. 2007b. Black swans and the domain of statistics. *American Statistician* 61:1–3.

Taleb, N., and C. S. Tapiero. 2010. Risk externalities and too big to fail. *Physica A* 389: 3503–3507.

Tapiero, C. S. 1988. *Applied stochastic models and control in management.* Amsterdam/New York: North-Holland.

———. 1998. *Applied stochastic models and control in finance and insurance.* Boston: Kluwer Academic Press.

———. 2004. *Risk and financial management: Mathematical and computational concepts.* Hoboken, NJ: John Wiley & Sons.

Tett, G. 2009. *Fool's gold.* New York: Free Press.

Wall Street Journal (Eastern edition). 2008. Japan's reserves top $1 trillion. March 8, B14.

CHAPTER 2

Applied Finance

OVERVIEW

This chapter provides a motivation for specific problems and issues that are considered throughout the book. Topics covered include insurance and finance; pricing and investing in securities (but also real investments such as in infrastructure, and their price); finance and the environment; finance and your pension fund; finance and the pricing of contracts (for example, a franchise contract); finance and the price of reliability and safety; and so forth. A retrospective evolution of financial theories and their application (most of which have garnered Nobel Prizes for their authors) is also presented. Finally, this chapter broadly outlines the extraordinary technological developments that are contributing to a growth of virtual financial enterprises, virtual markets, electronic trading, and the evolution of financial virtual universes that seem to usher in a new financial order. This chapter is mostly nonquantitative. Subsequent chapters are more specific and more technical.

FINANCE AND PRACTICE

Finance practice spans an extensive number of problems and issues, some of which are concerned with the question "At what price would we be willing to buy or sell an asset?" What is the market price? How can we manage and insure investment risks?

Risk Finance and Insurance

Insurance is used to substitute payments now for potential losses (to be reimbursed) later. It is based on a contractual agreement with one party (the insured) seeking to insure against part or all of a risk of loss by paying a premium to another party (the insurer). Such an exchange is based on both the preferences and information of the parties to the contract (insured and insurer, investors). Insurance firms, in addition, have capitalized on the pooling of risks and their financial management (by securitization, for example) to reduce their consequences (and thus their price) and increase their ability to bear risk. This is how markets for fire, theft, casualty, and life insurance, as well as health and unemployment insurance, have come to be as important as they are today. It is because of persons', investors', and firms' desires for *certainty* and to avoid too great a loss (even with small probabilities) that financial insurance contracts (based on various formulas for risk sharing) have expanded into a broad variety of specialized firms dealing in insurance (such as reinsurance, insurance brokers, etc.). Further, the growth of insurance as a counterparty to risk-averse financial institutions, trading in derivatives and risk-prone assets, has become essential for the sustenance of financial markets. Without such an insurance counterparty (part of which is assumed by hedge funds, however), a financial market that provides an opportunity to trade and exchange might not be possible. (See Chapter 10.)

The traditional approach to insurance is based on actuarial science—seeking to measure and calculate real risks, their statistical characteristics, and their consequences. However, a convergence of insurance and finance is contributing to the growth of financial insurance products. For example, the use of put options in financial trades (see Chapter 8) allows traders to limit their losses. In other cases, securitization of insurance portfolios (consisting in buying and selling incoming premium payments and insurance claims losses) has allowed a transfer of risk from individual banks to financial markets. As a result, some financial products have become broadly traded with their associated risks borne by insurance firms, while some insurance portfolios have also been securitized with some of the risks transferred to financial markets (see Chapter 10 on credit derivatives). The convergence of insurance and finance is thus leading to insurance being far more in tune with financial markets by augmenting significantly the expansion and scope of financial credit risks and their derivatives (Chapters 9 and 10).

Insurance is mostly based on sharing and shifting risks to some willing agent, and depends on insured behavior. For this reason, insurance firms use incentives to mitigate the insured's personal risk taking. For example, car insurance rates tend to be linked to a person's past driving record, leading to the use of *bonus-malus* (i.e., based on good and bad experience) insurance contracts. What is the price of such incentive contracts to insureds, and do they have a market price? Certain clients (or clients in certain geographical areas) might be classified as *high-risk* clients, required to pay higher insurance fees (the insurance risk premium), while others may be classified as low-risk and have correspondingly low fees. Inequities in insurance rates occur, however, because of an imperfect knowledge of the probabilities of loss and due to asymmetric information between insureds and insurers, resulting in a nonrational exchange of risk. These exchanges entail risks we call *moral hazard* and *adverse selection* risks (see Chapter 6). For example, situations may occur when fire insurance policies will be written for unprofitable plants, leading the managers of the overinsured plant to be unmotivated in preventing loss through fire. By the same token, universal health care insurance costs may turn out to be higher for those who are rich and able to pay more to subsidize those who are unable to pay. Such situations may counter the basic understanding of what we mean by a *fair* price for insurance, and thus are the subject of careful social and business scrutiny. While these issues are difficult to deal with in a purely financial context, the financial input of such insurance is essential to the sustainability of any health care insurance plan.

Infrastructure Finance

Local and regional authorities, municipalities, developing countries, and other governmental entities are increasingly seeking to tap financial markets to raise the resources required for their projects and infrastructures. Traditionally, infrastructure investments have been the domain of governments, with utilities acting as nationalized firms (or under full government control). This is changing, both because of a lack of public funds needed for such projects, technologies that have contributed to reduce natural monopolies in infrastructures, and the size and sophistication of financial products. Further, a growth of credit and debt instruments of various sorts (see Chapters 9 and 10) create more dollars in search of fewer investment alternatives. Market pricing and the marketing of infrastructure returns and risks have also made it possible to invest rationally in infrastructures, based on economic principles rather than ideological or political intent. At the same time, this has led to a growth of available funds for countries that do not have well-developed financial markets.

These developments are important, providing a greater opportunity to create a better life for more people and provide profitable financial opportunities. Governments such as France have also recognized that power monopolies are not sustainable and that unbundling of utilities services and their securitization is an economic necessity for their future growth and development within the EU framework. This practice is also pursued in other countries by outright complete or partial divestiture (privatization), selected stock issues, and other means that contribute to the liquidity of their assets. Infrastructure investments are not limited to power and energy only. Transportation, environmental quality, education, and a broad array of income-producing and social projects are the recipients of financial resources originating in local and global financial markets.

Finance, the Environment, and Exchange-Traded Funds Indexes

A clean environment costs money. Pollution abatement, energy-efficient products (such as environmentally friendly cars), recycling, and reengineering for a sustainable environment require investments. Financial markets have recognized that these investments are also financial opportunities for firms to retool environmentally derived industries. To share in such prospective profits, an exchange-traded fund (ETF) index, such as the Global Energy Innovation Index (GEIX), for example, was set up to allow investors to speculate and share in *environmental finance* investments. The GEIX is a currency-neutral financial index monitoring quoted companies in renewable energy and energy technology. It consists of 50 companies quoted on the world's major stock markets which derive at least half of their value from activities in renewable energy or low-carbon energy technology. Capitalization of these companies is in the tens of billions of dollars and is believed to have unlimited prospective opportunities. Both conservative investors, funds of various sorts, private equity, and other companies are increasingly interested in such indexes in order to profit from a prospective growth in *green innovation* (Bloomberg, www.newenergyfinance.com). The GEIX has at times performed far better than, say, the S&P index, providing far greater returns.

Of course, events such as oil at over $130, recurring weather disasters, the prospect of climate change, carbon emissions regulation and trading, and others have contributed to the financial activity in firms relating to renewable energy or firms that consume much energy. These along with other issues such as regulation, investment credits, new technologies (in wind, solar, ethanol), carbon credits and trading, and more, are opening opportunities. The success of these ventures will be amplified if they can be priced and traded to tap the resources required for their expansion. For example, if investors assume that the quality of the environment will be increasingly regulated and polluting firms penalized ever more, the price of carbon credits is likely to grow. Predictions for such markets are extremely difficult at this time, though. For example, the Kyoto Protocol, focusing on clean energy (renewable energy, energy efficiency, and switching to cleaner fuels), came into effect at the end of February 2005, with a volatile stock market effect on renewable energy technologies. The Kyoto Protocol depends, however, on global collaboration and an agreement between developed and undeveloped countries.

Finance and Your Pension

Pensions collateralized to financial market prices are becoming important because governments all over the world (as well as large corporate firms such as General Motors) are no longer willing or able to assume the obligations that pension payments entail. The post–World War II practice of pay-as-you-go (PAYGO) pension, where one generation assumes responsibility for the preceding one, has also reached a breaking point with aging postwar generations and the adoption of liberal political values, letting each one reach decisions that best suit individual needs.

Further, increasingly long indebtedness by governments (as is the case in the United States and as we have observed in the Euro-Greek crisis of 2010) may induce governments to spend less and increase the pressure to reduce pension payments. Individuation of pension funds associated to equity-linked or savings and assets indexation insured by large insurance firms may thus evolve to be part of your future pension. Modern attitudes toward pension planning presume that either no authority has the means to assume pension liabilities or that each of us knows best. One way or another, each potential pensioner must by necessity become financially savvy and understand the implications of his financial decisions, for both the short term and the long haul.

In line with pension schemes reappraisal, pension funds are reassessing their investment policies, which fall into three essential categories:

1. Market capitalization, with the current trend allowing a greater part to be invested in stocks.
2. Investment in fixed income and bonds, both drawn upon large firms or governments.
3. Investment in a broader class of fixed assets, in contrast to previous investment primarily in real estate.

Trends in pension fund portfolios, moving increasingly away from fixed (risk-free) investments toward securities, financial derivatives, and real estate investments, are also demanding greater competence in financial engineering. At the same time, pension funds are attempting to deal with a changing actuarial profile of their insureds, including, for example, their life expectancy, health care costs, savers' personal profiles, future inflationary pressures, and so forth. (Savers' personal profiles provide pension insurers a better assessment of the life expectancies—including potentially, in the future, their DNA signatures—and future needs.) At the same time, insurers impose limitations commensurate with what these profiles reveal. This results in a *disaggregation* and *individuation* of pensions' insurance portfolios and, as a result, a breakdown of traditional approaches to insurance based on risk aggregation and risk sharing. These issues are raising immense problems for pension funds and insurers, changing the core business of pension retirement finance. In these conditions, it is not clear how savings and future payments may be valued from an individual saver's point of view. Of course, utility theory and risk-bearing theories (Chapter 5) may be applied to value savers' contributions but are not easily applicable in pricing alternative retirement schemes.

Financial institutions (banks, insurance firms, and hedge funds) have realized that this new game plan is a challenging opportunity that they cannot afford to misunderstand and underestimate. The current state of affairs has, thus, an important effect on persons who do not have sufficient wealth to support their future needs and who rely mostly on pension withdrawals from their paychecks, made by employers, and payments made to social security. Further, the proliferation of so-called *pension firms* is leading to the marketing of new packaged-saving modes. Explicitly, the traditional pension saving approach consisting in investment in fixed-income obligations, generally issued and backed by the government, is currently amended to provide greater investment flexibility by indexing investment to equity investments and thereby to potential risks (although to a potential appreciation of the pension also). While this flexibility may be more responsive to market forces and better tailored to individual savers' needs, it remains a very risky proposition as the financial crisis of 2008–2009 has shown. Individuation of pension savings (partly or wholly) is an emerging fact, however. This is a global problem, each country defining its own game plan, each with its own social undertones and structure, each with its own price, risks, and their consequences.

There are other reasons for governments' disassociation from social and retirement pension funds and their active support of asset-backed pension plans. Some reasons include early retirement, a structural growth in unemployment, increased life expectancy, the inflow of more women into the labor market, a trend toward lower interest rates, and so on. These factors combine to increase the cost of national pension fund insurance. Further, the credo for smaller government, privatization and disengagement by governments, and the growth of global financial markets are also reducing the need for deficit financing through guaranteed payments to pension funds, which are an important source of budget deficit financing.

Contract Pricing and Franchises

Economic contracts and financial exchanges are made for profit. This general principle also underlies franchise contracts, outsourcing agreements, and joint partnerships, to name just a few. Franchises are basically a contract between two legally independent firms establishing a long-term relationship where the franchiser grants to the franchisee the right to use the franchiser's trademark. In exchange, the franchisee pays a lump-sum fee and annual royalties at an agreed percentage of sales. Over one-third of all retail sales in the United States occur through a franchise system. For example, production may be centralized while distribution may be franchised (e.g., car selling, some food and department stores, fast food, Benetton, etc.). In some cases, branding and advertising are centralized but production is decentralized, franchised to companies focused in manufacturing. The economic rationale arises due to very high set-up costs of marketing, selling, and logistic costs.

Typically, a franchise contract lasts for a definite or an indefinite period of time in which the owner of a protected trademark (brand) grants to another person or firm, for some consideration, the right to operate under this trademark for the purpose of producing or distributing a product or service (Caves and Murphy 1976). Franchise contracts involve, therefore, a sharing of tangible and intangible assets between independent firms. The value of such assets is defined by their use and is therefore difficult to price. Further, franchisee fees assume many forms, including royalties or commission, resale price, maintenance, exclusive territories, exclusive dealing, as well as exclusivity relationships of various sorts with reciprocal agreements for the conduct of mutual services. Traditionally, an expected utility framework based on the parties' utilities for money is used to value franchise contracts. Such an approach is subjective, expressing the individual value that each of the parties draws from the agreement. However, the parties' set financial price for the franchise is not the market price. A market price might be constructed to better appreciate the valuation of such agreements.

Catastrophic Risks, Insurance, and Finance

Global warming, population explosion, the sad growth of terrorism, and the yearly ritual of the hurricane season is an indication that catastrophic risks are no longer rare. Further, *securitization* of catastrophic insured risks, weather-related derivatives, cat bonds (or catastrophic bonds), and other financial products that transfer disaster-derived risks to financial markets have contributed to financial innovation, a trend expanding dramatically with global climatic change. At the same time, the insurance industry has also distinguished a variety of catastrophic events, leading insurers to develop product lines specifically tailored to particular catastrophic events and to capitalize on their potential profits. A survey of disasters in web sites such as www.emdat.net clearly points to the growth, breadth, and consequences of such events. Essentially, we distinguish between two types of disasters:

1. Natural and naturally derived disasters.
2. Man-made and derived disasters.

Natural disasters are essentially events that are not caused by people (but their consequences may importantly be amplified by the concentrations of man-made habitat) and are presumed to occur rarely but with dire financial consequences. Floods, extreme temperatures, extreme winds, earthquake, volcanoes, earth movements, forest fires, and the like are such disasters. For example, the 2004 Asia tsunami caused 226,408 deaths, and China's flood in 1931 (Yangtsekiang-Wuhan) had 400,000 victims.

Man-made disasters have multiple origins, reflecting the global activity humanity is involved in. For example, terror acts, technological disasters, air transport accidents, and ruinous swindles (such as Madoff's) may produce disasters of life, ecology, and finance. Technological disasters may originate in deadly chemical, gas, and radioactive gas emissions; industrial fires; collapsing mines; contaminated rivers and water sources; as well as environmental disasters (such as the effects of global warming, CO_2, and other pollutants). Transport disasters include airliners and trains crashing, Titanic-like ships sinking, and, not least, oil spills and their derived environmental disasters (the unfortunate BP Gulf disaster of 2010).

The number of disastrous rare events has increased over time for many reasons. Improved accounting of such events, a growth in the density of human settlements concentrated in specific parts of the world, technology, and the sophistication of military weapons have conspired to allow the few to tyrannize the many. The financial cost of such disasters is hardly accounted for, although costs sustained by Swiss Re, a leading reinsurer, indicated the growth of such costs resulting from such events. Swiss Re revenues have increased as well, however, with losses stimulating a growth in risk premiums for insurance and reinsurance. A similar phenomenon is observed in other financial cost-push industries.

Various countries have recognized the importance of these risks to their social and economic well-being. For example, agricultural insurance against the weather threats of crop destruction over large territories is subsidized by governments. The rationale for such insurance subsidies is due to the fact that such disasters are too great for the farmers to bear alone and at the same time might be disastrous for the country if it loses its capacity to produce food. Insuring against catastrophic and big-item risks is challenging financial engineering to contribute to alternative insurance approaches based on financial markets. For example, in France, the government assumes the coverage of all forms of catastrophic events (the law of July 13, 1982), although in August 1, 1990, the law was amended not to include storms, where insureds are required to take a special insurance contract. The cost of such a contract includes multiple risks and a co-participation and is determined by 12 percent of the asset coverage; 0.5 percent for cars; and a self initial participation of 380 euros for individuals, 1,150 euros for firms, and 1,530 and 3,060 euros in case of drought (for individuals and firms). Denmark assumes flood disasters by creating a special fund financed by insurance against fire. In the United States, flood insurance is sponsored by the federal government and in some states (such as Florida and New Jersey) such insurance is required by all homeowners. Pricing these risks opens the potential "for all of us to cover all of us."

The market price of insurance for such big items remains difficult to calculate, however. For publicly held and traded insurance firm securities, their price and their traded derivatives may reveal how the market assesses the risks an insurance firm is bearing (and thereby define implicitly what ought to be the risk premium price for such items). (See Chapters, 9, 10, and 11.)

The Price of Safety

Safety reflects a subjective state of mind, measured in terms of probabilities and their adverse consequences. Safety assumes many forms, such as the feeling of being protected versus being exposed to loss. Practically, it may refer to home safety with protective measures taken against external events (weather, home invasion, etc.); it may refer to computer safety and cyber security with actions taken to limit computer invasions; or it may refer to specific elements in use (stairs, cars, food, etc.). Safety depends on two factors: (1) the reliability of a product or a process designed to operate without default over a period of time, its fail-safe mechanisms, and the like; and (2) the user, whose safety depends on his own actions. For example, car safety depends on both the car and the driver of the car. Safety in such cases would preempt unintentional actions by the driver who would face adverse consequences.

A risk-sensitive pricing approach to financial safety may be implemented successfully if the risks can be accounted for, quantified, and translated into monetary terms. Financial methods provide a number of alternative avenues we may use, as will be discussed in Chapters 7 and 8.

The Price of Inventories

A broad range of parts, materials, commodities, and products that are used in industrial processes are also traded and priced by financial markets. Industrial managers dealing with both demands and price uncertainties may profit from such markets and price the resources and the inventories they use in their processes (rather than just consider these processes and inventories as costs). When both prices and demands are stochastic and dependent, Ritchken and Tapiero (1986) have pointed out the potential use of derivatives to manage inventory risks.

Such an approach underlies a common practice by certain firms who use commodities that are traded in speculative financial markets as an opportunity to profit in combination with the management of their inventories. In these situations, production-based activities are combined with hedging and speculations regarding their potential demand and the associated price of commodities. For example, manufacturers who use metals, energy-related products (oil, gas, heating fuel, electricity, etc.), agricultural goods (soybeans, orange juice, etc.), and other products may have an opportunity to manage orders in concert with financial hedges and speculations. Of course, an essential presumption in order for such strategies to profit through financial markets is that commodities are broadly traded and that markets are efficient allowing the pricing of these materials. Chapter 7 looks at a specific example to this effect.

Pricing Reliability and Warranties

When risks are due to the potential malfunction of a product, buyers can acquire warranties that may mitigate their risks as long as the warranty is alive. The price of such warranties is based on both insurance and financial issues, and they may therefore be priced explicitly or implicitly. Typically, such problems are treated from an engineering quantitative-statistical viewpoint. In such approaches, reliability and the warranty are well defined and an optimization of costs or profits is used to determine both the reliability function configuration and the terms of the warranty. A financial approach, by contrast, prices the future risks associated with both the reliability of the product or system and its consequential warranty costs. In a financial system, the price of risk for reliability or warranty is necessarily the same and therefore, one or the other reveals the price of the other. In the financial literature, such a presumption is used to price by replication one cash flow by another when the former flow is observable and therefore to price known.

For products sold with a warranty, their risks are defined by default events (their unreliability) and their severity. For example, let a warranty be defined for a period of time T and assume default at time t. Further, let $K(t)$ be the maximum warranty coverage at t and $\tilde{X}(t)$ be its random cost. A seller's warranty cost (revenue to the buyer) is then:

$$\tilde{W}(t) = Min\left(\tilde{X}(t), K(t)\right) = \tilde{X}(t) - Max(\tilde{X}(t) - K(t), 0), 0 < t \leq T \qquad (2.1)$$

Explicitly, when the cost is higher than warranted, $\tilde{W}(t) = K(t)$, otherwise it equals $\tilde{X}(t)$ (when cost is less than warranted). A warranty defined by both its expiration coverage, T and $K(t)$, can assume several forms though. For example, for a replacement warranty with unit price P, $K(t) = P$, while a warranty's gradual reduced coverage is $K(t) = P(1 - \alpha t/T)$ where α is a proportional reduction in the warranty's coverage.

Sellers may sell a product with or without a warranty. If a product is sold with its warranty, its price is effectively $P + p$ where p, the warranty price, is included in the product selling price. If a product is sold without a warranty, buyers may choose among an array of warranties with scheduled prices $p(T, K(t))$, $t \leq T$. Two alternative approaches are used to price warranties. A first approach is based on the expected utility arguments (see Chapter 5), expressing the individual risk attitude of the buyer, and on a market price approach (see Chapter 8).

The Price of Quality Claims

Claims are made to entice and attract customers. For these reasons, firms are often tempted to make claims that might or might not be met (for example, see Pfeifer et al. [2009], Tapiero [1981], and Welker [1995]). Ex ante, claims have a nonconformance risk. Examples abound. Drug manufacturers often make claims that are not fully tested, which can have disastrous financial consequences. By the same token, advertising claims for a product lifetime may turn out to be disappointing, with consequential costs that a claimant firm incurs knowingly (see Whisenant et al. 2003). For this reason, the reliability of a claim or a claimant is important.

To compensate for claim unreliability, firms may offer reassurance that their claims are well founded by providing signals, assurances, and warranties. For example, a car manufacturer assures clients of the proper function of their car over a given period of time or over a given mileage by assuming the risks that such claims are not met. Further, when claims are made, issues relating to who bears the risk and the responsibility for the claim are important since nonconforming performance can result from many causes. These causes may be internally induced (by false claims, by inappropriate training and documentation, etc.) or occurring externally (for example, by hazardous or uncontrollable events that affect the performance of the service or of the product).

The price of claims is therefore important to mitigate the risks that claims entail. In other words, firms' willingness to commit to specific claims has financial consequences and therefore a price to identify. For example, a firm overstating its claims may bear in the future financial consequences due to claims that turn out to be (for statistical or other reasons) false, while a firm underclaiming may both downgrade its value and underprice itself.

In financial services, hedge funds, corporate firms, and the like, claims are also made to entice customers to invest or to be positively predisposed toward these firms. For example, hedge funds stop reporting their results when these are becoming embarrassing, resulting in biased industry reports for the hedge funds index. Explicitly, for funds that ceased reporting, the average monthly rates of return in the six months that preceded their doing so was −0.56 percent, compared to an average monthly rate of return of 0.65 percent when they were reporting. As a result, poor results are dropped from the index reports, leading unsuspecting investors to invest in an index that is not as good as its claim. This practice is not limited to hedge funds, however. Aggregate performance of mutual funds and other assets can be distorted. These distortions—claims made by financial consultants and advisers, paid professionals advising drug companies, corporations, and CEOs—both true and false have an immense importance in financial markets that are fueled by a combination of legitimate information, gossip, and false claims that build up sentiments, intentions, and the propensity of financial actors to buy and sell.

FINANCIAL RISK PRICING: A HISTORICAL PERSPECTIVE

Financial theory has contributed immensely to the growth of finance. Starting with Markowitz's 1950 seminal paper on portfolio optimization (see Markowitz 1952, 1959, 1991), continuing through Sharpe's capital asset pricing model (CAPM) (see Sharpe 1964), to Arrow-Debreu's state preference theory, and to Merton, Black, and Scholes's option pricing formulas, there is a time line of seminal contributions that have been granted Nobel Prizes for their contribution. Following is a review of some of these contributions.

- *1950:* Harry Markowitz (Nobel Prize winner) puts forth a mean-variance analysis as a foundation for portfolio theory. Markowitz's contribution provided a rational foundation for diversification implied by a quadratic utility (see Chapter 5).
- *Late 1950s:* Kenneth Arrow and Gerard Debreu (both Nobel Prize winners) outline a *state preference theory* and show that security prices allocate risk efficiently. Further, they demonstrate that for an efficient allocation of resources and risks, we require a set of "complete" securities that permit agents to hedge all risks (Chapter 8). State preference theory is shown later to underlie the fundamental finance approach to asset pricing when markets are complete—namely in equilibrium, with buyers and sellers agreeing on one and only one price for a given asset.
- *1958:* Franco Modigliani and Merton Miller (both received Nobel Prizes on irrelevance theory) show that in an efficient market the value-price of a company is independent of its capital structure (equity, debt). In other words, the leverage of a firm has no effect on its security price. Since this is not the case in practice, this theory emphasizes the importance of hedging. This fallacy has recently increased concerns about leverage risks.

- *1960:* William Sharpe (1964) (Nobel Prize winner), building on Markowitz's contribution, develops the CAPM and demonstrates that financial markets compensate investors for accepting systematic or market risks but not for idiosyncratic risk (which is specific to an individual asset and can be eliminated through diversification). Sharpe's contribution has influenced financial risk management by emphasizing the need for investors to hedge, whether they can mitigate risks or not (see Chapters 3 and 5).
- *1973:* Fischer Black, Myron Scholes, and Robert Merton (Nobel Prizes were awarded to Scholes and Merton after Black died in 1995) work on the pricing of options. The technical pricing of derivatives (options) has allowed extraordinary growth of financial markets. Black, Scholes, and Merton's contributions are based wholly on the Arrow-Debreu state preference theory; their practical contribution is extremely important. Today options are used and priced in many financial markets. Chapter 7 outlines both the Arrow-Debreu framework and its use in pricing options.
- *1976:* Arbitrage pricing theory, developed by Stephen Ross, points out that the price of a security is driven by a number of factors including macroeconomic variables, indexes, and so forth. Ross's contribution has allowed the segmentation of CAPM systematic risks (see Chapters 3 and 5). The multiplicity of sources of risks is both practically and theoretically challenging.
- *1976:* John Cox, Stephen Ross (1976), and Mark Rubinstein suggest a binomial option pricing model treated analytically and practically. Such a contribution has simplified both the explanation of option prices and their financial engineering. The binomial option model and its extension to trinomial and other models are used in this book to maintain its simplicity (see Chapters 5 and 6).
- *1985:* Clifford Smith and René M. Stulz, in their work on underinvestment, point out that stockholders refuse to invest in low-risk, low-return assets to avoid shifting wealth from themselves to debt holders. As a result, they suggest that there is shareholder value in better risk management through better investment decisions. At the same time, shifting investments to high-risk assets may lead firms to be highly leveraged due to the returns spread they obtain by using debt (see Chapter 9). The financial crisis of 2008 has triggered a flight from risk, however, with consequences that have not yet been fully appreciated. For example, the flight from risk may entail a flight from investments in favor of short-term trades that seek to profit now compared to a potential risky and unpredictable future.
- *1993:* Kenneth Froot, David Scharfstein, and Jeremy Stein suggest a framework for risk management including hedging and risk as a corporate strategy. They suggest that the goal of risk management is to ensure that a company's liquidity for value-enhancing investments and maintain future obligations. The credit crisis of 2008 has confirmed in particular the paramount importance of managing liquidity risks (see also Chapter 10).

These contributions add up to the many extensions and tools that are now an essential part of financial engineering. These financial tools are extremely important to financial institutions that manage not only money and financial assets but also systems, people, and complex organizations.

The financial meltdown of 2008 has raised many questions, however, critically reviewing past theory and seeking to define the future of finance. The presumption of the fundamental approach to finance that "the future is now"—namely, that future risks are the determinants of current prices and, inversely, that current prices reflect future risks—has raised many critics. This is not new, however. St. Augustine in his *Confessions* (volume X) already claimed that we are always in the present: the present of the past, the present of the future, and the present of the present. In this context, there is only the here and now. A first and critical assessment of the fundamental approach proclaims that prices cannot be an expectation of their future if future risk manifestations are unknown and unlikely. In other words, the well-known adage that "the likely is unlikely—certain to occur but unpredictable" would eradicate the validity of the underlying assumption of fundamental finance. In other words, predictability of future states, a fundamental assumption of the fundamental financial asset pricing theory (see Chapter 7), can be wrong, pointing thereby to a major lacuna in our understanding of financial markets. This statement is, of course, not completely justified, since fundamental finance is a theory *of* and *in* economic equilibrium, rather than off-equilibrium. For this reason, finance has to reckon with off-equilibrium financial markets'. While fundamental theories have served us well when financial markets are reasonably predictable (i.e., have few states to reckon with), it fails us in turbulent, complex, rare, and unpredictable times. These are, however, situations in which risks matter most.

Financial markets, their prices, and their risks reflect our future environment and life. Present events and trends, already obvious today, are already pointing to (as stated in Chapter 1) five phenomena:

1. Globalization, interconnectedness, and the growth of risk.
2. A trend to a multipolar financial world promising far greater instability in financial markets, and greater difficulties in regulating and managing moral hazard risks (see Chapter 6) and outlier behaviors by financial parties.
3. Changing financial institutions. Over these past decades, banks and a large number of financial institutions have become marketers of financial products, rather than providers of liquidity.
4. Growth of information technology (IT) risks and IT finance because there are many more of us who are far more IT-savvy and far more aware, and with a far greater ability to affect the commons. This can lead to a tyranny of minorities, common extreme behavior fueled by excessive and unfiltered information far more apt to generate contagious behaviors and therefore financial runs.
5. The growth of complexity, and uncontrolled financial markets may yet become the rule rather than an exception. This means that the risk of recurrent chaos in financial markets is not far-fetched. Of course, our call for more or less regulation indicates such concerns. Whether regulation can in fact be effective remains to be seen.

While these risks are prevalent today in many forms in and out of the financial world, in the future the mix is likely to change. For example, environment and risk externalities, counterparty and litigation risks, safety and security risks, networks and IT, and so on, some of which have been raised here, are emerging as additional important candidates that will define the future of risk finance and how we manage financial risks.

ESSENTIALS OF FINANCIAL RISK MANAGEMENT

Financial risk management seeks to alter or favorably mitigate the outcomes a portfolio of financial and other assets may have and reduce their consequences to planned or economically desirable levels. To do so, we use a number of approaches and techniques designed to confront the risks elaborated in Chapter 1. These approaches include:

- Ex ante risk management or risk planning, controls and risk prevention, capital assets requirements such as value at risk (VaR—see Chapter 3), future contingencies, and so on.
- Ex post risk management or activities and investments pursued to augment the potential to recover from dire risk consequences and adapt to a changing environment. This includes as well a combined ex ante and ex post approach to financial management, which we imply in developing a robust financial engineering—seeking to design ex ante investments that are relatively insensitive to a broad array of multiple risks.
- Robust risk management to reduce a sensitivity to events that were not predicted or accounted for.
- Strategic risk management or counterparty financial risk management based on the growth of networked financial and business institutions, networked financial markets, information asymmetries that lead to moral hazard, and information and power risks for investors (Chapter 6).
- Managing risk externalities and regulation. An externality is a cost or benefit that is experienced by someone who is not a party to the transaction that produced it. There are both negative and positive externalities. For example, pollution is a negative externality while an investment in infrastructures yields positive externalities. These risks thus arise when a perpetrator of risk is not assuming its consequences. This is considered later in this chapter, with its implications to the growth of financial institutions to become too big to fail (TBTF) and their effects on a sustainable financial system.

Ex ante risk management consists in the prior application of various tools such as diversification, portfolio design to meet specific risk management specifications, preventive controls, preventive actions, insurance and risk sharing, information seeking, statistical analysis, and forecasting. *Ex post risk management* is a posterior and reactive set of measures taken when a risk event has occurred. These may include using collaterals to mitigate the effects of credit risk, option contracts to mitigate the effects of adverse movements in stock prices, and so forth. For example, call options would limit the downside risk. Such protection has a price, however, defined by the option price.

A *robust risk management,* unlike ex ante and ex post risk management, seeks hedges that are insensitive to a broad range of risks. Such an approach is presumed to protect a portfolio in broad circumstances. Stress testing by banks is applied by testing the financial strengths of banks under multiple financial scenarios. It may therefore be assumed to be a means to test the robustness of banks. Generally, robustness expresses the insensitivity of a process or a model to the randomness of parameters (or their misspecification). The search for robust processes, insensitive to risks, is an essential and increasingly important approach to managing financial risk.

Strategic risks and their management result from the risk consequences of exchange and collaboration between financial parties whose motivations may differ. These risks arise in OTC exchanges when traders, banks, and investors swap assets with each other and assume counterparty risks. Strategic risks may also lead to insider trading and other factors that undermine the proper function of financial markets.

Finally, the management of financial risk externalities is important for a number of reasons. When they exist, they are mostly important. When firms (banks for example) assume too much risk, and put the financial system at risk, they act in effect as polluters, putting everyone's well-being at risk. In such cases, the cost of risk externalities is a social cost defined by

$$\text{Social cost (SC)} = \text{private cost (PC)} + \text{external cost (EC)}$$

and in marginal cost terms, the marginal social cost (MSC) equals the marginal private cost (MPC) plus the marginal external cost (MEC), or

$$\text{MSC} = \text{MPC} + \text{MEC}$$

To manage these costs two approaches are prevalent. A first approach is due to Pigou and calls for the perpetrators of external costs to assume responsibility by *internalization* through taxation (or the Pigouvian tax), subsidies, and regulation. A second approach is based on Coase, who observed a key feature of externalities: that they are reciprocal in nature. This means that externalities are not simply the result of one person's action, but rather result from the combined actions of two or more parties. As a result, Coase calls as well for the victim of the risk externality to change his behavior rather than only for the polluter to do so. In Coase's spirit, if polluters are left free to pollute, they will continue to do so.

Let's take an example. The banking system causes a systemic loss of $20 trillion if it pursues investment policies that entail excessive risks. If it were to pursue reasonable risk management policies, the loss in returns would be $200 billion. It would cost clients of the banking system a loss of $100 billion if the banks were to pursue risk avoidance strategies and a total loss of their wealth if there was a systemic breakdown. Banks clients can, of course, move their wealth elsewhere into nontradable assets (and thus contribute to a reduction in market liquidity).

So which solution makes more sense—having investors change their investment habits, remove their wealth from banks, contribute to bank losses and to a reduction in market liquidity, or letting the banks pursue their quest for ever higher and risk-prone profits? From an efficiency perspective, it makes more sense for investors at large to pull out, because they can prevent banks from assuming the extraordinary risks they take. This is, of course, a loss avoidance strategy. For Coase, a solution to risk externalities can be reached if externality problems are solved efficiently through private transactions—namely, through banks and the behavior of investors.

Comprehensive Financial Risk Management

The growth of financial complexity and the dependence of financial firms networked and financial markets have ushered in a period that calls for a comprehensive approach to financial risk management. Financial crises and their aftermath are a reminder that financial firms and financial markets are dependent and subject to multiple sources of risks (some unpredictable) that can combine to launch a contagion of market failures. Comprehensive financial risk management (CFRM) *intentionality* is based on the following principles:

- Risk arises due to many interacting risk factors.
- Risk is nonlinear, in the sense that it cannot be predicted by a simple extrapolation of past events.
- Risks are hidden.
- The more important risks are unpredictable and might not be preventable. Their consequences may be mitigated, however, by a comprehensive and robust approach to financial risk management.
- Both prevention and recovery from extreme losses must be emphasized.

To apply these principles, financial risk management requires:

- Measuring and tracking global trends and macroeconomic risks.
- Reducing the complexity of financial products and financial services through greater transparency, traceability, and the control of risks and their rewards. Complexity increases nontransparency and contributes to information asymmetries and mispricing of financial assets.
- Seeking sustainable financial performance, based on long-term sustainability of short-term profitability.
- Providing an enforceable code of assurance based on equitable risk sharing for financial products, at the time financial products are bought, maintained, and sold through the many intermediaries of financial networks.
- Seeking not only to enrich the barons of finance but also the stakeholders of financial institutions.

TECHNOLOGY AND COMPLEXITY

Both finance and industry have experienced a parallel growth in technology and complexity that has altered the economics of both. The business and industrial revolution would not have happened without a revolution in the means and supply of credit. In fact, one could claim that a financial revolution preceded the first industrial revolution, a revolution that has made it possible for industrial entrepreneurs to take risks and contribute to economic development. Similarly, the insurers who back Lloyd's of London (also called *Names*, which consist of wealthy investors willing to assume risk for a price—the insurance premium) have made it possible to expand commercial navigation, exploration, and business by the growth of credit that has established new foundations for industry to assume risks it could not assume by itself. Simultaneously, business and industrial development have raised the need and demand for credit, which created new means to produce moneys. As a result, both industry and credit have grown hand in hand in size and complexity, contributing to:

- The growth of complementary and self-reinforcing needs by industry and credit.
- The needs of warring nations producing both more credit (bonds to finance their warring needs) and more financial technologies to produce credit and manage financial resources.
- Democratization of the political process and globalization, where each individual today has become an active and free participant in financial markets, whether willing or not.

For the financial industry, increasingly demanding consumers accelerate the demand for and use of financial technologies downstream the financial supply chain. Simultaneously, the expansion of financial markets to their global and multipolar scales necessitates an upstream growth and integration. These factors are contributing to a far greater complexity in managing both financial firms and financial resources, while at the same time rendering their regulation an almost impossible task. These trends have altered the structure of financial enterprises and their technologies.

Opportunities for financial and technological innovation are continuously challenging a transformation occurring everywhere and in everything. In finance, new trends have arisen. On the one hand, growth of the real sector (client-based and corporate firms) and its growing demand for credit, its variety, and its complexity have led to the engineering of complex derivatives. On the other, financial products have stimulated the growth of industrial entrepreneurship and innovation by providing broader opportunities to exchange and allowing many more investors to participate in business enterprises. Products such as options, credit default swaps (CDSs), collateralized debt obligations (CDOs), and so forth (see Chapters 9 and 10) have produced a financial supply chain and financial bazaars of extreme complexity where risk and insurance are intermingled—an insurance intent in one instant (a put option) becoming a speculative bet in another.

At the same time, global finance has evolved into a virtual machine where money and trades can be conducted from any place and at any time using electronic means. These opportunities are of great concern, however—they raise concerns about regulation, controls, safety, security, moral hazards, and uncontrolled insider trading of all sorts. Finance fueled by new virtual technologies has contributed to a global transformation and generated a process that no longer responds to regulation but transforms financial firms into increasingly financial virtual enterprises.

Finance is thus set into an explosive dynamics, feeding its own complexity with technology generating greater needs for greater controls. This observation is a consequence of the law of requisite variety in cybernetics (Ashby 1964), which states that controllers need to be more sophisticated than the object or person controlled in order for the controls to be effective. On the one hand, regulation agencies will require greater sophistication to meet the extreme sophistication of investment bankers, hedge fund managers, and financial institutions. On the other, controls require more measurements, more intelligent reporting, more technology, and therefore greater complexity. Can we do things in a simple manner? Can we be more preventive? At what costs? Technology in both industry and finance is thus naturally unstable, involving perpetual activities that require perpetual innovations to render subservient what has been constructed. An end is reached when this process can no longer be sustainable and reaches a state of meltdown—whether industrial or financial. Today, financial virtual and complex enterprises are real, expanding globally and exponentially in a broad variety of markets and across many financial products, driven by technology and the need of firms to obtain more credit, reduce costs, and do more with much less.

The benefits are also substantial. However, there are risks to be aware of and to mitigate. These include risks of complexity, risk to size, as well as risks of being engaged in an unsustainable innovation-complexity-technology cycle. Virtual financial enterprises are already altering the future of finance. Technology makes it possible for financial services to trade in any of the many global financial markets, using a broad variety of products and agents selected and driven by computer platforms, algorithms, and data analytic systems. Further, an expansion of financial consolidation and activity in the banking sector, combined with the maturation of financial technologies that cater to individuals and financial services, provides ample opportunities for the growth of financial virtual enterprises. These are some of the many professional challenges that financial engineers are most likely to confront in our financial future. Examples are considered next.

Retailing and Finance

A simple example suggested by Khoshafian (2010) illustrates a simple situation exploding into a myriad of virtual activities. Say that a consumer purchases a digital camera from a retail store. As soon as this purchase is consumed, a chain of virtual events is triggered that includes many firms in various and distant locations. To begin, the consumer's credit card is charged, computer-aided financial accounting in the retailer's back office is registered, and appropriate software might record the transaction (connected by intranet or Internet to other firms). Internally, the inventory database is updated, the manufacturer informed (triggering a whole range of exchanges and notifications in satellite computers), warranty and financial service are notified, parts suppliers in the factory are notified, and so forth. In fact, an enormous machine has been activated—a machine in many locations involving a variety of firms, agents, and parties in different ways. A simple transaction has thus triggered a complex process with potentially an enormous number of contractual relationships (some collaborating and some not), subject to potential cyber-security risks, human factor risks, and even strategic risks.

While these risks are mostly downplayed because of the benefits virtualization provides when it operates effectively, they exist nonetheless, and may have at times an important impact that requires both elaborate means of control and complex and reliable parallel control processes—to assure that no errors and no foul play endanger the transaction.

Finance, Cyber Risks, and Terrorism

In the past, while Washington's national security and financial systems have been operating independently, intelligence analysts have focused on explicit threats posed by cyber threats to the financial system. These have raised challenges due to the complexity of both the virtual security problems (Internet, networking, globalization) and the global financial infrastructure. Although approaches to security and to economic risks differ, their consequences are extremely important. For example, in August 2006 an unexplained decline in certain airline stocks took place shortly before the arrests in Britain of terrorists plotting to blow up transatlantic airliners. In addition, there are many other ways one may conceive of to foment economic troubles for both companies and countries.

IT and Madoff

The Madoff $65 billion Ponzi scheme has raised great awareness that the losses it caused could have been thwarted. Namely, fund-of-hedge-funds managers who lost big in the alleged fraud could have avoided the debacle if they had deployed technology to gather information and monitor the trading strategies and results from hedge funds they were invested in. Having a system that monitors compliance enforces a discipline.

Virtual Markets

Virtual markets define a virtual financial world as a community of investors linked up to online brokerages communicating electronically with exchanges. For example, NASDAQ, dubbed "the world's first electronic market," is an example of a virtual market where buyers and sellers meet electronically and are matched by algorithms. Purchases and sales are recorded using book-entry database methods for the clearing corporation. Only information expressing ownership is exchanged—not physical money or certificates. As late as the 1960s, buyers and sellers would have to physically meet at a physical place, where within a certain time, physical cash or checks would be exchanged for stock certificates. This is of course no longer the case.

Virtual Products

In 1981, when the Shad-Johnson Accord declared that cash-settled contracts were not a form of gambling, different kinds of financial products became popular. Prior to this time, cash-settled contracts were considered gambling (as affirmed by U.S. Supreme Court rulings). The reasoning implied that there cannot be a real delivery contract without delivering anything real. After Shad-Johnson, buyers and sellers were able to trade any virtual commodity represented by an agreed-upon number. Cash-settled stock index futures were first; today such contracts can be based on snowfall and temperature, future interest rate movements, stock volatilities, carbon pollution, and of course, whether a company will be able to pay its bills. For some, the virtual nature of the financial process may be a culprit for the recent problems that have plagued economies and markets everywhere. (Although these markets and products can no longer be ignored, Whalen 2008).

Virtual Markets Participants

Some buyers and sellers prefer to hide their identities. One reason may be to get a better price. Another may be to illegally manipulate a price. Today markets that support anonymous trading are a big business, called *dark pools* (Schmerken 2008).

Trading algorithms and high-frequency trading can also hide identity. Is the bid for 100 shares coming from Fidelity, George Soros, or the next-door neighbor? These are important questions to reckon with to maintain the integrity and the safety of trading.

Virtual Economic Universes

An example of a virtual economic universe is Second Life (secondlife.com), a web site with over 10 million users that supports an entire virtual economy based on a virtual currency, the Linden dollar. Trading in Linden dollars is not a game: There is a currency exchange for Linden dollars into real U.S. dollars. Many lose and make real money in such virtual enterprises by virtual trades.

The virtual financial world is of course rich in products, markets, and diversity and has commensurably raised many issues regarding operational risk (op risk); financial and financial institutions regulation that seeks compliance to reasonable (albeit questionable by some) standards; robustness of the financial sector; data and transactions security; and the maintenance of transparency and liquidity. These factors are also drivers of risks, which can, without controls, lead the promise of virtual financial (and nonfinancial) enterprises to falter. These new virtual risks include:

- Cybernetic risks, arising from technological complexity and control imbedded in the law of requisite variety indicated earlier.
- Contractual (counterparty) risks and strategic risks, arising from conflicting interests and risks and collaborating partners with asymmetric preferences and information.
- Security and opportunity (moral hazard) risks.
- Human factors and operational IT risks.
- Endogenous risks, internally generated by financial virtual enterprises.

MARKET MAKING AND PRICING PRACTICE

In practice, securities and their derivatives (options) are traded in stock and derivative exchanges (the NYSE, NASDAQ, CAC40, TASE25, FTSE, CBOE, Montreal

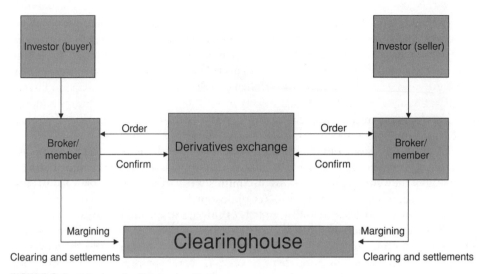

FIGURE 2.1 Market for Derivative Exchange

Derivative exchange, Philadelphia, etc.). A typical market for derivative exchange and trading is shown in Figure 2.1 and consists of:

- *Investors*—buy or sell side.
- *Brokers*—members of the exchange who execute for a fee the buy/sell orders.
- The *exchange*—usually supervised by a specialist. Each exchange has its own rules, procedures, and regulation.
- The *market maker* (specialist)—sets the trading price to provide market liquidity and profit.
- The *clearinghouse*—confirms the transactions.

Thus, buyers and sellers act mostly in a technology-supported environment through brokers who submit orders to the *derivative exchange* with transactions confirmed by the *clearinghouse*. As Figure 2.1 indicates, the market process is defined by financial supply and demand chains, with additional parties such as advisers, financial marketers, and the many others that make up the world of financial services. Each side of the chain is similar in the sense that it originates with investors, a selected broker (a member of the exchange), a market maker who sets the price for both buyers and sellers (bid and ask prices), and a clearinghouse to account for and manage these transactions. If all of these facets of the supply-demand chains are independent of one another and meet only on the exchange floor, then the orders (buy and sell) are only a function of latent risks, macroeconomic conditions, and the risk taking of investors and speculators.

Prices for buy and sell investors are defined by the market maker, who is a specialist in some securities or financial derivatives and whose role is to provide liquidity (and at times profit from such transactions). For example, say that an order to buy is set for a given day to be at any price below \$12, or $Min(\tilde{p}, 12)$ where $\tilde{p}$ is a day price. At the same time, assume that a seller's order is to sell at a minimum price of \$13 during a day, or $Max(\tilde{p}, 13)$. The market maker's role is to reconcile these seemingly different prices. Of course, there may be thousands of such orders on the buy and sell side, and therefore the market maker might select bid and ask prices that maximize the volume of orders transacted. Alternatively, the market maker may buy for his own account shares from the seller and sell them at a later time to buyers when he changes the price and the buyer is enticed to lower his expectations and buy at a higher price. In this case, the market maker uses *inventories* to allow financial exchanges (and thereby maintains the market liquidity).

This example is one of many that highlight both the complexity and the opportunities market makers have due to their intermediary positions and the informational advantages they can profit from. Adam Smith's work (*The Wealth of Nations*) underlies the economic and liberal market philosophy that presumes that markets are fully competitive and therefore ultimately transparent and liquid. In fact this may not be the case, although most financial markets seek to provide liquidity, transparency, and a fair exchange. The business of market making can differ from market to market, with competing specialist market makers that in practice define the price formation mechanism.

Market Makers, Market Liquidity, and Bid-Ask Spreads

Liquidity is defined by its financial immediacy to both buyers and sellers. A market maker's function in this case is that of an intermediary that facilitates the exchange and provides *immediacy*: buying from public sellers and selling to public buyers and profiting from the difference in bid and ask prices. For this reason, essential indicators of liquidity include the bid-ask spread, the time between an order made and the order fulfilled, as well as the volume of outstanding and waiting trades. For example, auction-rated securities (ARSs) were deemed to be an extremely liquid financial investment and were bought for that reason. However, in 2008 and in 2009, many such ARSs could not be redeemed and have kept investors locked in holding ARSs they could not sell. By the same token, credit markets in 2009 were believed to be illiquid in some sectors due to banks' refusal to grant credit to small businesses and individuals. Both situations resulted in a widening of the bid-ask prices. Liquid markets thus have narrow spreads while illiquid markets are signaled by a broadening of the bid-ask spread.

Bid-ask prices are quoted by market makers—bid prices for prospective investors and ask prices for prospective sellers. In some cases, market makers may also use the inventory of shares accumulated through past transactions to augment liquidity (or potentially speculate on the growth or the decline of the share price). Furthermore, they may keep a market book of orders, consisting of various types of orders such as limit orders to buy and sell, stop orders placed by market participants, and so forth. To perform their function and supply financial immediacy, market makers require large capital resources to meet the intermediate positions and the risks implied in the function they assume. Market makers are therefore large financial institutions or banks (particularly merchant and investment banks). They often have to buy large quantities of securities during a bear market phase, which they off-load later (implying the need for a healthy financial carrying capacity). At the same time, their unique position at the intersection between financial markets' demand and supply provides an information source, which they can use (and misuse) to make extremely large profits—often at the expense of their clients. They do so by trading in their dual capacity or by executing large orders away from the market (so-called *block* and OTC trades). These privileges are granted to attract market makers with sufficiently large capital resources in order to increase market liquidity. In a truly liquid and competitive environment, there are usually several competing market makers that specialize in a particular financial instrument, which contributes to market efficiency.

There has been an ongoing debate about whether intermediaries are needed to provide liquidity. Some say that electronic and algorithmic order matching is sufficient, while others believe that market makers are needed to bridge the spread inherent in buyers' and sellers' prices. For example, small-cap stocks are often thinly traded. A market maker intermediary may then bridge the spread gap to ensure that transactions occur within reasonable amounts of time and without large price variations. Trying to buy or sell a large block of securities creates a market imbalance. In such cases, market makers may buy or sell slices of the block, placing these slices within reasonable order sizes and in a timing that would contribute to the operation of a stable financial market.

Alternative Market Structures

Market structures are varied, and new market-clearing mechanisms arise with surprising frequency. Further, the credit and illiquidity crises of 2008–2009 has also raised the prospect and the importance of financial regulation to maintain transparency and avoid both conflicts of interest by market makers and the extraordinary advantages that some banks profit from due to their unique intermediary and at times almost monopolist positions in financial markets.

In principle, exchange in financial markets may differ according to the attributes of the traded assets, as well as in the location of the exchange, the time of the transaction, and the manner that the transaction takes place. Further, markets differ in the degree of participation of intermediaries and in the role they play in the market. Certain aspects of diversification are necessary due to the particular manner in which a given market operates (for example, the manner in which the market price is discovered). The variety of possible market organizations provides an opportunity to compare these markets. For an extensive study, see Economides and Siow (1985 and 1988); Economides and Schwartz (1995); Hann (2001); Klein and Quelch (1977a and b); Lin et al. (2002); Madhavan (1992); O'Hara (2001); Pagano and Roell (1990); Panayides and Charitou (2004); Spulber (1996); and Stern and El-Ansary (1992).

The New York Stock Exchange (NYSE) is the best-known example of a single market maker for a security (see Table 2.1 for a number of such markets). Dealers can compete for trades, buying and selling securities for their own account, but there is usually one market maker for a security (or for several securities). Traditionally dealers have competed in a central location, as is the case on the London Stock Exchange or the NASDAQ. Globalization is leading to greater competition and decentralization. Bonds, unlike securities for example, trade primarily through bilateral negotiations between dealers and customers while electronic markets are now used profusely, providing a mechanism for the automatic matching of orders. Today the majority of trading in global foreign exchange markets takes place over

TABLE 2.1 Market Structures

	Specialist	Dealer	Electronic
Equity	New York Stock Exchange	NASDAQ, London Stock Exchange	Stock Exchange of Hong Kong, Instinet, Paris Bourse
Bond		Bond dealers	Tradenet, EUREX
Foreign exchange		FX brokers	Reuters, EBS

electronic exchanges such as Reuters and Electronic Broking Services (EBS). Actual market making is based on structures and rules that dictate:

- What can be traded.
- Who can trade.
- When and how orders can be submitted.
- Who may see or handle the order.
- How orders are processed.

These rules affect the price formation process. Without financial markets and market makers, markets cease to exist and are replaced by individualized bilateral contracts.

Organization structures for financial markets and market making are numerous and can be studied directly by turning to the web sites of the financial markets (NYSE, CBOE, EURONEXT, etc.).

SUMMARY

This chapter has provided a cursory view of some of the faces of finance. These have included risks, their financial manifestations, their management, and their pricing. A broad historical line of financial concepts as well as the potential and intricate effects of technology on finance and market making were also outlined. In such contexts, application of finance and financial engineering is far reaching, spanning all facets of our economic and social activities. Finance is also a risky business, which requires that we apply it carefully and manage the risks that investors, traders, speculators, and society at large assume due to their and others' financial activities. The next chapter is technical and addresses the basic problems of seeking, analyzing, and making financial sense of data. In particular, estimation approaches to volatility and related problems are considered.

TEST YOURSELF

2.1 Define the following terms:
   a. Hazard risks.
   b. Intra-operational risks.
   c. Strategic risks.
   d. Risk externalities.

   e. Information and statistical risks.
   f. Information and power asymmetry risks.
   g. Legal risks.

2.2 Define the risk of a credit transaction in terms of the probability of default, the probability of the size loss, and the probability of the percentage that can be recovered. Can you provide a single measure to define practically (and therefore simply) a measure of the risk? Can you think how to compensate the credit firm that assumes such a risk?

2.3 Name four substantially different manners in which insurance firms, banks, and hedge funds manage their risks.

2.4 Explain the following approaches to risk management (but use several examples to demonstrate their use):
   a. Ex ante risk management.
   b. Ex post risk management and risk recovery.
   c. Robust risk management (in particular explain what robustness means to you).

2.5 What is a risk externality? Provide an example and suggest in the context of your example how you would attempt to manage it and why.

2.6 How do the concerns of financial risk management of an individual investor and a corporate firm (say an industrial and a corporate financial enterprise) differ? Provide two examples.

2.7 Technology in industry and finance—which comes first? (Be aware that there is evidently a strong interdependence, much like the chicken and egg dilemma.)

2.8 Technology in industry and finance—what are the differences and what are the similarities?

2.9 Virtual enterprises and technology—how do these concepts apply to financial credit and to financial management? Can you indicate five important challenges that virtual banking is confronted with?

2.10 What are the financial risk implications of complexity growth and increased intermediation? How do they influence finance and the financial risks individual and corporate firms face?

2.11 How does financial transparency and the quality of financial products affect their price and trading in financial markets?

2.12 What are the roles of technology in managing money and credit?

REFERENCES

Akkermans, A. H., and H. van der Horst. 2002. Managing IT infrastructure standardization in the networked firm. *International Journal of Production Economics* 75:213–228.

Ananth, Madhavan. 2002. Market microstructure: A survey. *Journal of Financial Markets* 3 (3):205–258.

Anwar, S. 2001. Government spending on public infrastructure, prices, production and international trade. *Quarterly Review of Economics and Finance* 41:19–31.

Arrow, K. J. 1965. *Aspects of the theory of risk-bearing.* Helsinki: Yrjo Jahnssonin Säätiö.

———. 1982. Risk perception in psychology and in economics. *Economics Inquiry* (January):1–9.

Ashby, W. R. 1964. *An introduction to cybernetics.* London: University Paperbacks.

Aschauer, D. A. 1989a. Is public expenditure productive? *Journal of Monetary Economics* 23:177–200.

———. 1989b. Does public capital crowd out private capital? *Journal of Monetary Economics* 24:171–188.

Barlow, R., and F. Proschan. 1965. *Mathematical theory of reliability.* New York: John Wiley & Sons.

Batten, D. F., and C. Karlsson, eds. 1996. *Infrastructure and the complexity of economic development.* Advances in spatial science series. Heidelberg and New York: Springer, 49–60.

Blair, R. D., and D. L. Kaserman. 1982. Optimal franchising. *Southern Economic Journal* 49 (2):494–505.

Black, F., and M. Scholes. 1973. The pricing of options and corporate liabilities. *Journal of Political Economy* 81:637–659.

Bloomberg. 2009. www.newenergyfinance.com.

Bradfield, J. 1982. Optimal dynamic behavior of a market-maker in choosing bid and asked prices. *Journal of Economics and Business* 34:303–316.

Brockett, P. L., and X. Xia. 1995. Operations research in insurance, a review. *Transactions Society of Actuaries* 47:7–82.

Campbell, John Y. 2000. Asset pricing at the millennium. *Journal of Finance* 55 (4): 1515–1567.

Caves, R. E., and W. E. Murphy. 1976. Franchising firms, markets and intangible assets. *Southern Economic Journal* 42 (April):572–586.

Coase, Ronald H. 1960 The problem of social cost. *Journal of Law and Economics* 3 (1).

Corbett, C., 2001. Stochastic inventory systems in a supply chain with asymmetric information: Cycle stocks, safety stocks, and consignment Stocks. *Operations Research* 49:487–500.

Corbett, C., and C. S. Tang. 1998. Designing supply contracts: Contract type and information asymmetric information. In *Quantitative Models for Supply Chain Management*, ed. Tayur et al. Dordrecht: Kluwer.

Corbey, M., 1991. Measurable economic consequences of investments in flexible capacity. *International Journal of Production Economics* 23 (1–3):47–57.

Cox, J. C., and S. A. Ross. 1976. The valuation of options for alternative stochastic processes *Journal of Financial Economics* 3 (1–2):145–166.

Cox, J. J., and N. Tait. 1991. *Reliability, safety and risk management.* London: Butterworth-Heinemann.

Debreu, G. 1959. *Theory of value: An axiomatic analysis of economic equilibrium.* New Haven and London: Yale University Press.

Economides, N., and R. A. Schwartz. 1995. Equity trading practices and market structure: Assessing asset managers' demand for immediacy. *Financial Markets, Institutions and Instruments* 4 (4).

Economides, N., and A. Siow. 1985. *Liquidity and the success of futures markets.* Working paper CSFM-118, Center for the Study of Futures Markets, Columbia Business School.

———. 1988. The division of markets is limited by the extent of liquidity. *American Economic Review* 78 (1):108–121.

Euronext. 2001. *Institutional Investors User Guide*, November.

Evans, P., and G. Karras. 1994. Are government activities productive? *Review of Economics and Statistics* 76:1–11.

Ford, R., and P. Poret. 1991. Infrastructure and private-sector productivity. *OECD Economic Studies* (17) (Autumn):63–89.

Froot, Kenneth A., David S. Scharfstein, and Jeremy C. Stein. 1993. Risk management: Coordinating corporate investment and financing policies. *Journal of Finance* 48 (5) (December):1629–1658.

Garman, M. 1976. Market microstructure. *Journal of Financial Economics* 3:257–275.

Gillen, D. W. 1996. Transportation infrastructure and economic development: A review of recent literature. *Logistics and Transportation Review* 32 (1):39–62.

Gramlich, E. M. 1994. Infrastructure investment: A review essay. *Journal of Economic Literature* 32 (3) (September):1176–1196.

Hann, R. 2001. The changing market microstructure of Dutch small- and midcaps. *NIB Capital* (December).

Hirschleifer, J., and J. G. Riley. 1979. The analysis of uncertainty and information: An expository survey. *Journal of Economic Literature* 17:1375–1421.

Holtz-Eakin, D., and A. E. Schwartz. 1994. Infrastructure in a structural model of economic growth. *National Bureau of Economic Research working paper* 4824 (August).

———. 1995. Infrastructure in a structural model of economic growth. *Regional Science and Urban Economics* 25 (2):131–151.

Kaihara, T. 2001. Supply chain management with market economies. *International Journal of Production Economics* 72:5–14.

Kaufmann, P. J., and R. P. Dant. 2001. The pricing of franchise rights. *Journal of Retailing* 77:537–545.

Kaufmann, P. J., and F. Lafontaine. 1994. Costs of control: The source of economic rents for McDonald's franchises *Journal of Law and Economics* 37 (2):413–453.

Khoshafian, S. 2010. www.pega.com/featured/SOE/ and www.webservicesarchitect.com.

Klein, L. R., and J. A. Quelch. 1977a. Business-to-business market making on the Internet. *International Marketing Review* 14 (5):345–361.

———. 1997b. *TRADE'ex: The stock exchange of the computer industry.* Harvard Business School Case N9-597-019.

Kogan, K., and C. S. Tapiero. 2007. *Supply chains, operations modeling and management.* Boston: Springer Verlag.

Lafontaine, F. 1992. Contract theory and franchising: Some empirical results. *Rand Journal of Economics* 23 (2):263–283.

Leach, J. C., and A. Madhavan, 1992. Intertemporal price discovery by market makers: Active versus passive learning. *Journal of Financial Intermediation* 2:207–235.

———. 1993. Price experimentation and security market structure. *Review of Financial Studies* 6 (2):375–404.

Madhavan, A. 1992. Trading mechanisms in securities markets. *Journal of Finance* 47:607–642.

Manecke, N., and P. Schoensleben. 2004. Cost and benefit of Internet support of business processes. *International Journal of Production Economics* 87:213–229.

Markowitz, H. M. 1952. Portfolio selection. *Journal of Finance* 7:77–99.

———. 1959. *Portfolio selection: Efficient diversification of investments.* New York: John Wiley & Sons.

———. 1991. Foundations of portfolio theory. *Journal of Finance* 46 (2):469–477 (reviews the 1950 paper as well).

Mathewson, G. F., and R. A. Winter. 1986. The economics of franchise contracts. *Journal of Law and Economics* 28 (October):503–526.

Merton, R. C. *Continuous-time finance.* 1990. Oxford, U.K.: Basil Blackwell. (Rev. ed., 1992.)

Modigliani F., and M. H. Miller. 1958. The cost of capital, corporation finance and the theory of investment. *American Economic Review* 48 (3) (June):261–297.

Munier, B., and C. S. Tapiero. 2008. Risk attitudes. In *Encyclopedia of quantitative risk assessment*, ed. Brian Everitt and Ed Melnick. Hoboken, NJ: John Wiley & Sons.

Munnell, A. H. 1992. Infrastructure investment and economic growth. *Journal of Economic Perspectives* 6 (4) (Fall):189–198.

O'Hara, M. 1995. *Market microstructure theory*. Malden, MA: Blackwell.

———. 2001. Overview: Market structure issues in market liquidity. *Market microstructure theory, market liquidity: Proceedings of a workshop held at the Bank of International Settlements*, Basel, April.

Pagano, M., and A. Roell. 1990. Trading systems in European stock exchanges. Discussion paper 75, Financial Markets Group, London School of Economics.

Panayides, M., and A. Charitou. 2004. The role of market maker in international capital markets: Challenges and benefits of implementation in emerging markets. Yale ICF working paper 04-04.

Parlar, M., and D. Perry. 1996. Inventory models of future supply uncertainty with single and multiple suppliers. *Naval Research Logistics* 43:191–210.

Pfeifer, C., K. Schredelseker, and G. U. H. Seeber. 2009. On the negative value of information in informationally inefficient markets: Calculations for large number of traders. *Euro Journal of Operations Research* 195:117, 126.

Pigou, A. C. 1920. *The economics of welfare*. London: MacMillan Co.

Posner, M., and C. S. Tapiero. 1988. The manufacturing quality density function and quality control. *International Journal of Production Research* 26.

Reisman, A., P. Ritchken, and C. S. Tapiero. 1986. Reliability, pricing and quality control. *European Journal of Operations Research*.

Rey, P. 1992. The economics of franchising. ENSAE paper, February. Paris: ENSAE.

Rey, P., and J. Tirole. 1986. The logic of vertical restraints. *American Economic Review* 76:921–939.

Reyniers, D. J., and C. S. Tapiero. 1995. The delivery and control of quality in supplier producer contracts. *Management Science* (October–November).

Ritchken, P., and C. S. Tapiero. 1986. Contingent claim contracts and inventory control. *Operations Research* 34:864–870.

St. Augustine. 1991. *Confessions*, vol. 10. Oxford's World Classic. London: Oxford University Press.

Sanchez-Robles, B. 1998a. Infrastructure investment and growth: Some empirical evidence. *Contemporary Economic Policy* 16 (1) (January):98–108.

———. 1998b. The role of infrastructure investment in development: Some macroeconomic considerations. *International Journal of Transport Economics* 25 (2) (June): 113–136.

Sanmay, Das. 2003. Intelligent market-making in artificial financial markets. *AI Technical Report/CBCL Memo 2003-005/226*. Cambridge, MA: Massachusetts Institute of Technology.

Schmerken, I. 2008. End game: Anti-gaming technology in dark pools tops buy-side agenda. Barclays Capital. http://advancedtrading.com/printableArticle.jhtml?articleID=210000386.

———. 2009. Fund-of-hedge funds lacked technology to avoid Madoff losses. *Advanced Trading*, January 8. http://www.advancedtrading.com/showArticle.jhtml?articleID=212701382.

Schreiber, P., and R. Schwartz. 1985. Efficient price discovery in a securities market: The objective of a trading system. In *Market making and the changing structure of the securities industry*, ed. Y. Amihud, T. Ho, and R. Schwartz. Lexington, MA: Lexington Books.

Sharpe, W. F. 1964. Capital asset prices: A theory of market equilibrium under risk. *Journal of Finance* 19:425–442.

Shelton, C., and N. T. Chan. 2001. *An electronic market-maker. Technical Report AI-MEMO2001-005.* Cambridge, MA: Massachusetts Institute of Technology, AI Lab.

Skinner, D. 1994. Why firms voluntarily disclose bad news. *Journal of Accounting Research* 32:38–60.

Smith, Adam. 2003. *The Wealth of Nations.* New York: Bantam Classics.

Smith, Clifford W., and René M. Stulz. 1985. The determinants of firms' hedging policies. *Journal of Financial and Quantitative Analysis* 20 (4):391–406.

Spulber, D. F. 1996. Market making by price-setting firms. *Review of Economic Studies* 63 (4):559–580.

Stern, L. W., and A. I. El-Ansary. 1992. *Marketing channels.* Englewood Cliffs, NJ: Prentice-Hall.

Stoll, H., and R. Huang. 1991. Major world equity markets: Current structure and prospects for change. Working paper, Vanderbilt University.

Tapiero, C. S. 1981. Optimal product quality and advertising. *INFOR* 19:311–318.

———. 1996. *The management of quality and its control.* London: Chapman and Hall.

———. 2000a. Ex-post inventory control. *International Journal of Production Research,* April.

———. 2000b. The NBD repeat purchase process and M/G/Infinity queues. *International Journal of Production Economics* 63:141–145.

———. 2004. Risk management. In *Encyclopedia on actuarial science and risk management,* ed. J. Teugels and B. Sundt. Hoboken, NJ and London: John Wiley & Sons.

———. 2005a. Reliability design and RVaR. *International Journal of Reliability, Quality and Safety Engineering* 12 (4) (August).

———. 2005b. Advertising and advertising claims over time. In *Optimal control and dynamic games: Applications in finance, management science and economics,* ed. C. Deissenberg and R. F. Hartl. Berlin: Springer.

———. 2006. *Risk and assets pricing.* In *Handbook of engineering statistics.* Berlin and New York: Springer Verlag.

———. 2009. *The market price of safety and economic reliability.* Working paper, Center for Risk Engineering, New York University Polytechnic Institute.

Welker, M., 1995. Disclosure policy, information asymmetry, and liquidity in equity markets. *Contemporary Accounting Research* 11 (2):801–827.

Whalen, Chris. 2008. New hope for financial economics: Interview with Bill Janeway. Institute of Risk Analysis, November 17. http://us1.institutionalriskanalytics.com/pub/IRAStory.asp?tag=323.

Whisenant, S., S. Sankaraguruswamy, and R. Raghunandan. 2003. Market reaction to disclosure of reportable events. *Auditing: A Journal of Practice and Theory* 22 (1):181–194.

Witt, R. C. 1986. The evolution of risk management and insurance: Change and challenge. Presidential address, ARIA. *Journal of Risk and Insurance* 53 (1):9–22.

Zabel, E. 1981. Competitive price adjustment without market clearing. *Econometrica* 49:1201–1221.

CHAPTER 3

Risk Measurement and Volatility

OVERVIEW

Financial practice is embedded in the measurement and the use of data, its interpretation, and its reconciliation with economic theories, trends, and insights that are used for financial decision making. Securities, bonds, and options' prices as well as financial and economic time series are used in many ways and for many purposes. They may be used to test the validity of financial models, to predict future prices, to reveal financial markets expectations, and so on. The focus of this chapter is on quantitative definitions and measurements of risk using statistical techniques. Our purpose is to familiarize students of financial engineering with these techniques to help them make sense of the extraordinarily abundant and complex financial data that is available from both public and private sources. The chapter's message is that financial decisions involve information, analysis, and interpretation; and that data contributes to a greater understanding of financial trends and to our ability to forecast the prices of securities and their derivatives and to make educated financial decisions.

RISK, VOLATILITY, AND MEASUREMENT

Finance is about money, expectations, prices, and financial consequences—whether adverse (in which case it is a risk) or not (in which case it is a profitable return). Price may be an insurance premium that an insured pays to an insurer, expressing both the insured's demand for risk protection and the insurer's price of bearing risk. Price is thus defined by the exchange between the two parties to such a transaction. For this reason, a price implies parties' needs, their information, and their attitudes toward risk taking. When one of the parties is a financial market consisting of many buyers and sellers trading under the same terms and the same price, then the price is a market price. For example, the market price of a corporate security signals financial prospects of the firm accounted for by its expected future returns and risks.

To account for this risk, a *risk premium* is paid to the buyer of the security to compensate the risk he assumes. The price of the security however implies a financial market valuation for the rights and the risks/rewards of holding the security. These rights include a legal right of the investor over a firm's (uncertain) revenues, its dividends, the right to vote at the firm's assembly, and optional rights embedded

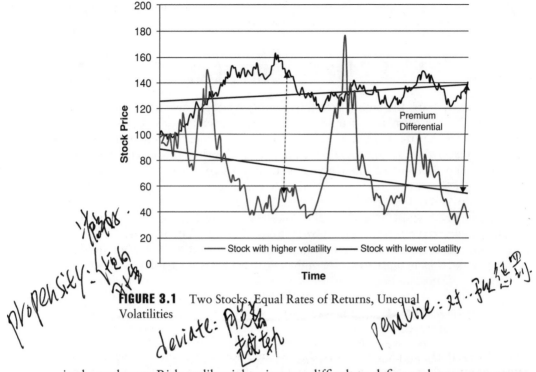

FIGURE 3.1 Two Stocks, Equal Rates of Returns, Unequal Volatilities

in the exchange. Risk, unlike rights, is more difficult to define and may mean many things to many people. Nonetheless, it is commonly agreed in practice that a security's volatility provides a proxy measurement for the risk of the security. *Volatility* is the propensity of a security's (or asset's) price to deviate from its expectation. For this reason, its measurement can be used to approximate—given an acceptable model that relates the risk premium and volatility—the price of risk.

To highlight the effects of volatility on a security's price, consider two securities with the same returns but with two different volatilities (see Figure 3.1). Their prices differ—the higher-volatility security (indicated by the lighter line) is penalized for its implied volatility risk: The higher the security's volatility, the lower the price, and vice versa. To appreciate this intuitive statement, assume that a security price is a function of its mean rate of return μ_i and its volatility σ_i given explicitly by a function: $S_i(\mu_i, \sigma_i, t)$, $i = 1, 2$. Say that the two securities have an identical rate of return, in which case $\mu_1 = \mu_2$. A technical analysis of this equation follows.

Assume that the volatility is not too large, such that an approximate two-term linear Taylor series expansion of the stock prices with respect to a zero-volatility stock (in effect, a risk-free bond whose price is $S(\mu_i, 0, t)$) is as follows:

$$S(\mu_i, \sigma_i, t) = S(\mu_i, 0, t) + \frac{\partial S(\mu_i, 0, t)}{\partial \sigma_i} \sigma_i, \quad \frac{\partial S(\mu_i, 0, t)}{\partial \sigma_i} > 0 \qquad (3.1)$$

We set the securities to have the same returns to focus on the volatility. Then $\mu_1 = \mu_2$ and $S(\mu_1, 0, t) = S(\mu_2, 0, t)$. In other words, a price differential between these two securities expresses a higher risk premium for the higher-volatility stock $S(\mu_2, \sigma_2, t)$ manifested by a lower security price, or:

$$S(\mu, \sigma_1, t) - S(\mu, \sigma_2, t) = \frac{\partial S(\mu, 0, t)}{\partial \sigma_1}(\sigma_1 - \sigma_2) < 0 \qquad (3.2)$$

Thus, as $\sigma_1 > \sigma_2$, the higher-volatility security's price is necessarily lower, and vice versa. The risk premium per unit volatility is thus given by $-\partial S(\mu, 0, t)/\partial \sigma_1$. In Figure 3.1 note that the solid vertical line denotes the average premium differential while the dotted vertical line connecting the two stock prices at a given time is the point premium differential. Explicitly, if a stock price goes down or up when the volatility increases or decreases, as previously presumed, then it is safe to believe that volatility and risk are closely associated. For example, say that the second asset is a risk-free bond whose rate of return is the risk-free rate R_f, and say that the first security rate of return is μ_1 whose volatility is σ_1. Then, considering a Taylor series expansion with respect to both the mean rate of return and the volatility about a risk-free bond reduces equation (3.1) to the following expansion:

$$S(\mu_1, \sigma_1, t) - B(R_f, t) = \frac{\partial B(R_f, t)}{\partial \mu_1}(\mu_1 - R_f) + \frac{\partial B(R_f, t)}{\partial \sigma_1}(\sigma_1 - 0) \qquad (3.3)$$

where $S(R_f, 0, t) = B(R_f, 0, t) = B(R_f, t)$ is the price of a default-free bond whose rate of return is the risk-free rate; while $\partial B(R_f, t)/\partial \sigma < 0$ is a fall in the price of the bond if it were to be a bond price subject to returns volatility; $\partial B(R_f, t)/\partial \mu > 0$ is the growth in the bond price if its rate of return increases; and finally, $\mu_1 > R_f$. In this case, equation (3.3) points out a lower price spread $S(\mu_1, \sigma_1, t) - B(R_f, t)$ if, for a fixed rate of return, the volatility of the security increases and if the security's rate of return decreases. Further, the price spread increases if the security's volatility declines and its rate of return increases. These observations are just technical, however, and do not imply any financial theory. We shall see in subsequent chapters that a financial theory is needed to explain both the reasons for such changes and their quantitative assessment.

From a financial investment viewpoint it is important to understand and appreciate the many reasons that volatility may increase or decrease. For example, market volatility may be due to macroeconomic variables (such as national statistics of GNP, GDP, interest rates, unemployment, etc.) that underlie the performance of corporate securities. A constant flow of information—both objective and subjective contribute to variations in security prices. Similarly, studies have shown that the corporate financial structure (its leverage or debt-to-equity ratio) appreciably affects the price and the volatility of a security. For example, if we accept equation (3.3), we note that leverage contributes on the one hand to a growth in rates of return on a firm's equity and, on the other, to volatility growth.

Some studies point to a determinant role of interest rates. A rationale for these observations is embedded in the presumption that firms that have a higher leverage will be more risky and therefore are more likely to shun investors who abhor risk—or equivalently, shy away from stock prices with greater volatility (although, greater leverage may imply greater rates of return and therefore have the opposite effect, attracting risk-seeking investors). The security markets and the bond markets (with prices determined by their underlying interest rates) are further in competition. When interest rates increase, new bond issues have a higher price (while older ones, at reduced interest rates, have a lower price), which attracts funds from securities to the bonds markets, and vice versa.

The explicit measurement of risk (aside from that defined by a security's volatility) is difficult. In practice, we use risk-derived measures, applied to reveal and price the consequences of risk. We saw above that risk can be derived from a stock price's volatility. However, risk may also be conceived by some as a disappointment, a deviation from an expected return or expected performance. For example, a hedge fund manager whose rate of return falls below a contracted investor minimal loss can be very costly and thus very disappointing (i.e., the manager incurs an ex post loss, which is performance dependent). In such cases, the risk borne by the hedge fund manager is that the investor may reclaim his investment.

Such disappointment can be measured in various manners, albeit personal. For example, a firm that is expected (based on analysts' estimates) to provide a rate of return on its stocks of 3 percent for a quarter may place its security price at risk if it reports a lower rate of return. This effect might be increased further due to the asymmetric effects of negative versus positive return reports. If (and this is of course only a hypothesis) the price of disappointment is substantially correlated to a security's volatility, then the measurement and pricing of volatility may provide a derived indicator for the security risks. In other words, this is a price an investor is willing to pay to avoid such a disappointment.

Trades in options are often interpreted as trades in volatility, the option price mirroring the volatility and vice versa, the volatility mirrored by the option price. Other measurements of risk may be important for the individual investor who adopts and uses them to tailor his risks based on a personal measurement and a risk preference and attitude. These personal factors are not traded, and their price can be determined only implicitly, revealed by the investor's trades in fact. Some of these measures will be considered later on (in particular, the range, the max, and the min statistics). These measurements may be personal and revealing but with a price that cannot be ascertained (directly or indirectly) because such measures are not agreed on by buyers and sellers and therefore cannot be defined as financial products about which traders can bet. The importance of well-defined and accepted standards for measuring risks cannot be understated. Therefore, defining acceptable and tradable risk measurements is a permanent financial engineering challenge.

MOMENTS AND MEASURES OF VOLATILITY

Certain returns have no risk! An investor will be paid what is expected by the certain return. In reality, however, all assets have more or less risk. For example, a U.S. dollar may seem certain for a U.S. citizen living in the United States, but it is less certain for a European citizen whose dollar returns are subject to the euro-dollar exchange rate. By the same token, Treasury bills (those U.S. government traded bonds) may feel safe to some but are a very risky investment for anyone who believes the United States will be faced with significant inflation in the coming years. The prospects of an asset price are thus measured in terms of future uncertain events and the probabilities we associate to these events. In this section, we consider essential measurements of prices, risks, and their statistical characteristics used both in theory and in practice.

Expectations, Volatility, Skewness, Kurtosis, and the Range

Let the time record of a stock price be S_t at day t (say at the stock exchange closing time). The day's rate of return of the stock realized at time t is a certain quantity based on the measurements of this day:

$$R_t = \frac{S_t - S_{t-1}}{S_{t-1}} = \frac{S_t}{S_{t-1}} - 1, t = 1, 2, 3, \ldots \tag{3.4}$$

At this time t, the next day's rate of return at time $t + 1$ is, however, random and given by:

$$\tilde{R}_{t+1} = \frac{\tilde{S}_{t+1} - S_t}{S_t} = \frac{\tilde{S}_{t+1}}{S_t} - 1, t = 1, 2, 3, \ldots \tag{3.5}$$

where "~" is used to denote random variables with a probability distribution function which we write by:

$$f\left(\tilde{R}_{t+1} | \Im_t\right)$$

Here $\Im_t$ is called a *filtration* and indicates that this distribution embeds all the information we have up to time t (see also Chapter 8). In other words, a filtration implies that the probability density function (PDF) is an estimate based on the sum total of all information available regarding the random variable. Two traders, each with his own information bias, will thus reach different conclusions regarding a returns distribution due to their filtration. Alternatively, we write for convenience:

$$f_t\left(\tilde{R}_{t+1}\right) = f\left(\tilde{R}_{t+1} | \Im_t\right)$$

Of course at time t, we have:

$$f_t\left(R_t\right) = 1$$

since the rate of return is known and uniquely defined. At time t, the expected rate of return at the next period $t + 1$ is thus a random variable whose mean and variance (with its root square denoting the volatility) are:

$$\hat{R}_{t+1|t} = E\left(\tilde{R}_{t+1} | \Im_t\right) = \int_{\Re} \tilde{R}_{t+1} f\left(\tilde{R}_{t+1} | \Im_t\right) d\tilde{R}_{t+1} \tag{3.6}$$

where $\Re$ is used to define the relevant sample space of the returns random variable, and:

$$\sigma_{t+1|t}^2 = E\left(\tilde{R}_{t+1} - \hat{R}_{t+1|t}\right)^2 = \int_{\Re} \left(\tilde{R}_{t+1} - \hat{R}_{t+1|t}\right)^2 f\left(\tilde{R}_{t+1}\,|\,\Im_t\right) d\tilde{R}_{t+1} \qquad (3.7)$$

By the same token, third and higher moments of the probability distribution can be defined. The third moment indicates asymmetry about its mean, defined by:

$$\xi_{t+1|t} = E\left(\tilde{R}_{t+1} - \hat{R}_{t+1|t}\right)^3 \qquad (3.8)$$

The corresponding (asymmetry) index of skewness of the distribution is:

$$\text{Index of skewness} = \frac{\xi_{t+1|t}}{\sigma_{t+1|t}^3} \qquad (3.9)$$

while the fourth moment of a distribution, the kurtosis, defines the distribution *flatness* and therefore the relative thickness of the tails, or:

$$\psi_{t+1|t} = E\left(\tilde{R}_{t+1} - \hat{R}_{t+1|t}\right)^4 \qquad (3.10)$$

It is also summarized by its index of kurtosis:

$$\text{Index of kurtosis} = \frac{\psi_{t+1|t}}{\sigma_{t+1|t}^4} \qquad (3.11)$$

The importance of these moments cannot be overstated. For example, say that a returns time series is shown empirically to have a normal probability distribution of mean and variance (μ, σ^2). Since the normal distribution is symmetric, its third moment (and thereby its index of skewness) is necessarily null. For this reason, such an index expresses a departure from the normal assumption, which has extremely important implications to financial theory and practice as will be seen in subsequent chapters. By the same token, the thickness of the tail—the index of kurtosis—is an indicator of a distribution's predictability. Thick tails mean that there are many more states that have an appreciable probability mass, and, therefore, predicting the distribution's states will be increasingly difficult. In other words, a data set exhibiting a very high kurtosis implies that prices are commensurably unpredictable.

For a standard normal probability distribution with constant mean and constant variance, we have the following moments:

$$E\left(\varepsilon\right) = \mu = 0, \; E\left(\varepsilon^2\right) = \sigma^2 = 1, \; E\left(\varepsilon^3\right) = 0, \; E\left(\varepsilon^4\right) = 3 \qquad (3.12)$$

And therefore, its index of skewness is null while its index of kurtosis is

$$\frac{\psi}{\sigma^4} = \frac{4}{\sqrt{\pi}}\Gamma\left(\frac{5}{2}\right) = 3$$

In other words, if we estimate the probability moments of a security's rates of return and observe that their third moment (skewness) is not null, this ought to point out that rates of return do not have a normal probability distribution. Similarly, if the fourth moment reveals a kurtosis that differs from that of the normal distribution, then again, the rates of return and their associated risks cannot be presumed to be normal. Such a distribution may have fatter tails than those of the normal probability distribution if its kurtosis is larger and, therefore, the presumption of price predictability, which is essential in fundamental finance (see Chapter 7) falters.

Finally, assume that a security's prices over n days are given by $S_t, S_{t-1}, \ldots, S_{t-n}$. Let the high and the low of the security prices over these n days be $H_t^{(n)}$ and $L_t^{(n)}$ respectively, or:

$$H_t^{(n)} = Max\{S_t, S_{t-1}, \ldots, S_{t-n}\}, \; L_t^{(n)} = Min\{S_t, S_{t-1}, \ldots, S_{t-n}\} \quad (3.13)$$

The range is defined over a time interval by:

$$\Re_t^{(n)} = H_t^{(n)} - L_t^{(n)} = Max\{S_t, S_{t-1}, \ldots, S_{t-n}\} - Min\{S_t, S_{t-1}, \ldots, S_{t-n}\} \quad (3.14)$$

These statistics are collected daily and advertised by financial markets at the end of a day. The range in particular indicates the high less its low price of the day, while other day prices (the open and closing prices) are time point observations of the price reported. The range statistic applied over a number of days is a function of the time interval selected and the underlying probability distribution. If we consider *moving* statistics $H_t^{(n)}$, $H_{t+1}^{(n)}$, $H_{t+2}^{(n)}$, ..., each of these statistic will depend on the others as they all use common records (of prices, returns, etc.) and require therefore a careful analysis.

Nevertheless, the range is a statistical measure complementary to volatility. It differs from volatility, although a large and increasing range may point to an increasing variance (or to the existence of outliers—those points that do not conform to statistically expected patterns). The interpretation of these statistics is a financial econometric challenge, however. In some cases, the range may detect volatility growth since an unexpected growth in the range points to volatility growth while a persistent range (continuously following a patterned change with little variation) may indicate a mean-reversion process (considered later in this chapter). In other words, once the range has increased due to an outlier, mean reversion (a counter-movement process, reducing a price after it has grown over its mean) will set in to stabilize prices about their mean. In some cases, the range-to-standard-deviation statistic of a security time series has also been used to point to departures from the normality of a time series (see Chapter 4). Such a statistic is often used by financial speculators as an index of chaos (see the Hurst Index in Chapter 4).

EXAMPLE: IBM RETURNS STATISTICS

Using a typical record of trades in IBM's security (or similar data) we calculated the mean and the volatility for IBM using an Excel program (see computer-aided resources at www.charlestapiero.com). These led to a mean of 0.001375 and a

TABLE 3.1 Standardized statistical characteristics of IBM day prices

Mean	0
Standard error	0.009150084
Median	−0.027020074
Mode	−0.027020074
Standard deviation	1.000041861
Sample variance	1.000083724
Kurtosis	9.919066518
Skewness	0.043580821

volatility of 0.01339. Furthermore, a calculation of other moments for normalized data over a long period of time indicated that there was almost no skewness but a strong kurtosis. In other words, the data set we used indicated almost symmetric returns and fat tails for the returns distribution (since the kurtosis index is 9.91 > 3 for normally distributed rates of returns). The data skewness was 0.043 (while it equals zero for a normal probability distribution). These statistics imply that rates of return of IBM calculated over many years are not normal (see Table 3.1 for a summary of such statistics). This fact is challenging theoretical finance that hinges on the normality assumption of rates of returns.

These statistics illustrate a common situation in financial markets. Daily returns distributions exhibit longer tails and a sharper peak than a normal distribution with the same standard deviation. This means that for large portions of time, returns fluctuate in a range smaller than that of a normal distribution.

EXAMPLE: MOMENTS AND THE CAPM

In Chapter 5, we consider the development of the capital asset pricing model (CAPM) in greater detail. This is a financial linear model that expresses a firm rate of return in terms of the ongoing risk-free rate and the market (or an appropriate market index) rate of return. Here, we use simple moment calculations to express the *beta*, a linear coefficient used profusely in financial practice. The underlying rationale for this model hypothesizes that the rate of return of a security is a linear function of the difference between a fully diversified portfolio (namely an index portfolio such as the S&P) and the risk-free rate. Such a regression can be formulated as a model that can be estimated by linear regression (see the next section). It is given by:

$$\tilde{k} = \alpha + \beta \left(\tilde{R}_m - R_f \right) + \tilde{\varepsilon}_k, \tag{3.15}$$

where $\tilde{k}$ is the security rate of return
$\tilde{R}_m$ is the index rate of return
R_f is the risk-free rate

Finally, $\tilde{\varepsilon}_k$ is assumed to be a zero mean and normally distributed random variable with known variance, while (α, β) are two model parameters estimated by $\left(\hat{\alpha}, \hat{\beta}\right)$.

A first-moment equality of (3.15) yields:

$$E\left(\tilde{k}\right) = \hat{\alpha} + \hat{\beta}\left(E\left(\tilde{R}_m\right) - R_f\right) \tag{3.16}$$

In particular, if the security is now a fully diversified portfolio, in other words, the expected rate of return of the portfolio is equated to that of the market rate of return, then:

$$E\tilde{k} = E\tilde{R}_m$$

and therefore,

$$E\tilde{R}_m = \hat{\alpha} + \hat{\beta}\left(E\tilde{R}_m - R_f\right) = \hat{\alpha} + \left(E\tilde{R}_m - R_f\right)$$

Thus, for a diversified portfolio, $\hat{\alpha} = R_f$. Equation (3.15) is thus replaced by:

$$\tilde{k} - R_f = \beta\left(\tilde{R}_m - R_f\right) + \tilde{\varepsilon}_k \tag{3.17}$$

A second moment for the rates of return, (3.15) or (3.17), yields:

$$\text{var}(\tilde{k}) = \beta^2 \text{var}(\tilde{R}_M) + \text{var}(\varepsilon_k) + 2\beta \text{cov}(\tilde{R}_M, \tilde{\varepsilon}_k) \tag{3.18}$$

where

$$\text{cov}(\tilde{R}_M, \varepsilon_k) = E\left(\left(\tilde{R}_M - \hat{R}_M\right)(\tilde{\varepsilon}_k - \hat{\varepsilon}_k)\right)$$

denotes the covariation for a fully diversified portfolio with rate of return $\tilde{R}_M$ and residual error term $\tilde{\varepsilon}_k$ given from (3.17) by

$$\tilde{\varepsilon}_k = \tilde{k} - \beta\tilde{R}_M - \left(R_f - \beta R_f\right)$$

Thus,

$$\text{var}(\tilde{\varepsilon}_k) = \text{var}\left(\tilde{k} - \beta\tilde{R}_M\right) = \text{var}(\tilde{k}) + \beta^2 \text{var}(\tilde{R}_M) - 2\beta\text{cov}(\tilde{k}, \tilde{R}_M) \tag{3.19}$$

Inserting $\text{var}(\tilde{k})$ from equation (3.18) into (3.19) we have:

$$\text{var}(\tilde{\varepsilon}_k) = \beta^2\text{var}(\tilde{R}_M) + \text{var}(\tilde{\varepsilon}_k) + 2\beta\text{cov}(\tilde{R}_M, \tilde{\varepsilon}_k) + \beta^2\text{var}(\tilde{R}_M) - 2\beta\text{cov}(\tilde{k}, \tilde{R}_M) \tag{3.20}$$

And therefore,

$$\begin{cases} 0 = \text{cov}(\tilde{R}_M, \tilde{\varepsilon}_k) + \beta\text{var}(\tilde{R}_M) - \text{cov}(\tilde{k}, \tilde{R}_M) \quad \text{or} \\ \text{cov}(\tilde{k}, \tilde{R}_M) = \text{cov}(\tilde{R}_M, \varepsilon_k) + \beta_k\text{var}(\tilde{R}_M) \end{cases} \tag{3.21}$$

However, for a portfolio that is fully diversified, $\text{cov}(\tilde{R}_M, \tilde{\varepsilon}_k) = 0$ and therefore the security's estimated beta, denoted now as β_k, is given by:

$$\beta_k = \frac{\text{cov}\left(\tilde{R}_M, \tilde{k}\right)}{\sigma_M^2} = \rho_{kM}\frac{\sigma_k}{\sigma_M} \tag{3.22}$$

where ρ_{kM} is the correlation factor between the security price and the portfolio index. Note that these calculations have not assumed the error term to be normally distributed. This is the case because the CAPM model is a 2 moments probability model.

Data analysis can provide alternative means to calculate a security's Beta. In particular, if returns data are skewed, we have (Christoffersen, Jacobs, and Vainberg 2008):

$$skew_k = \frac{E\left(\tilde{k} - E\left(\tilde{k}\right)\right)^3}{\sigma_k^3} = \frac{E\left(\alpha + \beta\left(\tilde{R}_m - R_f\right) + \tilde{\varepsilon}_k - E\left(\alpha + \beta\left(\tilde{R}_m - R_f\right) + \tilde{\varepsilon}_k\right)\right)^3}{\sigma_k^3}$$

$$= \frac{\beta^3 E\left(\tilde{R}_m - \hat{R}_m\right) + E\left(\tilde{\varepsilon}_k\right)^3}{\sigma_k^3} = \frac{\beta^3 skew_m \sigma_m^3 + skew_{\varepsilon,k}\sigma_{\varepsilon,k}^3}{\sigma_k^3} \tag{3.23}$$

As a result, a skew beta is:

$$\beta_k = \left(\frac{skew_k \sigma_k^3 - skew_{\varepsilon,k}\sigma_{\varepsilon,k}^3}{skew_m \sigma_m^3}\right)^{\frac{1}{3}} \tag{3.24}$$

However if the residual error is normal, then its skew is null and therefore, the beta is (in other words, data skewness affects the Beta estimate):

$$\beta_k^{(n)} = \left(\frac{skew_k}{skew_m}\right)^{\frac{1}{3}}\left(\frac{\sigma_k}{\sigma_m}\right) \tag{3.25}$$

PROBLEM 3.1: CALCULATING THE BETA OF A SECURITY

Consider a security price (such as IBM, Bank of America, or some other corporation). Calculate for a day-time record of one month the moments of the security and the moments of the S&P market index. Then, calculate the beta of the security using the method of moments. Subsequently, consider the residual error and check if the residual has a zero skew.

Modeling Rates of Return

A financial model is a simplified representation of some parts or aspect of a real financial process. Financial modeling, however, consists in determining a model that maps this real process into a meaningful financial context, which we can estimate empirically or treat mathematically to some useful end. When a model is *stochastic*, it requires as well that we distinguish and integrate the known with the unknown. These are difficult tasks that require that we find some mechanisms (such as intuition, common sense, judgment, and a deep appreciation of economic theories) to reconcile our knowledge with our lack of it. For this reason, financial modeling is not merely a technique but an art of blending the relevant aspects of a given problem or process, and its unforeseen consequences, with a descriptive yet tractable mathematical methodology.

Two approaches are pursued in financial modeling. The first is data based, seeking explanatory models from an economic data set (such as securities prices, financial indexes, interest rates, economic time series, etc.). The second approach is based on the construction of models that use both economic and behavioral rationales, tested by unfolding market prices and economic/financial events. This latter approach is considered in detailed in Chapter 5 using utility theory, while Chapter 8 uses an endogenous model of traders and investors in a financial market. Such models are based on a number of assumptions such as an economic equilibrium that defines a unique price, no arbitrage, and so on. In this section, we outline a number of elementary financial models for rates of return and prices. Subsequently, we consider a number of statistical estimation techniques that can provide statistical estimates for the parameters of such models.

Models of Rate of Returns

The rate of return (ROR) financial models we consider include:

- The constant rate of return (ROR) hypothesis.
- Mean reversion models.
- Implied (or inverse) financial models.

The Constant Rate of Return Hypothesis   Let the time record of a stock price be S_t at day t (say at the stock exchange closing time). The day ROR observed at a time t and its next-day (random) ROR are by definition:

$$R_t = \frac{S_t - S_{t-1}}{S_{t-1}} = \frac{S_t}{S_{t-1}} - 1, \, t = 1, 2, 3, \ldots \quad \text{and} \quad \tilde{R}_{t+1} = \frac{\tilde{S}_{t+1} - S_t}{S_t} = \frac{\tilde{S}_{t+1}}{S_t} - 1 \quad (3.26)$$

Note that $\tilde{R}_{t+1}$ is a random variable at time t. Assume that $R_j, \, j = 1, 2, \ldots, t$ are observed rates of returns. The constant ROR hypothesis states that the expected ROR of a security is some (statistical population) constant μ and defined by the following stochastic model:

$$\tilde{R}_{t+1} = \mu + \sigma\tilde{\varepsilon}_{t+1} \quad (3.27)$$

with

$$E\left(\tilde{R}_{t+1}\right) = \mu, \, E\left(\tilde{\varepsilon}_{t+1}\right) = 0, \, \text{var}\left(\tilde{\varepsilon}_{t+1}\right) = 1$$

where $\tilde{\varepsilon}_{t+1}$ denotes the random error assumed to be identically and independently distributed as a normal probability distribution with mean zero and variance 1. This model assumes that at all time periods, returns have statistically identical and independent returns (of previous periods), with mean μ and variance σ^2. Combining equation (3.26) and (3.6), we get the following model for the security price equation for a time interval of one day $\Delta t = 1$ lognormal model:

$$\frac{\tilde{S}_{t+1} - S_t}{S_t} = \frac{\Delta \tilde{S}_{t+1}}{S_t} = \tilde{R}_{t+1} = \mu + \sigma\varepsilon_{t+1}, S_0 > 0, t = 1, 2, 3, \dots . \qquad (3.28)$$

When the time interval is small, defined by Δt, we have, instead of (3.28), the following:

$$\frac{\Delta \tilde{S}_{t+1}}{S_t} = \mu\Delta t + \sigma\Delta W_t, \quad S_0 > 0, \quad t = 1, 2, 3, \dots . \qquad (3.29)$$

where ΔW_t is used to denote standard normally distributed and independent random variables with mean zero and a time linear variance. Thus for a small interval of time, the variance is linear in the time interval Δt. This can be verified by

$$E\left(\varepsilon_{t+\Delta t}\right) = E\left(\Delta W_t\right) = 0$$

and

$$\text{var}\left(\varepsilon_{t+\Delta t}\right) = \text{var}\left(\sigma\Delta W_t\right) = \sigma^2\Delta t$$

Equation (3.29) is a lognormal process since the derivative of security prices has linear normal returns. This can be verified by a natural logarithmic transformation of the security price, $h\left(S_t\right) = \ln\left(S_t\right)$. A Taylor series expansion with respect to the price at a previous instant of time (say the previous day price S_{t-1}) yields:

$$h\left(S_t\right) = h\left(S_{t-1}\right) + \frac{\partial h\left(S_{t-1}\right)}{\partial S_t}\left(S_t - S_{t-1}\right) + \frac{1}{2}\frac{\partial^2 h\left(S_{t-1}\right)}{\partial S_t^2}\left(S_t - S_{t-1}\right)^2$$

$$+ \frac{1}{2.3}\frac{\partial^3 h\left(S_{t-1}\right)}{\partial S_t^3}\left(S_t - S_{t-1}\right)^3 \qquad (3.30)$$

Applying the transformation, $h(S_t) = \ln\left(S_t\right)$, for a previous instant of time Δt, we have then:

$$\ln\left(S_t\right) = \ln\left(S_{t-1}\right) + \frac{S_t - S_{t-1}}{S_{t-1}} - \frac{1}{2}\left(\frac{S_t - S_{t-1}}{S_{t-1}}\right)^2 + \frac{1}{3}\left(\frac{S_t - S_{t-1}}{S_{t-1}}\right)^3 + \cdots . \qquad (3.31)$$

Or, using the fact that a normal probability distribution has no skewness and that $\text{var}(\sigma\Delta W_t) = \sigma^2\Delta t$, we have:

$$\Delta\left(\ln(S_t)\right) = \ln(S_t) - \ln(S_{t-\Delta t}) = \tilde{R}_t - \frac{1}{2}\left(\tilde{R}_t^2\right) + \frac{1}{3}\left(\tilde{R}_t^3\right) + \cdots.$$

$$= \mu\Delta t + \sigma\Delta W_t - \frac{1}{2}\left(\mu\Delta t + \sigma\Delta W_t\right) = \left(\mu - \frac{1}{2}\sigma^2\right)\Delta t + \sigma\Delta W_t$$

$$(3.32)$$

And finally,

$$\Delta\left(\ln(S_t)\right) = \left(\mu - \frac{1}{2}\sigma^2\right)\Delta t + \sigma\Delta W_t \qquad (3.33)$$

This model is widely used in financial modeling and underlies the Black-Scholes model (see Chapter 8).

Autoregressive Processes and Mean Reverting Models Some financial models are defined as autoregressive (AR) processes. Consider the simple AR(1) model defined here:

$$R_t = \alpha R_{t-1} + \varepsilon_t, \ |\alpha| < 1 \qquad (3.34)$$

where ε_t is assumed i.i.d. (independently and identically distributed) with mean zero and variance σ^2. A general AR(n) model, accounting for past returns as well, is written similarly by:

$$R_t = \sum_{i=1}^{n} \alpha_i R_{t-i} + \sigma\varepsilon_t, \ |\alpha_i| < 1 \qquad (3.35)$$

Other models can be developed, with a smaller number of parameters to estimate. Models that extend our assumptions include the mean reversion ROR and the AR models. Say that the current rate of return is a weighted function of past rate of return variations, which we denote by Δy_{t-i}. In other words, we rewrite equation (3.35) as follows:

$$R_t = \sum_{i=1}^{n} \mu_i \Delta y_{t-i}, \text{where} \quad \Delta y_{t-i} = \Delta R_{t-i} \quad \text{and} \quad \Delta R_{t-i} = \alpha\Delta t + \sigma\Delta W(t-i)$$

$$(3.36)$$

where μ_i, α, and σ are another set of parameters. For convenience, say that the current rate of return is a continuous time function exponentially decreasing as a function of all past rates of return variations (in discrete time, it corresponds to a geometric distribution):

$$R(t) = \int_{-\infty}^{t} e^{-\mu(t-\tau)} dy(\tau) \tag{3.37}$$

An equivalent expression to equation (3.37) is found by deriving this equation with respect to time t, or:

$$\Delta R(t) = -\mu \Delta t \int_{-\infty}^{t} e^{-\mu(t-\tau)} dy(\tau) + \Delta y(\tau) = \Delta y(t) - \mu R(t) \Delta t \tag{3.38}$$

Since perturbations in rates of returns are random and given by equation (3.36):

$$\Delta y(t) = \alpha \Delta t + \sigma \Delta W(t) \tag{3.39}$$

we obtain the following rates of returns process:

$$\Delta R(t) = \alpha \Delta t + \sigma \Delta W(t) - \mu R(t) \Delta t \tag{3.40}$$

which we rewrite as follows:

$$\Delta R(t) = \mu \left(\frac{\alpha}{\mu} - R(t) \right) \Delta t + \sigma \Delta W(t) \tag{3.41}$$

Such a process is the well-known mean reverting process and can be shown to be normally distributed as well. Such models appear in finance in various applications such as modeling interest rates (the Vacicek model) and others. Other variations of this model can be derived (see www.charlestapiero.com for extensions). If rates of return have a constant mean, then

$$E(\Delta R(t)) = 0$$

and therefore,

$$E(R(t)) = \frac{\alpha}{\mu}$$

Implied (or Inverse) Financial Modeling   Consider a call option whose strike price is \$55. The option expiry date is December 15, 2005. Its price is \$0.05, and the volume transacted is 1,005 contracts. This price is thus a bet that the buyer of the option makes with respect to the future price of the option's security. In particular, if a specific model is assumed a known probability model a further of volatility, then this information can be used by a trader to estimate of the volatility at the option expiry date. In this sense, option data reveals traders' current beliefs regarding the underlying stock price volatility at the date the option contract is to be exercised.

However, calculating the volatility using options data differs from the direct statistical calculations in two manners. First, it is based on the presumption that option prices can be modeled as a known function of volatility, in which case we can inverse the model to obtain a measurement of volatility (which is implied by the option price model and the actual option price), or:

$$\text{Option Price} = \text{Option Price Model (Data, Volatility)}$$

$$\Rightarrow \text{Volatility} = \text{Model}^{-1} (\text{Data, Option Price})$$

The volatility thus calculated is an assessment of current beliefs regarding the future (or forward-looking), which is embedded in the model we use to predict the future underlying price. Such information is useful to bankers who use this information to assess the current market belief regarding future prices; and it is a tool for traders, investors, and speculators who assume financial positions based on their beliefs and the information they have (which might differ from the current market beliefs). Such an approach differs substantially from the statistical approach based on past prices rather than beliefs regarding future ones. In Chapter 11, the inverse problem for determining the parameters of a probability distribution of an underlying security based on observable option prices is considered in detail.

STATISTICAL ESTIMATIONS

We introduce in this section the principles of three statistical approaches to estimate the parameters of a financial model. These include the least squares approach, maximum likelihood, and ARCH-GARCH techniques. Each of these approaches is useful, although for financial modeling the need to estimate simultaneously expected rates of return and their volatility has led to the application of ARCH and GARCH techniques developed by Engle and Bollerslev (Bollerslev 1986; Bollerslev et al. 1994; Engle 1982), with the former granted the Nobel Prize for his academic work.

Least Squares Estimation

Consider a constant rate of return model:

$$R_{t-i} = \mu + \varepsilon_{t-i}, i = 0, 1, 2, \ldots, n \tag{3.42}$$

The error term is thus

$$\varepsilon_{t-i} = R_{t-i} - \mu$$

If the model is statistically unbiased, it means that

$$E\left(\varepsilon_{t-i}\right) = E\left(R_{t-i}\right) - \mu_t = 0$$

and therefore, its mean estimate at time t based on the past k observations is

$$\mu_t = E\left(\mu \mid \Im_t\right) = \frac{1}{k} \sum_{i=0}^{k-1} R_{t-i}, \quad \Im_t \equiv \{R_t, R_{t-1} \dots R_{t-k}\} \tag{3.43}$$

where the data set consist of the rates of return over the past k periods. Least squares (LS) estimation calculates such an estimate by minimizing its least squares error, or:

$$\underset{\mu}{Min}\, E\left(\varepsilon_{t-i}\right)^2 = \sum_{i=0}^{k-1} \left(R_{t-i} - \mu\right)^2 \tag{3.44}$$

A first-order necessary condition is:

$$\frac{\partial E\left(\varepsilon_{t-i}\right)^2}{\partial \mu} = -2 \sum_{i=0}^{k-1} \left(R_{t-i} - \mu\right) = 0$$

and therefore

$$\hat{\mu} = \frac{1}{k} \sum_{i=0}^{k-1} R_{t-i}$$

as indicated in equation (3.43). This statistical estimate is written as follows:

$$\hat{\mu}_t = E\left(\mu \mid \Im_t\right)$$

with $\Im_t$ its filtration, including all the information we selected as relevant at time t. The variance estimate is found by:

$$\hat{\sigma}_t^2 = \frac{1}{k-1} \sum_{i=0}^{k-1} \left(R_{t-i} - \hat{\mu}_t\right)^2 \tag{3.45}$$

This expression, written equivalently in terms of the filter $\Im_t$, is as follows:

$$\hat{\sigma}_t^2 = E(\varepsilon_t^2 \mid \Im_t) = E(R_t^2 \mid \Im_t) - \hat{\mu}_t^2$$

which is explicitly given by:

$$\hat{\sigma}_t^2 = \frac{\hat{\mu}_t^2 k}{k-1} + \frac{1}{k-1} \sum_{i=0}^{k-1} \left(R_{t-i}^2\right) - 2\frac{\hat{\mu}_t}{k-1} \sum_{i=0}^{k-1} R_{t-i} \tag{3.46}$$

Of course, if returns vary over time (as it is indeed the case), then the assumption of constant rates of return may be doubtful, and another model is needed that better fits the data set at hand. Further, if rates of returns are not normally distributed, then these estimators may also be misleading.

Maximum Likelihood

Let an asset's returns at time t have probability distributions $f_t(R, t-i), i = 0, 1, 2, \ldots n$. And let R_{t-i} be the observed return at time $t-i$. The likelihood of these observations, assuming that they are independent, is given by the product probability:

$$L_t = \prod_{i=0}^{n} f_t(R_{t-i} \,|\, \mu_t, \sigma_t^2) \qquad (3.47)$$

where μ_t, σ_t^2 are the parameters that define the probability distribution. The most likely parameters for a given set of observed rates of returns $R_t, R_{t-1}, R_{t-2}, \ldots, R_{t-n}$ can be found by maximizing their likelihood or, equivalently, maximizing their Ln-likelihood. The parameter estimation problem is thus reduced to:

$$\underset{\mu_t, \sigma_t^2}{Max}\, Ln\,(L_t) = \sum_{i=0}^{n} \ln f_t(R_{t-i} \,|\, \mu_t, \sigma_t^2) \qquad (3.48)$$

For simplicity, say that $f_t(R_{t-i} \,|\, \mu_t, \sigma_t^2)$ assumes a normal probability distribution. Then:

$$\begin{cases} f_t(R_{t-i} \,|\, \mu_t, \sigma_t^2) = \dfrac{1}{\sqrt{2\pi\sigma_t^2}} \exp\left\{ \dfrac{1}{2}\left(\dfrac{R_{t-i} - \mu_t}{\sigma_t}\right)^2 \right\} \\[4mm] Ln\left\{ f_t(R_{t-i} \,|\, \mu_t, \sigma_t^2) \right\} = \dfrac{1}{2}\left(\dfrac{R_{t-i} - \mu_t}{\sigma_t}\right)^2 - \dfrac{1}{2}\ln\left(2\pi\sigma_t^2\right) \end{cases}, \qquad (3.49)$$

The maximum likelihood parameters are then found by solving:

$$\underset{\mu_t, \sigma_t^2}{Max}\, Ln\,(L_t) = \dfrac{1}{2}\sum_{i=0}^{k}\left(\dfrac{R_{t-i} - \mu_t}{\sigma_t}\right)^2 - \dfrac{1}{2}\sum_{i=0}^{k}\ln\left(2\pi\sigma_t^2\right) \qquad (3.50)$$

Optimal maximum likelihood estimate at time t for these two parameters has first-order conditions:

$$\begin{cases} \dfrac{\partial Ln\,(L_t)}{\partial \mu_t} = 0 \Rightarrow \sum_{i=0}^{k}(R_{t-i} - \mu_t) = 0 \text{ and } \hat\mu_t = \dfrac{1}{k+1}\sum_{i=0}^{k} R_{t-i} \\[4mm] \dfrac{\partial Ln\,(L_t)}{\partial \sigma_t^2} = 0 \Rightarrow \dfrac{1}{\sigma_t^4}\sum_{i=0}^{k}(R_{t-i} - \mu_t)^2 = \sum_{i=0}^{k}\dfrac{1}{\sigma_t^2} \text{ and } \hat\sigma_t^2 = \dfrac{1}{k+1}\sum_{i=0}^{k}(R_{t-i} - \mu_t)^2 \end{cases} \qquad (3.51)$$

Using this approach, we can construct a priori models defining an evolution of volatility as a function of past estimates. For example, the following estimates seek to capture the stochastic evolution of volatility and at the same time reduce the number of parameters that one may assume in defining an underlying volatility process. In particular, let

$$\hat{\sigma}_{t,k}^2 = E_t(r_t^2) = \sum_{i=0}^{k} w_t(t-i)r_{t-i}^2, r_{t-i} = R_{t-i} - \mu_{t-i} \qquad (3.52)$$

where $w_t(t-i)$ is the weight given at time t to past observations at $t-i$
r_{t-i} is a standardized return observed at time $t-i$. Assume $w(t-i) = w_t(t-i)$ with
$w(t-i) = 1/T, T = k+1$. This leads to the following estimate:

$$\hat{\sigma}_{t,k}^2 = E_t(r_t^2) = \frac{1}{k+1} \sum_{i=0}^{k} r_{t-i}^2 \qquad (3.53)$$

An extension that gives greater weight to immediate past observations compared
to more distant (past) observations consists in an exponential smoothing of past
variance measurements (such as a geometric declining memory) given by

$$w(t-i) = \theta^i(1-\theta)$$

which is a function of one parameter only. In this case, we obtain:

$$\hat{\sigma}_{t,k}^2 = E_t(r_t^2) = (1-\theta) \sum_{i=0}^{k} \theta^i r_{t-i}^2, r_{t-i} = R_{t-i} - \mu_{t-i} \qquad (3.54)$$

Alternatively, volatility models can be constructed that assume that volatility is
a stochastic process (expressed in terms of unknown parameters to be estimated)
that characterizes its uncertainty.

ARCH and GARCH Estimators

For normal returns with known mean and known volatility, an observation can be
written in terms of standard normal variates:

$$z_t = \frac{\tilde{R}_t - \mu_t}{\sigma_t} \sim N(0, 1) \qquad (3.55)$$

Thus, for mean returns estimated based on a data set consisting of returns normally
distributed, we can write

$$\tilde{R}_t = \mu_t + \sigma_t z_t$$

Such a mean can be estimated either by linear regression or by maximum likelihood. However, this procedure presumes that the standard deviation is known. If
the standard deviation (volatility) has to be estimated as well using the same data
set, there are statistical problems due to the dependence of both parameters on the
same data set.

It is these situations that have motivated estimation techniques coined autoregressive conditional heteroskedasticity (ARCH) and generalized ARCH (GARCH). Engle in particular has suggested that we remove this co-dependence between the mean and the variance estimators and thereby remove the heteroskedasticity of data. Note that a data set is homoskedastic if its residuals (once estimators are determined) are uniformly randomly distributed. When a data set exhibits nonuniformly distributed random residuals, and in particular a dependence, we call such a pattern heteroskedastic. Removing the dependence from the residual once a mean has been estimated and using the adjusted residuals to estimate the standard deviation defines the ARCH and GARCH approach.

The assumption of constant volatility, has repeatedly been contradicted in financial time series. Fluctuations in returns of actual assets tend to cluster. A turbulent trading day tends to be followed by another turbulent day, while a tranquil period tends to be followed by another tranquil period. This means that there are memory effects where past fluctuations in returns influence current and future fluctuations. The normal model assumes, however, that all information is contained within the current asset price.

EXAMPLE: THE AR(1)-ARCH(1) MODEL

The simplest model suggested by Engle is the AR(1)-ARCH(1) model, explicitly stated as follows. First, assume an autoregressive returns process AR(1) model defined earlier with parameters α and σ:

$$\tilde{R}_t = \alpha R_{t-1} + \varepsilon_t, \ |\alpha| < 1 \tag{3.56}$$

where ε_t are assumed i.i.d with mean zero and variance σ^2. Now let $\mathfrak{R}^{t-1}$ be a security returns time series observed and therefore available at time $t-1$, with $\mathfrak{R}^{t-1} = \{R_0, R_1, \ldots, R_{t-1}\}$. Assuming the AR(1) model, the returns expectation conditionally on the data set is:

$$E(\varepsilon_t) = 0, \ E(\tilde{R}_t \,|\, \mathfrak{R}^{t-1}) = \alpha R_{t-1} \tag{3.57}$$

while the variance estimator is also an unbiased estimator of the variance since, from equation (3.56),

$$\text{var}\left(\tilde{R}_t\right) = \alpha^2 \text{var}\left(R_{t-1}\right) + \text{var}\left(\varepsilon_t\right)$$

or

$$\text{var}\left(\tilde{R}_t\right) = \frac{\text{var}\left(\varepsilon_t\right)}{\left(1 - \alpha^2\right)} = \frac{\sigma^2}{\left(1 - \alpha^2\right)}$$

Thus,

$$\text{var}(\tilde{R}_t) = \frac{\sigma^2}{1-\alpha^2} \quad \text{while} \quad \text{var}(\tilde{R}_t \, |\Re^{t-1}) = E\left\{\left[\tilde{R}_t - E(\tilde{R}_t \, |\Re^{t-1})\right]^2 |\Re^{t-1}\right\} = \sigma^2 \tag{3.58}$$

Note that the variance estimators are constants over time. Further, these variances are independent of the information available up to time t, or $\{\Re^t, t \geq 0\}$. The need for conditioning the variance estimator on the information available (the time series) underlies ARCH and GARCH models. For the AR(1) model, Engle (1982) proposed that the error variance be set as a linear function of the past error, in which case:

$$E(\varepsilon_t \, |\Re^{t-1}) = 0 \, , \, \text{var}(\varepsilon_t \, |\Re^{t-1}) = \alpha_0 + \alpha_1\varepsilon_{t-1}^2 \, , \, \alpha_0 > 0, \alpha_1 \geq 0 \tag{3.59}$$

where the information available on hand is now

$$\Re^{t-1} = \{R_{t-1}, R_{t-2}, \ldots\} = \{\varepsilon_{t-1}, \varepsilon_{t-2}, \ldots\}$$

since by definition of the AR(1) process we have

$$\varepsilon_{t-i} = \tilde{R}_{t-i} - \alpha R_{t-1-i}$$

The parameter $|\alpha| < 1$ assumes that the R process is stationary at the second order while the positive values for α_0, α_1 guarantee that the conditional variance is positive. The AR(1) model with errors specified by the two preceding equations is known as the ARCH(1) model. The error estimate term is in this case:

$$v_t = \varepsilon_t^2 - \text{var}\left(\varepsilon_t \, |Y^{t-1}\right)$$

written by the AR(1) model:

$$\varepsilon_t^2 = \alpha_0 + \alpha_1\varepsilon_{t-1}^2 + v_t \tag{3.60}$$

Further, if $\alpha_1 < 1$, it is easy to show that

$$\text{var}(\varepsilon_t) = \alpha_0/(1-\alpha_1)$$

and as a result,

$$\text{var}(\varepsilon_t \, |\Re^{t-1}) - \text{var}(\varepsilon_t) = \alpha_1(\varepsilon_{t-1}^2 - \sigma^2) \tag{3.61}$$

Thus, the error variance is only a function of the information available up to this time. This approach can be generalized further by considering a general linear regression where the error term is also estimated. This brief introduction to ARCH and GARCH models highlights some of the considerations we must keep in mind when dealing with the estimation of an underlying process variance (its volatility).

EXAMPLE: A GARCH (1,1) MODEL

An alternative model for the volatility is provided by the GARCH model (Bollerslev 1986). It is specified by assuming that the conditional error term has a zero mean normal probability distribution with a model variance h_t, or

$$\left(\varepsilon_t \left| \Re^{t-1} \right.\right) \sim N(0, h_t)$$

where

$$h_t = \alpha_0 + \alpha_1 \varepsilon_{t-1}^2 + \alpha_2 \varepsilon_{t-2}^2 + \alpha_3 \varepsilon_{t-3}^2 + \cdots + \alpha_q \varepsilon_{t-q}^2 + \gamma_1 h_{t-1} + \gamma_2 h_{t-2} + \cdots + \gamma_p h_{t-p}$$
$$\alpha_0 > 0, \alpha_i \geq 0, i = 1, 2, \ldots, q \quad \text{and} \quad \gamma_j, j = 1, 2, \ldots, p$$

$$(3.62)$$

which defines a Garch (p,q) model. In this case, the model is estimated by:

$$z_t = x_t \beta + \varepsilon_t, t = 1, 2, \ldots, T \tag{3.63}$$

with a conditional error:

$$\left(\varepsilon_t \left| \Re^{t-1} \right.\right) \sim N(0, h_t)$$

HIGH-LOW ESTIMATORS OF VOLATILITY

The range statistic measures the difference between the high and the low of a security price over a given period of time (usually such data is available daily). The range, like the volatility, is an indicator of variability, albeit with different characteristics. For example, the range is more sensitive to outliers that generate spikes in financial time series. If an intraday day price probability distribution is specified in terms of only two parameters, then the range will necessarily be a function of the these two parameters as well. This simple observation has been applied to estimate financial series volatility including Parkinson (1980), Garman and Klass (1980), Roger and Satchell (1991), and Kunitomo (1995), as well as Yang and Zhang (2000). Here we treat the simplest case, which sets a relationship between the range and volatility for normally distributed data samples and summarize without proofs volatility estimates based on the range statistics.

Parkinson (1980) suggested the following estimate:

$$\hat{\sigma}_{Park,t}^2 = \frac{\left[\ln\left(H_t / L_t\right)\right]^2}{4\ln(2)} = \frac{\left[\ln\left(H_t\right) - \ln\left(L_t\right)\right]^2}{4\ln(2)} = \frac{r_t}{4\ln(2)}, \quad r_t = \ln\left(H_t\right) - \ln\left(L_t\right)$$

$$(3.64)$$

where H_t is the high of the day
        L_t is its low
        r_t is the range of the ln transformed high and low prices of the day

A proof of this result is based on an underlying normal process and a result of Feller (1951).

Garman and Klass (1980) improved on Parkinson's estimate by including as well the close and the open prices (however, both assume that data is standardized to be drift-free). In this case, the GK estimate is given by:

$$\hat{\sigma}^2_{GK,t} = \sum_{i=1}^{t} \left\{ \frac{1}{2} \left(\ln \frac{H_i}{L_i} \right)^2 - (2 \ln 2 - 1) \left[\ln \frac{C_i}{O_i} \right]^2 \right\} \tag{3.65}$$

Where C_i is the closing price and O_i is the open price, both at time i.

Roger and Satchell (1991), Kunitomo (1995), and Yang and Zhang (2000) expanded further the volatility estimate and consider the process drift as well. Their estimates which are given by the following:

$$\hat{\sigma}^2_{RS,t} = \frac{1}{t} \sum_{i=1}^{t} \left\{ \ln \frac{H_i}{C_i} \ln \frac{H_i}{O_i} + \ln \frac{H_i}{C_i} \ln \frac{H_i}{O_i} \right\} \tag{3.66}$$

$$\sigma^2_{K,t} = \frac{1}{nt} \left(\frac{6}{\pi^2} \right) \sum_{i=1}^{t} \left[\left(1 - \frac{i}{t} \right) \ln \frac{H_i}{O_i} \right]^2 \tag{3.67}$$

And the Yang and Zhang estimate, which takes into account overnight price differences, is as follows:

$$\hat{\sigma}^2_{YZ} = \frac{1}{n-1} \sum_{t=1}^{n} \left(\ln \left(\frac{O_t}{C_{t-1}} \right) - \bar{o} \right)^2 + k \frac{1}{n-1} \sum_{t=1}^{n} \left(\ln \left(\frac{C_t}{O_t} \right) - \bar{c} \right)^2 + (1-k) \hat{\sigma}^2_{RS} \tag{3.68}$$

EXTREME MEASURES, VOLUME, AND INTRADAY PRICES

Data are important and useful if they can be properly used. For example, if we use the closing price of a security to estimate the security's rate of return and its volatility, why should we then acquire data that exhibit as well its daily high and low? Why should the volume of transactions during a day be relevant? In principle, all the available data ought to be used to estimate the parameters of interest and predict the security price and its derivatives. Further, if rates of return have a normal probability distribution, then estimates of their mean and variance ought to characterize as well the highs and lows observed. A cursory verification of intraday data (i.e., the extremely large numbers of trades that occur during a trading day) will point out that price variations are not normal and therefore conventional statistical techniques might not be useful. Generally, if financial markets are not stable (i.e., with large and stochastic volatility), returns will not have a normal probability distribution. In such cases, can the high, the low, and other data routinely collected be useful?

In this section, we depart from our previous analyses and assume that rates of return do not have a normal probability distribution and investigate how additional data can be used to improve financial predictions—in particular, we use the volume, the high, and low statistics. To highlight our approach that combines the high, the low, and the volume transacted in any one day, we consider some examples on extreme statistics.

For simplicity we assume that intraday data have a common probability distribution (which need not be normal). The three statistics, high, low, and volume, define the data set for the intraday price distribution. Two cases arise. If markets are liquid (in which case the volume is large), the high and low distributions can be assumed to have an extreme limit distribution (as we shall see shortly) and thus facilitate the estimation of the parameters of the price distribution in that day. If the volume is small (implying that markets are not liquid), we may still be able to use order statistics to calculate some of the properties of the financial prices. In these and in other situations, the challenge to financial engineers is to maximize the use of relevant information to be concordant with financial markets observations, and thereby to improve our ability to understand, price, and predict financial prices.

Statistical Orders, Volume, and Prices

Consider the record of intraday trades with few transactions (namely a situation of low volume traded) and let the distribution of prices during a day be $F(x)$. Define the largest (high) and observed value of the day be:

$$Y_n = S_{(n)} = Max\{S_1, S_2, \ldots, S_n\}$$

where $\{S_1, S_2, \ldots, S_n\}$ are the recorded prices during the day. Assume that during the day trades are statistically independent (which is a simplification) and let $S_{(j)}$ be the jth order (price) statistic, with $S_{(1)} < S_{(2)} < S_{(3)} < \ldots < S_{(n)}$ over n prices. Let $F_j(S)$, $j = 1, 2, \ldots, n$ denote the density function of $S_{(j)}$. Then, the distribution function of the maximum $Y_n = S_{(n)}$ is given by:

$$F_n(S) = P\left\{S_{(n)} < S\right\} = P\left\{all\ \ S_i < S\right\} = [F(S)]^n \tag{3.69}$$

Similarly, for the minimum statistic $Y_1 = S_{(1)} = \min[S_1, S_2, \ldots, S_n]$ (low price of the day) we have,

$$F_1(S) = P\left\{S_{(1)} < S\right\} = 1 - \Pr\left\{S_{(1)} > S\right\} = 1 - \Pr\left\{all\ \ S_i > S\right\} = 1 - [1 - F(S)]^n \tag{3.70}$$

Generally, for the jth (price of the day) statistic,

$$F_{(j)}(S) = \sum_{j=i}^{n} \binom{n}{i} [F(S)]^i [1 - F(S)]^{n-i} \tag{3.71}$$

Therefore, by deriving with respect to S, we have the distribution:

$$f_j(S) = \frac{n!}{(j-1)!(n-j)!} f(S) [F(S)]^{j-1} [1 - F(S)]^{n-j} \tag{3.72}$$

In particular, for the maximum (high price) and the minimum (low price) statistics which is recorded each day, we have the following marginal probability distributions:

$$f_n(S) = nf(S) [F(S)] n - 1$$

and

$$f_1(S) = nf(S) [1 - F(S)]^{n-1} \tag{3.73}$$

The time records of the high and the low prices in a day provide thus two data samples that can be used to estimate the distribution of the day price (or return). Since these statistics are taken from the same sample, we have a joint bivariate order distribution (see Provasi 1996) given by:

$$f_{kj}(S_1, S_2) = \frac{n!}{(j-1)!(n-k)!(n-j)!} f(S_1) f(S_2) [F(S_1)]^{j-1} [F(S_2) - F(S_1)]^{k-j-1}$$
$$\times [1 - F(S_2)]^{n-k} - \infty < S_1 < S_2 < \infty \tag{3.74}$$

And therefore, for the joint distribution of the high and the low, we have $k = n$ and $j = 1$:

$$f_{12}(S_1, S_2) = nf(S_1) f(S_2) [F(S_2) - F(S_1)]^{n-2} [1 - F(S_2)], \quad -\infty < S_1 < S_2 < \infty \tag{3.75}$$

Their conditional probabilities are:

$$f_{2:1}(S_2 \,|S_1) = f(S_1, S_2)/f_1(S_1)$$

while moments of the range can be calculated using the joint distribution in equation (3.75).

These results depend on the statistical independence of prices within the time span used. This is of course a strong assumption. However, if we assume prices are identically and independently distributed within a day, then the joint probability distribution $f_{12}(S_1, S_2)$ is a function of the volume transacted within this day, the day price probability distribution with open and close prices recorded daily.

For some distributions, explicit and analytical results can be obtained. Otherwise, it is necessary to turn to numerical and simulation techniques. For large samples (i.e. very liquid markets), limit distributions for the high- and low-order statistics can be used (as is shown in examples later as well as in extensions to this chapter at www.charlestapiero.com).

PROBLEM 3.2: THE PROBABILITY OF THE RANGE

Let the order statistics $S_{(1)}$ and $S_{(n)}$ denote the smallest and the largest prices over n periods. We assume that each day, prices are identically and independently distributed. Show that for the range process we have

$$P(R \leq a) = P(S_{(n)} - S_{(1)} \leq a) = \frac{n}{n-1} \int\limits_{-\infty}^{\infty} [F(z+a) - F(z)]^{n-1} f(z) dz \qquad (3.76)$$

The study of dependent data (i.e., the prices are not identically distributed each day), as is usually the case in stochastic processes, is difficult. However, techniques such as copulas (see Chapter 4) can be used.

Intraday Prices and Extreme Distributions

Assume a very large day volume of n transactions with high (and low) statistics with probability distribution $F_{Y_n}(R) = [F_R(R)]^n$. At the limit, when n is large, this distribution converges to a family of extreme distributions. These distributions are given by three families:

$$\text{Gumbel}: F_Y(y) = \exp(-e^{-y}), \, y \in IR \qquad (3.77)$$

$$\text{Weibull}: F_Y(y) = \begin{cases} \exp\left(-(-y)^{-k}\right) & \text{for } y < 0 \, (k < 0) \\ 0 & \text{for } y \geq 0 \end{cases} \qquad (3.78)$$

$$\text{Frechet}: F_Y(y) = \begin{cases} 0 & \text{for } y \leq 0 \\ \exp(-y^{-k}) & \text{for } y > 0 \, (k > 0) \end{cases} \qquad (3.79)$$

Consider, for example, a two-parameter Weibull extreme distribution for the lowest price in a day,

$$f(s_{(1)} | \alpha, \beta) = \alpha \beta S_{(1)}^{a-1} e^{-\beta S_{(1)}^a}, \, S_{(1)} \geq 0, \beta, a > 0; F(S_{(1)}) = 1 - e^{-\beta S_{(1)}^a} \qquad (3.80)$$

The mean and the variance are then:

$$E(S_{(1)}) = \beta^a \Gamma\left(\frac{1}{a} + 1\right), \, \text{var}(S_{(1)}) = \beta^{2a} \left[\Gamma\left(\frac{2}{a} + 1\right) - \Gamma^2\left(\frac{1}{a} + 1\right)\right] \qquad (3.81)$$

To estimate these parameters, approximately, we can use the moments of a data sample, which is equated to the Weibull theoretical moments. This will result in an approximate estimate.

DATA TRANSFORMATION

When a data sample is transformed and used for estimation purposes, it has statistical implications. Assume a continuous function of the security price admitting first and second derivatives and given by $y_t = h(S_t)$. First note that a Taylor series expansion about $h\left(\hat{S}_t\right)$ where $\hat{S}_t = E(S_t)$ yields:

$$
\begin{aligned}
h(S_t) = h\left(\hat{S}_t\right) &+ \frac{\partial h\left(\hat{S}_t\right)}{\partial S_t}\left(S_t - \hat{S}_t\right) + \frac{1}{2}\frac{\partial^2 h\left(\hat{S}_t\right)}{\partial S_t^2}\left(S_t - \hat{S}_t\right)^2 + \\
&+ \frac{1}{1.2.3}\frac{\partial^3 h\left(\hat{S}_t\right)}{\partial S_t^3}\left(S_t - \hat{S}_t\right)^3 + \frac{1}{1.2.3.4}\frac{\partial^4 h\left(\hat{S}_t\right)}{\partial S_t^4}\left(S_t - \hat{S}_t\right)^4 + \cdots
\end{aligned}
\tag{3.82}
$$

Letting the error estimate be $\varepsilon_t = S_t - \hat{S}_t$, with $E(\varepsilon_t) = 0$ and $\mathrm{var}(\varepsilon_t) = \sigma^2$, we have:

$$
\begin{aligned}
E(h(S_t)) = h\left(\hat{S}_t\right) &+ \frac{\partial h\left(\hat{S}_t\right)}{\partial S_t}E(\varepsilon_t) + \frac{1}{2}\frac{\partial^2 h\left(\hat{S}_t\right)}{\partial S_t^2}E(\varepsilon_t^2) + \\
&+ \frac{1}{1.2.3}\frac{\partial^3 h\left(\hat{S}_t\right)}{\partial S_t^3}E(\varepsilon_t^3) + \frac{1}{1.2.3.4}\frac{\partial^4 h\left(\hat{S}_t\right)}{\partial S_t^4}E(\varepsilon_t^4) + \cdots
\end{aligned}
\tag{3.83}
$$

For example, if the residual has a normal probability distribution of zero mean and variance σ^2, then since $E(\varepsilon_t^3)=0$, and $E(\varepsilon_t^4) = 3\sigma^4$ we have:

$$
E(h(S_t)) = h\left(\hat{S}_t\right) + \frac{1}{2}\frac{\partial^2 h\left(\hat{S}_t\right)}{\partial S_t^2}\sigma^2 + \frac{1}{8}\frac{\partial^4 h\left(\hat{S}_t\right)}{\partial S_t^4}\sigma^4
\tag{3.84}
$$

By the same token, the variance expectation

$$
\mathrm{var}(h(S_t)) = E[h(S_t) - E(h(S_t))]^2
$$

based on the first three terms of a Taylor series expansion yields (with ξ_t denoting a standard normal probability random variable):

$$
\mathrm{var}(h(S_t)) = E\left[h\left(\hat{S}_t\right) + \frac{\partial h\left(\hat{S}_t\right)}{\partial S_t}\sigma\xi_t + \frac{1}{2}\frac{\partial^2 h\left(\hat{S}_t\right)}{\partial S_t^2}\sigma^2\xi_t^2 - h\left(\hat{S}_t\right) - \frac{1}{2}\frac{\partial^2 h\left(\hat{S}_t\right)}{\partial S_t^2}\sigma^2\right]^2
\tag{3.85}
$$

And as a result,

$$
\begin{aligned}
\operatorname{var}\left(h\left(S_{t}\right)\right) &= E\left[\frac{\partial h\left(\hat{S}_{t}\right)}{\partial S_{t}}\sigma\xi_{t}+\frac{1}{2}\frac{\partial^{2}h\left(\hat{S}_{t}\right)}{\partial S_{t}^{2}}\sigma^{2}\left(\xi_{t}^{2}-1\right)\right]^{2} \\
&= \left(\frac{\partial h\left(\hat{S}_{t}\right)}{\partial S_{t}}\sigma\right)^{2}E\left(\xi_{t}^{2}\right)+\left(\frac{1}{2}\frac{\partial^{2}h\left(\hat{S}_{t}\right)}{\partial S_{t}^{2}}\sigma^{2}\right)^{2}E\left(\xi_{t}^{2}-1\right)^{2} \\
&\quad +\frac{\partial h\left(\hat{S}_{t}\right)}{\partial S_{t}}\frac{\partial^{2}h\left(\hat{S}_{t}\right)}{\partial S_{t}^{2}}\sigma^{3}\left(E\xi_{t}^{3}-E\xi_{t}\right)
\end{aligned}
\tag{3.86}
$$

In particular, note that for the standard normal probability distribution we have $E\left(\xi_{t}\right)=0$, $E\left(\xi_{t}^{2}\right)=1$, $E\left(\xi_{t}^{3}\right)=0$, and $E\left(\xi_{t}^{4}\right)=3$. As a result,

$$
\operatorname{var}\left(h\left(S_{t}\right)\right)=\sigma^{2}\left(\frac{\partial h\left(\hat{S}_{t}\right)}{\partial S_{t}}\right)^{2}+\sigma^{4}\left(\frac{\partial^{2}h\left(\hat{S}_{t}\right)}{\partial S_{t}^{2}}\right)^{2}
\tag{3.87}
$$

For example, for $h(S_{t})=\ln\left(S_{t}\right)$, then

$$
\partial\ln\left(S\right)/\partial S=1/S,\ \partial^{2}\ln\left(S\right)/\partial S^{2}=-1/S^{2}
$$

and therefore,

$$
\operatorname{var}\left(\ln\left(S_{t}\right)\right)=\frac{\sigma^{2}}{S_{t}^{2}}\left(1+\frac{\sigma^{2}}{S_{t}^{2}}\right)
\tag{3.88}
$$

EXAMPLE: TAYLOR SERIES

A Taylor series expansion of $h\left(S_{t}\right)$ around its previous price S_{t-1} (rather than its mean) is:

$$
\begin{aligned}
h\left(S_{t}\right) &= h\left(S_{t-1}\right)+\frac{\partial h\left(S_{t-1}\right)}{\partial S_{t}}\left(S_{t}-S_{t-1}\right)+\frac{1}{2}\frac{\partial^{2}h\left(S_{t-1}\right)}{\partial S_{t}^{2}}\left(S_{t}-S_{t-1}\right)^{2} \\
&\quad +\frac{1}{2.3}\frac{\partial^{3}h\left(S_{t-1}\right)}{\partial S_{t}^{3}}\left(S_{t}-S_{t-1}\right)^{3}
\end{aligned}
\tag{3.89}
$$

For $h(S_{t})=\ln\left(S_{t}\right)$, show that:

$$
\ln\left(S_{t}\right)-\ln\left(S_{t-1}\right)=R_{t}-\frac{1}{2}\left(R_{t}^{2}\right)+\frac{1}{3}\left(R_{t}^{3}\right)+\cdots.
\tag{3.90}
$$

Show further that if the rate of return has a constant mean μ and variance λ^2, then

$$E\left(\Delta \ln\left(S_t\right)\right) = \mu - \frac{1}{2}\left(\lambda^2 + \mu^2\right) \tag{3.91}$$

and

$$E\left(\Delta \ln\left(S_t\right)^2\right) = E\left(R_t - \frac{1}{2}R_t^2\right)^2 = ER_t^2 - ER_t^3 + \frac{1}{4}ER_t^4$$

Additionally, say that the mean rate of return is constant and given by μ,

$$\text{var}\left(\Delta \ln\left(S_t\right)\right) = \lambda^2 + \mu^2 - ER_t^3 + \frac{1}{4}ER_t^4 - \left(\mu - \frac{1}{2}\left(\lambda^2 + \mu^2\right)\right)^2 \tag{3.92}$$

where $\left(ER_t^3, ER_t^4\right)$ are a function of the skewness and kurtosis of the returns.

VALUE AT RISK AND RISK EXPOSURE

The value at risk (VaR) is a measure of risk exposure that is used in practice extensively and consists in the following: For a given horizon time T and confidence level P_{VaR}, VaR is defined as the loss in value over the time horizon T that is exceeded with probability P_{VaR}. If ξ denotes a dollar change in a portfolio over a period of time T, then

$$P_{VaR} = P(\xi < -VaR) = \int_{-\infty}^{-VaR} P_T(\xi)d\xi \tag{3.93}$$

where $P_T(.)$ is the probability distribution of losses defined over the time period T.

Risk exposure relates to the volatility of the underlying process through its effect on the probability distribution of ξ. It is used for risk management purposes by setting aside an amount of reserve capital (called the value at risk, VaR) to meet excessive losses. Basel II financial regulation has used the VaR as a capital requirement that financial services must keep in risk-free and liquid accounts to meet their obligations. This regulation, shortly after its implementation, was changed following critics' pointing to its *risk measure incoherence* (for example, Artzner, Delbaen et al. 1997; Artzner 1999)—that is, its neglecting (and thus not accounting for) operational risks and dominant rare risks that are both important and unpredictable. In some cases, VaR has been accused of inducing financial firms to take more risks rather than fewer. For example, while AIG and Lehman Brothers have maintained plenty of cash and assets to avoid any failure, they were nonetheless struck by a financial meltdown in September 2008.

Failure of the VaR approach as an exclusive approach to managing a firm's financial liquidity risks has also been criticized. Other measures have thus been suggested, such as *shortfall* and *stop-loss measures*. A shortfall approach is defined by calculating a VaR as follows:

$$S_F = E(\xi \,|\, \xi \leq -VaR) = \int\limits_{-\infty}^{-VaR} \xi f_\xi(x)dx \qquad (3.94)$$

while the stop-loss measure (SL), which seeks to bound the losses of a portfolio, is:

$$S_{SL} = E\left(Max\left(\xi - SL, 0\right)\right) = \int\limits_{SL}^{\infty} (\xi - SL)\, f\,(\xi)d\xi \qquad (3.95)$$

where $f(\xi)$ is the loss probability distribution.

All these measures depend on our ability to define risks and their probability distributions. For this reason, the practical challenge to VaR applications resides in the estimation of potential losses. For example, if a portfolio's wealth is defined by a (thin-tail) normal probability distribution, risks are fairly predictable and therefore they do not matter much (as one may prevent, account, and compensate for these risks). Risks that are rare, mostly unpredictable, and extremely important do matter, however, but these risks are not easily identifiable and quantifiable. For this reason, numerous techniques including extreme distributions, Pareto-Levy processes (see the extreme distributions introduced earlier and in Chapter 4), and simulations (or a stress test based on many scenarios) are also used.

The commercial success of VaR is undeniable though. It provides a single and practical number applied easily by nontechnical managers. It provides a simple aggregate measure of risk (albeit with many concerns about its validity). More importantly, *value* and *risk* are business words well framed in the VaR concepts required for Basel II financial certification. At the same time, a misunderstood VaR can have many pitfalls. These include summarily:

- A bias that made it possible for banks to assume excessive risks and still meet VaR regulations—in particular, assuming risks through optional products that were not accounted for in banks' portfolios (particularly credit derivatives).
- Loss models with leptokurtic distributions, rare events, and so on, such that using exclusively the variance-covariance of a return process led to understating risk.
- Measurement problems arising when using exclusively historical data that reflects past risks. Risks are mostly the legacy of the future, revealed by markets' attitudes embedded in options price data, nonstationarity, multiple sources of interacting and dependent risks, and so forth. The exclusive use of optional products to insure these risks has also proved to be useless when financial markets failed and optional products could not priced or liquefied.
- Overstating VaR as the essential tool to manage risk exposure. This has led also to a biased approach rather than to a comprehensive financial risk management.

Next we consider simple examples of VaR application to highlight its meaningfulness.

VaR and Its Application

Assume a portfolio of six securities for which the price (or the rate of return) and the volatility of each are given. Risk exposure over a time interval T is calculated as follows. First, we determine the gains/losses of the portfolio over the period T defined by:

$$\xi_T = \sum_{j=1}^{m} \left(\sum_{i=1}^{T} \tilde{\pi}_{ij} n_j \right) \tag{3.96}$$

where n_j is the number of shares j (with m securities held) in the portfolio
$\tilde{\pi}_{ij}$ is the profits or losses at time i of a share j

If shares are assumed to be normally distributed or, alternatively, the portfolio risk is assumed to be function of its mean and variance only, then the following two parameters define essentially the portfolio over the period T:

$$\mu_T = E\left(\xi_T\right) = \sum_{j=1}^{m} \left(\sum_{i=1}^{T} E\left(\tilde{\pi}_{ij}\right) \right) n_j,$$

$$\sigma_T^2 = \mathrm{var}\left(\xi_T\right) = \mathrm{var} \sum_{j=1}^{m} \left(\tilde{\pi}_{1j} n_j + \tilde{\pi}_{2j} n_j + \tilde{\pi}_{3j} n_j \cdots + \tilde{\pi}_{Tj} n_j \right) \tag{3.97}$$

Note in this last expression some of the difficulties in calculating the portfolio variance. First, there may be dependent prices across the portfolio's shares; and second, the share prices may themselves be (and most probably, they are) autocorrelated. Additional risks (as outlined in Chapter 4) may increase this variance as well. If we simplify our analysis to one period, then for a portfolio of six shares with:

$$n_1 = 100, n_2 = 300, n_3 = 150, n_4 = 400, n_5 = 500, n_6 = 50$$

the expected loss is:

$$\mu_1 = E\left(\xi_1\right) = \sum_{j=1}^{6} \left(E\left(\tilde{\pi}_{1j}\right) \right) n_j = 100 E\left(\tilde{\pi}_{11}\right) + 300 E\left(\tilde{\pi}_{12}\right) + 150 E\left(\tilde{\pi}_{13}\right)$$

$$+ 400 E\left(\tilde{\pi}_{14}\right) + 50 E\left(\tilde{\pi}_{15}\right)$$

If the variances (given as a proportion of the means) and the matrix of correlations between these shares are given by:

$$\sigma_j^{2I} = \{0.6E(\tilde{\pi}_{11}), 1.3E(\tilde{\pi}_{12}), 0.7E(\tilde{\pi}_{13}), 0.5E(\tilde{\pi}_{14}), 1.0E(\tilde{\pi}_{15}), (0)E(\tilde{\pi}_1)\}$$

$$[\rho_{kj}] = \begin{bmatrix} 1 & 0.2 & 0.5 & -0.3 & -0.4 & 0.1 \\ & 1 & 0.3 & 0.6 & -0.2 & -0.3 \\ & & 1 & 0.2 & 0.15 & -0.4 \\ & & & 1 & 0.15 & -0.2 \\ & & & & 1 & 0.3 \\ & & & & & 1 \end{bmatrix}$$

then the portfolio gains/losses variance is:

$$\sigma^{2I} = \left\{ \sum_{j=1}^{6} n_j^2 \sigma_{1j}^2 + \sum_{k \neq j}^{6} \sum_{j}^{6} n_j n_i \rho_{kj} \sigma_{1,k} \sigma_{1,j} \right\} \tag{3.98}$$

If the gains/loss distribution has a known (or assumed) probability distribution, the VaR is:

$$P(\xi \leq -VaR) = \int_{-\infty}^{-VaR} f(\xi \mid \mu_1, \sigma^I) d\xi \tag{3.99}$$

and

$$P(\xi \leq -VaR) = \int_{-\infty}^{\frac{\mu_1 - (-VaR)}{\sigma^I}} f(.. \mid 0, 1) d.. = F_{STDN}\left(\frac{\mu_1 - (-VaR)}{\sigma^I}\right) \tag{3.100}$$

For example, if the risk exposure is limited to 5 percent (see Figure 3.2), then:

$$F_{STDN}\left(\frac{\mu_T - (-VaR)}{\sigma_T}\right) = 0.05$$

and the VaR is calculated by:

$$VaR = \mu_1 - \sigma^I F_{STDN}^{-1}(0.05) = \mu_1 - 1.96\sigma^I$$

In practice, a portfolio's gains and losses are recorded over time. The statistical treatment of these gains and losses provides then the probability distribution of gains and losses, which we have used here. While this is simplistic, it highlights the essentials of the VaR approach applied.

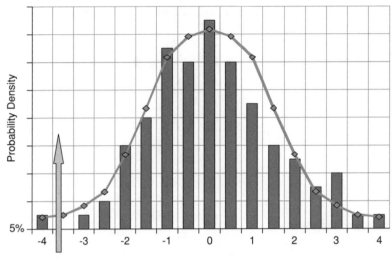

FIGURE 3.2   Definition of the VaR with 5 Percent Risk Exposure of the
Left Tail

EXAMPLE: VaR AND SHORTFALL

Let ΔX be the change in value (price) of a portfolio over a given period of time T
and let p be the portfolio's risk exposure. Thus, the VaR is defined by

$$\text{Prob}(\Delta X \leq -VaR) = p$$

Let W_t be the portfolio wealth state at time t and say $\Delta X = \tilde{W}_T - W_t$ is now
the portfolio gain/loss over the time interval $T - t$, the planning horizon used for the
VaR risk exposure analysis. Thus,

$$\text{Prob}\left(\tilde{W}_T \leq W_t - VaR\right) = p$$

and therefore,

$$\text{Prob}\left(\tilde{W}_T \leq W_t - VaR\right) = F_{\tilde{W}_T}(W_t - VaR) = p$$

or

$$W_t - VaR = F_{\tilde{W}_T}^{-1}(p) \tag{3.101}$$

and

$$VaR = W_t - F_{\tilde{W}_T}^{-1}(p)$$

Instead of a VaR risk exposure, consider an expected shortfall defined by:

$$S_d = E[\Delta X | \Delta X \leq -VaR] \text{ or } S_d = E[\tilde{W}_T - W_t | \tilde{W}_T \leq W_t - VaR] \qquad (3.102)$$

and explicitly,

$$E[\tilde{W}_T - W_t | \tilde{W}_T \leq W_t - VaR] = \int_{-\infty}^{W_t - VaR} (y - W_t) dF_{W_T}(y) \qquad (3.103)$$

Thus, the amount of capital set aside (the shortfall VaR, also distinguished from the VaR by EVaR) to meet contingent shortfalls may be much larger if the tail distribution is fatter. When the distribution is normal (which is in practice an overly optimistic case), we can then use the following partial moment equation to calculate the EVaR as well as its variance:

$$E[Z^n | Z \leq -v] = \frac{1}{\sqrt{2\pi}} \int_{-\infty}^{-v} Z^n e^{-\frac{1}{2}Z^2} dZ \qquad (3.104)$$

EXAMPLE*: VaR, NORMAL ROR, AND PORTFOLIO DESIGN

A portfolio consists of at most three securities and a bond. The rate of return (ROR), volatility, and the current price for each of these securities are given by:

Securities				
	1	2	3	Bond
ROR	0.05	0.09	0.06	0.04
(ROR) volatility	0.1	0.12	0.08	0
Current price	30	45	70	92

Let the current budget available be $1,000,000. How would you construct a portfolio that has a shortfall risk exposure of at most 15 percent of its capital over one year with a risk exposure of 5 percent? (Note that the three securities have a variance-covariance matrix given by:

$$\begin{vmatrix} 1 & 0.3 & -0.4 \\ - & 1 & 0.6 \\ - & - & 1 \end{vmatrix}$$

---

*Requires a slightly more advanced mathematical background; please see the Introduction.

This problem, unlike previous applications of VaR, seeks to design a portfolio that meets financial regulations' risk exposure and shortfall risk exposure. To solve this problem, assume that the evolution of each financial asset price is given by the following processes:

$$\frac{\Delta S_i}{S_i} = \alpha_i \Delta t + \sigma_i \Delta W_i, \tag{3.105}$$

Where $S_i(0)$ is given. Let,

$$\Delta \prod = \sum_{i=1}^{4} n_i \Delta S_i$$

be the gain/loss of the portfolio over the relevant period of time considered for the portfolio design. Then the Var and EVaR constraints are specified by:

$$F\left(\Delta \prod \leq -VaR\right) \leq p \ \text{ or } \ \int_{-\infty}^{-VaR} f\left(\Delta \prod\right) d\left(\Delta \prod\right) \leq p \tag{3.106}$$

and

$$\int_{-\infty}^{-EVaR} \Delta \prod f\left(\Delta \prod\right) d\left(\Delta \prod\right) \leq qW$$

where q is a proportion of the initial portfolio at risk with,
$p = 0.05, q = 0.15, W = 1,000,000$

If the objective of a portfolio is defined by (see Chapter 5 for justifications)

$$\underset{n_1, n_2, \dots}{Max} \ E\left(\Delta \prod\right) - \lambda \sqrt{\text{var}\left(\Delta \prod\right)} \tag{3.107}$$

then a VaR and EVaR regulation-consistent portfolio will result from a solution of:

$$\underset{n_1, n_2, \dots}{Max} \ E(\Delta \prod) - \lambda \sqrt{\text{var}(\Delta \prod)}$$

Subject to :

$$\Delta \prod = \sum_{i=1}^{4} n_i \Delta S_i = \sum_{i=1}^{4} n_i \left(\alpha_i S_i \Delta t + \sigma_i S_i \Delta W_i\right), \ \prod_0 = \sum_{i=1}^{4} n_i S_i \leq \prod_0 = W$$

$$F\left(\Delta \prod \leq -VaR\right) \leq p \ \text{ or } \int_{-\infty}^{-VaR} f(\Delta \prod) d(\Delta \prod) \leq p, \int_{-\infty}^{-EVaR} \Delta \prod f(\Delta \prod) d(\Delta \prod) \leq qW$$

$$\tag{3.108}$$

Note that if the gains/losses have a normal probability distribution then the VaR is given by:

$$VaR = E\left(\Delta \prod\right) - \sqrt{\text{var}\left(\Delta \prod\right)} Z_{1-p} \qquad (3.109)$$

which corresponds to the portfolio's objectives parameters (this is demonstrated in Chapter 5). In particular, if we set such a certain equivalent to:

$$CE = E\left(\Delta \prod\right) - \lambda\sqrt{\text{var}\left(\Delta \prod\right)} \qquad (3.110)$$

and

$$\lambda = \frac{E\left(\Delta \prod\right) - CE}{\sqrt{\text{var}\left(\Delta \prod\right)}} \text{ and } Z_{1-p} = \frac{E\left(\Delta \prod\right) - VaR}{\sqrt{\text{var}\left(\Delta \prod\right)}}$$

then,

$$\frac{\lambda}{Z_{1-p}} = \frac{E\left(\Delta \prod\right) - CE}{E\left(\Delta \prod\right) - VaR} \text{ or } \lambda = Z_{1-p}\frac{E\left(\Delta \prod\right) - CE}{E\left(\Delta \prod\right) - VaR} \qquad (3.111)$$

in which case, the objective of a VaR consistent portfolio has a *certain equivalent* which we specify by CE_{VaR}:

$$CE_{VaR} = \underset{n_1, n_2, \ldots}{Max} E\left(\Delta \prod\right) - Z_{1-p}\sqrt{\text{var}\left(\Delta \prod\right)}\frac{E\left(\Delta \prod\right) - CE}{E\left(\Delta \prod\right) - VaR} \qquad (3.112)$$

The numerical solution, although cumbersome, can be achieved using standard optimization software. Finally note, that if this is the certain equivalent of an outcome in one period, then its current value is discounted at a risk-free rate; or, replacing the certain equivalent CE:

$$CE_0 = \frac{1}{1 + R_f}\left\{\underset{n_1, n_2, \ldots}{Max} E\left(\Delta \prod\right) - Z_{1-p}\frac{\lambda\text{var}\left(\Delta \prod\right)}{E\left(\Delta \prod\right) - VaR}\right\} \qquad (3.113)$$

The Estimation of Gains and Losses

The statistics of the VaR approach are calculated in a number of ways including the historical data approach, variance-covariance, and the Monte Carlo simulation. Other approaches are based on extreme distributions and statistical models of various sorts. These approaches are briefly outlined next.

The Historical VaR Approach   The historical VaR generates scenarios directly from historical data. For each day, returns and associated risk factors are assessed and characterized probabilistically. This approach generates a number of errors though.

Markets may be nonstationary and therefore the scenarios may be difficult to characterize. This has the effect of overestimating the leptokurtic effect (the third-order moments of the distribution due to heteroskedasticity, the time dependence between the probability estimates). Application of the VaR using simulation instead tends to underestimate these effects because it uses theoretical distributions (such as the normal and lognormal distributions that are necessarily a simplification of a complex and unfolding reality).

The Analytic Variance-Covariance Approach   This approach while aggregating many risks, assumes the normality of returns given by a mean and a standard deviation as we have used it thus far. In trading rooms, application of the VaR, requires that the outcomes of multiple interacting risk factors (exchange rate risk, interest rates risk, stock price risks, etc.), which may be correlated as well, ought to be accounted for. Simplistically, their joint effects are assessed by the variance-covariance matrix. For example, a portfolio consisting of a long position in Deutsche marks and a short in yen with a bivariate normal distribution for two risk factors has a VaR that can be calculated with great ease. Let σ_1 and σ_2 be the standard deviations of two risk factors and let $\rho_{1,2}$ be their correlation. The resultant standard deviation of the position is thus:

$$\sigma_p = 0.5(\sigma_1^2 + \sigma_2^2 + 2 * \rho_{1,2}\sigma_1\sigma_2)^{1/2}$$

This is easily generalized to more than two factors. Problems arise, however, regarding the definition of multivariate risk distributions. Mostly, only marginal distributions are given while the joint multivariate distribution is not easily observable— theoretically and statistically. Recent studies have supported the use of copula and have given greater attention to the many risks that portfolios are subject to (see Chapter 4). These approaches are attracting much interest due to the interaction effects of multiple risk sources about which we have partial information.

Monte Carlo Simulation and VaR   Monte Carlo simulation techniques are both widely practiced and easy to apply. Their applications should be critically and carefully made. In simulation, one generates a large number of risk scenarios that follow the same underlying distribution. For each scenario the value of the position is calculated and recorded. The simulated values form a probability distribution for the value of a portfolio, which is used in deriving the VaR. In simulation, the essential questions remain: what model and what distribution to select? Monte Carlo simulation does not resolve these problems but provides a broader set of models and distributions we can select from.

VaR and Extremes Statistics   The usefulness of *extreme statistics* arises when extreme events are far more important than normal events. Normal events may underestimate the significant risks to confront or provide risk management principles insensitive to extreme losses. Extreme distributions are defined over the max or the min of a sample of random returns and have fatter tails than, say, the normal distribution. For example, say that a portfolio has a loss density function $F_R(x)$ while we seek the smallest profit (largest loss) over n periods as

$$Y_1 = Min\{R_1, R_2, \ldots, R_n\}$$

In this case, a target maximum loss VaR with risk specification p is

$$p = P(Y_1 < -VaR) = \int_{-\infty}^{-VaR} dF_1(\xi) \tag{3.114}$$

In probability terms, and as seen earlier, we have:

$$F_1(R) = P\{R_{(1)} < R\} = 1 - \Pr\{R_{(1)} > R\} = 1 - \Pr\{\text{all } R_i > R\} = 1 - [1 - F(R)]^n \tag{3.115}$$

and therefore,

$$p = \int_{-\infty}^{-VaR} d\left(1 - [1 - F(\xi)]^n\right) = \int_{-\infty}^{-VaR} n\frac{f(\xi)}{(1 - [F(\xi)])^{1-n}}d\xi \tag{3.116}$$

At the limit, when n is large, this distribution converges to Gumbel, Weibull, or a Frechet distributions as we saw earlier. This fact is an essential motivation for their use in VaR analyses. The VaR is then calculated simply since these distributions have analytical cumulative probability distributions as specified earlier.

SUMMARY

This chapter has introduced a fundamental challenge of risk engineering—using data, interpreting data, and seeking to measure fundamental statistics for financial analysis and decision making. The quantitative definition of risk and volatility, interpreting statistical moments, and estimating statistical parameters were the essential concerns of this chapter. They were introduced prior to an introduction to financial theory in order to motivate the students to the practical issues that they are likely to confront in practice. The usefulness of this chapter is increased when the student is required to apply the models and the statistical distributions defined to real-data financial problems (such as using time series on interest rates, on selected securities, etc., that are broadly and freely available).

TEST YOURSELF

3.1 Why do we need quantitative models in finance? Discuss their use to predict (e.g. stock prices and returns); to understand the financial process; to manage risks and make better decisions; and finally to value and price (e.g. price a bond, a security, or an option).

3.2 Discuss the following types of models and explain how they are similar, how they differ, or are compatible:

    a. A theoretical model (such as mathematical representation of a theory).
    b. An empirical representative model.
    c. A statistical model.
    d. An implied model for the probability of prices at a later date.

3.3 Compare the following types of model representation:

    a. Graphical (such as histograms to model frequency curves or probability distributions).
    b. Parametric models (used to characterize a theoretical distribution).

3.4 We have constructed in this chapter models for rates of return (constant rates of returns models and mean reversion models). Can you suggest such models to construct the rates of return of securities, interest rates, derivative prices, real estate markets? Explain which model would in your view be worth testing empirically.

3.5 You are given a typical financial data set (you are free to select any of the series on Bloomberg, www.yahoo.finance.com, or in www.charlestapiero.com).

    a. Graph each of the series.
    b. Calculate the rates of return and graph the day return series.
    c. Calculate and graph the weekly mean return.
    d. Calculate and graph the weekly standard deviation.
    e. Calculate and graph the weekly range.
    f. Calculate and graph the range-to-standard-deviation ratio.

Date	Open	Close	Low	High	Volume
11/2/98	34.52	34.52	34.1	35.05	3658
11/3/98	34.37	34.48	34.21	34.9	2714
11/4/98	35.44	35.09	34.86	36.16	4046
11/5/98	36.89	35.4	34.83	37.04	4936
11/6/98	37.27	36.66	36.66	37.61	3437
11/9/98	35.63	36.89	35.51	37.04	3125
11/10/98	34.94	33.91	33.79	35.17	2953
11/11/98	34.6	35.05	34.18	35.4	2556
11/12/98	33.68	34.02	33.37	34.75	3648
11/13/98	34.94	33.91	33.79	35.17	2953
11/16/98	35.35	35.63	35.05	35.97	3309
11/17/98	37.42	35.4	34.83	38.03	8411
11/18/98	37.77	37.38	36.39	37.77	4554
11/19/98	37.57	37.77	37.19	37.88	2899
11/20/98	37.84	37.57	37.54	38.15	4325
11/23/98	38.71	38.8	38.64	39.79	4317
11/24/98	39.6	39.71	39.48	40.86	4806

3.6 Repeat problem 3.5 by using a financial market index (Dow, NASDAQ, FTSE, CAC40, S&P, etc.).

3.7 Repeat problem 3.5 by using exchange rates data (dollar, euro, yen).

3.8 What is a sample space? Define formally a probability distribution. Why do we need probability theory in analyzing observed data? Compare and contrast the classical and frequency definitions of probability.

3.9 A stock increases with probability 0.45. The probability that it increases two days in a row is (0.2). What is the probability that it will increase given that it has increased in the previous day? Given that it has decreased in the previous day? If you need additional information to calculate these probabilities, assume what you need. Interest rates have just gone up—what is the probability that the market stock price of an insurance firm with significant real estate holdings will go up or down, or remain unchanged?

3.10 Is there a relationship between volume and price? between volume and rate of return? Use one of the series you have studied to answer this question (you do so by trying a number of alternative models and see which one fits best).

3.11 What are interest rates and why are they important? What are risk-free interest rates? What are interest rates on assets that are risky? And what do they measure? What happens if we borrow money for different periods of time? (For example, what is the interest rate for a mortgage of 5 years and that for 25 years, and how do such interest rates differ?) What is a spot interest rate? Discuss the modeling and estimation challenge of interest rates. In particular use a mean reversion model.

3.12 The autoregressive model is:

$$y_t = \beta_0 + \beta_1 x_{t-1} + \cdots + \beta_n y_{t-n} + \varepsilon_t$$

while the moving average model is

$$y_t = \beta_0 + \beta_1 \varepsilon_{t-1} + \beta_2 \varepsilon_{t-2} + \beta_3 \varepsilon_{t-3} + \cdots + \beta_n \varepsilon_{t-n} + \cdots + \varepsilon_t$$

How do they differ?

3.13 In 1973, Bernell K. Stone presented a class of risk measures that includes most of the empirical and theoretical class of risk measures. It is specified by the following:

$$R_t(W_0, k, A; f) = \left(\int_{-\infty}^{A} |W - W_0|^k f_t(W) dW \right)^{\frac{1}{k}}$$

Show that

$$R_t(\hat{W}, 2, \infty; f) = \text{Standard deviation}$$

and subsequently define and discuss derived measures. In particular:

$$R_{\alpha,t}(f) = \int_{-\infty}^{t} (t-W)^{\alpha} \, f(W)dW = \text{Fishburn's measure}$$

3.14 An individual insured has a claim distribution that is exponentially distributed with known mean of $25,000. The claim probability is $p = 0.05$. What is the expected claim amount if the self-participation of the insured is (1) a fixed amount $a = \$3,000$; (2) a proportion of the claim $q = 0.15$; (3) a combination of the two, both a fixed amount and a proportional self-participation? What is the variance of this latter claim distribution?

3.15 An insurance company is reinsuring parts of its claim in a stop-loss formula (over $250,000). What is the expected premium that the company must pay the reinsurer if the reinsurer covers all claims over $250,000? Assume that the loading factor used for reinsurance is known and given by $b = 0.20$ and that the distribution is approximately normal with known mean ($35,000) and variance equal to twice the mean (just write the equations). What is the expected amount that the insurer pays as claims? What is the claim variance for both the insurer and the reinsurer?

3.16 There are $n = 1,000$ insured in our portfolio. The probability of an accident for each person is 0.05. What is the mean number of accidents? What is its variance? What is the probability of having more than three accidents? What is the probability of obtaining a number of accidents between one and three?

3.17 A stock price grows each month at a geometric binomial distribution, with $p = 0.45$, the probability that the stock increases by 5 percent, and a probability of declining by 3 percent. The current stock price is $20. What is the probability distribution of the stock price in six months? What is its mean and what is its variance? Define the following term: $max[S(6) - 24,0]$. What is its expected value and what is its variance?

3.18 A stock price grows (or declines) in jumps of 4 percent per month over its previous monthly price. What is the probability of the number of times the stock has gone up, and the number the stock has gone down? What is the probability of the stock price at that time? Finally, what is the expected price and what is its variance? How would you write the evolution of such a price as an intertemporal stochastic difference equation?

3.19 A stock price has a rate of return that is constant and given by a while its volatility is b. What is the underlying stock price process? What is the probability distribution of returns over $(0, t)$? What is the probability distribution of the stock price? What is the mean price and its variance at a later time t? What is the solution of the underlying stock price process? Provide a binomial approximation to the underlying price process and discuss its implications for computational finance.

3.20 *In finance, we often use the capital asset pricing model (CAPM), which is defined as follows:

$$E\{R_i\} = R_f + \beta_i \left[E\{R_m\} - R_f \right]$$

where R_i is the rate of return of the ith security, R_m is a market rate of return (an index), and R_f is the risk-free rate. Theoretical analysis indicates that the beta factor is:

$$\beta_i = \frac{\text{cov}(R_i, R_m)}{\text{var}(R_m)}; \quad \beta_i = \frac{E(R_i - \hat{R}_i)E(R_m - \hat{R}_m)}{E(R_m - \hat{R}_m)^2}$$

a. If R_i and R_m are jointly and normally distributed with known means and known variances, what is the beta factor of the security?

b. Assume now a function of R_m, say $f(R_m)$, and show that

$$\text{cov}(R_i, f(R_m)) = E\{f'(R_m)\} \text{cov}(R_i, R_m)$$

3.21 *Assume that P is a stochastic inflation rate. Show that the beta adjusted for inflation is:

$$E\{R_i P\} = R_f E(P) + \beta_i E \left[R_m P - R_f P \right]$$

Since this is not so simple, verify the following development:

$$
\begin{aligned}
\text{cov}\{R_i P, R_m P\} &= E\{R_i\} E\{R_m\} \text{var}\{P\} + E\{R_i\} E\{P\} \text{cov}\{P, R_m\} \\
&\quad + E\{R_m\} E\{P\} \text{cov}\{P, R_i\} + E^2\{P\} \text{cov}\{R_i, R_m\} \\
&\quad + \text{cov}\{R_i, P\} \text{cov}\{R_m, P\} + \text{cov}\{R_i, R_m\} \text{var}\{P\}
\end{aligned}
$$

as well as

$$
\begin{aligned}
\text{var}\{R_m, P\} &= E^2\{R_m\} \text{var}\{P\} + 2E(P)E\{R_m\} \text{cov}\{P, R_m\} \\
&\quad + E^2\{P\} \text{var}\{R_m\} + \text{cov}^2\{P, R_m\} + \text{var}\{R_m\} \text{var}\{P\}
\end{aligned}
$$

and therefore that

$$\beta_{i, REAL} = \frac{\text{cov}\{R_i P, R_m P\}}{\text{var}\{R_m, P\}}$$

---

*Requires a slightly more advanced mathematical background; please see the Introduction.

3.22 Prove for the lognormal distribution

$$f_{LN}(x) = \frac{1}{x\sqrt{2\pi\sigma^2}} \exp\left[-\frac{\ln^2(x/x_0)}{2\sigma^2}\right]$$

that

$$E(x^n) = x_0^n e^{n^2\sigma^2/2}$$

Discuss why the lognormal is popular in finance and how it is usually represented as a model. Discuss the relationship between normally distributed rates of returns and lognormal stock prices.

3.23 Risk management consists in setting a number of rules that reduce risk. If individual claims are limited to a maximal amount of a, then the risk of N claims is:

$$X = \sum_{i=1}^{N} \min(y_i, a)$$

while their complements are insured by some insurer (who assumes this risk for a given premium that is negotiated between the first insurer and the reinsurer). What are the means and the variance of these claims?

3.24 For the extreme Weibull distribution show that:

$$f(\tau) = \frac{c}{\zeta}\left(\frac{\tau}{\zeta}\right)^{c-1} e^{-(\tau/\zeta)^c}, \tau \geq 0, \zeta, c > 0; \quad F(\tau) = 1 - e^{-(\tau/\zeta)^c},$$

$$E(\tau) = \zeta\Gamma\left(\frac{1}{c}+1\right), \text{var}(\tau) = \zeta^2\left[\Gamma\left(\frac{2}{c}+1\right) - \Gamma^2\left(\frac{1}{c}+1\right)\right]$$

Discuss when and why the Weibull distribution is useful. How fat are its tails? Define the VaR for a given risk exposure when losses over a given period of time have such a loss distribution. If the Weibull distribution defines instead the probability of a financial product defaulting over time, what is the conditional probability of default at a specific time t? What is the EVaR of losses given that they have a Weibull probability distribution?

3.25 The Pareto probability distribution is a fat-tail distribution given by

$$f_\alpha(x) \cong \alpha C_\pm^\alpha/(|x|^{1+\alpha}); \quad \text{for} \quad x \to \pm\infty$$

Show that such a distribution has an infinite variance. What are the financial implications of using such a distribution for asset prices?

3.26 Show that for a normal probability distribution with mean a and standard deviation σ that:

$$F(x) = \frac{1}{\sigma\sqrt{2\pi}} \int_{-\infty}^{x} e^{-(t-a)^2/2\sigma^2} \, dt = \frac{1}{2}\left[1 + erf\left(\frac{x-a}{\sigma\sqrt{2}}\right)\right]$$

while for a lognormal probability distribution, we have:

$$F(x) = \frac{1}{2}\left[1 + erf\left(\frac{\ln x - a}{\sigma\sqrt{2}}\right)\right]$$

3.27 The volume of stocks transacted in a day is assumed to have a Weibull probability distribution. Assume that a record of volumes for a given security is given over a period of 21 days. What are the maximum likelihood estimates of these parameters? Provide the equations to solve for these parameters rather than actually solving them (this will most likely be a set of nonlinear equations to be solved numerically).

3.28 Using a securities day time series (for example, using the IBM day prices time series over this past month), transform the data price by a logarithmic transformation, and calculate the average returns, the variance, the skewness, and the kurtosis. Repeat these calculations for another extremely volatile stock and compare your results by indicating how you would use such information when trading on these two stocks only. Further, indicate the approximations you make when using only the expected returns as your only estimate to calculate the expected ln transformation of prices.

3.29 The VIX fear index is a market index used to reflect what is defined as *fear* in financial markets by measuring the rate of change squared at any given time. The presumption of this index is that the larger the rate of change, the greater the volatility and therefore the greater the fear that financial markets are not stable, fluctuating into situations that will make it hard to price financial assets. Such an index is calculated by the following equation:

$$h(S_{t+1}) = (-1 + S_{t+1}/S_t)^2$$

Provide a three-terms Taylor series expansion of the VIX index with respect to the previous security price.

3.30 What are the advantages and the disadvantages when using value at risk and the expected shortfall as measures of risk exposure? Let the gains/losses of a portfolio have a mean rate of $10 million and a variance of 1.5 times the mean. Assume a normal probability distribution for the profit/loss and calculate the VaR for a risk exposure of 0.1, 0.05, and 0.01. Discuss what banks do to reduce VaR. Repeat your analysis by using the extreme Weibull probability distribution. How and why would your VaR results differ? How significant is your choice of the gains/loss probability distribution. (For your calculation, you will have to program on Excel the calculations of the Weibull parameters and calculate its corresponding VaR and EVaR.)

3.31 European Banks have suffered major damage due to U.S. Banks selling toxic mortgage-backed securities. Can you explain why? What was the role of the value at risk approach in managing risks and why did it fail European banks? (To answer this question, note first that optional products are not always properly accounted for as risky products in their portfolio.)

REFERENCES

Admati, A. R. P., and P. Pfleiderer. 1988. A theory of intraday patterns: Volumes and price volatility. *Review of Financial Studies* 1 (1):3–40.

Andersen, T. G. 1996. Return volatility and trading volume: An information flow interpretation of stochastic volatility. *Journal of Finance* 51:169–204.

Andersen, T., and T. Bollerslev. 1997. Intraday periodicity and volatility persistence in financial markets. *Journal of Empirical Finance* 4:115–158.

Andersen, T., T. Bollerslev, F. Diebold, and J. Wu. 2006. Realized beta: Persistence and predictability. In *Econometric analysis of economic and financial time series, Part B*, ed. T. Fomby and D. Terrel, 1–140. Volume 20 of Advances in econometrics series. New York: JAI Press.

Ang, A., J. Chen, and Y. Xing. 2006. Downside risk. *Review of Financial Studies* 19 (4):1191–1239.

Artzner, P. 1999. Application of coherent measures to capital requirements in insurance. *North American Actuarial Journal* 3 (2):11–25.

Artzner, P., F. Delbaen, J. M. Eber, and D. Heath. 1997. Thinking coherently. *RISK* 10:68–71.

Ball, C. A., and W. N. Torous. 1984. The maximum likelihood estimation of security price volatility: Theory, evidence, and application to option pricing. *Journal of Business* 57 (January):97–112.

Basak, S., and A. Shapiro. 2001. Value-at-risk-based risk management: Optimal policies and asset prices. *Review of Financial Studies* 14:371–405.

Basi, F., P. Embrechts, and M. Kafetzaki. 1998. Risk management and quantile estimation. In *Practical guide to heavy tails*, ed. R. Adler, R. Feldman, and M. Taqqu, 111–130. Boston: Birkhauser.

Beckers, S. 1996. A survey of risk measurement theory and practice. In *Handbook of Risk Management and Analysis*, ed. C. Alexander. New York: John Wiley & Sons.

Bollerslev, T. 1986. Generalized autoregressive conditional heteroskedasticity. *Journal of Econometrics* 31:307–327.

Bollerslev, T., R. F. Engle, and D. B. Nelson. 1994. ARCH models. In *Handbook of econometrics IV*, ed. R. F. Engle and D. L. McFadden, 2961–3038. Amsterdam: Elsevier Science.

Brailsford, T. J., and R. W. Faff. 1996. An evaluation of volatility forecasting techniques. *Journal of Banking and Finance* 20:419–438.

Brandt, M., and F. Diebold. 2006. A no-arbitrage approach to range based estimation of return covariances and correlation. *Journal of Business* 79:61–74.

Christoffersen, P., K. Jacobs, and G. Vainberg. 2008. Forward looking betas. Working paper, Department of Finance, McGill University, Montreal, Canada.

Corrado, C., and T. Su. 1996. Skewness and kurtosis in S&P 500 index returns implied by S&P 500 index option prices. *Journal of Derivatives* 4:8–19.

Eberlein, E., and U. Keller. 1995. Hyperbolic distributions in finance. *Bernoulli* 1:281–299.

Embrechts, P., C. Klupperberg, and T. Mikosch. 1997. *Modelling extremal events in insurance and finance.* Berlin/Heidelberg: Springer.

Engle, R. F. 1982. Autoregressive conditional heteroskedasticity with estimates of the variance of United Kingdom inflation. *Econometrica* 50:987–1007.

Feller, W. 1951. The asymptotic distribution of the range of sums of random variables. *Annals of Mathematical Statistics* 22:427–32.

Garman, Mark B., and Michael Klass. 1980. On the estimation of security price volatilities from historical data. *Journal of Business* 53 (1):67–78.

Gerber, H. U. 1979. An introduction to mathematical risk theory. Monograph 8, Huebner Foundation, University of Pennsylvania, Philadelphia.

Glosten, Lawrence R., Ravi Jagannathan, and David E. Runkle. 1993. On the relation between the expected value and the volatility of the nominal excess returns on stocks. *Journal of Finance* 48 (5):1779–801.

Gourieroux C., J. P. Laurent, and O. Scaillet. 2000. Sensitivity analysis of values at risk. *Journal of Empirical Finance* 7:225–245.

Hadar, Josef, and William R. Russell. 1969. Rules for ordering uncertain prospects. *American Economic Review* 59:25–34.

Jorion, P. 1997. *Value at risk: The new benchmark for controlling market risk.* Chicago: McGraw-Hill.

Kunitomo, N. 1995. Improving the Parkinson method of estimating security price volatilities. *Journal of Business* 65 (2):295–302.

Lundberg, O. 1940. *On random processes and their applications to sickness and accident statistics.* Uppsala, Sweden: Almquist and Wiksells.

Machina, Mark J. 1987. Choice under uncertainty: Problems solved and unsolved. *Journal of Economic Perspectives* 1:121–154.

Martens, M., and D. van Dijk. 2007. Measuring volatility with the realized range. *Journal of Econometrics* 138:181–207.

Morgan, J. P. 1995. *Introduction to RiskMetrics*™, 4th ed. New York: J.P. Morgan.

Ng, V. K., and S. C. Pirrong. 1994. Fundamentals and volatility: Storage, spreads and the dynamic of metals prices. *Journal of Business* 67:203–230.

Parkinson, M. 1980. The extreme value method for estimating the variance of the rate of return. *Journal of Business* 53 (1) (January):61–65.

Poon, S.-H. 2005. *Forecasting volatility in financial markets: A practical guide.* Hoboken, NJ: John Wiley & Sons.

Poon, S.-H., and C. Granger. 2003. Forecasting volatility in financial markets: A review. *Journal of Economic Literature* 41 (2) (June):478–539.

Provasi, Corrado. 1996. Using algebraic software to compute the moments of order statistics. *Computational Economics* 9:199–213.

Rogers, C., and S. Satchell. 1991. Estimating variance from high, low and closing prices. *Annals of Applied Probability* 1:504–512.

Roger C., S. Satchel, and R. N. Rodriguez. 1977. A guide to the Burr Type XII distributions. *Biometrika* 64:129–134.

Samuelson, P. A. 1965. Proof that properly anticipated prices fluctuate randomly. *Industrial Management Review* 6:41–49.

Schachter B. 2002. All about value at risk. www.GloriaMundi.org/var.

Söderlind, Paul, and L. E. O. Svensson. 1998. New techniques to extract market expectations from financial instruments. *Journal of Monetary Economics* 40 (2) (October):383–429.

Stein, E., and J. Stein. 1991. Stock price distributions with stochastic volatility: An analytic approach. *Review of Financial Studies* 4 (Winter):727–752.

Tapiero C. S. 2004. Risk management. In *Encyclopedia on actuarial and risk management*, ed. Jozef Teugels (Editor-in-Chief), Born Sundt (Editor-in-Chief). Hoboken, NJ and London: John Wiley & Sons.

———. 2005a. Reliability design and RVaR. *International Journal of Reliability, Quality and Safety Engineering* 12 (4) (August).

———. 2005b. Value at risk and inventory control. *European Journal of Operations Research* 163 (3):769–775.

Tse, Y. K. 1991. Stock returns volatility in the Tokyo Stock Exchange. *Japan and the World Economy* 3:285–298.

West, K. D., and D. Cho. 1995. The predictive ability of several models of exchange rate volatility. *Journal of Econometrics* 69:367–391.

Wiggins, James B. 1991. Empirical tests of the bias and efficiency of the extreme-values variance estimator for common stocks. *Journal of Business* 64 (3):417–432.

———. 1992. Estimating the volatility of S&P 500 futures prices using the extreme-value method. *Journal of Futures Markets* 12 (3):265–273.

Yang, D., and Q. Zhang. 2000. Drift independent volatility estimation based on high, low, open, and close prices. *Journal of Business* 73:477–492.

CHAPTER 4

Risk Finance Modeling and Dependence

OVERVIEW

Dependence arises because financial prices and events depend on one another, on latent and common macroeconomic factors, on other assets, on other securities, and on a broad array and many types of information. In some cases, events may also feed each other, leading to complex feedback relationships and to a contagion (for example, a contagion of defaulting loans, bank runs, the meltdown of financial markets and their security prices, etc.). Generally, dependence implies that assets tend to move in directions that are observed more or less to be concurrent—some movements may be causal, other spurious. Dependence may also be a signal and a symptom of common risk sources (such as macroeconomic factors affecting assets in a given portfolio) or result from real or statistical covariations between assets. Although dependence is fundamental for finance, it is loosely used, implying far more than is implied by a simple (noncausal) statistical covariation of asset prices and economic factors. The definition of financial models that seek to structure causally the dependence of financial prices are therefore important and are central to financial modeling, financial theory, and risk engineering in general. The purpose of this chapter is to focus attention to a number of approaches for quantitatively modeling dependence. This chapter seeks to motivate the student to appreciate the fact that dependence is complex and extremely important practically and theoretically. While some elements in this chapter require a prior statistical background, the topics considered are kept as simple as possible.

INTRODUCTION

Financial dependence occurs for many reasons. It may be due to the statistical covariation of prices that have no causal explanation. It may also be causal or endogenous, expressing the behavior of investors responding to past events (their memory).

This chapter requires that the reader have a slightly more advanced mathematical background.

For example, if a market is said to have momentum, it means that a price rise (or fall) would cause a further price rise (or fall). Inversely, a financial market price may be contrarian, reverting when a price movement occurs in one direction. Price contagion and mean reversion are manifestations of financial dependence. Technically, these processes are also called *persistent* and express an intertemporal and statistical dependency. *Contagious* processes may produce price upswings and then switch to price downswings. Further, at any one time, both effects may be active, interacting and producing price patterns that may be difficult to analyze a priori (after the fact, however, a price process may be explained one way or the other). When market processes are *self-stabilizing*, an equilibrium price may be reached, while when markets are contagious and unsustainable, they exhibit booms followed by busts. In other cases, there may be a dynamic *equilibrium* reflecting complex and dependent relationships coexisting and acting on the market mechanism, which are theoretically and empirically difficult to track.

Dependent price processes are therefore notoriously difficult to model causally and explain, so they provide a permanent source of challenging problems to financial engineers. When a process has a nonlinearly increasing variance over time (i.e., reflecting the increased intractability of future events), specific stochastic models (some called Levy processes, persistent and fractal stochastic models, etc.) are used to capture the model variability that is not explained. Some of these models are considered in this chapter in a simple expository manner; however, for further study, the reader ought to consult the bibliographical list at the end of this chapter.

For expository purposes, five types of dependence can be defined:

1. Independence, with asset prices statistically independent of one another.
2. Statistical dependence, with specific prices exhibiting a statistical covariation. Such situations testify to the effect that two securities' price movements seem to be statistically correlated without an explicit causal explanation of these movements.
3. Latent (or underlying) dependence, when two or more prices are subject to a common source of risk—whether arising due to rare events or not. In this case, the latent factor causes all prices to be affected at the same time, albeit in similar or other manners.
4. Short-term memory dependence (and temporal persistence), occurring when a price time path history determines subsequent unfolding probabilities for future prices.
5. Long-run memory dependence, when the long-past memory—or future expectations, singly or in concert—affects the evolution of prices, producing a nonlinear time growth in asset price variance. In such cases, in the long run, the variance of prices can be infinite and therefore prices are presumed to be unpredictable (or to have an extremely large variance).

Each of these facets of dependence contributes to our approach to modeling and to the rich literature for quantitatively modeling financial models. To model such time dependence we use probability and stochastic models to define events, their covariations, and their intertemporal causality. Some techniques were used in Chapter 3 and include linear, mean reverting, and other models, and of course empirical observations that point to specific covariations in asset prices.

Dependence and Probability Models

Multivariate probability distribution models are used to model the multiple sources of price variations and their covariations. Empirical evidence may point to covariations in some assets and may call for models with a greater explanatory power that captures this dependence. The number of approaches and techniques one uses are technically challenging. Some approaches are described here, and in more detail in the sections that follow.

- *Statistical functional dependence* (whether based on multiple asset prices or stochastic dynamic financial processes)—including for example, a linear rate of return (ROR) and mean reverting models considered in Chapter 3 with residual errors that might or might not indicate spurious correlations.
- *Copulas* (as a means to model complex dependent probability distributions by partial information—mostly their marginal probability distributions). Copula models are profusely used in credit risk portfolios and in value at risk to fit to empirical observations or simulate co-variate events.
- *Short-term memory models*. These are models that evolve based on the immediate time path preceding a random movement in a price. For example, if prices have increased in the past two days, what are the prospects of these prices to increase or decrease? How different are such prospects if the price would have decreased two days ago and increased in the past day? These models have complex probability structures and are implied in many practical trading strategies based on momentum and contrarian strategies (see also Vallois and Tapiero 2009 and 2010; Herman and Vallois 2010).
- *Long-run memory and fractal models*. These are models that account for a non-linear time variance in an underlying (stochastic) price process. These models are not based on a causal analysis of price variations but on empirical observations that the linear time growth of normal distributions (also called Brownian motion or Wiener processes in stochastic models) is too restraining. Such models include as well fat-tail probability distributions where tail variations are modeled to be larger than those observed in normal probability distributions.

STATISTICAL DEPENDENCE

A price index such as the NYSE Dow Jones stock index, the S&P 500, the CAC40 (France), the TASE 25 (Israel), and the like is a weighted portfolio of the largest stocks being traded in the stock exchange. The index is expressed by a weighted sum of these firms. For example, the S&P 500 index is composed of the 500 largest firms in the NYSE, while the TASE 25 is composed of its largest 25 firms. The stock prices of these firms are necessarily correlated, due to the common business environment they are subject to. This may also be due to the intricate business relationships these firms have, or due to their being part of a common index. There are advantages for firms to be part of an index, as many investment instruments, sizeable pension funds, and other financial institutions have adopted trading strategies based on such an index. Thus, by buying into an index, these investment firms essentially buy the stocks of the index member firms. As a result, it may be apparent that a given stock price's strength is due to the index strength rather than to the firm itself.

Questions of statistical dependence are thus intricate. Explicitly, does a stock price increase because of the index rise or decline, or does the index rise due to a stock price rise? Or both? Further, other factors may affect (unequally) an index and a firm's stock price. If an index is subject to a latent and macroeconomic risk, falling by 20 percent over one week, this may contribute to a drop in the stock price of the firm as well (when in fact, the adverse macroeconomic environment contributes to the firm's profits).

For these reasons, the mutual and dependence effects of an index and its component stock prices are to be carefully evaluated. Technically, this dependence can be stated as follows. Let the TASE 25 index, consisting of 25 stock prices, be given by:

$$\tilde{S}_{T25}(t) = \sum_{i=1}^{25} w_i \tilde{S}_i(t) \tag{4.1}$$

Where w_i is the weight of firm i in the index whose stock price at time t is a random variable $\tilde{S}_i(t)$. All variables are random except for the index weights. In normal times, assuming that returns are normal, the rate of return of the index can be written as follows:

$$\tilde{R}_{T25}(t) = \sum_{i=1}^{25} w_i \frac{\tilde{S}_i(t + \Delta t) - \tilde{S}_i(t)}{\tilde{S}_i(t)} = \sum_{i=1}^{25} w_i \tilde{R}_i(t) \tag{4.2}$$

And therefore, the mean rate of return and the returns variance of the weighted aggregate index are:

$$E\left(\tilde{R}_{T25}(t)\right) = \sum_{i=1}^{25} w_i E\left(\tilde{R}_i(t)\right) \tag{4.3}$$

$$\mathrm{var}\left(\tilde{R}_{T25}(t)\right) = \sum_{i=1}^{25} w_i^2 \mathrm{var}\left(\tilde{R}_i(t)\right) + 2\sum_{i=1}^{25}\sum_{j\neq i}^{25} w_i w_j \rho_{ij} \sqrt{\mathrm{var}\,\tilde{R}_i(t)}\sqrt{\mathrm{var}\,\tilde{R}_j(t)} \tag{4.4}$$

where correlations ρ_{ij}, define the statistical dependence between the 25 components of the index.

If all firms rates of returns are positively correlated, then holding on to an index would seem to be more risky than constructing one's own index, better suited to one's needs. Further, if the index is subject to a specific source of risk, say a latent factor, that other securities are not affected by, a drop in the index price will necessarily affect the price of each of these securities. However, if an index falls suddenly due to a member firm of the index that suddenly seeks bankruptcy proceedings, the holder of the index may be partially protected by his holdings due to the index's compensation effect (i.e., its safety in an aggregate holding of firms' securities). In practice, statistical dependence is not easily expressed in terms of asset price correlations and requires therefore other approaches—both empirically and modeling based. The CAPM model considered in Chapter 3 is an exception, based on a correlation between a security price and the market index assumed to be the rate of return (ROR) of a fully diversified portfolio. Examples and applications are considered in the next section.

Dependence and Quantitative Statistical Probability Models

Multivariate risks are the rule rather than the exception. For example, say that a bank lends K to a person and let the loan collateral that the bank requires be an asset whose current price is V_0. The loan is to be reimbursed including an interest charge r at a future date, say T. At the loan maturity let the price of the collateral be a random variable $\tilde{V}(T)$. If $\tilde{V}(T) < K(1+r)$ (the collateral is smaller than the person's debt) a loan default occurs if the debtor walks away from his collateral. In such cases, default is a random event defined by the probability $P\left(\tilde{V}(T) < K(1+r)\right)$ while the creditor (the bank) recovers the debtor collateral $\tilde{V}(T)$. Reimbursement of a loan is thus a random variable given by:

$$Min\left(K(1+r),\, \tilde{V}(T)\right) = K(1+r) - Max\left(0,\, K(1+r) - \tilde{V}(T)\right)$$

In other words, for the creditor, the payment of the loan at maturity equals the debt less the price of a put option whose strike is the debt. The bank (assuming that there are such options being traded in an efficient market) can then insure the debt payment by imposing on the debtor an additional fee at the time the loan is granted, equal to the option price. In an efficient world, there can be no risks if the bank decides to cover (i.e., hedge) the collateral price. Reality is more complex, however. For example, the future collateral price may depend on other risk factors not accounted for initially and therefore misprice the required hedge. Such risks, in extremis, may include the risk of the put option if the buyer is unable to meet the option's obligations (just as was the case when AIG could not meet its obligations in 2008). When the collateral loses a substantial part of its value, then both the person who has received the loan and the bank will necessarily be at risk.

For discussion purposes, let $\tilde{U}(T)$ be a random external event not accounted for initially by financial markets in pricing collaterals. The probability distribution of the collateral price, for a specific and conditional event $U(T)$, would, in fact, have a probability distribution $f_{V|U}\left(\tilde{V}(T)|U(T)\right)$. Since $\tilde{U}(T)$ is random with a probability distribution $f_U\left(\tilde{U}(T)\right)$, the joint probability distribution is:

$$f_{U,V}(\tilde{V}(T), \tilde{U}(T)) = f_{V|U}\left(\tilde{V}(T)|\tilde{U}(T)\right) f_U\left(\tilde{U}(T)\right) \tag{4.5}$$

As a result, the probability of the collateral defaulting is in fact:

$$P\left(\tilde{V}(T) < K(1+r)\right) = \int_{-\infty}^{K(1+r)} \int_{U \in U} f_{U,V}(\tilde{V}(T), \tilde{U}(T)) d\tilde{V}(T) d\tilde{U}(T) \qquad (4.6)$$

and

$$\begin{cases} \dfrac{f_{U,V}(\tilde{V}(T), \tilde{U}(T))}{f_V\left(\tilde{V}(T)\right) f_U\left(\tilde{U}(T)\right)} \neq 1 & \text{if dependent} \\[4mm] \dfrac{f_{U,V}(\tilde{V}(T), \tilde{U}(T))}{f_V\left(\tilde{V}(T)\right) f_U\left(\tilde{U}(T)\right)} = 1 & \text{if independent} \end{cases} \qquad (4.7)$$

These relationships are difficult to determine in practice, however. In some cases the external event may be a rare event with a small probability with dire consequences, covarying with the collateral price, which is difficult to assess explicitly. Although, as shown in the next section, we can use a copula to construct a model of such covariation. In some cases, explicit (and parametric) probability models are used that allow greater transparency in the modeling of covariations.

Many Sources of Normal Risk: Aggregation and Risk Factors Reduction

Say that a portfolio consists of n assets, priced $\tilde{V}_i(t), i = 1, 2, \ldots, n$, all of which are defined (for simplicity) by normal probability distributions with known mean and known variances. Say that these assets are dependent and let their joint probability distribution be normal with a known mean vector $\mathbf{M}(t)$ and a known variance-covariance matrix $\Sigma(t)$ that expresses their dependence. For these two assets, we have:

$$\mathbf{M}(t) = \begin{pmatrix} \hat{U}(t) \\ \hat{V}(t) \end{pmatrix} \text{ and } \Sigma(t) = \begin{pmatrix} \sigma_U^2 & \sigma_{UV} \\ \sigma_{UV} & \sigma_V^2 \end{pmatrix} \text{ and } \sigma_{UV} = \rho \sigma_U \sigma_V \qquad (4.8)$$

where ρ is the correlation between these two assets. If $\rho = 0$, these assets are independent. If $\rho > 0$ (or < 0) these assets are positively (negatively) correlated. The standard normal vector $\mathbf{Y}(t)$ has thus a joint and normal probability distribution:

$$f\left(\mathbf{Y}(t)\right) = \frac{1}{(2\pi)^{\frac{n}{2}} |\Sigma|^{1/2}} \exp\left\{-\frac{1}{2}\left(\mathbf{Y}(t) - \mathbf{M}(t)\right)^T \Sigma^{-1}\left(\mathbf{Y}(t) - \mathbf{M}(t)\right)\right\}, n = 2 \qquad (4.9)$$

This latter expression can be generalized further to a portfolio of n assets (or collaterals) with a joint normal distribution of n assets, with known mean vector and known variance-covariance matrix. If these assets (or collaterals) depend on an external and common event, say again $\tilde{U}(t)$, then the explicit portfolio asset prices joint probability distribution is:

$$f_{U,V_i}(\tilde{V}_1(t), \ldots, \tilde{V}_n(t), \tilde{U}(t)) = f_{V_i|U}\left((\tilde{V}_1(t), \ldots, \tilde{V}_n(t) | \tilde{U}(t))\right) f_U\left(\tilde{U}(t)\right) \qquad (4.10)$$

A portfolio of such assets will naturally be more complex to evaluate statistically than, say, a portfolio consisting of independent assets. Such problems recur often in credit risk and credit derivatives problems (Chapters 9 and 10) and are typically difficult to analyze because of the substantial amounts of information (which can be unreliable over time) that such analyses require.

EXAMPLE: RISK FACTORS AGGREGATION

When the number of risk sources is very large, it is possible to approximate these risks by reducing them to one or to a set of essential risk factors. Two approaches may be considered. A first approach is based on arguments of the central limit theorem in statistics, and the other on principal component analysis (PCA). Both approaches can be misleading, however, if the use of the normal probability distribution cannot be justified. For example, let $\mathbf{w}$ be a vector of n correlated random variables, all of which have a zero mean and a variance 1 (in other words, all random variables have been standardized). Let the correlation matrix be $\mathbf{Q} = [q_{ij}]$, i, $j = 1, \ldots, n$. Next, assume a portfolio of assets with rates of returns given by the following equation:

$$\tilde{R} = \mu + \sum_{i=1}^{n} a_i \tilde{w}_i \tag{4.11}$$

A first approximation consists in aggregating all sources of risks, replaced by one simple random variable for the portfolio. This results in mean and variance:

$$E \sum_{i=1}^{n} a_i \tilde{w}_i = 0,$$

$$\text{var}\left(\sum_{i=1}^{n} a_i \tilde{w}_i\right) = \sum_{i=1}^{n} a_i^2 \, \text{var}\,(\tilde{w}_i) + 2 \sum_{i>j}^{n} \sum_{j=1}^{n} a_i a_j \, E\left(\tilde{w}_i \tilde{w}_j\right) = \sum_{i=1}^{n} a_i^2 + 2 \sum_{i>j}^{n} \sum_{j=1}^{n} a_i a_j q_{ij} \tag{4.12}$$

A rate of return is then reduced to a normal random variable $\tilde{R}$, with a standard normal probability distribution for ξ:

$$\tilde{R} = \mu + \left(\sqrt{\sum_{i=1}^{n} a_i^2 + 2 \sum_{i>j}^{n} \sum_{j=1}^{n} a_i a_j q_{ij}}\right) \xi \tag{4.13}$$

This aggregation is based on the law of large numbers in statistics. Its use can be problematic in practice, however, as it confounds sources of risk. For example, if one risk is normal and the other is a rare event, such a normalized aggregation might be misleading.

The motivation to aggregate risk sources into *significant* risk factors whether selectively or based on an approximate reduction and aggregation into risk components, remains a difficult statistical problem. Next, we consider a risk factors reduction using the principal component analysis. This method uses the eigenvalues of the correlation matrix. For simplicity, we consider only two sources of risks to highlight the assumptions and the mathematical treatments implied in using PCA (see also www.charlestapiero.com for an extension).

EXAMPLE: PRINCIPAL COMPONENT ANALYSIS (PCA)

Principal component analysis is a statistical data analysis method that seeks to reduce the dimension of a matrix by using its redundancy, using the data matrix eigenvalues. The larger the eigenvalues the more such an eigenvalue accounts for the matrix variability (as will be shown here). As a result, it provides an approximation of a random vector by another random vector of smaller dimensions.

For example, assume a database consisting of time series of n variables (such as the rate of returns of securities). The rates of returns matrix of correlations can then be determined empirically. Let the resulting data matrix be **D**. PCA's purpose is to use fewer variables to replicate the variability of the data matrix. For example, if the price of water is a function of an extremely large number of sources, then seeking the three or four principal components that reasonably approximate water price's variability would result in a simplified model (with fewer factors to reckon with). The same idea applies to constructing market indexes or summarizing the variability of a term structure of interest rates (i.e., the variations in all interest rates) into a single factor.

Explicitly, PCA proceeds as follows: We define a vector of n parameters $\boldsymbol{\alpha} = (\alpha_1, \ldots \alpha_n)^T$ normalized such that

$$\sum_{i=1}^{n} \alpha_i = 1, \alpha_i \geq 0$$

Define the standardized vector (detrended) of all ROR by $\mathbf{z} = \mathbf{D}\boldsymbol{\alpha}$ where $E(\mathbf{z}) = 0$. The sum of errors squared, expressing the data variation, is then $\mathbf{z}^T\mathbf{z}$. The maximum sum of squares (accounting for the largest amount of variation in the data base) can then be determined by selecting the parameters

$$\sum_{i=1}^{n} \alpha_i = 1, \alpha_i \geq 0$$

that minimizes their least squares deviation,

$$\underset{\boldsymbol{\alpha} \geq 0}{Min} \quad \mathbf{z}^T\mathbf{z} = \boldsymbol{\alpha}^T\mathbf{D}^T\mathbf{D}\boldsymbol{\alpha} = \boldsymbol{\alpha}^T\left[\mathbf{D}^T\mathbf{D}\right]\boldsymbol{\alpha} \text{ Subject to: } \boldsymbol{\alpha}^T\boldsymbol{\alpha} = 1 \qquad (4.14)$$

Note that the matrix $\mathbf{A} = \mathbf{D}^T\mathbf{D}$ is now a square and invertible $n \times n$ matrix from which eigenvalues λ are found by solving $|\lambda I - \mathbf{A}| = 0$. Suppose that $\mathbf{x}$ is a nonzero vector in $\mathbf{R}^n$ and let λ be any nonzero scalar so that $\mathbf{A}\mathbf{x} = \lambda\mathbf{x}$. We call $\mathbf{x}$ an eigenvector of the matrix $\mathbf{A}$ and λ its *eigenvalue*. Since the matrix $\mathbf{A}$ is square and invertible, the determinant, $|\mathbf{A} - \lambda\mathbf{I}|$ (where $\mathbf{I}$ represents the unit matrix) is called the characteristic equation of $\mathbf{A}$ and admits solutions for eigenvalues.

The maximal sum of squares $\mathbf{z}^T\mathbf{z}$ (accounting for the maximal variability) defines the largest eigenvalue λ_1 of the matrix $\mathbf{D}^T\mathbf{D}$ and is proportional to the variance of the vector $\mathbf{z}$. The solution vector is called the characteristic vector $\boldsymbol{\alpha}$ of the data set $\mathbf{D}$. This procedure has thus defined one principal (largest) component.

Another component can be constructed in a similar manner to account for the remaining variability in the data set and be consistent with the largest component previously calculated. In particular, a second principal component can be defined by solving for another characteristic vector $\boldsymbol{\beta}$ (orthogonal to the vector $\boldsymbol{\alpha}$), or:

$$\underset{\boldsymbol{\beta} \geq 0}{Max} \quad \mathbf{z}_1^T\mathbf{z}_1 = \boldsymbol{\beta}^T\left[\mathbf{D}^T\mathbf{D}\right]\boldsymbol{\beta} \text{ Subject to: } \boldsymbol{\beta}^T\boldsymbol{\beta} = 1 \text{ and } \boldsymbol{\alpha}^T\boldsymbol{\beta} = 0 \qquad (4.15)$$

where $\boldsymbol{\alpha}^T\boldsymbol{\beta} = 0$ is the orthogonally additional constraint that ensures that the characteristic vectors are uncorrelated. Repeating this procedure, a set of characteristic vectors $(\boldsymbol{\alpha}, \boldsymbol{\beta}, \boldsymbol{\gamma}, \boldsymbol{\delta}, ...)$ are defined by their eigenvalues $(\lambda_1, \lambda_2, ...) = (\boldsymbol{\alpha}^T\boldsymbol{\alpha} = 1, \boldsymbol{\beta}^T\boldsymbol{\beta} = 1, \boldsymbol{\gamma}^T\boldsymbol{\gamma} = 1, \boldsymbol{\delta}^T\boldsymbol{\delta} = 1, ...)$ and are all orthogonal since $(\boldsymbol{\alpha}^T\boldsymbol{\beta} = 0, \boldsymbol{\alpha}^T\boldsymbol{\gamma} = 0, ..., \boldsymbol{\delta}^T\boldsymbol{\gamma}^T = 0, ...)$.

In summary, the eigenvector with the highest eigenvalue is the principal component of the data set, and has accounted for the most significant variability (as explained previously). Once eigenvectors are found from the covariance matrix, they are ordered by their eigenvalue, from highest to lowest. This procedure gives the components an order of significance. If we leave out some components, the final data set will have lower dimensions than the original, resulting in a reduction of the dimensionality of model factors. We can then form a matrix $\mathbf{P}$ by taking the eigenvectors that we want to keep from the list of eigenvectors in the columns. The final data will be obtained by multiplying the transpose of matrix $\mathbf{P}$ by the transpose of the adjusted initial data (the initial data from which we subtract the mean.

$$\text{Final Data} = \mathbf{P}^T \times (\text{Adjusted Data})^T \qquad (4.16)$$

A simple example for a bivariate data set is used next to highlight such an approach explicitly.

EXAMPLE: A BIVARIATE DATA MATRIX AND PCA

Define two random vectors $\mathbf{w}$ and $\mathbf{v}$ and let $\mathbf{Q}$ be the correlation matrix. Set $\mathbf{w} = \mathbf{Q}\mathbf{v}$. The correlation matrix is square and invertible; thus one random vector can be defined in terms of the other (and vice versa) by solving $\mathbf{Q}^{-1}\mathbf{w} = \mathbf{v}$. For example, for two sources of risk and a matrix:

$$\mathbf{Q} = \begin{pmatrix} q_{11} & q_{12} \\ q_{21} & q_{22} \end{pmatrix} \text{ and } \begin{pmatrix} w_1 \\ w_2 \end{pmatrix} = \begin{pmatrix} q_{11} & q_{12} \\ q_{21} & q_{22} \end{pmatrix}\begin{pmatrix} v_1 \\ v_2 \end{pmatrix} \text{ and } \begin{pmatrix} v_1 \\ v_2 \end{pmatrix} = \begin{pmatrix} q_{11} & q_{12} \\ q_{21} & q_{22} \end{pmatrix}^{-1}\begin{pmatrix} w_1 \\ w_2 \end{pmatrix}$$

$$(4.17)$$

For a correlation matrix, we have $q_{ii} = 1, q_{12} = q_{21}, i = 1, 2$ and therefore:

$$w_1 = v_1 + q_{12}v_2 \text{ and } w_2 = q_{12}v_1 + v_2 \text{ or } v_1 = \left(\frac{w_1 - w_2q_{12}}{1 - q_{12}^2}\right), v_2 = \left(\frac{w_2 - w_1q_{12}}{1 - q_{12}^2}\right)$$

(4.18)

To reduce the number of risk sources, we first determine the matrix Q eigenvalues $\lambda_j, j = 1, 2$. These are found by solving the determinant equation:

$$|Q - \lambda I| = 0 \text{ with } Q - \lambda I = \begin{pmatrix} q_{11} - \lambda & q_{12} \\ q_{21} & q_{22} - \lambda \end{pmatrix}$$

and

$$\begin{vmatrix} q_{11} - \lambda & q_{12} \\ q_{21} & q_{22} - \lambda \end{vmatrix} = (q_{11} - \lambda)(q_{22} - \lambda) - q_{12}q_{21} = 0$$

(4.19)

Solution for the eigenvalues $\lambda_i, i = 1, 2$ are then:

$$\lambda_1 = \frac{q_{22} + q_{11}}{2} + \sqrt{\left(\frac{q_{22} + q_{11}}{2}\right)^2 - q_{11}q_{22} + q_{12}q_{21}},$$

$$\lambda_2 = \frac{q_{22} + q_{11}}{2} - \sqrt{\left(\frac{q_{22} + q_{11}}{2}\right)^2 - q_{11}q_{22} + q_{12}q_{21}}$$

(4.20)

And for a correlation matrix, this is reduced to:

$$\lambda_1 = 1 + q_{12}, \lambda_2 = 1 - q_{12}$$

To determine the eigenvectors associated to each eigenvalue of this matrix, we solve the matrix equation:

$$Q\beta_j = \lambda_j\beta_j, j = 1, 2, , \ldots n$$

or explicitly:

$$\begin{pmatrix} q_{11} & q_{12} \\ q_{21} & q_{22} \end{pmatrix}\begin{pmatrix} \beta_1 \\ \beta_2 \end{pmatrix} = \begin{pmatrix} \lambda_1 & 0 \\ 0 & \lambda_1 \end{pmatrix}\begin{pmatrix} \beta_1 \\ \beta_2 \end{pmatrix}, \quad \text{eigenvector for } \lambda_1;$$

(4.21)

$$\begin{pmatrix} q_{11} & q_{12} \\ q_{21} & q_{22} \end{pmatrix}\begin{pmatrix} \beta_1' \\ \beta_2' \end{pmatrix} = \begin{pmatrix} \lambda_2 & 0 \\ 0 & \lambda_2 \end{pmatrix}\begin{pmatrix} \beta_1' \\ \beta_2' \end{pmatrix}, \quad \text{eigenvector for } \lambda_2$$

Generally, since the matrix Q is symmetric nonnegative definite, the eigenvalues are all nonnegative and the eigenvectors are all orthogonal to each other. Normalization of the eigenvectors yields $Q|\beta_j| = \sum \beta_{ij}^2 = \lambda_j j = 1, 2, \ldots, n$. If we order the eigenvalues in an increasing order such that $\lambda_1 \geq \lambda_2 \geq \lambda_3 \geq \ldots \lambda_n$ then β_1 is called the first principal component, and β_j is called the jth principal component. In our simple example, say that the first eigenvalue is larger than the second one, or $\lambda_1 \gg \lambda_2$, and say that we drop the second eigenvalue. Thus, the new data matrix (or correlation matrix Q_r if we decide to collapse such a matrix) can be defined in terms of the first principal component, or:

$$Q_r = \begin{pmatrix} \beta_1 \\ \beta_2 \end{pmatrix}^T \begin{pmatrix} q_{11} & q_{12} \\ q_{21} & q_{22} \end{pmatrix}^T \tag{4.22}$$

Practically, we may consider only the first few principal components to capture a data set essential variations of multiple risks, thereby reducing significantly the dimensionality of the risk sources to be accounted for.

EXAMPLE: A MARKET INDEX AND PCA

Does a market index based on a select number of firms measure the true evolution of the market price? Does an index based on the 25 largest firms out of the thousands traded provide an acceptable proxy measure of the market variation? In other words, from a matrix of thousands of firms' prices traded, what are the first 25 components and do they account for the thousands of firms' price variations? If this were the case, can we use the first 25 components as a market variability index? Such questions can be applied to numerous problems such as the price of water, which is not traded but is found to covary with hundreds of firms and other economic, geographic, and political variables.

Technically, a *multiple risks lognormal model* used to price an asset can be approximated by reducing its dimensionality, by reducing its number of risk sources through PCA. This is done as follows. Let a multiple risk model be defined by $Y_1 = \Sigma \Delta w$ where Δw_j, $j = 1, 2, \ldots, n$ are n sources of risk, defined by normally distributed random variables with mean zero and variance 1. In matrix notation, we have

$$Y_1 = \Sigma \Delta w$$

and therefore

$$\Delta w = \Sigma^{-1} Y_1$$

Using the eigenvalues, each of the individual risk sources can be written as follows:

$$\Delta w_j = \frac{1}{\lambda_j} \sum_{\ell=1}^{n} \beta_{\ell j} \Delta v_\ell \tag{4.23}$$

where Δv_ℓ are random variables (components) and Δw_j are independent random variables with mean zero, uncorrelated over time and variance $\Delta t = 1$. Equivalently:

$$\Delta v_\ell = \sum_{i=1}^{n} \beta_{\ell i} \Delta w_i, \ell = 1, 2, \ldots, n$$

Further if we select the components with the largest eigenvalues (that will account for most of the variation), that is, $\lambda_{k+1}, \lambda_{k+2}, \ldots, \lambda_{k+n} \ll \lambda_1, \lambda_2, \ldots, \lambda_k$, then:

$$\Delta v_\ell \approx \sum_{i=1}^{k} \beta_{\ell i} \Delta w_i, \ell = 1, 2, \ldots .k$$

And therefore, we can write:

$$\Delta w_j = \sum_{\ell=1}^{k} \beta_{\ell j} \Delta v_\ell \tag{4.24}$$

as well as:

$$\sum_{i=1}^{n} \sigma_{\ell i} \Delta w_i \approx \sum_{j=1}^{k} \sigma_\ell \beta_{\ell j} \Delta v_\ell$$

For example, assume a lognormal market index price that is subject to many risks:

$$\frac{\Delta S_\ell(t)}{S_\ell(t)} = \chi_\ell(t)\Delta t + \sum_{i=1}^{n} \sigma_{\ell i} \Delta w_i, S_\ell(0) > 0 \tag{4.25}$$

with a solution (to be seen in a subsequent chapter) by:

$$S_\ell(t) = \Phi_\ell(t) S_\ell(0) \exp\left\{ \sum_{i=1}^{n} \sigma_{\ell i} \Delta w_i \right\} \tag{4.26}$$

where $\Phi_\ell(t)$ is some deterministic function of time (to be defined subsequently when we consider Ito's stochastic calculus; see Chapter 8). This may be written in terms of far fewer random variables. Namely, for $k = 3$:

$$S_\ell(t) = \Phi_\ell(t) S_\ell(0) \exp\left\{ \sum_{j=1}^{3} \sigma_\ell \beta_{\ell j} \Delta v_j \right\} =$$
$$= \Phi_\ell(t) S_\ell(0) \exp\left\{ \sigma_\ell \beta_{\ell 1} \Delta v_1 + \sigma_\ell \beta_{\ell 2} \Delta v_2 + \sigma_\ell \beta_{\ell 3} \Delta v_3 \right\} \tag{4.27}$$

Thus, we can reduce the number of risk sources to the essential fewer and representative risk components.

DEPENDENCE AND COPULAS

When the underlying joint probability distributions of dependent events are complex, *copulas* can be used to model their joint distributional dependence. Copulas are algebraic structures (functional models) that represent technically the statistical dependence of joint distributions as a function of their marginal probability distributions. These models are used extensively in practice although they may be difficult to justify a priori. Their mathematical tractability and ease of use (in this case our ability to simulate extremely complex dependent probability structures) may be at odds with their actual representativeness. For this reason, their empirical verification prior to their use in practice is important.

For example, say that the price probability distributions of an index and a firm stock price are given at a given time by $f_S(S_1)$ and $f_M(M_1)$ respectively, while their cumulative distributions are:

$$F_S(S_1) = \int_{-\infty}^{S_1} f_S(x)dx \text{ and } F_M(M_1) = \int_{-\infty}^{M_1} f_M(y)dy \qquad (4.28)$$

A two-dimensional copula defines a joint cumulative distribution as an algebraic structure $C(u, v)$ of its respective cumulative distributions:

$$C(u, v) = P(U_S \leq F_S(S_1), U_M \leq F_M(M_1)), u = F_S(S_1) \ v = F_M(M_1) \qquad (4.29)$$

with u and v denoting the marginal cumulative distributions. Copulas $C(u, v)$ have of course the same properties as those of joint cumulative probability distributions, or:

$$0 \leq C(u, v) \leq 1; 0 \leq u \leq 1, 0 \leq v \leq 1,$$
$$C(0, u) = C(u, 0) = 0 \quad \text{and} \quad C(1, u) = C(u, 1) = u \qquad (4.30)$$

Due to their practical importance, Copulas have been the subject of considerable research and application in insurance, in VaR applications, and in credit risks and their derivatives (see also Chapters 9 and 10). For example, they are used to provide estimates of portfolio losses consisting of statistically dependent assets and securities that might be concordant with observable data sets.

There are numerous copulas, designed to meet a broad variety of modeling and statistical needs. For example the following three copulas exhibit specific statistical properties:

$$\begin{cases} 1. & \text{Mixture Copula}: & C(u, v) = (1 - \rho)uv + \rho \min(u, v), \rho > 0 \\ 2. & \text{Co} - \text{monotonic Copula}: & C_U(u, v) = \min\{u, v\} \\ 3. & \text{Counter} - \text{monotonic Copula}: & C_L(u, v) = (u + v - 1)^+ \end{cases}$$
$$(4.31)$$

A mixture copula refers to a mixture of two probability distributions while co-monotonic copulas point to probability distributions that move in tandem (or vice versa for counter-monotonic copulas). Other copulas can be defined to better fit observed empirical records of stocks, credit default, or any joint distributions. Their applications are indeed very large, and numerous publications document their characteristics (e.g., Nelsen 1999; Cherubini et al. 2004; Embrechts et al. 2002,

2003, 2007; McNeil, Frey, and Embrecht 2005; Patton 2009). Often used copulas include:

- *Gaussian (normal) copulas.* The copula of the n-variate normal distribution with linear correlation matrix R is

$$C_R(u) = \Phi_R^n(\Phi^{-1}(u_1), \dots, \Phi^{-1}(u_n)),$$

where Φ_R^n denotes the joint distribution function of the n-variate standard normal distribution function with linear correlation matrix R, and Φ^{-1} denotes the inverse of the distribution function of the univariate standard normal distribution. Such a copula has been used extensively in the past to price credit risk models (see the KMV model in Chapter 10). Since there is no closed-form expression for Φ^{-1} there is no closed-form expression Φ_R^n. In a bivariate case the Gaussian copula can be written in terms of the correlation matrix parameters as:

$$C_R(u, v) = \int_{-\infty}^{\Phi^{-1}(u)} \int_{-\infty}^{\Phi^{-1}(v)} \frac{1}{2\pi \left(1 - R_{12}^2\right)^{1/2}} \exp\left\{-\frac{s^2 - 2R_{12}st + t^2}{2(1 - R_{12}^2)}\right\} ds\, dt \tag{4.32}$$

Note that R_{12} is simply the usual linear correlation coefficient of the corresponding bivariate normal distribution. It can be shown that Gaussian copulas do not have upper and hence lower tail dependence (due to radial symmetry). This explains why multivariate normal distributions do not assign a high enough probability of occurrence to events that are subject to common and rare risk factors.

- *The Gumbel family copula.* Let $\varphi(t) = (-\ln t)^\theta$, where $\theta \geq 0$. The Gumbel family copula is used to model co-dependent extreme events. It is given by:

$$C_\theta(u, v) = \varphi^{-1}(\varphi(u) + \varphi(v)) = \exp\left(-\left[(-\ln u)^\theta + (-\ln v)^\theta\right]^{1/\theta}\right) \tag{4.33}$$

This copula has upper tail dependence and has been used in some value at risk (VaR) models where many extreme risks, some dependent, are used to determine a financial institution's capital adequacy ratio (CAR). (See also Chapter 3.)

- *The Frank family copula.* Let

$$\varphi(t) = -\ln \frac{e^{-\theta t} - 1}{e^{-\theta} - 1}$$

where $\theta \in [-\infty, \infty] \backslash \{0\}$. This leads to the Frank family copula:

$$C_\theta(u, v) = -\frac{1}{\theta} \ln \left(1 + \frac{(e^{-\theta u} - 1)(e^{-\theta v} - 1)}{(e^{-\theta} - 1)}\right) \tag{4.34}$$

- *The Clayton family copula.* Let $\varphi(t) = (t^\theta - 1)/\theta$, where $\theta \in [-1, \infty]\backslash\{0\}$. This is given by:

$$C_\theta(u, v) = \max\left([u^{-\theta} + v^{-\theta} - 1]^{-1/\theta}, 0\right) \qquad (4.35)$$

For $\theta > 0$ the copula is strict and simplifies to

$$C_\theta(u, v) = [u^{-\theta} + v^{-\theta} - 1]^{-1/\theta}$$

The Clayton family copula has lower tail dependence for $\theta > 0$.

EXAMPLE: THE GUMBEL COPULA, THE HIGHS AND THE LOWS

Extreme (Weibull, Gumbel, Frechet) probability distributions were used in Chapter 3 to model the high and the low intraday price distributions. Say that the joint cumulative probability distribution of the highs and the lows are modeled now by type A Gumbel distributions $[u(x), v(y)]$ with joint distribution:

$$F(x, y) = u(x)v(y) \exp\left(-\theta \left[\frac{1}{\ln u(x)} + \frac{1}{\ln v(y)}\right]^{-1}\right) \qquad (4.36)$$

where $u(x)$ and $u(x)$ are marginal Gumbel cumulative distributions. Note that for such a distribution,

$$u(x) = [x]^n \quad v(y) = 1 - [1 - y]^n$$

and since the high and the low prices are drawn from the same probability distribution, we have $y = x = F(S)$. Thus, the bivariate (high and low prices for a day) copula, where $u = u(x)$, $v = v(y)$, is:

$$C(u, v \,|\, x) = uv \exp\left(-\theta \left[\frac{1}{\ln u} + \frac{1}{\ln v}\right]^{-1}\right) \qquad (4.37)$$

And therefore,

$$C(x, y \,|\, S) = [x]^n \left(1 - [1 - y]^n\right) \exp\left(-\theta \left[\frac{1}{n \ln [x]} + \frac{1}{\ln \left(1 - [1 - y]^n\right)}\right]^{-1}\right)$$

$$x = y = F(S) \qquad (4.38)$$

which provides a joint cumulative distribution for the high and the low which can be tested against empirical data. Alternatively, a type B Gumbel given by (note that another parameter m has been inserted) is given by:

$$F(x, y) = u(x)v(y) \exp\left(\left[\left(\ln\frac{1}{u(x)}\right)^m + \left(\ln\frac{1}{v(y)}\right)^m\right]^{\frac{1}{m}}\right) \qquad (4.39)$$

where

$$m > 1, m = \frac{1}{\sqrt{1-\rho}}$$

with ρ being a coefficient of correlation between the high and the low. We can of course calculate the explicit joint probability distribution, using the fact that

$$f(x, y) = \frac{\partial^2 F(x, y)}{\partial x \partial y}$$

and simulate such a joint distribution using Monte Carlo techniques and calculate its moments (mean, variance, covariance, skewness, kurtosis, etc.).

EXAMPLE: COPULAS AND CONDITIONAL DEPENDENCE

Financial statistics are dependent both horizontally (across many securities and other economic variables) and conditionally, presenting complex intertemporal relationships. In some cases, their modeling can be simpler to formulate based on the conditional distributions. An alternative model to simple intertemporal relationships (exponential smoothing, autoregressive, mean reversion, etc.) may be the use of conditional copulas. For example, given two financial prices, it might be easier to use a joint copula in terms of the (statistical) conditional distributions of the price distributions. For example, postulate a joint cumulative distribution for two financial prices (S and C) by a bivariate copula:

$$C\left(F_S(S_1), F_C(c_1)\right) = \int_{-\infty}^{S_1} \int_{-\infty}^{c_1} f(x, y)dxdy \qquad (4.40)$$

It might be more intuitive to express price C conditional on another price distribution S rather than specifying directly their joint distribution. To do so, we proceed as follows: Let the first derivative of a bivariate copula with respect to its first (risk factor) argument u be

$$C_1(u, v) = \frac{\partial C(u, v)}{\partial u}$$

or

$$C_1(u, v) = \frac{\partial C(u, v)}{\partial u} = C_{2|1}(v \,|u) = C_{2|1}\left(F_C(c_1)\,|F_S(S_1)\right) \qquad (4.41)$$

This conditional copula defines the conditional cumulative probability distribution of $(c_1 | S_1)$ or

$$F_{c_1 | S_1}(c_1) = C\left(F_C(c_1) | F_S(S_1)\right)$$

The conditional probability distribution of the security C and that of S is thus:

$$\frac{\partial F_{c_1 | S_1}(c_1)}{\partial c_1} = f(c_1 | S_1) \tag{4.42}$$

In practice, additional knowledge, both qualitative and quantitative, is needed to define a copula. To this end, families of copulas have been studied, providing a library of relationships one may select from. Next, an example developed by Embrechts et al. (2002, 2003, 2007) is used to derive copulas from their condition (model) copulas.

EXAMPLE: COPULAS AND THE CONDITIONAL DISTRIBUTION

Say that a copula is given by

$$C(u, v) = \left[u^{-\alpha} + v^{-\alpha} - 1\right]^{-\frac{1}{\alpha}}, \alpha > 0$$

and calculate the derivative with respect to v. This results in a conditional copula,

$$C_{2|1}(v|u) = \frac{\partial C}{\partial u} = u^{-\alpha-1} \left[u^{-\alpha} + v^{-\alpha} - 1\right]^{-\left(\frac{1}{\alpha}+1\right)} \tag{4.43}$$

Now set the conditional copula $q = C_{2|1}(v|u)$ and solve for v. We obtain then the conditional density function given u, or

$$v = \left\{-1 + \left(u^{-\alpha} q^{-\frac{\alpha}{1+\alpha}}\right) - u^{-\alpha}\right\}^{-\frac{1}{\alpha}} = \left\{-1 + u^{-\alpha}\left(q^{-\frac{\alpha}{1+\alpha}} - 1\right)\right\}^{-\frac{1}{\alpha}} \tag{4.44}$$

In other words, in terms of security prices x_1 and x_2 we have, by definition of $v = F_2(x_2), u = F_1(x_1)$,

$$F_2(x_2) = \left\{-1 + (F_1(x_1))^{-\alpha}\left(q^{-\frac{\alpha}{1+\alpha}} - 1\right)\right\}^{-\frac{1}{\alpha}} \tag{4.45}$$

An explicit conditional copula is thus:

$$q = F_{2|1}(x_2 | x_1) = \left\{-1 + (F_1(x_1))^{\alpha}\left[(F_2(x_2))^{-\alpha} - 1\right]\right\}^{-\frac{1+\alpha}{\alpha}} \tag{4.46}$$

while the conditional probability distribution is given by:

$$
f_{2|1}(x_2|x_1) = \frac{\partial F_{2|1}(x_2|x_1)}{\partial x_2}
$$

$$
= (1 + \alpha) \frac{f_2(x_2)}{F_2(x_2)} \left(\frac{F_1(x_1)}{F_2(x_2)} \right)^{\alpha} \left\{ -1 + (F_1(x_1))^{\alpha} \left[(F_2(x_2))^{-\alpha} - 1 \right] \right\}^{-\left(\frac{1+2\alpha}{\alpha} \right)}
$$

(4.47)

In other words, given the security price x_1, the probability distribution function of the security price x_2 is given by equation (4.47). Generally, if we define the k-dimensional Copula,

$$
C_1(u_1) = u_1, C_2(u_1, u_2), \ldots\ldots, C_n(u_1, u_2, u_3, \ldots, u_n)
$$

(4.48)

with $C(u_1, u_2, u_3, \ldots, u_n) = C_n(u_1, u_2, u_3, \ldots, u_n)$, and the conditional copula is:

$$
C_k(u_k | u_2, u_3, \ldots, u_{k-1}) = P\{U_k \le u_k | U_2 = u_2, U_3 = u_3, \ldots, U_{k-1} = u_{k-1}\}
$$

(4.49)

and

$$
C_k(u_k | u_2, u_3, \ldots, u_{k-1}) = \frac{\dfrac{\partial^{k-1} C_k(u_1, u_2, \ldots, u_k)}{\partial u_1, \ldots\ldots \partial u_{k-1}}}{\dfrac{\partial^{k-1} C_{k-1}(u_1, u_2, \ldots, u_{k-1})}{\partial u_1, \ldots\ldots \partial u_{k-1}}}
$$

(4.50)

Thus, for k = 2, we have as seen earlier:

$$
C_2(u_2|u_1) = \frac{\dfrac{\partial C_2(u_1, u_2)}{\partial u_1}}{\dfrac{\partial C_1(u_1)}{\partial u_1}} = \frac{\dfrac{\partial C_2(u_1, u_2)}{\partial u_1}}{\dfrac{\partial}{\partial u_1} u_1} = \frac{\partial C_2(u_1, u_2)}{\partial u_1}
$$

(4.51)

Such models are, of course, only modeling tools that allow us to construct broader and more comprehensive models of dependence to reflect both our appreciation of security prices' covariation and their empirical evidence. Such models are in general extremely difficult to study analytically, but the structure of copulas provides ample opportunities for their simulation and study complex dependent relationships. For extensions of such an approach, we refer the reader to Embrechts et al. (2003) and Nelsen (1999) as well as to www.charlestapiero.com.

FINANCIAL MODELING AND INTERTEMPORAL MODELS

Probability modeling is extremely useful to rationalize the unknown by embedding it into a coherent framework, clearly distinguishing what we know with what we don't know. Yet the presumption that we can formalize our lack of knowledge may be hard to defend. At a more specific level, there seems to be some confusion regarding our understanding of randomness, uncertainty, and chaos—three essential concepts that underlie the modeling of uncertainty in finance and engineering.

These terms underlie the polemic regarding modeling cultures. For example, a majority of observed phenomena of randomness in nature cannot and should not be explained by a conventional probability theory. Rather, randomness is an expression of events unpredictability. A number of information theorists (for example, Jaynes 1957a and 1957b) defined randomness in terms of *nonuniqueness* and *nonregularity*. For example, a die has six faces and therefore it has nonuniqueness. Further, the expansion of $\sqrt{2}$ or of π provides an infinite string of numbers that appear irregularly, and can therefore be thought of as *random*. These particular characteristics have been used by simulation theorists to generate strings of random numbers for Monte Carlo simulations. By the same token, Nobel laureate Max Born stated in his 1954 inaugural address that randomness occurs when determinacy lapses into indeterminacy without any logical, mathematical, empirical, or physical argumentation (preceding, thereby, an important research effort on chaos). Statements such as "we might have trouble forecasting the temperature of coffee one minute in advance, but we should have little difficulty in forecasting it an hour ahead" by Edward Lorenz, a weather forecaster and one of the co-founders of chaos theory, reinforced the many dilemmas we must confront in probability modeling.

In financial forecasting, the accuracy of predictions does not always turn out to be any better than that of weather forecasts. Accrued evidence further points out that the assumptions made by probability models are in practice violated. Further, the use of predictive models based on past short-term and long-term memory data (and thereby implying that future prices are co-dependent with past prices) undermines the existence of martingales in finance (and thus contradicts the essential part of modern financial pricing theory—see Chapters 7 and 8). Can stock prices be modeled by stochastic differential equations? The question of whether we can assume that *noise* is a normal Brownian motion and similar questions, are some of the issues we confront.

Many research papers on the study of various nonlinear models seek to bridge a gap between traditional probability approaches and systems exhibiting non-normal behavior. We next consider some classical departures from the normal modeling of randomness and their effects on financial modeling. This discussion is meant to motivate the reader to appreciate that theory has its own limits and that reconciling theory and real processes is always challenging. The essential factors we consider are the effects of short-term memory and long-term memory. Both of these processes, if they do exist in financial time series, will violate the presumption that financial markets are complete (Chapter 7) and therefore call for careful application.

Time, Memory, and Causal Dependence

The fascination with time and memory is not new. Philosophers, psychologists, economists, historians, and statisticians, among many others, have come to grips with time and memory, each in their own way. Each contributes an important and unique point of view allowing a better understanding of how time, change, dependence, and memory affect our understanding of processes and how to model them. These considerations are essential to modeling financial time series. The questions of what is time, what is memory, and how do the two conjure to create and induce dependence and change, are fundamental to financial modeling.

Greek philosophers associated time with change. Aristotle's concept of time (in *Metaphysica*), for example, defines an objective, numerable time, as that associated to change and movement. In the Middle Ages, Saint Augustine (*Confessions*, Book X), suggests a more subjective approach to time and financial modeling, concluding that we are always in a *present* which consists of the present of the present, the present of the future, and the present of the past. Thus, past and future coexist in the here and now, defined by our memory of the past and our expectation of the thereafter. Some of our actions account for this explicitly, always implicitly. In other words, we may say that each one of our present acts is framed in a perspective of past and future time.

Technically, we may use our record of the past (the memory) to both assess our present (in which case, it is called by some *filtering*) and construct an expectation—a forecast of the future. Similarly, our expectations of a future define our present (as fundamental financial theory concludes in Chapter 7). In either case we may have different approaches to conceive of the past and conceive a present future. The two, past and future, define the process of change and must therefore be understood, constructed, and tested over time. For example, our ability to invest, to plan, and to predict stock prices is based on our ability to reproduce and understand the factors that determine changing prices. These issues are of course omnipresent and underlie conflicting approaches to finance, each approach (charting based on extrapolating past trends or based on a rational expectation of future prices or fundamental finance) entrenched in a set of assumptions that justify one, the other, or both.

If we causally order a set of events (to model a financial process, for example), we have in essence described an intertemporal dependence. Bertrand Russel, in his *Time and Experience*, distinguished two sources of our knowledge of time:

> *One is the perception of succession within one specious present, the other is memory. Remembering can be perceived, and is found to have a quality of greater or less remoteness, in virtue of which all my present memories can be placed in a time order. But this time is subjective, and must be distinguished from historical time. Historical time has to the present the relation of "preceding," which I know from the experience of change within one specious present. In historical time, all my present memories are now, but in so far as they are veridical they point to occurrences in the historical past.*
>
> —Bertrand Russel, *Time and Experience*, 216

Such an approach reflects, too, the underlying ideas expounded by Saint Augustine in Book XI of *Confessions*, as stated earlier. To develop such ideas in a scientific sense, psychologists such as the School of Janet (1920) Fraisse (1957), Piaget (1946), Wallis (1966), and many others have devised an experimental approach seeking to better understand time and memory and in particular in modeling the interactions of time-memory-change.

Piaget's *The Notion of Time in Infants* (1946) indicated that time is tied to the notion of memory and is parallel to our perception and awareness of elapsed time. As a result, a consciousness of time is registered in our memory. Without memory there is no perception of time, and therefore a coupling of time and memory is essential to construct the mechanism that explains how change unfolds (or in other words, to construct the process underlying change). For example, if a process is temporally unrecorded, then time, as a dimension along which our analysis is made and extrapolated, is simply not defined (this implies that without recording financial data there are no financial processes we can relate to). Conversely, without a sequence or patterning of time dependence, memory does not exist. For example, if a financial market is in equilibrium, it will not move from this equilibrium and therefore it will have no memory, nor change, since there will be no cause for change. This means that a market in equilibrium has no temporal causality. When a market is continuously fed by new and random information, it is perpetually in disequilibrium, and it has a memory of an equilibrium it seeks to return to (as is the case in contrarian and mean reverting models). When financial markets are subjected to shocks, innovations, and other interferences leading these markets to be out of equilibrium, then a change in equilibrium may be induced based on a switch to economic regimes, regulation, or political or technological change. In this sense, an equilibrium in financial markets may be *dynamic*—existing but always changing.

The fundamental theory of finance (Chapter 7) in particular presumes that current prices now are a *rational expectation of future prices* (of course, we should add that these prices are defined under a certain probability measure, its martingale, and are subject to a filtration, summarizing all the relevant and fully used information). In this case, the past is no guide to the future and therefore trading with technical charts is misguided. Some financial traders, anchored in their experiences, may prefer to use charting techniques, reflecting a future price based on an extrapolated memory of the past where the future prices are not considered explicitly. Statistical predictions of, say, a stock volatility are determined by statistical ARCH and GARCH techniques and are therefore a reflection of the past, to reveal a future volatility. Technically, we use models, whether deterministic or stochastic, to represent a hypothetical process of change. These are and will remain only models expressing our human intentionality, personal experience (memory) and the theoretical know-how we can apply to represent price processes and analyze their consequences. However, in practice, the proof of the pudding will remain the essential test that traders may apply to justify their model: Was their bet justified by the money they made or lost?

Quantitative Time and Change

Change measures are a quantitative expression of what has occurred between past and future, determined by their characteristics, the information, and so forth. In a timeless state there is no change, while in a period of perpetual innovation and volatility there is a great deal of change. An underlying price process that is not volatile exhibits little change in prices while a volatile price process has prices changing intently. Explicitly, if the stock price today is $36 and at the end of the day is it is $36.50, the change is relative to the current price and equals $0.50.

Change can be subjective, probabilistic, or psychological. Captain James Mulligan, Jr., a pilot captured during the war in Vietnam and years later released, was able to recall the precise date of every significant event during his long captivity. He knew the dates of various bombing raids, the dates when his colleagues had been captured or tortured, and the dates of occasional change in his prison life. Captain Mulligan was aware of time and its record, but only in terms of temporal milestones for which he had a memory. Change is then an expression of these memory states. For example, in a random walk, events occur independently of one another, and there is a change only relative to a current state. Thus change has no memory except of its current state, which has no effect on change.

When an event is memory dependent, higher-order processes than Markov ones are needed to model their behavior. If the probability of an event is a function of both its current state and its previous movement, then such a process has a higher-order memory. We shall call such processes *short memory*. A particular presumption of some financial traders is that such a short memory exists and is implied in their trading strategies, betting on a stock price momentum to buy more or less of a stock (while contrarians do exactly the opposite). In this case, a price growth feeds a price growth. Such processes, generalized random walks, are also called *persistent* random walks (Vallois and Tapiero 2007 and 2009).

When events are positively correlated over time, volatility increases and alters the expectation for change. In this sense, aversion to a volatile stock market is equivalent to an aversion to change, which implies conservative trading strategies (i.e., not only adverse to risk). As a result, by ignoring change, conservative trading can become extremely risky. For the long run, memory carried over many periods of time may lead to processes that have an infinite variance, while the long-run volatility of a memory-less process is scant by comparison. Therefore, long-run memory induces greater uncertainty regarding a process future (and, thereby, a greater future volatility). But of course, this makes sense only to the extent that information as it unfolds is not used to learn. Learning, therefore, is a means to counter the modeling volatility effects of dependence and change as they are manifested over time.

Persistence and Short-term Memory

Short-term memory models define explicitly an intertemporal causal dependence based on a past time path—that is, its explicit memory rather than its summary. In such models, the probability of a price increasing or decreasing is a function of both the current state of the price but also the prices assumed in the previous instants (that make up such an explicit memory). These models may be persistent, exhibiting local price contagions and nonlinear variance-volatility evolutions. Such models differ from long-run memory models or fractal models that are used to model a long-run time nonlinear growth in models' variance.

For example, consider a portfolio of a bank's loans. Does default of a loan alter the default probability of another loan? What about the default of two, three, and more loans? Is a bank failure, two banks failures, and so on, a signal to the failure to other banks? Are such bank failures contagious or not? Since finance is based on both real and prospective events, a broad number of future and potential scenarios or events may be open to interpretations that affect market price processes. Does removing an investment from a hedge fund affect the probability of another investor removing his investments as well? By the same token, do variations in exchange rate prices exhibit a contagious behavior or are they antipersistent? Do insurance claims by one insured affect the insured's propensity to make a claim the following year? And so on.

For example, let $(d_1, d_2, d_3, \ldots)$ be the number of banks' defaults at time $t = 1$, 2, 3, …. To what extent is the number of defaults (of, equivalently, the probability of default of a bank) at a later time determined by past defaults? Explicitly, at time $t = 4$, what is the meaning of the conditional probability $p_4\,(d_4\,|d_1, d_2, d_3\,)$ which expresses an explicit and conditional temporal event on past realizations (of banks' defaults)?

In these models, the probabilities of future events are a function of realized other events (rather than a statistical realization determined by past events—as is the case when Bayesian learning is included in a particular model). These are questions that underlie the existence or the nonexistence of a temporal causality that is termed *persistence*. Such processes may explain financial momentum in stock markets, based on a presumption that a stock price's growth furthers more growth in such prices (or the converse, a decline furthers continuing decline). These processes therefore differ and significantly from a Markov model where the probability of an event depends only on a process current state, rather than being anchored in the past and experienced history (although multiperiod models can be modeled in some cases as Markov models). In other words, rather than emphasize a dependence on where we are, memory dependence emphasizes where we came from as well, which determines the probabilities of subsequent movements. Empirical verification using security stock prices has shown that such memory is prevalent in intraday data (using minutes' traded prices) rather than in day prices or weekly averaged prices. The implication of this observation is that short-term memory may be useful for high-frequency trading with trades defined by the past change in prices over the past few minutes. In other words, short-term memory is dissipated in time series that record processes infrequently. (For further study, see Vallois, Tapiero [2007 and 2009], and Herman and Vallois [2010]).

Long-run memory, unlike short-term memory, assesses the probability of current events based on long-past events, each having individually and collectively an effect, which is summarized by a parametric (and mostly increasing) process variance. For finance, the evolution of the variability is extremely important but difficult to interpret and predict. For this reason, long-run memory that resists simple causal modeling turns out to be a convenient statistical model. Long-run memory has important implications for many of the paradigms used in modern financial economics. For example, optimal investment and portfolio decisions may become extremely sensitive to the investment horizon if stock returns were long-term dependent. Conclusions of more recent tests of the efficient market hypothesis (EMH) or stock market rationality also hang precariously on the presence or absence of long-term memory (Lo 1991 and 1997). If speculative prices exhibit dependency, then the existence of such dependency would be inconsistent with rational expectations and would thus make a strong case for technical forecasting on stock prices.

To model long-run memory, fractional Brownian motion is often used. This is a stochastic process defined by a *Brownian-normal-like* process, which we denote by $B_H(t)$, that has a zero mean and a nonlinear time variance growth (see the many references at the end of this chapter, including in particular Mandelbrot). Explicitly, for all real times $t, s \in \Re$, the fractional Brownian motion has the following properties:

$E[B_H(t)] = 0$ and covariance:

$$E[B_H(t)B_H(s)] = \frac{1}{2}\left\{|t|^{2H} + |s|^{2H} - |t-s|^{2H}\right\} \tag{4.52}$$

where H is the Hurst index (defined shortly). Thus, at time $t=s$ the variance is

$$E[B_H(t)^2] = |t|^{2H}$$

For example, if $H > 0.5$, the variance will grow at a positive nonlinear rate (contributing thereby to the unpredictability of future prices since it will have an infinite variance). By the same token, if the index $H < 0.5$, the variance will decline over time, leading to a process that is reverting to some steady state.

Fractional Brownian motion has also the following properties: First, it has the same distribution as a normal probability distribution $B(1)$ with mean zero and variance 1 (a standardized Brownian motion), $B_H(t) \sim t^H B(1)$. This means that the variance for any time interval s is equal to s^{2H} times the variance for the unit interval (Mandelbrot and Van Ness 1968):

$$B_H(t+s) - B_H(t) \underset{i.d.}{\rightarrow} s^H[B_H(t+1) - B_H(t)] \tag{4.53}$$

Second, increments of fractional Brownian motion are also fractional and are given by:

$$E\left[(B_H(t+\Delta) - B_H(\Delta))(B_H(s+\Delta) - B_H(\Delta))\right]$$

Furthermore, the increments variance is:

$$E\left[B_H(t+s) - B_H(t)\right]^2 = s^{2H}E\left[B_H(t+1) - B_H(t)\right]^2 \tag{4.54}$$

As with the R/S process described in the next subsection, if $H = 0.5$, the process has independent increments (corresponding to a Wiener process). If $H > 0.5$, the underlying stochastic process has long-range dependence. Namely, it is easy to show that:

$$\sum_{i=1}^{\infty} \text{cov}\left(B_H(1), B_H(i+1) - B_H(i)\right) = \infty \tag{4.55}$$

The implication of nonindependence—that is, $H \neq 0.5$—means that the process is non-Markovian. Further, the covariance between future and past increments is positive if $H > 0.5$ and negative if $H < 0.5$. It is interesting to note that the range of the fluctuations increases as H increases. Fractional Brownian motion has attracted much interest in finance. For references and further study see the numerous references to Mandelbrot as well as many other authors who sought to reconcile the physical observation of data and the commonly used normal process.

THE R/S INDEX

In Chapter 3, we note that the range of a security's price over one day is used by Parkinson, Garman, and others to calculate the process volatility. Empirical use of range statistics as a proxy for volatility is to be used carefully, however (albeit, it might be complementary), as there are important differences between the range and volatility. Essentially, estimates of volatility are more robust than the range, being far more sensitive to extreme variations. The ratio of range-to-standard-deviation (R/S) for a standardized series, or the Hurst index to characterize these series, is often used by financial analysts as an indicator of volatility and chaos and is useful if this caveat is recognized. The Hurst index, an exponent (Hurst 1951), seeks to quantify the statistical bias in a series, arising from self-similarity power laws in time series. It is also known as range/scale analysis and defined through rescaling the range into a dimensionless factor leading to the following observation (which has been verified in many situations and shown to be fairly robust):

$$\frac{R_T}{S_T} = \underset{T \to +\infty}{\cong} (\alpha T)^h \qquad (4.56)$$

where T is time—the length of a series sample that we use to calculate the statistics R_T and S_T

h is the Hurst exponent

α is a constant

Over many samples, a linear regression provides an estimate of the Hurst index[*]:

$$\ln\left(\frac{R_T}{S_T}\right) = \alpha + h\ln(T) \qquad (4.57)$$

The origins of the Hurst exponent are due to Hurst (1951), who began working on the Nile River Dam project and studied the random behavior of the influx of water from rainfall over the thousand years that data have been recorded (these data have been accumulated since the time of the Pharaohs and used to tax farmers based on the presumptions that high levels of the Nile would produce necessarily richer crops). These observations indicated that if the series were random, the range would increase with the square root of time. This result was confirmed empirically for many time series and theoretically for normal processes. Hurst noted explicitly that most natural phenomena follow a biased random walk and thus characterized it by the parameter h, expressing as well a series' dependence, coined by Mandelbrot

---

[*]For a more precise statistical procedure and applications, see Greene and Fielitz (1977 and 1980); Beran (1994); Booth et al. (1982); Diebold and Rudebusch (1989); Duncan (2006 and 2009); Duncan, Hu, and Pasik-Duncan (2000); Mandelbrot (1963, 1972, and 1974); Mandelbrot and Van Ness (1968); Mandelbrot and Wallis (1968 and 1969) Vallois and Tapiero (1995a, 1995b, 1996a, 1996b and 1996c).

the "Joseph effect" after the man who interpreted Pharaoh's dreams as pointing to seven abundant years to be followed by seven meager years. Thus, when the Hurst index equals 0.5 the series is subject to random variations (or *normal noise*). When it is larger than 0.5 it exhibits a *herd effect* (or a persistence with volatility stampeding over time), while for values smaller than 0.5, volatility is tampered over time.

Technically, the basic idea of long-run memory is that in a sample of size n, the sample mean will decay at a rate proportional to $1/n^\alpha$ while the sample correlation $\rho(n)$ decays to zero proportionately to $1/n^\alpha$, $0 < \alpha < 1$. Beran (1994) thus defines long-run memory as follows: Let there be a stationary process for which there exists a real number $\alpha \in (0, 1)$ and a constant such that

$$\lim_{n \to \infty} \frac{\rho(n)}{C_\rho n^{-\alpha}} = 1$$

In this case, the stationary process is said to be with long-run memory or long-range dependence. With this definition in hand, Beran points to a relationship between the sample volatility and the Hurst exponent, or:

$$\lim_{n \to \infty} \frac{\mathrm{var}\left(\sum_{i=1}^{n} X_i\right)(n)}{C_\rho n^{2H}} = \frac{1}{H(2H-1)} \tag{4.58}$$

As a result, the evolution of a forecast error from period to period will indicate the fractal character of the series as well as the existence of long-run memory. Thus, if $H = 0.5$, the disjoint intervals are uncorrelated. For $H > 0.5$, the series are correlated, exhibiting a memory effect (which tends to amplify persistent patterns in time series). For $H < 0.5$, these are called *antipersistent* time series. Such analyses require large samples, however, which might not be always available. For this reason, R/S analyses were used primarily for long time series such as sunspots, water levels of rivers, intraday trading stock market ticker data, and so forth.

The implications of the Hurst index can be interpreted in a number of ways. For example, if the range increases over time much faster than the standard deviation, it could imply that the series is *chaotic* (in the sense that a rapidly augmenting range preludes estimates of a growing volatility). These relative effects, if well understood, can be used profitably for detection and departure of the Gaussian-normal hypothesis. There are some problems in using R/S statistics, however, because of the extreme sensitivity to recent observations and, in particular, outliers that can lead to jumps in the range process that may not be detected as much by standard deviation statistics. These and other difficulties have been the source of concern in applying the R/S statistic. Further, given that both the R and S statistics provide information regarding a time series variability and since they have differing sensitivities to short- and long-term memory, a study of their ratio should be combined with a concurrent and separate analysis of the range and variance processes.

This facet of the R/S statistic has long been recognized in the detection of outliers. Irwin in 1925 pointed out the implications to outlier rejection using R/S analysis on identically and independently distributed samples. When the standard deviation is known and given by σ, he proposed the following statistic (in Barnett and Lewis 1994) for testing upper outliers in a sample of size n where $x_{(i)}$ is the ith ordered statistic (see also Chapter 3):

$$\lfloor x_{(n)} - x_{(n-1)} \rfloor / \sigma \text{ and } \lfloor x_{(n-1)} - x_{(n-2)} \rfloor / \sigma$$

Subsequently, a number of related approaches have been devised. Of particular interest is the range/spread (standard deviation) statistic, which is defined in fact by the R/S statistic:

$$\left[x_{(n)} - x_{(1)} \right] / s$$

The study of R/S in continuous time series and models is difficult, however. Feller as early as 1951 remarked that it is difficult to compute the range distribution in a symmetric random walk. Subsequently, Imhof (1985 and 1992) as well as Vallois (1993) and Vallois and Tapiero (1995a, 1995b, 1996a, and 1996b) have studied this process and have characterized the basic statistical properties of the range process that can be used fruitfully for the study of volatility in stochastic processes. Since then, many such applications have been made.

In summary, the range process is important for a number of reasons. First, it provides a statistic for the second-order variation of a process. Thus, a process that exhibits extremely large variation can be detected by estimating the process range. Of course, the process standard deviation provides such information as well, as we saw earlier, but volatility estimates are slower in reflecting bursts in volatility growth. Second, by noting that the standard deviation process is more robust than the range process, a combination of the two processes can provide some useful statistics based on the speed at which they evolve whenever the process parameters change. These differences underlie the R/S analysis and the definition of the Hurst exponent for time series, which is particularly important for the study of volatility of time series.

SUMMARY

This chapter has addressed the important financial issue of dependence. A number of approaches and statistical probability approaches were outlined, providing a broad appreciation of terms such as *statistical correlation, copulas, short-term memory* and *persistence, long-term dependence, R/S analysis,* and *fractional Brownian motion.* These notions are important as they underlie the many quantitative techniques we use to model stochastic-probability events, their risks, and their financial consequences. This chapter, although introductory, is relevant to an understanding of many problems in financial modeling and in interpreting financial time series. Applications include the high and low statistics and the Hurst index, default of loans and other credit instruments over time, the evolution of prices, and others. This chapter was starred as it requires a far greater use of quantitative and statistical tools than is possible in the scope of this book. Nevertheless an intuitive understanding of the concepts outlined in this chapter is practically important as they help us appreciate the many issues we might be confronted with when financial markets are incomplete.

TEST YOURSELF

This chapter being of an advanced nature, problems and applications are included in extensions of this chapter at www.charlestapiero.com.

REFERENCES

Alizadeh, S., M. W. Brandt, and F. X. Diebold. 2002. Range based estimation of stochastic volatility models. *Journal of Finance* 47:1047–1092.

Anderson, T. G., R. A. Davis, J. P. Kreiss, and T. Mikosch, eds. 2009. *Handbook of financial time series*. Berlin: Springer-Verlag.

Baillie, R., and T. Bollerslev. 1992. Prediction in dynamic models with time dependent conditional variances. *Journal of Business Economics and Statistics* 5:91–113.

Barnett, V., and T. Lewis. 1994. *Outliers in statistical data*, 3rd ed. New York: John Wiley & Sons.

Beran, Jan. 1994. *Statistics for long-memory processes*. London: Chapman and Hall.

Bollerslev, T. 1986. Generalized autoregressive conditional heteroscedasticity. *Journal of Econometrics* 31:307–327.

Bollerslev, T., R. F. Engle, and D. B. Nelson. 1994. ARCH models. In *Handbook of econometrics IV*, ed. R. F. Engle and D. L. McFadden, 2961–3038. Amsterdam: Elsevier Science.

Booth, G., F. Kaen, and P. Koveos. 1982. R/S analysis of foreign exchange rates under two international monetary regimes. *Journal of Monetary Economics* 10:407–415.

Bouchaud, J. P., and M. Potters. 2003. *Theory of financial risks and derivatives pricing from statistical physics to risk management*, 2nd ed. London: Cambridge University Press.

Brandt, M. W., and F. X. Diebold. 2006. A no-arbitrage approach to range-based estimation of return covariances and correlations. *Journal of Business* 79:61–74.

Brock, W. A, D. A. Hsieh, and B. LeBaron. 1992. *Nonlinear dynamics, chaos and instability*. Cambridge, MA: MIT Press.

Cartea, A., and S. Howison. 2003. Distinguished limits of Levy-Stable processes, and applications to option pricing. University of Oxford, Mathematical Institute. http://www.finance.ox.ac.uk/file_links/mf_papers/2002mf04.pdf.

Chen, X., and Y. Fan. 2006. Estimation and model selection of semiparametric copula-based multivariate dynamic models under copula misspecification. *Journal of Econometrics* 135:125–154.

Cherubini, U., Elisa Luciano, and Walter Vecchiato. 2004. *Copula methods in finance*. Hoboken, NJ: John Wiley & Sons.

Davis, M., and V. Lo. 2001. Infectious default. *Quantitative Finance* 1:382–387.

Diebold, F., and J. A. Lopez. 1995. *Modeling volatility dynamics*. Federal Reserve Bank of New York.

Diebold, F., and G. Rudebusch. 1989. Long memory and persistence in aggregate output. *Journal of Monetary Economics* 24:189–209.

Duncan, T. E. 2006. Some bilinear stochastic equations with a fractional Brownian motion. In *Stochastic processes, optimization, and control theory: Applications in financial engineering, queueing networks and manufacturing*, ed. H. Yan, G. Yin, and Q. Zhang, 97–108. Berlin: Springer Science + Business Media.

————. 2009. Some topics in fractional Brownian motion. *Risk and Decision Analysis* 1 (3):1–17.

Duncan, T. E., Y. Z. Hu, and B. Pasik-Duncan. 2002. Stochastic calculus for fractional Brownian motion I: Theory. *SIAM Journal on Control and Optimization* 36: 582–612.

Embrechts, P., H. Furrer, and R. Kaufmann. 2007. Different kinds of risk. In *Handbook of financial time series*, ed. T. G. Andersen, R. A. Davis, J.-P. Kreiss, and T. Mikosch. Berlin: Springer Verlag.

Embrechts, P., A. Höing, and A. Juri. 2003. Using copulae to bound the value-at-risk for functions of dependent risks. *Finance & Stochastics* 7:145–167.

Embrechts P., T. Mikosch, and C. Kluppelberg. 1997. *Modeling extremal events for insurance and finance*. Berlin: Springer Verlag.

Embrechts, P., A. McNeil, and D. Straumann. 2002. Correlation and dependence properties in risk management: Properties and pitfalls. In *Risk management: Value at risk and beyond*, ed. M. Dempster. Cambridge, UK: Cambridge University Press.

Engle, R. 1982. Autoregressive conditional heteroskedasticity with estimates of the variance of U.K. inflation. *Econometrica* 50:987–1008.

———. 2002. Dynamic conditional correlation: A simple class of multivariate GARCH models. *Journal of Business Economics and Statistics* 20:339–350.

Fang, K. T., S. Kotz, and K. W. Ng. 1987. *Symmetric multivariate and related distributions*. London: Chapman & Hall.

Feller, W. 1951. The asymptotic distribution of the range of sums of independent random variables. *Annals of Mathematical Statistics* 22:427–432.

Fraisse, P. 1957. *La psychologie du temps*. Paris: Presses Universitaires.

Frees, E., and E. Valdez. 1998. Understanding relationships using copulas. *North American Actuarial Journal* 2:1–25.

Fung, H. G., and W. C. Lo. 1993. Memory in interest rate futures. *Journal of Futures Markets* 13:865–873.

Fung, Hung-Gay, Wai-Chung Lo, and John E. Peterson. 1994. Examining the dependency in intra-day stock index futures. *Journal of Futures Markets* 14:405–419.

Gleick, J. 1987. *Chaos: Making a new science*. New York: Viking Press.

Gopikrishnan, P., M. Meyer, L. A. N. Amaral, and H. E. Stanley. 1998. Inverse cubic law for the distribution of stock price variations. *European Physical Journal B* 3:130–143.

Grandmont, J., and P. Malgrange. 1986. Nonlinear economic dynamics: Introduction. *Journal of Economic Theory* 40.

Granger, C. 1980. Long memory relationships and the aggregation of dynamic models. *Journal of Econometrics* 14:227–238.

Granger, C. W., and T. Trasvirta. 1993. *Modelling nonlinear economic relationships*. Oxford: Oxford University Press.

Green, M. T., and B. Fielitz. 1977. Long term dependence in common stock returns. *Journal of Financial Economics* 4:339–349.

———. 1980. Long-term dependence and least squares regression in investment analysis. *Management Science* 26 (10) (October):1031–1038.

Helms, B., F. Kaen, and R. Rosenman. 1984. Memory in commodity futures contracts. *Journal of Futures Markets*. 4:559–567.

Hermann, Samuel, and P. Vallois. 2010. From persistent random walks to the telegraph noise. *Stochastic Processes and Their Applications*. Forthcoming.

Hsieh, D. A. 1991. Chaos and nonlinear dynamics application to financial markets. *Journal of Finance* 46:1839–1877.

Hurst, H. E. 1951. Long term storage of reservoirs. *Transaction of the American Society of Civil Engineers* 116.

Imhoff, J. P. 1985. On the range of Brownian motion and its inverse process. *Annals of Probability* 13 (3):1011–1017.

Jaynes, E. T. 1957a. Information theory and statistical mechanics. *Physical Review* 106: 620.

———. 1957b. Information theory and statistical mechanics II. *Physical Review* 108:171.

Joe, H. 1997. *Multivariate models and dependence concepts*. London: Chapman & Hall.

Johnson, N., and S. Kotz. 1972. *Distributions in statistics: Continuous multivariate distributions.* New York: John Wiley & Sons.

Jorion, P., and G. Zhang. 2007. Good and bad credit contagion: Evidence from credit default swaps. *Journal of Financial Economics* 84:860–881.

Levy, P. 1937. *Théorie de l'addition des variables aléatoires.* Paris: Gauthier-Villars.

———. 1951. Wiener random functions and other Laplacian random functions. Proc. 6th Berkeley Symposium on Probability Theory and Mathematical Statistics, 171–186.

Li, D. X. 1999. On default correlation: A copula function approach. Working paper 99–07, RiskMetric Group.

Lo, Andrew W. 1991. Long term memory in stock market prices. *Econometrica* 59 (5) (September):1279–1313.

———. 1997. Fat tails, long memory and the stock market since 1960s. *Economic Notes* 26:213–245.

Mandelbrot, B. B. 1963. The variation of certain speculative prices. *Journal of Business* 36:394–419.

———. 1972. Statistical methodology for non-periodic cycles: From the covariance to R/S analysis. *Annals of Economic and Social Measurement* 1:259–290.

———. 1974. Intermittent turbulence in self-similar cascades: Divergence of high moments and dimension of the carrier. *Journal of Fluid Mechanics* 62:331–358.

Mandelbrot, B., and M. Taqqu. 1979. Robust R/S analysis of long run serial correlation. *Bulletin of the International Statistical Institute* 48 (Book 2):59–104.

Mandelbrot, B. B., and J. W. Van Ness. 1968. Fractional Brownian motions, fractional noises and applications. *SIAM Review* 10:422–437.

Mandelbrot, B., and J. Wallis. 1968. Noah, Joseph and operational hydrology. *Water Resources Research* 4:909–918.

———. 1969. Computer experiments with fractional noises. *Water Resources Research* 5:228–267.

Marshall, A., and I. Olkin. 1988. Families of multivariate distributions. *Journal of the American Statistical Association* 83:834–841.

McNeil, R., A. J. Frey, and P. Embrechts. 2005. *Quantitative risk management.* Princeton, NJ: Princeton University Press.

Medio, Alfredo. 1992. *Chaotic dynamics.* Cambridge: Cambridge University Press.

Mzasoliver, Jaume, J. M. Porra, and G. H. Weiss. 1992. The continuum limit of a two dimensional persistent random walk. *Physica A* 182:593–598.

Nelsen, R. B. 1999. An introduction to copulas. Lecture Notes in Statistics 139. New York: Springer Verlag.

Oakes, D. 1994. Multivariate survival distributions. *Journal of Nonparametric Statistics* 3:343–354.

Otway, T. H. 1995. Records of the Florentine proveditori degli cambiatori: An example of an antipersistent time series in economics. *Chaos, Solitons and Fractals* 5:103–107.

Patton, Andrew J. 2009. Copula-based models for financial time series. In *Handbook of financial time series*, ed. T. G. Andersen, R. A. Davis, J.-P. Kreiss, and T. Mikosch. Berlin: Springer Verlag.

Peter, Edgar E. 1995. *Chaos and order in capital markets.* New York: John Wiley & Sons.

Piaget, J. 1946. *La notion du temps chez l'enfant.* Paris: Presses Universitaires de France.

RiskMetrics Group. 1997. CreditMetrics—technical document. www.riskmetrics.com/research.

Russel, Bertrand. 1915. On the experience of time. *Monist* 25:212–33.

Schweizer, B. 1991. Thirty years of copulas. In *Advances in probability distributions with given marginals*, ed. G. Dall'Aglio, S. Kotz, and G. Salinetti, 879–885. Dordrecht: Kluwer Academic Publishers.

Sklar, A. 1959. Fonctions de répartition à n dimensions et leurs marges. *Publications de l'Institut de Statistique de l'Université de Paris* 8:229–231.

Stanley, M. H. R., L. A. N. Amaral, S. V. Bulkdyrev, S. V. Havlin, H. Leschron, P. Mass, M. A. Salinger, and H. E. Stanley. 1996. Scaling behavior in the growth of companies. *Nature* 379:804–806.

Starr, M. K., and C. S. Tapiero. 1975. Linear breakeven analysis under risk. *Operation Research Quarterly* 26:847–856.

Szász, Domokos, and Bálint Tóth. 1984. Persistent random walks in a one dimensional random environment. *Journal of Statistical Physics* 37:27–38.

Tapiero, C. S., and P. Vallois. 2000. The inter-event range process and testing for chaos in time series. *Neural Network World* 10 (1–2):89–99.

———. 2010. *Short term memory in intraday financial data*. Working paper, Department of Finance and Risk Engineering, New York University Polytechnic Institute, Brooklyn.

Taqqu, M. S. 1986. A bibliographical guide to self similar processes and long range dependence. *In Dependence in Probability and Statistics*, ed. E. Eberlein and M. S. Taqqu, 137–165. Boston: Birkhuser.

Tóth, Bálint. 1986. Persistent random walks in random environments. *Probability Theory and Related Fields* 71:615–662.

Vallois, P. 1993. Diffusion arrêtée au premier instant où le processus de l'amplitude atteint un niveau donné. *Stochastics and Stochastic Reports* 43:93–115.

———. 1995. *On the range process of a Bernoulli random walk*. Proceedings of the Sixth International Symposium on Applied Stochastic Models and Data Analysis, vol. II, ed. J. Janssen and C. H. Skiadas, World Scientific, 1020–1031.

———. 1996. The range of a simple random walk on Z. *Advanced Applied Probability* 28:1014–1033.

Vallois, P., and C. S. Tapiero. 1995. Moments of an amplitude process in a random walk. *Recherche Operationnelle/Operation Research (RAIRO)* 29 (1):1–17.

———. 1996. The range process in random walks: Theoretical results and applications. In *Advances in Computational Economics*, ed. H. Ammans, B. Rustem, and A. Whinston. Dordrecht: Kluwer Publications.

———. 1996. *Run length statistics and the Hurst exponent in random and birth-death random walks Chaos, Solitons and Fractals*. September.

———. 1997. Range reliability in random walks. *Mathematics Methods of Operations Research* 45 (3).

———. 2007. Memory-based persistence in a counting random walk process. *Physica A*, October.

———. 2009. A claims persistence process and insurance. *Insurance Economics and Mathematics* 44 (3) (June):367–373.

Wallis, R. 1966. *Time: Fourth Dimension of the Mind*. New York: Harcourt Brace and Jovanovich.

CHAPTER 5

Risk, Value, and Financial Prices

OVERVIEW

The utility approach provides an economic foundation to financial decision making and risk management. The capital asset pricing model (CAPM) model and the stochastic discount factor (SDF) or kernel pricing and many aspects of corporate finance are essentially based on utility theory. This chapter begins with an introduction to value and price, risk and money, and subsequently introduces fundamental contributions of utility theory to finance. In practice, utility in finance is important for portfolio theory, pricing, financial risk management, risk sharing, insurance, and the many areas of financial analysis and financial management.

VALUE AND PRICE

Value is derived from needs and the ability to meet these needs. A price, however, reflects the complex and interacting forces of demand and supply of a security being traded. J. B. Say, a French economist, as early as the seventeenth century pointed out that price is a clearing mechanism, at which an equilibrium is reached between demand and supply. Say that many investors want to buy IBM shares, while other and fewer investors are willing to sell their shares. An excess demand will contribute then to an increase in the price of IBM's shares, until an equilibrium price, equating the demand for IBM shares and their supply, is reached. Prices, in both real and financial markets, are thus relative to the many buyers and sellers participating in these markets, their alternatives, their needs, and their willingness to buy and sell. Some items or securities, however, have a price regulated by an authority or one that is due to their special characteristics. The air we breathe is a priceless asset without which we could not survive, although the presumption that it is plentiful leads to, perhaps, mispricing it. By the same token, the price of water is increasingly concerning financial markets as the demand for water increases while its quality and quantity are becoming more erratic, uncertain, and at times insufficient. For these reasons, an increased attention is directed toward the valuation and the pricing of water and similar commodities.

Both value and price are intimately related to risk. If investors abhor uncertainty, then rewards for holding the risky asset ought to be higher than that of a riskless asset in order to compensate the buyers of such an asset. The price of the asset will then be determined by the propensity of investors to commit investments for the rewards that asset may promise. If investors seek a flight from risk, the price will be lower; if investors seek rewards (however uncertain these rewards may be), the price will increase. Our concern in this and the following chapter is to define the value of an uncertain prospect to a party (a person or a firm) based on the personal information the party has and his personal risk attitude (i.e a predisposition to bear risk). Subsequently, we shall be concerned with the relationship of value to a market price (or rather, a synthetic price that has the same mathematical characteristics of a market price implied by the financial model of complete markets; see Chapters 7 and 8). We consider two approaches: the expected utility framework and the fundamental finance approach, outlined and contrasted in Chapters 5 and 7.

The fundamental finance approach prescribes that prices result from an exchange between buyers—needy investors—and sellers of such needs through an exchange in a financial market. However, personal prices set by buyers (bids) and sellers (asks) express the many factors that define their needs, their risk attitudes, their information, and the external economic conditions at the time the exchange is made. When there is only one buyer and one seller, exchange terms are based on their mutual interests defining the contract price and its clauses agreed on to assure that the agreement will be maintained (and if not, to provide the means to ensure its enforcement). Contractual agreements, whether traded in a financial market or privately exchanged, may vary. Some include principal assets or their derivatives, priced in various manners as well. Some approaches use a subjective valuation such as a *utility measurement of money* (introduced in this chapter). Others seek to determine a synthetic price equivalent to a market price which is assumed to be unique (see Chapters 7 and 8).

Market prices are real and liquid in the sense that they can be observed and traded from second to second. Fundamental theories of finance seek to explain such prices by theoretical constructs that justify these prices and their movement by an implied *rationality* shifting when information accrues and future expectations change. In this sense, a market price is an imputation to informational states and investors', traders', or speculators' expectations and attitudes toward these states. If prices are determined in this manner and are unique, we then presume that there is no arbitrage. Practically, this means that financial profits cannot be made without assuming risks. This statement is important in finance and will be defined formally and substantively in Chapter 7. Such markets are called *complete* or *efficient*.

Practically, the price of a security in the stock market is determined by a *market maker* whose function is to provide market liquidity by setting a price at which bid and ask prices can be reconciled and at which exchange occurs. Market makers, reacting of course to both supply and demand, provide the liquidity for the security for which they assume a responsibility. When markets are not liquid, it implies that there are no buyers and sellers that can agree on an exchange price. In such a case, prices may be determined through individual negotiations that may or may not result in an agreement and its price. This price determines then the *utility* each of the parties draws from such an agreement.

Prices are derived from the benefits, the risks, and the future prospects they grant to parties agreeing to an exchange. Uncertainty regarding the terms associated with the agreement may be mitigated, however, by many financial products, such as insurance, options priced by financial markets, and so forth. Markets that trade in such options are abundant and include, among others, the NYSE, LSE, and CBOE. There are other markets, trading in real assets and nonfinancial items, such as eBay, which has built person-to-person (P2P) e-markets; e-transport markets (where buying and selling space on transport ships through intermediaries is achieved through an intermediate e-commerce firm); and others. In this sense, the concept of *market* is broadly accepted and practiced, although financial markets are by far bigger than almost any existing market and trade all goods and commodities that can be denoted by money. The real valuation of assets and their prices imputed by buyers and sellers, compared to their prices in financial exchanges, is thus important. This chapter and the next are focused on a real utility approach to valuation, which is a personal approach to valuation.

The utility financial approach to valuation is based on the following terms:

- *Preference*, expressing rationally a need or a want by buyers and sellers.
- *Uncertainty*, defining a state of knowledge in terms of events and their probabilities.
- An *intertemporal* preference for money, or "substituting returns and payments now for later".
- *Exchange*, expressing our wants (utilities), the wants of others, their willingness, and their ability to pay and to share risks and rewards.

These essential facets of utility and its valuation interact often in extremely complex manners that can provide a better understanding of the mechanisms through which securities' and real assets' prices are determined. Each of these is considered here in a utility framework.

UTILITY, RISK, AND MONEY

Risk is an adverse consequence, valued explicitly or latent in the objectives, the information, and the attitudes that investors have. Measured risks and their cash value are not always easy to calculate, however. For example, industrial risk applications have mostly avoided risk valuation and focused instead on the measurement of variations (standard deviation, variance, range, etc.) to characterize risk, while lacking a market for an exchange of these variations and thus being unable to price these variations. Their presumptions are that the standard deviation of a process is correlated to risk and, therefore, reducing (controlling) one reduces the other. The utility approach, instead, combines both decision makers' risk attitudes and their valuation of money embedded in a parametric utility function. While the functional form of a utility function is used to capture a personal rationality, its parameters provide a specific estimate of such a rationality based on both experimentation and observed behaviors.

Utility expresses an *individual* or *subjective* valuation of money. When an asset has an uncertain value, its expected utility provides a unique value that measures the desirability of the uncertain financial prospect. In practice, people do not value money in the same manner nor do they value money equally. Both an attitude toward money and the willingness to take risks originates in a person's initial wealth, information, emotional states, and the pleasure or fear evoked by risk. When persons abhor risk, they seek to prevent, manage, and be protected from these risks. Do we insure our house against fire? Do we insure our belongings against theft? Should we insure our exports against currency fluctuations or against payment default by foreign buyers? Do we invest in foreign lands without seeking protection from national takeovers? How can we prevent the risks of a demand shortfall for a product or the risks of not meeting a demand? In such situations, risk is often exchanged, or transferred from one party to the other, who in turn might transfer it to some other parties (as it is the case in mortgage transactions). In recent years, increased use is made of financial markets to sell portfolios of contracts, in whole or in part, as securities—better known as securitization.

Of course, how much a person is willing to pay and how much risk he is willing to bear allows us to assess the person's attitude toward risk. Similarly, just as a speculator is willing to pay a small amount of money to earn a very large and very uncertain return, a risk-averse person would equally be willing to pay a small amount of money to seek protection from a loss, even if the probability of that loss is very small. In both cases, expected payoff as a sole criterion breaks down—for otherwise there would be no casinos and no insurance firms. Further, if expected payoff was a criterion applied by all uniformly, all investors would make the same decisions—namely, buy the security with the largest potential returns—which is not the case. Due to the integral role utility theory plays in economics and finance, it is important to appreciate its normative principles.

Utility's Normative Principles: A Historical Perspective

The expected utility framework underlies a number of theoretical approaches to financial pricing. In a doctoral dissertation titled *Theory of Investment Values*, John Burr Williams in 1937 suggested that the price of a stock is calculated by the long-run present value of its dividend payments, subsequently called the *dividend discount model*. Assuming that all investors reason in the same manner, all investors will buy the same security. The test of the market has refuted this presumption and has led to the rise of risk and its price as an essential element to reckon with. In this case, markets, because of investors' and traders' broadly different risk attitudes, are motivated to exchange, and markets can exist. Imagine a world in a flight from risk where no party is willing to assume any risk. There cannot be then a financial market, and there cannot be liquidity to allow trades.

An important contribution, based on existence of risk/rewards in financial decision making, was pointed out in 1950 by Harry Markowitz, a Nobel Prize winner. Markowitz (1959) suggested a mean-variance analysis as the foundation for a personal approach to portfolio management that provided a rational foundation for risk diversification as a management strategy—namely, one does not invest all of one's eggs in the same (security) basket! Rather, investors' decisions are determined in a (mean-variance) returns space, where deviations from expected returns imply a risk. Markowitz's portfolio did not include a risk-free asset (say a bond) that may have provided a price relative to a risk free asset (or the price of a spread).

An extension to this effect by Tobin (1956) (see also Sharpe, Lintner, and Mossin in the 1960s) and including a risk-free asset led to the celebrated capital asset pricing model (CAPM). The particular importance of the CAPM is both its simplicity and its defining the risk premium, relative both to the risk-free rate and to a fully diversified index. Practically, the CAPM allowed a simple econometric approach to estimate the excess returns of stock prices based on available financial stocks' time series and financial market indexes. Excess returns were shown theoretically to compensate for excess market risks (but not for idiosyncratic risk, which is specific to an individual asset and can be eliminated through diversification). The contribution of CAPM to financial practice is important and has influenced financial risk management by emphasizing the need for investors to hedge, whether they can or cannot mitigate risks. Extension to a multiperiod and to a multifactor framework, coined *intertemporal* CAPM (ICAPM) and the asset price theory (APT) have linked the excess returns of risky assets to both the market returns over time and other indexes or macroeconomic factors. These ideas resulted in Kernel pricing (or stochastic discount factors (SDF)) based on the utility of consumption, and the APT (to be considered subsequently).

The utility of the consumption-based approach to pricing was developed in 1970, based on John Maynard Keynes' fundamental analysis of national product, investment, and consumption. It resulted on the consumption-based capital asset pricing model (CCAPM), extended importantly in the 1990s to kernel pricing or the stochastic discount factor (SDF) (Campbell 2000; Cochrane 2001). This approach provides also a rationale for linking the inter-temporal utility of consumption and the market pricing approach, as we shall see in this and in the next chapter.

Using extensive financial data, analyses based on the CCAPM were not able to explain financial prices, however, unless extremely conservative and unrealistic assumptions were made. Among these is the important *equity premium puzzle* (see Mehra and Prescott 1985 and Chapter 6). Following these observations, a number of utility functions were suggested, richer and more able to accommodate the empirical evidence we have. These resulted in important contributions and extensions of the expected utility approach, which is now far more attuned to market prices.

In the early 1950s, Arrow and Debreu (both Nobel Prize winners) derived a *state-preference theory* that underpins derivative and asset pricing and shows that the ultimate role of stock markets is to allocate risk efficiently. State-preference theory essentially demonstrates that for an efficient allocation of resources and risks, we require a set of *complete* securities that permit agents to hedge all risks. (This is considered further in Chapter 7.) Both approaches are important and underlie the remaining chapters of this book.

There is a technical relationship between these approaches, which points out to a relationship between a subjective valuation of risk and an implied risk-neutral probability distribution that underscores the Arrow-Debreu framework (see this chapter and Chapters 6 and 11 for computing implied risk neutral probability distributions).

Prelude to Utility and Expected Utility

Risk attitudes underlie decisions made under uncertainty and an implied *axiomatic rationality*. Common objectives preceding the expected utility approach that express explicitly or implicitly a risk attitude have mostly been discarded (although they reappear and are used in some contexts). These include:

- *The expected value (or Bayes') objective.* Preferences for financial alternatives are reached by sorting in an increasing order their expected monetary values.
- *Principle of insufficient reason (Laplace in the sixteenth century as well as Bayes).* When the probabilities of future states are not known, we assume that they are equally likely. In other words, utmost ignorance is replaced by assigning to each state the same probability!
- *The minimax (maximin) objective.* This consists in selecting the decision that will have the least loss, regardless of what future (state) may occur. It is used when we seek protection from the worst possible state and expresses an attitude of abject pessimism. The minimax criterion takes the smallest of the available maximums (usually costs). Maximin is a loss-averse mind set. As long as we do get the best of all worst possible outcomes the investor is satisfied.
- *The maximax (minimin) objective.* This objective is an optimist's criterion, banking on the best possible future yielding the hoped-for largest possible profits. It is based on the belief or the urge to profit as much as possible, regardless of the probabilities of desirable or other events. The minimin criterion is a pessimist's point of view. Regardless of what happens, only the worst case can happen! On the upside, such a point of view leads only to upbeat news.
- *The minimax regret or Savage's regret objective.* The previous objectives are before-the-fact evaluations of payoffs and their consequences. In practice, payoffs and probabilities are not easily measured. Thus, these criteria express a philosophical outlook rather than an objective on which to base a decision. Ex post (after the fact) unlike ex ante decisions are reached once information is revealed and uncertainty is resolved. Each decision has then a regret defined by the difference between the gain made and the gain that could have been realized had we selected the best decision (associated to the event that actually occurs). An expected-regret decision seeks to minimize the expectation for such a regret, while a minimax regret decision seeks to select the decision providing the least maximal regret. The cost of a decision's regret thus represents the difference between the ex ante payoffs that would be received with a given outcome and as the maximum possible ex post payoff received. Bell (1995) has pointed out the relevance of this criterion by suggesting that decision makers may select an act by minimizing the regrets associated to the potential decisions they may reach. Behaviorally, such a criterion would be a characteristic of persons who are attached to their past. Their past mistakes haunt their present day! Hence, they do the best they can to avoid them in the future.

These criteria, albeit easy to apply, have been found insufficient to meet the theoretical problems that decision making under uncertainty requires. As a result, considerable research and attention were directed to a concept of utility on the basis of which decision making under uncertainty and risk can be set on firmer rational foundations. Next we consider theoretical assumptions and practical implications of the utility approach to the valuation of uncertain prospects and its applications to finance.

LOTTERIES AND UTILITY FUNCTIONS

What is the price π of a simple digital lottery $\tilde{\pi}_1$ consisting in winning a reward R with probability p, or losing one's investment π? Lotteries of this sort appear in many instances. A speculator buys a stock, expecting to make a profit (in probability), but such an investment might also result in a loss. A person can buy a lottery because there is another party who is willing to sell this lottery. It is their differences (and risk attitudes) that allow such an exchange and contribute to the functioning of financial markets.

If a person is oblivious to risk, then money may be valued as a simple expectation. In this case, the worth of the lottery (its fair price) is based on calculating its expected value $\pi = E(\tilde{\pi}_1)$. Evidence indicates that this is not the case, however. Rather, buyers of lotteries are implicitly willing to pay far more than the expected value of a prospective large gain, even if it has a very small probability of materializing. Why is this the case? However irrational it may seem at first, many people do so because they value the prospect of winning big, even with a small probability, much more then the prospect of losing small, even with a large probability. We call such persons *risk lovers* or *risk takers*. Inversely, people who abhor risk may prefer the safe returns of U.S. Treasury bills compared to bets on a casino's roulette wheel. We call such persons risk averters.

This uneven valuation of money means that we are unable to compare two expected lotteries equally. People are different in many ways, not least in their needs, their attitudes, and their preferences for outcomes that are uncertain. An understanding of human motivations and decision making is thus needed to reconcile observed behavior in a predictable and theoretical framework. This observation is fueling the renewed interest of financial analysis in behavioral finance. This is also what expected utility theory purports to do. Explicitly, it seeks to define a scale of money values, called the utility function $u(.)$, whose expectation provides the means for comparing alternative and uncertain prospects, and thereby reach a choice based on such comparisons. Defining such a function is of course a perpetual and challenging task.

In this framework, the larger the expected utility, the *better* it is. For example, assuming that there is such a function $u(.)$, then two sums (R) and (0), defining a lottery, can be transformed into utilities $u(R)$ and $u(0)$ and be compared using their (scaled) utilities. The presumption that expected utility is the true scale for valuing the uncertain prospect, although criticized, is generally accepted when lacking a better alternative. The utility of the lottery would then be $u(R)$ if we win with a probability p and $u(0)$ if we lose with probability $1 - p$. The expected utility (Eu) worth of this lottery would then be:

$$Eu(\tilde{\pi}_1) = pu(R) + (1 - p)u(0) \tag{5.1}$$

since the values of lotteries with the same expected utility are equivalent. The fair price, by the utility equivalence, can then be determined. Say that the price is π, a certain quantity; then:

$$u(\pi) = Eu(\tilde{\pi}_1) \tag{5.2}$$

In money terms, the certain amount we are willing to pay for the uncertain prospect is thus (assuming an invertible utility function):

$$\pi = u^{-1}\left(Eu(\tilde{\pi}_1)\right) \tag{5.3}$$

We call π a *certain equivalent* to the uncertain prospect $\tilde{\pi}_1$. This amount expresses the money that an investor may be willing to part from in order to acquire the uncertain prospect that is offered by some other investor (who prefers the risk-free prospect). If the prospect is riskless, then its expectation-worth is $E(\tilde{\pi}_1)$ while the difference

$$E(\tilde{\pi}_1) - \pi = E(\tilde{\pi}_1) - u^{-1}\left(Eu(\tilde{\pi}_1)\right)$$

denotes the *risk premium* associated to the uncertain prospect. The price of risk in a lottery is therefore its risk premium.

EXAMPLE: THE UTILITY OF A LOTTERY *forego; 付清 ....*

Consider the lottery in Figure 5.1. We want to determine the premium of such a lottery and compare it to the actual price paid for it. Let $u(.)$ be the utility of money and assume that the initial wealth is W. In order to participate in the lottery, a price is to be paid, say π, for an uncertain prospect $\tilde{X}$, given by \$10,000 or nothing. Let x^* be the amount one is willing to forego to participate in the lottery. If this is larger than the price π, then of course buying the lottery is rational. These lotteries are equivalent if:

$$u(W - x^*) = Eu(W + \tilde{X} - \pi) = pu(W + 10,000 - \pi) + (1 - p)u(W - \pi) \tag{5.4}$$

where $W - x^*$ is the certain equivalent of the lottery with:

$$x^* = W - u^{-1}\left(pu(W + 10,000 - \pi) + (1 - p)u(W - \pi)\right) > \pi \tag{5.5}$$

if you buy the lottery.

Note that there may be a difference between the certain equivalent x^* and the premium π. If it were a *fair* price (in an expected sense), then of course $x^* - \pi = 0$. In practice it may be that for some, $x^* \neq \pi$ and therefore some would buy the lottery and some would not. This is also a proof that risk attitudes are important. If the buyer of the lottery is willing to pay more than it is worth, then $x^* > \pi$, in which case we might associate to the buyer a risk-loving attitude, a gambler who wants to

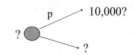

FIGURE 5.1 A Simple Lottery

win big and cares relatively little about the loss of investment in the lottery. National lotteries are fully aware of these attitudes and their contribution to profits.

Quadratic Utility and Portfolio Pricing

The quadratic utility function is important and commonly used in finance and expresses its expected value in terms of two essential financial statistics: the mean return and its volatility. For example, say that wealth is random and given by $\tilde{w}$ while the utility function is:

$$u(\tilde{w}) = \tilde{w} - \rho(\tilde{w} - \hat{w})^2$$

This implies that expected returns are preferred while variations about the expected returns are not, where the parameter ρ defines an index of risk (volatility) aversion as we shall see shortly. The expected utility is then

$$Eu(\tilde{w}) = \hat{w} - \rho\sigma^2$$

with mean and variance given by $(\hat{w}, \sigma^2)$. The certain equivalent is determined by:

$$u(CE) = Eu(\tilde{w})$$

and therefore by

$$CE - \rho(\hat{w} - CE)^2 = \hat{w} - \rho\sigma^2$$

Let the risk premium be $\pi = \hat{w} - CE$ (expressing an expected return less its utility-equivalent risk-free return). We can write this expression as a quadratic equation:

$$F(\sigma^2, \pi) = \rho\left[\sigma^2 - \pi^2\right] - \pi = 0$$

and thereby define its risk premium by the solution of the preceding quadratic equation:

$$\pi^* = -\frac{1}{2\rho} \pm \sqrt{\left(\frac{1}{4\rho}\right)^2 + \sigma^2} \tag{5.6}$$

When an investor is infinitely risk averse, then $\rho \to +\infty$ and $\pi^* = \sigma$, while when the investor is infinitely risk loving ($\rho \to -\infty$) we have $\pi^* = -\sigma$ and therefore, the risk premium for all investors can be written as follows:

$$\pi^* = \lambda\sigma, \lambda \in [-1, +1]$$

When the risk aversion index ρ is small, then $\pi \approx 0$. As a result, it is convenient to write:

$$CE = \hat{w} - \pi \quad \text{or} \quad CE = \hat{w} - \lambda\sigma, \quad \lambda \in [-1, +1] \tag{5.7}$$

For example, consider as a special case a portfolio of financial assets, say n shares of a stock whose current price is S and a bond whose price is B. The current worth of the portfolio is $W = nS + B$ while we estimate that its next period price is random with a stock rate of return $\tilde{R}$ and risk-free rate of return R_f for an investment in a risk-free bond:

$$\tilde{W} = nS(1 + \tilde{R}) + B(1 + R_f) \tag{5.8}$$

Thus, the expected next period portfolio price is:

$$E\left(\tilde{W}\right) = nS\left(1 + E\left(\tilde{R}\right)\right) + B(1 + R_f) \tag{5.9}$$

While the certain equivalent at the next period is:

$$CE_1 = nS\left(1 + E\left(\tilde{R}\right)\right) + B(1 + R_f) - \lambda nS\sqrt{\operatorname{var}\left(\tilde{R}\right)} \tag{5.10}$$

Its present value, discounted at the risk-free rate (since it is a certain equivalent), is thus:

$$CE_0 = \frac{CE_1}{1 + R_f} = B_0 + \frac{nS_0\left(1 + E\left(\tilde{R}\right) - \lambda\sigma\left(\tilde{R}\right)\right)}{1 + R_f} \tag{5.11}$$

If there is no arbitrage, then the risk-free rate necessarily equals the certain equivalent rate and:

$$R_f = E\left(\tilde{R}\right) - \lambda\sigma\left(\tilde{R}\right)$$

or $$\tag{5.12}$$

$$E\left(\tilde{R}\right) - R_f = \lambda\sigma\left(\tilde{R}\right)$$

Further, if we replace $CE_0 = B_0 + nS_0$ in equation (5.11) we get also equation (5.12).

Utility and an Insurance Exchange

An exchange is made between two specific parties. Say that one party, an insurance firm, charges for a given random insured loss $\tilde{X}$ a premium π. Should the insured take it? What is the premium that the insurer should quote? To respond to this question, an expected utility framework can be used (if these utilities can be defined, of course). Let the insured wealth be w and assume two possibilities, insure (with utility $u(w - \pi)$) or not (with expected utility $Eu(w - \tilde{X})$). An exchange occurs then, when:

$$\text{Insured: } u(w - \pi) \geq Eu(w - \tilde{X}); \quad \text{Insurer: } U(W - \pi) \leq EU(W - \tilde{X}) \tag{5.13}$$

where U is the utility function of the insurer and W is its capital

Pricing in such cases is based on a negotiated (or imposed) settlement between the parties, each privy to its own information, needs, and means. In practice, insurance firms, through aggregation of insured risks and diversified portfolios, are actually facing less risk than the individual insured. For this reason, it pays for an insurance firm to insure, since it will collect a risk premium that is larger than the risk premium it will assume for the same risk. Further, the more it insures independent risks, the more it is diversified.

Negotiations occur between an insured and an insurer when there are alternative insurance means (for example, by turning to financial markets, by turning to other forms of risk management, etc.) and when the insurer might be willing to reduce the insurance premium to retain the insured. In practice, selecting a premium policy is complicated both because of difficulties in assessing the actual demand for insurance as a function of the premium policy and in assessing the actuarial costs of claims for each insured risk category. As a result, there are many formulas, defined mostly a priori or based on the experience of insurers as to what premium might bring greater profit. For example, the loading factor policy is an expected-cost-plus policy, consisting in assessing in a risk category the number of claims times their expected dollar value and loading this expectation by a parameter (for example, 20 percent). In this case, the premium demanded equals:

$$P(t) = (1 + L)E(N(t))E(\tilde{X}) \tag{5.14}$$

where $N(t)$ is the number of insureds in the portfolio at a given time; $\tilde{X}$ is the aggregate claims for the portfolio given by the sum of individual claims:

$$\tilde{X} = \sum_{j=1}^{\tilde{M}(t)} \tilde{x}_j$$

where $\tilde{M}(t) \leq N(t)$ is the number of claims (a random variable); and L is the loading factor. Other approaches recommend the use of specific utility functions, such as the logarithmic and exponential utility function to be defined shortly.

Selecting the premium policy depends therefore on the manner in which we define the insured risk, the risk sustained by the insurance firm, and the relationship in place between the insured and the insurer. In practice, insurance firms are businesses that ask as much money as they can and will receive. Even when they do so, they often turn to securitize their portfolios and sell them at a profit to willing financial markets. For big-ticket items (or group collective insurance schemes), the premium policy is negotiated and the premium defined by negotiations between the insured and the insurer. In the past few years, the securitization of insurance portfolios has contributed to defining a market price for insurance.

EXAMPLE: THE POWER UTILITY FUNCTION

Let a utility function be a power function $u(\pi) = \pi^{\alpha}$ where

$$Eu(\tilde{\pi}_1) = E\left(\tilde{\pi}_1^{\alpha}\right) = PG(\alpha)$$

Thus, the certain equivalent π is found by:

$$\pi^\alpha = PG(\alpha)$$

or

$$\pi = [PG(\alpha)]^{\frac{1}{\alpha}}$$

The risk premium is thus:

$$E\left(\tilde{\pi}_1\right) - \pi = E\left(\tilde{\pi}_1\right) - [PG(\alpha)]^{\frac{1}{\alpha}}$$

If $\tilde{\pi}_1 = (100, 80)$ with probabilities $(p, 1 - p) = (0.4, 0.6)$, the expected value is

$$E\left(\tilde{\pi}_1\right) = 100{*}0.4 + 80{*}0.6 = 94$$

while:

$$E\left(\tilde{\pi}_1^\alpha\right) = 0.4{*}100^\alpha + 0.6\,(80)^\alpha = PG(\alpha)$$

and therefore,

$$\pi = \left[E\left(\tilde{\pi}_1^\alpha\right)\right]^{\frac{1}{\alpha}} = [PG(\alpha)]^{\frac{1}{\alpha}} = (0.4{*}100^\alpha + 0.6\,(80)^\alpha)^{\frac{1}{\alpha}}$$

Thus, the risk premium equals

$$28 - [PG(\alpha)]^{\frac{1}{\alpha}} = 28 - (0.4{*}100^\alpha + 0.6\,(80)^\alpha)^{\frac{1}{\alpha}}$$

which is necessarily a function of the utility parameter α.

EXAMPLE: VALUATION AND THE PRICING OF CASH FLOWS

When cash flows are random, we can use the expected utility of the random cash flow to calculate its present value by discounting the certain equivalent with a risk-free discount rate or by discounting with a *risk-adjusted* discount rate. Explicitly, for a two-periods problem, let $\tilde{C}$ be an uncertain cash flow in the next period with expected utility $E\left(u(\tilde{C})\right)$. Its certain equivalent is $CE = u^{-1}(Eu(\tilde{C}))$. Since CE is a sure quantity, the discount rate applied to value such a quantity one period hence is (as seen earlier) the risk-free rate R_f. In this case,

$$PV = \frac{CE}{1 + R_f} = \frac{u^{-1}(Eu(\tilde{C}))}{1 + R_f} = \frac{E(\tilde{C}) - P}{1 + R_f} \qquad (5.15)$$

where P is the risk premium. Equivalently, we can calculate the PV by using the expected cash flow but discounted at a rate k (incorporating the risk inherent in the cash flow). Namely,

$$PV = \frac{E(\tilde{C})}{1+k} = \frac{CE}{1+R_f} = \frac{E(\tilde{C}) - P}{1+R_f} \tag{5.16}$$

As a result, we see that the risk-free rate and the risk premium combine to determine the risk-adjusted rate as follows:

$$1 - \frac{P}{E(\tilde{C})} = \frac{1+R_f}{1+k} \rightarrow k - R_f = (1+k)\frac{P}{E(\tilde{C})} \text{ or } k = \frac{1+R_f}{1 - P/E(\tilde{C})} - 1 \tag{5.17}$$

In particular, note that $k - R_f$ defines the *spread*. This is the rate of return needed to compensate for the uncertainty in the cash flow $\tilde{C}$ in the next period.

Now let the risk-free rate be 0.05 and let a project yield for one period be 0.08. Then the proportional risk premium (per expected dollar to be collected, $P/E(\tilde{C})$, a period hence) is:

$$k = \frac{1+R_f}{1 - P/E(\tilde{C})} - 1 \text{ or } 0.08 = \frac{1+0.05}{1 - P/E(\tilde{C})} - 1 \text{ and } \frac{P}{E(\tilde{C})} = \frac{0.03}{1.08} = 0.0277 \tag{5.18}$$

A first generalization of this approach consists in the following: If prospects for a project i are defined in terms of alternative and discrete events j, each with outcome r_{ij}, $j = 1, 2, \ldots, n$ and probability (r_{ij}, p_{ij}), we have instead the following expected utility:

$$U_i = \sum_{j=1}^{n} p_{ij} u(r_{ij}) \text{ and } R_{CE(i)} = U_i^{-1}\left(\sum_{j=1}^{n} p_{ij} u(r_{ij})\right) \tag{5.19}$$

and the certain equivalent is:

$$R_P = \sum_{j=1}^{n} p_{ij} r_{ij} - R_{CE(i)} \tag{5.20}$$

EXAMPLE: RISK AND THE FINANCIAL MELTDOWN

Say that a bank has assembled a portfolio of risky obligations with random returns $\tilde{X}$. Let the bank capital be W. Assume further that $EU(W + \tilde{X}) \geq U(W)$, which justifies the bank's holding of such obligations. Now assume that the bank seeks to sell a portion of these obligations, given by $(1 - \alpha)\tilde{X}$, which provides a fixed return

$\pi_{1-\alpha}$. Such a strategy is economical if:

$$EU(W + \pi_{1-\alpha} + \alpha \tilde{X}) \geq U(W + \tilde{X}) \tag{5.21}$$

In this case, the least certain equivalent sell price of these obligations is:

$$EU(W + \pi_{1-\alpha} + \alpha \tilde{X}) = U(CE_{1-\alpha}), EU(W + \tilde{X}) = CE_1 \text{ and } CE_{1-\alpha} \geq CE_1 \tag{5.22}$$

Now assume that the bank divides the portfolio of obligations into two tranches, each of different characteristics, defined by $\tilde{X}_1$ and $\tilde{X}_2$, and sells these tranches, each providing an income to the bank. The resulting premium would then be:

$$EU\left(W + \pi_{1:1-\alpha} + \pi_{1:1-\beta} + \alpha \tilde{X}_1 + \beta \tilde{X}_2\right) = U\left(CE_{1-\alpha;1-\beta}\right) \tag{5.23}$$

In order to augment the cash revenues and convince buyers to buy loan portfolios, financial institutions have bought and sold insurance on these same portfolios. For example, say that in order to sell a share of the second tranche portfolio, $(1 - \beta)\tilde{X}_2$, the bank offers to sell insurance to protect buyers. In this case, they collect a premium $\lambda_{2\beta,K}$ for an option which is $Max\left((1 - \beta)\tilde{X}_2 - K, 0\right)$. The bank's utility is then:

$$EU\left\{W + \pi_{1:1-\alpha} + \pi_{1:1-\beta} + \lambda_{2\beta,K} + \alpha \tilde{X}_1 + \beta \tilde{X}_2 - Max\left((1 - \beta)\tilde{X}_2 - K, 0\right)\right\} \tag{5.24}$$

Note that the option is not accounted for in the books of the bank and, therefore, the added premium has increased its capital while maintaining its risk nontransparent. Such nontransparency lets it expand its risk portfolios and pretend that in fact it does not own these portfolio risks (since they are not accounted for). Such an approach can be amplified, of course, if the entire loan portfolio was sold and reinsured, in which case, we have:

$$EU\left[W + \pi_1 + \pi_2 + \lambda_1 + \lambda_2 - Max\left(\tilde{X}_1 - K, 0\right) - Max\left(\tilde{X}_2 - K, 0\right)\right] \tag{5.25}$$

where $\pi_1 + \pi_2 + \lambda_1 + \lambda_2$ are the profits resulting from selling the two tranches and reinsuring them. If options are not listed as risk because they occur in the future, then the *visible utility* of the bank is:

$$U\left(W + \pi_1 + \pi_2 + \lambda_1 + \lambda_2\right) \tag{5.26}$$

. . . which is all profit!

Repeating infinitely such a procedure leads to an extraordinary balance sheet and huge risks that are not accounted for. Such strategies have resulted in the demise of some celebrated institutions when the value of assets insured have crashed and the risks returned to haunt these same institutions.

UTILITY RATIONAL FOUNDATIONS

The assumptions implied in expected utility are justified if the following conditions are met:

1. Prospects can be compared.
2. Prospects can be ranked such that preferred alternatives have greater utility.
3. Prospects are strongly independent.
4. Prospect preferences are transitive.
5. Alternatives prospects are indifferent if their utilities are equal.

These are, of course, extremely strong assumptions and have been profusely criticized. Nevertheless, they remain workable hypotheses in many financial problems. Assuming that a function $u(.)$ meets these assumptions, then in an expected utility framework:

- $u(\pi) = Eu(\tilde{\pi})$ implies an indifference between two prospects.
- $u(\pi) < Eu(\tilde{\pi})$ implies a preference for the uncertain prospect.
- $u(\pi) > Eu(\tilde{\pi})$ implies a preference for the certain prospect.

Further:

1. The higher the utility, the more desirable the outcome, or $u'(.) > 0$.
2. For three potential investment alternatives, if alternative A is preferred to B, and B is preferred to C, then necessarily A is preferred to C. This is also called the transitivity axiom.
3. For indifferent outcomes, their expected utilities are equal, and vice versa; given two prospects with equal expected utilities, an investor would be indifferent in choosing one or the other.

These three assumptions underlie the rational framework of expected utility that supposedly eliminates the uncertainty from pricing, and bring it to a problem under certainty (risk-free), where prices are known. There remains the nagging question: What are, and how can we define, such utility functions?

The Risk Premium

Say that $\{\tilde{R}, P(.)\}$ is a set of rewards $\tilde{R}$ defined by a continuous probability distribution $P(.)$ and define a utility function $u(.)$ for such rewards. The expected utility provides a scale for the valuation of the rewards $\tilde{R}$, and its certain (risk-free) equivalent R_{CE} is then:

$$E\left(u(\tilde{R})\right) = \int_{r \in \Re} u(r)P(r)dr \text{ and } R_{CE} = u^{-1}\left(E\left(u(\tilde{R})\right)\right) \text{ an its mean } \hat{R} = E\left(\tilde{R}\right)$$

$$(5.27)$$

The difference $\hat{R} - R_{CE}$ can be interpreted, as stated earlier, as the amount to compensate the holder of the uncertain prospect for the risk he is assuming, also called the risk premium, or:

$$P = \hat{R} - R_{CE} \qquad (5.28)$$

If there is no arbitrage, then the certain equivalent is necessarily the risk-free rate of return (since it is a certain quantity) and therefore:

$$R_f = R_{CE}, \ \hat{R} = R_f + P \text{ and } \hat{R} - R_f = P \qquad (5.29)$$

is the spread.

For example, say a stock is earning a rate of return of 10 percent, when the risk-free alternative is 7 percent. This implies that a risk premium of 3 percent is needed to compensate the holder of the stock. These relationships are important as they point to alternative measures of the risk premium (which is in such cases the price of the risk attitude of the investor). If this is the case, securities' premium rates of return ought to be the same—whether we use market prices to calculate them or if we use other approaches. If these prices are not the same, this will mean that there may be something else that we are missing when calculating the risk premium. This was observed in fact by Mehra and Prescot (1985) who pointed out a substantial difference between the equity premium using financial time series of stocks and using a utility model based on investors' preferences for future consumption. This difference (although there are many papers and studies that seek to reconcile these differences) is called the *equity premium puzzle*. It highlights the necessity to reconcile the validity of financial models we use with the financial data at hand. When these cannot be reconciled, it implies that the model fails to explain what it purports to explain in the first place.

Utility and Its Behavioral Derivatives

Say that an uncertain prospect is given by:

$$\tilde{R} = \hat{R} + \tilde{\varepsilon}, \quad \mathrm{var}(\tilde{\varepsilon}) = \sigma^2, \quad E(\tilde{\varepsilon}) = 0$$

where σ^2 is the payoff variance. The payoff expected utility is then $Eu(\hat{R} + \tilde{\varepsilon})$, which equals the utility of the certain equivalent, or

$$u(R_{CE}) = u(\hat{R} - P)$$

A marginal analysis based on a Taylor series valuation relative to the expected return yields then:

$$E(u(\tilde{R})) = E\left(u(\hat{R} + \tilde{\varepsilon})\right) = E\left(u(\hat{R}) + \tilde{\varepsilon}u'(\hat{R}) + \frac{\tilde{\varepsilon}^2}{2}u''(\hat{R})\right) = u(\hat{R}) + \sigma^2\frac{u''(\hat{R})}{2}$$

$$(5.30)$$

By definition of the certainty equivalent $u(R_{CE}) = E(u(\tilde{R}))$ we have:

$$u(R_{CE}) = E(u(\tilde{R})) \Rightarrow u(\hat{R}) - Pu'(\hat{R}) = E(u(\tilde{R})) = E\left(u(\hat{R} + \tilde{\varepsilon})\right) = u(\hat{R}) + \sigma^2 \frac{u''(\hat{R})}{2}$$

(5.31)

Equating these two terms, the risk premium is given by:

$$P = -\frac{1}{2}\sigma^2 \frac{u''(\hat{R})}{u'(\hat{R})}$$

(5.32)

Note that $u'(\hat{R}) > 0$ and therefore a premium is positive if $u''(\hat{R}) < 0$ and vice versa for a risk-loving investor. In this spirit, a risk attitude is embedded in the utility function's derivatives, leading to the definition of an index of risk aversion, called the Arrow-Pratt index of risk aversion and given by:

$$A_P(\hat{R}) = -\frac{u''(\hat{R})}{u'(\hat{R})} \quad \text{or } P = \frac{1}{2}\sigma^2 A_P(\hat{R})$$

(5.33)

This index expresses the quantity by which a fair bet must be altered by a risk-averse decision maker in order to be indifferent between accepting and rejecting the bet.

Analysis of risk aversion has indicated that there may be other indexes indicative of such attitudes. For example, an index of prudence and temperance was suggested by Kimball (1990) and by Eeckhoudt, Gollier, and Schlesinger (1996) based on the third derivative of the utility function. A quantitative treatment of measures of risk attitude and their correspondence between mean-variance and expected-utility approaches can be found in Eichner and Wagener (2005) (see also Munier and Tapiero [2008]). Measurements of absolute risk attitudes are characterized by a utility function $u(.)$ as follows:

$$A_k \equiv -\frac{u^{k+1}(W)}{u^k(W)}, \ W \in \Re, k \in \mathrm{N}$$

(5.34)

where W is the investor's wealth and $u^k(W)$ denotes the kth derivative with respect to wealth. Particular measurements of risk attitudes consist thus of A_1, which is the Arrow-Pratt measure of absolute risk aversion defined earlier. Similarly, A_2 and A_3 are used to denote a quantitative estimate of absolute prudence and absolute temperance. When $k \geq 3$, a number of studies have suggested a meaning embedded in a "mixed risk aversion" (Eichner and Wagener 2005) and given by:

$$B_k \equiv -z\frac{u^{k+1}(W+z)}{u^k(W+z)}$$

(5.35)

For $k = 1$ this yields a partial relative risk aversion, while for $k = 2$ and $k = 3$, these can be used as measurements of partial prudence and partial temperance.

If the expected utility is subject to another source of risk, and if it is appreciably insensitive to this source of risk, it will be said to be robust. A prudent investor, for example, will reach an investment decision based on a utility that reflects this prudence-robust attitude. For example, an investor with a precautionary motive will tend to save more to hedge against the uncertainty that arises from additional sources of risk not accounted for by the expected utility of uncertain returns. This notion of prudence was, as stated earlier, first defined by Kimball (1990) and by Eeckhoudt and Kimball (1991) subsequently and is associated to the optimal utility level (measured by the relative marginal utilities invariance), which is or could be perturbed by other sources of risk. For example, say that $(W, \tilde{R})$ are the wealth of a person and the random payoff that results from some investment. If we use the expected marginal utility, then at the optimum:

$$Eu'(W + \tilde{R}) > u'(W) \tag{5.36}$$

if u' is convex and

$$Eu'(W + \tilde{R}) < u'(W)$$

if u' is concave. A risk premium calculated as shown earlier and whose purpose is to value the premium ψ to pay for prudence can then be applied. In other words, ψ is the amount of money required to maintain the marginal utility levels at a known level—that is, to buy insurance so that we maintain the same portfolio risk performance. Or:

$$u'(W - \psi) = Eu'(W + \tilde{R}) \tag{5.37}$$

and

$$\psi = W - u'^{-1}\left(Eu'(W + \tilde{R})\right)$$

Proceeding as before (by using a first-term Taylor series approximation on the marginal utility), we find that the prudence premium equals:

$$\psi = \left[-\frac{u'''(W)}{u''(W)}\right] = A_3(W) \tag{5.38}$$

The squared bracket term is called the *degree of absolute prudence*. For a risk-averse decision maker, the utility second-order derivative is negative ($u'' \leq 0$) and therefore prudence will be positive (negative) if the third derivative u'' is positive (negative). Further, Kimball (1990) also shows that if the risk premium is positive and decreases with wealth, w, then $\psi > \pi$. As a result, $\psi - \pi$ is a premium one would pay to render the expected utility of an investment invariant under other sources of risk (meaning a robustness of the utility with respect to other sources of risk it may depend on). These terms—*expected utility, certainty equivalent, risk premium, Arrow-Pratt index of risk aversion*, and *prudence*—are used profusely in insurance, economics and financial applications as we shall see subsequently.

EXAMPLES: SPECIFIC UTILITY FUNCTIONS

Example 1: Assume an exponential concave utility function $u(w) = 1 - e^{-aw}$, $a > 0$ with $u'(w) = ae^{-aw} > 0$, $u''(w) = -a^2 e^{-aw} < 0$. This implies that the greater the wealth, the greater the utility. The rate of growth of this utility is declining with increasing wealth (specified by the negative second-order derivative). Its index of risk aversion is a constant, or $R_A(w) = -u''/u' = a > 0$. For the logarithmic utility function $u(w) = \log(\beta + \gamma w)$, $\beta > 0, \gamma > 0$, the index of risk aversion is decreasing in wealth since $R_A(w) = \gamma/(\beta + \gamma w)$ while for the hyperbolic absolute risk aversion (HARA) utility function:

$$u(w) = \frac{1-\gamma}{\gamma} \left[\frac{aw}{1-\gamma} + b \right]^{\gamma} \quad u' = a \left[\frac{aw}{1-\gamma} + b \right]^{\gamma-1} > 0,$$

$$u'' = -a^2 \left[\frac{aw}{1-\gamma} + b \right]^{\gamma-2} < 0 \quad (5.39)$$

Its index of risk aversion and risk premium are given by:

$$A_P(w) = \frac{a}{b + aw/(1-\gamma)} > 0 \text{ and } P = \frac{a\sigma^2}{2(b + aw/(1-\gamma))} \quad (5.40)$$

Example 2: Say that you are offered an investment for a year, at the end of which the rate of return will be (0.18, –0.05) with probabilities (0.3, 0.7). Assume a logarithmic utility function. The rate of return that the bank may then offer to entice you to leave the money in the bank is found as a simple application of the expected utility principle:

$$\ln(W(1 + R_{Bank})) = 0.30 \ln(W(1 + 0.18)) + 0.70 \ln(W(1 - 0.05))$$

and finally,

$$1 + R_{Bank} = (1 + 0.18)^{0.30}(1 - 0.05)^{0.70}$$

Example 3: Let the utility of consumption be $u(c) = c^{1-\gamma}/(1-\gamma)$. Then $u'(c) = c^{-\gamma}, u''(c) = -\gamma c^{-\gamma-1}$. The Arrow-Pratt index of absolute risk aversion is

$$A(c) = -u''(c)/u'(c) = -\left(-\gamma c^{-\gamma-1}\right)/c^{-\gamma} = \gamma/c$$

Example 4: In many instances, calculation of the expected utility is difficult. However, expected utility bounds provide a first approximation. For risk-averse investors with utility function $u(.)$ and $u''(.) \leq 0$ we can bound the expected utility from above. This is known as *Jensen's inequality*, and it is given by:

$$E(u(\tilde{R})) \leq u(\hat{R}) \text{ when } u''(.) \leq 0 \text{ and } E(u(\tilde{R})) \geq u(\hat{R}) \text{ when } u''(.) \leq 0 \quad (5.41)$$

and vice versa when the utility function represents a risk-loving investor (i.e., $u''(.) \geq 0$). When rewards have known mean and known variance, Willassen (1981 and 1990) has shown that for a risk-averse decision maker, the expected utility can be bounded from below and above by:

$$u(\hat{R}) \geq Eu(\tilde{R}) \geq \hat{R}^2 u(\alpha_2/\hat{R})/\alpha_2; \quad \alpha_2 = E(\tilde{R}^2) \tag{5.42}$$

The first inequality is, of course, Jensen's inequality while the second provides a best lower bound on expected utility. It is possible to improve on this estimate by using the best upper and lower Tchebycheff (or Chebychev) bounds on expected utility (Willassen 1990). This inequality is particularly useful when we interpret and compare the effects of uncertainty on the choice of financial decisions. When returns are skew we can generalize these expressions by taking higher-order derivatives in approximating the expected utility function of returns by a Taylor series, expanded about its means.

Utility functions, of a more general functional form, have been suggested as well to account for other dimensions of risk, such as their intertemporal effects. For example, failure to explain the equity premium puzzle has led several authors to seek a more general utility function that can better fit equity premiums over time with the actually observed data (as discussed earlier). One such attempt is the general expected utility (GEU) suggested by Epstein and Zin (1989 and 1991). They propose that the current utility of consuming a certain asset at a given time t is defined in terms of both a risk aversion and an intertemporal substitution of consumption now versus later (emphasizing thereby that in an intertemporal framework both risk aversion and time depend on one another in some fashion). A model that would consider such elements is as follows:

$$u_t^{1-\rho} = \left[c_t^{1-\rho} + \beta \left(E_t u_{t+1}^{1-\alpha} \right)^{\frac{1-\rho}{1-\alpha}} \right] \tag{5.43}$$

where α is a measure of relative risk aversion, $1/\rho$ is a measure of the elasticity of the intertemporal (preference for consumption) substitution, and $u_t^{1-\rho}$ is a utility of consumption now and consumption later (in the next period). A detailed analysis of this model follows in a later section. For example, if we assume that there is no risk aversion and no time substitution for consumption, then $\alpha = 0$ and $\rho = 0$ and therefore:

$$u_t = c_t + \beta \left(E_t u_{t+1} \right)$$

Other models have sought to extend this approach by suggesting that consumption is a function of habits and therefore the utility at any time depends on the consumption in the previous period. The utility of consumption can then be defined as follows:

$$U_t(c_t) = E_t \sum_{i=0}^{\infty} \beta^i u(c_{t+i} - \lambda c_{t+i-1}), \lambda > 0 \tag{5.44}$$

where $\lambda > 0$ is an index of habit formation and $u(c_{t+i} - \lambda c_{t+i-1})$ is the utility of the consumption change, given by these authors by $u(v_{t+i})$ earlier. Analysis of these equations and their implications can be found in References in this chapter and in the next chapter relating to the equity premium puzzle.

THE PRICE AND THE UTILITY OF CONSUMPTION

The problem we consider next is based on an intertemporal optimization problem, establishing a relationship between the price of current consumption and savings for future consumption. Such an approach underlies the CCAPM or kernel pricing method. Say that an investor has a wealth of $\$W$ (say \$100,000) and a wealth utility $u(W) > 0$. If the investor consumes some of his wealth today, say c_0, and invests his remaining wealth $(W - c_0)$ for future consumption, at a rate of return $\tilde{R}$, the consumption at the next period is then $c_1 = (W - c_0)(1 + \tilde{R})$. The utility of wealth that accounts for consumption in both periods is then

$$EU(W_0, W_1) = U(W_0) + \beta EU(W_1)$$

where β is some discount factor. Generally, at time t, we have rate of return $\tilde{R}_t$, and

$$c_{t+1} = (1 + \tilde{R}_t)(W_t - c_t)$$

and in terms of utilities of consumption rather than wealth, we have:

$$\underset{c_t}{Max}\, u(c_t) + \beta Eu(c_{t+1}),\, c_{t+1} = (1 + \tilde{R}_t)(W_t - c_t) \tag{5.45}$$

A utility optimal consumption allocation is thus found by:

$$u'(c_t) = \beta E\left[(1 + \tilde{R}_t)u'\left((1 + \tilde{R}_t)(W_t - c_t)\right)\right] \text{ or } u'(c_t) = \beta E\left[(1 + \tilde{R}_t)u'(c_{t+1})\right] \tag{5.46}$$

which we can write as follows:

$$1 = E\left[\left(\beta\frac{u'(c_{t+1})}{u'(c_t)}\right)(1 + \tilde{R}_t)\right] = E\left[\tilde{M}_t(1 + \tilde{R}_t)\right] \text{ with } \tilde{M}_t = \beta\frac{u'(c_{t+1})}{u'(c_t)} \tag{5.47}$$

In this formulation, $\tilde{M}_t$ is called the kernel price. It is an alternative means to construct models that can help us define empirically the price of risk. If an asset's price is risk-free, then an investment of \$1 will bring the certain rate of return R_f. Inserting this observation in the kernel price equation, we have:

$$1 = E\left[\tilde{M}_t(1 + \tilde{R}_t)\right] \equiv E\left[\tilde{M}_t(1 + R_f)\right] = (1 + R_f)E\left[\tilde{M}_t\right] \tag{5.48}$$

And therefore, the risk-free discount rate equals the expected kernel price, or:

$$E\left[\tilde{M}_t\right] = 1/(1 + R_f)$$

This allows rewriting the kernel pricing formula for a risky asset by:

$$1 = E\left[\tilde{M}_t\left(1 + \tilde{R}_t\right)\right] = E\left[\tilde{M}_t\right]E\left[\left(\tilde{M}_t / E\left(\tilde{M}_t\right)\right)\left(1 + \tilde{R}_t\right)\right]$$

and thereby:

$$1 + R_f = E\left[\frac{\tilde{M}_t}{E\left(\tilde{M}_t\right)}\left(1 + \tilde{R}_t\right)\right]. \tag{5.49}$$

In other words, expectation of the pricing kernel is equal to the risk-free discount rate. For a security whose current price is S_0 and its future price and return are a random variable $\tilde{S}_1$ and $\left(1 + \tilde{R}\right)$, priced initially by $(1 + k)$, we have

$$(1 + k) = E\left\{\left(1 + \tilde{R}\right)\tilde{M}_1\right\}$$

while for the security we have:

$$S_0 = E\left\{\tilde{M}_1\tilde{S}_1\right\} \text{ and } S_0 = \frac{1}{1 + R_f}E\left\{\frac{\tilde{M}_1}{E\left\{\tilde{M}_1\right\}}\tilde{S}_1\right\} \tag{5.50}$$

which can be written as follows:

$$S_0 = \frac{1}{1 + R_f}E^{M_1}\left\{\tilde{S}_1\right\} \tag{5.51}$$

where expectation $E^{M_1}\left\{\tilde{S}_1\right\}$ is taken with respect to a risk-neutral probability measure $\{M_1\}$ or a numéraire (to be expanded on in Chapter 7). The definition of such a measure is an essential problem that underlies the pricing of financial assets in complete markets. Of, course if we define by $E^P\{.\}$ an expectation taken with respect to a probability distribution while $E^{M_1}\{.\}$ is an expectation taken with respect to the measure $\{M_1\}$, then equating equations (5.50) and (5.51) leads to:

$$S_0 = \frac{1}{1 + R_f}\int_{\Re}\left\{\frac{\tilde{M}_1}{E\left\{\tilde{M}_1\right\}}\tilde{S}_1\right\}f^P(\tilde{S}_1)d\tilde{S}_1 = \frac{1}{1 + R_f}\int_{\Re}\left\{\tilde{S}_1\right\}f^{M_1}(\tilde{S}_1)d\tilde{S}_1 \tag{5.52}$$

And therefore,

$$f^{M_1}\left(\tilde{S}_1\right) = \frac{\tilde{M}_1}{E\left\{\tilde{M}_1\right\}}f(\tilde{S}_1) \text{ or } \frac{f^{M_1}\left(\tilde{S}_1\right)}{f(\tilde{S}_1)} = \frac{\tilde{M}_1}{E\left\{\tilde{M}_1\right\}} \tag{5.53}$$

In such cases, we say that the market is complete and prices are calculated with respect to the (measure or numéraire) probability distribution by expectation of the future price, discounted at the risk-free rate. If there is such a probability measure, then equation (5.48) holds.

$$\frac{f^Q(S_1)}{f^P(S_1)} = \frac{M_1}{E\{M_1\}} = (1+R_f)M_1 \tag{5.54}$$

$$\frac{f^Q(S_1)f^P(S_1) - f^{P'}(S_1)f^Q(S_1)}{[f^P(S_1)]^2} = (1+R_f)\frac{u''(W_1)}{u'(W_0)} \tag{5.55}$$

which provides a unique relationship between the subjective probability distribution $f^Q(\tilde{S}_1)$ and the risk-neutral probability distribution that prices assets by an expected value of $f^Q_{\tilde{S}_1}(\tilde{S}_1)$. It can be written as:

$$\frac{d}{dS_1}\left(\frac{f^Q(S_1)}{f^P(S_1)}\right) = (1+R_f)\frac{u''(W_1)}{u'(W_0)}$$

which can be rearranged as follows:

Using the Arrow-Pratt index of risk aversion, $A_P(S_1)$, this is reduced to:

$$A_P(S_1) = \frac{d}{dS_1}\left[\ln\frac{f^P(S_1)}{f^Q(S_1)}\right], \quad A_P(S_1) = -\frac{u''(W_1)}{u'(W_1)} \tag{5.56}$$

This latter equation provides a clear interpretation for the ratio of a risk-neutral and a subjective price distribution of an investor whose utility is $u(.)$. Further, it provides a relationship that relates three essential elements that determine prices, with any two defining the third. These are:

1. Private information, defined by $f^P(S_1)$.
2. Market implied information, defined by $f^Q(S_1)$.
3. The risk attitude, embedded in the Arrow-Pratt index of risk aversion $A_P(S_1)$.

These can be used to determine the implied relationships between the subjective market estimate of the prices' probability distribution, the market risk-neutral measure, and the implied risk attitude embedded in these distributions.

A broad number of techniques, statistical and otherwise, are applied to estimate and reveal the implied risk attitude of decision makers using these relationships. Some of these techniques include models embedded in an explicit utility function, which is in turn estimated using market price data. In other cases, attitudes are determined through the implied preferences of the utility function of a person, investor, trader, or risk manager. These studies amplify the fact that in finance, risk attitudes or a person's beliefs and preferences combine through an exchange of agents to determine the price of risk (implied in a risk-neutral distribution and based on the presumption that markets are always reflecting a rational behavior and a risk attitude revealed by asset prices). In this sense, the financial price of risk is similar to that of the risk premium implied in utility functions. These models are of course just models, in the sense that they are limited, focusing on some parts of reality, and reflecting the model builder's understanding of behavioral and economic attitudes, limitations, and bounded rationality, and thereby attitudes toward specific events.

EXAMPLE: KERNEL PRICING AND THE EXPONENTIAL UTILITY FUNCTION

Let the utility of an investor be of the exponential type, then,

$$\frac{f^Q(S_1)}{f^P(S_1)} = \left(1 + R_f\right)e^{-\rho(W_1 - W_0)}$$

while

$$\rho = \frac{d}{dS_1}\left[\ln\frac{f(S_1)}{f^Q(S_1)}\right] \qquad (5.60)$$

where ρ is the investor's utility index of risk aversion. Thus, if the utility of an investor is known, his personal forecast of the future price reveals (again assuming the investor's rationality and implied complete markets) the security's future market prices. Similarly, let the utility function of consumption be logarithmic, then $u'(c) = \ln(c)$, $u'(c) = 1/c$ and

$$M_{t+1} = \beta\frac{c_t}{c_{t+1}}$$

or

$$\tilde{R}_{t+1} = \beta\frac{\frac{1}{\beta}c_{t+1} - c_t}{c_t}$$

and further,

$$\frac{p_t}{c_t} = \beta E_t\left[\frac{\tilde{x}_{t+1}}{c_{t+1}}\right] \qquad (5.61)$$

Thus, for

$$\pi_t = \frac{p_t}{c_t}; \tilde{\pi}_{t+1} = \frac{\tilde{x}_{t+1}}{c_{t+1}}$$

we have:

$$\pi_t = \beta E_t\left(\tilde{\pi}_{t+1}\right)$$

EXAMPLE: THE PRICING KERNEL AND THE CAPM

Assume that the pricing kernel is a linear function of a price index (for example the S&P 500, the Dow Jones index, etc.). Thus, $M_1 = a + bR_m$. Inserting this equation in the pricing equation for a dollar invested in some stock, we have:

$$1 = E\{(1 + R_i)M_1\} = E\{(1 + R_i)(a + bR_m)\}$$

where R_i is the stock rate of return. Simple manipulations point out:

$$1 = E\{(1 + R_i)(a + bR_m)\} = E(1 + R_i)E(a + bR_m) + \text{cov}\{(1 + R_i), (a + bR_m)\} \tag{5.62}$$

Since $E(a + bR_m) = E(M_1) = 1/(1 + R_f)$, with:

$$1 - \text{cov}\{(1 + R_i), (a + bR_m)\} = \frac{1}{1 + R_f}E(1 + R_i)$$

and

$$1 + E(R_i) = (1 + R_f)[1 - \text{cov}\{(1 + R_i), (a + bR_m)\}]$$

the security spread is:

$$E(R_i) - R_f = -(1 + R_f)\,\text{cov}\{(1 + R_i), (a + bR_m)\} =$$

$$= \frac{\text{cov}\{(R_i - R_f), (R_m - R_f)\}}{Var(R_m - R_f)}E(R_m - R_f) = \beta_i E(R_m - R_f) \tag{5.63}$$

where β_i is the security's beta, given by:

$$\beta_i = \frac{\text{cov}\{(R_i - R_f), (R_m - R_f)\}}{Var(R_m - R_f)} \tag{5.64}$$

Namely, we have reduced the pricing kernel to that of a CAPM:

$$E(R_i) - R_f = \beta_i E(R_m - R_f) \tag{5.65}$$

What if the kernel is nonlinear, a quadratic function in the index (i.e., a function of its volatility as well)? What if we select two or more indexes such as the S&P 500 and a foreign index? These and other questions pertain to issues of more than one source of information that require more refined pricing models. This kernel pricing approach can be generalized in many ways, notably by considering multiple periods and various agents (heterogeneous or not) interacting in financial markets to buy, sell, and transact financial assets.

EXAMPLE: KERNEL PRICING AND THE HARA UTILITY FUNCTION

An alternative approach to defining a relationship between a utility, the private, and the market probability distributions based on a utility maximization problem is considered next. Assume an asset whose current price is \$1 and whose future price is random given by W_T. The investor's rationale is to optimize his expected utility subject to the payment now (which he is willing to forego) for such an investment. This is reduced in our case to the following optimization problem:

$$\underset{W}{Max}\, E^P u(W_T) \text{ Subject to: } 1 = \frac{1}{\left(1 + R_f\right)^T} E^Q (W_T) \tag{5.66}$$

where E^P is an expectation of the utility taken using the investor's personal-subjective probability distribution, while E^Q is a market pricing expectation that uses a risk-neutral probability distribution (since the price now is a risk-free discounted value of the next-period expected price). A solution is straightforward and leads to (as seen earlier):

$$f^Q(W_T) = e^{R_f(T-t)} \frac{u'(W_T)}{u'(W_t)} f^P(W_T) \text{ And } A_r(W_T) = \frac{d}{dW_T} \left(\ln \frac{f^P(W_T)}{f^Q(W_T)} \right) \tag{5.67}$$

where $f^P(.)$ and $f^Q(.)$ are the subjective and the risk-neutral distributions. If the investor's utility function is of the HARA type, with

$$u'(W_T) = a \left[\frac{a W_T}{1 - \gamma} + b \right]^{\gamma - 1}$$

we can show that:

$$\frac{f^Q(W_T)}{f^P(W_T)} = e^{R_f(T-t)} \frac{u'(W_T)}{u'(W_t)} = e^{R_f(T-t)} \left(\frac{a W_t + b(1 - \gamma)}{a W_T + b(1 - \gamma)} \right)^{1-\gamma} \tag{5.68}$$

Or, in terms of the Arrow-Pratt index of absolute risk aversion:

$$0 < A_P(W_T) = \frac{a}{b + a W_T/(1 - \gamma)} = \frac{d}{dW_T} \left(\ln \frac{f^P(W_T)}{f^Q(W_T)} \right) \tag{5.69}$$

and

$$\exp \left\{ \int A_P(W_T)\, dW_T \right\} = \exp \left\{ \int \frac{a}{b + a W_T/(1 - \gamma)}\, dW_T \right\} = \frac{f^P(W_T)}{f^Q(W_T)} \tag{5.70}$$

or

$$f^Q(W_T) = f^P(W_T) \exp \left\{ -\int A_P(W_T) \, dW_T \right\} \qquad (5.71)$$

For the HARA case, we note that:

$$\exp \left\{ \int \frac{1}{b + a W_T/(1-\gamma)} dW_T \right\} = \exp \left\{ \frac{1-\gamma}{a} \ln(b + a W_T/(1-\gamma)) \right\}$$

$$= [b + a W_T/(1-\gamma)]^{\frac{1-\gamma}{a}} \qquad (5.72)$$

And therefore,

$$f^Q(W_T) = f^P(W_T) \left[b + \frac{a}{1-\gamma} W_T \right]^{\frac{a}{1-\gamma}} \qquad (5.73)$$

On the basis of these results, we can also calculate (as a function of the utility function parameters) the differences between the mean price forecasts of the investor and those believed by investors and speculators in financial markets.

Extensive research, both theoretical and empirical, has extended this approach and indicated a number of important results. For example, risk attitude is not only state varying but is time varying as well. Further, it clearly sets out the concept of risk attitude in terms of a distance between the subjective and the risk-neutral (market) distributions. For notational simplicity, set:

$$g(W_T) = \ln \left(\frac{f^P(W_T)}{f^Q(W_T)} \right) \text{ then: } \frac{g''(W_T)}{g'(W_T)} - g'(W_T) = A_\pi \text{ or } g''(W_T) = (A_\pi + A_P) A_P$$
$$(5.74)$$

In this equation, we clearly see the relationship between the risk-neutral, the subjective, and the risk attitude of the investor with respect to both the index of absolute risk aversion and the investor's prudence.

The Price and Demand for Insurance

People buy insurance to protect themselves from adverse consequences. Their demand for insurance is therefore a function of their risk attitude embedded in their utility for money. In this section we develop a financial-utility approach to pricing the demand for insurance based on the definition of insurance as a risk-sharing scheme that involves a transfer of some money (the risk insurance premium) from one party—the insured—to the insurer (Tapiero 2010a). Extensions to collateralized debt obligations (CDOs) are considered in Chapter 10.2.

Say that an individual has a utility function $u(.)$ and let W be his initial wealth. Consider a prospective individual risk $\tilde{x}_t$, a random variable, for which an insurance contract is sought. Insurance contracts are defined, as seen earlier, by a premium P

paid to the insurer. Such a contract is made by the insured if $u(W - P) \geq Eu(W - \tilde{x}_t)$. At equality, $W - P$ is a certain equivalent since $W - P \geq u^{-1}Eu(W - \tilde{x}_t)$, otherwise $P \leq W - u^{-1}Eu(W - \tilde{x}_t)$. This premium, as noted earlier, is not a price but expresses the amount of money that the insured would be willing to pay to insure his risk. In general, insurance contracts are risk-sharing agreements when the insured assumes part of the risk, insures the remaining risk, and pays an amount of money, demanded and agreed on, to the insurer. Let $\tilde{x}_t^{(a)}$ be the risk assumed by the insured and its complement $\tilde{y}_t^{(a)}$ the demand for insurance, assumed by an insurer whose price is P_a. We set:

$$\tilde{x}_t^{(a)} = \min(\tilde{x}_t, a) \text{ and } \tilde{y}_t^{(a)} = \min(\tilde{x}_t - a, 0) \tag{5.75}$$

The insured expected utility whose wealth is W and private information is $f^P(\tilde{x}_t)$ is then

$$E^P u\left(W - P_a - \tilde{x}_t^{(a)}\right)$$

Similarly, the insurer utility whose risk capital (including its assets and insurance liabilities) is a random variable, which we denote by $\tilde{W}_F$, and a private information given by $f^I\left(y_t^{(a)} \mid \tilde{W}_F\right)$, is then:

$$E^I U\left(\tilde{W}_F + P_a - \tilde{y}_t^{(a)}\right)$$

In this case, assuming that the insured and the insurer select their decisions simultaneously, the demand for insurance and its price are given by the solution of the following equation (where K is the insured real assets capital and $\tilde{Z}_t$ is its potential losses from other insurance contracts):

$$\underset{a \geq 0}{Max} \, E^P u\left(W - P_a - \tilde{x}_t^{(a)}\right) \geq E^P u(W - \tilde{x}_t)$$

$$\underset{P_a \geq 0}{Max} \, E^I U\left(K - \tilde{Z}_t + P_a - \tilde{y}_t^{(a)}\right) \geq U^I\left(\tilde{W}_F\right) \tag{5.76}$$

with $\tilde{W}_F = K - \tilde{Z}_t$. If, in addition, we assume that the market price defined by the insurer is consistent with his utility and personal information, then using the kernel pricing method, we have for a terminal wealth state $\tilde{W}_t = K - \tilde{Z}_t + P_a - \tilde{y}_t^{(a)}$ the following result:

$$\underset{a \geq 0}{Max} \, E^P u\left(W - P_a - \tilde{x}_t^{(a)}\right) \geq E^P u(W - \tilde{x}_t) \quad \text{Subject to: } P_a = e^{-R_f t} E^Q\left(\tilde{y}_t^{(a)}\right) \tag{5.77}$$

where the insurer index of risk aversion is

$$A_r\left(\tilde{W}_t\right) = \frac{d}{dW_t}\left(\ln \frac{f^I\left(\tilde{W}_t\right)}{f^Q\left(\tilde{W}_t\right)}\right), \, A_r\left(\tilde{W}_t\right) = -\frac{U''\left(\tilde{W}_t\right)}{U'\left(\tilde{W}_t\right)}$$

and the insurer terminal wealth at the end of the insurance contract is a random variable determined by $\tilde{W}_t = K - \tilde{Z}_t + P_a - \tilde{y}_t^{(a)}$. While such a problem may appear difficult to solve, its solution is simplified by the fact that it depends on one parameter only—that of the co-participation that the insured determines and expresses his risk bearing (with its complement, the demand for insurance).

Typically, insurers have far more statistical information about insureds, and therefore the price of insurance is resolved as a Stackelberg (leader-follower) game, defined as follows:

$$\underset{P_a \geq 0}{Max}\, E^I U \left(K - \tilde{Z}_t + P_a - \tilde{y}_t^{(a)} \right) \geq U^I \left(\tilde{W}_F \right) \quad \text{with } \tilde{W}_F = K - \tilde{Z}_t$$

Subject to: $\hspace{8cm}$ (5.78)

$$\underset{a \geq 0}{Max}\, E^P u \left(W - P_a - \tilde{x}_t^{(a)} \right) \geq E^P u \left(W - \tilde{x}_t \right)$$

Such games consist, as stated in equation (5.78), in the insured selecting the amount of insurance to bear given its price. The demand for insurance is thus the amount of risk that the insured does wish to self-insure. The insurer, knowing the insured's willingness to pay schedule, optimizes the price of insurance (which in turns defines the co-participation of the insured). The co-participation first defined by $a^* = a^* (P_a)$ is then used by the insurer to determine the inverse demand for insurance $P_a^* \left(a^* \left(P_a^* \right) \right)$. (See www.charlestapiero.com for extensions.)

When pricing kernels are well defined, an implied and presumed market risk aversion can be estimated. If investors are indifferent to risk, the corresponding personal probabilities would be the same as those of a risk-neutral distribution (RND) (which is used to characterize the market probability distribution of future prices). In fact, the RND is adjusted upward (or downward) for all states in which the dollars are more (or less) highly valued. Hence, the higher the risk aversion, the more different the RND and the subjective probability will be. The risk aversion can thus be estimated from the joint observation of the two densities as we saw earlier through a simple two-periods problem. In other words, the index of absolute risk aversion A_P can be written as a functional relationship: $A_P = f(RND, \text{Subjective Probability})$.

This was exploited by Ait-Sahalia and Lo (2000) in extracting a measure of risk aversion in a standard dynamic exchange economy (Lucas 1978). Such a relation can be defined simply by maximizing the expected utility of a portfolio at a future date whose current price is one dollar and using the investor's probability distribution when valuing the utility of financial prospects. In this formulation, risk attitude is a function of the risk-neutral and the investor's subjective probability distributions. Given any two of these elements, the third can then be inferred. This has led to empirical applications where the implied risk attitude can be determined on the basis of market option prices (where the implied risk-neutral distribution can be determined using option prices, for example; see Chapter 11). And vice versa: Prices may be explained by their implied risk attitudes—which, if not confirmed or pointing to incoherence between observed and implied risk attitudes will lead necessarily to puzzling questions regarding the models we use.

SUMMARY

Utility theory underlies a rational approach to valuation, defined in terms of a number of hypotheses (axioms). Valuations of uncertain prospects are defined in terms of expected utilities. Terms such as *certain equivalents*, *risk aversion*, and implied behavioral assumptions in a utility function were used to formulate and deal with numerous economic insurance and financial problems. Empirical and behavioral data have pointed out that such rationality may not always be justified, which has led to the growth of a behavioral approach to finance. In the next chapter, applications are considered that maintain the validity of the utility approach. Nonetheless, important applications including derivation of the kernel pricing method and its application have also been used to establish a conceptual linkage between personal-utility-based valuation and market pricing. This linkage implies that the financial market process, the individual's rationality (or the Arrow-Pratt index of risk aversion), and information are intimately related.

TEST YOURSELF

5.1 For the lottery in the accompanying diagram, what is the premium you would be willing to pay if your utility is $u(.)$?

What is the certain equivalent of this lottery? What is the risk premium of this lottery? What is the maximal amount you will be willing to pay for such a lottery? What is the Arrow-Pratt index of risk aversion of this lottery?

5.2 If the discount rate for a risk-free investment is 0.08 and if the risk premium equals 10 percent of the expected return, what is the risk-adjusted discount rate?

5.3 You are offered an investment for a year, at the end of which the rate of return will be (0.18, –0.05) with probabilities (0.30, 0.70). Assuming that you have a logarithmic utility function, what is the rate of return the bank has to offer you to entice you to leave your money in the bank?

5.4 Assume next that the utility of the insured is exponential and that of the insurer is of the HARA type. What would be the effects on the premium that the insurer can ask for and the insured will be willing to pay if the insurer is much, much richer than the insured?

5.5 An investor has a HARA utility function given by

$$u(w) = \frac{1-\gamma}{\gamma}\left[\frac{aw}{1-\gamma} + b\right]^{\gamma}$$

What is the index of risk aversion? What is the certainty equivalent? What is the risk premium? If the return w is uncertain, how would you respond to the same questions? If the risk-free rate is 0.05, what is the risk-adjusted rate? What is the index of prudence? Calculate it for the HARA and explain its importance (or unimportance).

5.6   Use a discount rate of 0.12 for the time value of money and calculate the present value of a payment stream that increases by 15 percent per year for five years and with a terminal payment of $100,000. If the payment needed to buy such a return initially is $180,000, what is the internal rate of return (IRR)? What is the difference between the IRR and the discount rate?

5.7   An insurance company insures 10,000 people, and the average payment to insured was $1,200. What is the premium per contract if the loading factor is q? How does such a approach differ from an insurance portfolio traded in the stock market? Can you suggest what would be the price of the insurance contract?

5.8   Say that a person has an exponential utility function $u(x) = 1 - \exp(-\rho x)$. Assume that x is a measure of wealth one period hence (say one year). What is the present value of this wealth? Assume a known risk-free rate (for example, 7 percent) and say that x is known for sure, given by $3,000. Assume at present that x has a normal probability distribution with known mean and known variance. What is the expected utility? Now assume that the expected return μ is known while the rate of return of the firm equals 40 percent more than the risk-free rate. What would then be the risk premium? If the risk premium equals 20 percent of the mean return, what is the rate of return?

5.9   What is a risk-free rate and what is a risk-adjusted discount rate? How do you think they ought to differ? Explain why.

5.10 What is the net present value of an income of $500 per month for two years if the discount rates are 3 percent, 5 percent, and 8 percent annually?

5.11 How much would you pay for an annuity that gives you $1,000 each month for five years and then $25,000 at the end of the fifth year? Assume a yearly discount rate of 5 percent, 9 percent, and 12 percent.

5.12 Investment in a port requires $100 million over five years. The port authority has decided to market a bond of par value of $X with a coupon payment of $1 million every year, starting the fifth year, until maturity in 20 years.

   a. The current market rates are for 1 to 5 years equal to 5 percent; for 5 to 10 years, 5.5 percent; and finally, for 10 to 20 years they equal 6 percent. What is the face value of the bond to be issued?
   b. What is the current yield of the bond?
   c. After one year the short (1 to 5 years) remains unchanged but the rates for 5 to 20 years increase by 12 percent. What is the yield after one year?

5.13 An annuity pays the holder a scheduled payment over a given amount of time (finite or infinite). Determine the value of such an annuity using bond values at the current time. What would this value be in two years using current observed rates? What will be the value of an annuity that starts in T years and will be paid for N years afterwards? How would you write this annuity if the annuity is terminated at the time the annuity holder passes away (assuming that all payments are then stopped)?

5.14   Say that we have an obligation whose nominal value is $1,000 at the fixed rate of 10 percent with a maturity of three years, reimbursed in five. In other words, the firm obtains a capital amount of $1,000 whose cost is 10 percent. What is the financial value of the obligation? Now, assume that just after the obligation is issued the interest rate falls from 10 to 8 percent. The firm's cost of finance could have been smaller. What is the value of the obligation (after the change in interest rates) and what is the loss to the firm?

5.15   An insured has an exponential utility function with a known index of risk aversion. What is the maximum premium he would be willing to pay if the risk he is insuring is normal with the mean $\mu = \$10,000$ and variance $\sigma^2 = k\mu$, $k = 1$, and his wealth is $100,000?

   a. What is the optimal and proportional amount he would prefer to self-insure?
   b. If the insurer is a large firm and fully diversified, how much do you believe it would ask the insured to pay for a premium?
   c. How is this question related to the health insurance debate?
   d. How is the insurance premium related to financial markets activity?

5.16   What is the difference between a risk exchange between two firms (or investors) and their trading in financial markets?

5.17   An investor portfolio consists of an investment in two risk assets and a risk-free one. The portfolio current price is $1,000,000. The rates of return for the stocks' prices are random and given by 8 and 12 percent with variances equal to $8k_1$ and $12k_2$ percent. The correlation between these stocks is ρ_{12}. The risk-free bond has a rate of return of 5 percent. How much would you invest in each of those securities if you have an exponential utility function? If you have a power utility function? If you have a logarithmic utility function? When do you have a perfect diversification of your portfolio? When there is no diversification? If the spot, risk-free rate changed by $?R_f$, by how much would your asset allocation change?

5.18   What is the certain equivalent of a logarithmic utility $\ln(a + bw)$? Of an exponential utility $-\exp(-aw)$? What is the risk premium for these two utilities? For these cases, assume that payments are made in a year. What is their current value if the risk-free rate is given? What is the risk-adjusted rate? What is the relationship between these rates for both utilities? Explain their differences.

REFERENCES

Ait-Sahalia, Yacine, and Lo, Andrew W. 2000. Nonparametric risk management and implied risk aversion. *Journal of Econometrics* 94 (1–2):9–51.

Alexander, C. 1998. *Risk management and analysis*, vols. 1 and 2. New York: John Wiley & Sons.

Allais, M. 1953. Le comportement de l'homme rationnel devant le risque: Critique des postulats et axiomes de l'école americaine. *Econometrica* 21:503–546.

———. 1979. The foundations of a positive theory of choice involving risk and a criticism of the postulates and axioms of the American School. In *Expected utility hypothesis and the Allais paradox*, ed. M. Allais and O. Hagen. Dordrecht, Holland: D. Reidell.

Arrow, K. J. 1951. Alternative approaches to the theory of choice in risk-taking situations. *Econometrica* (October).

———. 1965. *Aspects of the theory of risk-bearing*. Helsinki: Yrjo Jahnssonin Säätiö.

———. 1982. Risk perception in psychology and in economics. *Economics Inquiry*, January, 1–9.

Bell, D. 1995. Risk, return and utility. *Management Science* 41:23–30.

Campbell, J. Y. 2000. Asset pricing at the millennium. *Journal of Finance* LV (4):1515–1567.

Cochrane, John H. 2001. *Asset pricing*. Princeton, NJ: Princeton University Press.

Doherty, Neil A. 2000. *Integrated risk management: Techniques and strategies for managing corporate risk*. New York: McGraw-Hill.

Eeckhoudt, L., C. Gollier, and H. Schlesinger. 1996. Changes in background risk and risk taking behavior. *Econometrica* 64:683–689.

Eeckhoudt, L., and M. Kimball. 1991. Background risk prudence and the demand for insurance. In *Contributions to insurance economics*, ed. G. Dionne. Boston: Kluwer Academic Press.

Eichner, T., and A. Wagener. 2005. Measures of risk attitude and correspondence between mean variance and expected utility. *Decisions in Economics and Finance* 28: 53–67.

Ellsberg, D. 1961. Risk, ambiguity and the savage axioms. *Quarterly Journal of Economics*, November: 643–669.

Epstein, Larry G., and Stanley E. Zin. 1989. Substitution, risk aversion and the temporal behavior of consumption and asset returns: A theoretical framework. *Econometrica* 57:937–969.

———. 1991. Substitution, risk aversion and the temporal behavior of consumption and asset returns: An empirical analysis. *Journal of Political Economy* 99:263–286.

Fama, Eugene F. 1996. The CAPM is wanted, dead or alive. *Journal of Finance* 51 (December): 1947–1958.

Fishburn, P. C. 1970. *Utility theory for decision making*. New York: John Wiley & Sons.

Friedman, M., and L. J. Savage. 1948. The utility analysis of choices involving risk. *Journal of Political Economy*, August.

———. 1952. The expected utility hypothesis and the measurability of utility. *Journal of Political Economy*, December.

Froot, Kenneth A., David S. Scharfstein, and Jeremy C. Stein. 1993. Risk management: Coordinating corporate investment and financing policies. *Journal of Finance* 48 (5) (December): 1629–1658.

Gollier, C. 2000. *The economics of risk and time*. Cambridge, MA: MIT Press.

Grossman, S., and O. Hart. 1983. An analysis of the principal-agent model. *Econometrica* 51:7–46.

Gul, Faruk. 1991. A theory of disappointment aversion. *Econometrica* 59:667–686.

Hadar, Josef, and William R. Russell. 1969. Rules for ordering uncertain prospects. *American Economic Review* 59:25–34.

Hirschleifer, J., and J. G. Riley. 1979. The analysis of uncertainty and information: An expository survey. *Journal of Economic Literature* 17:1375–1421.

Holmstrom, B. 1979. Moral hazard and observability. *Bell Journal of Economics* 10:74–91.

Ivan, Mirela, and C. S. Tapiero. 2010a. A financial approach to reliability pricing of warranties. Working paper, New York University Polytechnic Institute.

———. 2010b. Water supply risk, demand uncertainty and the price of water and water shortage. Working paper, New York University Polytechnic Institute.

Kahnemann, D., and A. Tversky. 1979. Prospect theory: An analysis of decision under risk. *Econometrica*, March: 263–291.

Kimball, M. 1990. Precautionary saving in the small and in the large. *Econometrica* 58:53–78.

Lintner J. 1965a. The valuation of risky assets and the selection of risky investments in stock portfolios and capital budgets. *Review of Economic and Statistics* 47:13–37.

———. 1965b. Security prices, risk and maximum gain from diversification. *Journal of Finance* 20:587–615.

Lucas, Robert E., Jr. 1978. Asset prices in an exchange economy. *Econometrica* 46 (6):1429–1445.

Machina, M. J. 1982. Expected utility analysis without the independence axiom. *Econometrica*, March, 277–323.

Markowitz, Harry M. 1952. Portfolio selection. *Journal of Finance* 7:77–99.

———. 1959. *Portfolio selection: Efficient diversification of investments.* New York: John Wiley & Sons.

Mehra, R., and E. C. Prescott. 1985. The equity premium: A puzzle. *Journal of Monetary Economics* 15:145–161.

Merton, R. C. 1990. *Continuous time finance.* Cambridge, MA: Blackwell.

Modigliani, F., and M. Miller. 1958. The cost of capital and the theory of investment. *American Economic Review* 48 (3) (June):261–297.

Mossin J. 1966. Equilibrium in a capital asset market. *Econometrica* 34:768–783.

Munier, B., and C. S. Tapiero. 2008. Risk attitudes. In *Encyclopedia of quantitative risk assessment*, ed. Brian Everitt and Ed Melnick. Hoboken, NJ: John Wiley & Sons.

Myers, Stewart. 1984. The capital structure puzzle. *Journal of Finance* 39 (3) (July): 575–592.

Pratt, J. W. 1964. Risk aversion in the small and in the large. *Econometrica* 32:122–136.

———. 1990. The logic of partial-risk aversion: Paradox lost. *Journal of Risk and Uncertainty* 3:105–113.

Rabin, M. 1998. Psychology and economics. *Journal of Economic Literature* 36:11–46.

Samuelson, Paul A. 1963. Risk and uncertainty: A fallacy of large numbers. *Scientia* 98:108–163.

Sharpe, W. F. 1964. Capital asset prices: A theory of market equilibrium under risk. *Journal of Finance* 19:425–442.

———. 1966. Mutual fund performance. *Journal of Business* 39:119–138.

Siegel, A. 1995. Measuring systematic risk using implicit beta. *Management Science* 41:124–128.

Siegel, Jeremy J., and Richard H. Thaler. 1997. The equity premium puzzle. *Journal of Economic Perspectives* 11:191–200.

Smith, Clifford W., and René M. Stulz. 1985. The determinants of firms' hedging policies. *Journal of Financial and Quantitative Analysis* 20 (4):391–406.

Taleb, N. 2007. *The black swan: The impact of the highly improbable.* New York: Random House.

Tapiero C. S. 2004. Risk management. In *Encyclopedia on actuarial science and risk management*, ed. J. Teugels and B. Sundt. Hoboken, NJ and London: John Wiley & Sons.

———. 2008. Orders and inventory commodities with price and demand uncertainty in complete markets. *International Journal of Production Economics* 115:12–18.

———. 2010a. The demand and the price of insurance. Working paper, New York University Polytechnic Institute.

———. 2010b. The price of quality claims. Applied Stochastic Models in Business and Industry, forthcoming.

————. 2010c. The price of safety and economic reliability. In *Safety and risk modeling and its applications*, ed. Pham Hoang. Springer Verlag, forthcoming.

Tapiero, C. S., and K. Kogan. 2009. Risk-averse order policies with random prices in complete markets and retailers' private information. *European Journal of Operations Research* 196:594–599.

Tobin, J. 1956. The interest elasticity of the transaction demand for cash, *Review of Economics and Statistics* 38:241–247.

Willassen, Y. 1981. Expected utility, Chebychev bounds, mean variance analysis. *Scandinavian Economic Journal* 83:419–428.

————. 1990. Best upper and lower Tchebycheff bounds on expected utility. *Review of Economic Studies* 57:513–520.

CHAPTER 6

Applied Utility Finance

OVERVIEW

Utility theory underlies the foundations of traditional finance. Portfolio theory, developed by Harry Markowitz (who shared the Nobel Prize in 1990), is based on a mean-variance valuation that implies a quadratic utility function. Similarly, topics and models such as the capital asset pricing model (CAPM), kernel pricing or stochastic discount factor (SDF), and their many applications to financial theory and practice are themselves applications of utility. These concepts are both important and have been applied to many financial issues seeking to value, price, and reach better decisions. This chapter highlights a sample of such applications including the valuation of portfolios, the valuation of infrastructures, and so forth. These applications emphasize the intricate and complementary relationships between value and price. Value is ascribed by persons' (or firms') needs while price is a mechanism that is set by risk sharing between parties of various needs and means in a personal exchange or in a market exchange.

RISK AND THE UTILITY OF TIME

Discounting is used to price future prospects, whether risk-free or not. A question such as, "What is the value (now) of a dollar next year?" epitomizes the value of time and its price—the discount factor. Valuation of payments is generally time- and risk-dependent, defined in terms of the payments, their uncertainty, as well as the information relevant to these payments at any given instant of time. Earlier we used discount rates without discussing their utility implications (except through some simple examples pertaining to the utility of consumption). In this section, the utility of time is discussed further.

Expected Utility and the Time Utility Price of Money

Let w_t, w_{t+1} be the wealth of an investor at two consecutive instants of time, and define by $u(w_t, w_{t+1})$ the utility of over two periods. There is a time preference for a money increment Δw now over an instant of time later if the utility now of this increment is larger than its utility later. A utility expression for this statement is as follows:

$$u(w_t + \Delta w, w_{t+1}) > u(w_t, w_{t+1} + \Delta w), \quad \frac{\partial u(w_t, w_{t+1})}{\partial w_t} > 0, \quad \frac{\partial u(w_t, w_{t+1})}{\partial w_{t+1}} > 0 \qquad (6.1)$$

The first derivatives indicate that at all times, more money is better. For a constant two-period utility function, $u(w_t, w_{t+1}) = \bar{u}_t$, an implicit differentiation yields a rate of substitution between money now versus money later, or:

$$\frac{dw_t}{dw_{t+1}} = -\frac{\frac{\partial u(w_t, w_{t+1})}{\partial w_{t+1}}}{\frac{\partial u(w_t, w_{t+1})}{\partial w_t}} < -1 \qquad (6.2)$$

Thus, exchanging a dollar at time t for a dollar at time $t + 1$ will cost something, given by the time preference and the risk attitude of the investor defined by his utility function. This time substitution denotes the discount rate or equivalently the interest rate $r(w_t, w_{t+1})$ applied to time valuation, which is a function of the two prospects at times t and $t + 1$:

$$1 + r(w_t, w_{t+1}) = -\frac{dw_t}{dw_{t+1}} \qquad (6.3)$$

If the utility for money is additive over time, a simplification is reached, namely:

$$u(w_t, w_{t+1}) = u_t(w_t) + u_{t+1}(w_{t+1}) \text{ and } 1 + r(w_t, w_{t+1}) = \frac{\partial u(w_{t+1})/\partial w_{t+1}}{\partial u(w_t)/\partial w_t} \qquad (6.4)$$

The discount factor is thus an expression of the marginal utility's time substitutions.

Risk, Safety, and Reliability

Safety is a risk consequence that can be objective, measured in terms of probabilities and their consequences; or it can be perceptive, reflecting a state of mind. As a result, safety assumes many forms, such as being protected from consequential events or from being exposed to something that causes a loss. Although safety is an important part of our concern, its price is difficult to determine as it is not negotiated or traded in financial markets. Yet we spend money to buy safety! It is these expenditures that reveal what is the price we are willing to pay to live safely. The purpose of this application is to demonstrate one procedure, based on the utility approach to calculate such a price.

Say that the reliability of a process or product is $R(.)$—that is, the probability of no failure over the time interval $[0, t]$ is $R(t) = 1 - F(t)$. Let its selling price be π. A person using the system or product has, however, a probability p of using the system safely. The probability of a safe and reliable use of the system is random with expectation $Q(t) = pR(t)$ while the probability of a default is $1 - pR(t)$. The variance of a safe use is thus $\text{var} Q = R(t) p (1 - R(t) p)$. This implies that in any sale there is a counterparty risk since the seller and the buyer have both a responsibility and a stake in reliability and in safety. The producer's responsibility is to provide a reliable product and information and education for the system and its proper use, while the user's responsibility is to learn how to use the product and use it safely (although some users might seek the means to have the product fail, as will be seen in later sections of this chapter). The transaction leading to an exchange between a buyer and a seller is therefore an exchange that implies mutual responsibility, with both parties potentially liable wholly or partly for the costs associated with an unsafe consequence.

For example, a car well designed with a number of safety gadgets can be very unsafe if these safety gadgets are misunderstood and poorly used. Further, while the producer may only design the product-system reliability, it is the user whose behavior defines the product safety by his own actions (and therefore reliability). The reliability–safety design problem thus requires that we consider as well the risk/safety consequences of both the product design and the consumer-user behavior when using this product.

To account for such a situation, we define the probability of an adverse event, an unreliability due as well to the use of the product with probability $1 - \tilde{p} R(.)$ where $\tilde{p}$, now a random variable, expresses a heterogeneous distribution of users. We also define a random event failure cost $\tilde{Z}$. The firm's effective problem consists then in the selection of a reliability that meets now both the reliability and profitability constraints and that recognizes the risk consequences of users. From a firm's viewpoint, its profit is

$$\tilde{\prod} = \pi D - \Phi(R(t), D) - \sum_{j=1}^{\tilde{M}} (1 - \theta) \tilde{Z}_j \tag{6.5}$$

where D is the total number of units sold, $\Phi(R(t), D)$ is the cost of production when the reliability is $R(t)$, while

$$\sum_{j=1}^{\tilde{M}} (1 - \theta) \tilde{Z}_j, 0 \le \tilde{M} \le D$$

and θ is the user's share of default costs. Assume $\tilde{p}$ has a mean and variance, $\hat{p} = E(\tilde{p})$, $\sigma_p^2 = \text{var}(\tilde{p})$. Therefore, the number of defaulting units is a binomial (Lexian) mixture with mean and variance given by:

$$\tilde{M} \sim \binom{D}{j} (1 - \hat{p} R(.))^j (\hat{p} R(.))^{D-j}$$

with the following moments:

$$E(\tilde{M}) = D(1 - \hat{p} R(.)), \quad \text{var}(\tilde{M}) = D \hat{p} R(.) (1 - \hat{p} R(.)) + D(D - 1) R^2(.) \sigma_p^2 \tag{6.6}$$

The expected profit a period later of the firm and its standard deviations are thus:

$$
\begin{cases}
E\left(\tilde{\Pi}\right) = (1 + R_f)\left[\pi D - \Phi(R(.), D)\right] - (1 - \theta)E\left(\tilde{M}\right)E\left(\tilde{Z}_j\right) \\[2ex]
\sigma\left(\tilde{\Pi}\right) = (1 - \theta)\sqrt{\mathrm{var}\left(\sum_{j=1}^{\tilde{M}}\tilde{Z}_j\right)} = (1 - \theta)\sqrt{\left\{E(\tilde{M})\mathrm{var}\left(Z_j\right) + \mathrm{var}(\tilde{M})\left[E\left(Z_j\right)\right]^2\right\}}
\end{cases}
$$

$$(6.7)$$

Assuming a quadratic utility function as considered in the previous chapter, the firm certain equivalent is thus (see Chapter 5 for the development of this relationship):

$$
CE_0 = \frac{1}{1 + R_f}\left\{E\left(\tilde{\Pi}\right) - \lambda\sigma\left(\tilde{\Pi}\right)\right\} \tag{6.8}
$$

A firm maximizing its profits present estimate yields

$$
\frac{\partial CE_0}{\partial R(.)} = 0 \Rightarrow \frac{\partial E\left(\tilde{\Pi}\right)}{\partial R(.)} = \lambda\frac{\partial\sigma\left(\tilde{\Pi}\right)}{\partial R(.)} \text{ and } \lambda = \frac{\partial E\left(\tilde{\Pi}\right)}{\partial R(.)}\bigg/\frac{\partial\sigma\left(\tilde{\Pi}\right)}{\partial R(.)} \tag{6.9}
$$

Therefore, the firm optimal and current certain equivalent, embedded in its process (or product) design is:

$$
CE_0^* = \frac{1}{1 + R_f}\left\{E\left(\tilde{\Pi}\right) - \left(\frac{\partial E\left(\tilde{\Pi}\right)}{\partial R(.)}\bigg/\frac{\partial\sigma\left(\tilde{\Pi}\right)}{\partial R(.)}\right)\sigma\left(\tilde{\Pi}\right)\right\} \tag{6.10}
$$

Such a price depends of course on the individual buyer's propensity to default (even if the process is reliable). The cost of such default is embedded in the share of the default cost of the individual buyer and the share paid by the firm. For this reason, firms seek to produce designs that are *robust*, implying that they are relatively insensitive to default use by the individual buyer, and at the same time seek to limit the warranties they provide for processes while attending and educating their buyers to limit a potential liability for faults that they have not made. (See also www.charlestapiero.com)

ASSET ALLOCATION AND INVESTMENTS

Portfolio asset allocation deals with an individual investor's valuation and allocation of wealth. Portfolio strategies that speculate, hedge, and allocate funds to both financial and real assets are indeed one of the essential activities of financial managers.

Given the information of a number of candidate assets to invest in, the problem can be formulated by:

$$\underset{0 \leq y_i \leq 1, \sum_{i=1}^{n} y_i = 1}{Max} \quad E\left(u(\tilde{W}_1)\right) \tag{6.11}$$

where

$$\tilde{W}_1 = \sum_{i=1}^{n} \tilde{r}_i \, (y_i \, W)$$

where W denotes the initial wealth of the investor and $\tilde{W}_1$ denotes the uncertain wealth that results from an investment apportioning a proportion y_i of one's wealth to an asset i for a return of $\tilde{r}_i \, (y_i \, W)$, one period hence. This problem assumes many forms and there are many approaches to its solution. Essential approaches are due to Markowitz (1959), Sharpe, and Lintner. Almost all asset managers have a Markowitz-based portfolio computer optimization program that assumes a quadratic utility, which reduces a portfolio valuation to be a function only of its first two statistical moments. Yet the financial crisis has shown the danger of not recognizing tail events—in particular because mean-variance pushed asset prices higher as their tail event was ignored, thereby contributing partly to creating such a tail event.

Markowitz's premise, based on the first two moments of a portfolio, states that an investment portfolio ought to have two objectives: a maximal expected return on the one hand and a least variance on the other. These are summarized as follows:

$$\begin{cases} Max \ E(\tilde{W}_1) \ \text{Subject to:} & Var(\tilde{W}_1) \leq \lambda, \ \sum_{i=1}^{n} y_i = 1, 0 \leq y_i \leq 1 \\ Min \ Var(\tilde{W}_1) \ \text{Subject to:} & E(\tilde{W}_1) \geq \mu, \ \sum_{i=1}^{n} y_i = 1, 0 \leq y_i \leq 1 \end{cases} \tag{6.12}$$

In other words, optimal portfolios can be expressed in terms of a mean return and minimum risk constraint subject to variance and return constraints, respectively. Let all optimal portfolios prices be defined by $\Pi \, (\lambda, \mu)$. A portfolio is then dominant in a mean-variance sense if and only if $E(\tilde{W}_1) \geq \mu^*$ and $Var(\tilde{W}_1) \leq \lambda^*$. Thus, if preferences for a specific investor's portfolio can be specified by some function $\Pi \, (\lambda^*, \mu^*)$, continuous in (λ^*, μ^*) with:

$$\frac{\partial \Pi \, (\lambda^*, \mu^*)}{\partial \mu} \geq 0 \ \text{and} \ \frac{\partial \Pi \, (\lambda^*, \mu^*)}{\partial \lambda} \leq 0 \tag{6.13}$$

then the investment portfolio dominates any other portfolio (again, in a mean and variance sense) if:

$$\Pi \left(Var(\tilde{W}_1), E(\tilde{W}_1)\right) \geq \Pi \, (\lambda^*, \mu^*) \tag{6.14}$$

This is the essential contribution of the Markowitz approach, which is compatible with a quadratic utility. A simple example demonstrates the technical application of the Markowitz approach.

EXAMPLE: A TWO-SECURITIES PROBLEM

For a two-securities portfolio, let the portfolio return be:

$$\underset{\substack{Portfolio \\ return}}{\tilde{r}_P} \quad = \quad \underset{\substack{Portfolio \\ weight}}{y_1} \quad \underset{Risk\ 1}{\tilde{r}_1} + \quad \underset{\substack{Portfolio \\ weight}}{y_2} \quad \underset{Risk\ 2}{\tilde{r}_2} \tag{6.15}$$

Thus, the portfolio mean and variance are

$$\hat{r}_P = y_1\hat{r}_1 + y_2\hat{r}_2, \, y_2 = 1 - y_1$$

and

$$\sigma_p^2 = y_1^2\sigma_1^2 + y_2^2\sigma_2^2 + 2y_1y_2\sigma_{12}$$

with assets correlation

$$\rho_{12} = \frac{\sigma_{12}}{\sigma_1\sigma_2}$$

These assets are said to be perfectly diversified if $\rho_{12} = -1$ in which case,

$$\sigma_p^2 = y_1^2\sigma_1^2 + y_2^2\sigma_2^2 - 2y_1y_2\sigma_{12}$$

while no diversification is possible if $\rho_{12} = +1$ in which case $\sigma_p = y_1\sigma_1 + y_2\sigma_2$. Assets that are less than perfectly correlated contribute to a variance reduction. Set $y = y_1$ and consider the return constraint $\hat{r}_P = y(\hat{r}_1 - \hat{r}_2) + \hat{r}_2$. And

$$y = \frac{\hat{r}_P - \hat{r}_2}{\hat{r}_1 - \hat{r}_2}$$

or

$$1 - y = \frac{\hat{r}_1 - \hat{r}_P}{\hat{r}_1 - \hat{r}_2}$$

The variance constraint is then

$$\sigma_p^2 = y^2\sigma_1^2 + (1 - y)^2\sigma_2^2 + 2y(1 - y)\sigma_{12}$$

Inserting the proportion invested in the first asset, we have:

$$\sigma_p^2 = \left(\frac{\hat{r}_P - \hat{r}_2}{\hat{r}_1 - \hat{r}_2}\right)^2\sigma_1^2 + \left(\frac{\hat{r}_1 - \hat{r}_P}{\hat{r}_1 - \hat{r}_2}\right)^2\sigma_2^2 - 2\left(\frac{\hat{r}_P - \hat{r}_2}{\hat{r}_1 - \hat{r}_2}\right)\left(\frac{\hat{r}_P - \hat{r}_1}{\hat{r}_1 - \hat{r}_2}\right)\sigma_{12} \tag{6.16}$$

Set:

$$F(\sigma_p^2, \hat{r}_P) = 0 = -\sigma_p^2 + \left(\frac{\hat{r}_P - \hat{r}_2}{\hat{r}_1 - \hat{r}_2}\right)^2 \sigma_1^2$$

$$+ \left(\frac{\hat{r}_P - \hat{r}_1}{\hat{r}_1 - \hat{r}_2}\right)^2 \sigma_2^2 - 2\left(\frac{\hat{r}_P - \hat{r}_2}{\hat{r}_1 - \hat{r}_2}\right)\left(\frac{\hat{r}_P - \hat{r}_1}{\hat{r}_1 - \hat{r}_2}\right)\sigma_{12} \qquad (6.17)$$

Note that the function $F(\sigma_p^2, \hat{r}_P)$ in (6.17) denotes the set of investment possibilities, expressing the returns/risk substitution consistent with the constraints specifications. The curve $(\hat{r}_P, \sigma_p^2)$ defining these substitutions is called the *efficiency curve*. By implicit differentiation, we have the marginal substitution between variance and mean return of the portfolio:

$$\frac{d\sigma_p^2}{d\hat{r}_P} = -\frac{\partial F(\sigma_p^2, \hat{r}_P)/\partial \hat{r}_P}{\partial F(\sigma_p^2, \hat{r}_P)/\partial \sigma_p^2} \qquad (6.18)$$

providing thereby a map, substituting returns for risk (variance), on the basis of which we can select the desirable portfolio and, vice versa, substituting risk for returns. An individual selecting a specific return/risk profile will do so based on his individual utility. For example, let an investor's expected utility be given by the quadratic utility

$$U(\hat{r}_P, \sigma_p^2) = \hat{r}_P - \lambda \sigma_p^2$$

expressing an investor's preference of more returns and less variance. Then a risk-minimizing investor selecting an optimal return level would be given by:

$$\frac{\partial U(\hat{r}_P, \sigma_p^2)}{\partial \hat{r}_P} = 1 - \lambda \frac{d\sigma_p^2}{d\hat{r}_P} = 1 - \lambda \frac{\partial F(\sigma_p^2, \hat{r}_P)/\partial \hat{r}_P}{\partial F(\sigma_p^2, \hat{r}_P)/\partial \sigma_p^2} = 0 \qquad (6.19)$$

For an investor with an index of risk aversion λ^*, the optimal return and corresponding risks are set by:

$$\lambda^* = \frac{\partial F(\sigma_p^2, \hat{r}_P)/\partial \sigma_p^2}{\partial F(\sigma_p^2, \hat{r}_P)/\partial \hat{r}_P} \qquad (6.20)$$

and

$$U(\hat{r}_P, \sigma_p^2) = \hat{r}_P - \sigma_p^2 \frac{\partial F(\sigma_p^2, \hat{r}_P)/\partial \sigma_p^2}{\partial F(\sigma_p^2, \hat{r}_P)/\partial \hat{r}_P} = \hat{r}_P - \sigma_p^2 \frac{d\hat{r}_P}{d\sigma_p^2} = \hat{r}_P\left(1 - \frac{d\hat{r}_P}{\hat{r}_P}\frac{\sigma_p^2}{d\sigma_p^2}\right)$$

$$= \hat{r}_P\left(1 - \frac{\frac{d\ln\hat{r}_P}{d\hat{r}_P}}{\frac{d\ln\sigma_p^2}{d\sigma_p^2}}\right) \qquad (6.21)$$

In this case, note that for risk neutrality we have

$$\frac{d \ln \hat{r}_P}{d \hat{r}_P} = 0$$

while for a risk-averse investor

$$\frac{d \ln \hat{r}_P}{d \hat{r}_P} < \frac{d \ln \sigma_p^2}{d \sigma_p^2}$$

In our special two-assets case, we have set:

$$0 - \sigma_p^2 + \left(\frac{\hat{r}_P - \hat{r}_2}{\hat{r}_1 - \hat{r}_2}\right)^2 \sigma_1^2 + \left(\frac{\hat{r}_P - \hat{r}_1}{\hat{r}_1 - \hat{r}_2}\right)^2 \sigma_2^2 - 2 \left(\frac{\hat{r}_P - \hat{r}_2}{\hat{r}_1 - \hat{r}_2}\right) \left(\frac{\hat{r}_P - \hat{r}_1}{\hat{r}_1 - \hat{r}_2}\right) \sigma_{12} \quad (6.22)$$

$$\frac{d \hat{r}_P}{d \sigma_p^2} = \frac{1}{2} \frac{(\hat{r}_1 - \hat{r}_2)^2}{(\hat{r}_P - \hat{r}_2) \sigma_1^2 + (\hat{r}_P - \hat{r}_1) \sigma_2^2 - 2 \left(\hat{r}_P^2 - \frac{\hat{r}_1 + \hat{r}_2}{2}\right) \sigma_{12}} \quad (6.23)$$

$$U(\hat{r}_P, \sigma_p^2) = \hat{r}_P - \frac{1}{2} \frac{(\hat{r}_1 - \hat{r}_2)^2 \sigma_p^2}{(\hat{r}_P - \hat{r}_2) \sigma_1^2 + (\hat{r}_P - \hat{r}_1) \sigma_2^2 - 2 \left(\hat{r}_P^2 - \frac{\hat{r}_1 + \hat{r}_2}{2}\right) \sigma_{12}} \quad (6.24)$$

If the second asset is risk free, then:

$$U(\hat{r}_P, \sigma_p^2) = \hat{r}_P - \frac{1}{2} \frac{(\hat{r}_1 - R_f)^2 \sigma_p^2}{(\hat{r}_P - R_f) \sigma_1^2} = \hat{r}_P - \frac{1}{2} \frac{(\hat{r}_1 - R_f)^2 y_1^2}{(\hat{r}_P - R_f)} = \hat{r}_P - \frac{1}{2} (\hat{r}_P - R_f)$$

$$= \frac{1}{2} (\hat{r}_P + R_f)$$

where $\sigma_p^2 = y_1^2 \sigma_1^2$ and $y = \frac{\hat{r}_P - \hat{r}_2}{\hat{r}_1 - \hat{r}_2}$ $\quad (6.25)$

EXAMPLE: A TWO-STOCKS PORTFOLIO

Assume that a portfolio is to be constructed from two assets, each with mean return and variance given in the following table. In addition, we assume that these assets are correlated with a correlation factor of 0.2.

Stock	Mean Return	Variance
A	0.18	0.1
B	0.12	0.05

The set of feasible investments is given by:

$$\sigma_p^2 = \left(\frac{\hat{r}_P - 0.12}{0.18 - 0.12}\right)^2 \sigma_1^2 + \left(\frac{\hat{r}_P - 0.18}{0.18 - 0.12}\right)^2 \sigma_2^2$$

$$- 2\frac{(\hat{r}_P - 0.18)(\hat{r}_P - 0.12)}{(0.18 - 0.12)^2}\left(.2\sqrt{0.1 * 0.05}\right)$$

In this case, we note that to a portfolio return, there corresponds a portfolio variance. For example, if the desired rate of return is 0.15, the corresponding variance would be:

$$\sigma_p^2 = \left(\frac{0.03}{0.06}\right)^2 (0.1)^2 + \left(\frac{0.03}{0.06}\right)^2 (0.05)^2 + 2\frac{(0.03)(0.03)}{(0.06)^2}\left(.2\sqrt{0.1 * 0.05}\right)$$

$$\sigma_p^2 = .25\left[0.0125 + \left(.2\sqrt{0.005}\right)\right] = 0.00661$$

In this manner, each point in the return-variance curve will provide a set of feasible investments.

PROBLEM 6.1: THE EFFICIENCY FRONTIER

Repeat these calculations for rates of return between 0.12 and 0.18, and graph your results.

	$\hat{r}_p$	σ_p^2	$\hat{r}_p$	σ_p^2
1	0.125	0.00661	0.145	
2	0.13		0.15	
3	0.135		0.16	
4	0.14		0.165	

When we graph the efficiency frontier (calculated by Excel software), we have the results shown in Figure 6.1.

The introduction of a risk-free asset in the composition of the Markowitz portfolio is of both theoretical and practical importance. Using the risk-free asset as a reference asset, it is possible to price a risky asset relative to that of a risk-free asset as well as in reference to some other (say synthetic or index price). Such an observation underlies the basic CAPM for pricing risky assets. Consider a portfolio that consists of a stock and a risk-free asset (a bond), or:

$$\tilde{W}_1 = y W_0 (1 + R_f) + (1 - y) W_0 (1 + \tilde{R}_i) \tag{6.26}$$

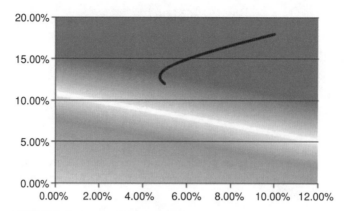

FIGURE 6.1   The Efficiency Frontier

where y is the proportion of one's wealth invested in the risk-free asset with its remaining part invested in a security. In this case, the portfolio rate of return and its variance are reduced (where we set $\hat{r}_2 = R_f$ and $\sigma_2 = 0$), as shown earlier, to:

$$\sigma_p = \left(\frac{\hat{r}_P - R_f}{\hat{r}_1 - R_f} \right) \sigma_1$$

or

$$\frac{\sigma_p}{\sigma_1} = \frac{\hat{r}_P - R_f}{\hat{r}_1 - R_f}$$

and

$$\hat{r}_1 - R_f = \frac{\sigma_1}{\sigma_P} \left(\hat{r}_P - R_f \right) \tag{6.27}$$

The Markowitz model is important for three essential reasons. First, it justifies the well-known belief that it is not optimal to put all one's eggs in one basket (or the principle of diversification). Second, a portfolio value is expressed in terms of its means returns and its variance, which can be measured by using financial statistical techniques. Further, the lower the correlation, the lower the risk. In fact, two highly and negatively correlated assets can be used to create an almost risk-free portfolio. Third and finally, for each asset, there are two risks, one diversifiable through a combination of assets and the other nondiversifiable to be borne by the investor and for which there may be a compensating return. Markowitz's (1959) contribution cannot be overstated. It laid the foundations for portfolio theory whereby rational investors determine the optimal composition of their portfolio on the basis of the expected returns, standard deviations of return, and the correlation coefficients of rates of return.

PROBLEM 6.2: A TWO-SECURITIES PORTFOLIO

Solve the following optimization-efficient frontier–minimum variance portfolio problem:

$$\text{Min } f(y_1, y_2) = \sigma_1^2 y_1^2 + \sigma_2^2 y_2^2 + 2\rho_{12}\sigma_1\sigma_2 y_1 y_2 \text{ Subject to: } y_1 + y_2 = 1 \quad (6.28)$$

and show that its solution is:

$$y_1^* = \frac{\sigma_2^2 - \rho_{12}\sigma_1\sigma_2}{\sigma_1^2 + \sigma_2^2 - 2\rho_{12}\sigma_1\sigma_2}, \quad y_2^* = \frac{\sigma_1^2 - \rho_{12}\sigma_1\sigma_2}{\sigma_1^2 + \sigma_2^2 - 2\rho_{12}\sigma_1\sigma_2} \quad (6.29)$$

Subsequently, consider an investment in three companies, A, B, and C. A forecast for each of these companies is given and summarized by a mean-variance return as well as a correlation between these companies holding for a period during which you are to construct a portfolio. For that same period, the risk-free rate is 7 percent. The data are given in the following with their correlation matrix.

Company	Mean Rate of Return	Standard Deviation
A	12%	6%
B	9%	4%
C	18%	12%

Find the minimum variance portfolio subject to a required rate of return equal to the risk-free rate.

Graph the value of a minimum variance portfolio when the risk-free rate increases from 5 to 18 percent. (*Note:* This problem can be solved in Excel program.)

In practice, investors have found that multiple sources of risk seem to matter, some of these risks accounting for risks ignored in the CAPM (see Chapters 3 and 5), such as credit risk, macroeconomic risk, informational asymmetries, and so forth. This led to a generalization of sorts of the CAPM, which consists in assuming that there may be more than one factor at play in influencing the stock returns. For example, in addition to the factor state, the gross domestic product (GDP), expected inflation, interest rate movements, and the like, may be important as well.

In this case, to capture these effects the asset pricing theory (APT) approach suggests that the following relationship may be determined:

$$\tilde{k} = \hat{k} + \beta_{GDP}(GDP) + \beta_{IR}(IR) + \varepsilon_k \quad (6.30)$$

where β_{GDP} is a beta factor associated to the factor GDP sensitivity. Similarly, β_{IR} expresses the returns' sensitivity to the interest rates factor, while ε_i represents stock-specific random events. The expected returns of the stock can then be represented as a multiple-factor equation that is regressed on the factors' premiums, or:

$$\hat{k} - R_f = \beta_{GDP}(RP_{GDP}) + \beta_{IR}(RP_{IR}) \tag{6.31}$$

with RP_k denoting the risk premium associated to the risk factor k. A number of examples can then be considered, highlighting the generality of the APT approach. For example, if we consider a well-diversified portfolio, then:

$$R_P = E(R_P) + \beta_P(F) + \varepsilon_P \tag{6.32}$$

where F is the factor and $\varepsilon_P \to 0$ (since it is fully diversified). As a result, we obtain a model similar to the CAPM since in this case:

$$E(R_P) - R_f = \beta_P(RP_F) \tag{6.33}$$

By the same token, consider a market-indexed portfolio. In other words:

$$E(\tilde{R}_M) - R_f = \beta_P E(RP_M) = \beta_P \left(E(\tilde{R}_M) - R_f \right)$$

thus, as expected,

$$\beta_M = 1 \tag{6.34}$$

The APT approach is important in practice. It is essential, however, that the important factors be determined and selected to be statistically orthogonal (to assure that statistical results are meaningful). Further, the number of factors ought to be small to avoid covariations.

In practice, investors will want alphas, a riskless return, because money is made for sure, at no risk. What does it mean to chase alphas? This means that markets are incomplete and therefore some investors are managing to make money even though there is risk. When alphas are hard to come by, what do we look for? We look for large betas. But then this may be indicative of too much risk. As a result, if investors want more income and there are too many funds chasing alphas, in the end, markets will be more efficient and thereby added income will happen only if there is more risk. Some firms are therefore switching from open-end to closed-end funds in pursuing larger incomes.

CONDITIONAL KERNEL PRICING AND THE PRICE OF INFRASTRUCTURE INVESTMENTS

The kernel pricing method can be applied in various ways as we saw in Chapter 5. In this section, such an approach is extended to a specific real infrastructure investment problem (for an approach to a real inventory problem, see the next problem and Tapiero [2008]). These problems are faced with both price and demand uncertainty and consist in selecting an infrastructure investment both to meet future needs and at the same time assure that such an investment has sustainable benefits. To do so, both demand and the price (whether explicit or implicit) that users pay for such an infrastructure are assumed to be unknown at the time the investment is made.

Unlike previous approaches to such a problem, we consider here a financial approach based on a personal future (forecast) price distribution $f^P(\pi)$. The conditional mean demand and the variance of the demand for such an infrastructure are assumed also, given by $E(D|\pi) = \mu(\pi)$ and $\text{var}(D|\pi) = \sigma^2(\pi)$ with a probability distribution of

$$f^P_{D|\pi}(D|\pi)$$

For example, if an air route is launched between two regions (say A and B), the demand estimate in the mean (and its variability) is a function of the price of transport between these routes. Let the net future revenues resulting from the infrastructure investment Q be

$$R = (1 - \tau)\, Min(D,\, Q)\, \pi$$

where τ is a tax rate paid to the authority investing $C(Q)$ in such an infrastructure. Assuming that that there is a Q distribution for such tax returns, we have then a return at time $t > 0$ given by:

$$C_0(R_t) = e^{-R_f t} E^Q\left(\tilde{R}_t\right), \quad \tilde{R}_t = \tau\pi\, Min\left(\tilde{D}_t(\pi),\, Q\right) \tag{6.35}$$

Summing these returns over n periods (the useful life of the infrastructure), we have then:

$$C(Q) = \sum_j^n C_0(R_j) = e^{-R_f t} \sum_j^n E^Q(\tilde{R}_t), \quad \tilde{R}_j = \tau\pi_j\, Min\left(\tilde{D}_j(\pi_j),\, Q\right), \, j = 1, 2 \ldots n \tag{6.36}$$

For simplicity, say that the probability is mean conditional on price, or

$$f_{D|\pi}(D_j) = \frac{1}{\mu_j(\pi_j)} \exp\left(-\frac{D_j}{\mu_j(\pi_j)}\right), \, 0 \le D_j < \infty \tag{6.37}$$

Then,

$$\tilde{R}_j = \tau\pi_j\, Min\left(\tilde{D}_j(\pi_j),\, Q\right) = \begin{cases} \tau\pi_j \tilde{D}_j(\pi_j) & \text{if } \tilde{D}_j(\pi_j) \le Q_j \\ \tau\pi_j Q_j & \text{if } \tilde{D}_j(\pi_j) \ge Q_j \end{cases} \tag{6.38}$$

and

$$C(Q) = \sum_j^n C_0(R_j) = e^{-R_f t} \sum_j^n \tau \int_0^\infty \int_0^{Q_j} \pi_j \tilde{D}_j(\pi_j) f_{D|\pi}^P(\tilde{D}_j) f^Q(\pi_j) d\pi_j d\tilde{D}_j$$

$$+ e^{-R_f t} \sum_j^n \tau Q_j \left[\int_0^\infty \pi_j \int_0^{Q_j} f_{D|\pi}^P(\tilde{D}_j) d\tilde{D}_j \right] f^Q(\pi_j) d\pi_j \qquad (6.39)$$

Or:

$$C(Q) = \sum_j^n C_0(R_j)$$

$$= e^{-R_f t} \sum_j^n \tau \int_0^\infty \frac{\pi_j}{\mu_j(\pi_j)} \left[\int_0^{Q_j} \tilde{D}_j(\pi_j) \exp\left(-\frac{D_j}{\mu_j(\pi_j)}\right) d\tilde{D}_j \right] f^Q(\pi_j) d\pi_j$$

$$+ e^{-R_f t} \sum_j^n \tau Q_j \left[\int_0^\infty \frac{\pi_j}{\mu_j(\pi_j)} \int_0^{Q_j} \exp\left(-\frac{D_j}{\mu_j(\pi_j)}\right) d\tilde{D}_j \right] f^Q(\pi_j) d\pi_j \quad (6.40)$$

Using the integral equations:

$$\int_0^Q D \exp\left(-\frac{D}{\mu}\right) dD = \mu^2 \left(1 - e^{-Q/\mu}(1 + Q/\mu)\right);$$

$$\int_0^Q e^{-D/\mu(\pi)} dD = \mu(\pi) \left(1 - e^{-Q/\mu(\pi)}\right) \qquad (6.41)$$

we obtain, instead of equation (6.39):

$$C(Q) = \sum_j^n C_0(R_j)$$

$$= e^{-R_f t} \sum_j^n \tau \int_0^\infty \left[\pi_j \mu_j(\pi_j) \left(1 - e^{-Q_j/\mu_j(\pi_j)} \left(1 + \frac{Q_j}{\mu_j(\pi_j)}\right)\right) \right] f^Q(\pi_j) d\pi_j$$

$$+ e^{-R_f t} \sum_j^n \tau Q_j \left[\int_0^\infty \pi_j \left(1 - e^{-Q_j/\mu_j(\pi_j)}\right) \right] f^Q(\pi_j) d\pi_j \qquad (6.42)$$

Say that the mean demand is large compared to the capacity Q, then a first-order Taylor series approximation:

$$e^{-Q_j/\mu_j(\pi_j)} \approx 1 - Q_j/\mu_j(\pi_j)$$

leads to:

$$C(Q) = \sum_j^n C_0(R_j) = e^{-R_f t} \sum_j^n \tau(Q_j) \int_0^\infty \pi_j f^Q(\pi_j) d\pi_j$$

$$+ e^{-R_f t} \sum_j^n \tau Q_j^2 \left[\int_0^\infty \frac{\pi_j}{\mu_j(\pi_j)} \right] f^Q(\pi_j) d\pi_j \qquad (6.43)$$

and therefore to:

$$C(Q) = \tau \sum_j^n Q_j \pi_{j,0} \left(1 + \frac{Q_j}{\mu_j(\pi_{j,0})} \right) = \tau \sum_j^n Q_j \pi_{j,0}$$

$$\text{with } \pi_{j,0} = e^{-R_f t} \int_0^\infty \pi_j f^Q(\pi_j) d\pi_j \qquad (6.44)$$

Of course, since an infrastructure can be used by many persons and firms, the benefits to the investor in infrastructure can be substantial (albeit their costs can be large as well).

CONDITIONAL KERNEL PRICING AND THE PRICING OF INVENTORIES

Inventory problems are generally beset by both price and demand uncertainty. They consist in selecting an inventory order policy that minimizes expected inventory cost. To do so, we need both demand and price forecasts. Here, a financial approach is considered (for further study see, Tapiero [2008]). Say that $f^P(\pi)$ is a personal forecast probability distribution of prices while the conditional probability distribution of the demand for a product on the price is

$$f^P_{D|\pi}(D|\pi)$$

When markets are complete and the price distribution can be calculated, we let the price probability distribution be $f^Q(\pi)$. In this case, the private and the market price joint demand—price distributions are:

$$f^P(D, \pi) = f^P_{D|\pi}(D|\pi) f^P(\pi)$$

and

$$f^Q(D, \pi) = f_{D|\pi}^P(D|\pi) f^Q(\pi) \tag{6.45}$$

In some cases, only the marginal demands and prices are assumed known and therefore the joint distribution can be calculated only by approximation or by combining it with subjective and empirical analysis. Practically, the conditional dependence of demand in prices may be only in the mean and/or in its moments. Namely, the probability distribution of demand $f_{D|\pi}(D|\pi)$ depends only on the mean and variance, $E(D|\pi) = \mu(\pi)$ and $\text{var}(D|\pi) = \sigma^2(\pi)$. For example, if the demand has an exponential distribution with its mean a function of the price, we have then $f_{D|\pi}^P(D|\pi)$ as given in equation (6.37).

Next assume that the returns from inventory management are given by the quantity sold at the market price and at the end of the period, while the costs include inventory costs (of either excess order or under ordering) accounted for at the end of the period and the initial purchase costs. These are summarized by the following equation (where the risk-free rate is assumed null):

$$\Lambda(D, \pi|Q, \pi_0) = \pi Min(Q, D) - q Max(Q - D, 0) - h Max(D - Q, 0) \tag{6.46}$$

where the holding cost per unit is q and the shortage cost per unit is h. These costs imply a risk attitude and therefore are a special utility function $u(.)$. First note that the conditional payoff (including inventory costs) is:

$$U(\pi|Q, \pi_0) = E_D \Lambda(D, \pi|Q, \pi_0) = \int_0^\infty (\Lambda(D, \pi|Q, \pi_0)) f_{D|\pi}^P(D) dD$$

$$= \pi \int_0^Q D f_{D|\pi}^P(D) dD - q \int_0^Q (Q - D) f_{D|\pi}^P(D) dD$$

$$- h \int_Q^\infty (x - Q) f_{D|\pi}^P(D) dD \tag{6.47}$$

For the exponential demand distribution, this expression can be computed analytically. It is a simple exercise to show that in this case:

$$U(\pi|Q, \pi_0) = \mu(\pi)(\pi + q)\left[1 - e^{-Q/\mu(\pi)}\right] - qQ - (h + q)\mu(\pi) e^{-Q/\mu(\pi)} \tag{6.48}$$

which we rewrite for convenience as follows:

$$U(\pi|Q, \pi_0) = \mu(\pi)(\pi + q) - \mu(\pi)(\pi + 2q + h) e^{-Q/\mu(\pi)} - qQ \tag{6.49}$$

As a result, assuming that the an inventory manager maximizes the expected costs, initially, we have:

$$\underset{Q \geq 0}{Min}\, U(\pi|Q, \pi_0) \text{ leading to: } Q = \mu(\pi) \ln \frac{(\pi + 2q + h)}{q} \tag{6.50}$$

And therefore, the minimum cost of the inventory policy is:

$$U^*(\pi \mid Q, \pi_0) =$$

$$\mu(\pi)\left((\pi + q) - (\pi + 2q + h)\exp\left(-\ln\frac{(\pi + 2q + h)}{q}\right) - q\ln\frac{(\pi + 2q + h)}{q}\right)$$

$$(6.51)$$

while the current price (at a risk-free rate equal to zero) is $E^Q U^*(\pi \mid Q, \pi_0)$, which requires the risk-neutral probability distribution of prices.

The pricing of options on a commodities market order provides an opportunity to assess an implied risk-neutral distribution (see Chapter 11) that would allow the calculation of the inventory price given the preceding equation (in this case, the inventory problem pertains to ordering traded commodities). Related problems (see for example, Ritchken and Tapiero [1986] and www.charlestapiero.com) point out further that the costs of an inventory policy can be reduced if option orders (call and puts) are integrated in the inventory policy. In other words, if the inventory policy consists of a portfolio of a physical order quantity Q combined with a number of n of call and m puts with current prices (π_0, C_0, P_0), then meeting future demands can be mitigated by adding such contracts to the tools used by inventory managers.

AGENCY AND UTILITY

Agency problems recur where there are two parties: a principal and an agent (PA). For example, while stockholders (through their representatives on the board of directors and their voting shares) may be the principals of a corporation, the CEO is an *agent*, paid to provide returns to the principals. Similar situations arise between the owner of a hedge fund and its traders, between financiers and hedge fund managers, and so on. The PA problem may be defined by how to motivate and provide incentives for the agent to invest sufficient efforts to earn returns for the principal without giving away the whole house (i.e., assuming excessive risks). Risk arises because the actions taken by the agent may be observed only imperfectly, since performance observed by the principal is the outcome of the agent actions (known only to the agent), and therefore the information observed is perturbed by some randomness—known or unknown to the principal.

Formally, the principal agent problem consists then in determining the rules for sharing the outcomes obtained through such an organization based on the asymmetry of information and power that coexist in such relationships. Such information asymmetry leads to a moral hazard risk. Such problems are pervasive throughout financial industries—for example, designing appropriate incentive compensation, regulating financial services through capital adequacy requirements (CAR), and so forth. The expected utility framework is applied to provide a first-order approach to this problem and obtain a better understanding of the intricacies of the principal-agent (PA) problem. Practically, the PA problem is a difficult one, involving both information and power asymmetries and producing both financial and strategic risks arising from the preferences—their intentionality, the risk attitudes, and the resulting games that such associations or relationships entail.

For simplicity, consider an example based on the *first-order approach*. For convenience, let $\tilde{x}$ be a random variable, which represents the gross return obtained by a hedge fund manager—in this case presumed to be the principal with a trader acting as an agent. The trader's returns are assumed to be a function of some variable a, expressing the trader's effort, which is not observed by the principal. In other words, the returns distribution is some density function $f(\tilde{x}, a)$, where a is statistically independent of the returns.

Next assume a sharing rule given by $y(\tilde{x}, a)$. The principal-agent problem consists in determining the amount transferred to the agent by the principal in order to compensate him for the efforts he performs on behalf of the principal (the hedge fund manager). To do so, assume that the agent utility is separable and given by:

$$V(y, a) = v(y) - w(a); v' > 0, v'' \leq 0, w' > 0, w'' > 0 \tag{6.52}$$

Further, in order to assure the agent's participation, it is necessary to provide at least an expected utility:

$$EV(y, a) \geq 0 \text{ or } Ev(y) \geq w(a) \tag{6.53}$$

In this case, the utility of the principal is

$$u(\tilde{x} - y), u' > 0, u'' \leq 0$$

EXAMPLE: A LINEAR RISK-SHARING RULE

The problems we formulate depend then on the information distribution between the principal and the agent. Again for simplicity, assume that the agent's effort a is observable by the principal (in other words, focusing on the power effects of the principal over the agent). In this case, the problem of the principal is formulated by optimizing both a and, of course, the transfer. That is,

$$\begin{array}{l} \underset{a, y(.)}{Max} \, Eu(\tilde{x} - y(\tilde{x})) \\ \text{Subject to:} \\ Ev(y(\tilde{x}) - w(a)) \geq 0 \end{array} \tag{6.54}$$

By applying the conditions for optimality, the optimal solution is found to be:

$$\frac{u'(\tilde{x} - y(\tilde{x}))}{v'(y(\tilde{x}))} = \lambda \tag{6.55}$$

This yields a sharing-rule based on the agent and the principal marginal utility functions, a necessary condition for Pareto optimal risk sharing. A differentiation of the sharing rule indicates that:

$$\frac{dy}{dx} = \frac{u''/u'}{u''/u' + v''/v'} \quad \text{or} \quad \frac{dy}{dx} = \frac{A_u}{A_u + A_v} \tag{6.56}$$

For example, if we assume exponential utility functions with constant risk aversion indexes A_u and A_v, then risk sharing is defined by a linear sharing rule:

$$y = \frac{A_u}{A_u + A_v} x + K \tag{6.57}$$

INFORMATION ASYMMETRY: MORAL HAZARD AND ADVERSE SELECTION

Information asymmetry has special importance, providing a trading advantage to traders who have more, more timely, and better information. Insider trading, managers trading in their company shares, and so forth are of course particularly acute issues with which regulators have been concerned. By the same token, counterparty risk is often extremely sensitive to such asymmetry. Such situations result in markets being incomplete since the basic assumptions regarding fair competition are violated.

In general, the presumption that information is commonly shared is also often violated. Some information may be truthful, some may not be. Truth in lending for example, is an important legislation passed to protect consumers, which is, in most cases, difficult to enforce. Courts are filled with litigation on claims and counterclaims, leading to a battle of experts on what and where truth may lie. Environmental litigation has often led to a battle of PhDs expounding alternative and partial pearls of knowledge. In addition, positive, negative, informative, partial, asymmetric, and other types of information have different effects on both decision makers and markets. For example, firms and funds are extremely sensitive to negative information regarding their stock, their products, as well as their services. Pharmaceutical firms may be bankrupted upon adverse publicity, whether true or not, regarding one of their products. For example, the Food and Drug Administration (FDA) warning about the content of benzene in Perrier's sparkling water has more than tainted the company's image, its bottom-line profits, and, at a certain time, its future prospects.

Information asymmetry may lead to parties' opportunistic behavior such as cheating. For example, some consumer journals may receive money in various forms (mostly advertising dollars) not to publish certain articles and thereby manage information in a way that does not benefit the public. For this reason, regulatory authorities are needed in certain areas. A used car salesman may be tempted to sell a car with defects unknown to the prospective buyer. In some countries, importers are not required to inform clients of the origin and the quality (state) of a product and of parts used in the product sold. As a result, a product claimed to be new by the seller may not be really new.

These questions arise on Wall Street in many ways. Should analysts buy shares of companies they cover? Are investors duped by raters catering to banks' claims of quality for certain financial products when in fact they are not? And so on.

Following the financial meltdown of 2008–2009 the extraordinary profits made consistently by banks (and in particular Goldman Sachs) have raised questions regarding the informational advantage banks have and how they use it to profit (often at the expense of their clients). In a comprehensive article regarding "Tenacious G" (Goldman Sachs), in *New York* magazine (August 3, 2009), numerous issues are raised regarding the firm's incredible financial performance and its persistence, pointing to potential information asymmetries and conflicts of interest. For example, because it deals both as a trading house for huge institutional investors and as a fee-based adviser to the companies being traded, the firm has become a huge repository for information, with a view into what everyone is doing. So if a big investor wants to buy, say, the energy markets, Goldman Sachs, by virtue of its knowledge of what other big investors are trading and what its corporate energy clients are doing (on Goldman's own advice), can offer a highly accurate view of what's likely to happen with the energy market. It can also do very well on its own energy trades—in fact, before the market crashed the firm made vast profits on proprietary trading by bets made on its own balance sheets.

The questions is then how legal such trades should be. Further, should access to proprietary information be allowed to provide as well advantage in proprietary trading? Are such trades *insider trading*, whether legal or not? While claims were made by Goldman Sachs that its trading and advisory functions are separate, some clients have indicated that in some cases, Goldman trades were against their own interests. Goldman's profiting from this ethical gray area was exemplified by the real estate market and the subprime mortgage collapse: Goldman Sachs sold subprime mortgage investments to its clients for years, but then in 2006 began trading against subprime on its own balance sheet without informing its clients, a hedge that ultimately let it profit when the real estate market cratered.

Similar information asymmetries issues due to high-frequency trading software have come to the public attention and were raised in numerous journals. Such software takes information—primarily real-time share prices—and uses proprietary algorithms to predict the next twitch in the stock market. Using such software, a bank or a hedge fund can buy and sell stocks in fractions of seconds and make money on every movement of the stock price. While the use of such algorithms (developed by quant financial engineers) is not illegal, the growth of large databases, some proprietary and some publicly available, provide an immense advantage to banks at the expense of other investors. These information problems are the subject of extensive study, both for practical and theoretical reasons. Their risk implications are summarized by two sources of risk: *adverse selection* and *moral hazard*.

ADVERSE SELECTION

Adverse selection occurs when securities of different qualities are uniformly priced. Risk is assumed because information may be hidden. For example, buying a securitized asset may hide risks or obligations riskier than presumed by the buyer. Banks and financial institutions may themselves be unaware of the risks they are selling and trading in, or perhaps just content to act as irresponsible intermediaries. Akerlof's seminal paper (1970) demonstrated that the average investments in profitable enterprises (or not) might still be a function of their price, but for various investors, they may not be priced equally. Similarly, in the 1980s, persons who discovered that they had AIDS were very quick in taking out very large life insurance policies (before insurance firms knew what it really entailed and therefore were at first less informed than the insured). Buying bonds or stocks of various qualities (but of equal ratings) is sometimes difficult to discern for an individual investor. For this reason, rating agencies tracking and following firms have an important role to play, compensating the problems of information asymmetry and making markets more efficient. This role is not always properly followed, as demonstrated by evidence emerging from the Enron debacle where changing accounting practices had in fact hidden information from the public. For these reasons, the price of a security can often be skewed by such information asymmetry and by the many firms and mechanisms that portend to compensate such an informational state.

Information asymmetry may thus explain the desires of consumers to buy service warranties or product warranties to protect themselves against failures, or to favor firms who possess service organizations (in particular when the products are complex or involve some up-to-date technologies). The potential for adverse selection may also be used to protect national markets. Antidumping laws, nontariff trade barriers, and national standards and approvals of various sorts are some of the means used to manage problems of adverse selection on the one hand and manage market entries to maintain a competitive advantage on the other. Finance and insurance abound with applications and examples where asymmetry induces an uncertainty that has nothing to do with what nature does but with what people do.

Problems of adverse selection can sometimes be overcome by compulsory insurance regulation requiring all homeowners to insure their homes or requiring everyone to take out medical insurance, for example. Some employers insure all their employees as one package to avoid adverse selection problems. If everyone is insured, high-risk individuals will be better off (since they will be insured at a lower premium than justified by the risks they carry) and would in fact be free-riders. Whether low-risk individuals are better off under this scheme depends on how risk averse they are as the insurance they are offered is not actuarially fair.

THE MORAL HAZARD PROBLEM

Exchange entails risks that depend on the behavior and the information of the parties; these risks are called *moral hazard*. For example, the cost of insurance depends on the behavior of drivers. Similarly, the cost of warranties depends on both the information each has regarding the product to be bought and consumed and the ex post behavior of each of the parties. Such behaviors, however, cannot always be observed directly. As a result, a price cannot accurately be based on the behavior, although prices and costs do depend on such behavior. In this case, equilibrium cannot always be the best and rational optimum and, as a result, some form of controls (interventions, regulation, etc.) may be required to reach a best solution. For example, should car insurance be obligatory? How do purchasers react after buying insurance? How do markets behave when there is moral hazard and how can it be compensated?

Imperfect monitoring of fund managers, for example, can lead to moral hazard because a fund manager cannot be observed, and therefore he may use this fact to its advantage—and not deliver the right level of performance. Of course, if we contract the delivery of a given level of returns and if the fund manager knowingly does not maintain the terms of the contract, he would be cheating. We can deal with such problems with various sorts of controls combined with incentive contracts to create an incentive not to cheat or lie and to perform in the interest of the investor. If a fund manager were to cheat or lie, and if he were detected, he would then be penalized accordingly (following the terms agreed on in the contract). For some, transparency (i.e., sharing information) is essential to provide a signal that they operate with the best of intentions. For example, some restaurants might open their kitchen to their patrons to convey a message of truthfulness insofar as cleanliness is concerned; a trader will make all its transactions known; a supplier will let the buyer visit the manufacturing facilities as well as reveal procedures relating to quality, machining controls, and the production process in general; a fund manager will provide regulators truthful reports regarding the fund's state and strategy, and so on.

For these reasons, moral hazard pervades some of the most excruciating problems of finance. The problem of deposit insurance and the too-big-to-fail syndrome encourages excessive risk taking. As a result of implicit governmental guarantee, banks enjoy a lower cost of capital, which leads to the consistent underpricing of credit. Swings in economic cycles are thus accentuated. The Asian crisis of 1998 is a case in point. The extent of its moral hazard is difficult to measure but with each bailout by governments and the International Monetary Fund (IMF), the trend for excessive risk taking is reinforced. At a more mundane level, moral hazard is pervasive. For example:

- An overinsured driver may drive recklessly. Thus, while the insured motorist is protected against any accident, this may induce him to behave in a nonrational manner and cause accidents that are costly to society.
- In 1998, the NYSE at last, belatedly (since the practice was acknowledged to have been going on from 1992), investigated charges against floor brokers for *front-running* or *flipping*. This is a practice in which the brokers used information obtained on the floor to trade and earn profits on their own behalf. One group of brokers was charged with making $11 million.
- The removal of responsibility from employees may induce a moral hazard. It is for this reason that incentives, performance indexation, and accountability are important.

Throughout these examples, there are negative inducements to good performances. To control or reduce these risks, it is necessary to proceed in a number of manners. Today's concern for firms' organizational design, the management of traders, and their compensation packages is a reflection of the need to construct relationships that do not induce counterproductive acts. Some of the steps that can be followed include:

- Detecting signals of various forms and origins to reveal agents' behaviors, rationality, and performances. A greater understanding of agents' behavior can lead to a better design of the workplace and to appropriate inducements of all parties involved in the firm's business.
- Managing and controlling the relationship between business partners, employees, and workers. This means that no relationship can be taken for granted. Earlier, we saw that information asymmetry can lead to opportunistic behavior such as cheating, lying, and being counterproductive, just because there may be an advantage to doing so without having to sustain the consequences of such behavior.
- Developing an environment that is cooperative, honest, and open. This leads to a frank exchange of information and optimal performances.

All these actions are important. It is therefore not surprising that many of the concerns of managers deal with people, communication, simplification, and the transparency of everything firms do.

SIGNALING AND SCREENING

In conditions of information asymmetry, one of the parties may have an incentive to reveal some of the information it has. The seller of an outstanding concept for a start-up to invest in will certainly have an interest in making his concept transparent to the potential venture capitalist (VC) investor. He may do so in a number of ways, such as pricing it high and therefore conveying the message to the potential VC that it is necessarily (at that price) a dream concept that will realize an extraordinary profit in an initial public offering (IPO)—but then, the concept seller may also be cheating! The seller may also spend heavily on advertising the concept, claiming that it is an outstanding one with special technology that it is hard to verify—but then the seller may also be lying! Claiming that a start-up concept is just "great" may be insufficient. Not all VCs are gullible. They require and look for signals that reveal the true potential of a concept and its potential for making large profits.

Pricing, warranties, and advertising are some of the means used by well-established firms selling a product to send signals. For example, the seller of a lemon with a warranty will eventually lose money. Similarly, a firm that wants to limit the entry of new competitors may signal that its costs are very low, such that if others decide to enter, they are likely to lose money in a price battle. Advertising heavily may be recuperated only through repeat purchase and, therefore, overadvertising may be used as a signal that the overadvertised products are of good quality. For start-ups, the game is quite different. Venture capitalists look for the signals leading to potential success, such as good management, proven results, patentable ideas, and a huge potential, combined with hefty growth rate in sales. Still, these are only signals, and more sophisticated investors actually get involved in the start-ups they invest in to reduce further the risks of surprise.

Uninformed parties, however, have an incentive to look for and obtain information. For example, shopping and comparing, searching for a job, and so forth, are instances of information seeking by uninformed parties. Such activities are called *screening*. A life insurer requires a medical record history; a driver who has a poor accident record is likely to pay a greater premium (if he can obtain insurance at all). If characteristics of customers are unobservable, firms can use *self-selection* constraints as an aid in screening to reveal private information. For example, consider the phenomenon of rising wage profiles where workers get paid an increasing wage over their careers. An explanation may be that firms are interested in hiring workers who will stay for a long time. Especially if workers get training or experience, which is valuable elsewhere, this is a valid concern. The firms will then pay workers below the market level initially so that only loyal workers will self-select to work for the firm.

The classic example of signaling was first analyzed by Spence (1974), who points out that high-productivity individuals try to differentiate themselves from low-productivity ones by the amount of education they acquire. In other words, only the most productive workers invest in education. This is the case because the signaling cost to the productive workers is lower than that to low-productivity workers. Therefore firms can differentiate between these two types of workers due to their making different choices.

Uninformed parties can screen by offering a menu of choices or possible contracts to prospective (informed) trading partners who self-select one of these offerings. Such screening was pointed out in insurance economics, for example, showing that, if the insurer offers a menu of insurance policies with different premiums and amounts of coverage, the high-risk clients self-select into a policy with high coverage. This can lead to insurance firm portfolios with bad risk crowding out the good ones. Insurance companies that are aware of these problems create risk groups and demand higher premiums from members in the bad-risk portfolio as well as introducing a number of clauses that require sharing responsibility for payments in case claims are made.

SUMMARY

Utility theory offers a theoretical framework providing a greater understanding of risk and financial decision making. Applications include financial pricing, risk management, and financial theory. Applications require, however, information regarding the risk attitude expressing the decision maker's risk preferences and the probability distribution of the uncertain events underlying the problem at hand. In some cases, such information is not available. For this reason, such an approach to financial decision making is not always deemed practical. Nonetheless, lacking a better alternative, it is profusely used. The emergence of behavioral finance in financial practice is a testament to the resilience—albeit still imperfect—of the subjective approach to finance.

TEST YOURSELF

6.1 Consider an insured, an insurer, and a reinsurer, each faced with the following returns:

$$\text{Insured:} \quad R_i(\tilde{x}\,|a\,,q) = \begin{cases} \tilde{x} & \tilde{x} \le a \\ a + (1-q)(\tilde{x}-a) & \tilde{x} \ge a \end{cases}$$

$$\text{Insurer:} \quad R_I(\tilde{x}\,|a,b,q) = \begin{cases} 0 & \tilde{x} \le a \\ q(\tilde{x}-a) & a < \tilde{x} \le b \\ q(b-a) & \tilde{x} > b \end{cases}$$

$$\text{Reinsurer:} \quad R_r(\tilde{x}\,|ab,q) = \begin{cases} 0 & \tilde{x} \le b \\ q(\tilde{x}-b-a) & \tilde{x} \ge b \end{cases}$$

What is the expected utility of each and what each one would optimize?

6.2 What is the relationship between individual preferences and discounting?

6.3 Discuss the following pricing concepts:
- Price as an equilibrium of demand and supply.
- Price as a relative measurement, and relative to what? Would that be equivalent to insurance taken to remove uncertainty from uncertain cash flows of future dividends?

- Price as a means of exchange (contracted or not). The market price expresses the willingness of an individual to pay for a product, a service, or a security.

6.4 What are the effects of asset (statistical) dependency on the risk of a portfolio?

6.5 What is diversification and when and why is it important in managing a portfolio risk?

6.6 Two firms get together to share the risk of developing a new product. The development cost is $50 million. The potential payoff in terms of current value (albeit uncertain) is double that amount. How should the firms split the profits in order for each share's to be a function of the amount each invested?

6.7 What is the difference between a risk exchange between two firms (or investors) and their trading in financial markets?

6.8 Consider an insured, an insurer, and a reinsurer. How do they share risk? What ought to be the premium paid and received by each? How does securitization contribute to a greater efficiency of risk allocation?

6.9 A portfolio consists of an investment in two securities and a risk-free bond. The portfolio's current price is $1,000,000. The rates of return for the stocks are random and given by 8 and 12 percent with variances equal to 8 and 12 percent. The correlation between these stocks is $\rho_{12} = 0.3$. The bond has a rate of return of 5 percent. How much would you invest in each if you have an exponential utility function? When can you have a perfect portfolio diversification? If the spot, risk-free rate changes by ΔR_f, by how much would your allocation change?

6.10 Consider a portfolio with a quantile risk (value at risk) constraint: Some portfolio problems are designed to meet a quantile (or value at risk) risk regulation constraint with which the investor is concerned. Assume a portfolio consists of two assets with $\tilde{\pi}(y_1, y_2) = \tilde{r}_1 y_1 + \tilde{r}_2 y_2$ where

$$E\tilde{r}_1 = \mu_1, \ E\tilde{r}_2 = \mu_2, \ \text{var}\,\tilde{r}_1 = \sigma_1^2, \ E\tilde{r}_2 = \sigma_2^2, \ \text{cov}(\tilde{r}_1, \tilde{r}_2) = \rho\sigma_1\sigma_2$$

Specify the risk constraint:

$$P\{\tilde{\pi}(y_1, y_2) \leq -VaR\} \leq \xi$$

where $-VaR$ is the amount of money set aside to meet potential losses in the portfolio, which is constrained to a quantile risk ξ. What is the optimal portfolio?

6.11 Consider again the portfolio $\tilde{\pi}(y_1, y_2) = \tilde{r}_1 y_1 + \tilde{r}_2 y_2$ from question 6.10, and let $\Pi(y_1, y_2) = R_1 y_1 + R_2 y_2$ be the returns realized (R_1, R_2) from an asset allocation (y_1, y_2). A *regret* expresses the disparity between the realization of returns and some expected or planned expected returns. It will be convenient for this example to assume that regret is measured relative to a certain equivalent investment that yields the risk-free rate. In this case, if either or both $(R_1 \leq R_f, R_2 \leq R_f)$, there will be a regret, while if $(R_1 > R_f, R_2 > R_f)$ there will be an *elation*. These assumptions can then lead to a portfolio design problem, which we can formulate as follows:

$$\alpha y_1 \left(R_1 - R_f\right)^+ + \alpha y_2 \left(R_2 - R_f\right)^+ - \beta y_1 \left(R_f - R_1\right)^+ - \beta y_2 \left(R_f - R_2\right)^+, \alpha < \beta$$

How does such a portfolio compare to the Markowitz portfolio selection problem? In particular, assume that returns are random, defined by the following states:

$$\tilde{r}_1 = \{r_{11}, r_{12}, r_{13}\}, \tilde{r}_2 = \{r_{21}, r_{22}\}$$

Reduce the portfolio selection problem to the solution of a linear program.

6.12 Discuss the utility effects of the following and alternative approaches to risk management:

- Diversification (perhaps powerful but can be misleading, in particular in periods of high volatility and therefore relative unrobustness).
- Use of derivative products (which transfer risk and provide protection for downside risk and are therefore preventive in some specific sense).
- Value at risk (VaR) (widely used—the Basel Committee, J.P. Morgan, etc.— but with inherent issues to contend with rendering it at times overly conservative).
- Using alternative risk-transfer tools (such as insurance, financial engineering, etc.).

REFERENCES

Akerlof, G. 1970. The market for lemons: Quality uncertainty and the market mechanism. *Quarterly Journal of Economics* 84:488–500.

Bell, D. E. 1982. Regret in decision making under uncertainty. *Operations Research* 30:961–981.

———. 1985. Disappointment in decision making under uncertainty. *Operation Research* 33:1–27.

———. 1995. Risk, return and utility. *Management Science* 41:23–30.

Chew, Soo H., and Larry G. Epstein. 1989. The structure of preferences and attitudes towards the timing of the resolution of uncertainty. *International Economic Review* 30:103–117.

Eeckhoudt, L., and M. Kimball. 1991. Background risk prudence and the demand for insurance. In *Contributions to Insurance Economics*, ed. G. Dionne. Boston: Kluwer Academic Press.

Ellsberg, D. 1961. Risk, ambiguity and the Savage axioms. *Quarterly Journal of Economics*, November:643–669.

Epstein, Larry G., and Stanley E. Zin. 1989. Substitution, risk aversion and the temporal behavior of consumption and asset returns: A theoretical framework. *Econometrica* 57:937–969.

———. 1991. Substitution, risk aversion and the temporal behavior of consumption and asset returns: An empirical analysis. *Journal of Political Economy* 99:263–286.

Fama, Eugene F. 1992. The cross-section of expected stock returns. *Journal of Finance* 47:427–465.

Fothergill, M., and C. Coke. 2001. Funds of hedge funds: An introduction to multi-manager funds. *Journal of Alternative Investments* (Fall):7–16.

Friedman, M., and Savage, L. J. 1948. The utility analysis of choices involving risk. *Journal of Political Economy*, August.

———. 1952. The expected utility hypothesis and the measurability of utility. *Journal of Political Economy*, December.

Grossman, S., and O. Hart. 1983. An analysis of the principal agent model. *Econometrica* 51:7–46.

Gul, Faruk. 1991. A theory of disappointment aversion. *Econometrica* 59:667–686.

Henker, T. 1998. Naïve diversification for hedge funds. *Journal of Alternative Investments* (Winter):32–42.

Hirschleifer, J. 1970. Where are we in the theory of information. *American Economic Review* 63:31–39.

Hirschleifer, J., and J. G. Riley. 1979. The analysis of uncertainty and information: An expository survey. *Journal of Economic Literature* 17:1375–1421.

Holmstrom, B. 1979. Moral hazard and observability. *Bell Journal of Economics* 10 (1):74–91.

Kahnemann, D., and A. Tversky. 1979. Prospect theory: An analysis of decision under risk. *Econometrica*, March, 263–291.

Kreps, David M., and Evan L. Porteus. 1978. Temporal resolution of uncertainty and dynamic choice theory. *Econometrica* 46:185–200.

———. 1979. Dynamic choice theory and dynamic programming, *Econometrica* 47:91–100.

Laibson, David. 1997. Golden eggs and hyperbolic discounting. *Quarterly Journal of Economics* 112:443–477.

Lintner, John. 1965. The valuation of risk assets and the selection of risky investments in stock portfolios and capital budgets. *Review of Economics and Statistics* 47 (1): 13–37.

Loomes, G., and R. Sugden. 1982. Regret theory: An alternative to rational choice under uncertainty. *Economic Journal* 92:805–824.

———. 1987. Some implications of a more general form of regret theory, *Journal of Economic Theory* 41:270–287.

Machina, M. J. 1982. Expected utility analysis without the independence axiom. *Econometrica*, March, 277–323.

———. 1987. Choice under uncertainty, problems solved and unsolved. *Economic Perspectives*, Summer:121–154.

Markowitz, Harry M. 1959. *Portfolio selection: Efficient diversification of investments*. New York: John Wiley & Sons.

Mossin, Jan. 1969. A note on uncertainty and preferences in a temporal context. *American Economic Review* 59:172–174.

Quiggin, J. 1985. Subjective utility, anticipated utility and the Allais paradox. *Organizational Behavior and Human Decision Processes*, February, 94–101.

Rabin, Matthew. 1998. Psychology and economics. *Journal of Economic Literature* 36: 11–46.

Riley, J. 1975. Competitive signalling, *Journal of Economic Theory* 10:174–186.

Reyniers, D. J., and C. S. Tapiero. 1995a. The delivery and control of quality in supplier producer contracts. *Management Science*, October–November.

———. 1995b. Contract design and the control of quality in a conflictual environment. *European Journal of Operations Research* 82 (2):373–382.

Ritchken, P., and C. S. Tapiero. 1986. Contingent claim contracts and inventory control. *Operation Research* 34:864–870.

Rogerson, W. P. 1985. The first order approach to principal agent problems. *Econometrica* 53:1357–1367.

Sharpe, W. F. 1964. Capital asset prices: A theory of market equilibrium under risk. *Journal of Finance* 19:425–442.

Siegel, Jeremy J., and Richard H. Thaler. 1997. The equity premium puzzle. *Journal of Economic Perspectives* 11:191–200.

Spence, A. M. 1977. Consumer misperceptions, product failure and product liability. *Review of Economic Studies* 44:561–572.

Spence, M. 1974. *Market signaling.* Cambridge, MA: Harvard University Press.

Tapiero, C. S. 2008. Orders and inventory commodities with price and demand uncertainty in complete markets. *International Journal of Production Economics* 115:12–18.

———. 2010. The demand and the market price for insurance. Working paper, Department of Finance and Risk Engineering, New York University Polytechnic Institute.

Tapiero, C. S., and L. Jacque. 1987. The expected cost of ruin and insurance premiums in mutual insurance. *Journal of Risk and Insurance* LIV (3) (September).

Tapiero, C. S., L. Jacque, and Y. Kahane. 1986. Insurance premiums and default risk in mutual insurance. *Scandinavian Actuarial Journal* 1986:82–97.

Tapiero, C. S., and K. Kogan. 2009. Risk-averse order policies with random prices in complete markets and retailers' private information. *European Journal of Operations Research* 196:594–599.

CHAPTER 7

Derivative Finance and Complete Markets

Discrete States

OVERVIEW

The fundamental theory of finance. Spurred by seminal contributions by Kenneth Arrow, Gerard Debreu, Robert Lucas, Paul Samuelson, Robert Merton, Fischer Black, and many other economists and financial theorists has provided applied and theoretical finance an extraordinary boost. Under certain well-defined conditions it has made it possible to price derivatives of various sorts and augmented importantly the observable information regarding market price processes. Unlike the utility approach, based on a personal valuation of real financial states, fundamental theory is utility free and has replaced real states with implied market states priced by bets of buyers and sellers. In the fundamental finance approach, market states (specific and well-defined gains or losses) are priced by the bets made by buyers and sellers, resulting in state prices that define the market equilibrium. When such equilibrium exists fueled by information, market liquidity, and the many economic and noneconomic factors that determine the financial market environment, markets are said to be complete; when it does not exist, markets are said to be incomplete.

When markets are in *equilibrium*, defined by a single price, a current price implies future state prices. Inversely, future states and their prices imply a current price. For example, the current price of an option implies a belief about future option prices (and thereby the underlying asset) and vice versa: Any change in beliefs regarding future asset prices is reflected in a change of the current option's price.

In this sense, market prices can be interpreted, rationalized, and at times used to predict the beliefs of buyers and sellers regarding market prices. The idea of *complete markets* underlies this chapter, which introduces the fundamental approach to asset pricing and its implications with numerous applications treated. The chapter maintains a simple discrete time framework, and elaborates the elements underpinning modern financial theory. Examples and cases are outlined to maintain the relevance of the concepts introduced to financial practice.

THE ARROW-DEBREU FUNDAMENTAL APPROACH
TO ASSET PRICING

When markets are complete, the fundamental financial approach to asset pricing states that the current price is unique, implied by the sum of future states and their corresponding unique state prices. Financial pricing requires then that future states, expressing gains and losses associated to each state, be explicitly defined and that bets be taken on each of these states by an abstract assembly of buyers and sellers trading in these states. In equilibrium, a price results and is defined for each of these states. In this sense, real uncertainty is removed and replaced by an exchange of those abstract buyers and sellers that make up the financial population (including, investors, traders, banks, firms, etc.).

For investors, seeking protection against future states they deem undesirable, there must also be investors or speculators willing to bet on these states that are deemed now desirable. Without such a population of financial parties, there is no market exchange, and therefore there is no market liquidity. The assumptions made and needed for markets to be complete are therefore stringent, as will be discussed later on. It is nonetheless simple, applicable, and revealing of financial markets' price processes. Unlike games of chance (such as roulette), with players gambling against "the bank," in a financial market all players are both gamblers and bank, providing the funds that determine the price of states and playing against all other players who assume the same role. In such a game, the game is fair: No player is discriminated against, and no player dominates the market's information or lacks information (all players are equally informed).

In practice, this is not always the case, and therefore markets are mostly incomplete, although because market incompleteness presumably cannot be sustained, there are forces that contribute to markets returning to a state of completeness. Arbitrage and many diverse and contradictory trading techniques are based on information and beliefs that markets are incomplete, seeking to profit from such market states until they become complete again.

Assume that a security's future states are well defined and that there is a demand and a supply for each of these states. We let these states be defined by gains or losses $S_j(1)$, $j = 1, 2, \ldots, n$ about which bets are taken (i.e., bought by the many financial parties that make up the financial security market). A market with two states is called *binomial*, with three states *trinomial*, and so forth. In equilibrium, each of these states has an associated price, resulting from the exchange between buyers and sellers betting on each of these states. We assume that these prices are π_j, $j = 1, 2, \ldots, n$. The current price of this security is (in the Arrow-Debreu framework) a price implied by these states, explicitly given by their sum:

$$S(0) = \sum_{j=1}^{n} S_j(1)\pi_j \tag{7.1}$$

Since this price can be observed, it is in fact *information* regarding the future states and their prices. In this sense, both current prices and future states and their processes imply each other—the former observable and therefore real, the other not observable and therefore implied.

The fundamental approach to asset pricing is based on four factors:

1. An equilibrium theory about all asset states and their state prices.
2. States are explicitly (or implicitly) well defined.
3. Each state price is defined uniquely.
4. The current (and real) asset price implies the aggregate future states and their price.

A violation of these statements means that markets are incomplete. $Violation: 违反$

The practical and financial engineering implications of this theoretical framework, although justifiably criticized for many reasons, are both widely accepted and used (albeit increasingly criticized). Many problems and questions are raised that may invalidate its application. It is nevertheless robust, based on relatively few assumptions (compared to competing theories). For example: What if the states are not well defined? How can one define the state prices? What if we do not have sufficient information to define the implied states and their prices (i.e., the financial market is not information rich enough)? What if the market has agents that are better informed compared to others, or agents more powerful than others, able to exercise their power to change market prices? What if information is purposely misleading? And so on.

For example, a market may be extremely volatile and unpredictable (technically defined by an implied fat-tails distribution of future states, some of which are unpredictable). In such cases, markets are incomplete. However, the market may appear to be complete if *all* buyers and sellers do not have this information and therefore would not bet on states they are not aware of. Nevertheless, there is, in such a case, mispricing of the asset as its current price does not imply rare and unknown events. Of course, from time to time, as informed investors and traders become aware that there may be such a state, prices will change to reflect this new state that defines now future asset states and their resulting prices. By the same token, if a market assumes many states (due to a large volatility), determining the corresponding state prices will require much supporting information, which might not be available. In such cases, markets tend to be less attractive to investors and traders who abhor such volatility. In this case, too, market liquidity declines, or again, financial pricing theory falters in its quest to define a unique market price.

When an asset's future state is unique, all bets are made about this state, and therefore there is one and only one state price. For example, say that there exists a riskless bond whose current price is $B(0)$. The bond pays for sure, at some specific date, one payment and only one payment known to be $B(T)$. In this case, the Arrow-Debreu price is implied by $B(0) = B(T)\pi_T$. Alternatively, we can define the future bond price in terms of its rate of return, or

$$B(T) = B(0)(1 + R_f(0, T))^T$$

which leads to a discount factor applied to the future state, defining the state price:

$$\pi_T = \left(1 + R_f(0, T)\right)^{-T}$$

Next, assume there exists an asset with two future states, one paying $15 and the other $10. Each of these states has implied state prices (π_1, π_2). The current price implied by these states and their prices is then $S(0) = 15\pi_1, +10\pi_2$. If these prices (π_1, π_2) are unique, the current price is also unique, called the *market price.* If these prices are not unique (i.e., there is no equilibrium price regarding each of these states), then the market price is incomplete, and the Arrow-Debreu framework fails to price uniquely the asset price. However, even if the asset price is unique, the state prices (π_1, π_2) defined by the price $S(0)$ consist of two unknowns in one equation.

To determine these state prices, additional pertinent information is needed. Evidently, the larger the number of states, the more information pertinent to the asset price will be needed. For this reason, financial information is valuable, as it provides the means to define state prices and thereby the asset's current market price. One pertinent source of information (but by no means the only one) is given in the price of a bond whose current price is $B(0)$, and its next state is the bond payment made for sure in the next period, $B(1)$. This payment is made in both states priced (π_1, π_2). Using again the Arrow-Debreu prices, the bond price can be written as follows:

$$B(0) = B(1)\pi_1 + B(1)\pi_2 = B(1)(\pi_1 + \pi_2)$$

which provides a second equation for the state prices. Their solution, using the numbers above, yields the state prices:

$$\pi_2 = 3\frac{B(0)}{B(1)} - \frac{1}{3}S(0) \text{ and } \pi_1 = \frac{1}{3}S(0) - 2\frac{B(0)}{B(1)}$$

Alternatively and equivalently, the risk-free bond can be used to standardize the definition of state prices by defining these prices in terms of a synthetic probability distribution, which we call a risk-neutral probability distribution (although it does not reflect any real uncertainty, as it is the case with actuarial probabilities used in insurance). For simplicity, assume a riskless bond whose current price is $B(0)$ and whose risk-free rate of return is known, given by R_f. In this case, regardless of the future states 1 and 2, the future price of this bond is:

$$B(0) = B(0)(1 + R_f)\pi_1 + B(0)(1 + R_f)\pi_2 = B(0)(1 + R_f)(\pi_1 + \pi_2) \quad (7.2)$$

and therefore,

$$\pi_1 + \pi_2 = \frac{1}{1 + R_f} \quad (7.3)$$

As a result, since:

$$S(0) = 15\pi_1, +10\pi_2 \quad (7.4)$$

The current price is:

$$S(0) = \frac{1}{1 + R_f} \left(15 p^Q + 10 \left(1 - p^Q \right) \right) \tag{7.5a}$$

and

$$p^Q = \frac{\pi_1}{\pi_1 + \pi_2} \tag{7.5b}$$

And generally,

$$S(0) = \frac{1}{1 + R_f} \left(p^Q S^+(1) + \left(1 - p^Q \right) S^-(1) \right) = \frac{1}{1 + R_f} E^Q \left(\tilde{S}(1) \right) \tag{7.6}$$

where E^Q is an expectation with respect to the synthetic (risk-neutral) probability distribution with p^Q its unique remaining parameter whose solution is implied by the current asset price, the current rate of return of the risk-free asset (the bond), and future states. A synthetic interpretation is given to p^Q because it is not a probability but merely an expression that reflects the future equilibrium of assets' state prices.

In a rich and liquid financial market, providing abundant pertinent information on current and future prices, such synthetic distributions can be constructed to account for a larger number of states. Alternatively, financial models can be constructed as well, resulting in the reduction of explicit state prices by defining state prices in terms of parametric functional forms. For example, for a synthetic probability distribution $p_i^Q, i = 1, 2, \dots$ consisting of an extremely large number of states, a continuous parametric probability distribution may be used with parameters to be defined by the pertinent information that can be applied to revealing the distribution's parameters. The financial model reliability may then be tested against empirical evidence ex post when market information reveals observed prices. The need for reliable financial models and the pertinent information needed to reveal these parameters justifies the immense investments that financial firms devote to acquiring information, developing financial models, and learning how to use and manage these models and information to price assets. Information and financial models are then what makes it possible to determine the future market state prices implied by the Arrow-Debreu financial theory.

This approach differs significantly from the expected-utility approach, which has emphasized a personal risk preference and risk attitude combined with subjective (private) information to value an asset—a personal rather than a market price. For this reason, the "utility price" implies only the persons' (investor or trader) willingness to bear the price of an asset risk. The utility approach is therefore mostly applied when markets are incomplete, infusing in valuation an attitude and information that compensates for the volatility and the nonuniqueness of asset prices. When markets are complete, the financial theory is then a better predictor of asset prices.

The Arrow-Debreu framework is extremely important from both theoretical and empirical viewpoints, justified by a robust economic rationale. Its pricing framework can be standardized relative to other asset prices—in particular, risk-free assets, as we have shown earlier—and lead to a synthetic probability distribution with current prices equal to their expected future price discounted at the risk-free rate. We shall see that other pertinent information can be used and prices measured with respect to other reference assets, also called *Numéraire*. Such reference assets may include market indexes and other probability measures. Standardization of state prices and their transformation into synthetic probability distributions result from the information we possess and resolve the indeterminacy of states and state prices. When a reference asset is known for sure (such as a risk-free asset, a zero-coupon bond), the Arrow-Debreu state prices can be standardized to a risk-neutral pricing framework, as previously seen.

EXAMPLE: GENERALIZATION TO n STATES

Assume a zero-coupon bond whose price one period hence is $1, or $B(1) = \$1$, in a financial world with n future state prices π_j, the current price of a bond is:

$$B(0) = \sum_{j=1}^{n} \pi_j B_j(1) = \sum_{j=1}^{n} \pi_j, \, B_j(1) = 1, \forall j \tag{7.7a}$$

However, $1 for sure in the next period is now worth its discounted value at the risk-free rate R_f. Therefore,

$$B(0) = \frac{1}{1 + R_f}$$

or

$$\frac{1}{1 + R_f} = \sum_{j=1}^{n} \pi_j \tag{7.7b}$$

Using this information (of the risk-free market), we consider next the price of a security whose current price is $S(0)$ and future states $S_j(1)$ and future state prices π_j:

$$S(0) = \sum_{j=1}^{n} S_j(1)\pi_j = \frac{\sum_{j=1}^{n} S_j(1)\pi_j}{(1 + R_f)\sum_{j=1}^{n} \pi_j} = \frac{1}{1 + R_f}\sum_{j=1}^{n} S_j(1)\left(\frac{\pi_j}{\sum_{j=1}^{n} \pi_j}\right) \tag{7.8}$$

Adjusted standardized state prices, called *risk-neutral probabilities*, are then defined by:

$$p_j^Q = \frac{\pi_j}{\sum_{j=1}^{n} \pi_j}, 0 \leq p_j^Q \leq 1$$

and

$$\sum_{j=1}^{n} p_j^Q = 1 \tag{7.9}$$

In other words, the security price, written relative to the risk-neutral probabilities p_j^Q, is:

$$S(0) = \frac{1}{1 + R_f} \sum_{j=1}^{n} S_j(1) p_j^Q$$

Or:

$$\frac{S(0)}{B(0)} = \frac{1}{B(0)(1 + R_f)} E^Q(S(1)) = E^Q\left(\frac{S(1)}{B(1)}\right) \qquad (7.10)$$

where E^Q means that expectation is taken with respect to *a probability measure* defined by the risk-neutral probabilities p_j^Q, $j = 1, 2, \ldots, n$.

An equivalent expression for this equality is given by *deflating prices* for both periods, resulting in deflated prices of equal expectations with respect to the risk-neutral measure, or:

$$\frac{S(0)}{B(0)} = E^Q\left(\frac{S(1)}{B(1)}\right) \qquad (7.11)$$

and since we also have:

$$\frac{S(1)}{B(1)} = E^Q\left(\frac{S(2)}{B(2)}\right)$$

and therefore,

$$\frac{S(0)}{B(0)} = E^Q\left(\frac{S(1)}{B(1)}\right) = E^Q\left(\frac{S(2)}{B(2)}\right) = \ldots = E^Q\left(\frac{S(n)}{B(n)}\right) = \ldots \qquad (7.12)$$

explicitly:

$$\frac{S(0)}{1} = \frac{1}{(1 + R_f)} E^Q(S(1)) = \frac{1}{(1 + R_f)^2} E^Q(S(2)) = \ldots = \frac{1}{(1 + R_f)^n} E^Q(S(n)) = \ldots$$

$$(7.13)$$

This mathematical property underlies a fundamental and important property: the martingale of financial prices in complete markets. In other words, the current price equals the expected value of the stock price with an expectation taken with respect to a probability measure—defined by the risk-neutral probabilities. We develop this approach in greater detail later in this chapter. The definition of martingales is further extended in Appendix A of this chapter.

The Arrow-Debreu framework indicates that a state price is associated to an event state and not to its payout magnitude. Thus, if a state has a payout of $10 and its state price is 0.4, $(S_1(1) = 10, \pi_1 = 0.4)$; or a payout is $6 with state price 0.5

$(S_2(1) = 6, \pi_3 = 0.7)$, then the current price is:

$$S(0) = (\pi_1 + \pi_2)\left(10\frac{\pi_1}{\pi_1 + \pi_2} + 6\frac{\pi_2}{\pi_1 + \pi_2}\right) = \frac{1}{1 + R_f}\left(10p_1^Q + 6p_2^Q\right)$$

where　　　　　　　　　　　　　　　　　　　　　　　　　　　　　　　　　　(7.14)

$$\pi_1 + \pi_2 = \frac{1}{1 + R_f}, \; p_1^Q + p_2^Q = 1$$

Thus,

$$0.9 = \frac{1}{1 + R_f} \text{ and } R_f = 0.11$$

and

$$S(0) = \frac{1}{1 + 0.11}(10 * 0.4444 + 6 * 0.5555) = 6.9369$$

where the risk neutral probabilities are (0.3636, 0.4545) and the implied current price is 6.9369.

EXAMPLE: BINOMIAL OPTION PRICING

Option prices are derived from a security price and therefore share their state prices (but not the payments defined by each state). As a result, given the state prices or, equivalently, their risk-neutral probabilities, the option prices are uniquely defined when a market is complete. At the same time, in a complete market, option prices are also revealing future state prices and can be used to define these prices. Explicitly, let there be two states for a security whose current price is $S(0)$ and whose states at time $t = 1$ are $S(1) = \left(S_1^+, S_1^-\right)$. With two states, and relative to a risk free-bond, we have:

$$S(0) = \frac{1}{1 + R_f}E^Q(S(1)) = \frac{1}{1 + R_f}E^Q\left(p_1^Q S_1^+ + p_2^Q S_1^-\right)$$ (7.15)

Let a call option's maturity be also at time $t = 1$ with a strike K and $C(1) = \left(C(S_1^+, K), C(S_1^-, K)\right)$. Since state prices are shared by the option's underlying, we have necessarily:

$$C(0) = \frac{1}{1 + R_f}E^Q(C(1)) = \frac{1}{1 + R_f}\left(p_1^Q C(S_1^+, K) + p_2^Q C(S_1^-, K)\right)$$ (7.16)

For example, if $K = 8$, $R_f = 0.11$, and option maturity is at time $t = 1$, we have, for a call option, payouts at maturity of:

$$C(1) = \left(Max(S_1^+ - K, 0), MaxC(S_1^- - K, 0)\right)$$

As a result,

$$C(0) = \frac{1}{1 + R_f} \left(p_1^Q Max(S_1^+ - K, 0) + (1 - p_1^Q) Max(S_1^- - K, 0) \right) \qquad (7.17)$$

Since $p_1^Q = 0.4444$, we have a call option price which is defined uniquely:

$$C(0) = \frac{1}{1 + 0.11} \left(p_1^Q Max(10 - 8, 0) + (1 - p_1^Q) Max(6 - 8, 0) \right)$$

$$= \frac{2p_1^Q}{1 + 0.11} = \frac{2(0.444)}{1 + 0.11} = 0.800 \qquad (7.18)$$

PROBLEM 7.1: THE IMPLIED RISK-NEUTRAL PROBABILITY

Assume that the price of an underlying is $S_0 = 20$ while the next two states of the underlying are prices $S_{11} = 20(1 + 0.3)$ and $S_{12} = 20(1 - 0.2)$, respectively. The risk-free rate is $R_f = 0.06$. Show that $p^Q = 0.72$ and show that the price of a call option with maturity in the next period (year) with strike 22 equals $C(0, 22) = 2.7961$.

EXAMPLE: THE PRICE OF A CALL OPTION

Let a stock price be $S_1(0)$ while a time period later it is defined by the stock future states $S_1(0) \rightarrow (S_{1,1}(1), S_{1,2}(1))$. If markets are complete, the Arrow-Debreu state prices are defined by:

$$S_1(0) = \pi_1 S_{1,1}(1) + \pi_2 S_{1,2}(1), \ \pi_1 + \pi_2 = \left(1 + R_f \right)^{-1} \qquad (7.19)$$

or

$$S_1(0) = \frac{1}{1 + R_f} \left[p_1^Q S_{1,1}(1) + p_2^Q S_{1,2}(1) \right]$$

When this is the case,

$$S_1(0) = \frac{1}{1 + R_f} E^* \left(S_1(1) \right) \qquad (7.20)$$

with

$$p_1^Q = \frac{(1 + R_f) S_1(0) - S_{1,2}(1)}{S_{1,1}(1) - S_{1,2}(1)} \ \text{and} \ p_2^Q = 1 - p_1^Q \$$$

Given these probabilities, we can calculate the price of assets derived from the security (in other words, subject to the same state prices). For a call option whose strike is K and whose cash flow at its maturity is given by:

$$C_1(1) = \begin{cases} C_{11}(1) = Max\,(S_{1,1}(1) - K, 0) & \text{Std State 1 price } p_1^Q \\ C_{12}(1) = Max\,(S_{1,2}(1) - K, 0) & \text{Std State 2 price } p_2^Q \end{cases} \tag{7.21}$$

the current price of the option is:

$$C_1(0) = \frac{1}{1 + R_f} \left\{ p_1^Q C_{1,1}(1) + p_2^Q C_{1,2}(1) \right\} \tag{7.22}$$

where $\{C_{1,1}(1), C_{1,2}(1)\}$ are the option states at time $t = 1$ and $C_1(0)$ is the current option price, which is calculated using the risk-neutral probabilities $p_i^Q, i = 1, 2$, or

$$C_1(0) = \frac{1}{1 + R_f} \left\{ p_1^Q (C_{1,1}(1) - C_{1,2}(1)) + C_{1,2}(1) \right\} \tag{7.23}$$

Since

$$p_1^Q = \frac{(1 + R_f)\,S_1(0) - S_{1,2}(1)}{S_{1,1}(1) - S_{1,2}(1)} \quad \text{and} \quad p_2^Q = 1 - p_1^Q$$

we have:

$$C_1(0) = \frac{1}{1 + R_f} \left\{ \frac{(C_{1,1}(1) - C_{1,2}(1))\left[(1 + R_f)\,S_1(0) - S_{1,2}(1)\right]}{S_{1,1}(1) - S_{1,2}(1)} + C_{1,2}(1) \right\} \tag{7.24}$$

Say that the call option price is given by $C_{1,1}(1) = S_1(1) - K$ while $C_{1,2}(1) = 0$, then:

$$C_1(0) = \frac{1}{1 + R_f} \frac{(S_1(1) - K)\left[(1 + R_f)\,S_1(0) - S_{1,2}(1)\right]}{S_{1,1}(1) - S_{1,2}(1)} \tag{7.25}$$

In other words, if $S_1(0) = 20$, $S_{1,1}(1) = 24$, $S_{1,2}(1) = 18$, $K = 22$, and $R_f = 0.1$, then:

$$C_1(0) = \frac{1}{1 + R_f} \frac{(24 - 22)\left[(1 + R_f)\,20 - 18\right]}{24 - 18} = \frac{1}{1 + R_f} \frac{2 + 20 R_f}{3} = 1.2121 \tag{7.26}$$

EXAMPLE: A GENERALIZATION TO MULTIPLE PERIODS

A generalization to n periods is neither straightforward nor evident. Say that a stock price can either increase or decrease from period to period. In an Arrow-Debreu framework, at time t, the current prices of an underlying and, say, call and put option prices with strikes K and V are:

$$S(t) = \frac{1}{1 + R_f(t, t+1)} E^{Q(t)}\left(\tilde{S}(t+1)\right)$$

$$C(t) = \frac{1}{1 + R_f(t, t+1)} E^{Q(t)}\left(Max\left(\tilde{S}(t+1) - K, 0\right)\right)$$

$$= \frac{1}{1 + R_f(t, t+1)} E^{Q(t)}\left(\tilde{C}(t+1)\right), t \leq T_C - 1 \tag{7.27}$$

$$P(t) = \frac{1}{1 + R_f(t, t+1)} E^{Q(t)}\left(Max\left(V - \tilde{S}(t+1), 0\right)\right)$$

$$= \frac{1}{1 + R_f(t, t+1)} E^{Q(t)}\left(\tilde{P}(t+1)\right), t \leq T_P - 1$$

where T_C and T_P are the options' call and put maturities and $R_f(t, t+1)$ is the one-period term structure risk-free rate. Note that at time t, the synthetic (risk-neutral) probability distribution is altered by new information, new states, new state prices to be determined, and so forth. In this context the price of, say, a call option whose maturity is at time T_C is given by a recursive system of equations:

$$C(t) = \frac{1}{1 + R_f(t, t+1)} E^{Q(t)}\left(\tilde{C}(t+1)\right), t \leq T_C - 1$$

$$C(T_C) = Max\{S(T_C) - K), 0\} t \leq T_C - 1 \tag{7.28}$$

Thus, over two periods, before the exercise of the call option, we have:

$$C(T_C - 1) = \frac{1}{1 + R_f(T_C - 1, T_C)} E^{Q(T_C-1)}\left(\tilde{C}(T_C)\right)$$

$$= \frac{1}{1 + R_f(T_C - 1, T_C)} E^{Q(T_C-1)}\left(Max\{\tilde{S}(T_C) - K), 0\}\right)$$

$$C(T_C - 2) = \frac{1}{1 + R_f(T_C - 2, T_C - 1)} E^{Q(T_C-2)}\left(\tilde{C}(T_C - 1)\right) \tag{7.29}$$

$$= \frac{1}{1 + R_f(T_C - 2, T_C - 1)} \frac{1}{1 + R_f(T_C - 1, T_C)} E^{Q(T_C-2)}\left(Max\{\tilde{S}(T_C) - K), 0\}\right)$$

Note that in this case, one period before the option's maturity, the expectation is taken with respect to a measure about the asset states and state prices (or in this case, risk-neutral probabilities) that differ from period to period. Moving from period to period thus alters the reference information with respect to which risk-neutral probability distributions are calculated. An alternative manner to write the evolution of options' prices is, therefore, conditional on a filtration as discussed in Chapter 3. Or,

$$C(t) = \frac{1}{1 + R_f(t, t+1)} E^Q\left(\tilde{C}(t+1) \,|\, \Im_t\right), \, t \le T_C - 1$$

$$C(T_C) = Max\left\{S(T_C) - K\right\}, 0\} \, t \le T_C - 1$$

(7.30)

In other words, properly pricing options and other assets over time entails an important growth of parameters one has to consider. For this reason, financial models are needed to reduce the number of variables and parameters to reckon with.

To do so, consider a binomial security whose price from period to period has a rate of return equal to 2 or 1 percent. The security's current price is $10 while the risk-free rate is 8 percent. We want to determine the (risk-neutral) probability distribution of the stock price in six months. First note that the underlying price process is binomial, as shown in Figure 7.1.

As a result, the price at the sixth period is:

$$S_6 = (1+h)^i(1-d)^{6-i} S_0 \text{ wp} \binom{6}{i} (p^Q)^i (1-p^Q)^{6-i} \text{ or}$$

$$S_6 = 10(1+0.2)^i(1-0.01)^{6-i} \text{ wp} \binom{6}{i} (p^Q)^i (1-p^Q)^{6-i}$$

(7.31)

The price is therefore:

$$(a)\, S_0 = \left(\frac{1}{1+R_f}\right)^6 E^Q(S_6)$$

$$= \left(\frac{1}{1+R_f}\right)^6 \sum_{i=0}^{6} \binom{6}{i} \left[p^Q(1+h)\right]^i \left[(1-d)(1-p^Q)\right]^{6-i} S_0$$

(7.32)

$$(b)\, 1 = \left(\frac{1}{1+0.08/12}\right)^6 \sum_{i=0}^{6} \binom{6}{i} \left[p^Q(1.02)\right]^i \left[(0.99)(1-p^Q)\right]^{6-i}$$

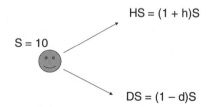

FIGURE 7.1   Binomial Price Process

The prices of a call and put option with maturities at time $t = 6$, each with strikes K_1 and K_2 respectively, are then:

(a) $C_0 = \left(\dfrac{1}{1 + R_f}\right)^6 E^Q (Max\,(S_6 - K_1, 0))$

$= \left(\dfrac{1}{1 + R_f}\right)^6 \displaystyle\sum_{i=0}^{6} \binom{6}{i} (p^Q)^i\,(1 - p^Q)^{6-i}\,Max\,((1 + h)^i(1 - d)^{6-i} S_0 - K_1, 0)$

(b) $P_0 = \left(\dfrac{1}{1 + R_f}\right)^6 E^Q (Max\,(K_2 - S_6, 0))$

$= \left(\dfrac{1}{1 + R_f}\right)^6 \displaystyle\sum_{i=0}^{6} \binom{6}{i} (p^Q)^i\,(1 - p^Q)^{6-i}\,Max\,(K_2 - (1 + h)^i(1 - d)^{6-i} S_0, 0)$

$$(7.33)$$

Note that since p^Q is assumed constant from month to month, a solution over one month is given by:

$$p^Q = \frac{[(1 + R_f) - (1 - d)]}{(1 + h) - (1 - d)} = \frac{R_f + d}{h + d} = \frac{0.08/12 + 0.01}{0.02 + 0.01} = 0.5555$$

With this risk-neutral probability, we can then calculate the current price of derivatives of the current stock as well as the prices investors and speculators will be expecting in two, three, four, five, and six months. Explicitly, the price of a European call on the underlying binomial stock if the exercise date is one month, two months, six months, and one year is given as follows. Let the strike price be $10.5. After one month, the option price is:

$$C_H = Max\,[0, (1 + h)S - K] = Max\,[0, (1 + 0.02)10 - 10.5] = 0$$
$$C_D = Max\,[0, (1 - d)S - K] = C_H = Max\,[0, 0.09*10 - 10.5] = 0$$
$$\text{Option Price} = 0$$

After one year, the price $S(12)$ and the call option are:

$$\tilde{S}_{12} = 10\,[1.02]^i\,[1 - 0.01]^{12-i} \; wp \; \binom{12}{i} [p^Q]^i\,[1 - p^Q]^{12-i}; \; p^Q = 0.55; S_0 = 10$$

and

$$\left\{ \begin{array}{l} C_0(12, K) = \dfrac{1}{(1 + R_f/12)^{12}} E^Q Max\,\{\tilde{S}_{12} - K_1, 0\}, \\[2ex] \tilde{S}_{12} = 10\,[1.02]^i\,[1 - 0.01]^{12-i} \geq K_1, \; i \geq i^* = \dfrac{\ln\left(K_1/10*0.99^{12}\right)}{\ln\left[\dfrac{1.02}{0.99}\right]} \\[3ex] C_0(12, 10.5) = \dfrac{\left[S_0 \displaystyle\sum_{i=i^*}^{12} (1.02)^i(0.99)^{12-i} - 10.5\right] \binom{12}{i} [0.55]^i\,[1 - 0.55]^{12-i}}{(1 + 0.08/12)^{12}} \end{array} \right.$$

where $C_0(12, 10.5)$ is the price of a call option whose strike is $10.50 and exercise time is 12 months.

What are the requirements for no arbitrage? First, we can use these requirements to construct a model that will give us the price of a call option when the underlying is binomial and whose option has a strike 1.2 times the current market price, while the futures are either 1.5 or 0.8 times the current market price. Assume that the option exercise time is one year and the risk-free rate for this year is 8 percent. If it were a put option whose strike is 1.1, the current market price is calculated similarly. Using $K_2 = \$47$, $n = 6$ months, $R_f = 0.12$, and $S = \$45$, $S_H = (1 + h)S$, $h = 0.10$, then $S_L = (1 - l)S$, $l = 0.12$ will provide the option price. The question one may ask then is why would we use derivatives and why not? Rather, if we were to trade with derivatives, what should we be aware of and be careful to do? The answers to these questions underlie the controversy regarding the use of derivatives, which we highlight later in this book. Nevertheless, the extraordinary growth of derivatives finance and its uses in the many financial markets of the world are a clear testimony to their usefulness.

PROBLEM 7.2: OPTIONS AND THEIR PRICES

1. What are the prices of a European call option and a put option on the underlying binomial stock if the exercise date is one month, two months, six months, and one year? Let the strike price for the call be $10.50 and that of the put be $12. Further assume that the risk-free rate is 12 percent annually and that the stock goes up or down with increments of 5 percent or 4 percent per month.
2. The current price of a stock is $30. A call on this stock for the next period has a price of $5 for a strike of $32. The risk-free rate is 10 percent. The price of the stock can either go up to a high value or fall to a low value of $25. What is the risk-neutral probability? Why is it implied? What is the high price that you are using to calculate this risk-neutral probability?
3. A trinomial random walk has state and state prices given by $\left(S^+, \pi_1; S^0, \pi_2; S^-, \pi_3\right)$. The risk-free rate is R_f. In addition, the prices of the underlying security and a call option are also given. What are the state prices? And what are the risk-neutral probabilities?

PUT-CALL PARITY

Assume that we buy a stock but, and at the same time, borrow (at the risk-free rate) the present value of an option's strike. Such a portfolio would be equal at time $t = 0$ to:

$$\Pi(0) = S(0) - K/(1 + R_f)^T \tag{7.34}$$

The terminal payoff of this portfolio, $\Pi(T)$ is then equivalent to buying a call and selling a put, or $C(T) - P(T)$. In other words,

$$\Pi(T) \equiv C(T) - P(T) \tag{7.35}$$

which leads to a put-call (price) parity identity that holds when the market is complete, or:

$$C(0) - P(0) = S - K/(1 + R_f)^T \qquad (7.36a)$$

As noted earlier, the price of the call and the put are a function of the underlying security price, the strike, the time to maturity, and the risk-free rate. Assume for discussion purposes that at a specific instant of time the prices of the call and put are written as $C(t) = C(t, S_t)$ and $P(t) = P(t, S_t)$. The put-call parity equation is then:

$$C(t, S_t) - P(t, S_t) = S_t - K/(1 + R_f)^{(T-t)} \qquad (7.36b)$$

In this case, if markets are complete, a change in the underlying price over two consecutive instants of time ought to maintain such a put-call parity. If this is not the case, the assumption of market completeness may be questioned. In other words, if we consider partial derivatives of the call and put option prices $\partial C(t, S_t)/\partial S_t$ and $\partial P(t, S_t)/\partial S_t$, one derivative ought to be a predictor of the other if markets are complete. These derivatives are discussed in detail subsequently and are called the *Greeks*, expressing the sensitivity effects of financial prices to specific variation in the underlying and other factors determining the prices of options. These Greeks provide an additional source of information which is helpful to better understand the evolution of market prices.

PROBLEM 7.3: PROVING THE PUT-CALL PARITY

Given the price of a call and its strike, calculate the price of a corresponding put (use the put-call-parity) and demonstrate why this parity holds. What are the implications to financial markets if put-call parity does not hold? In your view, why wouldn't such parity hold?

EXAMPLE: PUT-CALL PARITY AND DIVIDEND PAYMENTS

Construct the following two portfolios at time t:

Time t	Time T	
	$S_T < K$	$S_T > K$
$c + Ke^{-R_f(T-t)}$	$\begin{vmatrix} K \\ K = (K - S_T) + S_T \end{vmatrix}$	$\begin{vmatrix} (S_T - K) + K = S_T \\ S_T \end{vmatrix}$
$p + S_t$		

We see that at time T, the two portfolios yield the same payoff $Max(S_T, X)$ which implies the same price at time t. Thus:

$$c + Ke^{-R_f(T-t)} = p + S_t$$

If this is not the case, then there would be some arbitrage opportunity. In this sense, computing European option prices is simplified since knowing one leads necessarily to knowing the other. When we consider dividend-paying options, the put-call parity relationships are slightly altered. Let D denote the present value of the dividend payments during the lifetime of the option (occurring at its ex-dividend date). Then: $c > S - D - Ke^{-R_f(T-t)}$ and $p > D + Ke^{-R_f(T-t)} - S$. Similarly, for put-call parity in a dividend-paying option, we have the following bounds:

$$S - D - K < C - P < S - Ke^{-R_f(T-t)}$$

PROBLEM 7.4: OPTIONS PUT-CALL PARITY

Show that for put-call parity the following relationships hold:

$$c + Ke^{-R_f(T-t)} = p + S = Max(S_T, X)$$

$$\frac{\partial c}{\partial S} = 1 + \frac{\partial p}{\partial S}, \frac{\partial^2 c}{\partial S^2} = \frac{\partial^2 p}{\partial S^2}, \frac{\partial c}{\partial K} + e^{-R_f(T-t)} = \frac{\partial p}{\partial K}$$

and

$$\frac{\partial c}{\partial \tau} - KR_f e^{-R_f \tau} = \frac{\partial p}{\partial \tau}, \ \tau = T - t$$

Can such information be used to test market completeness?

THE PRICE DEFLATOR AND THE PRICING MARTINGALE

We noted earlier in equation (7.11) that $S(t)/B(t)$ denotes a series of random variables of equal mean defined by:

$$\frac{S(0)}{B(0)} = E^Q\left(\frac{S(t)}{B(t)}\right) = \ldots = E^Q\left(\frac{S(T)}{B(T)}\right) = \ldots \ldots \tag{7.37}$$

Over time, expectations are updated as evidence regarding market prices and other relevant information accrues. An appropriate manner to write this is:

$$\frac{S(0)}{B(0)} = E^Q\left(\frac{S(t)}{B(t)} \bigg| \Im_0\right) = \ldots = E^Q\left(\frac{S(T)}{B(T)} \bigg| \Im_0\right) = \ldots \ldots \tag{7.38}$$

where $|\Im_0$ denotes explicitly the conditional dependence of an accrued evidence $\Im_0$ at time $t = 0$, called a *filtration*. In other words, price estimates are formed by the information accrued that changes from moment to moment, and thereby alters the price continuously. For example, an instant of time later, when new information is obtained, we have:

$$\frac{S(1)}{B(1)} = E^Q\left(\frac{S(t)}{B(t)}\,|\Im_1\right) = \ldots = E^Q\left(\frac{S(T)}{B(T)}\,|\Im_1\right) = \ldots. \tag{7.39}$$

where $S(1)$ is now the current observed price (rather than a random future price), an estimate obtained with respect to a new filtration $|\Im_1$. In other words, as information accrues revealing future and prospective market conditions, these revelations are integrated in the current price through the new filtration. Since it is impossible to predict future information, it is impossible by the same token to predict for sure what future filtrations will be and, thereby, to predict security prices with any certainty. In this sense, stock market prices are not predictable, except in a conditional sense that changes from one instant to another.

In complete markets, any asset price equals its risk-free rate discounted expectation under the risk-neutral distribution. For this reason, much effort is expended, theoretically and practically, in determining the appropriate risk-neutral distribution that can be used to determine asset prices (and, by implication, a broad variety of derived prices). When the underlying price process is a martingale and risk-neutral pricing of financial assets applies, then the price of a cash flow S_n realized at time n is:

$$\frac{S_0}{B(0)} = E^Q\left(\frac{S_n}{B(n)}\,|\Im_0\right)$$

Hence the forward price is,

$$S_0 = B(0)E^Q\left(\frac{S_n}{B(n)}\,|\Im_0\right) \tag{7.40}$$

where $\Im_0$ is a filtration. Expectation of the stock price is taken then with respect to a measure—which is in this case the reference (risk-free) bond. If K is the exercise price of a call option for exercise at some time T, then, the price C_t of such an option (as well as a broad variety of other options) under risk-neutral pricing is:

$$\frac{C(t)}{B(t)} = E^Q\left(\frac{C(T)}{B(T)}\right)$$

or

$$C(t) = \frac{B(t)}{B(T)}E^Q\left(\max\left(S_T - K, 0\right)|\Im_t\right) \tag{7.41}$$

Such an approach applies to both discrete and continuous time and state models. The practical importance of a martingale representation for asset pricing arises from two essential results:

1. The Harrison-Pliska martingale no-arbitrage theorem states that under risk-neutral pricing, the price process is a martingale.
2. A martingale can be defined by a change of measure (with respect to which an expectation is taken). Appendix A introduces both essentials of martingale mathematics and change of measures. Such an approach is extremely useful in pricing financial assets when markets are assumed to be complete.

Martingale and the concept of market completeness are intimately connected—in a complete market, prices define a martingale (Harrison and Pliska 1981). The inverse is not true, however: A martingale is not necessarily a market price process.

If price processes follow a martingale, it implies that only the information available today is relevant to make a prediction on future prices. In other words, the present price has all the relevant information embedding investors' expectations. This means that in practice (the weak form efficiency) past prices should be of no help in predicting present prices or, equivalently, prices have no memory. When any of a number of hypotheses (martingale, rationality, no arbitrage, etc.) cannot be validated, the Arrow-Debreu framework is no longer applicable in its simple form. In such a case, prices can no longer be unique, and markets are said to be incomplete.

PRICING AND COMPLETE MARKETS

In financial equilibrium, a market is complete. This means that there are no arbitrage opportunities. An investor cannot profit if he does not assume risk. Profits are thus the rewards that investors reap for the risks they assume (as they, therefore, potentially assume losses as well). When there is no opportunity for arbitrage, the exchange price is unique and thus an investor cannot buy a share and immediately resell it at another price. Inversely, when states and state prices are not known or are ill defined, prices are not unique, and markets are said to be incomplete. In such markets, it is difficult for investors to agree on a price at which they would be willing to trade, providing thereby a potential for arbitrage.

The relevance of both complete and incomplete markets to financial practice is extremely important. Complete markets are usually used as a reference price while incomplete markets express prices off the financial market price equilibrium (and are notoriously difficult to predict). Traders, investors, speculators, arbitrageurs, and others, seek profit opportunities by detecting incompleteness in the market or by identifying the mispricing of an asset they can capitalize on and profit from. If markets are complete, this will imply four things:

1. Future prices are implied in the current price. In this sense, past prices are not relevant to determining the current price. This latter statement should be pondered carefully, as past prices may be used in predicting the future market states.
2. There is a unique price.
3. Complete markets imply that *all* the information available regarding the security and its price is available to all (so that no one can profit individually from insider trading or privy information, or assume an unfair advantage compared to other investors).
4. Investors will not be able to earn above-average returns without taking above-average risks. In such a situation, there are no arbitrage opportunities and therefore there is no free lunch.

In a complete market, prices are defined by *rational expectations*. This is a term coined by John Muth (1961), who formulated it as a decision-making hypothesis in which agents are informed, constructing a model of the economic environment and using all the relevant and appropriate information available to them at the time a decision is made (see also Magill and Quinzii 1996, 23):

> *I would like to suggest that expectations, since they are informed predictions of future events, are essentially the same as the predictions of the relevant economic theory.... We call such expectations "rational."... This hypothesis can be rephrased a little more precisely as follows: that expectations (or more generally, the subjective probability distribution of outcomes) tend to be distributed, for the same information set, about the prediction of the theory (the objective probability of outcomes).*

In other words, if investors are smart, their subjective beliefs are the same as those of the real (market) world—they are neither pessimistic nor optimistic. When this is the case and rational expectations equilibrium holds, we say that markets are complete or efficient. Samuelson pointed out in 1965 that these market prices have the martingale property. This observation led Fama (1965) and Lucas (1978) to characterize such properties as *market efficiency*.

There is disagreement among economists, however, on whether markets are efficient or not. Some believe that markets are efficient (and therefore complete), and some do not. Obviously, market efficiency fails to account for market anomalies such as bubbles and bursts, rare events, the relationship of firms' performance to size, information and power asymmetries, thinly traded markets, markets of poor liquidity, and so on. For example, information asymmetries, insider trading, and advantages of various sorts can provide an edge to individual investors and thereby violate the basic tenets of market efficiency—that no individual can profit above normal profits without assuming a commensurate risk. When these situations are not overwhelming, market prices may be representative of an approximate complete market, and financial prices can be trusted. When this is not the case, financial markets, as a trusted means to trade and exchange fairly, are not sustainable. Market meltdowns and a lack of financial liquidity become probable occurrences.

The dependent interaction of markets (as is the case in a global economy) can lead also to market mispricing and financial instabilities due to very rapid and positive feedback between markets, reacting to misinformation, fears, and rumors. Such virtual situations lead to a growth of volatility, instabilities, and perhaps in some special cases to chaos. Nonetheless, whether the hypothesis that markets are complete is right or wrong, it seems to work sometimes. When it does not work and it is presumed to work nonetheless (i.e., it is implied to work), prices are adjusted accordingly to reflect such situations. Prices are then implied by the model we use and its parameters based on actual prices. Price estimates and actual prices may differ, however, accounting for statistical variations and model errors.

To confront these challenging situations, other approaches, both theoretical and practical, are needed. Numerous approaches are also suggested. For example, behavioral finance provides an alternative dogma (based on psychology) to explain the behavior of financial markets. These approaches are based on the explanation of individuals' and herd behaviors as well as limits of rationality presumed by investors (and their quantitative formulations). Whether these approaches will converge to a general financial-economic-quantitative theory of financial markets remains yet to be seen. Currently, some believe that the current price includes all future information, and they therefore believe in the existence of Arrow-Debreu prices. And some assume that the past and individuals' behaviors can be used to predict future prices. If the test is to make money, then the verdict is far from reached. Richard Roll, a financial economist and money manager, argues (as quoted in a Burton Malkiel article in the *Wall Street Journal*):

> *I have personally tried to invest money, my clients' and my own, in every single anomaly and predictive result that academics have dreamed up. And I have yet to make a nickel on these supposed market inefficiencies. An inefficiency ought to be an exploitable opportunity. If there is nothing that investors can exploit in a systematic way, time in and time out, then it's very hard to say that information is not being properly incorporated into stock prices. Real money investment strategies do not produce the results that academic papers say they should . . . but there are some exceptions including long-term performers that have over the years systematically beat the market.*
> —Burton Malkiel, *Wall Street Journal*, December 28, 2000

Risk-Neutral Pricing and Market Completeness

Synthetic probability distributions (such as the risk-neutral distribution) are models constructed to price assets that are coherent with the Arrow-Debreu theory. All these distributions are based then on a unique set of probabilities that depends on a number of assumptions. These include:

- No arbitrage opportunities.
- No dominant trading strategies.
- Law of the single price.

No arbitrage occurs, as stated earlier, when it is not possible for an agent to make money for sure without having to invest any in the first place. The *single price hypothesis* was elaborated by Modigliani and Miller (1958), stating that two prospective future cash flows with identical risks must be priced equally. In other words, if we can replicate an asset price by a synthetic portfolio whose value can be ascertained to be identical to the asset, then if there is no arbitrage, the prices of the asset and of the synthetic portfolio are necessarily the same. This implies market completeness and requires:

- No transaction costs (generally, a frictionless market).
- No taxes.
- Infinitely divisible assets.
- The ability of agents to borrow or lend at the same rates.
- No information asymmetry regarding future state prices.
- No short sales.
- Rational investors.

Any violation or restrictions that will violate market completeness will open for the initiated and well-informed investor an opportunity for arbitrage. Although in practice at least one of these assumptions is often violated. However, for many fundamental and useful results in financial theory, the assumption of no arbitrage is maintained. When this is not the case, and the assumption of market completeness is violated, it is no longer possible to obtain a unique set of *risk-neutral probabilities* (there may be several sets of such risk-neutral probabilities, none of which defines the pricing martingale, however).

To determine a risk-neutral pricing framework, we might follow a number of approaches, falling in two essential categories:

1. Price by replication of a cash flow by another (whose price is known and therefore apply the law of the single price).
2. Price by finding the unique pricing martingale.

In the first case, we construct a portfolio with a known price to replicate an asset's cash flows we seek to price. When such a portfolio can be defined and the market is complete, the asset price is then determined uniquely. In the second case, we usually imply that markets are complete and find the corresponding martingale that prices the underlying asset. In such cases, a price is defined with respect to a *probability measure* that defines the martingale, or:

$$\text{Price} = \text{E}^{\text{Probability Measure}} \{\text{Future Cash Flows}\}$$

Using the pricing martingale, the underlying process is driftless. Finding the pricing martingale is not easy, however. (See Chapter 11.)

The fundamental theorem of risk-neutral pricing is stated without proof as follows:

Fundamental Theorem of Risk Neutral Pricing
Assume that the market admits no arbitrage portfolios and that there exists a riskless lending/borrowing at rate R_f. Then, there exists a probability measure (risk-neutral) defined on the set of feasible market outcomes (1,2, ... M) such that the value of any security is equal to the expected value of its future cash flows discounted at the riskless lending rate.

To calculate these risk-neutral probabilities, we use, as indicated earlier, a portfolio to replicate the security prices or assume the martingale property for the underlying asset, or apply implied risk neutral distributions (Chapter 11).

Definition: Complete Markets
A securities market with M states is said to be complete *if, for any cash flow, there exists a portfolio of traded securities $(n_1, n_2, \ldots n_N)$ which has a cash flow associated to each state $j \in [1, \ldots M]$ it assumes. Thus, market completeness implies that:*

$$\sum_i S_{ij}(1) = \pi_j, \ j \in [1, \ldots M]$$

has a solution $\mathbf{n} \in \mathfrak{R}^N$ for any $P \in \mathfrak{R}^M$. This is equivalent to the matrix rank condition: rank $|M|$.

Thus, if a portfolio can be replicated uniquely, it has a single price and complete markets can exist. Inversely, the uniqueness of asset prices determines a complete market. This is summarized by the following proposition:

Proposition: Uniqueness and Complete Markets
Suppose that the market is complete. Then there is a unique set of state prices
$(\pi_1 \ldots \pi_M)$ *and hence a unique set of risk neutral probabilities. Conversely, if there is a unique set of state prices, then the market is complete with risk-neutral probabilities* $(p_1^Q \ldots p_M^Q)$.

The generality of these results is maintained in intertemporal and continuous-time (dynamic) asset pricing as well. When there is an opportunity for arbitrage, it is possible to define a trading strategy that costs nothing to form, never generates losses, and, with positive probability, will produce strictly positive gains at some time. Of course, if there is no potential for arbitrage, then such a trading strategy cannot exist. Applications to a broad variety of other pricing problems are considered in the next chapter. In the next section, a variety of option payouts at their maturity are outlined.

OPTIONS GALORE

Options are financial tools designed to meet a broad variety of needs. They can be used to speculate, to insure, to invest, and so on. There are, as a result, a vast number of options of various types, categories, and characteristics, traded both in financial markets and over the counter (OTC). A partial summary of option types includes the following:

- *Packaged options* are usually expressed and valued in terms of plain vanilla options and are used to generate desired risk properties and profiles. Options strategies such as covered call, protective put, bull and bear spreads, calendar spread, butterfly spread, condor, lap and flex, warrants (options on a firm's equity), and others are such examples to be introduced in this chapter and in Chapter 8.
- *Compound options* are derived options based on exercise prices that may be uncertain (for example, warrants, options on corporate bonds, etc.) In this case, the option is a derived asset twice, first on the underlying asset and then on some other variable on the basis of which the option is constructed.
- *Forward starts* are options with different states, awarding the right to exercise the option at several times in the future.
- *Path-dependent options* depend on the price and the trajectory of other variables. Asian options, knockout options, and many other option types are of this kind, as we shall see subsequently.
- *Multiple assets options* involve options on several and often correlated risky assets (such as exchange options, etc.).

In addition, there are options on currencies, on commodities, on future climatic conditions, on carbon emissions, on firms' equity (also called warrants), and so forth.

When warrants are exercised, firms issue new stock, thereby diluting the current stockholders' equity holdings. The price of such warrants ought to include therefore the price of dilution in case they are exercised. The number of options used in practice is therefore very large and expanding to meet new needs and provide new opportunities to profit. In the next subsection we consider a number of options and their payout at maturity. Given a pricing martingale or an appropriate risk-neutral distribution, the prices of such options can be determined using the Arrow-Debreu framework.

Options' payouts at their maturity are essential to determine their current price (once a risk-neutral probability distribution is defined). There are various options such as packaged and binary options, look-back, Asian, exchange, chooser, and other options. Their payout terms are outlined here.

Packaged and Binary Options

Packaged options are varied. Consider first binary options. A payoff for binary options occurs if the value of the underlying asset at maturity T, say $S(T)$, is greater than a given strike price K. The amount paid may be constant or a function of the difference $S(T) - K$ (as is the case for a call option). The variety of options that pay nothing or pay something can be summarized by:

- *Cash or nothing*: Pays an amount of cash A if $S(T) > K$.
- *Asset or nothing*: Pays $S(T)$ if $S(T) \geq K$, otherwise it pays nothing.
- *Gap*: Pays $S(T) - K$ if $S(T) \geq K$ (as in a call option).
- *Supershare*: Pays $S(T)$ if $K_L \leq S(T) \leq K_H$ (the price is within two specified bounds) or pays nothing.
- *Switch*: Pays a fixed amount for every day that the stock trades above a given level K in a period $[0, T]$, or pays nothing.
- *Corridor* (or *range notes*): Pays a fixed amount for every day that the stock trades above a level K and below a level L in a period $[0, T]$, or pays nothing.

EXAMPLE: LOOK-BACK OPTIONS

Floating-strike look-back options provide a payout based on a look-back period, equaling the difference between the largest value during the period and the current price. Thus, at maturity, we have for a min and a max look-back option:

$$Min : V(T) = \max(0, S(T) - S_{\min})$$
$$Max : V(T) = \max(0, S_{\max} - S(T)) \tag{7.42}$$

EXAMPLE: ASIAN OPTIONS

Asian options are calculated by replacing the strike price by the average stock price in the period. Let the average price be:

$$\bar{S}(T) = \frac{1}{T} \int_0^T S(t)dt; t \in [0, T] \tag{7.43}$$

Then the value of the call and put with strike of an Asian option is simply:

$$Put : V(T) = \max\left(0, \bar{S}(T) - K\right);$$
$$Call : V(T) = \max\left(0, K - \bar{S}(T)\right) \tag{7.44}$$

EXAMPLE: EXCHANGE OPTIONS

These are multiasset options that provide the possibility of a juxtaposition of two assets (S_1, S_2) given by $Max(S_2(T) - S_1(T), 0)$. Such options can also be used to construct options on the maximum or minimum of two assets. For example, buying the option to exchange one currency (S_1) with another (S_2) leads to:

$$\begin{cases} V(T) = \min\left(S_1(T), S_2(T)\right) = S_2(T) - Max(S_2(T) - S_1(T), 0) \\ V(T) = \max\left(S_1(T), S_2(T)\right) = S_1(T) + Max(S_2(T) - S_1(T), 0) \end{cases} \tag{7.45}$$

EXAMPLE: CHOOSER OPTIONS

These provide an option to buy either a call or a put. Explicitly, say that (T_1, T_2) are the maturity dates of call and put options with strikes (K_1, K_2). Now assume that an option is bought on either of the options with maturities $T \leq (T_1, T_2)$. The payoff at maturity T is then equal to the max of a call $C(S(T), T_1 - T; K_1)$ and the put $P(S(T), T_2 - T; K_2)$:

$$\max\left(C(S(T), T_1 - T; K_1), P(S(T), T_2 - T; K_2)\right) \tag{7.46}$$

EXAMPLE: BARRIER AND OTHER OPTIONS

Barrier options have a payoff contingent on the underlying assets reaching some specified level before expiry. These options have knock-in features (namely *in-barrier*) as well as knock-out features (*out-barrier*).

We can also consider barrier options with exotic and other features such as options on options, calls on puts, calls on calls, puts on calls, and so forth, as well as calls on forwards and vice versa. These are compound options and are written using both the maturity dates and strike prices for both the assets involved. For example, consider a call option with maturity date and strike price given by (T_1, K_1). In this case, the payoff of a call on a call with maturity date T and strike K is a compound option given by:

$$C_c(T_1, K_1) = Max(0, C(S(T), T_1 - T, K_1) - K_1) \tag{7.47}$$

where $C(S(T), T_1 - T, K_1)$ is the value at time T of a European call option with maturity $T_1 - T$ and strike price K_1. By the same token, a compound put option on a call pays at maturity:

$$P_c(T_1, K_1) = Max(0, K - C(S(T), T_1 - T, K_1)) \tag{7.48}$$

Practically, the valuation of such options is straightforward under risk-neutral pricing since their value equals their present discounted terminal payoff (at the exercise time).

EXAMPLE: PASSPORT OPTIONS

These are options that make it possible for the investor to engage in short/long (sell/buy) trading of his own choice while the option writer has the obligation to cover all net losses. For example, if the buyer of the option takes positions at times t_i, $i = 1, \ldots, n - 1$, $t_0 = 0$, $t_n = T$ by buying or selling European calls on the stock, then the passport option provides the following payoff at time T, the option exercise time:

$$Max \left(\sum_{i=0}^{n-1} u_i \left[S(t_{i+1}) - S(t_i) \right], 0 \right) \tag{7.49}$$

where u_i is the number of shares (if bought, it is positive; if sold, it is negative) at time t_i and resolved at period t_{i+1}. In this case, the period profit or loss would be $[S(t_{i+1}) - S(t_i)]$. Particular characteristics can be added such as the choice of the asset to trade, the number of trades allowed, and so on.

OPTIONS AND THEIR REAL USES

Options allow investors flexibility, the value of which is embedded in the option price. For example, say that a utilities firm is considering reconverting its facility from one strictly dependent on fuel oil to one that can burn either fuel oil or coal—whichever is more advantageous. Value will then be derived by switching from one technological capability to another—as a function of fuel and coal prices. Other properties are also providing values, including the flexibility embedded in the exercise of the option; the mixing of inputs or outputs in an industrial process; the option to stop a project; as well as the option to outsource, to initiate, to change a program's sequence and so forth. These are extremely important and practical uses of options, and they therefore justify our focus on such applications.

Similarly, an investor uses options to manage risks. Consider for example a call option, which provides the holder or the buyer of the option, the right, but not the obligation, to buy an underlying security at a fixed price before the expiration date of the option. In this case, the gain is not limited while the loss is limited to the price of the call or the premium. Usually the options contract is made of 100 calls and expires on the third Friday of the month. However, the existence of sellers is necessary to conclude the contract, and the seller of a call option must then be ready to deliver the underlying asset (since he has the obligation to sell the asset when the buyer desires to exercise his option). The seller is more exposed to risk because his loss is open-ended and could reach any value if the stock falls, while his gain is limited to the *premium* or the price of the call.

By contrast, a put option gives the holder of the option the right to sell an underlying asset at a fixed price before the expiration of the option. His gain is open, and his loss is limited to the premium. The seller of the put option is then obliged to buy the assets when the holder decides to exercise the option. His gain is limited to the premium, and his loss is open. We represent these profit-loss opportunities later with diagrams for a number of particular trading strategies. Trades in options are therefore not riskless—one or the other of the parties involved in such transactions always assumes a risk that the other is willing to forgo or pay for.

A by-product of derivatives, particularly those traded on organized markets, is *price discovery*. Namely, information is public and therefore a derivatives exchange provides price transparency of investors' expected beliefs regarding future prices. In that sense, a derivatives exchange can serve as a data hub for price discovery. Further, when a derivative market is liquid it may be considered as proxy to the cash market. This dual relationship is ensured if the organized derivatives exchange is liquid. A breakdown in liquidity will, of course, lead to mispricing and cause exchange markets to falter. In 2008 we witnessed the problems caused by a lack of liquidity and a fallout in some options markets, which have necessitated massive government intervention.

Options are thus traded because of their usefulness, providing utility to the investor, to the trader, to the speculator, to public financial agencies, to risk managers, and so forth. Some investors buy options because of their leverage effect. This effect is based on the fact that participation requires only the option premium and not buying the full title on the security (or some other assets). To properly trade in derivatives, three separate issues must be considered: (1) how well the buyer understands the derivative gains and losses; (2) what the derivative will be used for (hedging, speculating); and (3) the inherent risks of the derivative. Failure to understand these risks can lead to numerous and unexpected losses, as derivatives relate to both beliefs and future expected conditions that may change over time and are therefore sensitive to market moods and psychology. Risks associated with trading in derivatives include, importantly, a system risk that can undermine the stability of the economy. Nonfinancial firms need to be aware of three main risks when using derivatives: (1) a market derivative price risk; (2) a basis risk, or the risk associated with payments incurred to offset price changes in the derivative (when the value of the underlying asset falls, the value of the derivative may not rise by the expected amount); and (3) a credit or *counterparty* risk, which arises when the institution concerned (the party to the contract) will not be able to pay its dues.

Derivative risks are therefore explicit, implicit, and perceived, as Figure 7.2 indicates. While credit derivatives have mushroomed into a huge financial market, it

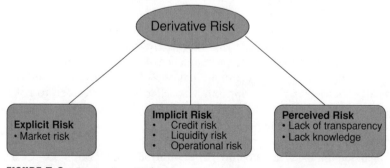

FIGURE 7.2 Derivatives Risks

is also a market that one has to approach with great care. Pricing issues relating to credit derivatives and complex and structured products are considered in Chapters 9 and 10.

For example, implicit and nontransparent risks are often ill perceived and not accounted for, yet in times of crisis they can become overwhelming. A lack of knowledge or education regarding traded financial products; and complexity, which requires both controls and a careful usage of derivatives all contribute to nontransparency. Thus, for derivatives, exchange transparency and liquidity are important to attract many agents and complete a market as much as possible. In addition, a derivative market has to provide a safe trading environment and an efficient clearing mechanism.

FIXED-INCOME PROBLEMS

Fixed-income problems entail promissory notes by the seller of these notes. For example, a coupon-paying bond is also a promise to pay regularly a given sum (the coupon) over a given period of time with a notional settlement at the bond maturity. Obligations to pay a fixed income to the bondholder do not depend on the firm's performance but on the bond covenant that regulates the amount, the terms, and the conditions for such payments. In the following examples, we consider a number of such fixed-income contracts and their derivatives. In particular, we shall price some of these contracts.

EXAMPLE: PRICING A FORWARD

A forward rate is an agreement made between two parties seeking generally to protect or hedge themselves against a future interest rate or price movement, for a specific hedging period, by fixing a future interest rate or price at which they will buy or sell for a specific principal sum in a specified currency. It requires that settlement be effected between the parties in accordance with an established formula. Typically, forward contracts, unlike future contracts, are not traded and can therefore be tailored to specific needs. This means that contracts tend to be much greater in size, far less liquid, and less competitively priced, but suffer from no basis risk.

The price at time t of a forward contract at time T in the future can be written by $B(t, T)$ or by $B(t, t + x)$, $x = T - t$ and is defined by (delivery) price whose value at delivery is null under risk-neutral pricing.

$$E(\text{Future Spot Rate} - \text{Forward Rate}) = 0$$

The relationship between forward rates and spot prices is a matter of intensive research and theories. For example, the fundamental financial theory suggests that we equate the expected future spot rate to the current forward rate—that is (as indicated from the previous equation),

$$\text{Forward Rate} = E(\text{Future spot rate})$$

For example, if s_t is the logarithm of spot price of a currency at time t and f_t is the logarithm of a one-month forward, the expectation hypothesis means that:

$$f_t = E(s_{t+1}) \tag{7.50}$$

Note that if S_t is the spot price at time t, $\Delta S_t = S_{t+1} - S_t$, then the rate of change, expressing the rates of return $\Delta S_t / S_t$, is given by $\Delta \left(\log S_t \right)$ with $s_t = \log S_t$. Empirical research has shown, at least for currencies forward, that this is misleading; therefore additional and alternative theories are often devised that introduce concepts of risk premium as well as the expected rate of depreciation to explain the incoherence between spot and forward market values and risk-neutral pricing.

Forward and future contracts are not only used in financial and commodities markets. For example, a transport futures exchange has been set up on the Internet to help solve forward planning problems faced by truckers and companies shipping around the world. The futures exchange enables companies to purchase transport futures, helping them to plan their freight requirements and shipments by road, rail, and possibly barge. The exchange allows truckers and manufacturers to match transport capacity to their shipments and to match their spot requirements, buy and sell forward, and speculate on future movements of the market. This market completes other markets where one can buy and sell space on ocean-going ships. For example, London's Baltic Exchange handles spot trades in dry cargo carriers and tankers.

EXAMPLE: PRICING A FIXED-RATE BOND

Let the present value of a coupon paying \$$c$ at some time T be $cB(t, T)$ where $B(t, T) = 1$. Next, let N be the principal and let $t(i)$ be the payment date of the ith coupon (paid every 6 months). The price of a bond with n coupon payments left is thus:

$$B(t) = \sum_{i=1}^{i=n} B(t, t + 0.5i)c + B(t, t + 0.5n)N \qquad (7.51)$$

For example, let the coupon payment be \$4 million, and let \$100 million be the notional amount. The coupon payments are in 3, 9, and 15 months. Then:

$$B(t, t + 0.25) = 0.97531$$
$$B(t, t + 0.75) = 0.924271$$
$$B(t, t + 1.25) = 0.824894$$

The price of the bond (in million \$) is therefore:

$$93.3873 = (0.97531 \times 4) + (0.924271 \times 4) + (0.824894 \times 4) + (0.824894 \times 100)$$

Pricing a Term Structure of Interest Rates

Forward rates, as previously indicated, represent a relationship between time to maturity and interest rates. A forward rate is also agreed on at time t but for payments starting to take effect at the future time t_1 and for a certain amount of time $t_2 - t_1$. Such rates are denoted by $f(t, t_1, t_2)$. A relationship between forward rates and spot rates exists, but it hinges on an arbitrage argument. Roughly, this argument states that two equivalent investments (from all points of view) have necessarily the same returns. Explicitly, say that at time t we invest \$1 for a given amount of time $t_2 - t$ at the available spot rate (yield). The price of such an investment in discrete and continuous time is then:

$$B_1(t, t_2) = B_f(t, t_2) = \left[1 + R_f(t, t_2)\right]^{-(t_2 - t)}$$
$$B_1(t, t_2) = B_f(t, t_2) = \exp\left\{-R_f(t, t_2)(t_2 - t)\right\} \tag{7.52}$$

Alternatively, we could invest this \$1 for a certain amount of time $t_1 - t, t_1 \leq t_2$ at which time the moneys available will be reinvested at a forward rate for the remaining time interval $t_2 - t_1$. The price of such an investment in discrete time will then be

$$B_2(t, t_1, t_2) = B_2(t, t_1)\left[1 + f(t, t_1, t_2)\right]^{-(t_2 - t_1)} \tag{7.53}$$

or

$$B_2(t, t_1, t_2) = B_2(t, t_1)\exp\left[-f(t, t_1, t_2)(t_2 - t_1)\right]$$

No *arbitrage*, in this case, means that if these investments are equivalent (i.e., have the same risk), then their value must be the same, or $B_1 = B_2$, and therefore in discrete and continuous time we have:

$$\begin{cases} B_1(t, t_2) = B_f(t, t_2) = B_2(t, t_1, t_2) = B_f(t, t_1)\left[1 + f(t, t_1, t_2)\right]^{t_2 - t_1} \\ B_1(t, t_2) = B_f(t, t_2) = B_2(t, t_1, t_2) = B_f(t, t_1)\exp\left[-f(t, t_1, t_2)(t_2 - t_1)\right] \end{cases} \tag{7.54}$$

leading to, in discrete time:

$$\left[1 + f(t, t_1, t_2)\right]^{t_2 - t_1} = \frac{B_f(t, t_2)}{B_f(t, t_1)} = \frac{\left[1 + R_f(t, t_2)\right]^{t_2 - t_1}}{\left[1 + R_f(t, t_1)\right]^{t_1 - t}} \tag{7.55}$$

and in continuous time:

$$f(t, t_1, t_2) = -\frac{1}{(t_2 - t_1)}\ln\left(\frac{B_f(t, t_2)}{B_f(t, t_1)}\right) = \frac{R_f(t, t_2)(t_2 - t) - R_f(t, t_1)(t_1 - t)}{t_2 - t_1}$$

$$\tag{7.56}$$

This is a general equation that can be specialized to specific periods. In particular, let f_k denote the k period forward rate, expressing the rate agreed on at time t for k periods hence (and for all subsequent periods of time). In this case, it is simple to verify that in discrete time:

$$1 + f_k = \frac{\left[1 + R_f(t, t + k + 1)\right]^{k+1}}{\left[1 + R_f(t, t + k)\right]^{k}}$$

as well as

$$\left[1 + R_f(t, T)\right]^{T-t} = \prod_{k=0}^{T-t-1}(1 + f_k) \tag{7.57}$$

which provides a relationship between the spot and the forward interest rates. In this sense, in a perfect market where arbitrage is not possible, the spot rate (yield) contains all the information regarding the forward market interest rate, and vice versa. Similarly, in continuous time, note that:

$$B_f(t, t_1) = e^{-R_f(t,t_1)(t_1-t)}, t_1 > t$$
and
$$B_f(t, t_1, t_2) = e^{-f(t,t_1,t_2)(t_2-t)} = \frac{B_f(t, t_2)}{B_f(t, t_1)} = \frac{e^{-R_f(t,t_2)(t_2-t)}}{e^{-R_f(t,t_1)(t_1-t)}} \tag{7.58}$$

Thus,

$$f(t, t_1, t_2) = \frac{1}{t_2 - t_1} \ln\left[\frac{B_f(t, t_1)}{B_f(t, t_2)}\right] \tag{7.59}$$

Further, the spot rate is given by:

$$f(t, t_1) = f(t, t_1, t_1) = \lim_{\varepsilon \to 0} f(t, t_1, t_1 + \varepsilon) = \lim_{\varepsilon \to 0} \frac{1}{\varepsilon} \ln\left[\frac{B(t, t_1 + \varepsilon)}{B(t, t_1)}\right] \tag{7.60}$$

As a result, the forward rate is given by:

$$f(t, t_1) = f(t, t_1, t_1) = -\frac{d}{dt_1} \ln B(t, t_1) = -\frac{1}{B(t, t_1)} \frac{d}{dt_1} B(t, t_1) \tag{7.61}$$

EXAMPLE: THE TERM STRUCTURE OF INTEREST RATES

The term structure of interest rates varies according to the bond lifetime:

	1 year	2 years	3 years	4 years	5 years
$Y(0,t)$	0,0527	0,053	0,0537	0,0543	0,0551
$Y(1,t)$	—	0,0533	0,0542	0,0548	0,0557
$Y(2,t)$	—	—	0,0551	0,0556	0,0565
$Y(3,t)$	—	—	—	0,0561	0,0572
$Y(4,t)$	—	—	—	—	0,0583

These numbers are calculated as follows. Note first that forward yields in complete markets are calculated by noting that if there is no arbitrage then a dollar invested at time 0 for t periods has the same value as a dollar invested for s periods and then reinvested for the remaining $t - s$ periods. In other words, in complete markets:

$$[1 + y(0, t)]^t = [1 + y(0, s)]^s [1 + y(s, t)]^{t-s} \tag{7.62}$$

leading to

$$y(s, t) = \left(\frac{[1 + y(0, t)]^t}{[1 + y(0, s)]^s} \right)^{\frac{1}{t - s}} - 1 \tag{7.63}$$

For example, say that we are currently in the year 2000. This means that we have to insert the term structure rates of year 2000 in our equation in order to calculate the current bond price, or:

$$B_{100}(0, 5) = 100 \left[\frac{1}{(1 + 0, 0527)} + \frac{1}{(1 + 0, 053)^2} + \frac{1}{(1 + 0, 0537)^3} + \frac{1}{(1 + 0, 0543)^4} \right]$$

$$+ 1100 \frac{1}{(1 + 0, 0551)^5} = 1192, 84 \tag{7.64}$$

A year later: How much could it be worth? (Note that we have to change the interest rate applied to payments.)

$$B_{100}(1, 5) = 100 \sum_{k=1}^{4} \left[\frac{1}{1 + y(1, k)} \right]^k + 1000 \frac{1}{[1 + y(1, 5)]^T} = 1155, 72 \tag{7.65}$$

PROBLEM 7.5: ANNUITIES AND OBLIGATIONS

1. An annuity pays the holder a scheduled payment over a given amount of time (finite or infinite). Determine the value of such an annuity using bond values at the current time. What would this value be in two years using current observed rates?
2. What will be the value of an annuity that starts in T years and will be paid for N years afterwards? How would you write this annuity if the annuity is terminated at the time the annuity holder passes away (assuming that all payments are then stopped)?
3. Say that we have an obligation whose nominal value is $1,000 at the fixed rate of 10 percent with a maturity of three years, reimbursed in five. In other words, the firm obtains a capital sum of $1,000 whose cost is 10 percent. What is the financial value of the obligation? Next, assume that just after the obligation is issued the interest rate falls from 10 to 8 percent. The firm's cost of finance could have been smaller. What is the value of the obligation (after the change in interest rates) and what is the perceived loss to the firm?

OPTIONS TRADING, SPECULATION, AND RISK MANAGEMENT

Options trading can be risky. In some cases, traders may gain if their bets turn out to be right, and lose when their bets falter. In most cases, however, options are used to hedge and mitigate risks by providing an opportunity to construct desired risk profiles.

Options may also be used for diversification. Despite the recent innovation in financial technology, no derivatives exist for directly hedging significant sources of business risk like inflation and recession. Therefore, options by themselves may not provide a fool-proof hedge. Some well-known and frequently used option trading strategies have specific risk and hedging characteristics and specific names, which we will outline briefly. Below, we define essential terms used when trading:

- A *covered position* consists in selling a call contract while owning the underlying asset.
- A *naked position* consists in selling a call contract while not owning the under- lying asset. The broker may require the seller of the option to post a margin that serves as a collateral to the transaction. The initial amount posted to the broker is known as the *initial margin*.
- *Opening transactions* occur if we initiate a transaction (for example, buy- ing or selling a call for the first time or increasing our interest in a given position).
- *Closing transactions* occur if we close the transaction or *exercise* the option.
- *Hedging* is a set of financial activities we turn to when we proceed to reduce risk through financial transactions (buying and selling insurance and credit deriva- tives, for example).
- Speculating arises when we purchase investments that present the possibility of large profits, but with higher-than-average possibility of loss.

These transactions are defined as well by various *types of orders*, including:

- *Market order*: Used for equities. An order to buy or sell a set amount of securities at the most advantageous price obtainable (after the order is made in the trading crowd).
- *Limit order*: An order to buy a stock at or below a specified price, or to sell a stock at or above a specified price. For instance, one may call a broker and ask to "buy 100 shares of XYZ Corp. at $8 or less" or "sell 100 shares of XYZ at $10 or better." The customer specifies a price, and the order is executed only if the market reaches or betters that price. A conditional trading order is designed to avoid the danger of adverse unexpected price changes.
- *Stop-loss order*: An order to sell a stock when the price falls to a specified level.
- *Stop-limit order*: A stop order that designates a price limit. Unlike the stop-loss order, which becomes a market order once the stop is reached, the stop-limit order becomes a limit order.
- *Stop order* (or *stop*): An order to buy or sell when a definite market price is reached, either above (on a buy) or below (on a sell) the price that prevailed when the order was given.

Trading, investing, and speculating differ essentially in the types of orders made and the steps taken to mitigate the risk consequences of such orders.

Option Trading Strategies

We shall use the following terminology:

S = the prevailing price of a stock
X = the exercise price of the option contract
C_0 = the call premium
Intrinsic value of a call = $S - X$
Intrinsic value of a put = $X - S$

If the intrinsic value is positive the option is *in-the-money* (ITM) and the option contract is exercisable, while when the intrinsic value is negative the option is *out-of-the-money* (OTM) and is not exercisable. If the intrinsic value equals zero the option is *at-the-money* (ATM). The time value of an option is the value over and above the intrinsic value that the market places on the option. It is considered as a value (price) for a continuing exposure to movements in the underlying stock. The price on this time value depends on a number of factors including the remaining time to expiry, the volatility of the stock, the risk-free interest rate, and expected dividends. When these parameters change, the option price will also change. An option's sensitivity to these changes is measured in terms of *Greeks*. These are parameters that measure the marginal change in the option price as a function of these parameters and are used when trading and hedging with options. We shall study these Greeks subsequently.

A portfolio defines an investment and a hedging strategy implied in the portfolio's composition of assets, some of which are more or less risky. For example, a portfolio that includes options long or short, on some future date, is necessarily a bet regarding the future with risks associated to their future payments. Similarly, options may have speculative or hedging purposes. Given the number of optional products and their broadly different characteristics, financial managers may tailor a portfolio to many of the needs that investors and speculators may want. Essential option portfolio strategies we are concerned with here include the following as well as other strategies designed to meet specific trading and hedging needs:

- The long and short covered call.
- The long and short protective put.
- The covered call.
- The protective put.

Each strategy expresses a belief held by an investor or trader-speculator regarding future market conditions, who then bets (thus assumes risks) on these beliefs. These strategies are used by both private investors, mutual funds, hedge funds, banks, and financial services. Some investors buy long shares and assume the risk associated with these shares, but they may also buy or sell optional products to mitigate the risks they assume in such trades (and provide a cushion in case the market changes direction). Other strategies use stock market futures and options to protect their portfolio against a slump, and so forth. The number of possibilities is indeed very large, summarized by profit and loss (P/L) diagrams to highlight the particularities of any specific strategy. These diagrams are a plot of the profit (the payoff less the necessary investment in such an optional strategy) arising from the strategy as a function of the value of the underlying asset at the option expiration.

The Long Call Trade A long call trade consists of the following: Buy a call with an exercise price of X. An investor may do so when he expects the market to be bullish or expects volatility to be bullish. The more bullish the expectation, the further OTM (higher strike) the purchased call should be. When this is the case, a long call combines limited downside exposure (limited to the premium paid for the option) with an unlimited profit in a rising market. A quantitative pricing for a long call in a complete market (i.e., using the risk-neutral distribution) is given by

$$C_{X,T}(0) = e^{-R_f T} E^Q (Max(S(T) - X, 0)) \qquad (7.66)$$

where $S(T)$ is the underlying asset price at its exercise time and X is the option exercise price. A graphical representation of the profit/loss of a long call is outlined in Figure 7.3. The longer the time to expiry, the higher the P/L curve. By contrast, the short call trade consists in selling a call option and assumes the risk of having to sell, at expiry, the stock at the strike price. To compensate for this risk, the short side of the option collects a premium.

The Long Put The long put consists in buying a put in the market. Investors do so when they expect the market price or the volatility to be bearish. Thus, the more bearish the expectation, the further out-of-the-money (lower strike) the purchased put should be. A long put combines limited upside exposure with protection in a falling market. The price is then given by $P_{X,T}(0)$:

$$P_{X,T}(0) = e^{-R_f T} E^Q Max(X - S(T), 0) \qquad (7.67)$$

The profit/loss graph is shown in Figure 7.4.

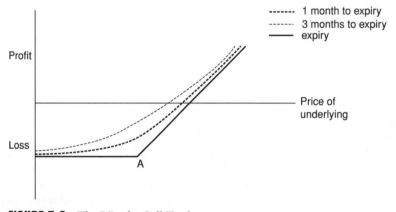

FIGURE 7.3 The P/L of a Call Trade

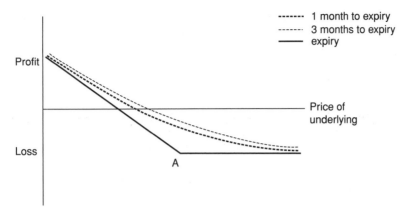

FIGURE 7.4 The P/L Graph of a Long Put

The Covered Call The covered call is an option strategy that is used to limit portfolio losses if the underlying price rises above the option strike. Such a strategy consists in buying long a stock and selling (short) a call. The portfolio position is then:

$$\Omega(0) = S(0) + C(0)$$

At maturity, the covered call position is given by:

$$\Omega(T) = S(T) - C(T) = S(T) - Max\,(S(T) - X, 0) \text{ Or } \Omega(T) = Min\,[S(T), X]$$
$$(7.68)$$

In other words, the portfolio is assured at least the strike. Explicitly, we have:

$$\begin{aligned} &\text{If } S(T) < X, \Omega(T) = S(T) + 0 = S(T) \\ &\text{If } S(T) > X, \Omega(T) = S(T) - (S(T) - X) = X \end{aligned} \tag{7.69}$$

And therefore, the current price of this strategy is $\Omega(0)$:

$$\Omega(0) = e^{-R_f T} E^Q \{Min\,[S(T), X)]\} = e^{-R_f T} E^Q \{S(T)\} + e^{-R_f T} E^Q \{Max\,(S(T) - X, 0)\}$$
$$(7.70)$$

Thus,

$$\Omega(0) = S(0) - C(0) \tag{7.71}$$

which assures the holder of the portfolio at least the strike (in case the underlying falls below the strike). Such strategies are therefore used as an insurance against market risk. The P/L graph of the covered call strategy is given in Figure 7.5.

The Protective Put The protective put is used when we want to protect an investment against a potential drop in prices. Of course one may buy from an insurer insurance against such a drop, but assuming markets are complete, one may turn to

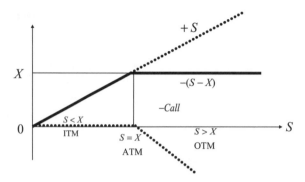

FIGURE 7.5   The P/L of a Covered Call

a protective put strategy. This strategy consists in buying a stock (long) and buying a put (long). The price of such a portfolio is then $S(0) - P(0)$ where the put strike is X. At maturity, the portfolio price is:

$$\Omega(T) = S(T) + P(T) = S(T) + Max\,(X - S(T), 0) \tag{7.72}$$

In this case, the conditional profits/losses are:

$$
\begin{aligned}
&\text{If } S(T) < X, \Omega(T) = S(T) + X - S(T) = X \\
&\text{If } S(T) > X, \Omega(T) = S(T) + 0 = S(T)
\end{aligned}
\tag{7.73}
$$

which implies a terminal price, guaranteed at initial price X or $\Omega(T) = Max\,(X, S(T))$ and therefore:

$$
\begin{aligned}
&\Omega(T) = Max\,(X, S(T)) \text{ or} \\
&\Omega(0) = S(0) - P_{X,T}(0) = e^{-R_f T} E^Q S(T) + e^{-R_f T} E^Q Max\,(X - S(T), 0)
\end{aligned}
\tag{7.74}
$$

PROBLEM 7.6: PORTFOLIO STRATEGIES

What will be the implications of buying a call and selling a put, each with a different strike but with the same exercise time? At the exercise time, the money collected (or paid) will be:

$$C(T) - P(T) = Max\,(S(T) - K_1, 0) - Max\,(K_2 - S(T), 0) \tag{7.75}$$

The payoff would then be (say $K_1 < K_2$):

$$
C(T) - P(T) = \begin{cases} -(K_2 - S(T)) & if & S(T) < K_1 \\ 2S(T) - K_1 - K_2 & K_1 < S(T) < K_2 \\ S(T) - K_1 & S(T) > K_2 \end{cases}
\tag{7.76}
$$

which points to its profitability if the market is indeed bullish. Say that interest rates are 8 percent for a year, and let the exercise time be in six months, while the stock's price is currently \$35. The monthly growth or loss rates are given by 2 percent and

1.5 percent, respectively, while the strikes are $K_1 = 33$, $K_2 = 38$. In this case, what would be the price of these options? To do this calculation, use the multiperiod binomial model.

The Long and Short Straddle   A *straddle* consists in buying (long) a call and a put, each having the same strike at maturity T. Such a strategy is essentially a bet by the investor who believes markets are likely to be highly volatile. However, when markets are stable, the portfolio will be a loss. A straddle is indeed a gamble seeking to beat market expectations (on the high and the low ends) and capitalize on directional moves or increases in volatility. At its expiry, profits would be unlimited in case of an increase or decrease in the underlying, while the loss will be limited to the premium paid in establishing the position. The price of such a portfolio position is $\Omega(0) = C(0) + P(0)$, while at its exercise, it equals:

$$\Omega(T) = C(T) + P(T) = Max\left(S(T) - X, 0\right) + Max\left(X - S(T), 0\right) \qquad (7.77)$$

The conditional prices are:

$$\begin{aligned} If\ S(T) > X,\ \Omega(T) &= S(T) - X \\ If\ S(T) < X,\ \Omega(T) &= X - S(T) \end{aligned} \qquad (7.78)$$

with a price:

$$\Omega(0) = e^{-R_f T} E^Q \Omega(T) = e^{-R_f T} E^Q \left(C(T) + P(T)\right) \qquad (7.79)$$

The *short straddle* consists in selling a put and a call at the same strike. Investors may use such a strategy when they have an expectation that market prices will be neutral while volatility is bearish. The potential profit of such a strategy is limited to the credit received by establishing the position. The profit is then highest if the market settles at the current (initial) price. Losses are unlimited when there is either an increase or a decrease in the underlying. Breakeven is reached if the underlying rises or falls from the strike X by the same amount as the premium received from establishing the position.

The Spread   A spread strategy consists in selling a call (short) and buying a (long) call on the same stock with different exercise prices or time to maturity. The rationale for such a strategy is based on the investor's belief that the stock is going up, but at the same time, seeking some protection if this does not turn out to be the case. Downside losses would then be less than a simple call. Thus, the spread price is initially

$$\Omega(0) = -C(K_1, 0) + C(K_2, 0)$$

while at maturity:

$$\Omega(0) = e^{-R_f T} E^Q \Omega(T) = e^{-R_f T} E^Q \left(C(K_1, T) - C(K_2, T)\right) \qquad (7.80)$$

where $\Omega(T)$ is the price at maturity. If the price at maturity is $S(T)$, there are three possibilities:

If $S(T) < K_1$ then $\Omega(T) = S(T) - K_1$

If $K_1 < S(T) < K_2$ then $\Omega(T) = S(T) - K_1 - (S(T) - K_2) = K_2 - K_1$ (7.81)

If $S(T) > K_2$ then $\Omega(T) = S(T) - K_2$

Note that in this case there is no loss at the exercise, but there is a payment, which is incurred necessarily at the time the spread option is written.

The Strip Strategy In a strip, unlike a spread, the investor makes two unequal bets on market prices with the presumption that these may go up or down. Such a portfolio consists in buying (long) a call and two (long) put options. In this case, we have at maturity:

$$\Omega(T) = C(K, T) + 2P(K, T) \tag{7.82}$$

Thus,

$$\begin{aligned} &\text{If } S(T) < K \text{ then } \Omega(T) = 0 + 2(K - S(T)) \\ &\text{If } K < S(T) \text{ then } \Omega(T) = S(T) - K \end{aligned} \tag{7.83}$$

We use a strip when we believe the market to be volatile and potentially increasing or falling. Such a strategy incurs a loss as long as the market price remains stable. Nevertheless, it is a costly strategy involving the premium price paid for buying both the calls and the puts.

The Strap Strategy The strap, unlike the strip, makes an unequally weighted bet on whether the markets goes down or up by buying two (long) call option plus a (long) put. Thus, at maturity the payoff is

$$\Omega(T) = 2C(K, T) + P(K, T) = 2Max(S_T - K, 0) + Max(K - S_T, 0) \tag{7.84}$$

The Long Strangle The long strangle consists in buying a put and a call at a higher strike. Such a strategy is used when the holder of the strangle expects a major movement in market prices but is unsure of its direction. A larger directional move is needed than in a straddle in order to yield a profit, but if the market stagnates, losses will be smaller. The profit potential is unlimited although a substantial directional movement is necessary to yield a profit in case of both the expected rise or fall in the underlying. However, a loss, limited to the premium paid for the position taken, occurs when market prices are static.

The Short Strangle The short strangle consists in selling a put at strike price A and selling a call at a higher strike B. Such a position, unlike the long strangle, is taken when market expectations are bearish with neutral volatility. In other words, the holder of such a position expects low volatility and no major directional move. It is more cautious than a straddle as profit potential spans a larger range, although the maximum potential profits will be lower. The position's profit is then limited to the premium received. The profit will be highest if the underlying remains within the market level *A–B*. The loss is unlimited, however, for a sharp move of the underlying in either direction. A breakeven is reached if the underlying falls below the strike *A* or rises above the strike *B* by the same amount as the premium received in establishing the position.

Short Put Spread versus Call   A short put spread versus call strategy consists in selling a put at strike *B*, buying a put at a lower strike (*A*), and buying a call at any strike (*C*) (generally, the long call will be at a higher strike than both puts). The profile is similar to that of a short put spread, but the long call provides unlimited profit potential should the underlying rise above C. Such a strategy is a bet that the market will be bullish and volatility bullish. In this case, the profit is unlimited in a rising market while the loss is limited in a falling market. A breakeven is reached if the position is opened at a net credit, and when the underlying falls below strike B by the premium received. If the position is opened at a net debit, breakeven is reached when the underlying rises above strike A by the amount of premium paid.

Short Call Spread versus Put   This trading strategy consists in selling a call at strike *B*, buying a call at a higher strike (*C*), and buying a put at any strike; the long put will generally be at a strike lower than both calls (*A*). This spread has a similar profile to the short call spread, but the long put provides unlimited profit potential in a falling market. Such a trade is made when the expectations are of a bearish market and a bearish volatility. Thus, the profit and loss at expiry are profit-unlimited in a falling market and loss-limited in case of a rising market. Breakeven occurs if the position is created at a net debit and the underlying falls below strike *C* by the net amount of premium paid. If the position is opened at a net credit, breakeven occurs when the underlying rises above strike B by the net premium received.

Long Call versus Put   The trade: Buy a call at strike *B*, sell a call at higher strike (*C*), and sell a put at any strike; the short put will generally be at a strike lower than both calls (*A*). This spread has a similar profile to the long call spread, but the short put reduces the cost of the strategy due to the intake of premium. The long call versus the put has the following characteristics: Expectations are that the market is bullish and volatility bearish. Further, profits are limited in a rising market while losses are unlimited in a falling market. If the position is opened at a net debit, breakeven occurs when the underlying rises above strike *B* by the net amount of the premium paid. If the position is created at a net credit, breakeven is reached when the underlying falls below the strike *B* by the same amount as the premium received.

Long Put Spread versus Call   This trade consists in buying a put at strike *B*, selling a put at a lower strike (*A*), and selling a call at any strike; the short call will generally be at a higher strike than both puts (*C*). The profile is similar to that of a long put spread, but with greater intake of premium due to the short call. In a long put spread versus call, market expectations are for both a bearish market and volatility. Further, profits are limited in a falling market, and losses are unlimited if the market rises. If the position is created at a net debit, breakeven is reached when the underlying falls below a strike *B* by the net amount of premium paid. If the position is opened at a net credit, breakeven occurs when the underlying rises above strike A by the premium received.

Long Straddle versus Call The trade: Buy a call at strike A, buy a put at the same strike, and sell a call at any strike; the short call will generally be at a strike higher than the straddle (B). This spread provides similar exposure to the long straddle, but with less initial outlay due to the premium received from the short call. The long straddle versus call has a market-neutral expectation and a bullish volatility. Further, profits are unlimited in a falling market and limited in a rising market, while losses are limited in a static market. Breakeven is reached when the underlying moves in either direction by the net amount of premium paid.

Long Straddle versus Put The trade: Buy a call at strike B, buy a put at the same strike (B), sell a put at any strike; generally the short put will be at a strike lower than the straddle (A). This spread offers similar exposure to the long straddle, but at a cheaper cost because of the premium taken in from the short put. In a long straddle versus put, expectations are for the market to be neutral to bullish and a bullish volatility. At expiry, profits are unlimited in a rising market and limited in a falling market, while breakeven is reached when the underlying moves in either direction by the amount of the premium paid.

Short Straddle versus Call The trade: Sell a call at strike A, sell a put at the same strike (A), buy a call at any strike; the long call will generally be at a higher strike than the straddle (B). The profile is similar to that of a short straddle, but loss in a rising market is limited by the long call. For the short straddle versus call, expectations are for market neutral and bearish volatility while at expiry, profits are limited in a static (nonvolatile) market while losses are limited if the market rises and unlimited in a falling market. Breakeven is reached when the underlying moves in either direction by the amount of the premium received.

Short Straddle versus Put The trade: Sell a call at strike B, sell a put at the same strike (B), buy a put at any strike; generally the long put will be at a strike lower than the straddle (A). This spread offers similar exposure to the short straddle, but the long put limits risk in a falling market. In the short straddle versus put, expectations are also for a neutral market and bearish volatility. However, at expiry, profits are limited in a static market while losses are limited if the market falls and unlimited if the market rises. Breakeven is reached when the underlying moves in either direction by the amount of premium received.

Long Butterfly Spread with Calls The trade: Buy a put (or call) at strike A, sell two puts (or calls) at a higher strike B, buy a put (or call) at an equally higher strike C. Market expectations are then to be direction neutral, and for volatility to be bearish. In this case, the holder expects the underlying to remain close to the strike B, or anticipate a fall in implied volatility. This position is less risky than selling straddles or strangles as there is a limited downside exposure. At expiry, the maximum profit is limited to the difference in strikes between A and B less the net cost of establishing the position (and maximized at midstrike B). Maximal losses are limited to the net cost of the position for either a rise or a fall in the underlying. Breakeven is reached where the intrinsic value of the lower-strike option equals the net cost of establishing the position, or when the intrinsic value of the higher-strike call equals the net cost of establishing the position.

Short Butterfly The trade: Sell a put (or a call) at strike *A*, buy two puts (or calls) at strike *B*, and sell a put (or call) at strike *C*. Market expectation is for a neutral market and bullish volatility. In this case the holder of the trade expects a directional move in the underlying, or a rise in implied volatility. At expiry, profit is defined by the net credit received in establishing the position and occurs if there is a sufficient directional move of the underlying, in either direction. The loss is limited to the difference in strikes between *A* and *B*, plus (minus) the net credit (debit) in establishing the position. Breakeven is reached where the intrinsic value of the lower-strike option equals the net credit in establishing the position, or when the intrinsic value of the higher-strike option equals the net credit in establishing the position.

Long Condor The trade: Buy a put (call) at strike price *A*; sell a put (call) at two equally higher strikes *B* and *C*; buy a put (call) at yet higher strike *D*. The long condor expects direction-neutral markets and a bearish volatility. A long condor allows for a greater degree of volatility and hence a wider band of profit potential than a long butterfly. At expiry, profits are maximized when the underlying settles between the two exercise prices *B* and *C*, but declines as the market rises or falls beyond these strikes. Losses occur if the underlying rises toward strike *D* or falls toward strike *A*. Loss will be limited to the cost of establishing the position for either a rise or a fall in the underlying. Finally, a lower breakeven point is reached when the underlying reaches the lower strike price *A* plus the cost of establishing the spread, and a higher breakeven arises when the underlying reaches the level of the higher strike *D* minus the cost of establishing the spread.

Short Condor The trade: Sell a put (call) at strike *A*; buy a put (call) at two equally higher strikes *B* and *C*; sell a put (call) at yet higher strike *D*. Expectations are for a direction-neutral market and a bullish volatility. The holder of the trade expects that the market will move significantly, or volatility will rise, but is uncertain of its direction. However, short condor will require a larger directional move than that of a butterfly in order to yield a profit. At expiry, the profit is limited and occurs if the market moves above the highest strike (*D*) or below the lower strike at *A*, while maximum losses are limited and occur if the market remains between the exercise prices *B* and *C*. Finally, breakeven is reached when the intrinsic value of the lower-strike option equals the net credit in establishing the position, or when the intrinsic value of the higher-strike option equals the net credit in establishing the position.

SUMMARY

The complete market's financial dogma is the result of an extraordinary and sustained effort by leading economic and financial theorists that has provided a theoretical pricing framework, which is also applied profusely. The uses and the trades of derivatives, once they have been priced, have increased at an extraordinary rate, providing liquidity and the means for investors and speculators to design strategies tailored to their needs. This chapter has introduced the rationale of such a pricing framework and has used simple examples to demonstrate its applications. Technically, pricing derivatives is based on portfolio replication as well as on finding a pricing martingale, namely, the martingale that allows us to price assets within the complete market framework. The next chapter emphasizes a variety of applications, derivative financial products, and problems priced by this important approach. Although the assumptions that underlie complete markets have been criticized due to their occasional failings, it remains a powerful financial tool for financial engineers.

APPENDIX A: MARTINGALES

Essentials of Martingales

A discrete stochastic process $\{x_n, n = 0, 1, 2, 3, \ldots\}$ is a martingale if for $n = 0, 1, 2, 3, \ldots$ the following property holds:

$$E\{|x_n|\} < \infty \text{ and } E\{x_{n+1} | x_n, x_{n-1}, x_{n-2}, \ldots\} = x_n \tag{A.1}$$

namely, that the conditional next-period (deflated) price is equal to its current (deflated) price. Note that the martingale is defined with respect to the process realization (a filtration), which is represented in this case by the process's past information, $x_n, x_{n-1}, x_{n-2}, \ldots$. But it may be measured relative to some other process with respect to which the (filtration) process $\{y_n, n = 0, 1, 2, 3, \ldots\}$ defines a martingale if:

$$E\{x_{n+1} | y_n, y_{n-1}, y_{n-2}, \ldots\} = x_n \tag{A.2}$$

A number of examples will highlight the martingale property. Let the stock price process be defined in terms of a Bernoulli event where stock prices grow from period to period at rates $a > 1$ and $b < 1$ with probabilities defined as follows:

$$S_t = \begin{cases} aS_{t-1} \ w.p. \ \dfrac{1-b}{a-b} \\[2ex] bS_{t-1} \ w.p. \ \dfrac{a-1}{a-b} \end{cases} \tag{A.3}$$

This process is a martingale. First it can be summed and, further, we have to show that this a constant mean process with:

$$E(S_{t+1} | S_t, S_{t-1}, \ldots, S_0) = E(S_{t+1} | S_t) = S_t \tag{A.4}$$

Explicitly, we have:

$$E(S_{t+1} | S_t) = aS_t \frac{1-b}{a-b} + bS_t \frac{a-1}{a-b} = S_t \frac{b(a-1) + a(1-b)}{a-b} = S_t$$

Whether this is a price observed reflecting a market price is totally another question (and probably it is not). By the same token, we can show that there are many other processes that have the martingale property. Consider the trinomial (birth-death) random walk defined by:

$$
\begin{cases}
S_{t+1} = S_t + \varepsilon_t, \, S_0 = 0 \\
\varepsilon_t = \begin{cases} +1 \, \text{w.p.} \, p \\ 0 \, \text{w.p.} \, r \\ -1 \, \text{w.p.} \, q \end{cases} ; \quad p \geq 0, q \geq 0, r \geq 0, p + q + r = 1
\end{cases}
\tag{A.5}
$$

Of course it is not a martingale, as it has a drift rate of $(p - q)$. However, it is easy to show that the driftless process $(S_t - t(p - q); t \geq 0)$ is a martingale. To verify this assertion, note that:

$$
\begin{aligned}
E\left(S_{t+1} - (t+1)(p-q)/\Phi_t\right) &= E\left(S_t + \varepsilon_t - (t+1)(p-q)/\Phi_t\right) = \\
&= S_t - (t+1)(p-q) + E(\varepsilon_t) = S_t - (t+1)(p-q) + (p-q) = \\
&= S_t - t(p-q)
\end{aligned}
\tag{A.6}
$$

where $\Phi_t \equiv (S_0, S_1, S_2, \ldots, S_t)$ resumes the information set available at time t. Further,

$$
\left(S_t^2 - t(p-q); t \geq 0\right), \left\{\left(S_t^2 - t(p-q)\right)^2 + t\left((p-q)^2 - (p+q)\right); t \geq 0\right\}
\tag{A.7}
$$

and

$$
\left\{\lambda^{x_t}, \lambda = q/p, t \geq 0\right\}, \, p > 0
$$

are also martingales. The proof is straightforward. By the same token, we can also consider processes that are not martingales and then find a transformation or another process that will render the original process a martingale. In this sense, a price process might not be a martingale but we might find a reference asset relative to which the relative price process is a martingale.

Consider next a stock price; then under a martingale measure, we have:

$$
\frac{S(0)}{B(0)} = E^Q\left(\frac{S(1)}{B(1)}\right)
\tag{A.8}
$$

and for a call option,

$$
\frac{C(0)}{B(0)} = E^Q\left(\frac{C(1)}{B(1)}\right)
$$

Generally, for an option whose maturity is at t and whose strike is K, the call price is:

$$
\frac{C(0 : t, K)}{B(0)} = E^Q\left(\frac{C(t; K)}{B(t)}\right) = E^Q\left(\frac{(S(t) - K)^+}{B(t)}\right)
\tag{A.9}
$$

The Change of Measures and Martingales

How do we find a measure and how do we change a measure? These are the questions we encounter when we apply the martingale approach to asset pricing. This requires that we define and use Novikov's condition, the Radon Nikodym derivative, and Girsanov's theorem.

Essentially, Novikov's condition states that a price process be of bounded variance. For a change of measure in discrete time, the idea is as follows. Consider two martingale measures defined by a deflator with respect to a risk-free bond and another with respect to a market index. This means that:

$$\frac{S(0)}{B(0)} = E^Q\left(\frac{S(1)}{B(1)}\right) \text{ and } \frac{S(0)}{M(0)} = E^M\left(\frac{S(1)}{M(1)}\right) \tag{A.10}$$

where E^Q is an expectation relative to the risk-neutral process and E^M is an expectation with respect to the market index. A relationship between these two measures can be found by noting that the martingale property means that:

$$S(0) = B(0)E^Q\left(\frac{S(1)}{B(1)}\right) = M(0)E^M\left(\frac{S(1)}{M(1)}\right)$$

or

$$\frac{B(0)}{M(0)}E^Q\left(\frac{S(1)}{B(1)}\right) = E^M\left(\frac{S(1)}{M(1)}\right) \tag{A.11}$$

which can be written as follows:

$$E^Q\left(S(1)\frac{1/M(0)}{B(1)/B(0)}\right) = E^Q\left(\frac{S(1)}{M(1)}\frac{M(1)/M(0)}{B(1)/B(0)}\right) = E^M\left(\frac{S(1)}{M(1)}\right) \tag{A.12}$$

or

$$E^Q\left(\frac{S(1)}{M(1)}\Omega(B, M)\right) = E^M\left(\frac{S(1)}{M(1)}\right) \text{ where } \Omega(B, M) = \frac{M(1)/M(0)}{B(1)/B(0)} \tag{A.13}$$

As a result, the functional relationship $\Omega(B, M)$ provides a means to change Numéraire. Note that if we do not change the risk-neutral Numéraire then of course, $\Omega(B, M) = 1$. Inversely, under the market M Numéraire, we have:

$$E^M\left(S(1)\frac{1/B(0)}{M(1)/M(0)}\right) = E^M\left(\frac{S(1)}{B(1)}\frac{B(1)/M(0)}{M(1)/M(0)}\right) = E^M\left(\frac{S(1)}{B(1)}\Omega^{-1}(B, M)\right)$$

$$= E^Q\left(\frac{S(1)}{B(1)}\right) \tag{A.14}$$

This latter equality is essentially the Radon Nikodym derivative and is valid for all instants of time (since both expressions define a martingale with their appropriate probability measures). This equation provides a relationship between the two probability measures. Explicitly, let a random variable be defined by S^Q under the probability measure Q. By the same token let S^M be a random variable under the probability measure M, then a change of measure does not change the random price but transforms the probability measure from one set of probabilities to another and such that the following holds:

$$Law\left(S^Q | Q\right) \equiv Law\left(S^M | M\right) \tag{A.15}$$

This particular characteristic is used in the next chapter when dealing with continuous time and stochastic underlying processes. The solution of the Radon Nikodym derivative, providing a change in probability measure to define the pricing martingale, is due to Girsanov, known as the Girsanov theorem.

EXAMPLE: CHANGE OF MEASURE IN A BINOMIAL MODEL

Assume a binomial price model with the probabilities p of a price increase and $1 - p$ of a price decrease. The binomial states are

$$S_0 \Rightarrow \left(S^+; S^-\right) = (S_0(1+h); S_0(1-\ell))$$

To transform this process into a martingale we deflate the stock price (namely, we price with respect to the deflator), say, by a bond with a risk-free rate of return. A deflated stock price is thus:

$$\frac{S(0)}{B(0)} = E^{Q_R}\left(\frac{S(1)}{B(1)}\right) = \frac{S_0(1+h)}{B(0)(1+R_f)} p_1^* + \frac{S_0(1-\ell)}{B(0)(1+R_f)} p_2^* \tag{A.16}$$

or

$$\frac{S_0}{1} \Rightarrow \left(\frac{S^+}{1+R_f}; \frac{S^-}{1+R_f}\right) = \left(S_0\frac{1+h}{1+R_f}; \frac{1-\ell}{1+R_f}S_0\right) \text{ or } \frac{S_0}{1} = S_0^* \Rightarrow \left(S^{*+}; S^{*-}\right) \tag{A.17}$$

By the same token, under another measure, say a market M, we have:

$$\frac{S(0)}{M(0)} = E^M\left(\frac{S(1)}{M(1)}\right) = \frac{S_0(1+h)}{M(0)(1+h_M)} q_{1,M}^* + \frac{S_0(1-\ell)}{M(0)(1-\ell_M)} q_{2,M}^* \tag{A.18}$$

and therefore,

$$\begin{aligned}
\frac{B(0)}{M(0)} E^Q\left(\frac{S(1)}{B(1)}\right) &= \frac{S_0(1+h)}{B(0)(1+R_f)} p_1^* + \frac{S_0(1-\ell)}{B(0)(1+R_f)} p_2^* \\
&= E^M\left(\frac{S(1)}{M(1)}\right) = \frac{S_0(1+h)}{M(0)(1+h_M)} q_{1,M}^* + \frac{S_0(1-\ell)}{M(0)(1-\ell_M)} q_{2,M}^*
\end{aligned} \tag{A.19}$$

Using

$$\frac{S(0)}{M(0)} = E^M \left(\frac{S(1)}{M(1)} \right) = E^Q \left(\frac{S(1)}{M(1)} \frac{M(1)/M(0)}{B(1)/B(0)} \right) \tag{A.20}$$

we have explicitly,

$$\frac{S(0}{M(0)} = E^M \left(\frac{S(1)}{M(1)} \right) = E^{Q_R} \left(\frac{S(1)}{M(1)} \frac{M(1)/M(0)}{B(1)/B(0)} \right) =$$

$$= \frac{S_0(1+h)}{M(0)(1+h_M)} q_{1,M}^* + \frac{S_0(1-\ell)}{M(0)(1-\ell_M)} q_{2,M}^* =$$

$$E^{Q_R} \left(\frac{S(1)}{M(1)} \frac{M(1)/M(0)}{B(1)/B(0)} \right) = E^{Q_R} \left(\begin{array}{c} \dfrac{S_0(1+h)}{M(0)(1+h_M)} \dfrac{M(0)(1+h_M)/M(0)}{B(0)(1+R_f)/B(0)} p_1^* + \\ \dfrac{S(0)(1-\ell)}{M(0)(1-\ell_M)} \dfrac{(1-\ell_M)/M(0)}{B(0)(1+R_f)/B(0)} p_2^* \end{array} \right) \tag{A.21}$$

which is reduced to:

$$1 = \frac{(1+h)}{(1+h_M)} q_{1,M}^* + \frac{(1-\ell)}{(1-\ell_M)} q_{2,M}^* = \left(\begin{array}{c} \dfrac{(1+h)}{(1+h_M)} \dfrac{(1+h_M)}{(1+R_f)} p_1^* + \\ \dfrac{(1-\ell)}{(1-\ell_M)} \dfrac{(1-\ell_M)}{(1+R_f)} p_2^* \end{array} \right)$$

$$= \frac{(1+h)}{(1+R_f)} p_1^* + \frac{(1-\ell)}{(1+R_f)} p_2^* \tag{A.22}$$

In this case, note that the Radon Nikodym derivative is:

$$\frac{p_1^*}{q_{1,M}^*} = \frac{1+R_f}{1+h_M} \text{ and } \frac{p_2^*}{q_{2,M}^*} = \frac{1+R_f}{1-\ell_M} \text{ or } \xi_1^{-1} = \frac{1+R_f}{1+h_M} \text{ and } \xi_2^{-1} = \frac{1+R_f}{1-\ell_M} \tag{A.23}$$

Further,

$$\frac{1-p_1^*}{1-q_{1,M}^*} = \frac{1+R_f}{1-\ell_M}$$

and therefore,

$$\frac{p_1^*}{q_{1,M}^*} = \frac{1+R_f}{1+h_M} \text{ and } \frac{1-p_1^*}{1-q_{1,M}^*} = \frac{1+R_f}{1-\ell_M}$$

as well as:

$$\left(1 - \ell_M - q_{1,M}^* \frac{(1+R_f)(1-\ell_M)}{1+h_M} \right) = (1+R_f) - (1+R_f) q_{1,M}^* \tag{A.24}$$

which leads to:

$$q^*_{1,M} = \frac{(R_f + \ell_M)(1 + h_M)}{(1 + R_f)(h_M + \ell_M)} \qquad (A.25)$$

and to

$$q^*_{2,M} = 1 - \frac{(R_f + \ell_M)(1 + h_M)}{(1 + R_f)(h_M + \ell_M)} = \frac{(1 - \ell_M)(h_M - R_f)}{(1 + R_f)(h_M + \ell_M)}$$

The challenging problem is how to determine a measure with respect to which the price process just outlined is a martingale. To do so, we set the current price to its expected value (and, therefore, render the binomial process driftless). To this end, assume the risk-neutral probability measure p^* defined by $S^*(0) = E^*(S^*(1))$ and therefore

$$p^*_1 = \frac{R_f + \ell}{h + \ell}$$

as seen earlier. For example, let $R_f = 0.05$, $h = 0.10$, $\ell = 0.05$ while for a market index, $(h_M, \ell_M) = (0.07, 0.03)$. Then under the risk-neutral measure, we have:

$$p^*_1 = \frac{R_f + \ell}{h + \ell} = \frac{0.05 + 0.05}{0.15} = 0.66$$

But

$$\frac{p^*_1}{q^*_{1,M}} = \frac{1 + R_f}{1 + h_M} = \frac{1 + 0.05}{1 + 0.07} \text{ and } q^*_{1,M} = \frac{(1.07)0.66}{1.05}$$

and

$$\frac{1 - p^*_1}{q^*_{2,M}} = \frac{1 + R_f}{1 - \ell_M} = \frac{1 + 0.05}{0.97} \text{ and } q^*_{2,M} = \frac{(0.97)0.33}{1.05}$$

EXAMPLE: A TWO-STAGE RANDOM WALK AND THE RADON NIKODYM DERIVATIVE

In this example (due to Shreve) we proceed to a change of measure using the Radon Nikodym derivative. Consider the following binomial process $(p, 1 - p)$ relative to a measure P, which we seek to transform to another binomial process (a martingale) with probabilities $(p^*, 1 - p^*) = (\frac{1}{2}, \frac{1}{2})$. Over two periods, we have the following set of possibilities: The security increases twice, once, and none, or (HH, HL, LH, LL).

The probabilities are $(p, 1 - p) = \left(\frac{1}{3}, \frac{2}{3}\right)$ and $(p^*, 1 - p^*) = \left(\frac{1}{2}, \frac{1}{2}\right)$, the probability transform of the P process into a Q process, a martingale. Thus, relative to the Q martingale process, the probability that there are two successive price increases is:

$$P\left(\frac{H_P H_P}{H_Q H_Q}\right) : \frac{\left(\frac{1}{2}\right)\left(\frac{1}{2}\right)}{\left(\frac{1}{3}\right)\left(\frac{1}{3}\right)} = \frac{9}{4} \tag{A.26}$$

where

$$P\left(\frac{H_P H_P}{H_Q H_Q}\right)$$

denotes the ratio of the probabilities for this specific event. For all events, we summarize the calculation of the Radon-Nykodim derivatives:

$$\left(HH : \frac{\left(\frac{1}{2}\right)\left(\frac{1}{2}\right)}{\left(\frac{1}{3}\right)\left(\frac{1}{3}\right)} = \frac{9}{4}; HL : \frac{\left(\frac{1}{2}\right)\left(\frac{1}{2}\right)}{\left(\frac{1}{3}\right)\left(\frac{2}{3}\right)} = \frac{9}{8}; LH : \frac{\left(\frac{1}{2}\right)\left(\frac{1}{2}\right)}{\left(\frac{2}{3}\right)\left(\frac{1}{3}\right)} = \frac{9}{8}; \right.$$

$$\left. LL : \frac{\left(\frac{1}{2}\right)\left(\frac{1}{2}\right)}{\left(\frac{2}{3}\right)\left(\frac{2}{3}\right)} = \frac{9}{16} \right) \tag{A.27}$$

And as a result, the ratio of the measures yields:

$$\left(\xi(HH) : \frac{\left(\frac{1}{2}\right)\left(\frac{1}{2}\right)}{\left(\frac{1}{3}\right)\left(\frac{1}{3}\right)} = \frac{9}{4}; \xi(HL) : \frac{\left(\frac{1}{2}\right)\left(\frac{1}{2}\right)}{\left(\frac{1}{3}\right)\left(\frac{2}{3}\right)} = \frac{9}{8}; \right.$$

$$\left. \xi(LH) : \frac{\left(\frac{1}{2}\right)\left(\frac{1}{2}\right)}{\left(\frac{2}{3}\right)\left(\frac{1}{3}\right)} = \frac{9}{8}; \xi(LL) : \frac{\left(\frac{1}{2}\right)\left(\frac{1}{2}\right)}{\left(\frac{2}{3}\right)\left(\frac{2}{3}\right)} = \frac{9}{16} \right) ; \tag{A.28}$$

Or $\xi(w) = \dfrac{\mathbf{P}_{\frac{1}{2}}}{\mathbf{P}_{\frac{1}{3}}}$

In this case,

$$\xi(w) = \frac{\mathbf{P}_{\frac{1}{2}}}{\mathbf{P}_{\frac{1}{3}}}, \mathrm{E}\left(\xi(w)\mathbf{P}_{\frac{1}{3}}\right) = E\left(\mathbf{P}_{\frac{1}{2}}\right)$$

Define the following prices:

$$
\left(
\begin{array}{c}
HH : S(1+h)^2, \xi(HH) : \dfrac{\left(\frac{1}{2}\right)\left(\frac{1}{2}\right)}{\left(\frac{1}{3}\right)\left(\frac{1}{3}\right)} = \dfrac{9}{4} \quad HL : S(1+h)(1-\ell), \xi(HL) : \dfrac{\left(\frac{1}{2}\right)\left(\frac{1}{2}\right)}{\left(\frac{1}{3}\right)\left(\frac{2}{3}\right)} = \dfrac{9}{8} \\[4mm]
LH : S(1-\ell)(1+h), \xi(LH) : \dfrac{\left(\frac{1}{2}\right)\left(\frac{1}{2}\right)}{\left(\frac{2}{3}\right)\left(\frac{1}{3}\right)} = \dfrac{9}{8} \quad LL : S(1-\ell)^2, \xi(LL) : \dfrac{\left(\frac{1}{2}\right)\left(\frac{1}{2}\right)}{\left(\frac{2}{3}\right)\left(\frac{2}{3}\right)} = \dfrac{9}{16}
\end{array}
\right);
$$

$$(A.29)$$

APPENDIX B: FORMAL NOTATIONS, KEY TERMS, AND DEFINITIONS

In many cases a more formal language is used to present and explain the quantitative results we have outlined. This appendix defines some key terms. In most models of asset pricing we use a set of states Ω, with associated probabilities to characterize the model underlying uncertainty. Such a set may be finite or infinite. A set of events is then expressed by $\Im$, also called a tribe and by some a sigma-algebra. $\Im$ is a collection of subsets of Ω that can be assigned a probability $P(A)$ denoting the probability of a specific event A. In an intertemporal framework defined by dates $0,1,\ldots,T+1$, there is at each date a tribe $\Im_t \subset \Im$, corresponding to the events based on the information available at that time t. Any event in $\Im_t$ is known at time t to be true or false. The convention $\Im_t \subset \Im_s$, $t \leq s$ is used whenever we mean that events are never forgotten and therefore information obtained over time provides an ever-expanding knowledge. For simplicity, we let events in $\Im_0$ have probability 0 or 1, meaning that there is no information at time $t = 0$.

A filtration is defined by $\Phi = \{\Im_0, \Im_1, \Im_2, \ldots, \Im_T\}$, sometimes called an information structure, representing how information is revealed over time. For any random variable Y, we thus use at time t:

$$E_t(Y) = E(Y|\Im_t)$$

to denote the conditional expectation of Y given $\Im_t$. For notational simplicity, we also let $Y = Z$ for any two random variables Y and Z, if the probability that $Y \neq Z$ is zero.

An adapted process, defined by a sequence $X = \{X_0, X_1, X_2, \ldots, X_T\}$ such that, for each t, X_t is a random variable with respect to $(\Omega, \Im_t)$ means, informally, that X_t is observable at time t. An important characteristic of such processes in asset pricing is that an adapted process X is a martingale if for any times t and $s > t$, we have $E_t(X_s) = X_t$. For example, if the conditional expectation of an asset price equals the currently observed price, then the adapted price process is a martingale. For this reason, important facets of financial asset pricing revolve around the notion of martingales.

Another term of importance we use with respect to stochastic price processes is *non-anticipating*. This means that for any time $t < s$ the function (price) is statistically independent of the future uncertainty. Or, the current price is independent of the future Wiener process $W(s) - W(t)$. These mathematical properties are extremely useful in proving basic results in the theoretical analysis of financial markets. However, in practice, underlying processes might not be martingales and further be anticipative processes. Of course, this will also imply that our theoretical and financial constructs may be violated.

A security is then a claim to an adapted (and non-anticipating) dividend process, say D, with D_t denoting the dividend paid by the security at time t. Each security has an adapted security-price process S, so that S_t is the price of the security, ex dividend, at time t. That is, at each time t, the security pays its dividend D_t and is then available for trade at price S_t. This convention implies that D_0 plays no role in determining ex-dividend prices. The cum-dividend security price at time t is $S_t + D_t$. A trading strategy is an adapted process **n** in $\Re^N$. Here, n_t represents the portfolio held after trading at time t. The dividend process $D^{\mathbf{n}}$ generated by a trading strategy **n** is thus defined by

$$D_t^{\mathbf{n}} = n_{t-1}(S_{t-1} + D_t) - n_t S_t$$

with n_{-1} taken to be zero by convention. Consider a portfolio consisting in investing of our wealth in the security and in a bond B_{t-1}. Say that at time $t-1$, the portfolio wealth state is given by:

$$X_{t-1}^{\mathbf{n},m} = n_{t-1}S_{t-1} + m_{t-1}B_{t-1}. \tag{B.1}$$

We then state that a strategy is said to be self-financing if:

$$X_t^{\mathbf{n},m} - X_{t-1}^{\mathbf{n},m} = n_{t-1}(S_t - S_{t-1}) + m_{t-1}(B_t - B_{t-1}) \tag{B.2}$$

For example, a bonds-only strategy is defined by $n_{t-1} = 0$, while buy and hold (long) strategies (that do not depend on time) imply that $n_{t-1} = n > 0$. A short position is defined when $n_{t-1} < 0$. Finally, a strategy consisting in maintaining a constant proportion of our wealth in bonds and stock means that:

$$n_t S_t / X_t^{\mathbf{n},m} = \alpha \text{ while } m_t B_t / X_t^{\mathbf{n},m} = 1 - \alpha \tag{B.3}$$

TEST YOURSELF

7.1 Answer the following: What is an option? What is a European option? What is an American option? What is a compound option? What is an underlying asset? What is a call option? What is the strike price of a call option? What is the payoff of a call? What is the call option premium? What is a put option? What is the strike price of a put option? What does the payoff from a put represent? What is the premium of a put?

7.2 What does in-the-money indicate? What is the descriptive word used when the spot price exceeds the strike price for a put option? What is the theoretical value of an option?

7.3   Give three reasons you would use to buy an option (any option) and three reasons why you would sell that option.

7.4   What is an index option and how do such options differ from options on securities and options on corporate bonds?

7.5   What are the implications of buying a portfolio whose initial price is null and has, with a positive probability, a positive return in the next period?

7.6   Say that the risk-free rate is R_f and let the bond be risk-free as well; further assume that the underlying security is binomial. Express in this case, in mathematical notation, the potential for arbitrage. (Answer: At least one of the following two alternatives must hold strictly: $n_1 s_{1,H} + B(1 + R_f) \geq 0$ and $n_1 S_{1,L} + B(1 + R_f) \geq 0$.) If there is no arbitrage, what will the risk neutrality be? What is the difference between a historical probability and a risk-neutral probability?

7.7   Consider an investor buying two European put options with strike price of $40 and one European call option with strike price $50 on the same stock S with the same expiry date N. The total price of these options is $10. Show that the gain-loss function of this portfolio is $\Lambda(S_N) = 2(40 - S_N)^+ + (S_N - 50)^+ - 10$ where $S(N)$ is the price of the asset at time N. Two situations arise: If $S(N) < 40$ then the put options are exercised and the call option is not, in which case, $\Lambda(S_N) = 2(40 - S_N)^+ - 10 = 70 - 2S_N$ and a profit is earned if $S_N < 35$. If $\Lambda(S_N) = (S_N - 50)^+ - 10 = S_N - 60$ then none of the options are exercised and the premium is lost. Show also that if the price is larger than 50, then only the call option is exercised. And a profit is earned if the price is larger than 60.

7.8   Assume a portfolio of two securities and a bond, and set the portfolio price to be initially $P_0 = n_1 S_0 + n_2 V_0 + B$. Say that this portfolio price is null. What are the conditions for your constructing an arbitrage portfolio? Show how you would obtain such a portfolio by linear programming.

7.9   What is the payoff from the exercise of a one-year call option with a strike price of $170 and a premium of $1.00, given an underlying price of $172?

7.10   What is the P/L from the exercise of a one-year European call option with a strike price of $190 and premium of $4.50 given an underlying asset price of $235.50?

7.11   What is the P/L from an asset sold at $150 if the spot price moves to $100?

7.12   What is the payoff from the exercise of a one-year European put option with a strike price of $150 and a premium of $1.00, given that its underlying asset price is $123?

7.13   What is the payoff from the exercise of a one-year European call option with a strike price of $170 and a premium of $1.00, given an underlying asset price of $172?

7.14   Which option has the greatest value?

   a. A one-year European call option with a strike price of $95, a spot price of $95, volatility of 10 percent, and an interest rate of 5 percent.

    b. A two-year European call option with a strike price of $95, a spot price of $95, volatility of 10 percent, and an interest rate of 5 percent.

    c. A three-year European call option with a strike price of $95, a spot price of $95, volatility of 10 percent, and an interest rate of 5 percent.

    d. All options are equal in value.

7.15 How do interest rates affect the value of an option?

7.16 What are the variables that affect the value of an option?

7.17 What is the intrinsic value of an option?

7.18 How is the time value of an option calculated?

    a. Total option value minus intrinsic value.

    b. Intrinsic value minus total option value.

    c. Total option value minus time remaining to maturity.

    d. Intrinsic value minus time remaining to maturity.

7.19 What is the time value for a one-year European put with a strike price of $122 and an option value of $7.10 when the spot price of the underlying asset is $115.50?

7.20 Why does the value of an option decay over time, all things held constant?

7.21 What positions are bearish (i.e., they profit when underlying prices decline)?

7.22 What is a trading strategy? Define the different trading strategies, their characteristics, and which strategies you would prefer if expectations are for a bearish or bullish volatility.

7.23 Compare the following trading strategies: covered calls and protective puts. Why would you use one or the other?

7.24 What are spread strategies? When would you use these strategies? What are the prices of these strategies?

7.25 What are combination strategies? When would you use these strategies?

7.26 How did Barings Bank lose so much money in January 1994? Following the Kobe earthquake on January 17, the Nikkei plunged by over 1,000 points, leading to large losses of the puts in the straddle portfolio. Barings Bank, seeking to double-or-nothing its bet, responded in the subsequent weeks by massively increasing its holding of long futures on the Nikkei. A further fall in the Nikkei increased the losses on the puts and led to huge margin requirements on the futures, wiping out Barings. The failure of Barings was thus due to sour bets and to a failure of corporate risk management. Explain why it is true or false.

7.27 Compare the returns and the losses of two portfolios: Portfolio A—a long call option with maturity and strike K with an option price C; and Portfolio B—a single security S held long and borrowing of the present value of the strike, or $PV(K)$, for repayment at time T, the option's expiration date, with a cost of $S - PV(K)$. As a result, $C = S - PV(K) + IV(C)$. Adding and subtracting K, we have then the following equality:

$C = (S - K) + (K - PV(K)) + IV(C)$ or explicitly in words we have Call Price = Intrinsic Value + Time Value + Insurance Value.

7.28 Prove the put-call parity equation $C = PV(K) = P + S$ and discuss its importance for financial trading. (In particular, discuss how it can be used to replicate optional characteristics from one option to another)

7.29 In your view, what are potential reasons for put-call parity not to hold?

REFERENCES

Amin, K. 1993. Jump diffusion option valuation in discrete time. *Journal of Finance* 48:1833–1863.

Arrow, K. J. 1963. Aspects of the theory of risk bearing. YRJO Johansson Lectures. Reprinted in *Essays in the theory of risk bearing*. Chicago: Markham, 1971.

Blair, R. D., and D. L. Kaiserman. 1982. Optimal franchising. *Southern Economic Journal* 49(2):494–505.

Boyle, P. P. 1992. *Options and the management of financial risk*. New York: Society of Actuaries.

Brennan, M. J. 1979. The pricing of contingent claims in discrete time models. *Journal of Finance* 1:53–63.

Caves, R. E., and W. E. Murphy. 1976. Franchising firms, markets and intangible assets. *Southern Economic Journal* 42(April):572–586.

Cox, J. C., S. A. Ross, and M. Rubenstein. 1979. Option pricing approach. *Journal of Financial Economics* 7:229–263.

Cox, J., and M. Rubinstein. 1985. *Options markets*. Englewood Cliffs, NJ: Prentice Hall.

Dennis, P., and S. Mayhew. 2002. Risk neutral skewness: Evidence from stock options. *Journal of Financial and Quantitative Analysis* 37:471–493.

Easley, D., and M. O'Hara. 1987. Price, quantity, and information in securities markets. *Journal of Financial Economics* 19:69–90.

Fama, E. 1965. The behavior of stock market prices. *Journal of Business* 38:34–105.

———. 1970. Efficient capital markets: A review of theory and empirical work. *Journal of Finance* 25:383–417.

Friedman, M. 1953. *Essays in positive economics*. Chicago: University Press.

Girsanov, I. V. 1960. On transforming a certain class of stochastic processes by absolutely continuous substitution of measures. *Theory Probability and Its Applications* 5:285–301.

Harrison, J. M., and D. M. Kreps. 1979. Martingales and arbitrage in multiperiod security markets. *Journal of Economic Theory* 20:381–408.

Harrison, J. M., and S. R. Pliska. 1981. Martingales and stochastic integrals with theory of continuous trading. *Stochastic Processes and Applications* 11:261–271.

Karatzas, I., J. Lehocsky, S. Shreve, and G. L. Xu. 1991. Martingale and duality methods for utility maximization in an incomplete market. *SIAM Journal on Control and Optimization* 29:702–730.

Karlin, S., and H. M. Taylor. 1981. *A second course in stochastic processes*. San Diego: Academic Press.

Kaufmann, P. J., and R. P. Dant. 2001. The pricing of franchise rights. *Journal of Retailing* 77:537–545.

Kaufman, P. J., and F. Lafontaine. 1994. Costs of control: The source of economic rents for McDonald's franchises. *Journal of Law and Economics* 37(2):413–453.

Lafontaine, F. 1992. Contract theory and franchising: Some empirical results. *Rand Journal of Economics* 23(2):263–283.

Levy, P. 1948. *Processus stochastiques et mouvement Brownien*. Paris: Gauthier-Villars.

Lucas, R. E. 1978. Asset prices in an exchange economy. *Econometrica* 46:1429–1445.

Malliaris, A. G. 1981. Martingale methods in financial decision making. *SIAM Review*.

Mathewson, G. F. and R. A. Winter. 1986. The economics of franchise contracts. *Journal of Law and Economics* 28 (October):503–526.

Magill, M., and M. Quinzii. 1996. *Theory of incomplete markets*, vol. 1. Boston: MIT Press.

Malkiel, Burton G. 2000. Are markets efficient? Yes—Even if they make errors. *Wall Street Journal* (Eastern edition), December, A10.

Merton, R. C. 1990. *Continuous time finance*. Cambridge, MA: Blackwell.

Modigliani, F., and M. H. Miller. 1958. The cost of capital, corporation finance and the theory of investment. *American Economic Review* 48(3) (June):261–297.

Muth, J. 1961. Rational expectations and the theory of price movements. *Econometrica* 29:315–335.

Pfeifer, C., K. Schredelseker, and G. U. H. Seeber. 2009. On the negative value of information in informationally inefficient markets: Calculations for large number of traders. *European Journal of Operations Research* 195:117, 126.

Pliska, S. 1986. A stochastic calculus model of continuous trading: Optimal portfolios. *Mathematics of Operations Research* 11:371–382.

Posner, M., and C. S. Tapiero. 1988. The manufacturing quality density function and quality control. *International Journal of Production Research* 26.

Rey, P., and J. Tirole. 1986. The logic of vertical restraints. *American Economic Review* 76:921–939.

Ross, Stephen A. 1976. Options and efficiency. *Quarterly Journal of Economics* 90 (February): 75–89.

———. 1976. The arbitrage pricing theory of capital asset pricing. *Journal of Economic Theory* 13:341–360.

Rubin, P. H. 1978. The theory of the firm and the structure of the franchise contract. *Journal of Law and Economics* 21 (April):223–233.

Rubinstein, M. 1994. Implied binomial trees. *Journal of Finance* 69 (July):771–818.

Samuelson, P. 1965. Proof that properly anticipated prices fluctuate randomly. *Industrial Management Review* 6:41–49.

Sen, K. C. 1995. The use of initial fees and royalties in business format franchising. *Managerial and Decision Economics* 14(2):175–190.

Shreve S., 2005. *Stochastic Calculus for Finance I: The Binomial Asset Pricing Model*. New York, Springer.

Smith, C.W. 1976. Option pricing: A review. *Journal of Financial Economics* 3:3–51.

Tapiero, C. S. 1996. *The management and the control of quality*. London: Chapman and Hall.

———. 2005. Advertising and advertising claims over time. In *Optimal control and dynamic games, applications in finance, management science and economics*, ed. C. Deissenberg and R. F. Hartl. Berlin: Springer.

———. 2009. The market price of safety and economic reliability. Working paper, Department of Finance and Risk Engineering, New York University Polytechnic Institute, New York.

———. 2010. The financial price of quality claims. Working paper, Department of Finance and Risk Engineering, New York University Polytechnic Institute, New York.

Whisenant, S., S. Sankaraguruswamy, and R. Raghunandan. 2003. Market reaction to disclosure of reportable events. *Auditing: A Journal of Practice and Theory* 22(1):181–194.

Welker, M. 1995. Disclosure policy, information asymmetry and liquidity in equity markets. *Contemporary Accounting Research* 11(2):801–827.

CHAPTER 8

Options Applied

OVERVIEW

This chapter focuses on applications of the Arrow-Debreu theory, highlighting its many uses. A large variety of problems are treated including trading, immunization of portfolios, and short-selling as well as problems of pricing options, assets, and financial contracts. In addition, insurance contracts, infrastructure investments, pricing loans, and other problems are treated. The number of potential applications is extremely large and expanding in response to both needs and opportunities by and for investors and speculators. The chapter also provides an extension of the discrete state models considered in the previous chapter to the Black-Scholes continuous time lognormal model. Extensions to other models are profusely published and may be found in many standard financial engineering books as well as at the web site www.charlestapiero.com (where some of the problems outlined in this book are expanded). In addition, this chapter provides an introduction to the Greeks and their applications.

OPTION APPLICATIONS

To price assets we use essentially two techniques. One is based on replicating an asset to be priced by a portfolio whose price can be ascertained. Assuming that markets are complete, the law of the single price applies and therefore the asset and its replicating portfolio have necessarily the same price. In this sense, the price is only a construct indicative of the wants of buyers and sellers and the existence of an equilibrium based on the assumption of no arbitrage. A second approach is based on seeking a pricing martingale—namely, an arbitrage-free price process defined by a martingale. Applications of these approaches are numerous indeed and include the pricing of trading strategies, pricing particular industrial contracts, pricing pollution and carbon trading policies, pricing cooperatives, pricing health care insurance packages, pricing water and infrastructure investments, and so forth. Proper and fair pricing introduces greater efficiency in an economy since it allows the existence of a market and the definition of a price at which exchanges occur. If there is no efficient financial market, prices become arbitrary or result from some institutional decision processes (political, power based, etc.). The applications treated here span a broad range and outline a method for dealing with pricing various problems.

Risk-Free Portfolios and Immunization

Immunization strategies are often used in risk management and consist in the construction of a portfolio that replicates risk-free returns. In this case, immunization provides an alternative approach to commercial insurance by turning to financial markets (instead of using an insurance firm). This means that a portfolio whose current price is one dollar and whose next-period price is ensured and thus predictable with certainty with a price equal a risk-free investment.

For example, let a risk-free investment have cash flow (Q_0, Q_1) with $Q_0 = 1$ and $Q_1 \equiv 1 + R_f$. Let the replicating portfolio consist of the underlying and a call option where (a, b) are parameters denoting the number of shares in the underlying security and the call option. In this case, $Q_0 = a S_0 - b C_0 = 1$. A period later, replicating portfolio idols:

$$Q_{11} \equiv a S_{11} - b C_{11} = 1 + R_f, \quad Q_{12} \equiv a S_{12} - b C_{12} = 1 + R_f \tag{8.1}$$

which defines two equations in a and b, the parameters of the replicating portfolio with a solution:

$$a^* = \frac{(1 + R_f)(C_{11} - C_{12})}{(C_{11} - C_{12}) S_{11} - C_{11} (S_{11} - S_{12})}, \quad b^* = \frac{(1 + R_f)(S_{11} - S_{12})}{(C_{11} - C_{12}) S_{11} - C_{11} (S_{11} - S_{12})} \tag{8.2}$$

Thus, $a^* S_0 - b^* C_0 = 1$ and $C_0 = b^{*-1} - a^* b^{*-1} S_0$. Explicitly, inserting in the initial portfolio price, we obtain the discount factor:

$$\frac{1}{1 + R_f} = \frac{S_0 (C_{11} - C_{12})}{(C_{11} - C_{12}) S_{11} - C_{11} (S_{11} - S_{12})} - \frac{C_0 (S_{11} - S_{12})}{(C_{11} - C_{12}) S_{11} - C_{11} (S_{11} - S_{12})} \tag{8.3}$$

The option price implies then the risk-free discount rate (alternatively, we may interpret the risk-free rate as one implied by the portfolio consisting of the security and its underlying option). By the same token, for the option price

$$C_0 = \frac{S_0 (C_{11} - C_{12})}{(S_{11} - S_{12})} - \frac{1}{1 + R_f} \left(\frac{(C_{11} - C_{12}) S_{11}}{S_{11} - S_{12}} - C_{11} \right) \tag{8.4}$$

In particular, for a call option with $C_{12} = 0$ and $C_{11} = S_{11} - K$:

$$C_0 = (S_{11} - K) \left\{ \frac{S_0}{(S_{11} - S_{12})} + \frac{1}{1 + R_f} \left(1 - \frac{S_{11}}{S_{11} - S_{12}} \right) \right\} \tag{8.5}$$

For example, let a stock whose current price is $S_0 = 48$ assume two states, $S_{11} = 54$ and $S_{12} = 45$ one period later. The risk-free rate is 0.06 while a call option with an exercise in the next period is marketed whose strike is $K = 51$. Thus:

$$a^* = \frac{1 + R_f}{45}, b^* = \frac{1 + R_f}{15} \tag{8.6}$$

while the price of such a portfolio is:

$$48a^* - b^*C_0 = 1 \text{ and } 48\frac{1 + R_f}{45} - \frac{1 + R_f}{15}C_0 = 1 \text{ or } C_0 = 15(1.066 - 0.9433)$$

$$= 1.8495 \tag{8.7}$$

Selling Short

Short-selling is a practice that consists in selling assets, usually securities, that have been borrowed from a third party with the intention of buying identical assets back at a later date to be returned to the lender. The third party may have an interest in lending their assets for two reasons: They collect some cash and they move their assets off their balance sheet (in particular when these are toxic assets). This was practiced by Lehman Brothers and other financial firms during the financial crisis of 2008.

When there are such parties, a short-seller can profit from such a transaction by betting on the asset decline, bought at its lower price, and restoring the asset to the third party (with a hefty profit for the short-seller). Conversely, the short-seller will lose his bet if the price of the asset rises.

However, short-selling can be implemented through derivatives. For example, say that shares in the ABC Company currently sell for $10 per share. A short-seller would borrow 100 shares of ABC and then immediately sell those shares for a total of $1,000. If the price of ABC shares later falls to $8 per share, the short-seller would then buy 100 shares back for $800, return the shares to their original owner, and make a $200 profit (minus borrowing fees). This practice has the potential for losses as well. For example, if the shares of ABC that one borrowed and sold would increase to $25, the short-seller would have to buy back all the shares at $2,500, losing $1,500.

Because a short is the opposite of a long transaction, everything is the mirror opposite of a typical trade: The profit is limited but the loss is unlimited. Since the stock cannot be repurchased at a price lower than zero, the maximum gain is the difference between the current stock price and zero. However, because there is theoretically no ceiling on how much the stock price can go up (thereby costing short transactions money in order to buy the stocks back), an investor can theoretically lose a substantial amount of money if a stock continues to rise. In actual practice, however, as the price of the ABC Company would rise, the short-seller would eventually receive a margin call from the brokerage, demanding that the short-seller either cover his short position or provide additional cash in order to meet the margin requirement for ABC Company stock.

Short-sellers were blamed for the Wall Street Crash of 1929. Regulations governing short-selling were implemented in the United States in 1929 and in 1940. Political fallout from the 1929 Crash led Congress to enact a law banning short-sellers from selling shares during a declining market. This was in effect until

July 3, 2007, when it was removed by the SEC (SEC Release No. 34-55970). President Herbert Hoover and other public officials have condemned short-sellers in the past and during the 2008–2009 financial meltdown. In September 2008 short-selling was seen as a contributing factor to undesirable market volatility and subsequently was prohibited by the SEC for 799 financial companies for three weeks in an effort to stabilize those companies.

Future Prices

Say that we want to price a forward contract, consisting in buying for sure an asset whose current spot price is now $\$S$, at a price $\$F_T$ at time T. Let R_f be the period's riskless lending rate. The price of such a contract (since it is a riskless contract) is:

$$F_0 = e^{-R_f T} F_T$$

The return from such a transaction is therefore $Q = S - F_0$. Since no money has changed hands, there can be no profit; that is, $Q = 0$ and therefore $S = F_0$ and as a result the forward price is

$$F_T = Se^{R_f T}$$

Of course, the assumption of a unique price of assets with identical characteristics is necessary for such a result to be valid. If this is the case, then the market is complete.

A *future price*, unlike the forward price, consists in determining an agreed-on price at some future date where at all intermediate periods, a cost is incurred, called *marking to market*, to compensate for variation in the future prices over time. Thus, a future price at time $t = 0$ for a period later, time $t = 1$, $F(0,1)$, is equal to the forward price for that time, since no cost is incurred. In other words, $F(0,1) = F(1)$. Now consider the future price two periods hence, or $F(0,2)$. If the price increases to $S(H)$, the future price turns out to be the future price one period hence, which equals the one period forward price, or $F(H,1)$ (since only one more period is left till the exercise time). Similarly, if the price decreases to $S(L)$, the future price is now $F(L,1)$. As a result, the cash flow payments at the first and the second period are given in Figure 8.1.

Initially, *the value of these flows is worth nothing, since nothing is spent and nothing is gained*. As a result, the cash flows associated to time $t = 0$, time $t = 1$,

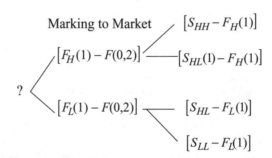

FIGURE 8.1   A Binomial Cash Flow

and time $t = 2$ are:

$$0 = \frac{1}{1 + R_f} \left[\alpha \left(F_H(1) - F(0, 2) \right) + \beta \left(F_L(1) - F(0, 2) \right) \right]$$

$$+ \frac{1}{(1 + R_f)^2} \left[\begin{array}{l} \alpha^2 \left(S_{HH} - F_H(1) \right) + \alpha\beta \left(S_{HL} - F_H(1) \right) + \\ \alpha\beta \left(S_{HL} - F_L(1) \right) + \beta^2 \left(S_{LL} - F_L(1) \right) \end{array} \right] \quad (8.8)$$

where α and β are parameters denoting the cash flow in case the future market price increases or decreases. This equation indicates that there is one equation in three unknowns. However, noting that for one-period future (forward) prices, we have:

$$F_H(1) = S_H \left(1 + R_f \right), \quad F_L(1) = S_L \left(1 + R_f \right) \quad (8.9)$$

inserting in the previous equation, we have:

$$0 = \frac{1}{1 + R_f} \left[\alpha \left(S_H \left(1 + R_f \right) - F(0, 2) \right) + \beta \left(S_L \left(1 + R_f \right) - F(0, 2) \right) \right]$$

$$+ \frac{1}{(1 + R_f)^2} \left[\begin{array}{l} \alpha^2 \left(S_{HH} - S_H \left(1 + R_f \right) \right) + \alpha\beta \left(S_{HL} - S_H \left(1 + R_f \right) \right) + \\ \alpha\beta \left(S_{HL} - S_L \left(1 + R_f \right) \right) + \beta^2 \left(S_{LL} - S_L \left(1 + R_f \right) \right) \end{array} \right] \quad (8.10)$$

and therefore,

$$F(0, 2) = \left(1 + R_f \right) \left[\alpha S_H + \beta S_L \right] + \frac{1}{(1 + R_f)} \left[\alpha^2 S_{HH} + 2\alpha\beta S_{HL} + \beta^2 S_{LL} \right]$$

$$- \left[\alpha^2 S_H + \alpha\beta S_H + \alpha\beta S_L + \beta^2 S_L \right] \quad (8.11)$$

Since

$$S(1 + R_f) = \left[\alpha S_H + \beta S_L \right],$$

$$S_H(1 + R_f) = \left[\alpha S_{HH} + \beta S_{HL} \right],$$

$$S_L(1 + R_f) = \left[\alpha S_{LH} + \beta S_{LL} \right] \quad (8.12)$$

as well as

$$S_H(1 + R_f) = \left[\alpha S_{HH} + \beta S_{HL} \right], \quad S_L(1 + R_f) = \left[\alpha S_{LH} + \beta S_{LL} \right] \quad (8.13)$$

we have:

$$F(0, 2) = \left(1 + R_f \right)^2 S + \frac{1}{(1 + R_f)} \left[\alpha \left(\alpha S_{HH} + \beta S_{HL} \right) + \beta \left(\alpha S_{HL} + \beta S_{LL} \right) \right]$$

$$- \left[\alpha^2 S_H + \alpha\beta S_H + \alpha\beta S_L + \beta^2 S_L \right] \quad (8.14)$$

which leads to the same price as that of the forward price found earlier: $F(0, 2) = \left(1 + R_f \right)^2 S$.

PROBLEM 8.1: PRICING A MULTIPERIOD FORWARD

Assume that the current price of an asset is S. Prove by induction that its future price n periods hence is $F(0, 2) = (1 + R_f)^n S$.

Security prices as well as their derivatives can also reveal future states rather than just the state prices. Next we consider such a problem in the context of an insurance pricing problem.

Pricing and New Insurance Business

Consider an insurance firm whose stock is quoted. It seeks to define a new insurance business to be marketed to insureds. What would be the market price of the new insurance business? Some ingredients to help us deal with this question include:

- The insurance firm receives a premium, which it invests—and therefore it has a known return from such an investment.
- The insurance firm faces the uncertainty of future losses associated with this business, although mitigated by the terms of the insurance contracts (such as co-participation agreements, excess of loss reinsurance terms, etc.).
- If the insurance firm chooses to be an intermediary, it may apply for reinsurance and share the insured risk and its insurance premium. Or the insurance firm may instead turn to financial markets to price and sell the new insurance contract and collect intermediaries' profits without risk (but be paid for its know-how and efforts).

A simple example can convey this approach. Let S_0 be the insurance firm price and let $S_0 + \pi$ be the firm's price inclusive of the insurance contract and its contingencies, where π is a premium collected per share. Our purpose is to determine the price π (albeit under simple assumptions and merely to highlight the approach used). To do so, assume that the firm is large and broadly traded with call and put options on the insurance firm's stock price as underlying. Potential losses from the new business are assumed to be catastrophic, affecting the stock price significantly. In this sense, insurance is an exchange between the insurer that receives the premium and the risks of the insured in case any catastrophic event occurs. As is shown in the following calculations, the premium the insurer will ask for (if markets are complete) is then determined by the beliefs of the investors and speculators trading on the firm call and put options.

Assuming complete markets, and therefore the existence of a risk-neutral probability p^Q, we have for the call and put options prices:

$$C_\pi = \frac{1}{1 + R_f} \left(p^Q C_\pi^+ + (1 - p^Q) C_\pi^- \right); P_\pi = \frac{1}{1 + R_f} \left(p^Q P_\pi^+ + (1 - p^Q) P_\pi^- \right)$$

$$(8.15)$$

while the underlying is:

$$S_0 + \pi = \frac{1}{1 + R_f} \left(p^Q (1 + h) (S_0 + \pi) + (1 - p^Q)(1 - \ell_\pi) (S_0 + \pi) \right) \qquad (8.16)$$

where $\ell_\pi = \ell + \ell^*$ is the stock-effect loss due to a normal loss (ℓ) and due to the new business catastrophic loss (ℓ^*). In this case:

$$1 = \frac{1}{1 + R_f} \left(p^Q(1 + h) + (1 - p^Q)(1 - \ell_\pi) \right) \tag{8.17}$$

and we have three equations with three unknowns. These are the insurance risk premium π, the risk-neutral probability p^{*Q}, and the predicted catastrophic loss ℓ^*. These equations result in a risk-neutral probability:

$$p^Q = \frac{R_f + (\ell + \ell^*)}{h + \ell + \ell^*} \tag{8.18}$$

We insert the call and put option prices and obtain two unknowns, the insurance premium to be received to face a stock loss return of ℓ^*. Namely,

$$\frac{R_f + (\ell + \ell^*)}{h + \ell + \ell^*} = \frac{C_\pi \left(1 + R_f\right) - C_\pi^-}{\left(C_\pi^+ - C_\pi^-\right)}; \frac{R_f + (\ell + \ell^*)}{h + \ell + \ell^*} = \frac{P_\pi \left(1 + R_f\right) - P_\pi^-}{\left(P_\pi^+ - P_\pi^-\right)} \tag{8.19}$$

For example, set

$$R_f = 0.05, \ell = 0.1, h = 0.2, C_\pi = 5, C_\pi^+ = Max(S_0(1 + h) - K, 0), C_\pi^- = 0,$$

and

$$P_\pi = 7, P_\pi^+ = 0, P_\pi^- = Max\left(Q - S_0(1 - \ell - \ell^*), 0\right)$$

where the strikes for the call and put options are known. Thus

$$p^Q = \frac{R_f + (\ell + \ell^*)}{h + \ell + \ell^*} = \frac{0.05 + 0.1 + \ell^*}{0.2 + 0.1 + \ell^*} \tag{8.20}$$

and therefore:

$$\frac{0.05 + 0.1 + \ell^*}{0.2 + 0.1 + \ell^*} = \frac{C_\pi \left(1 + R_f\right) - C_\pi^-}{\left(C_\pi^+ - C_\pi^-\right)} = \frac{C_\pi \left(1 + R_f\right)}{C_\pi^+}$$

$$= \frac{1.05 C_\pi}{(S_0 + \pi)(1 + h) - K}$$

$$\frac{0.05 + 0.1 + \ell^*}{0.2 + 0.1 + \ell^*} = \frac{P_\pi \left(1 + R_f\right) - P_\pi^-}{\left(P_\pi^+ - P_\pi^-\right)} = \frac{P_\pi^- - P_\pi \left(1 + R_f\right)}{P_\pi^-}$$

$$= \frac{Q - (S_0 + \pi)(1 - \ell - \ell^*) - 1.05 P_\pi}{Q - (S_0 + \pi)(1 - \ell - \ell^*)} \tag{8.21}$$

Further,

$$p^Q = \frac{C_\pi \left(1 + R_f\right)}{C_\pi^+} = \frac{\left(1 + R_f\right) C_\pi}{(S_0 + \pi)(1 + h) - K}$$

$$p^Q = \frac{P_\pi^- - P_\pi \left(1 + R_f\right)}{P_\pi^-} = \frac{Q - (S_0 + \pi)(1 - \ell - \ell^*) - \left(1 + R_f\right) P_\pi}{Q - (S_0 + \pi)(1 - \ell - \ell^*)} \quad (8.22)$$

As a result, the insurance premium per share is:

$$\pi = \frac{p^Q K + \left(1 + R_f\right) C_\pi}{1 + h} - S_0 = \frac{Q(1 - p^Q) + \left(1 + R_f\right) P_\pi}{(1 - p^Q)(1 - \ell - \ell^*)} - S_0 \quad (8.23)$$

while the implied belief regarding the (stock price) loss of the insurance firm (if losses materialize) is:

$$\frac{p^Q K + \left(1 + R_f\right) C_\pi}{1 + h} = \frac{Q(1 - p^Q) + \left(1 + R_f\right) P_\pi}{(1 - p^Q)(1 - \ell - \ell^*)} \quad (8.24)$$

Inserting our problem parameters and the implied risk-neutral probability p^{*Q}, we have:

$$1.05 * 5(0.9 - \ell^*) - 1.02 Q - 1.05 * 1.02 * 7$$

$$= \left(\frac{0.05 + 0.1 + \ell^*}{0.2 + 0.1 + \ell^*}\right)^2 K(0.9 - \ell^*) - \frac{0.05 + 0.1 + \ell^*}{0.2 + 0.1 + \ell^*}$$

$$\times \left\{1.02 Q - K(0.9 - \ell^*) + 1.05 * 5(0.9 - \ell^*)\right\} \quad (8.25)$$

This is one equation in ℓ^* when the options strikes traded are specified. This example indicates that derivatives markets reveal (or imply) the market assessment of future events (including the security and derivatives effects of future events—Katrina, tornados, disasters, etc.). The probabilities defined are not what dictate happenings, but they express the bets that the market is willing at a specific time to assume if these losses occur. It is a huge gambling casino where nature is the roulette of events made by men and women trading their risk preferences. In other words, the premium is a bet against, or for, the profit/loss outcome.

EXAMPLE: OPTIONS IMPLIED INSURANCE PRICING

An insurance firm insures an aggregate portfolio whose potential loss is binomial, namely a loss of $3 per share held by the firm when its current price is $125. All the insurance assets are invested in assets that have a rate of return of 10 percent in case of a gain and 2 percent in case of a loss. The risk-free rate is 6 percent. What is the price of insurance (the insurance risk premium) if the price of a call option on the firm underlying price is $4 with a strike of $128, while the option price is $3 with a strike of $126? In this problem, note that the insurance premium, once received, is invested with the insurance firm's portfolio. Thus,

$$125 + \pi = \frac{1}{1. + 0.06} \begin{pmatrix} (125 + \pi) (1. + 0.10) \, p^Q(1 - q) \\ + (125 + \pi) (1. - 0.02) (1 - p^Q) (1 - q) \\ + [(125 + \pi) (1. + 0.10) - 3] \, qp^Q \\ + [(125 + \pi) (1. - 0.02) - 3] \, q(1 - p^Q) \end{pmatrix} \tag{8.26}$$

The call option price is:

$$4 = \frac{1}{1. + 0.06} \begin{pmatrix} ((125 + \pi) (1. + 0.10) - 128)^+ \, p^Q(1 - q) \\ + [(125 + \pi) (1. - 0.02) - 128]^+ \, (1 - p^Q) (1 - q) \\ + [(125 + \pi) (1. + 0.10) - 128 - 3]^+ \, qp^Q \\ + [(125 + \pi) (1. - 0.02) - 128 - 3]^+ \, q(1 - p^Q) \end{pmatrix} \tag{8.27}$$

while the put option price is:

$$3 = \frac{1}{1. + 0.06} \begin{pmatrix} [126 - (125 + \pi) (1. + 0.10)] \, p^Q(1 - q) + \\ + [126 - (125 + \pi) (1. - 0.02)] \, (1 - p^Q) (1 - q) \\ + [126 - (125 + \pi) (1. + 0.10) + 3] \, qp^Q \\ + [126 - (125 + \pi) (1. - 0.02) + 3] \, q(1 - p^Q) \end{pmatrix} \tag{8.28}$$

These provide three equations in (π, p^Q, q) which we can solve.

Option Pricing in a Trinomial Random Walk

Consider an underlying trinomial security whose current price is S, while the prices it can assume in the following period are (S_H, S, S_L). The problem we have is to price a call option whose maturity is one period and whose strike is K. As discussed earlier, we cannot construct a portfolio consisting of the underlying security and a riskless bond only. In other words, the risk-free market does not provide sufficient information to determine the state prices. An additional source of information is therefore needed.

For this reason, consider a portfolio that consists of the underlying security, the riskless bond, and in addition we choose another call option whose strike is Q rather than K—the call option we seek to price (in fact we could have taken other derivatives such as a put option). Both options assume the following prices at maturity: (C_K^H, C_K, C_K^L) and (C_Q^H, C_Q, C_Q^L). The portfolio price is then

$$P_0 = n_1 S + B + n_2 C_Q^0$$

where C_Q^0 is the current price of such an option with a strike Q. Of course, replicating the call option with strike K, we require $C_K^0 = P_0$ initially, and at maturity:

$$C_K^H = P_1^H = n_1 S_H + B(1 + R_f) + n_2 C_Q^H$$
$$C_K = P_1 = n_1 S + B(1 + R_f) + n_2 C_Q$$
$$C_K^L = P_1^L = n_1 S_L + B(1 + R_f) + n_2 C_Q^L \tag{8.29}$$

or

$$
\begin{bmatrix} C_K^H \\ C_K \\ C_K^L \end{bmatrix} = \begin{bmatrix} P_K^H \\ P_K \\ P_K^L \end{bmatrix} = \begin{bmatrix} S_H & (1+R_f) & C_Q^H \\ S & (1+R_f) & C_Q \\ S_L & (1+R_f) & C_Q^L \end{bmatrix} \begin{bmatrix} n_1 \\ B \\ n_2 \end{bmatrix}
$$

And in matrix notation, its solution is:

$$
[C_K] = [\Lambda][n]^T \text{ and } [\Lambda]^{-1}[C_K] = [n]^T \tag{8.30}
$$

This system of three equations with three unknowns—the components of the replicating portfolio—can be solved if the matrix is invertible (i.e., it is of full rank). An explicit solution can be found by inverting the matrix (assuming that it is of full rank). If we reduce the number of variables to only two, we obtain the following system of equations:

$$
C_K^H - C_K = n_1(S_H - S) + n_2(C_Q^H - C_Q), \quad (C_K - C_K^L) = n_1(S - S_L) + n_2(C_Q - C_Q^L) \tag{8.31}
$$

The solution of these equations is then:

$$
n_1^* = \frac{(C_K^H - C_K)(C_Q - C_Q^L) - (C_K - C_K^L)(C_Q^H - C_Q)}{[(S_H - S)(C_Q - C_Q^L) - (S - S_L)(C_Q^H - C_Q)]}
$$

$$
n_2^* = \frac{(C_K^H - C_K)(S - S_L) - (C_K - C_K^L)(S_H - S)}{[(C_Q^H - C_Q)(S - S_L) - (C_Q - C_Q^L)(S_H - S)]} \tag{8.32}
$$

And therefore, the bond B share in the replicating portfolio is:

$$
B^* = \frac{C_K^H - n_1^* S_H - n_2^* C_Q^H}{1 + R_f} \tag{8.33}
$$

The option price whose strike is K and whose maturity is the next period is thus:

$$
C_K^0 = n_1^* S + B^* + n_2^* C_Q^0 \tag{8.34}
$$

Note that the solution we found is dependent on the price of the option with maturity Q. Therefore, the selection of the completing asset to the portfolio must be made carefully to assure its price availability. The approach we followed is nonetheless important as it clearly outlines the relationships between the number of states an asset can assume and the quantity of information needed to obtain a complete market price. The greater the number of states, the greater the amount of information we require. For these reasons, when the future is less predictable, defined by an ever-increasing number of states, volatility increases, and the price of the asset is more difficult to determine. For example, say that $S = 100$, $S_H = 110$, $S_L = 95$, $R_f = 0.08$, $Q = 103$, $K = 105$, $T = 1$. Note as well that for $C_Q = 0$, $C_Q^L = 0$, $C_Q^H = 7$,

$C_K^H = 5$, $C_K^L = 0$, $C_K = 0$. Thus, $B^* = (5 - 7)/1.08 = -2/1.08$ and:

$$n_1^* = \frac{(5)(0) - (0)(5)}{[(S_H - S)(C_Q - C_Q^L) - (S - S_L)(C_Q^H - C_Q)]} = 0;$$

$$n_2^* = \frac{(5)(100 - 95) - (0)(S_H - S)}{[(5)(100 - 95) - (0)(S_H - S)]} = 1 \qquad (8.35)$$

and finally,

$$C_K^0 = -\frac{7}{1.08} + C_Q^0$$

In other words, given the price of one option, the price of the other is also determined. In our case, say that $C_Q^0 = 10$; then

$$C_K^0 = 10 - \frac{7}{1.08} = 10 - 8.48 = 3.518 \qquad (8.36)$$

Pricing and Spread Options

Consider two binomial securities, potentially dependent one on the other. The current prices for each are $(S_1(0), S_2(0))$ while a period later the state prices these two securities assume are:

$$(S_1(0), S_2(0)) \Rightarrow \begin{cases} (S_1^+(1), S_2^+(1)) \\ (S_1^+(1), S_2^-(1)) \\ (S_1^-(1), S_2^+(1)) \\ (S_1^-(1), S_2^-(1)) \end{cases} \qquad (8.37)$$

We seek to price a spread option, consisting in paying $(S_1(1) - S_2(1) - K, 0)$ at its maturity—at period 1. The price of such an option (as we shall see here) is independent of the risk-free rate. To prove that this is the case, we construct a replicating portfolio consisting of two call options, each with strikes q_i, $i = 1, 2$ with current prices of $(C_1(q_1), C_2(q_2))$ where $S_1^-(1) < q_1 < S_1^+(1)$ and $S_2^-(1) < q_2 < S_2^+(1)$. Let the price of the current portfolio be:

$$\pi_0 = n_1 S_1(0) + n_2 S_2(0) + n_3 C_1(q_1) + n_4 C_2(q_2) \qquad (8.38)$$

Thus, ex post, at time $t = 1$, we have the following equalities:

$$\left(S_1^+(1) - S_2^+(1) - K, 0\right) = \pi_1(1) = n_1 S_1^+(1) + n_2 S_2^+(1) + n_3\left(S_1^+(1) - q_1\right)$$
$$+ n_4\left(S_2^+(1) - q_2\right)$$
$$\left(S_1^+(1) - S_2^-(1) - K, 0\right) = \pi_2(1) = n_1 S_1^+(1) + n_2 S_2^-(1) + n_3\left(S_1^+(1) - q_1\right)$$
$$\left(S_1^-(1) - S_2^+(1) - K, 0\right) = \pi_3(1) = n_1 S_1^-(1) + n_2 S_2^+(1) + n_4\left(S_2^+(1) - q_2\right)$$
$$\left(S_1^-(1) - S_2^-(1) - K, 0\right) = \pi_4(1) = n_1 S_1^-(1) + n_2 S_2^-(1) \qquad (8.39)$$

This is a system of four linear and independent equations in four unknowns, which can be solved for (n_1, n_2, n_3, n_4). In matrix notation, we have:

$$
\begin{bmatrix} \pi_1(1) \\ \pi_2(1) \\ \pi_3(1) \\ \pi_4(1) \end{bmatrix} = \begin{bmatrix} S_1^+(1) & S_2^+(1) & S_1^+(1) - q_1 & S_2^+(1) - q_2 \\ S_1^+(1) & S_2^-(1) & S_1^+(1) - q_1 & 0 \\ S_1^-(1) & S_2^+(1) & 0 & S_2^+(1) - q_2 \\ S_1^-(1) & S_2^-(1) & 0 & 0 \end{bmatrix} \begin{bmatrix} n_1 \\ n_2 \\ n_3 \\ n_4 \end{bmatrix} \tag{8.40}
$$

and therefore,

$$
\begin{bmatrix} n_1^* \\ n_2^* \\ n_3^* \\ n_4^* \end{bmatrix} = \begin{bmatrix} S_1^+(1) & S_2^+(1) & S_1^+(1) - q_1 & S_2^+(1) - q_2 \\ S_1^+(1) & S_2^-(1) & S_1^+(1) - q_1 & 0 \\ S_1^-(1) & S_2^+(1) & 0 & S_2^+(1) - q_2 \\ S_1^-(1) & S_2^-(1) & 0 & 0 \end{bmatrix}^{-1} \begin{bmatrix} \pi_1(1) \\ \pi_2(1) \\ \pi_3(1) \\ \pi_4(1) \end{bmatrix} \tag{8.41}
$$

The solutions $n_i^*, i = 1, 2, 3, 4$ are inserted in the pricing portfolio to determine the option price π_0 uniquely and independently of the risk-free rate.

Self-Financing Strategy

A *self-financing trading strategy* is a portfolio trading strategy such that, once money is invested, no money is added or taken out and all returns are reinvested in the portfolio. Let the price of a portfolio at time t be:

$$
\pi(t) = \sum_{i=1}^{n} S_i(t) n_i(t) \tag{8.42}
$$

where $n_i(t)$ is the number of shares held of an asset i whose current price is $S_i(t)$ at time t. The portfolio return over one period resulting from the portfolio appreciation (or depreciation) is $\Delta \pi(t) = \pi(t+1) - \pi(t)$. As a result, portfolio appreciation (or depreciation) is given by:

$$
\Delta \pi(t) = \sum_{i=1}^{n} n_i(t) \Delta S_i(t) + \sum_{i=1}^{n} S_i(t) \Delta n_i(t) \tag{8.43}
$$

where $\Delta n_i(t)$ expresses a change in the portfolio composition that contributes to the change effected on the portfolio by the investor (for example, selling shares and taking the money out for consumption). If all transactions are made but all the proceeds are kept in the portfolio, the portfolio growth (or loss) in value cannot be due to the portfolio composition. In this case, we say that the portfolio is self-financing and:

$$
0 = \sum_{i=1}^{n} S_i(t) \Delta n_i(t) \tag{8.44}
$$

As a result, for a self-financing portfolio, the random returns are:

$$\Delta \pi(t) = \sum_{i=1}^{n} n_i(t)\Delta S_i(t) \tag{8.45}$$

A self-financing portfolio is also useful to define both an arbitrage opportunity and the lack of it. Explicitly, if a self-financing portfolio has a null initial value, or $\pi(0) = 0$, an arbitrage opportunity arises if $P\{\pi(T) > 0\} > 0$ and $P\{\pi(T) < 0\} = 0$. In other words, if there is an arbitrage opportunity we can make money with no initial investment on our part. By negation, there is no arbitrage if no such opportunity exists.

The search for profits by traders and investors is then motivated by a search for arbitrage opportunities. This is of course a rational behavior, for in the presence of arbitrage opportunities, a rational investor would profit from arbitrage without limit and at no cost. Markets cannot long sustain such disequilibrium, however, and would (assuming that markets are stable) return to an equilibrium (and no arbitrage) state. The notion of no arbitrage (expressing a market equilibrium state) is thus fundamental and must be understood and applied to asset pricing.

RANDOM VOLATILITY AND OPTIONS PRICING

Random volatility arises for many reasons and poses at times important challenges to the pricing of derivatives. Technically it augments the sources of uncertainty (i.e., it augments the number of state prices we have to reckon with when pricing such a derivative). As a result, it requires additional information to compensate this increased variability.

The following example outlines an approach by portfolio replication to solve such problems. For demonstration purposes, assume that the underlying process is represented by a binomial underlying with the volatility assuming two possible values as well. The number of state prices is therefore $2 \times 2 = 4$, which requires far more information than that needed to price a deterministic volatility option price. However, as we are constructing a model of stochastic volatility (which is also information!), we may reduce the number of states. In other words, modeling a process can be used as well as an information source. For example, let:

$$x_{t+1} = x_t + \tilde{\alpha}_t x_t \varepsilon_t; \quad \varepsilon_t = \begin{cases} h & p \\ -\ell & q \end{cases}; \quad \tilde{\alpha}_t = \begin{cases} 1 & p_\alpha \\ 0 & q_\alpha \end{cases} \tag{8.46}$$

where $\tilde{\alpha}_t$ indicates a stochastic volatility. The underlying process is thus a trinomial random walk, resulting from the interaction between two sources of risk—the underlying process and its volatility (see Figure 8.2).

Assume that such a stock is being traded. In addition, say that both call and put options on this stock are traded, and finally say that we want to determine the risk-neutral probabilities and the price of a put option on this stock. For this purpose, we construct a replicating portfolio consisting of *a* shares of the stock, a risk-free bond, and *s* call options with strike K and exercise in the next period on the same stock.

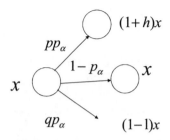

FIGURE 8.2 A Volatility,
Two Sources of Risk Process

The replicating portfolio is:

$$\pi_0 = ax + B + sC(0) \tag{8.47}$$

For the portfolio to replicate the put, it ought to replicate state by state and time by time the cash flow of the put. Replicating each of the future values of the portfolio, we have:

$$\pi_1 = ax(1+h) + B(1+R_f) + s\,[x(1+h) - K]$$
$$\pi_2 = ax + B(1+R_f) + s\,[0]$$
$$\pi_2 = ax(1-\ell) + B(1+R_f) + s\,[0] \tag{8.48}$$

Let the put option price be P_0. By replication, we have $\pi_0 = P_0$ as well as:

$$\pi_1 = P_1 = Max\,[Q - x(1+h), 0] = 0$$
$$\pi_2 = P_2 = Max\,[Q - x, 0] = 0$$
$$\pi_3 = P_3 = Max\,[Q - x(1-\ell), 0] = Q - x(1-\ell) \tag{8.49}$$

and therefore,

$$\pi_1 = ax(1+h) + B(1+R_f) + s\,[x(1+h) - K] = P_1 = 0$$
$$\pi_2 = ax + B(1+R_f) + s\,[0] = P_2 = 0$$
$$\pi_2 = ax(1-\ell) + B(1+R_f) + s\,[0] = P_3 = Q - x(1-\ell) \tag{8.50}$$

which leads to the portfolio composition:

$$a = \frac{x(1-\ell) - Q}{x\ell}; \quad s = \frac{h\,[x(1-\ell) - Q]}{\ell\,[K - x(1+h)]}; \quad B = -\frac{x(1-\ell) - Q}{\ell(1+R_f)} \tag{8.51}$$

As a result, the put option price $P_0 = ax + B + sC(0)$ is found to be:

$$P_0 = \frac{x(1-\ell) - Q}{\ell} \left\{ \frac{R_f}{1+R_f} + \frac{hC_0}{[K - x(1+h)]} \right\} \tag{8.52}$$

The put option price can also be written in terms of the risk-neutral probabilities by solving the system of equations:

$$P_0 = \frac{1}{1 + R_f} \left\{ p_1^Q P_1 + p_2^Q P_2 + p_3^Q P_3 \right\},$$

$$x = \frac{1}{1 + R_f} \left\{ p_1^Q (1 + h)x + p_2^Q x + p_3^Q (1 - \ell)x \right\}$$

$$p_1^Q + p_2^Q + p_3^Q = 1, \, p_i^Q \geq 0, i = 1, 2, 3 \tag{8.53}$$

with

$$P_1 = 0, \, P_2 = 0, \, P_3 = Q - x(1 - \ell)$$

and, for this example,

$$h = 0.10, \, \ell = 0.05, \, x = 20, \, Q = 21, \text{ and } R_f = 0.03, \, K = 19$$

The replicating portfolio is:

$$a = \frac{x(1 - \ell) - Q}{x\ell}, s = \frac{h\left[x(1 - \ell) - Q\right]}{\ell\left[K - x(1 + h)\right]}, B = -\frac{x(1 - \ell) - Q}{\ell(1 + R_f)}$$

$$a = \frac{20(1 - 0.05) - 21}{20(0.05)} = -2, s = \frac{3.2}{3} = 1.66, B = \frac{2}{0.0515} = 38.835 \tag{8.54}$$

The put option price is thus:

$$P_0 = -2x + \frac{2}{0.0515} + \frac{3.2}{3}C(0) = -40 + 38.835 + 1.06C(0)$$

$$= -1.165 + 1.06C(0) \tag{8.55}$$

REAL ASSETS AND REAL OPTIONS

Real options are not a recent invention. Copeland and Keenan (1998) argue that the account of a real option can be found in the writings of Aristotle, who describes how Thales, the sophist philosopher, after having divined an exceptionally good olive harvest within six months, paid a small fee to owners of olive presses for the right to rent their presses at a price set currently. After the harvest, Thales rented olive press capacity at a premium fee while paying the standard rate agreed upon six months in advance. Should the exceptional harvest not have occurred, Thales would have only incurred the original cost paid to book capacity. Thales had a real option written on capacity. To price real options, we essentially have to find a mechanism that allows us to calculate an asset's economic value based on its derivative that can be traded (and thereby have a market price set for it).

Real assets (and real options) are providers of value. For example, owning a house provides a value to its owner for it maintains a roof over his head. Real options are derived from the value an asset or a contract provides. Value with no price is, from an exchange point of view, worthless—or at least its market is so incomplete that it is difficult to determine what its price is. Pricing such assets, whether real, contractual, or financial, is therefore practically important. For example, a firm seeks to contract the right to discontinue development project. What should be its price? By the same token, an airline company contracts the acquisition (or the option to acquire) a new (technology) plane at some future time. The contract may involve a stream or a lump-sum payment to the contractor (say Boeing or Airbus) in exchange for the delivery of the plane at a specified time. Since payments are often made prior to the delivery of the plane, a number of (optional) clauses are added in the contract to manage the risks sustained by each of the parties if any of the parties were to deviate from the contract's stated terms (for example, late deliveries, technological obsolescence, etc.).

Similarly, a manufacturer can enter into binding bilateral agreements with a supplier by which agreed (contracted) exchange terms are set. This can involve future contractual prices, delivery rates at specific times (to reduce inventory holding costs), and of course a set of clauses intended to protect each party against possible failure by the other in fulfilling the terms of the contract.

Throughout these cases just described, the advantage resulting from negotiating a contract is to reduce, for one or both parties, the uncertainty concerning future exchange, operating, and financial conditions. Since for each contract there must be at least one buyer and one seller, the price of the contract can be interpreted as the outcome of a negotiation process where both parties have an inducement to enter into a contractual agreement. For example, the buyer and the seller of an option can be involved in a game, the benefits of which are implied in the risk premium (and vice versa—the option premium implying the future returns and losses to the parties privy to the contract). Note that the utility of entering into a contractual agreement is always positive ex ante for all parties; otherwise there would not be a contractual agreement. When the number of buyers and sellers of such contracts becomes extremely large, transactions become impersonal and it is the market price that defines the value of the contract. Strategic behaviors tend to break down, the larger the group, and prices tend to become more efficient.

Real options have assumed a growing importance due to both the increased complexity of industrial and business contracts and the ever-present need to manage risks. Following is an outline a number of such contracts.

- *Options to defer an investment* (whose price is derived potentially from the reduction of uncertainty as time passes and better forecasts can be determined). Such options are based on the premise that while the investment is delayed, additional information, reducing the future uncertainties associated to such an investment, will provide a better assessment of the investment price. Such knowledge is certainly worth money, which denotes the value price of such an option.
- *Options allowing staged investments.* Such options provide an added flexibility to managers to discontinue a given investment, an R&D development program, and so forth. For example, technology innovation beset by uncertainty and competition might be faced with new competing technologies rendering the development efforts useless. It is certainly worthwhile to have an option that allows discontinuing such a development.

- *Options based on operating conditions.* Having the option to shut down a plant, to contract a plant output, to restart production, to discontinue suppliers' contracts under certain operating conditions, is of value to industrial and corporate managers. These options are certainly worth money, which is the price of the option on the real operations of the enterprise.

There are of course many other options, such as *options to abandon* (for example, for a supplier, if demand does not materialize, if prices increase too much, if a new technology enters the market, etc., then abandoning an investment has value). Growth options, multiple interacting options, capacity switching between countries, valuing manufacturing flexibility, joint ventures as options to expand or options to acquire platforms of future development, options to defer closure of factories, options as capabilities-capacities, options on international alliances, and so forth, are examples that many authors have dealt with. By the same token, franchise contracts have an option value that can be priced, providing thereby a more precise assessment of the franchise worth and, thus, its fair price. In all circumstances, a better price estimate of clauses in negotiated contracts, and an appropriate market price of real assets and their derived benefits, can only improve the quality of the decisions made by entrepreneurs, investors, and corporate managers.

Say that a firm seeks to value the option to terminate a supply contract with a locked in price and switch to a supply based on market prices only. Conversely, a counterparty may value the option to terminate an investment in production capacity in case demand for its product turns out to be smaller than previously expected (or a desired bid does not materialize). Such problems recur often in investments in logistics infrastructure (ports, airports, highways, etc.). They may, for example, use the fact that at known or unknown future dates, information will be revealed that will necessarily change the risk premium to be paid for investments that may, conditionally on this information, turn very profitable or even useless.

The Option to Acquire the License for a New Technology

To appreciate the basic rational of real options, consider the case of an option to acquire a license for a new technology, discussed by Bowman and Moskowitz (2001) consisting in the purchase of a license for a new technology to be developed by another party. The following information is supplied:

- The initial cash outlay of the project is $900: $100 for purchasing the license and $800 for investing in a manufacturing facility to produce the product with the new technology.
- For the sake of simplification, there is a unique cash inflow, two years after the initial investment, estimated at $1,000.
- Assuming a risk-free rate of 5 percent and a risk premium of 5 percent, the project would traditionally be assessed with the net present value (NPV) criterion.

A calculation of the NPV indicates that the project would be rejected as its NPV is negative:

$$NPV = \frac{1,000}{(1.1)^2} - 900 = -73 \tag{8.56}$$

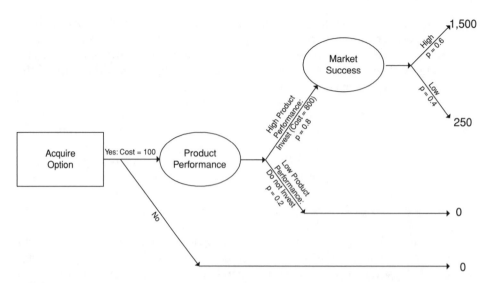

FIGURE 8.3 A Real Option and the Price of a License

The real option approach calculates instead the expected present value (EPV) of the option as the discounted value of the expected payoffs from owning the underlying asset given the probability of exercising the option, or:

$$EPV_{option} = 0.8 \times \left(0.6 \times \frac{1500}{1.05^2} + 0.4 \times \frac{250}{1.05^2} - \frac{800}{1.05} \right) + 0.2 \times 0 = 116 \quad (8.57)$$

In this case, the EPV of the option (116) is superior to the cost of the option (100), and the decision should be to purchase the license. It is common in the literature to define a project's strategic NPV as the difference between the EPV and the cost of the option. By purchasing the license, the company acquires the right, but not the obligation, to exploit commercially the product in a year's time. Given the current perception of uncertainty (probabilities in Figure 8.3), owning this option adds value to the firm.

THE BLACK-SCHOLES VANILLA OPTION[*]

The Black-Scholes model is a simple and widely applied model for pricing call and put options. The basic assumption of this model is that security rates of return are linear with a mean rate of return μ and a volatility σ, as stated in Chapter 3. In other words,

$$R(t) = \frac{\Delta S(t)}{S(t)} = \mu \Delta t + \sigma \Delta W(t), \ S(0) > 0 \quad (8.58)$$

where $W(t)$ denotes a Brownian motion, which is essentially an independent normally distributed random variable with mean zero and variance t. Thus, $E(\Delta W(t)) = 0$,

---

[*] Requires a slightly more advanced mathematical background; please see the Introduction.

$\text{var}(\Delta W(t)) = \Delta t$, $E(\Delta W(t)\Delta W(\tau)) = 0$, $\forall t \neq \tau$, and:

$$\Delta \ln S(t) = \left(\mu - \frac{1}{2}\sigma^2\right)\Delta t + \sigma \Delta W(t), \; S(0) > 0 \tag{8.59}$$

The ln transformation can be verified by a Taylor series approximation, as indicated in Chapter 3. In this case,

$$\Delta \ln S(t) = \frac{1}{S(t)}\Delta S(t) - \frac{1}{2}\frac{1}{S^2(t)}(\Delta S(t))^2 = \frac{\mu S(t)\Delta t + \sigma S(t)\Delta W(t)}{S(t)} - \frac{1}{2}\frac{\sigma^2 S^2(t)\Delta t}{S^2(t)} \tag{8.60}$$

This proves equation (8.59). This equation, however, is not a market price process. A number of approaches can be used to transform this equation into a market price process, however. These are shown next. Essentially, we consider first a binomial discretization of such a process and subsequently apply directly techniques of replication.

The Binomial Process as a Discrete Time Approximation

The binomial approximation to the Black-Scholes model can be defined in a number of ways. A common example consists in setting the mean-variance binomial approximation:

$$\Delta(\ln S(t)) = \begin{cases} \left(\mu - \frac{1}{2}\sigma^2\right)\Delta t + \sigma\sqrt{\Delta t} & wp \quad \frac{1}{2} \\ \left(\mu - \frac{1}{2}\sigma^2\right)\Delta t - \sigma\sqrt{\Delta t} & wp \quad \frac{1}{2} \end{cases} \tag{8.61}$$

and therefore:

$$E(\Delta \ln S(t)) = \left(\mu - \frac{1}{2}\sigma^2\right)\Delta t, \; \text{var}\left(\Delta \ln S(t)\right) = \sigma^2 \Delta t. \tag{8.62}$$

For a risk-neutral price process (with probability p^Q) with binomial states $\left(\mu - \frac{1}{2}\sigma^2\right)\Delta t \pm \sigma\sqrt{\Delta t}$, we have:

$$S(t) = e^{-R_f \Delta t} E^Q(S(t+\Delta t)) = S(t)p^Q e^{\left(\mu - \frac{1}{2}\sigma^2 - R_f\right)\Delta t + \sigma\sqrt{\Delta t}}$$
$$+ S(t)(1-p^Q)e^{\left(\mu - \frac{1}{2}\sigma^2 - R_f\right)\Delta t - \sigma\sqrt{\Delta t}} \tag{8.63}$$

which yields the risk-neutral probability:

$$0 < p^Q = \frac{1 - e^{\left(\mu - \frac{1}{2}\sigma^2 - R_f\right)\Delta t - \sigma\sqrt{\Delta t}}}{e^{\left(\mu - \frac{1}{2}\sigma^2 - R_f\right)\Delta t + \sigma\sqrt{\Delta t}} - e^{\left(\mu - \frac{1}{2}\sigma^2 - R_f\right)\Delta t - \sigma\sqrt{\Delta t}}}$$

$$= \frac{\left(e^{-\left(\mu - \frac{1}{2}\sigma^2 - R_f\right)\Delta t} - e^{-\sigma\sqrt{\Delta t}}\right)}{\left(e^{+\sigma\sqrt{\Delta t}} - e^{-\sigma\sqrt{\Delta t}}\right)} < 1 \tag{8.64}$$

If we assume that the time intervals are small, then

$$0 < p^Q = \frac{1}{2}\left(1 - \left(\lambda - \frac{1}{2}\sigma\right)\sqrt{\Delta t}\right), 1 - p^Q = \frac{1}{2}\left(1 + \left(\lambda - \frac{1}{2}\sigma\right)\sqrt{\Delta t}\right),$$

$$\lambda = \frac{(\mu - R_f)}{\sigma} \tag{8.65}$$

Note that λ is a risk premium. To price a call option at time T, with strike K, the binomial distribution can be used with a call option price:

$$C(0 \,|\, K, T) = e^{-R_f T} E^Q \, Max\,(S(T) - K, 0),$$

$$S(T) \sim S(0) \binom{T/\Delta t}{i} \left(p^Q e^{(\mu - \frac{1}{2}\sigma^2 - R_f)\Delta t + \sigma\sqrt{\Delta t}}\right)^i \left((1 - p^Q) e^{(\mu - \frac{1}{2}\sigma^2 - R_f)\Delta t - \sigma\sqrt{\Delta t}}\right)^{T/\Delta t - i}$$

$$\tag{8.66}$$

In the case of a lognormal price process such an approximation is not needed as we are able to calculate the risk-neutral distribution analytically. Nevertheless, this approximation is used here as an example, and it may be applied in a similar manner to other problems where we are not able to obtain analytical solutions.

The Black-Scholes Model Option Price and Portfolio Replication[*]

Consider the pricing of a call option at time t, $C(t)$, whose exercise price at time T is $C(T)$, $0 \le t \le T$. Its initial price is $C(0)$. Let $P(t), 0 \le t \le T$, be the price of an equivalent and replicating portfolio at time t. Assume that both the portfolio and the option prices are functions that accept first and second derivatives. A replicating portfolio is then defined by the time-state equivalence of the portfolio and the option price we seek to determine. If these two are equivalent, then necessarily, their price and their price change over time are equal during the option's life. Or,

$$C(t) \equiv P(t), \text{ and } \Delta C(t) \equiv \Delta P(t) \text{ in } 0 \le t \le T \tag{8.67}$$

The selection of the replicating portfolio is not evident, however. In particular, for a call option, assume that its price depends on its underlying security (whose price at time t is $S(t)$) or $C(t) \equiv C(S, t)$. Consequently, the portfolio designed is also a function of both the underlying security and time, or $P(t) = P(S, t)$. Let the portfolio consist of a linear combination of risk-free zero-coupon bond and an underlying security:

$$P(S, t) = B(t) + aS(t), \quad a = ?$$
$$\Delta B(t) = R_f B(t)\Delta t, \quad B(0) = ? \tag{8.68}$$

---

[*] Requires a slightly more advanced mathematical background; please see the Introduction.

where the portfolio is specified by the parameters $(a, B(0))$. A price variation is thus:

$$\Delta P(S, t) = \Delta B(t) + a\Delta S(t) \tag{8.69}$$

A replicating portfolio means that the call option and the portfolio are identical for each state and for each time period—that is:

$$C(t \mid S(t), T) \equiv P(t) \tag{8.70}$$

Letting for convenience $C(t \mid S(t), T) \equiv C(S, t)$, two equations define the call option in terms of the replicating portfolio:

$$C(S, t) \equiv B(t) + aS(t), \text{ and } \Delta C(t) \equiv \Delta B(t) + a\Delta S(t) \text{ in } 0 \leq t \leq T \tag{8.71}$$

However,

$$dB(t) = R_f B(t)dt = R_f (C(t) - aS(t))\, dt, \quad dC(t) \equiv R_f (C(t) - aS(t))\, dt + adS(t) \tag{8.72}$$

Or

$$dC(t) - R_f C(t)dt \equiv a \left(dS(t) - R_f S(t)dt\right) \text{ in} 0 \leq t \leq T \tag{8.73}$$

which can be written as follows: $\Delta \left(e^{-R_f t}C(t)\right) = a\Delta \left(e^{-R_f t}S(t)\right)$.

To determine the parameter a, we proceed as follows. First note that a two-terms Taylor series expansion of the option price $C(t, S)$ yields

$$\Delta C(t, S) = \frac{\partial C}{\partial t}\Delta t + \frac{\partial C}{\partial S}\Delta S + \frac{1}{2}\frac{\partial^2 C}{\partial S^2} (\Delta S)^2 \tag{8.74}$$

As a result:

$$\frac{\partial C}{\partial t}\Delta t + \frac{\partial C}{\partial S}\Delta S + \frac{1}{2}\frac{\partial^2 C}{\partial S^2} (\Delta S)^2 - R_f C(t)\Delta t = a \left(\Delta S(t) - R_f S(t)\Delta t\right) \tag{8.75}$$

which we rearrange into an equation consisting of two parts, a deterministic and a stochastic part:

$$\left\{\frac{\partial C}{\partial t}\Delta t + \frac{1}{2}\frac{\partial^2 C}{\partial S^2} (\Delta S)^2 - R_f C(t)\Delta t + a R_f S(t)\Delta t\right\} + \left(\frac{\partial C}{\partial S} - a\right)\Delta S = 0 \tag{8.76}$$

If the underlying security is defined as a (general) stochastic differential equation:

$$\Delta S(t) = f(S, t)\Delta t + \Lambda(S, t)\Delta W, S_0 > 0 \tag{8.77}$$

which we insert in the partial differential equation (PDE) price for the call option, or:

$$\left\{ \frac{\partial C}{\partial t} + \frac{1}{2}\frac{\partial^2 C}{\partial S^2}\Lambda^2(S, t) - R_f C(t) + a R_f S(t) + \left(\frac{\partial C}{\partial S} - a\right) f(S, t) \right\} \Delta t$$

$$\left(\frac{\partial C}{\partial S} - a\right) \Lambda(S, t)\Delta W = 0 \text{ and therefore } \frac{\partial C}{\partial S} = a \tag{8.78}$$

Replacing a by $\frac{\partial C}{\partial S}$ in the first part of the equation (in dt), we obtain a second-order PDE:

$$\frac{\partial C}{\partial t} + \frac{1}{2}\frac{\partial^2 C}{\partial S^2}\Lambda^2(S, t) + R_f S(t)\frac{\partial C}{\partial S} - R_f C(t) = 0 \tag{8.79}$$

This equation defines the price of a call option at times $0 \leq t < T$. For an exercise time T and strike K, the price at the option maturity is $Max\,[0, S(T) - K]$. Thus, the options' boundary conditions:

$$C(0, t) = 0, \forall t \in [0, T)\,; C(S, T) = Max\,[0, S(T) - K] \tag{8.80}$$

Note that exercise of the option is worth nothing prior to its exercise, or $C(0, t) = 0, \forall t \in [0, T)$. Such an option is called a *European option*. This does not mean that holding or selling the option is worthless, as the intrinsic value of its exercise at time T may be worth something to a trader or investor. The solution of the PDE together with its boundary (the exercise price of the option at its maturity) will provide the intrinsic price of the call option at each time t.

For the Black-Scholes model, this is reduced to:

$$\frac{\partial C}{\partial t} + \frac{1}{2}\frac{\partial^2 C}{\partial S^2}\sigma^2 S^2(t) + R_f S(t)\frac{\partial C}{\partial S} - R_f C(t) = 0,$$

$$C(0, t) = 0, \forall t \in [0, T)\,; C(S, T) = Max\,[0, S(T) - K] \tag{8.81}$$

The solution of this equation, a second-order PDE, can be verified to be:

$$C(S, t) = S\Phi(d_1) - Ke^{-R_f t}\Phi(d_2) \tag{8.82}$$

$$\Phi(y) = (2\pi)^{-1/2} \int_{-\infty}^{y} e^{-u^2/2}du; d_1 = \left[\frac{\log(S/K) + (T - t)(R_f + \sigma^2/2)}{\sigma\sqrt{T - t}}\right];$$

$$d_2 = d_1 - \sigma\sqrt{T - t},$$

There are many computer programs that compute these option prices as well as their sensitivities to variations in any of these parameters—these are the Greeks (as will be seen shortly). A call option price requires five parameters, however, four of which can be observed routinely while the fifth—the volatility—is more difficult to determine and has to be estimated statistically (in which case it reflects past prices) or determined implicitly. In this latter case it reflects future beliefs regarding the option's prices and volatility. For these reasons, if the Black-Scholes model is used, the price of the option implies the volatility, and inversely, the volatility would imply the option price—one implies the other. Thus, trading in options means trading the volatility and implies (reveals) the options traders' beliefs regarding the future volatility. The remaining four observable parameters include the stock price, the exercise price, the time to expiration, and the risk-free rate for the time to maturity. The dependence of the option price and its volatility justifies the common wisdom that trading in options and trading in volatility are in fact two sides of the same coin.

Risk-Neutral Pricing and the Pricing Martingale[*]

When the underlying price process is a martingale and risk-neutral pricing of financial assets applies (as we saw in Chapter 7), then the price of a cash flow S_T realized at time T is:

$$S_0 = e^{-R_f T} E^Q (S_T),$$

hence the forward price is: (8.83)

$$S_0 e^{R_f T} = E^Q (S_T | \Im_0)$$

where $\Im_0$ is a filtration, representing the initial information on the basis of which the expectation is taken (under the risk-neutral distribution with expectation denoted by $E^Q (*)$). Generally, at any time $t < T$, we have:

$$S_t e^{-R_f t} = e^{-R_f T} E^Q (S_T | \Im_t) \text{ or } S_t = e^{-R_f (T-t)} E^Q (S_T | \Im_t) \qquad (8.84)$$

where $\Im_t$ is the a filtration at time t, expressing all the price-relevant information (commonly available to all traders and investors) that is accumulated by time t. If an underlying asset is not risk-free, then it will be priced to reflect the price of risk. Such a pricing scheme applies to the security and to its derivatives as well.

A person's personal information and assessment are not sufficient to define the probability distribution $f^Q (S_T | \Im_t)$ with respect to which future prices are defined. Such a distribution has to reflect the exchange between buyers and sellers in a complete market that brings price to a uniquely defined equilibrium state. The mathematical property of such equilibrium prices has then a martingale property. Inversely, if there is such a martingale, and thus prices are in equilibrium, expectation with respect to this martingale provides the price of the current asset, since for a martingale, at all times, the expectation discounted at the risk-free rate is stationary, or:

$$S_0 = S_0 e^{-R_f (0)} = e^{-R_f t} E^Q (S_t | \Im_0) = e^{-R_f (t+\Delta t)} E^Q (S_{t+\Delta t} | \Im_0) = \cdots \cdots$$
$$= e^{-R_f T} E^Q (S_T | \Im_0) \qquad (8.85)$$

or at time t, for its derivative, it is given by:

$$V(S_t) e^{-R_f t} = e^{-R_f T} E^Q (V(S_T) | \Im_t) \text{ and } V(S_t) = e^{-R_f (T-t)} E^Q (V(S_T) | \Im_t) \qquad (8.86)$$

---

[*] Requires a slightly more advanced mathematical background; please see the Introduction.

If K is the strike price of a call option whose exercise time is T, then the price C_t of such an option under the martingale measure (in this case the risk-neutral pricing measure) is:

$$C_t = e^{-R_f(T-t)} E^Q (\max(K - S_T, 0) \,|\, \mathfrak{I}_t) \qquad (8.87)$$

Such an approach applies to both discrete (as seen in the previous chapter) and continuous time and state models. It also provides a broad avenue for practical applications based on two simple premises:

1. If markets are presumed complete, then finding the martingale that defines the complete market price process is feasible by extracting such information by observing market prices. This is usually called the implied martingale or the implied risk-neutral probability distribution (see Chapter 11).
2. If there is a mathematical expression that defines the pricing martingale, then prices of underlying assets and their derivatives can be calculated by expectations with respect to the martingale (price) measure. When models are assumed indeed to have the martingale property, a Monte Carlo simulation with respect to the risk-neutral distributions can be used to price assets and their derivatives since a price is calculated by an average (the expectation) of such simulated prices. The applications we consider in this section assume that there is such a price process.

The examples we treat are selected and used to highlight cursorily application of the martingale approach to asset pricing. As a first example, consider a digital option, which pays a fixed amount, say A, if the security price at its maturity is greater than a strike K. In this case, the price of such an option is $A\mathbf{1}_{S(T) \geq K} = V(T)$ with:

$$\frac{V(0)}{B(0)} = A E^Q \left(\frac{V(T)}{B(T)} \right) \qquad (8.88)$$

and therefore,

$$V(0) = B(0) A E^Q \left(\frac{\mathbf{1}_{S(T) \geq K}}{B(T)} \right) = \frac{B(0)}{B(T)} A E^Q \left(\mathbf{1}_{S(T) \geq K} \right) = A \frac{B(0)}{B(T)} \Pi^Q (S(T) \geq K)$$

$$= A \frac{B(0)}{B(T)} \Pi^Q \left(\frac{K}{S(T)} \leq 1 \right) \qquad (8.89)$$

where

$$\mathbf{1}_{S(T) \geq K} = \begin{cases} 1 & \text{if } S(T) > K \\ 0 & \text{if } S(T) \leq K \end{cases}$$

Since the risk-neutral process of the security price is:

$$\frac{\Delta S(t)}{S(t)} = R_f \Delta t + \sigma W^Q(T), \, S(0) > 0$$

leading to: $\qquad (8.90)$

$$S(T) = S_0 e^{R_f T - \frac{1}{2}\sigma^2 T + \sigma W^Q(T)}$$

we can write:

$$1 \geq \frac{K}{S(T)} = \frac{K}{S_0 e^{R_f T - \frac{1}{2}\sigma^2 T + \sigma W^Q(T)}} \text{ or } \ln(K) \leq \ln(S_0) + R_f T - \frac{1}{2}\sigma^2 T + \sigma W^Q(T)$$

(8.91)

Thus,

$$\Pi^Q\left(\frac{K}{S(T)} \leq S(T)\right) \equiv \Pi^Q\left(\frac{\ln(K) - \ln(S_0) - R_f T + \frac{1}{2}\sigma^2 T}{\sigma} \leq W^Q(T)\right) \qquad (8.92)$$

since

$$V(0) = A\frac{B(0)}{B(T)}\Pi^Q\left(\frac{K}{S(T)} \leq 1\right) = A\frac{B(0)}{B(T)}\Pi^Q\left(\frac{\ln\left(\frac{K}{S_0}\right) - R_f T + \frac{1}{2}\sigma^2 T}{\sigma\sqrt{T}} \leq \varepsilon^Q(T)\right)$$

(8.93)

where $\varepsilon^Q(T)$ is now a standard normal distributed random variable with mean zero and variance 1. The price of such a digital option is then:

$$V(0) = A\frac{B(0)}{B(T)}\left(1 - F_N^Q\left(\frac{\ln\left(\frac{K}{S_0}\right) - R_f T + \frac{1}{2}\sigma^2 T}{\sigma\sqrt{T}}\right)\right) \qquad (8.94)$$

A second example considers a call option with an exercise time T and strike K:

$$Max(0, S(T) - K)) = S(T)\mathbf{1}_{S(T) \geq K} - K\mathbf{1}_{S(T) \geq K} = V_1(T) - V_2(T) \qquad (8.95)$$

where $V_1(T)$ and $V_2(T)$ can be priced by choosing the appropriate measure. Pricing $V_1(T)$ with respect to the underlying security and $V_2(T)$ with respect to the underlying bond, we have:

$$\frac{V_1(0)}{S(0)} = E^S\left(\frac{V_1(T)}{S(T)}\right) \text{ and } \frac{V_2(0)}{B(0)} = KE^B\left(\frac{V_2(T)}{B(T)}\right), \qquad (8.96)$$

In the first case, we have:

$$V_1(0) = S(0)E^S\left(\frac{V_1(T)}{S(T)}\right) = S(0)E^S\left(\frac{S(T)\mathbf{1}_{S(T) \geq K}}{S(T)}\right)$$

$$= S(0)E^S\left(\mathbf{1}_{S(T) \geq K}\right) = S(0)\Pi^S\left(\frac{K}{S(T)} \leq 1\right) = S(0)\Pi^S\left(S(T) \geq K\right) \qquad (8.97)$$

$$V_2(0) = B(0)KE^B \left(\frac{1_{S(T) \geq K}}{B(T)} \right) = \frac{B(0)}{B(T)} KE^B \left(1_{S(T) \geq K} \right)$$

$$= K \frac{B(0)}{B(T)} \Pi^B \left(S(T) \geq K \right)$$

$$= K \frac{B(0)}{B(T)} \Pi^B \left(\frac{K}{S(T)} \leq 1 \right) \tag{8.98}$$

The option price is therefore:

$$\frac{V_1(0)}{S(0)} - \frac{V_2(0)}{B(0)} = S(0)\Pi^S \left(S(T) \geq K \right) - \frac{K B(0)}{B(T)} \Pi^B \left(\frac{K}{S(T)} \leq 1 \right) \tag{8.99}$$

As a result,

$$\frac{V_1(0)}{S(0)} - \frac{V_2(0)}{B(0)} = S(0)\Pi^S \left(S(T) \geq K \right) - K \frac{B(0)}{B(T)} \Pi^B \left(\frac{K}{S(T)} \leq 1 \right) \tag{8.100}$$

Now we introduce:

$$S(T) = S_0 e^{R_f T - \frac{1}{2}\sigma^2 T + \sigma W^Q(T)}$$

into these equations and obtain:

$$V_1(0) - V_2(0) = S(0)\Pi^S \left(W^Q(T) \geq \Psi \right) - \frac{K B(0)}{B(T)} \Pi^B \left(W^Q(T) \leq \Psi \right) \tag{8.101}$$

where

$$\Psi = \frac{\ln \left(\frac{K}{S_0} \right) - R_f T + \frac{1}{2}\sigma^2 T}{\sigma} \tag{8.102}$$

which provides an explicit solution to the option price since $\Pi^S \left(W^Q(T) \geq \Psi \right) = 1 - \Pi^S (\Psi)$ and $\Pi^B \left(W^Q(T) \leq \Psi \right) = \Pi^B (\Psi)$ are the cumulative normal probability distributions. This is also, of course, the Black-Scholes formula without having to solve its associated partial differential equation.

THE GREEKS AND THEIR APPLICATIONS

Portfolios and option prices are a function of a number of parameters that define the portfolio or the option. Some of these parameters are determined by market forces, some of which are observable and some of which are not. Other parameters are contracted. Some parameters change—both in time and due to random events reflecting economic and other conditions. As a result, option prices change as these parameters change, providing important information that can be used for risk management and trading purposes. Options' sensitivity to parametric changes, termed the *Greeks*, are thus needed to manage both portfolios and options. These Greeks are letters that expresses selectively the sensitivity of the option price with respect to specific parameters.

Explicitly, let an option price be given in terms of its parameters by:

$$C \equiv C(S, \tau, \sigma, R_f \,|\, T, K), \tau = T - t \tag{8.103}$$

A Taylor series expansion based on first-order (and second-order terms for randomly varying parameters) is then:

$$\Delta C = \frac{\partial C}{\partial S} \Delta S + \frac{\partial C}{\partial \tau} \Delta t + \frac{\partial C}{\partial \sigma} \Delta \sigma + \frac{\partial C}{\partial R_f} \Delta R_f + \frac{1}{2} \frac{\partial^2 C}{\partial S^2} (\Delta S)^2 \tag{8.104}$$

Or, in terms of Greek letters, we write:

$$\Delta C = \delta \Delta S + \theta \Delta t + v \Delta \sigma + \rho \Delta R_f + \frac{1}{2} \Gamma (\Delta S)^2; \tag{8.105}$$

with

$$\delta = \frac{\partial C}{\partial S}, \theta = \frac{\partial C}{\partial t}, v = \frac{\partial C}{\partial \sigma}, \rho = \frac{\partial C}{\partial R_f}, \Gamma = \frac{\partial^2 C}{\partial S^2} \tag{8.106}$$

Each of these terms is meaningful and used in a broad set of circumstances. A summary of their meanings is as follows:

- *Delta* or $\delta = \frac{\partial C}{\partial S}$ defines the theoretical change in an option price when its underlying stock price changes (per unit variation in the underlying price).
- *Theta* or $\theta = -\frac{\partial C}{\partial \tau}$ expresses the change in the option's value as the time to maturity decreases. We generally expect that options will become less valuable with the passage of time. Writing T as the option's remaining time to maturity, we set θ equal to the negative of the derivative of the option price with respect to T:
- *Vega or* $v = \frac{\partial C}{\partial \sigma}$ measures the sensitivity of the option price to the standard deviation of the underlying stock's return σ (the stock price volatility). Given the Black-Scholes formula, calls and puts have the same vega.
- *Gamma* or $\Gamma = \frac{\partial^2 C}{\partial S^2}$ is the second derivative of the option's price with respect to the underlying stock. Gamma gives the convexity of the option price with respect to the stock price. For options priced by the Black-Scholes formula, the call and put have the same gamma.
- *Rho* or $\rho = -\frac{\partial C}{\partial R_f}$ measures the change in an option price when the rate changes.

The Greeks are therefore marginal changes in the option price and are valid if the deviations in the economic parameters are not too great. Inserting these Greeks into the Black-Scholes partial differential equation, we obtain the following relationship, defining the call option price in terms of the Greeks and relevant parameters:

$$\Theta + R_f S \Delta + \frac{\sigma^2 S^2}{2} \Gamma = R_f C \qquad (8.107)$$

Evidently, this equation will differ from one derived asset to another (for example, for a bond, a currency, a portfolio of securities, etc., we will have an equation that expresses the parameters at hand and, of course, the underlying partial differential equation of the derived asset). These Greeks are extremely important in financial options practice. Table 8.1 summarized trading strategies based on the Greeks. Each

TABLE 8.1 The Greeks and Portfolio Strategies

Delta	Gamma	Theta	Strategy	Implementation
Positive	Positive	Negative	Long call	Purchase long call option.
Negative	Positive	Negative	Long put	Purchase long put option.
Neutral	Positive	Negative	Straddle	Purchase call and put, both with same exercise and expiration date.
Neutral	Positive	Negative	Strangle	Purchase call and put, each equally out-of-the-money, and write a call and a put, each further out-of-the-money, and each with the same expiration date.
Neutral	Positive	Negative	Condor	Purchase call and put, each equally out-of-the-money, and write a call and a put, each further out-of-the-money than the call and put that were purchased. All options have the same expiration date.
Neutral	Negative	Positive	Butterfly	Write two at-the-money calls, and buy two calls, one in-the-money and the other equally far out-of-the-money.
Positive	Neutral*	Neutral*	Vertical spread	Buy one call and write another call with a higher exercise price. Both options have the same time to expiration.
Neutral*	Negative	Positive	Time spread	Write one call and buy another call with a longer time to expiration. Both options have the same exercise price.
Neutral*	Positive	Negative	Back spread	Buy one call and write another call with a longer time to expiration. Both options have the same exercise price.
Neutral	Neutral	Neutral	Conversion	Buy the underlying security, write a call, and buy a put. The options have the same time to expiration and exercise price.

*Per Wilmott.
Source: Wilmott (2001).

recommendation, corresponding to a shift in the Greek, is of course based on the meaning that such a Greek points to in a complete financial market.

SUMMARY

This chapter has introduced a number of options pricing applications including the Black-Scholes model. Typical applications have included pricing options with a stochastic volatility, pricing real options, pricing with multiple sources of risk, and so forth. We have also introduced the Greeks. Greeks, as stated in the text, denote the sensitivity of option prices to their parameters and are in practice extremely useful, both in designing trading strategies and in providing an added source of information that we can use to better assess financial market prices. The last section in this chapter are therefore an introduction to options and their uses.

TEST YOURSELF

8.1 When is the trinomial random walk model applicable? In particular, discuss the case of slow-moving stock prices.

8.2 Assume that in an underlying trinomial random walk the current price is $10 while the future (next period) prices are (15, 10, 8). The price of a call option whose strike is $12 and whose strike is in the next period is known and equals $2. The risk-free rate is 6 percent. We seek to price a call option whose strike is $10. In this case, solve for the portfolio replicating composition, by setting

$$
\begin{bmatrix} 5 \\ 0 \\ 0 \end{bmatrix} = \begin{bmatrix} 15 & 1.06 & 3 \\ 10 & 1.06 & 0 \\ 8 & 1.06 & 0 \end{bmatrix} \begin{bmatrix} n_1 \\ n_2 \\ n_3 \end{bmatrix} \Rightarrow \begin{bmatrix} n_1^* \\ n_2^* \\ n_3^* \end{bmatrix} = \begin{bmatrix} 15 & 1.06 & 3 \\ 10 & 1.06 & 0 \\ 8 & 1.06 & 0 \end{bmatrix}^{-1} \begin{bmatrix} 5 \\ 0 \\ 0 \end{bmatrix}
$$

Show that the price of such an option $C(10,1)$ is: $C_0(10, 1) = 10n_1^* + n_2^* + 2n_3^*$ where (n_1^*, n_2^*, n_3^*) are solutions of the system of three linear simultaneous equations given in these data.

8.3 Answer the following:
   a. What is a naked option?
   b. What is a covered call? Explain why such a position is a hedge.
   c. What is a margin account? How does an obligation vary between the buyer and the seller of the option?

8.4 What is a bid-ask spread in options? Further, open a recent financial newspaper and provide the bid-ask prices for a security and corporate bond you may want to buy.

8.5 What is a commission? Discuss how you believe the commission (transaction cost) will affect your trading in options. Further, what are the commissions you have to pay for trading in options? Compare the commissions paid for the underlying security and the option, expressed as a percentage of their price. Why are options commissions bigger than securities commissions?

8.6   Which position has limited upside potential and unlimited downside risk?

    a. Long call.

    b. Short call.

    c. Long put.

    d. None of the above.

    Draw the option chart.

8.7   Which of the following risk parameters are inherent in a long put?

    a. Unlimited upside potential, limited downside risk.

    b. Limited upside potential, unlimited downside risk.

    c. Upside potential limited only to the extent that an asset price cannot fall below zero; limited downside risk.

    d. None of the above.

    Draw the option chart for the long put.

8.8   What does theta measure?

8.9   What is the effect on theta as the maturity of an option approaches?

8.10 What does delta measure?

8.11 When does delta approach 100 percent?

8.12 When does delta approach 0.00 percent?

8.13 What happens to delta at maturity of an option?

8.14 What does gamma measure?

8.15 What does vega measure?

8.16 What is the theoretical value of an option?

8.17 What do a call option's delta and a put option's delta represent? How are they similar and how do they differ?

8.18 What does a change in the delta of a call option mean, and what does it mean for a put option?

8.19 What are the values of the delta if the underlying is large compared to the strike? What if the underlying is small compared to the strike? Repeat these considerations for a put option.

8.20 What is a delta-neutral strategy? When would you use such a strategy? When would you adopt a positive or negative delta strategy? Finally, explain how you would implement such a strategy in various circumstances. To answer this question, use the data supplied for question 8.2.

8.21 How would you use the delta to construct a dynamic replicating strategy of a forward?

8.22 What is a gamma-neutral strategy? When and why would you use such a strategy? And how would you implement this strategy? Repeat your analysis for a positive and a negative gamma strategy.

REFERENCES

Admati, A. R., and P. Pfleiderer. 1988. A theory of intraday patterns: Volume and price variability. *Review of Financial Studies* 1:3–40.

Aït-Sahalia, Y., and A. Lo. 1998. Nonparametric estimation of state-price densities implicit in financial asset prices. *Journal of Finance* 53:499–547.

———. 2000. Nonparametric risk management and implied risk aversion. *Journal of Econometrics* 94:9–51.

Amihud, Y., and H. Mendelson. 1980. Dealership market: Market making with inventory. *Journal of Financial Economics* 8:31–53.

Bank, D. 1996. Middlemen find ways to survive cyberspace shopping. *Wall Street Journal* 12 (December):B6.

Bowman, E. H., and G. T. Moskowitz. 2001. Real options analysis and strategic decision making. *Organization Science* 12 (6) (November–December):772–777.

Brennan, Michael, and Eduardo Schwartz. 1980. Analyzing convertible bonds. *Journal of Financial and Quantitative Analysis* 15:907–932.

Copeland, Thomas E., and Philip T. Keenan. 1998. Making real options real. *McKinsey Quarterly* 2:38–49.

Demetz, H. 1968. The cost of transacting. *Quarterly Journal of Economics* 82:33–55.

Geske, R. 1978. The pricing of options with stochastic dividend yield. *Journal of Finance* 33 (2):617–625.

———. 1979. The valuation of compound options. *Journal of Financial Economics* 7: 63–81.

Giaccotto, G., G. M. Goldberg, and S. P. Hedge. 2007. The value of embedded real options: Evidence from consumer automobile lease contracts. *Journal of Finance* 62:411–445.

Grenadier, Steven R. 1995. Valuing lease contracts: A real-options approach. *Journal of Financial Economics* 38:297–331.

Harris, L. 1986. A transaction data study of weekly and intraday patterns in stock returns. *Journal of Financial Economics* 16:99–118.

Hasbrouck, J. 1988. Trades, quotes, inventories, and information. *Journal of Financial Economics* 22:229–252.

———. 1991. Measuring the information content of stock trades. *Journal of Finance* 46:178–208.

Hull, J. 2000. *Options, futures and other derivatives.* Englewood Cliffs, NJ: Prentice-Hall International.

Lee, W. Y., J. D. Martin, and Senchack, A. J. 1982. The case for using options to evaluate salvage values in financial leases. *Financial Management* 11 (3):33–41.

Margrabe, W. 1978. The value of an option to exchange one asset for another. *Journal of Finance* 33 (1):177–186.

McCleary, R., and R. A. Hay. 1980. *Applied time series analysis for the social sciences.* Beverly Hills, CA: Sage Publications.

McConnell, John J., and James S. Schallheim. 1983. Valuation of asset leasing contracts. *Journal of Financial Economics* 12:237–261.

McDonald, R., and D. Siegel. 1985. Investment and the valuation of firms when there is an option to shut down. *International Economic Review* 26 (2):331–349.

Ritchken, Peter H., and C. S. Tapiero. 1986. Contingent claims contracting for purchasing decisions in inventory management. *Operations Research* 34 (6) (November–December): 864–870.

Stoll, H. 1989. Inferring the components of the bid-ask spread: Theory and empirical tests. *Journal of Finance* 44:115–134.

Trigeorgis, L. 1991. A log-transformed binomial numerical analysis method for valuing complex multi-option investments. *Journal of Financial and Quantitative Analysis* 23 (3):309–326.

———. 1993a. The nature of option interactions and the valuation of investments with multiple real options. *Journal of Financial and Quantitative Analysis* 28 (1):1–20.

———. 1993b. Real options and interactions with financial flexibility. *Financial Management* 22 (3):202–224.

———. 1995. *Real options: Managerial flexibility and strategy in resource allocation.* Cambridge, MA: MIT Press.

Wilmott, Paul. 2001. *Paul Wilmott Introduces Quantitative Finance*, paperback. Chichester, UK: John Wiley & Sons.

CHAPTER 9

Credit Scoring and the Price of Credit Risk

OVERVIEW

Credit risk has emerged as one of the most important problems of finance. "Credit is a disposition of one man to trust another" (Walter Bagehot, nineteenth century). It is a trust that one bestows on a party to meet commitments negotiated a priori. Credit risk exposure arises when there is a lack of trust and credit contract parties may face adverse consequences. For example, lending money requires the belief and a trust that the borrower will both pay its debt and pay on time. When parties exchange (swap) assets and default occurs, a credit risk event occurs if one or both parties do not meet the terms set by the contract. Credit risk is thus the consequence of a change in terms, time of payment, or whether payments are not made or are made partly. Pricing and managing credit risk are thus important. This chapter focuses on individual credit risk, credit scoring, and credit granting, while the next chapter addresses credit risk and derivatives. These topics are likely to be of increased interest due to the attention that financial institutions are devoting to control their risk and more carefully select credit applicants.

CREDIT AND MONEY

Finance is about money—a means of exchange that provides value to the parties engaged in such an exchange. Money assumes many forms. For example, in antiquity and in the Middle Ages, money was a minted metal—bronze, silver, and gold. The holding and hoarding of such metals provided wealth to the holder. The discovery of the Americas and the huge quantities of gold and silver brought from the new to the old world by Spain, combined with a growth of global-euro exchanges, initiated a decline of minted metals in favor of a new type of exchange. On the one hand, the metal was a source of political power needed for financing wars and policies that required ever-greater quantities of metal (and thus providing excessive metal liquidity). On the other, the volume of business required more *money*, independent of the supply of minted metals.

These historical forces at play ushered in the decline of the Spanish Empire and the rise of empires based on paper money (as credit obligations). Banking families in Italy as well as traders in Holland and subsequently in England thus arose to become economically and politically dominant, assuming the roles of credit guarantors. A new financial system arose based on the implicit fiduciary trust in a banking system that has provided the required liquidity and guarantees to paper money. Today, these guarantees assume many forms such as certificate of deposits (CDs) that may or may not be safe, FDIC insurance in some banks for up to $250,000, and so forth. In Italy, banking houses were at the origin of the powerful Medici family (in Firenze), as well as the rising power of the dukes of Venice, with whom debt, credit, and finance became an essential fact of economies and personal lives.

Foundations for credit and banking may be due to Leonardo of Pisa (Italy, although living in Algeria), known as Fibonacci, who integrated Indian-Arab mathematics in calculation in his seminal *Book of Calculations* (1202)—a first book on financial engineering. Fibonacci allowed one to calculate debt repayment and present values, and thereby provided the means to calculate "implied" interest rates as a basic price of credit. It was in Italy and subsequently in Holland that credit markets were created. This allowed an extraordinary growth in the supply of money and its use for business transactions and economic development. At the same time, paper money trumpeted the decline of other means of exchange, emphasizing the strong relationship between power, paper money, and the credit granted through financial transactions. Nations with no money and no credit, from a historical perspective, will lose their standing (important lessons in light of the financial meltdown of 2008 in Europe and the United States).

The need to supply, hedge, and secure the holders of money (in any denomination) led also to institutional banking services (the central bank) and rules set up first in England to secure the growth of credit. Such rules were based on fractional deposits by members' banks, as will be seen later in this chapter. These rules are applied to this day, albeit they assume different names.

Since paper money is merely a promissory note guaranteed by the central bank, financial transactions are credit transactions. It is our trust in the government's commitment to meet the obligations associated with paper money that induces us to use this means of exchange. In this sense, credit and money are intimately related, one defining the other.

The creation of paper money paralleled a growth of economies that were able to provide credit. Banks (originally in England) have contributed to the expansion of credit by using one's deposit as collateral, used to provide loans—the primary form of credit. Banks, using a fractional reserve obligation to transfer to a central bank (say, the Bank of England, or the Fed in the United States) a percentage of the loan granted, allowed the granting of even more loans. Fractional reserves, aggregated over many depositing banks, provided a reserve for the banking system as a whole and a mitigation of the banking system's risk exposure as well as insurance against individual banks' default. Fractional reserves have thus allowed banks to expand credit by leveraging their capital.

Explicitly, let X be the bank capital loaned to a client at an interest rate r. Let y be the fraction put in reserve at the central bank. There remains $(1 - y)X$, which can be loaned at that same interest rate to a second client and $(1 - y)X - (1 - y)^2 X = y(1 - y)X$ to be loaned to a third client, and so on. Thus, for a loan of one dollar, reprocessed in loans n times, money in circulation increased by

$$\sum_{i=0}^{n}(1-y)^i = \frac{1-(1-y)^{n-1}}{y}$$

In other words, if the fractional deposit is only 5 percent, the amount of available credit has increased by a factor of $20\,(1-(.95)^{n-1})$. When n, the number of depositing banks, is large, a one-dollar credit could be increased twentyfold! Fractional reserves have thus allowed banks to expand credit by leveraging their capital.

Today, credit is expanded further by the use of optional products and credit derivatives. The creation, marketing, and management of such products underlies credit's extraordinary power and the growth of American financial institutions. In other words, finance has grown in importance together with its ability to provide credit and manage the money tree and their consequential risks. The current challenge is to manage the credit beast and allow an expansion of credit in tune with the economic values created by a global economic activity. At the same time, a failure to provide credit for economies' growth and expansion can contribute to their contraction. The future of finance is thus in a continuous state of change, fueled by new financial products that allow greater leverage to investors and firms and require more insurance for their liquidity.

The rise of central banking took place following the legal rights and trust that nations gave to their bankers to handle the supply and management of money for their good and the common good. As a result, central banks rather than governments are entrusted with managing responsibly the monetary policy—not to be used for their own selfish needs but for the betterment of society and the supply of credit needed for its proper functioning. The behavior of some banks and the greed of financial institutions prior to and during the financial meltdown of 2008 may have violated this trust and thereby contributed to the greatest threat to the future of finance. Credit risk scenarios are numerous, but imagine a world without banking or a world with a curtailed ability to provide credit. Such scenarios are equivalent to bringing the business of money back to the Middle Ages, when exchange was based on barter.

Governments capitalize on paper money and credit as a means to finance needs (public works, wars, etc.). They do so by printing money and issuing bonds and other obligations. It is these obligations that have created an extraordinary growth in money and credit and defined their price by the risk-free rate (since they were assumed risk-free). All wars and kingly projects throughout the past five centuries have led to a systematic growth in government obligations—better known as Treasury notes—and have expanded the amount of money traded. This led as well to the growth of the bond market as the largest and most important financial market. Modern-day options and future products have expanded these markets enormously, providing far more money and credit for business, and reducing drastically the impact of governments on these markets (except in some special cases through the interest rate set by central banks and in some places by regulation of these instruments). This has also contributed to global financial markets, allowing an expanded supply of money and credit that today reaches every corner of the world. In this sense, credit is *global money*, controlled by no one and needed by all.

The modern era of money and credit is far more sophisticated and complex than traditional banking. Securitized debts, mortgage-backed securities (MBSs), options, credit default swaps (CDSs), credit derivatives, complex and multi-name credit derivatives, and other financial instruments have ushered in a new era and a new financial environment where money is omnipresent, in everything and everywhere. Credit and credit markets are at the same time global, complex, and virtual. The world of credit, credit risk, credit derivatives, and credit management has thus both assumed a far greater importance and poses a great challenge to financial managers.

CREDIT AND CREDIT RISK

Credit risk consequences include a financial loss, a disappointment, and in some cases, business failure. These risks motivate credit buyers and sellers to seek credit risk reports (such as objective ratings and risk assessments to mitigate the effects of information asymmetry), to demand collateral from borrowers, to price and manage these collaterals and their associated risk, and finally (but most importantly) to buy insurance. Insurance may be contracted with insurance firms or by buying and selling derivatives in financial markets. All credit risk management strategies have a price and assume some risks, whether implicit or explicit. The importance of insurance in credit markets has transformed the role of insurance firms, providing new opportunities for profit or for losses (as was the case with AIG in 2008).

When credit risk is too great, its price is commensurably high. In this case, loans are not granted, or are granted at a very high price, which leads to a reduction in debt volume transacted and thus to reduced liquidity. In such an environment, businesses' transactions are reduced and may even falter. Without credit, all transactions are necessarily based on barter (for example, buying a table in exchange for agricultural products), in which case money loses its function and thereby its value.

Although we still use paper money in many daily transactions, its use has declined significantly with the increased use of financial technology and products that have replaced paper money by moneys of various sorts which are used to trade credit risks. Derivatives, debt obligations, credit card transactions, swaps, and the like are both real and virtual money alternatives. Money has thus changed from a physical reality (as is the case in bartering) to promissory notes (paper money), to future promises and credit agreements. In other words, money is *reengineered*, expressed in terms of and as a function of promises regarding real and financial assets. Further, credit derivatives and financial instruments that derive their value from credit contracts are themselves traded and treated as money. Governments, businesses, and individuals have capitalized on this process, leading to an extraordinary growth in credit and money. For example, in allowing the sale of government obligations (bonds) prior to their exercise and letting them be treated as equivalent to money, far more money was created that could be loaned, borrowed, saved, and invested. Similarly, corporate and rated bonds and their derivatives as well as engineered packages (such as securitized financial assets) in lieu of money were added to a plethora of financial products that are substantial in both absolute and relative money terms.

Credit risk refers to the financial consequences due to upgrading or downgrading of a borrower's creditworthiness or due to default of all or a part of a borrower's credit obligations. It consists of multiple risks, summarized by:

- *Default risk*, defined in terms of its sources, its legal and operational definitions, and how it is measured—explicitly, or implicitly by a price that financial markets ascribe to it. Default risk is thus a function of markets, counterparty, and latent risks.
- *Recovery risk*, defined by the potential recovery of losses. Such risks vary broadly from country to country and are based on the type of obligations the holder of the credit risk owns and the legal framework and practices that these risks are subjected to.
- *Collateral risk*, or risks associated with assets used to insure the underlying credit transaction. For example, a home used as collateral to a loan may have a value that fluctuates over time. The risk associated with the liquidity and the pricing of the collateral defines the collateral risk.
- *Third-party guarantee risk*. One of the external parties to a financial credit transaction may default (as was the case with AIG in 2008).
- *Legal risks* pertain to contracts in which credit recovery depends on the legal resolution of the contract in case of default. These risks and their price vary from court to court and from country to country. In some countries, borrowers may be overprotected and therefore may act in an opportunistic manner. In others, the borrower may be seized and put in jail even for a slight delay in payments.
- *Risk exposure to substantial losses of a credit portfolio*. Such risks underlie the Basel II regulations regarding capital adequacy ratio (CAR) and value at risk (VaR).
- *Macroeconomic and external (latent) real risks* that affect globally a credit portfolio—for example, risks associated with the cyclical behavior of the economy, or sudden jumps in economic variables (such as the financial meltdown of 2008). These risks are particularly important because they affect the credit portfolio as a whole and its underlying mortgages, loans, collaterals, and so forth. Some risks may be insured ex ante, but ex post risk recovery (even with insurance) may be challenging.
- *Counterparty risk*, or the risks inherent in information and power asymmetries of the parties to a credit contract. These risks are latent in over-the-counter (OTC) contracts but latent also in securitized and nontransparent portfolios. Increased attention is given by regulatory agencies to provide greater transparency and risk sharing by all the financial parties a securitized portfolio.

In general, the terms of credit define the financial borrowing/lending agreement. In practice, however, OTC contracts are not uniform. As a result, attempts are made to standardize credit products, improve their transparencies, and make the trades in financial markets fair. To do so and to protect themselves, corporate and financial firms turn to rating agencies (such as Standard & Poor's, Moody's, Fitch Investor Service, Nippon Investor Service, Duff and Phelps, Thomson Bank Watch, etc.) to certify the risk assumed by financial products as well as to rate corporate firms. Even rating does not reduce risk, however. Banks and financial institutions aware of these inadequacies of rating may proceed to reduce these risks by applying other risk management tools. The number of such tools is also varied. For example, limiting the level of obligations, seeking collateral, netting, recouponing, insurance, syndication, securitization, diversification, swaps, and so on, are some of the tools financial firms and banks use to mitigate their credit risk.

In the 2008 financial meltdown, credit risks, fueled by extremely leveraged firms (assuming very high debt-to-equity ratios), have become prominent, impacting financial markets and igniting global deflationary forces. *Wild money*, borrowed by hedge funds faster than it can be reimbursed to banks, created an unsustainable financial environment that was confronted with a credit crunch. Regulatory distortions, either insufficient or excessive, were also a persistent theme raised by media and the academic world. Overregulation hampers economic activity and thereby the creation of wealth, while underregulation (in particular in emerging markets with cartels and few economic firms managing the economy) can lead to speculative markets and financial distortions. The economic, accounting, regulatory, and financial professions have been marred with such problems.

Some banks cannot meet international standards for capital adequacy ratio (CAR). For example, Daiwa Bank, one of Japan's largest commercial banks, has withdrawn from all overseas business partly to avoid having to meet international capital adequacy standards.

To meet these difficulties, the Chicago Mercantile Exchange (CME) launched a new bankruptcy index contract (for credit default), working on the principle that there is a strong correlation between credit charge-off rates and the level of bankruptcy filings. The data for such an index is based on bankruptcy court data.

Complex financial products including mortgage-backed securities (MBSs) and other securitized assets (such as home mortgages, personal and business loans, credit cards, bonds, corporate loans, government loans, etc.) have expanded further the means to produce money and credit. Modern-day insurance (derivatives-based) contracts, credit default swaps (CDSs), multi-name credit derivatives (such as collateralized debt obligations and their variants), have made it possible for U.S. consumers to consume for the past decades as much as they have, at an unprecedented pace in history. However, the lack of credit, following the recent financial crisis, was due to a *process default* in these instruments. This was expressed by a fall in liquidity, banks hoarding cash, and investors refusing to buy securitized loans as they have done so gingerly in the past. Even after receiving billions of dollars from governments to stimulate the credit markets, banks were reluctant to lend money! The relative ineffectiveness of government intervention is a testament to the fact that the new economic and financial environment, defined in terms of new financial and information technologies, globalization, dependence, and the virtuality of financial transactions, has created a family of credit risks hitherto presumed to be unimportant. Nevertheless, credit risk instruments are far too important to be discontinued. While names may change, the credit process will most likely remain an important part of finance and economic growth.

PRICING CREDIT RISK: PRINCIPLES

Pricing credit risk and its management raises both modeling and financial challenges that resort to some simplifications. However, these simplifications can lead to errors and mispricing. In this chapter and the next, we outline three essential approaches:

1. Real credit pricing based on statistical and actuarial techniques (some commonly applied by insurance firms and banks, some specific to the credit risk business). Such techniques include credit scoring and granting based on models and rules practiced and experienced over long periods of time; rating of business and financial enterprises by rating agencies that have access to both company, economic, and financial data and have acquired the know-how to evaluate the ability of firms to meet their obligations.
2. Applications of fundamental finance (Arrow-Debreu) to price credit transactions. This approach uses, as indicated in Chapters 7 and 8, animated pricing framework. Techniques such as replication by a portfolio of assets with known prices and selecting a pricing martingale are also used. This latter approach is also the topic of Chapter 11 on implied volatility and implied risk-neutral distributions. These are approximate distributions that allow us to calibrate the parameters of a financial model and price credit assets using the risk-neutral framework.
3. The utility and implied utility approach. Such an approach is based on implied risk attitudes (and thus risk preferences). Such an approach was outlined in Chapters 5 and 6, while applications to credit risk are considered in this chapter and in Chapter 10 as well.

In simple terms, credit risk is defined in terms of *event risks* with specific probabilities attached to these events—whether we use real or implied financial pricing. When events are *real*, they are statistically and actuarially defined. When they are *implied*, they result from a risk-neutral financial model or from application of utility-based concepts that account for the propensity of buyers and sellers of credit to buy or sell at a given price. For example, in *real finance*, a borrower defaulting on a payment is predicted on the basis of a *credit score* determined on the basis of extensive statistical and mathematical analyses of borrowers' profiles and their credit history. When the default probability is defined in terms of the credit spreads (observed in credit markets), then given an appropriate pricing (risk-neutral) model, the price of credit risk is defined implicitly by model parameters.

By the same token, rating agencies (such S&P, Moody's, Fitch, etc.) assign ratings to business and financial enterprises as well as to some complex financial products, expressing probabilities of the firms' or products' to default (i.e., their financial strength and ability to meet their financial obligations). In such cases, event risks are defined by real or actuarial probabilities. Inversely, if a borrower's premium price is used to calculate the probability of the default event risk, this approach takes for granted the efficiency of financial markets and thus defines its implied default by an appropriate probability model. Such an approach will be used in the next chapter.

Pricing credit risk is important to determine how much to charge a borrower and manage financial credit transactions. Credit scoring, credit granting, the interest rates to charge loans, loans covenant and credit derivatives, and managing collateral are all part of a plethora of techniques that credit risk firms and bank managers use to control their credit risks. Some of the tools include:

- Insurance of credit transactions. In this case, either one or both parties or a third party will act as guarantor to some or all of the risk implied in a credit transaction. Insurance is an important element for enticing credit risk parties to engage in an exchange.
- Managing collaterals and hedging their values to maintain the collateral's effective use as a guarantor of the loan given to a borrower.
- Designing and securitizing credit risk portfolios. Such an approach is deemed important as it increases the marketability of credit risk products and the distribution of credit portfolio risk across many parties. On the downside, such portfolios may be nontransparent and difficult to price.
- Diversifying credit risk across different borrowers (as is commonly practiced by insurance firms). By lending to statistically independent borrowers, the resulting statistical properties of the portfolio may be less risky. In some cases, loan repayment may depend on macroeconomic variables such as interest rates, gross domestic product (GDP), and hurricanes or rare and catastrophic events (such as black swans). This may cause credit portfolios to lose significant value (for example, by a lack of liquidity, by a fall in underlying securities prices, etc.). A lack of diversification opportunities limits the amount of credit that firms can give and leads to economic contraction and a fall in portfolio prices. The risk of rare and catastrophic events is also very difficult to price, with few financial means that allow their full hedging.
- Loan underwriting standards (i.e., loan covenants and procedures applied to safeguard loan reimbursements). Standardized loan transactions are needed to create both greater liquidity and greater transparency in credit markets (and thus obtain prices that are more coherent with the market price of risk, and at the same time protect buyers and sellers from credit risk and moral hazard risk).
- Pricing and managing collaterals and credit derivatives. For example, securitization or techniques that repackage a pool of collateral assets on the balance sheet of a bank into securities that can be sold to investors in capital markets may be both nontransparent and difficult to price. While securitization has significantly augmented financial markets' liquidity, providing an economic stimulus to economic expansion, it has also contributed to the ability of firms to leverage excessively their financial activities, augmenting their average returns on equity but also appreciably increasing their risks. Securitization of MBSs and loans, for example, have unlocked liquidity, allowing more money to be loaned. At the same time it has led to an expansive financial supply chain of credit risks where banks no longer assume any risk but profit as intermediaries.
- Managing credit portfolios to mitigate the adverse consequences of macroeconomic trends. For example, periods of strong economic growth are sometimes accompanied by robust credit growth, followed by an increase in default rates, possibly as a consequence of imbalances generated in these periods (Bonfim 2009).
- Managing the counterparty risk. Several problems occur when credit transactions, involve as well a third external party. For example, a rating firm defining the credit quality of a portfolio, and an insurance firm insuring the portfolio,

are such parties. Issues arise such as, is the rating firm providing a high rate to a bank's portfolio because they profit from rating or because they may be engaged in other businesses with the bank? Is the insurance firm a traditional insurance firm or a financial and speculating enterprise branded as an insurance and financially safe firm? Is it a hedge fund providing a loan and seeking the firm to default to take it over cheaply?

The pricing and the management techniques of credit risks are thus challenging and require both research and a careful application of tools briefly outlined in this and in the next chapter.

CREDIT SCORING AND GRANTING

An individual credit risk (or that of a corporate firm) is defined in terms of its ability to meet a financial commitment. To do so, a personal and financial profile is summarized by a credit score (or a rating for a firm) that provides an estimate of the probability of default. The score assigned determines also the risk premium to be paid by the borrower. For example, a borrowing firm rated highly is likely to have easier access to credit, pay less for it, and may be required to provide lesser collateral. Similarly, a borrower with a low credit score, seeking a mortgage to buy a house, may be turned down or assessed highly by the bank to access credit (think of the penalties and the interest you pay when using your credit card when drawing a loan of $100 or failing to meet the payment by an hour). Determining a score (or a rating) is thus of great interest to banks and financial lending institutions who seek to score individuals' and firms' credit demands.

What Is an Individual Credit Score?

Credit scoring is a system creditors use to help them determine whether to give you credit, based on information about your personal and financial profile and based on your credit experience. Using a statistical program, your profile and credit performance and history are compared to borrowers with similar profiles, to assess your statistical probability of default. A credit scoring system awards points for each factor that defines your profile; techniques are devised to award points for each factor that helps predict who is most likely to default. The total number of weighted points (the *credit score*) is presumed to predict how creditworthy a person is—that is, the likelihood that an individual will repay a loan and meet the payments due (or the probability of default). Such an approach is based on the assumption that databases and their analyses are more reliable than subjective or judgmental methods (although loan officers also make a subjective evaluation of your loan request). In some cases, this scoring process is supplemented by interviews.

The personal profiles used are varied and include, among many items, such things as:

- Your bill-paying history.
- The number and type of accounts you own.
- Your late payments history.

- Outstanding collection actions or outstanding debt.
- The age of your accounts.
- Some personal information.

This information is used to create a credit report, which is filed with your credit application.

To develop a model, a creditor selects a random sample of borrowers, or a sample of similar borrowers if their sample is not large enough, and analyzes it statistically to identify characteristics that relate to creditworthiness. Each creditor may use different scoring models for different types of credit, or a generic model developed by credit scoring consultants. Under the Equal Credit Opportunity Act, a credit scoring system may not use certain characteristics like race, sex, marital status, national origin, or religion as factors. However, creditors are allowed to use age in properly designed scoring systems. But any scoring system that includes age must give equal treatment to elderly applicants.

Scoring systems calculate three quantitative factors applied in determining whether to grant credit:

1. Default, usually expressed by a probability calculated in some manner. This is called the probability of default (PD).
2. Recovery (recovery risk), which is a function of the collateral risk or third-party guarantee risk, legal risks, and the ability of the borrower to meet his commitments in case of defaults. This is also called the loss given default (LGD).
3. Risk of loss (or risk exposure), which includes both the individual and the economic (macroeconomic) risks that are associated with the credit granted. For example, a loan with various clauses indexed on interest rates may be exposed to interest rates fluctuations. To manage risk exposure, banks are required to set aside a certain amount of money to meet contingent losses with a specified probability (the value at risk, or VaR, regulation, described in Chapter 3).

To manage these risks, either voluntarily or through regulation, financial institutions manage the granting decision, the quality of collaterals, and the quality of guarantees. Insurance—through a third party or by hedging through optional products that use an underlying portfolio of credit products as collateral—is also used. The end result is for financial institutions to become intermediaries in a financial supply chain rather than bear their lenders' risk.

Bonds Rating or Scoring Business Enterprises

Bonds are binding obligations by the bond issuer to pay the bondholder (buyer) certain amounts of money at given dates. Some bonds may be subject to default, however, and to various sources of uncertainty. Several economists have studied and suggested models to price default bonds (e.g., Merton 1974; Moody's 1992; Standard and Poor's 1999; Chance 1990; Longstaff and Schwartz 1995; Jarrow and Turnbull 1995; Jarrow, Lando, and Turnbull 1997). Default bonds (as well as firms) are rated to provide a guideline to investors and creditors and the ability to assess and price the risks of rated firms, rated bonds, and generally rated financial instruments. The rating of bonds by firms such as Standard and Poor's or Moody's, thus provides an estimate of a bond quality.

The literature on such problems is extremely large, based on two classes of models, some proprietary and some based on well-known approaches including structural (exogenous) and endogenous models (e.g., Belkin et al. 1998; Black, Derman, and Toy 1990; Brennan and Schwartz 1979; Duffie 1999; Duffie and Kan 1996; Duffie and Lando 2001; Duffie and Singleton 1997; Elton et al. 2001; Heath, Jarrow, and Morton 1992; Das and Tufano 1996; Kijima and Kumoribayashi 1998). Default may assume many forms. Some bonds may default or delay on the coupon payout, or they may default at redemption (wholly or partly, with part of a loss recovered by the creditor).

The valuation and analysis of default bonds is based on the rating matrix, expressing the probable transition from one rate to another over a given period of time (mostly a year), and is defined by the rating agencies. In this case, the bond pricing problem uses the term structure of risk-free rates to calculate the discount rates to be applied to each rating (or alternatively, determine how a credit spread—as traded in a complete financial market—provides an estimate of the probability of default). These ratings can have important direct and indirect consequences. For example, if, as expected in 2012, a three-year period will begin in which more than $700 billion in risky high-yield corporate (bonds) debt will become due, the confluence of such sums with an already extremely large public debt may then contribute to a credit glut in the debt market. Such a situation can lead to a down-rating of the U.S. credit rating with far-reaching consequences for the U.S. financial market and for markets in general.

In discrete time, the full-term structure of interest rates may be needed to construct a risk-neutral framework to price a default bond. It might not be available, however, and thus defaulting bonds can turn out to be difficult to price. For example, for a (discrete time) bond with 15 rating classes and a maturity of two years, the relevant forward spans only the two years, which leads to an underdetermination of the equations needed to value the 15 ratings bond classes that a bond can theoretically assume. By the same token, a bond with four ratings and a maturity of 30 years with (assuming they exist) a published term structure of 30 rates leads to a gross overspecification of the equations needed to value the short (one-year) rating discount rate. For these reasons, term structure interest models are difficult to predict and their use in predicting the probability of default of bonds is at best an approximation. Lacking an ideal system for pricing rated firms, they are often used nonetheless (for a technical extension to pricing rated bonds see www.charlestapiero.com as well as subsequent examples in this and the next chapter).

Scoring/Rating Financial Enterprises and Financial Products

Firms that need and demand credit may also be rated, or scored. These scores are better known as credit ratings given by rating companies such as S&P, Moody's, and others whose business is to provide, for a fee, a firm rating. Rating of firms is based on both published financial data and intrafirm committees that analyze and

TABLE 9.1   A Rating Matrix

	Yr. 1	Yr. 2	Yr. 3	Yr. 4	Yr. 5	Yr. 6	Yr. 7	Yr. 8	Yr. 9	Yr. 10
AAA	0.00	0.00	0.03	0.07	0.11	0.20	0.30	0.47	0.54	0.61
AA	0.01	0.03	0.08	0.17	0.28	0.42	0.61	0.77	0.90	1.06
A	0.05	0.15	0.30	0.48	0.71	0.94	1.19	1.46	1.78	2.10
BBB	0.36	0.96	1.61	2.58	3.53	4.49	5.33	6.10	6.77	7.60
BB	1.47	4.49	8.18	11.69	14.77	17.99	20.43	22.63	24.85	26.61
B	6.72	14.99	22.19	27.83	31.99	35.37	38.56	41.25	42.90	44.59
CCC	30.95	40.35	46.43	51.25	56.77	58.74	59.46	59.85	61.57	62.92

discuss industry-specific trends to establish a semiobjective rating for the company. Ratings have been applied in the past few years to complex financial products (such as CDOs), hedge funds, and other financial entities that are far more secretive than publicly quoted firms and therefore far more difficult to assess. The reliability of such ratings can therefore be dubious—and can include opportunities for moral hazard (see Chapter 6). Raters may at times be overgenerous and may thus mislead investors. For example, the MBS crisis has raised serious doubts regarding the trustworthiness of rating firms, which profited hugely by rating as AAA securitized portfolios that were in fact based on risky mortgage obligations.

The rating score of a business firm can fall into a number of categories, such as AAA, AA, B, C, and so forth. The rating matrix constructed by the rating agency, based on global and industry (and some historical) data, provides an estimate of the probabilities that a rated entity (say AA) will switch within the year to another rating (AAA, A, B, C, etc.). An example is shown in Table 9.1, summarizing three essential risks:

1. Sovereign or environmental risk (industry-wide, macroeconomic, etc.).
2. Business risks.
3. Financial risks.

A firm rated AAA might be considered safe and carry a risk premium close to the risk-free rate, while a firm rated C may be assumed risky with a substantial risk premium paid to compensate its presumed risk. The process of determining the rating matrix is mostly qualitative, based on information exchanges, analysis of the rating firm, as well as the corporate rating firm procedures that evaluate firms individually and collectively (with respect to global industrial trends and macroeconomic conditions). This process contrasts the credit scoring and the estimation of a probability of default associated to an individual consumer credit score (which are statistically based on a cross-section and aggregate information regarding borrowers' ability to pay and environmental macroeconomic conditions). Nevertheless, the rating of a firm is extremely important and a determinant of its cost of finance. For example, financial products such as CDOs, while in fact risky, may have been overrated AAA and, as a result, may have induced investors to assume far greater risks than intended.

The determinants of business risk analysis include numerous factors:

- Industry characteristics such as maturity, growth potential, the business niche of the firm to be rated, cyclical considerations regarding the business of the firm, barriers to entry, and so forth.
- The firm competitive position, including:
  - Its market position (the market share, the product and sale diversity, operational flexibility and diversity, assets flexibility and diversity, etc.).
  - Its business stability.
  - The regulatory environment.

For example, Ganguin and Bilardello (2004) suggest the following case for forest products:

Keys to Success	Operating Measures of Success
Diversity	Product segments as percentage of total sales
	Geographic distribution of sales/production capacity
Attractive market position	Market size, supply/demand fundamentals
	Product price volatility
	Degree of client consideration
Low cost position	Relative input costs
	Economies of scale/capacity utilization
	Transportation costs
Vertical integration	Percentage of fiber self-sufficiency
	Percentage of energy self-sufficiency

Such analyses provide then a rating for a firm, spanning AAA (meaning the highest quality) to BBB+ (meaning an adequate payment capacity) to B+ (meaning high-risk obligations) to CCC (meaning a vulnerability to default). Potential relevant factors to the rating process are thus applied to define an overall rating. For example, for the forest products sector, Ganguin and Billardello (2004) point to the following essential sector's characteristics: unfavorable in relative terms for creditors; capital intensive; cyclical—boom and bust sector; chronic overcapacity. These do not exclude to have clear winners however within this sector, that is, firms that for some specific reasons are rated favorably while others may not be rated favorably. A credit rating is in this case an opinion about the capacity and willingness of a debtor to pay its financial obligations in a timely manner characterized by the scale set by the rater.

Rates, scores, analysis, audits, and so on are applied generally to assess a firm's ability to meet its obligations and its propensity to default, quantified as the *probability of default* (PD). The issues we confront are far more complex, however, and our ability to predict a firm's demise is at best tenuous. One approach, known as the *Z-score*, is based on an extensive statistical analysis of a database of firms (see Altman [1989]; Altman and Kishore [1996]; and Altman et al. [2003] references and applications of this approach). Difficulties in predicting bankruptcy arise due to the many factors that can lead to bankruptcy and their dependence on macroeconomic and external factors that are also hard to predict. Essentially, we tend to use factors originating in three sources:

1. *Market factors* such as the value of the asset and its collateral, its volatility (risk), the pricing of liabilities, the market liquidity (in particular when the firm is highly leveraged and depends on the market liquidity to refinance its debt), and so on.
2. *Operations and accounting factors* such as profitability of the firm, fixed and variable operations costs, and so on.
3. *Information and transparency*, such as the transparency of the firm's statistical data, rogue trading, and so on.

Further, while a combination of any or all factors may contribute to a firm's demise, there is usually one specific factor that causes a firm to implode. For example, if the price of a firm falls below a certain level, it may lead bondholders (with the option right to exercise the reimbursement of the firm debt) to demand that the firm meet its debt obligation immediately—leading to bankruptcy if there is no liquidity, even if the firm is asset-rich. By the same token, when a firm signals that it has no control over its own business (because of a serious breach of security, faulty products, grand larceny, etc.), it may ignite a contagious distrust and a run on the firm, leading to its being bankrupted. In this sense, while there may be many factors contributing to a firm's demise, it is generally one specific event that triggers the actual act of bankruptcy.

CREDIT SCORING: REAL APPROACHES

There are numerous approaches to individual credit scoring. These approaches are in general data intensive, based on large and common statistical databases combined with firms' specific databases. The analysis of such data includes, among many other techniques, application of logistic regressions (and their related extensions) and numerical and probability techniques (such as the separatrix) to predict the probabilities of individuals defaulting.

However, a score is only one element that determines the decision whether to grant credit. Consider, for example, an individual applying to a bank for a mortgage loan, which may or may not be granted. When the mortgage is granted, a bank may do so under specific conditions. These include the payment of an insurance premium, penalties for not meeting payments when they are due, the provision of collaterals, guarantors who may be pursued in case the borrower does not meet his commitments, and so forth. By the same token, the borrower may ask for and obtain (at a price) the right to reimburse the loan prior to its maturity, to renegotiate the terms at some future date, and their like. Such transactions and terms of credit are determined partly by the terms of the loan contracts, the quality of the collateral, the economic environment, and so on. If the collateral is excellent and is deemed to cover the loan, the credit score might be considered less important.

For example, prior to 2008, banks granted mortgages to all borrowers based on the presumption (which turned out to be false) that having the house as collateral in an environment of increasing housing prices would provide a safe insurance for the mortgage transaction. Supplementing such transactions by securitization and trading the credit obligations provided an additional source of profit that banks used liberally. Because the presumption of safety based on collateral turned out not to be accurate, as demonstrated in 2008, the credit score may return to its prior importance in the decision as to whether to approve credit and at what terms (creditors may ask a much higher price for credit and more collateral). Next we consider such approaches cursorily to provide only a basic understanding. Their applications, however, require careful and extensive statistical analysis and validation.

The Statistical Estimation of Default

A Binomial Model   A common statistical approach to define a borrower score is the logit model, defined as follows: Let a score be calculated in terms of a number of factors—questions and information a borrower is required to respond to. Let x_{ij} be the specific score of a person i on a specific item j (a factor). Such information is assembled through questionnaires that borrowers fill out when they apply for credit. Let a_j be a set of weights to be applied to each of the items recorded. Given these weights (estimated using a logit or other models), an aggregate score for a person i is then found to be

$$S_i = \sum_{j=1}^{p} a_j x_{ij}$$

To determine the weights to apply to an individual's profile, the logit model assumes that the probability of default of an individual is a function of his credit score:

$$PD_i = F(S_i) = F\left(\sum_{j=1}^{p} a_j x_{ij}\right) \tag{9.1}$$

where $F(S_i)$ is the probability that a borrower with score S_i defaults. Say that a number of M loans made in the past indicate, by 1 and 0, default and nondefault respectively of a particular borrower. Assuming that borrowers are statistically independent and if there are k defaults out of M, then the likelihood of default of the k borrowers is:

$$L_k = \prod_{i=1}^{k} F(S_i) \prod_{i=k+1}^{M} [1 - F(S_i)] = \prod_{i=1}^{k} F\left(\sum_{j=1}^{p} a_j x_{ij}^*\right) \prod_{i=k+1}^{M} \left[1 - F\left(\sum_{j=1}^{p} a_j x_{ij}^*\right)\right]$$

$$\tag{9.2}$$

where the first k records denote defaulting borrowers and the remaining $M - k$ denotes the nondefaulting borrowers, with each borrower profile given by x_{ij}^*. In other words, the logarithm of the likelihood function (ln-likelihood) is:

$$
ln(L_k) = \sum_{i=1}^{k} F\left(\sum_{j=1}^{p} a_j x_{ij}^*\right) + M - k - \sum_{i=k+1}^{M} F\left(\sum_{j=1}^{p} a_j x_{ij}^*\right) \tag{9.3}
$$

The score maximizing the ln-likelihood is thus found by the optimization problem:

$$
\frac{\partial ln(L_k)}{\partial a_j} = \sum_{i=1}^{k}\left(\sum_{j=1}^{p} x_{ij}^*\right) f\left(\sum_{j=1}^{p} a_j x_{ij}^*\right) - \sum_{i=k+1}^{M}\left(\sum_{j=1}^{p} x_{ij}^*\right) f\left(\sum_{j=1}^{p} a_j x_{ij}^*\right) = 0
$$
$$\tag{9.4}$$

which defines a system of p nonlinear equations in the parameters a_j.

$$
\sum_{i=1}^{k}\left(\sum_{j=1}^{p} x_{ij}^*\right) f\left(\sum_{j=1}^{p} a_j x_{ij}^*\right) = \sum_{i=k+1}^{M}\left(\sum_{j=1}^{p} x_{ij}^*\right) f\left(\sum_{j=1}^{p} a_j x_{ij}^*\right), \ j = 1, 2, \ldots p
$$
$$\tag{9.5}$$

Assuming that solutions a_j^* are found (say by standard numerical techniques such as Newton Raphson iteration techniques), then for any borrower whose profile is $x_{\ell j}$ the borrower score is defined by:

$$
S_\ell = \sum_{j=1}^{p} a_j^* x_{\ell j}
$$

A decision to grant or not grant credit will then be defined by a critical score S^*. Such a score is based on considerations of statistical risks that the creditor is willing to assume.

The Logit Model   A case of particular interest consists in setting the probability of default as a logistic probability distribution:

$$
PD_i = F(S_i) = \frac{e^{S_i}}{1 + e^{S_i}} = \frac{1}{1 + e^{-S_i}}, \ \frac{\partial PD_i}{\partial S_i} = \frac{e^{-S_i}}{\left(1 + e^{-S_i}\right)^2} > 0 \tag{9.6}
$$

and

$$
f(S_i) = \frac{\partial PD_i}{\partial S_i} = \frac{e^{-S_i}}{\left(1 + e^{-S_i}\right)^2} > 0 \tag{9.7}
$$

In this case, the higher the score, the larger the probability of default, while a loan is granted if:

$$S_\ell = \sum_{j=1}^{p} a_j^* x_{\ell j} < S^*$$

And vice versa, a loan is rejected if:

$$S_\ell = \sum_{j=1}^{p} a_j^* x_{\ell j} \geq S^*$$

Note that the weights a_j^* defined here are reduced to the following system of equations:

$$\sum_{i=1}^{k} \left(\sum_{j=1}^{p} x_{ij}^* \right) \frac{e^{-\sum\limits_{j=1}^{p} a_j x_{ij}^*}}{\left(1 + e^{-\sum\limits_{j=1}^{p} a_j x_{ij}^*}\right)^2} = \sum_{i=k+1}^{M} \left(\sum_{j=1}^{p} x_{ij}^* \right) \frac{e^{-\sum\limits_{j=1}^{p} a_j x_{ij}^*}}{\left(1 + e^{-\sum\limits_{j=1}^{p} a_j x_{ij}^*}\right)^2}, \, j = 1, 2, \ldots p$$

(9.8)

An alternative statistical approach, based on linear regression consists in setting:

$$\ln PD_i = S_i - \ln \left(1 + e^{S_i}\right); \ln(1 - PD_i) = -\ln \left(1 + e^{S_i}\right)$$ (9.9)

Thus, the ln of the odds of the probability of default, equals the credit score:

$$\ln \left(\frac{PD_i}{1 - PD_i} \right) = S_i = \sum_{j=1}^{p} a_j x_{ij}$$ (9.10)

Given a cross-section of borrowers with profiles x_{ij}^*, a regression of the following type can be used to estimate the weights to be applied to each factor:

$$\ln \left(\frac{PD_i}{1 - PD_i} \right) = \alpha + \sum_{j=1}^{p} \alpha_j x_{ij}^* + \tilde{\varepsilon}_i, E(\varepsilon_i) = 0, \text{var}(\varepsilon_i) = \sigma^2$$ (9.11)

where ε_i is a normal random variable with mean zero and variance σ^2 providing the means to estimate the parameter weights $a_j^* = \hat{a}_j$. In this case, note that scores are assumed to have a normal probability distribution with mean

$$\hat{\alpha} + \sum_{j=1}^{k} \hat{\beta}_j X_{ij}$$

and variance σ^2, or :

$$\ln\left(\frac{PD_i}{1-PD_i}\right) \sim N\left(\hat{S}_i; \sigma^2\right) = N\left(\hat{\alpha} + \sum_{j=1}^{k} \hat{\beta}_j X_{ij}; \sigma^2\right) \tag{9.12}$$

while the expected odds of a probability of default is found by:

$$\left(\frac{PD_i}{1-PD_i}\right) \sim e^{\tilde{S}_i}, \text{ and } \Omega = E\left(\frac{PD_i}{1-PD_i}\right) = E\left(e^{\tilde{S}_i}\right) \tag{9.13}$$

A loan is then granted only to scores that have odds of default smaller than, say, Ω^*. In other words, $E\left(e^{\tilde{S}_i}\right) \leq \Omega^*$. Note that since the score is normally distributed, we have:

$$E\left(e^{\tilde{S}_i}\right) = e^{\hat{S}_i - \frac{1}{2}\sigma^2}$$

and therefore

$$\ln e^{\hat{S}_i - \frac{1}{2}\sigma^2} = \hat{S}_i - \frac{1}{2}\sigma^2 \leq \ln \Omega^* \text{ and } \hat{S}_i \leq \ln \Omega^* + \frac{1}{2}\sigma^2$$

This model is one of many approaches, however. For example, the *probit* model, unlike the logit model, assumes that the probability of default is given by a cumulative normal probability distribution, defined by:

$$PD_i = F(S_i) = \int_{-\infty}^{S_i} \frac{1}{\sqrt{2\pi}} e^{-\frac{1}{2}x^2} dx \tag{9.14}$$

Other models can be constructed. These models have to be treated carefully, however, because the data available to banks that use such methods is truncated by the fact that it is based only on clients to whom a loan has been granted. Further, models that concentrate only on borrowers' statistical profiles, ignoring the collateral associated with these loans and the macroeconomic environmental variables, may be misleading. For example, a person with a great credit score may be invested in financial markets when these markets are unwinding, or be fired from a high-paying job due to his firm's failure. Further, GDP, interest rates, market liquidity, and many other related financial variables may also affect the probability of default and ought to be accounted for in making a decision to grant or not grant a loan. For this reason, there is a continuous search on how to proceed and determine the proper model to use. Of course, when a probability estimate of default is determined, it can be used in our previous examples in calculating the risks of loans and managing their corresponding risks. Other approaches including linear discriminant analysis, models of discrete choice, probit, and numerous other techniques and models (including artificial intelligence, data mining, and data analytic techniques) are also used.

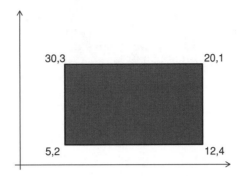

FIGURE 9.1 A Two-Attributes Profile

The Separatrix   We saw previously that credit granting based on a score can be defined simplistically in terms of a single score by relating this score to odds that a loan granted will default. Next we consider credit granting in terms of multiple factors (or scores). For simplicity, say that applicants for credit are defined in terms of two attributes (factors) with applicants' total score based on their score for each of these attributes. Our problem consists in determining a *separatrix* that can distinguish (and thus predict) between good and bad applicants, using the applicants' attribute profiles (scores). This is generally a complex numerical problem that seeks to separate good from bad applicants and obtain better credit performance predictions.

To keep our problem simple, assume two potential responses for the two attributes. In this case, we have $2^2 = 4$ possible profiles. For three attributes (scores), we have $2^3 = 8$ possibilities, while for 100 attributes we would have 2^{100} potential score profiles (which renders the problem of selecting a separatrix a challenging one). For two attributes, consider Figure 9.1. Each corner of the square represents an applicant's profile in terms of the number of loans granted at this profile and the number of defaults corresponding to this profile. For example, to a profile (1,1), there correspond 20 applicants with 1 defaulting. For three attributes there are eight possibilities, as indicated in Figure 9.2.

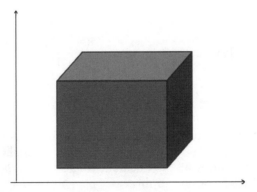

FIGURE 9.2 A Three-Attributes Applicant's Profile

The separatrix we seek consists in selecting a subset of profiles to which we grant credit while refusing credit to other profiles. For example, if we grant credit to profile (1,0) and (1,1), we will have 50 borrowers with 4 defaulting (or an 8 percent default rate expected from applicants that will be granted credit). However, we would have to turn down 17 applicants, 6 of whom would default, with an expected proportion of $(17 - 6)/17 = 11/6$ of nondefaulting applicants. How many to accept or how many to reject, knowing that not all will default, is therefore both a statistical and an economic question. For three attributes the problem remains the same but is of course more difficult due to the increased dimensionality.

Generally, when profiles are collected on both quantitative and qualitative scales, the problem of determining the separatrix is much more complex. For k attributes, let $X = (x_1, x_2, \ldots, x_k), x_i = 1, 0$ be the set of potential values that a score can take, and divide the space of credit taking clients into two types: G (good) and B (bad) on the basis of past performance. As a result, we have two subsets $G \in X$ and $B \in X, G \cup B = X$. Thus $P(G \in X)$ and $P(B \in X)$ are the probabilities of granting credit, while $P(D|G \in X)$ and $P(ND|B \in X)$ are the two risk probabilities. For the two-attributes case, with credit granted to score (1,1), we have:

$$P(D|G \in X) = \frac{1}{20}, 1 - P(D|B \in X) = 1 - \frac{9}{47} = 1 - 0.19 = 81\% \qquad (9.15)$$

EXAMPLE: A SEPARATRIX

A separatrix can be constructed using desired risk and economic objectives. Define two profile subsets A_G and A_B as "grant credit" and "do not grant credit" with $A \equiv A_G \cup A_B$,

$$A \Rightarrow \begin{cases} A_G : \text{Grant credit} \\ A_B : \text{Do not Grant Credit} \end{cases}; \quad A \equiv A_G \cup A_B \qquad (9.16)$$

Explicitly, let $X = \{x_1, x_2, x_3\}, x_i = 1, 0$ define the set of all profiles of all potential applicants, and assume a separatrix that allocates profiles to one or the other set $\{A_G, A_B\}$. Define the probabilities:

$$\begin{aligned} p(x|A_G) &= \frac{p(x, A_G)}{p(A_G)} = \frac{p(A_G|x)p(x)}{p(A_G)} \\ p(x|A_B) &= \frac{p(x, A_B)}{p(A_B)} = \frac{p(A_B|x)p(x)}{p(A_B)} \end{aligned} \qquad (9.17)$$

where $p(x|A_G)$ is the probability that a profile x applicant that has been granted credit defaults, and $1 - p(x|A_B)$ is the probability that an applicant with attributes x who is not granted credit would not default, where $\{p(A_G), p(A_B)\}$ are the probabilities of granting credit or not. In this case, $p(x|A_G)$ and $1 - p(x|A_B)$ are type I and type II risks for the creditor. To translate these probabilities into subjective expected losses, let L be a loss if credit is granted and let D be the loss of business cost under a given separatrix, then the expected cost is:

$$ECost = L \sum_{x \in A_G} p(x|A_G) p(A_G) + D \sum_{x \in A_B} (1 - p(x|A_B)) p(A_B) \qquad (9.18)$$

EXAMPLE: THE SEPARATRIX AND BAYESIAN PROBABILITIES

Consider the following three attributes with the separatrix that sets the first three profiles for credit granting while the remaining profiles are refused credit. For each of these profiles, prior data has indicated the following percentages of defaults: (2, 4, 3, 8, 9, 7, 4, 6). What are the expected costs of such a separatrix? And what are its average type I and II risks? What are the costs and the risks if the proportional number of 1,000 credit applicants are distributed in the eight potential profiles as follows: (5, 8, 20, 12, 10, 20, 15, 10)?

X_1	X_2	X_3	Quality
1	1	1	G
1	1	0	G
1	0	1	G
1	0	0	B
0	1	1	B
0	1	0	B
0	0	1	B
0	0	0	B

Over time and when empirical information is accumulated, the quality of the separatrix may be questioned and its predictive qualities improved in light of new evidence. The Bayes approach may then be used to update the default probabilities. In particular, note that:

$$p(A_G|x) = \frac{p(x|A_G)p(A_G)}{p(x|A_G)p(A_G) + p(x|A_B)p(A_B)},$$

$$p(A_B|x) = \frac{p(x|A_B)p(A_B)}{p(x|A_G)p(A_G) + p(x|A_B)p(A_B)} \qquad (9.19)$$

For example, let the prior predictive probability of default when granting or not granting credit be $\{p(A_G), p(A_B)\} = \{0.05, 0.12\}$ and let the number of profiles x that we have observed in a given period's default be 7 and 20 percent, respectively. Then, given this information, we have the following new posterior predictive probabilities:

$$p(A_G|x = 0.07) = \frac{(0.07)(0.05)}{(0.07)(0.05) + (0.20)(0.12)}$$

$$p(A_B|x = 0.20) = \frac{(0.20)(0.12)}{(0.07)(0.05) + (0.20)(0.12)} \qquad (9.20)$$

Or

$$p(A_G \,|x = 0.07) = .5932, \quad p(A_B \,|x = 0.20) = 0.4067 \tag{9.21}$$

PROBABILITY DEFAULT MODELS

Loan default portfolios depend often on the price of collateral that banks require to compensate their credit risks. The construction of default models is in general difficult due to the complexity and the many sources of risk that portfolios are subject to. Default models based on the joint probability distribution of two or more assets defaulting are thus needed (see also Chapter 4 for an introduction to dependent risk models). Next, we consider some simple examples to highlight the importance and the effects of risk dependence on portfolio credit risk.

Assume that the marginal probabilities of default (1) or no default (0) of two assets are given by:

$$f\,(y_i = 1 \,|\alpha_i) = \alpha_i \text{ and } f\,(y_i = 0 \,|\alpha_i) = 1 - \alpha_i, \quad i = 1, 2 \tag{9.22}$$

For two loans, the joint probability of default is assumed to be $f(y_1 = 1, \ y_2 = 1 \,|\psi) = \psi$. To construct a joint probability model of loan default, we first use the marginal moments

$$E\,(y_i \,|\alpha_i) = \alpha_i, \quad \text{var}\,(y_i \,|\alpha_i) = \alpha_i\,(1 - \alpha_i), \quad i = 1, 2$$

while for co-variation:

$$E\,(y_i y_j \,|\psi) = \psi \text{ and } \text{cov}\,(y_1, y_2 \,|\psi) = \psi - \alpha_1 \alpha_2$$

On the basis of these observations, say that the joint distribution is a joint Bernoulli distribution of the following type:

$$f\,(y_1, y_2 \,|\xi_1, \ \xi_2, \theta) = (\xi_1 \theta)^{y_1}\,(1 - \xi_1)^{1-y_1}\,(\xi_2 \theta)^{y_2}\,(1 - \xi_2)^{1-y_2}, \theta = \theta\,(\xi_1, \xi_2, \lambda)$$
$$\tag{9.23}$$

Note that:

$$f_i\,(y_i, |\xi_1, \ \xi_2, \theta) = (\xi_i \theta)^{y_i}\,(1 - \xi_i)^{1-y_i}\,\big(1 - \xi_j(1 - \theta)\big), \theta$$
$$= \theta\,(\xi_1, \xi_2, \lambda), \quad i = 1, 2, j \neq i \tag{9.24}$$

$$f_1\,(1 \,|\xi_1, \ \xi_2, \theta) = \xi_1 \theta\,(1 - \xi_2(1 - \theta) = \alpha_1, \ f_2\,(1 \,|\xi_1, \ \xi_2, \theta)$$
$$= \xi_2 \theta\,(1 - \xi_1(1 - \theta) = \alpha_2 \tag{9.25}$$

And finally:

$$f(1, 1 \,|\xi_1, \ \xi_2, \theta) = \xi_1\xi_2\theta^2, \theta = \theta\,(\xi_1, \xi_2, \lambda) \tag{9.26}$$

These moments' equality provides three equations for the joint Bernoulli distribution parameters, which can be solved by substitution or numerically.

When data is available, the parameters of the distribution $f(y_1, y_2\,|\xi_1, \ \xi_2, \theta)$ can be estimated either by least squares or by maximizing the data maximum likelihood (see also Chapter 3). For example, consider the maximum likelihood approach and let (y_{1i}, y_{2i}) be a data set, then the maximum likelihood estimators are found by:

$$L = Max \prod_{i=1}^{n} f(y_{1i}, y_{2i}\,|\xi_1, \ \xi_2, \theta) \text{ or } Max \sum_{i=1}^{n} \ln f(y_{1i}, y_{2i}\,|\xi_1, \ \xi_2, \theta)$$

$$= Max \sum_{i=1}^{n} \{y_{1i} \ln(\xi_1\theta) + (1 - y_{1i})\ln(1 - \xi_1) + y_{2i}\ln(\xi_2\theta) + (1 - y_{2i})\ln(1 - \xi_2)\} \tag{9.27}$$

Optimal estimators are then:

$$\sum_{i=1}^{n} \left\{ \frac{y_{1i}}{\xi_1} - \frac{1 - y_{1i}}{1 - \xi_1} + \frac{y_{1i} + y_{2i}}{\theta} \frac{\partial\theta}{\partial\xi_1} \right\} = 0;$$

$$\sum_{i=1}^{n} \left\{ \frac{y_{2i}}{\xi_2} - \frac{1 - y_{2i}}{1 - \xi_2} + \frac{y_{1i} + y_{2i}}{\theta} \frac{\partial\theta}{\partial\xi_2} \right\} = 0;$$

$$\sum_{i=1}^{n} \left\{ (y_{1i} + y_{2i}) \frac{\partial\theta}{\partial\lambda} \right\} = 0 \tag{9.28}$$

By assuming an appropriate functional form for θ, and deriving with respect to its parameters, we obtain a system of three equations in three unknowns.

For three or more assets/loans, we may then calculate a recursive equation. The parameters needed to model such dependence for two, three, four, and more random variables denoting a higher order of dependence requires a greater number of parameters (which renders such an approach unrealistic). For this reason, some other approaches are used to represent and capture the dependence and at the same time maintain the model tractable. To generalize this approach by assuming multivariate dependent Bernoulli default probabilities, with parameters that capture the higher-order dependence, we have:

$$f(y_i = 1\,|\xi_{1i}) = \alpha_{1i}$$
$$f(y_i = 1, y_j = 1\,|\xi_{2ij}) = \alpha_{2ij}, \quad i, j = 1, \ldots n; \quad i \neq j$$

$$\ldots\ldots\ldots$$

$$f(y_i = 1, y_j = 1, \ldots., y_m = 1\,|\xi_{k,i,j,\ldots m}) = \alpha_{k,i,j,\ldots m} \tag{9.29}$$

Note that the last expression stands for the probability of all loans defaulting at the same time. Since these are binary random variables, we have for any two pairs:

$$E\left(y_i \,|\xi_{1i}\right) = \alpha_{1i}, \; E\left(y_i y_j \,|\xi_{2ij}\right) = \alpha_{2,ij},$$

$$\mathrm{cov}\left(y_i, y_j \,|\xi_{2i}, \xi_{1i}, \xi_{1i}\right) = \alpha_{2,ij} - \alpha_{1i}\alpha_{1j}; \quad i \neq j \; \text{ and}$$

$$\rho_{ij}\left(y_i, y_j\right) = \frac{\alpha_{2,ij} - \alpha_{1i}\alpha_{1j}}{\alpha_{1i} - \alpha_{1i}\alpha_{1j}} \tag{9.30}$$

These properties are then used to estimate their parameters based on empirical observations of default.

EXAMPLE: A BIVARIATE DEPENDENT DEFAULT DISTRIBUTION

Say that the probability of two loans defaulting is:

$$f\left(y_1, y_2 \,|\alpha_1, \; \alpha_2, \psi\right) = \frac{(\alpha_1)^{y_1} \left(1 - \alpha_1\right)^{1-y_1} (\alpha_2)^{y_2} \left(1 - \alpha_2\right)^{1-y_2} \psi^{\,y_1 y_2}}{1 + \alpha_1 \alpha_2 (\psi - 1)},$$

$$\theta = \frac{\psi}{1 + \alpha_1 \alpha_2 (\psi - 1)} \tag{9.31}$$

The marginal distributions are:

$$f\left(y_1 \,|\alpha_1, \; \alpha_2, \psi\right) = \frac{(\alpha_1)^{y_1} \left(1 - \alpha_1\right)^{1-y_1}}{1 + \alpha_1 \alpha_2 (\psi - 1)} \left(1 - \alpha_2 + \alpha_2 \psi^{\,y_1}\right) \text{ and } f\left(1 \,|\alpha_1, \; \alpha_2, \psi\right)$$

$$= \frac{1 + \alpha_1}{1 + \alpha_1 \alpha_2 (\psi - 1)} - 1$$

$$f\left(y_2 \,|\alpha_1, \; \alpha_2, \psi\right) = \frac{(\alpha_2)^{y_2} \left(1 - \alpha_2\right)^{1-y_2}}{1 + \alpha_1 \alpha_2 (\psi - 1)} \left(1 - \alpha_1 + \alpha_1 \psi^{\,y_2}\right) \text{ and } f\left(1 \,|\alpha_1, \; \alpha_2, \psi\right)$$

$$= \frac{1 + \alpha_2}{1 + \alpha_1 \alpha_2 (\psi - 1)} - 1 \tag{9.32}$$

while the probability of both loans defaulting is:

$$f\left(1, 1 \,|\alpha_1, \; \alpha_2, \psi\right) = \frac{\alpha_1 \alpha_2 \psi}{1 + \alpha_1 \alpha_2 (\psi - 1)} \tag{9.33}$$

If we set:

$$1 + a = \frac{1 + \alpha_1}{1 + \alpha_1 \alpha_2 (\psi - 1)}, \, 1 + b = \frac{1 + \alpha_2}{1 + \alpha_1 \alpha_2 (\psi - 1)}, \, \frac{\alpha_1 \alpha_2 \psi}{1 + \alpha_1 \alpha_2 (\psi - 1)} = c$$

$$\tag{9.34}$$

this defines three equations with three unknowns.

Next say that the probability of two loans defaulting at the same time is given by 0.05 while the probability of the first loan defaulting is 0.08 and the second loan has a probability of 0.10. What are the distribution parameters? A solution would be a solution of the system of simultaneous equations (9.34).

Now assume that a data set consists of the following record of defaults: $(0, 0), (0, 0), (0, 0), (1, 1), (1, 0), (1, 0), (0, 1), (0, 0), (1, 0)$. How can we use this data set to calculate the underlying parameters of the joint distribution function? A simple solution would consist in applying ln-likelihood estimation to our probability model given by:

$$\ln \prod_{j=1}^{n} f\left(y_{1j}, y_{2j} \mid \alpha_1, \alpha_2, \psi\right)$$

$$= \ln \prod_{j=1}^{n} \left\{ \frac{(\alpha_1)^{y_{1j}} (1-\alpha_1)^{1-y_{1j}} (\alpha_2)^{y_{2j}} (1-\alpha_2)^{1-y_{2j}} \psi^{y_{1j} y_{2j}}}{1 + \alpha_1 \alpha_2 (\psi - 1)} \right\} \quad (9.35)$$

$$= \sum_{j=1}^{n} \begin{pmatrix} y_{1j} \ln(\alpha_1) + (1-y_{1j}) \ln(1-\alpha_1) + \\ y_{2j} \ln(\alpha_2) + (1-y_{2j}) \ln(1-\alpha_2) + \\ y_{1j} y_{2j} \ln \psi \end{pmatrix} - n \ln(1 + \alpha_1 \alpha_2 (\psi - 1))$$

and maximize with respect to the joint distribution parameters. This leads to a system of three equations with three unknowns which can be solved numerically:

$$\sum_{j=1}^{n} y_{1j} - \frac{\alpha_1}{1-\alpha_1} \sum_{j=1}^{n} (1 - y_{1j}) = n \frac{\alpha_1 \alpha_2 (\psi - 1)}{1 + \alpha_1 \alpha_2 (\psi - 1)}$$

$$\sum_{j=1}^{n} y_{2j} - \frac{\alpha_2}{1-\alpha_2} \sum_{j=1}^{n} (1 - y_{2j}) = n \frac{\alpha_1 \alpha_2 (\psi - 1)}{1 + \alpha_1 \alpha_2 (\psi - 1)}$$

$$\frac{1}{\psi} \sum_{j=1}^{n} y_{1j} y_{2j} = n \frac{\alpha_1 \alpha_2}{1 + \alpha_1 \alpha_2 (\psi - 1)} \quad (9.36)$$

EXAMPLE: A PORTFOLIO OF DEFAULT LOANS

Let a portfolio consist of n loans and let the probability of default of a specific loan be defined by the binary random variables $\tilde{y}_i, i = 1, \ldots, n$. The statistical properties of the portfolio can be defined by the aggregation of the portfolio's assets and their statistical averages. In this case, the expected probability of default is:

$$\bar{P} = E\left(\tilde{P}\right) = \frac{1}{n} E\left(\tilde{y}_i\right) = \frac{1}{n} \sum_{i=1}^{n} \alpha_{1i} \quad (9.37)$$

while the variance of such an average default is:

$$\text{var}\left(\tilde{P}\right) = \frac{1}{n^2} \text{var}\left(\sum_{i=1}^{n} \tilde{y}_i\right) = \frac{1}{n^2} \left(\sum_{i=1}^{n} \text{var}\left(\tilde{y}_i\right) + \sum_{i=1}^{n} \sum_{j \neq i}^{n} \text{cov}\left(\tilde{y}_i, \tilde{y}_j\right)\right) \quad (9.38)$$

Letting any two assets be co-dependent, as indicated in our previous joint distribution, we have:

$$\text{var}\left(\tilde{P}\right) = \frac{1}{n^2}\left(n\bar{P} - \sum_{i=1}^{n}(\alpha_{1i})^2 + \sum_{i=1}^{n}\sum_{j\neq i}^{n}(\alpha_{2,ij}) - \sum_{i=1}^{n}\sum_{j\neq i}^{n}(\alpha_{1i}\alpha_{1j})\right) \qquad (9.39)$$

Thus, the standard deviation of the probability of default can be calculated easily, which we denote for convenience by $\sigma\left(\tilde{P}\right)$. Given the set of all co-variances, the probability of any asset of the portfolio defaulting has a mean and variance given by $\left(\bar{P}, \sigma\left(\tilde{P}\right)\right)$. Further, the probability of k assets defaulting has a Lexian mixture binomial probability distribution with mean and variance (irrespective of the probability distribution of default as seen in Chapter 2) given by:

$$E(D) = n\bar{P}; \quad \text{var}(D) = n\bar{P}\left(1 - \bar{P}\right) + n(n-1)\sigma^2\left(\tilde{P}\right) \qquad (9.40)$$

If the cost of each default is a random variable, independent of the cost of other defaults, with known mean and variance, then the total cost of default is:

$$E\left(\sum_{q=1}^{\tilde{n}}\tilde{c}_q\right) = E(\tilde{n})E(\tilde{c}_q) = n\bar{P}E(\tilde{c}_q)$$

$$\text{var}\left(\sum_{q=1}^{\tilde{n}}\tilde{c}_q\right) = (E(\tilde{n}))^2\,\text{var}\left(\tilde{c}_q\right) + \text{var}\left(\tilde{n}\right)E\left(\tilde{c}_q\right)$$

$$= \left(n\bar{P}E(\tilde{c}_q)\right)^2\,\text{var}\left(\tilde{c}_q\right) + \left(n\bar{P}\left(1 - \bar{P}\right) + n(n-1)\sigma^2\left(\tilde{P}\right)\right)E\left(\tilde{c}_q\right)$$

$$(9.41)$$

Note that when the losses $\tilde{c}_q$ are statistically dependent on the number of losses, then the variance of the loss will have to account for such dependence.

EXAMPLE: A PORTFOLIO OF DEPENDENT DEFAULT LOANS

Assume a portfolio consisting of 50 loans, each with an expected probability of default given by $\alpha_i = \{0.02, 0.05, 0.07, 0.02, 0.01, \ldots\}$. Default loans are separated into two classes, high and low risk (high risk with individual default probabilities of 0.04 and higher, and low risk with default probabilities less than 0.04). These classes indicate that the mean default probabilities of loans in the high and the low risk categories are 0.06 and 0.03, respectively, while in both cases their variance equals the mean in their risk class. Assume at first that these variances are null while the default correlation is 0.4. In this case, we see that the first class (high risk) is defined by the random variable y_1 whose parameter is $\alpha_1 = 0.06$ while the second class (low risk) is a random variable y_2 whose parameter is $\alpha_2 = 0.03$. The correlation from the model in equation (9.30) is:

$$E(y_1 | \xi_1) = \alpha_1 = 0.06; E(y_2 | \xi_1) = \alpha_2 = 0.03, E(y_1 y_2 | \xi_{12}) = \alpha_{12};$$

$$\rho_{12}(y_i, y_j) = 0.4 = \frac{\alpha_{12} - \alpha_1 \alpha_2}{\alpha_1 - \alpha_1 \alpha_2} = \frac{\alpha_{12} - 0.018}{0.02 - 0.018} = \frac{0.8}{2} = 0.4 \qquad (9.42)$$

with $\alpha_{12} = 0.018 + 0.002 * 0.4 = 0.018 + 0.0008 = 0.0188$ defining the last parameter.

PROBLEM 9.1: THE JOINT BERNOULLI DEFAULT DISTRIBUTION

Say that the following data is available to you:

$$(j = 1{:}y_{1j} = 0, \quad y_{2j} = 1), (j = 2{:}y_{1j} = 1, \quad y_{2j} = 1), (j = 3{:}y_{1j} = 1, \quad y_{2j} = 0)$$
$$(j = 4{:}y_{1j} = 0, \quad y_{2j} = 0), (j = 5{:}y_{1j} = 1, \quad y_{2j} = 1)$$

What are the parameters of the joint Bernoulli distribution? What is the index of correlation?

CREDIT GRANTING

The need to price credit is imperative and intimately associated to the decision to grant credit. The approaches we consider next will highlight both the real-actuarial and risk-neutral approaches. The financial price of a credit product, whether real or implied, is then a determinant factor when the decisions are made whether to grant credit and at what price. To make this determination, we shall define a number of models in terms of the following parameters:

Parameters defined or to be specified:
- The size of the loan (in dollars or in another currency).
- The credit score of the borrower or the rating of the corporate entity seeking credit.
- The collateral applied, or needed, to secure wholly or partly the loan.

The credit risk consequences, summarized by the following:
- The default probability (PD).
- The loss given default (LGD).
- The credit recovery rate, in case of default.

Financial decisions, consisting of:
- Whether to grant credit or not.
- At what price (interest charges and other payments) to grant credit.
- What and how much collateral and insurance to require from a party.

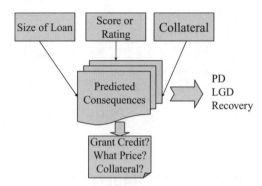

FIGURE 9.3   The Parameters of Credit Granting

These parameters are summarized in Figure 9.3. Subsequently we shall be concerned with the management of the credit granted, securitization, and the risk transfer of portfolios based on such credits through credit derivatives and related products such as CDS, CMOs, CDOs, and so forth in Chapter 10.

Define for convenience the following variables:

Π = The size of the loan requested at time $t = 0$
$\tilde{\Pi}_1$ = The borrower debt at time $t = 1$, the loan maturity
S = The score (or the rating) of the borrower
M_0 = The price of the collateral when the loan is made at $t = 0$
$\tilde{M}_1$ = The price of the collateral at $t = 1$, the loan maturity date

The academic literature and its practice abound with examples emphasizing what banks want and buy from consultants and what works. These approaches can be categorized in terms of the following types of approaches:

- Financial economic valuation emphasizing an implied financial approach consisting of:
  - Financial discounting of exogenous risks based on the credit spread, implying the probability of default (with an applicable implied risk-neutral measure).
  - Implied financial pricing based on credit risk and credit derivative prices that determine the implied risk-neutral distribution that allows pricing of loans (debt) and all their derivatives.
  - Endogenous financial valuation based on the collateral price. This approach defines credit risk in terms of firms' (or individuals') solvency implied by their collateral assets, equity, and their debt obligations.

The management of these risks is then based on:

- Risk exposure and insurance.
- Collateral pricing and management.
- Financial market pricing, credit intermediation, and credit risk transfer.

- Real-risk probabilities modeling and approaches based on statistical models (including data analytic methods), and granting credit based on scores and their economic implication.

A credit rate of a firm or a credit score (combined with a collateral) may then be used to reach a decision to grant credit or not. If the price of a collateral is likely to grow for the foreseeable future at an appreciable rate, it would justify and fuel giving credit to all borrowers (as it was the case with MBS). In practice, loan officers have provided credit as long as they believe they can secure their loan repayment through both insurance surcharges and collaterals. When an aggregation of loans into portfolios with various components (payments and obligations at various times) made it possible to securitize these portfolios and pass them on to other accepting parties, the credit risk responsibilities moved from the creditor to other willing parties (with rating firms rating such risky portfolios as AAA). Creditors (banks) have failed nonetheless, either by treating these rated portfolios as AAA-rated (which they were not) or by selling the portfolios as securitized products and selling insurance to protect investors from portfolio risk. In the latter cases, some banks such as Goldman Sachs, expecting prices to fall, bought bets that would make them more money if the real estate mortgage market were to fail, thus profiting three times: from the sale of mortgages to unsuspecting mortgage seekers, from their securitization, and from the contrarian bet they took against the real estate market.

For simplicity, we consider these approaches through simple examples, while more realistic and complex cases are treated in Chapter 10.

While in the past, credit scoring based on statistical and other techniques was used, in the past ten years, economic and financial approaches to credit granting and securitization have dominated the business of credit risk and its management.

EXAMPLE: CREDIT GRANTING AND CREDITOR'S RISKS

The decision to grant credit is binary: 1 for grant credit, 0 for do not grant credit, as Figure 9.4 indicates. The creditor decision is then based on the applicant score, the collateral, an insurance that the creditor buys (and has the borrower pay for), and general economic conditions.

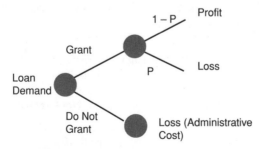

FIGURE 9.4 Credit Granting and Probabilities of Gain and Loss

When credit is granted, the borrower may or may not default, with consequent losses to both the creditor and the borrower. In this sense, the credit decision, whether it is based on a contractual relationship between the individual borrower and a bank or between a bank and a corporate entity, or a contractual exchange between two financial firms, involves risks to both parties. In summary, the decision to grant credit involves:

- A prospective and uncertain return, which can be positive or negative for either the creditor or the borrower (including repayment of the loans and his related collateral).
- A risk of granting the loan to a borrower who has been misjudged as a reliable borrower when in fact he has a propensity to default (also called a type I risk).
- A business loss risk of not granting the loan to an applicant borrower who, although his credit score indicated otherwise, could have been a good borrower who meets his commitments (also called a type II risk).
- A counterparty risks, based on false or partial information provided by either party, overstating expectations and uses of power and information asymmetries by both parties. In this case, risks are strategic, resulting from the personal (and conflicting) motives of the creditor and the borrower.

The decision to grant credit and its quantification underlies these concerns. The formulation we present next is a framework that highlights these concerns.

Say that the decision to grant a loan is weighed statistically and based on a model as in Table 9.2. Let x be a consumer's individual score. This score is classified in one of two (or more) classes, say $x \in \{X^*\}$ where X^* denotes the class of loans presumed safe and therefore reliably granted. Alternatively, say that $x \notin \{X^*\}$ means that the demand for credit is deemed unsafe and to be rejected. This is represented by the following binary statement:

$$u = \begin{cases} 1 & if \ x \in \{X^*\} \\ 0 & if \ x \notin \{X^*\} \end{cases} \tag{9.43}$$

while the risks a creditor has when granting credit are:

$$Type \ \mathrm{I}: P_I = P\{D|x, x \in \{X^*\}\} \ \text{and}$$

$$Type \ \mathrm{II}: P_{II} = 1 - Q\{D|x, x \notin \{X^*\}\} \tag{9.44}$$

TABLE 9.2 The Credit Granting Risk Probabilities

	$x \in X^*$ **Credit Granted**	$x \notin X^*$ **Credit Not Granted**
Default (D)	$P_I = P\{D|x, \{x \in X^*\}\}$ **Type I Risk**	$1 - P_{II} = Q\{D|x, x \notin X^*\}$ **Type II Risk**
No default (ND)	$1 - P_I = P\{ND|x, \{x \in X^*\}\}$	$P_{II} = 1 - Q\{D|x, x \notin X^*\}$

where $P_I = P\{D|x, x \in X^*\}$ is the conditional probability of granting credit to an applicant based on his score and the applicant defaulting, while $P_{II} = 1 - Q\{D|x, x \notin X^*\}$ is the conditional probability of not granting credit and the applicant would, presumably, not default. These two probabilities express two types of risks, type I and type II risks. These define quantitatively the probabilities of making a wrong decision when granting credit and when the decision is made not to grant credit. An elementary and risk-sensitive rule that determines the decisive credit score based on these risks consists then in selecting the risk probabilities that creditors are willing to assume and selecting the scores for which credit will be granted. This is explicitly stated by the following process (summarized in Table 9.2) where α and β are the risk constraints specified by the creditor.

$$
\begin{array}{lll}
\text{Find } \{x \in X^*\} & \text{The credit granting space} & \\
\quad \text{subject to :} & & \\
P_I = P\{D|x, \{x \in X^*\}\} \le \alpha & \text{The type I risk} & (9.45) \\
P_{II} = 1 - Q\{D|x, x \notin X^*\} \le \beta & \text{The type II risk} &
\end{array}
$$

Elementary application of (Bayes) probability calculus indicates that the joint probability of a default (or nondefault) and whether the credit granting decision was made or not is given by:

$$
\begin{aligned}
P(D, x \in X^*) &= P\{D|x \in X^*\} G(x \in X^*) = G(x \in X^*|D) P(D) \\
P(ND, x \in X^*) &= P\{ND|x \in X^*\} G(x \in X^*) = G(x \in X^*|ND) P(ND) \\
P(D, x \notin X^*) &= Q\{D|x \notin X^*\} G(x \notin X^*) = G(x \notin X^*|D) P(D) \\
P(ND, x \notin X^*) &= Q\{ND|x \notin X^*\} G(x \notin X^*) = G(x \notin X^*|ND) P(ND)
\end{aligned}
$$

$$(9.46)$$

where

$g(x)$ is the probability that an applicant has a score x

$G(x \in X^*) = \int_{\{x \in X^*\}} g(x)dx$ is the probability that credit is granted

$G(x \notin X^*) = \int_{\{x \notin X^*\}} g(x)dx$ is the probability that credit is not granted

$P(D, x \in X^*)$ is the probability that a borrower with score x and granted credit defaults

$Q(ND, x \notin X^*)$ is the probability that a borrower not granted credit would not have defaulted

The probabilities $P(D)$ and $Q(ND)$ are prior and subjective probabilities (based on previous data, information, and the current state of the credit markets and macroeconomic variables) that the applicant whose score is x defaults or not. A relationship between these probabilities is provided by Bayes' theorem (we consider only one case of the four states defined in Table 9.2), or:

$$P\{(D, x) | x \in X^*\}$$

$$= \frac{P(x \in X^* | (D, x)) P(D, x)}{P(x \in X^* | (D, x)) P(D, x) + P(x \in X^* | (ND, x)) P(ND, x)} \quad (9.47)$$

EXAMPLE: A BAYESIAN DEFAULT MODEL

Assume an individual applicant with score 600, when all scores above 500 are granted loans. Historical data points out that with such a rule in effect, 3 percent of loans granted have defaulted, while industry data has indicated that in the current economic conditions 5 percent of such applicants will default. In this case, the probability of default with such a score is given by

$$X = P(x \in X^* | (D, x)) = P(600 > 500 | (D, 600)) \quad (9.48)$$

or

$$0.03 = \frac{XP(D, 600)}{XP(D, 600) + (1 - X)P(ND, 600)}, \; X = P(600 > 500 | (D, 600))$$

$$(9.49)$$

and

$$0.03 = \frac{0.05X}{0.05X + (1 - X)0.95}$$

or

$$X = P(500 \in 600 | (D, 600)) = 0.370$$

In other words, $X = 0.37$ while the probability of granting credit and defaulting is $0.37 \times (0.03) = 0.111$

Next, assume that for all scores above the granting score, 6 percent have defaulted while the prior probability of default remains 5 percent. In this case the portfolio probability of default is:

$$P\{D | x \in X^*\} = \frac{P(x \in X^* | D) P(D)}{P(x \in X^* | D) P(D) + P(x \in X^* | ND) P(ND)} \quad (9.50)$$

The probability $P(x \in X^* | D)$ of the granted credit that will default is:

$$0.06 = \frac{P(x \in X^* | D) * (0.05)}{P(x \in X^* | D) * (0.05) + (1 - P(x \in X^* | D)) 0.95}$$

or

$$P\left(x \in X^* \,|\, D\right) = \frac{0.95}{0.97} = 0.979 \tag{9.51}$$

We now extend our analysis to a scored population.

EXAMPLE: A FINANCIAL APPROACH

Let $\left(\Pi, \tilde{\Pi}_1\right)$ be a loan (debt) granted to a borrower at a given initial time with a maturity of one period, at which time the debt is reimbursed and the creditor collects $\tilde{\Pi}_1$, a random variable we shall define shortly. If the borrower does not default, the creditor collects $\Pi\left(1 + R(S)\right)$ where $R(S)$ is the rate of interest charged by the creditor to a borrower whose score is S. By the same token, let $\left(M_0, \tilde{M}_1\right)$ be the prices of the collateral initially and at the time the loan matures and has to be repaid. If default of a loan is defined solely by the price of the collateral compared to the debt due at maturity, then the creditor collects the collateral at maturity if it is smaller than debt. Namely,

$$\begin{aligned} \tilde{\Pi}_1 &= Min\left\{\Pi\left(1 + R(S)\right), \tilde{M}_1\right\} \text{ or} \\ \tilde{\Pi}_1 &= \Pi\left(1 + R(S)\right) - Max\left\{\Pi\left(1 + R(S)\right) - \tilde{M}_1, 0\right\} \end{aligned} \tag{9.52}$$

For example, a person borrowing to buy a house with the obligation to repay the loan and its interest charge the next year, might decide to default if the house bought with the loan has a price smaller than that of the loan. In this case, a person's score has no impact on default. The amount of money collected by the creditor at maturity is then random, as previously defined, depending on the collateral price. If the collateral is traded in financial markets, then, as we see in equation (9.52), the amount of money collected by the creditor has, under the risk-neutral pricing Q measure, a current price of:

$$\begin{aligned} \bar{\Pi}_1 &= \frac{1}{1 + R_f} E^Q\left(\tilde{\Pi}_1\right) \\ &= \frac{1}{1 + R_f}\left\{\Pi\left(1 + R(S)\right) - E^Q\left(Max\left\{\Pi\left(1 + R(S)\right) - \tilde{M}_1, 0\right\}\right)\right\} \end{aligned} \tag{9.53}$$

and

$$\bar{\Pi}_1 = \frac{\Pi\left(1 + R(S)\right)}{1 + R_f} - Put\left(\Pi\left(1 + R(S)\right), 1 \,|\, M_0\right) \tag{9.54}$$

If markets are complete, then $\bar{\Pi}_1 = \Pi$ and therefore, the size of the loan granted is a solution of the pricing equation:

$$\Pi = \frac{1}{1 + R_f}\Pi\left(1 + R(S)\right) - Put\left(\Pi\left(1 + R(S)\right), 1 \,|\, M_0\right) \tag{9.55}$$

An explicit expression in terms of the spread, the put option price, and the collateral is given as follows:

$$\Pi = \frac{1 + R_f}{R(S) - R_f} Put\left(\Pi\left(1 + R(S)\right), 1 \,|\, M_0\right) \tag{9.56}$$

Replacing the put option by put-call parity, we have:

$$Put\left(\Pi\left(1 + R(S)\right), 1 \,|\, M_0\right) = Call\left(\left(\Pi\left(1 + R(S)\right), 1 \,|\, M_0\right)\right) + \frac{\Pi\left(1 + R(S)\right)}{1 + R_f} - M_0 \tag{9.57}$$

And an alternative expression for the loan granted as a function of the loan's contractual parameters is:

$$\Pi = M_0 - Call\left(\left(\Pi\left(1 + R(S)\right), 1 \,|\, M_0\right)\right) \tag{9.58}$$

If the collateral price is a lognormal process with volatility σ, then the call option price with strike $\Pi(1 + R(S))$ and exercise one period later (and generally, the debt maturity of the borrower) has a price given by (see Chapters 7 and 8):

$$Call_0 = M_0\Phi(d_1) - \Pi(1 + R(S))e^{-R_f}\Phi(d_2) \tag{9.59}$$

where

$$\Phi(y) = (2\pi)^{-1/2} \int_{-\infty}^{y} e^{-u^2/2} du;$$

$$d_1 = \left[\frac{\ln\left(\frac{M_0}{\Pi(1 + R(S))}\right) + (R_f + \sigma^2/2)}{\sigma}\right]; \quad d_2 = d_1 - \sigma \tag{9.60}$$

As a result,

$$\Pi = M_0 - M_0\Phi(d_1) + \Pi(1 + R(S))e^{-R_f}\Phi(d_2) \tag{9.61}$$

Dividing by the collateral initial price and the price of the loan, we have

$$\frac{M_0}{\Pi(1 + R(s))} = \frac{\left(1 - (1 + R(S))e^{-R_f}\Phi(d_2)\right)}{(1 + R(s))\left(1 - \Phi(d_1)\right)} \tag{9.62}$$

Define

$$x = \ln\left(\frac{M_0}{\Pi(1 + R(S)))}\right)$$

Then we obtain one equation in one unknown, for x, explicitly given by:

$$e^x = \frac{\left(1 - (1 + R(S))e^{-R_f}\Phi\left(\frac{x + R_f - \sigma^2/2}{\sigma}\right)\right)}{(1 + R(s))\left(1 - \Phi\left(\frac{x + R_f + \sigma^2/2}{\sigma}\right)\right)} \tag{9.63}$$

And as a result,

$$x = \ln\left(\frac{1 - (1 + R(S))e^{-R_f}\Phi\left(\frac{x + R_f - \sigma^2/2}{\sigma}\right)}{(1 + R(s))\left[1 - \Phi\left(\frac{x + R_f + \sigma^2/2}{\sigma}\right)\right]}\right)$$

$$\Phi(y) = (2\pi)^{-1/2} \int_{-\infty}^{y} e^{-u^2/2} du \tag{9.64}$$

In other words, two parameters define the conditions of the loan, defined by equation (9.64). The first parameter is the proportion of the collateral to the loan granted, and the second is the interest surcharge imposed on the loan. We can verify that the higher the surcharge (and therefore, the larger the spread), the smaller the required collateral, and vice versa—the smaller the surcharge, the larger the required collateral. In this sense, collateral-rich borrowers will pay less for debt while collateral-poor borrowers (and usually having a lower credit score or rating) will pay more for their debt. This equation is meaningful, however, only if the collateral is traded and financial markets are complete. For example, a corporate firm rated A that is in need of a loan, by putting its stock as collateral, may have to pay the interest rate $R(A)$, particular to its rating and at the same time deposit a quantity of stock collateral commensurate with the loan asked for and granted.

If a home currently priced at P_0 is put up as a collateral and the lender requires a proportion of self-financing of k times the price of the home, then letting the house be the collateral we have $M_0 = P_0$ while the loan granted is $\Pi = (1 - k)P_0$ with a surcharge a function of k, or $R(k, S)$. In other words, we have then:

$$e^x = \frac{P_0}{(1 - k)P_0(1 + R(k, S)))} = \frac{1}{(1 - k)(1 + R(k, S)))} \tag{9.65}$$

or

$$x = -\ln(1 - k) - \ln(1 + R(k, S))$$

For example, if a home mortgage is 90 percent of the price of the house, then $x(1 + R(k, S)) = 1/0.90$ and therefore, the required interest surcharge is found by a solution of:

$$
\ln\left(\frac{1}{0.90}\right)
$$

$$
= \ln\left(1 - (1 + R(.90, S))e^{-R_f}\Phi\left(\frac{\ln\left(\frac{1}{0.90}\right) - \ln(1 + R(0.90, S)) + R_f - \sigma^2/2}{\sigma}\right)\right)
$$

$$
- \ln\left(1 - \Phi\left(\frac{\ln\left(\frac{1}{0.90}\right) - \ln(1 + R(0.90, S)) + R_f + \sigma^2/2}{\sigma}\right)\right) \qquad (9.66)
$$

EXAMPLE: AN APPROXIMATE SOLUTION

Consider the equation

$$
\ln\left(\frac{1}{k}\right) = \ln\left(1 - (1 + R(k, S))e^{-R_f}\Phi\left(y - \frac{\sigma}{2}\right)\right) - \ln\left(1 - \Phi\left(y + \frac{\sigma}{2}\right)\right) \qquad (9.67)
$$

where

$$
y = \frac{\ln\left(\frac{1}{k}\right) - \ln(1 + R(k, S)) + R_f}{\sigma}
$$

$$
\Phi(z) \approx 1 - \left(\frac{0.34802}{1 + 0.47047z} - \frac{0.9587}{(1 + 0.47047z)^2} + \ldots\right)e^{-z^2} \qquad (9.68)
$$

and assume a risk-free rate of 0.05 and a volatility of 0.1. Then:

$$
\ln\left(\frac{1}{k}\right) = \ln\left(1 - (1 + R(k, S))e^{-R_f}\Phi\left(\ln\left(\frac{1}{k(1 + R(k, S))}\right)^{10}\right)\right)
$$

$$
- \ln\left(1 - \Phi\left(\ln\left\{e\left(\frac{1}{k(1 + R(k, S))}\right)^{10}\right\}\right)\right) \qquad (9.69)
$$

A numerical solution for the required spread as a function of k, the co-participation of the borrower in the price of the home, may be calculated.

PROBLEM 9.2: THE RATE OF RETURN OF LOANS

Begin with the following assumption: $k = 0.90$, 0.80, 0.70, 0.60, 0.50, 0.40, 0.30, 0.20, 0.10. Calculate the corresponding rate of return R. These values will point to the extraordinary returns that a creditor will have in charging the interest surcharge to subprime borrowers and then reselling these same mortgages dressed in a securitized portfolio.

THE REDUCED FORM (FINANCIAL) MODEL

The reduced form approach consists essentially in constructing a model for default and calculating the probability of default implied in a credit spread. The default asset risk spread, reflecting the demand and the supply for the asset, implies a discount that we relate (through a simple probability model) to a probability distribution of default. In other words, real default is *virtual* and might not indicate the real probability of default, but only a *market consensus* regarding the asset's potential default.

A simple introduction to such an approach can be shown by pricing a default bond. This approach makes no attempt to define default as an endogenous event (arising from a low level of firm value or cash flow, or the manner in which a firm is managed). Rather, default is specified exogenously. Issues such as leverage are not addressed explicitly, but only implicitly by buyers' and sellers' assessment of the leverage implication to default risk. These models were expounded on by numerous financial economists such as Duffie and Singleton (2003); Jarrow and Turnbull (1995); Jarrow, Lando and Turnbull (1997); Schönbucher (2003)and others. The model of Jarrow, Lando, and Turnbull (1997), for example, assumes that the value of a default-free zero-coupon bond, paying one dollar at maturity at time T, is known at time t. Let $B(t, T)$ be the price of this bond (paying one dollar at maturity time T). It is given by:

$$B(t, T) = e^{-R_f(t, T)(T-t)}, \ B(T, T) = 1 \qquad (9.70)$$

where $R_f(t, T)$ is the risk-free rate. Now assume the bond may default (for some external reasons) in the remaining time interval (t, T). Let the default event occur at time t with a probability distribution $f_D(\tau \,|\, \Im_t)$ where $\Im_t$ is a filtration at time t, or:

$$1_{\tau > t} = \begin{cases} 1 & \text{If default occurs in } (t, T) \\ 0 & \text{If no default occurs} \end{cases} \qquad (9.71)$$

Let $B_D(t, T)$ be the price of such a default bond defined by financial markets. This price is in fact the amount of money that the bondholder collects at maturity (expressing an implied discount applied to the bond due to a potential default). Thus, since $[1 - F_D(T \,|\, \Im_t)]$ is an implied probability denoting the probability that no default occurs, its default bond current price is by definition:

$$B_D(t, T) = E\left(B(t, T)\mathbf{1}_{\tau > T}\right) = B(t, T)\left[1 - F_D(T \mid \Im_t)\right]$$

$$= e^{-R_f(t, T)(T-t)}\left(1 - F_D(T \mid \Im_t)\right) \tag{9.72}$$

We can rewrite this expression in terms of a hazard rate, expressing the conditional probability of default at time t, given that there was no prior default until that time. The rationality of such an approach is that it allows us to express the money effects of a default as a discount rate augmenting the discount rate accounting for default at some future (and random) date. This is given by:

$$h_D(t) = \frac{f_D(t)}{1 - F_D(t)} = -\frac{\partial}{\partial t} \ln\left[1 - F_D(t)\right]$$

$$-\int_t^T h_D(s)ds = \ln\left[1 - F_D(t)\right] \text{ and } 1 - F_D(t) = e^{-\int_t^T h_D(s)ds} \tag{9.73}$$

If we are at time t, the probability of no default in the time interval (t, T) is written as follows:

$$1 - F_D(T \mid \Im_t) = e^{-\int_t^T h_D(s)ds} \text{ and } B_D(t, T) = e^{-\left(\int_t^T (R_f(s,T))ds + \int_t^T h_D(s)ds\right)} \tag{9.74}$$

The implied discount rate applied to the default bond is thus

$$\left(\int_t^T (R_f(s, T))ds + \int_t^T h_D(s)\, ds\right)$$

The discount rate used thus implies the price of the bond, and vice versa. The difference between a default and a risk-free bond $B_D(t, T) - B(t, T)$ is the risk premium for the default bond.

EXAMPLE: CALCULATING THE SPREAD OF A DEFAULT BOND

Say that the risk-free rate is set by the Fed to 6 percent. The price of a zero-coupon bond with maturity in one year is then $1/(1 + 0.06) = 0.94$. By comparison, consider a corporate bond that is selling for each dollar in the same conditions (one-year maturity) at \$0.80. The spread—the premium charged for a potential default of the issuing firm—is thus $0.94 - 0.8 = 0.14 = 14$ percent. The bond discount is thus calculated as follows.

For simplicity, say that the probability distribution of default is exponential and thereby, its hazard rate is constant and given by the parameter μ. The corporate bond price is thus:

$$0.80 = (1)\, e^{-0.06(1) - \int_0^1 \mu dx} = e^{-0.06 + \mu} \tag{9.75}$$

and

$$\mu = \ln\left(\frac{1}{0.80}\right) - 0.06 = 0.163144$$

Next, assume that if the corporate bond defaults, it will be only a partial loss with a recovery rate of 40 percent. In this case, the bond price at maturity is:

$$\begin{aligned} E\left(\tilde{B}_D^C(T)\right) &= (1)(1 - F_D(T)) + 0.6\,(F_D(T)) \\ &= (1)(1 - F_D(T)) + 0.6\,(F_D(T)) + 0.6 - 0.6 \\ &= (1 - 0.6)(1 - F_D(T)) + 0.6 \end{aligned} \tag{9.76}$$

and therefore,

$$E\left(\tilde{B}_D^C(T)\right) = 0.60 e^{-0.06} + .4 e^{-0.06 - \mu} \tag{9.77}$$

which equals 0.88506. If the price of such a bond (with 60 percent recovery) is now \$0.90, then the implied hazard default rate is:

$$0.90 = 0.60 e^{-0.06} + .4 e^{-0.06 - \mu} \text{ and } \mu = \ln\frac{0.4}{0.90 - 0.60 e^{-0.06}} - 0.06 \tag{9.78}$$

EXAMPLE: THE LOAN MODEL AGAIN

We consider again the pair (loan and debt repayment) $(\Pi, \tilde{\Pi}_1)$. Say that the debt repayment assumes two values only $\tilde{\Pi}_1 = (\Pi_1^+, \Pi_1^-)$ where $\Pi_1^+ = \Pi(1 + R(S))$. Thus, under risk-neutral pricing (see also Chapter 8), we have:

$$\Pi = \left(p^* \Pi_1^+ + (1 - p^*)\Pi_1^-\right) e^{-R_f} \tag{9.79}$$

Let PD be a function of a score and given by $F(S)$, the borrower score. Then the probability of no default is $1 - F(S)$ and thus, the hazard rate is

$$h(S) = \frac{f(S)}{1 - F(S)} \text{ or } 1 - F(S) = e^{-\int_s h(s)ds} \tag{9.80}$$

And therefore, the implied price (with continuous time discounting) is:

$$\Pi = e^{-R_f}\left((1 - F(S))\Pi_1^+ + F(S)\Pi_1^-\right) = e^{-R_f}\left(e^{-\int_s h(s)ds}\Pi_1^+ + \left(1 - e^{-\int_s h(s)ds}\right)\Pi_1^-\right)$$

$$= e^{-\left(R_f + \int_s h(s)ds\right)}\left(\Pi_1^+ - \Pi_1^-\right) + e^{-R_f}\Pi_1^- \tag{9.81}$$

In this case, the loan and its collateral (Π, M_0) implies the probability of default associated to a credit score (or rating). In particular, if $\Pi_1^- = 0$ is a total loss in case of default, then:

$$\Pi = e^{-\left(R_f + \int_s h(s)ds\right)}\Pi_1^+ = \Pi e^{R(S)} \text{ and } R(S) = R_f + \int_S h(s)ds \tag{9.82}$$

This approach to pricing default is, of course, fundamentally different from actuarial risk pricing. In actuarial pricing, objective statistical data and probability models are used to assess and predict mortality, default claims, and so forth, based on data and on models that are based on the hypotheses made regarding the underlying process. Hedging is then sought through insurance or reinsurance or by other mechanisms for risk sharing. A financial approach to default pricing relies instead on financial market transactions, reflecting the bets that buyers and sellers (investors, speculators, pension funds, etc.) are making on the default asset being traded. In this sense, the default price implies the exchanges (swaps) of markets participants, their risk attitudes, and their financial needs (hedging, speculating, etc.). Hedging in such a context is necessarily determined by the optional portfolios that are constructed to reflect individual preferences for profits and risk but are priced by the market.

When actuarial risks are aggregated into portfolios traded in financial markets, these actuarial risks become securitized and priced by the market. Such procedures only transfer the risk of the portfolio to a market rather than have it owned by a financial institution (which becomes an intermediary). This provides the holder of the actuarial risk a market valuation, however, which may entice him to assume (or not assume) these risks. Such situations are beset by information asymmetry, nontransparency of some of the risks traded, opportunities of adverse selection and moral hazard risks, and what are labeled counterparty risks.

EXAMPLE: PRICING DEFAULT BONDS

Let a default bond $B_D(t, T)$ have a recovery rate $K < 1$ at default. In other words, when the bond is redeemed, we collect $(1 \text{ or } K)$ which is equal to $(1)1_{\tau > T} + K1_{\tau \leq T}, K < 1$, or in expectation:

$$B_D(t, T) = B(t, T)\{[1 - F_D(t, T)] + K F_D(t, T)\}$$

$$= B(t, T)\{K + (1 - K)[1 - F_D(t, T)]\} \tag{9.83}$$

and finally,

$$B_D(t, T) = B(t, T)\{K + (1 - K)H(t, T)\}, \quad H(t, T) = e^{-\int_t^T h(s)ds} \tag{9.84}$$

In other words, the price of a default bond is priced by a risk-free bond and an added discount that takes into account the probability of default.

To determine the default parameters, however, we may consider explicitly the returns from a derived distribution, which reflect buyers' and sellers' beliefs regarding the future event at hand. Let the risk premium for a bond insuring a least recovery of K be π. Then,

$$B_D(0, T) = B(0, T) - \pi = B(0, T)\{K + (1 - K)H(0, T)\} \tag{9.85}$$

and therefore,

$$-\ln\left(1 - \frac{\pi}{B(0, T)(1 - K)}\right) = -\ln\left(1 - \frac{\pi e^{R_f(0, T)T}}{1 - K}\right) = H(0, T) \tag{9.86}$$

Similarly, put or other options on the bond can be used to determine the integral of the hazard rate. For example, say that $R_f(0, T) = 0.02$, $T = 2$, $K = 0.8$, $\pi = 0.15$, then:

$$-\ln\left(1 - \frac{0.15e^{0.04}}{0.2}\right) = \ln\left(\frac{1}{1 - 0.75e^{0.04}}\right) = \int_0^2 h(s)ds \tag{9.87}$$

If we construct a model for the hazard rate (based on an extreme Weibull probability distribution), then $h(t) = \alpha\lambda t^{\alpha-1}$ and

$$\frac{1}{1 - 0.75e^{0.04}} = e^{2^\alpha\lambda}$$

which provides one equation in two parameters. Another derivative would then be required to calculate the second parameter. These parameters are not defined by statistical means but rather are defined by the market price for the default bond.

EXAMPLE: PRICING DEFAULT BONDS AND THE HAZARD RATE

For a riskless bond, the discount used is the risk-free rate. At time $t = 0$, for a bond that gives \$1 at time T (a zero-coupon bond), the price of the bond is

$$B_f(0, T) = e^{-R_f T}$$

Now consider a bond that may default prior to time T and therefore would pay nothing. Let this price be $B_D(0, T)$. Clearly:

$$B_D(0, T) = \begin{cases} 1 & \text{if there is no default} \\ 0 & \text{if there is default} \end{cases} \tag{9.88}$$

In other words, the discount factor applied to the default bond is

$$R_f T + \int_0^T h(s) ds$$

and the price of the default bond implies its default, or:

$$R_f + \frac{1}{T} \int_0^T h(s) \, ds = \frac{1}{T} \ln\left(\frac{1}{B_D(0, T)}\right) \tag{9.89}$$

while the spread due to the default is:

$$\frac{1}{T} \int_0^T h(s) \, ds = \frac{1}{T} \ln\left(\frac{1}{B_D(0, T)}\right) - R_f \tag{9.90}$$

Note again that unlike real assets, this is a virtual default probability for financial assets, which is a function of traders' beliefs and their attitudes toward the consequences of a potential default event. If $h(t) = h_0$ then $h_0 t = -\ln R(t)$, $R(t) = e^{-h_0 t}$. Then the effective discount rate of the default bond would be $R_f + h_0$ and the spread will be therefore the *hazard rate* defined by:

$$h_0 = \frac{1}{T} \ln\left(\frac{1}{B_D(0, T)}\right) - R_f \tag{9.91}$$

Let $R_f = 0.05$, $B_f(0, 1) = e^{-(0.05)} = 0.955$, and let the price of a default bond be $B_D(0, 1) = 0.092$. Then

$$0.092 = e^{-(0.05 + h_0)}$$

and $h_0 = \ln(1/0.092) - 0.05 = 2.3359$. Other distributions can be constructed providing a richer family of default probability events that we may be able to use as implicit discount factors that account for risk of default.

EXAMPLES

In this section, we consider various problems and their solutions. Our purpose is to apply techniques introduced in this chapter.

EXAMPLE: THE BANK INTEREST RATE ON A HOUSE LOAN

Consider the buyer of a house whose price P is \$1 million. The buyer has $V = $700,000$ savings and requires a loan of $L = $300,000$ to buy the house. Say that the bank grants the loan to the borrower for one year with the loan reimbursed with an interest rate of ρ. A number of possibilities are then open to the bank, one of which is to buy insurance from a third party (an insurance firm). In other words, let the insurance firm demand a premium of $\pi = $25,000$ to secure the payment by the borrower. In this case, the bank's charge (assuming that it is fair and priced at the market price), is:

$$L + \pi = \frac{1}{1 + R_f} L(1 + \delta)$$

where the risk-free rate is 5 percent. Therefore, the interest charged by the bank is:

$$\delta = \left(1 + \frac{\pi}{L}\right)(1 + R_f) - 1 = \left(1 + \frac{25{,}000}{300{,}000}\right)(1 + 0{,}05) - 1 = 0{,}1375$$

EXAMPLE: BUY INSURANCE TO PROTECT THE PORTFOLIO FROM LOAN DEFAULTS

In this case, for simplicity, say that all loans are to be repaid in a year with a fixed rate of return (the interest rate ρ_i the bank charges for the loan). If the cost of insurance is I then, assuming that the bank rate is applied uniformly to all loans, we have:

$$CE_0 = \sum_{i=1}^{N} L_i = -I + \frac{\sum_{i=1}^{N} L_i (1 + \rho_i)}{1 + R_f} = -I + \frac{(1 + \rho) \sum_{i=1}^{N} L_i}{1 + R_f} \qquad (9.92)$$

and

$$\rho = 1 - (1 + R_f)\left(1 + \frac{I}{\sum_{i=1}^{N} L_i}\right) \qquad (9.93)$$

Thus, the price is determined by the cost of insurance. If the bank charges a rate larger than ρ, it will make an arbitrage profit. In practice, some loans include an addition to this rate to account for the cost of insurance, which leads to banks acting as intermediaries between borrowers and insurers who assume the risk of the (loans) portfolio. This practice has led to an ever-expanding business for insurance firms and the granting of credit to all borrowers, regardless of their credit score!

PROBLEM 9.3: USE THE PORTFOLIO AS AN UNDERLYING AND BUY OR SELL DERIVATIVES ON THIS UNDERLYING

In such problems, the portfolio is securitized and its statistical properties defined. Further, put options bought in financial markets on indexes that are strongly correlated with the underlying portfolio (for example, an index of real estate prices if this is a portfolio of mortgages) can be bought and sold. Such an approach is similar to the insurance that is financed by derivatives. For example, a loan secured by a collateral whose price is $V(t)$ at time t with a debt of $\$L(1 + \rho)$ due at time T can be insured by selling a put option with the collateral (or a portfolio of collaterals, if it is possible, or if an index correlated to that collateral can be determined—as is the case for an index on housing prices) as its underlying security.

Consider a loan of $100,000 with a duration (T) of one year. Assume that the collateral has a growth rate of 1 percent and a volatility of 3 percent with risk-free rates of 5 percent. How would we construct the equation that will provide the interest rate applied by the bank who assumes no risk (except that of illiquidity in the options markets)?

PROBLEM 9.4: LENDING RATES OF RETURN[*]

Suppose that the government passes a usury law that prohibits lending at more than 5 percent interest when market rates are much higher (due to inflation indexes). Assume that Mr. ABC wants to borrow $80,000 at 15 percent interest and can use his house as collateral, currently priced at $100,000. Rather than refusing ABC's demand, the bank decides to create a five-year contract with the following terms: The bank will hold title to the house and receive the right to sell to Mr. ABC the house for K at the end of five years. If the banks decides to sell, Mr. ABC must buy back the house at the agreed-on price of $100,000. In return, the bank loans $80,000 in cash and the right to buy the house from the bank for the price of K at the end of five years (the loan maturity). If Mr. ABC exercises his right, the bank must sell. How can this contract provide the bank a 15 percent yearly rate of return on its $80,000 loan? (Solution: The strike will have to be set to $160,909.)

CREDIT RISK AND COLLATERAL PRICING

Default, or the propensity to default, results from an imbalance between the debt and its collateral equity (or, equivalently, from a debt that cannot be met by the price of its collaterals or the debtor's ability to service the debt). In this case, when equity is insufficient to meet bondholders' requirements, default may occur, in which case bondholders have prior claim to the residual wealth of the firm. Such an approach,

---

[*]From T. S. Ho and E. O. Vieira.

based on a seminal paper by Merton (1974), has also been used to price a first generation of credit derivatives, as will be seen in Chapter 10.

Merton's approach consists in letting the price of equity be equivalent to that of a call option. Explicitly, let a firm value be V and its bond obligation B. Equity is thus defined by (since bondholders have priority on the firm's assets):

$$E = \begin{cases} V - B & V > B \\ 0 & V < B \end{cases}$$

or

$$E = Max\,(V - B, 0) \tag{9.94}$$

at time $T = 1$. From the bondholder viewpoint, we note that the price of the firm's obligation at time $T = 1$ is then:

$$V_B = \begin{cases} B & V > B \\ V & V < B \end{cases} \text{ or } V_B = Min\,(B, V) = V - E = V - Max(V - B, 0) \tag{9.95}$$

For example, say that in a binomial model, values in the next period are given by (V^+, V^-). Thus, equity and bond prices are:

$$\begin{aligned} (E^+, E^-) &= \left\{ (V^+ - B)^+, (V^- - B)^+ \right\} \\ (V_B^+, V_B^-) &= \left\{ \min\,(V^+, B), \min\,(V^-, B) \right\} \end{aligned} \tag{9.96}$$

To price corporate firm liabilities, V_B, construct a portfolio consisting of the firm's leverage and borrowing. Let the firm leverage be N and let b be the amount borrowed at the risk-free rate. Then a replication of corporate liability priced at time $T = 0$ is given by $V_B = NV - b$. One period later, at time $T = 1$, we have:

$$\text{Time T} = 0:\ V_B = NV - b \Leftrightarrow \begin{cases} NV^+ - b = V_B^+ = \min\,(V^+, B) \\ NV^- - b = V_B^- = \min\,(V^-, B) \end{cases} \text{Time T} = 1 \tag{9.97}$$

A solution for the replicating portfolio parameters is:

$$N = \frac{V_B^+ - V_B^-}{V^+ - V^-}, b = \frac{V^- V_B^+ - V^+ V_B^-}{(V^+ - V^-)\,(1 + R_f)} \tag{9.98}$$

For no arbitrage, we have:

$$V_B = NV - b = \left(\frac{V_B^+ - V_B^-}{V^+ - V^-} \right) V - \frac{V^- V_B^+ - V^+ V_B^-}{(V^+ - V^-)\,(1 + R_f)} \tag{9.99}$$

Or

$$V_B = \left(\frac{V_B^+ - V_B^-}{V^+ - V^-}\right) \left\{ V - \frac{V^- \min\left(V^+, B\right) - V^+ \min\left(V^-, B\right)}{\left(V_B^+ - V_B^-\right)\left(1 + R_f\right)} \right\} \qquad (9.100)$$

For another example, assume the debt principal is $B = 100$, the risk-free rate is 0.08, and the firm value is 110, which may increase or decrease to 125 and 75, respectively, corresponding to rates of return of 13.63 percent and –31.18 percent. Then we can calculate $NV - B$ as replicating the corporate liabilities and subsequently calculate the corporate equity, as previously indicated, by $E = V - V_B$. Specifically, we have:

$$V_B = \left(\frac{100 - 75}{125 - 75}\right) \left\{ 110 - \frac{75\,(100) - 125\,(75)}{(100 - 75)\,(1 + 0.08)} \right\} = 89.7$$

$$E = 110 - V_B = 110 - 89.7 = 20.3 \qquad (9.101)$$

If we have 100 equity shares, the price per share without debt is $e_0 = 10/100 = 0.1$ while with debt it equals $e_1 = 20.3/100 = 0.203$. This gain is of course at the expense of the bondholders who have invested \$100 million and are left after such an investment with a value of \$89.7 million (a loss of \$10.3 million). In other words, equity holders have more than doubled their equity price by incurring a \$100 million debt. They have done so, however, at the price of an increased risk of defaulting on payment of the debt and losing their equity. These simple observations explain the amount of debt that certain speculative investors assume in order to make as much money as possible. Table 9.3 repeats such calculations for different leverage levels, highlighting the payoff to the bondholder and to the equity holder. Explicit calculations are then given.

$$V_B(90) = \left(\frac{1}{50}\right) \left\{ 110(15) - \frac{75\,(90) - 125\,(75)}{1.08} \right\};$$

$$V_B(80) = \left(\frac{1}{50}\right) \left\{ 110\,(5) - \frac{75\,(80) - 125\,(75)}{1.08} \right\};$$

$$V_B(70) = \left(\frac{1}{50}\right) \left\{ 110\,(0) - \frac{75\,(70) - 125\,(70)}{1.08} \right\};$$

$$V_B(60) = \left(\frac{1}{50}\right) \left\{ 110\,(0) - \frac{75\,(60) - 125\,(60)}{1.08} \right\} \qquad (9.102)$$

TABLE 9.3 The Rate of Return (ROR) on Equity and Debt

Equity T=0	Debt	Equity T=0+	Debt T=0+	ROR Equity	ROR on Debt
10	100	20.3	89.7	190.3%	–10.3%
20	90	28.39	81.61	41.95%	–9.3%
30	80	36.5	73.5	21.6%	
40	70	45.19	64.81	12.82%	
50	60	54.45	55.55	8.9%	–7.47%

and therefore $V_B(90) = 81.61$; $V_B(80) = 73.5$; $V_B(70) = 64.81$; $V_B(60) = 55.55$. These results point, therefore, to a significant increase in the rate of return (ROR) of the firm with debt.

EXAMPLE: HEDGE FUNDS RATES OF RETURN

A hedge fund manager owns 10 percent of a $1 billion fund. The manager's returns are (20,2), which are 20 percent of the profit made by the manager during the year and 2 percent of the investors' capital (whether trading is profitable or not). The current price of the fund is obviously $1 billion with the fund manager owning 10 percent of the fund (his equity). Assume that the fund price can take either of two values a year later, denoted by V^+ (a gain of money) and V^- (a loss of money). Assuming that financial markets are complete, we have:

$$V_0 = \frac{1}{1 + R_f} \left(p^Q V^+ + (1 - p^Q) V^- \right)$$

or

$$p^Q = \frac{V_0 \left(1 + R_f \right) - V^-}{V^+ - V^-} \tag{9.103}$$

The investors' profit (in case of a gain) is then:

$$\Delta V_I = \frac{1}{1 + R_f} \left(p^Q k(V^+ - V_0)(1 - 0.20) + (1 - p^Q)k(V^- - V_0) - 0.02(k)V_0 \right),$$
$$k = 0.90 \tag{9.104}$$

The investors' rate of return is thus:

$$\frac{\Delta V_I}{k V_0} = \frac{1}{1 + R_f}$$
$$\times \left(\frac{(1 + R_f) - v^-}{v^+ - v^-} \left\{ (v^+ - 1)(1 - 0.20) - (v^- - 1) \right\} + (v^- - 1) - 0.02 \right) \tag{9.105}$$

where

$$v^+ = \frac{V^+}{V_0}, v^- = \frac{V^-}{V_0}$$

while the gain of the hedge fund manager and his rate of return are:

$$\Delta V_{HF} = \frac{k}{1+R_f} \left(p^Q (V^+ - V_0)(0.20) + 0.02\, V_0 \right)$$

$$+ \frac{(1-k)}{1+R_f} \left(p^Q(V^+ - V_0) + (1 - p^Q)(V^- - V_0) \right) \qquad (9.106)$$

$$\frac{\Delta V_{HF}}{(1-k)V_0} = \frac{1}{1+R_f} \left(\frac{k}{1-k} \left(p^Q(v^+ - 1)(0.20) + 0.02 \right) \right.$$

$$\left. + \left(p^Q(v^+ - 1) + (1 - p^Q)(v^- - 1) \right) \right) \qquad (9.107)$$

or

$$\frac{\Delta V_{HF}}{(1-k)V_0} = \frac{1}{1+R_f} \left(p^Q(v^+ - 1)\left(\frac{0.20k}{1-k}\right) + \frac{0.02k}{1-k} + (1 - p^Q)(v^- - 1) \right)$$

$$(9.108)$$

Thus, if

$$R_f = 0.08,\, k = 0.90,\, v^+ = 1.15,\, v^- = 0.95$$

then:

$$\frac{\Delta V_{HF}}{0.10\,V_0} = \frac{1}{1.08} \left(0.15 p^Q (18) + 1.8 - (1 - p^Q)0.05 \right) = 2.963\, p^Q + 1.620$$

$$(9.109)$$

Since

$$p^Q = \frac{(1 + R_f) - v^-}{v^+ - v^-} = \frac{(1 + 0.08) - 0.95}{1.15 - 0.95} = \frac{0.13}{0.2} = 0.65 \qquad (9.110)$$

we obtain a rate of return for the hedge fund manager-owner of 35.4 percent:

$$\frac{\Delta V_{HF}}{V_0} = 0.10\,(2.963(0.65) + 1.620) = 0.354 \qquad (9.111)$$

EXAMPLE: EQUITY-LINKED LIFE INSURANCE

Single premium equity-linked life insurance is a contract that enables its holder to receive the greater values of a portfolio of assets at the maturity of the contract, provided that the holder of the contract survives to the exercise date. For example, if $G(T)$ is a guaranteed amount at time T and $P(T)$ is the price of a portfolio at time T, then, if a person survives to time T, he collects $Max\,(P(T), G(T))$. The insured portfolio can be based on a single payment or on agreed-on contributions paid over time. The residual portfolio in case of death prior to maturity may also be negotiated.

In some cases, insurance firms may augment the guaranteed payment if the insured loses all rights to the portfolio if he dies prior to the exercise date T. In other cases, the insurance firm may pay a certain amount (indexed or not) to the insured in case of death prior to time T. Such contracts are in general difficult to price, essentially due to the length of time T implied and the lack of optional and traded products that have such long maturities.

Theoretically, such contracts can be modeled as follows. Let the price of a portfolio be $P(t), t \leq T$. Let the rate of return of the portfolio be α and σ be its volatility. We assume in addition that the insured has an additional contribution rate π (a premium) to pay as long $t \leq T$. Then the portfolio price process is:

$$\Delta P(t) = (\alpha P(t) + \pi)\, \Delta t + \sigma P(t)\Delta W(t), \ P(0) > 0 \tag{9.112}$$

where $P(0) > 0$ is the insured initial contribution to the portfolio. Two cases arise. Let $\tau > T$ be the time of death of the insured with survival probability $1 - F(\tau)$ and let the terms of the contract point to a payment at maturity be $Max(P(T), G(T))$. Since

$$1 - F(T) = \exp\left(-\int_0^T h(t)dt\right)$$

with $h(t)$ the hazard rate of the death probability distribution, the price of such a contract for an insured (assuming risk-neutral pricing—that is, a risk-neutral martingale for the portfolio price process) is:

$$V(t) = e^{-R_f(T-t)-\int_t^T h(x)dx} E^Q Max(P(T), G(T)) \tag{9.113}$$

While this model outlines a means to express an insurance contract in finance terms, it is only a theoretical construct. In practice, the death time of a person is not traded in financial markets and thus such contracts might not be perfectly hedged. Technically, this implies that there might not be a risk-neutral martingale to price it. Nevertheless, insurance firms sell such contracts (and mostly at a profit and an appreciable growth rate) because of both their potential variety and firms' ability to tailor such contracts to individual needs. For example, equity-indexed annuities, variable annuities, asset-value guarantees, portfolios indexed on currencies, financial markets indexes, and so on are of the equity-linked type. Commensurably, an extensive literature to this effect has been developed, ushering a greater convergence between the business of finance and insurance (e.g., Alexander Melnikov and Yuliya Romanyuk 2008).

EXAMPLE: DEFAULT AND THE PRICE OF HOMES

This example explains partly a financial market's markdown in asset prices due to default arising from a drop in the price of homes, defaulting when they were over-leveraged. It explains as well the phenomenon we witnessed prior to September 2008, that in a world where home prices are increasing at 5 to 6 percent a year compared to a median income rise of 1.5 percent, all credit seekers have actually received the credit they asked for. Credit was granted even if their ability (their credit score) to repay the loan was not considered a factor in the granting of the loan. This means of course that creditors, while granting the loan, were in fact speculating on the growth of the collateral—which turned out to be wrong, with dramatic consequences. In other words, creditors were selling to borrowers a put option that paid either the collateral or the loan taken plus its interest, or $Min(K(1 + R), S(T))$ where $S(T)$ is the collateral price at the time the loan is to be paid. This can be written as follows:

$$K(1 + R) + Min(0, S(1) - K(1 + R))$$

The ability to write the price of a loan as a put option that is perceived to be in-the-money may have incited creditors to augment the credit they provide, and to securitize their loans since financial markets would be willing to pay for these loans (in addition, these securitized loans were rated AAA). In other words, had housing prices kept increasing, there would not have been any credit failure. Of course, in such circumstances, and as seen in Chapter 7, the current price of such a put over one period is:

$$K = \frac{K(1 + R)}{1 + R_f} + \frac{p(S(1) - K(1 + R))}{1 + R_f} \tag{9.114}$$

where $p = P(S(1) \geq K(1 + R))$, and therefore,

$$R_f + p(1 + R) - R = +\frac{pS(T)}{K} \tag{9.115}$$

Let the price of a call option on the collateral be C with a strike Q, or:

$$C = \frac{1}{1 + R_f} p\{S(1) - Q\}$$

and

$$p = \frac{C(1 + R_f)}{S(1) - Q} \tag{9.116}$$

As a result,

$$R_f + \frac{C(1 + R_f)}{S(1) - Q}(1 + R) - R = \frac{C(1 + R_f)}{S(1) - Q}\frac{S(1)}{K} \tag{9.117}$$

which requires an interest rate to be imposed on the loan equal to:

$$R = \frac{R_f + \dfrac{C\left(1 + R_f\right)}{S(1) - Q}\left(\dfrac{S(1)}{K} - 1\right)}{\left(1 - \dfrac{C\left(1 + R_f\right)}{S(1) - Q}\right)} \tag{9.118}$$

and for $K = S(1)$ for

$$1 - \frac{C\left(1 + R_f\right)}{S(1) - Q} = \frac{R_f}{R} < 1$$

EXAMPLE: A BANK'S PROFIT FROM A LOAN

The next problem uses the same methodology to calculate how much money banks were in fact making in such transactions. Here again, we shall see that the credit score was not relevant for their decisions since they had the means, through financial markets, to become intermediaries rather than the holder of the mortgage and its associated risk.

A bank's loan of $100,000 is based on the home collateral currently valued at $120,000. The loan has to be repaid in full next year including an interest rate of 5 percent. House prices are expected to increase at a rate of 3 percent; however, a house's value might decline at a rate of 6 percent. A parallel market for the house allows other persons to buy the house in the following year at a price of $115,000. The price of this option is $1,500. The risk-free rate today is 4 percent. Calculate the probability of a loan default based on these values. What is the spread that the bank is using in granting such a loan? How much money is the bank making?

To solve this problem, we calculate first the probability that the option is exercised, corresponding to the price increasing by 3 percent. In this case,

$$p = \frac{C\left(1 + R_f\right)}{S(1) - K} = \frac{1,500(1 + 0.04)}{120,000 * (1.03) - 115.000} = \frac{1,560}{8,600} = 0.1814 \tag{9.119}$$

As a result, the implied probability of default is

$$1 - \frac{C\left(1 + R_f\right)}{S(1) - K} = 1 - 0.1814 = 0.8186$$

For the bank, the following states are implied. It receives $105,000 at the end of the year or it recuperates the house whose price, in case of default, is $120,000 \times (1 - 0.06) = \$112,800$. Using the market probability p, the present value of this transaction is:

$$PV = \frac{1}{1 + 0.04}\left((0.1814)(120,000 * 1.03) + (0.8186) * 112,800\right)$$
$$= 11,884 + 88,786 = 100670 \tag{9.120}$$

The bank's profit is therefore equal only to $670. Note that if the loss was greater than 6 percent, say 10 percent, then $120.000 \times (1 - 0.20) = \$96,000 < \$105,000$, in which case there will be a default and the bank will collect the collateral—the house (incurring probably additional costs since banks will have to resell the house at potentially an additional discount).

Consider again the bank spread of $670, and assume that it is able to transfer (sell to another institution) the loan of $100,000 with its collateral. In this case, there are no reasons for the bank not to repeat such transactions with an endless number of mortgage seekers (since it assumes no responsibility toward these mortgage holders and merely collects the spread) and to make an apparently riskless profit. Banks have in fact used this mechanism, but at the same time they have also sought to profit from the insurance premium they would collect by providing insurance for the house collateral! Namely, mortgage lender-banks provided an insurance against default of such mortgages in the form of put options that allowed them to collect an additional premium with no accounting of the options obligations they acquired (and therefore, not accounting in their books the risk of house prices). This procedure, apparently extremely profitable in a market of rising collateral, became disastrous when the market turned out to be otherwise.

RISK MANAGEMENT AND LEVERAGE

As a result of the 2008 crisis, firms that were highly leveraged have been challenged due to the liquidity crisis that ensued. At the same time, firm leverage is an important source of both profit and credit risk. Greater leverage provides an opportunity to increase the returns of a firm while posing greater risks at the same time. For example, hedge funds might assume highly leveraged bets that can yield extraordinary returns if the bet is a successful one and extremely large losses if the bet sours. Leverage is therefore a crucial factor in assessing the credit risk of a firm. It is also subject to manipulations and to management as financial markets and research analysts are very sensitive to this factor and to firms' published (and unpublished) statistical information.

For simplicity, assume that a firm's working capital consists of its own equity and the debt it assumes. In particular, assume that there are two sources of risks: liquidity risk (or the inability of a firm to service its debt) and the risk of default on a financial contractual agreement made with the creditor (for example, a debt incurred based on a firm rated AAA to be reimbursed in totality if it is down-rated; the contracted requirement which requires that the firm maintain an appreciable and well-defined ratio of equity to debt, etc.). In case such a contracted agreement for the terms of the debt is violated, the firm may be financially penalized in different ways. For example, bondholders can demand a larger coupon payment, demand immediate reimbursement of the debt, or have the right to take over the firm or put it into Chapter 11 bankruptcy proceedings. The purpose of a variety of such contractual agreements is to mitigate both the credit and counterparty risks, incite firms to act reasonably insofar as the use of debt, and of course to protect the safety of bondholders' reimbursements.

For example, say that a firm whose equity is worth $100 million is leveraged to a $1 billion firm, strapped with a $900 million loan to service by a yearly coupon payment of 10 percent. Assume that the firm can operate as long as it can pay $90 million a year and is bankrupt (taken over by bondholders) if it is unable to make the coupon payment commitment. Such a firm, which has no other financial covenant, acting malevolently, may decide simply upon receiving the $900 million loan to pay equity holders $500 million and service the debt with its remaining capital of $500 million. Of course, if the firm is extremely profitable, coupon payments may be sustainable. The probability that such a firm can sustain a debt repayment of $90 million on a working capital of $500 million is questionable, however. After a few years, say over five or six years, the firm may exhaust its capital (including the debt contracted) and be put into bankruptcy (with the CEO of the firm who has contracted such debt long gone with a hefty severance payment).

This extreme example may manifest itself in different ways by firms' and CEOs' actions. Similarly, extraordinary payments (whether they are performance based or not) to banks' CEOs and traders granted by a bank's board of directors might induce extreme leverage by banks and therefore irrational risks. The billions paid to such CEOs and traders, whether in good times or bad, can distort the impact of leverage risks.

A typical example is AIG's English division with a staff of 300 derivatives traders in mortgage-backed securities and credit derivatives bringing the company down to its knees—with close to $100 billion in direct and indirect losses—while providing extraordinary benefits to the culprit of such dismal performance. The same phenomenon was noted in the banking sector, however (Merrill Lynch, Bear Stearns, etc.), with payments to executives providing an incentive to excessive leverage and excessive risk taking. Such scenarios have recurred to some extent during the recent financial crisis when financial firms continued extraordinary payments to some of their employees regardless of the firm's financial health. For this reason, granting debt and managing the debt granted, through the many financial covenants that it might be necessary to append to credit, is a necessary element of credit risk management (both for the creditor and the borrower).

These problems are compounded further by various debt obligations with various maturities, which have to be met by firms either by substantial cash payments or by refinancing. In some cases, such refinancing is both costly and unavailable when credit markets are not liquid. For example, if a bond is to be redeemed at time T, the firm's cash position (or its capacity for credit) might meet such a commitment. Failure to meet such a commitment can lead to bankruptcy. By the same token, for a stream of bond maturities, such problems are just more complex and require therefore a careful management of debt redemption and its synchronization with both cash savings and credit assurances.

Explicitly, a firm defaults if either (1) it has no liquidity to meet payments to bondholders (i.e. no ability to service debt redemption and servicing) or (2) the price of its stock plus its liquid assets is less than an agreed-on proportion of the nominal debt. This latter condition can be part of a financial covenant setting a lien to the assets by the lender-bondholder or specifying that the borrowing firm maintain an agreed-on debt-to-equity (plus liquidity) ratio. This latter covenant provides, of course, a means to mitigate counterparty risk and potentially mitigates as well the propensity of firms to assume more risk that they ought to.

SUMMARY

This chapter has proposed an overview of individual credit risk, credit scoring, and credit granting. The importance of credit for an economy and for the proper operation of businesses was emphasized. Techniques for determining a credit score, whether for an individual borrower, for a firm, or for a financial product, were presented. Firms such as S&P, Moody's, Fitch, and others have specialized businesses to rate firms, providing guidelines to credit granting firms to both grant and price the credit they give to prospective borrowers. A number of particular techniques were suggested and briefly outlined, including logistic regressions, probability models to estimate the probability of default, and others.

The decision to grant credit to an individual borrower is intimately related to his credit score in theory and, in some cases, in practice. However, the current practice of requiring collateral to assure the safety of loans (and of securitizing these loans and collaterals, as we shall see in the next chapter) have reduced the importance of the credit score. Credit granting techniques are varied, some based on statistical models, others on Bayesian probability decision models, and some based on proprietary software that financial lenders acquire or develop in-house.

Finally, two approaches to pricing were introduced: a statistical-actuarial approach (see also Chapters 3 and Chapter 4); a risk-neutral approach (see Chapter 7 and Chapter 8). In this sense, credit risk, its assessment, analysis, granting, pricing, and management involve all facets of risk valuation and financial management. Given the importance of credit risk in a modern economy, it is likely to remain a topic of great importance in financial management.

TEST YOURSELF

9.1 What is your credit score? What is the meaning of such a question and what are the elements that make up your credit score? Limit yourself to 10 such elements (you may want to go to a bank and ask them to fill in a demand for credit and observe what their questionnaire for credit includes).

9.2 What is the *logit* approach and how is it used to determine relative weights to apply to a particular set of credit attributes in determining what credit score to apply to you?

9.3 What is a *probability of default* and how is it determined based on your credit score? Explain in particular the role of the logistic probability distribution of credit scores in determining this probability.

9.4 Clients that were granted credit in the past were put in the following eight categories (potential responses to a three-attributes questionnaire). The number of applicants granted credit in each category as well as the proportion defaulting (given in parentheses) was 200 (0.02); 150 (0.04); 500 (0.03); 50 (0.06); 100 (0.09); 75 (0.06); 20 (0.07); 60 (0.10). On the basis of these numbers answer the following:

X_1	X_2	X_3	Quality
1	1	1	G
1	1	0	G
1	0	1	G
1	0	0	B
0	1	1	B
0	1	0	B
0	0	1	B
0	0	0	B

a. Calculate the probability of default for all clients.

b. If each client has a return of 7 percent if he does not default, and a loss of 20 percent in case of default, what category of applicants would you grant credit in the future and what category would you not grant credit?

c. On the basis of your decisive rule, calculate the conditional probability that a client granted credit defaults; and the probability that a client not granted credit would not have defaulted.

9.5 The probability of default of any particular loan in a portfolio is presumed to have a beta probability distribution with mean and variance given by 0.05 and 0.08. The loan portfolio has 1,000 such loans. What is the expected number of loans to default and what is the variance of such an estimate if the loans are statistically independent? What are the effects of the size of the portfolio on the portfolio defaults variance? Why would you construct a portfolio with this many loans, and why not? On the basis of your answers, how would you organize the portfolio into four groups of an equal number of loans? To do so, assume that each loan (based on the score given to the loan) has a known probability of default. In other words, you are given 1,000 probabilities denoted by $p_i, i = 1, 2 ..., 1000$. Once you have formulated such a problem, can you construct a spreadsheet program to structure your portfolio into these four groups if you were to be supplied with these probabilities?

9.6 In a group of 250 loans, the current estimate of default probabilities is 0.10 with an equal variance. The probability distribution of the default probabilities is still a beta probability distribution. However, the number of actual defaults for this group turns out to be twice as much as expected (in other words, 50 loans defaulting). On the basis of this information, what have you learned and what is the updated (posterior) probability distribution of default, what is the expected number of defaults, and what is its variance? (Hint: To do these calculations, note that they are for a beta probability distribution.)

9.7 The probability distribution of scores of a loans portfolio has a Weibull probability distribution given by:

$$f(S) \approx \frac{c}{\zeta} \left(\frac{S}{\zeta} \right)^{c-1} e^{-(S/\zeta)^c}, S \geq 0, \zeta, c > 0; F(S) = 1 - e^{-(S/\zeta)^c}$$

where the higher the score, the better. The mean and the score variance of the loans population is thus:

$$E(S) = \zeta\Gamma\left(\frac{1}{c}+1\right), \text{var}(S) = \zeta^2\left[\Gamma\left(\frac{2}{c}+1\right) - \Gamma^2\left(\frac{1}{c}+1\right)\right]$$

The granting score is assumed to equal X while the probability of the number of defaults is a function of the score. What is the probability that an applicant drawn at random from this population obtains credit? What is the probability that an applicant with a random score gets credit if the decisive score is the 1.5 times the mean credit score? If the mean score is 500 and the parameter $c = 1$, what is probability of an applicant with a score of 600 obtaining credit if the decisive score is 500? 650? The probability of default today (based on industry data) is 5 percent while in the past, all applicants with a score of $S = 600$ have defaulted only with a probability of 3 percent. What is the probability that an applicant scored 600 and granted credit will default? What is the probability of default of applicants with a score larger than 800?

9.8 What are the essential risk factors that lenders use to reach the decision to grant credit or not? Explain in a few words how each factor is (or could be) managed by the lender. What are the risks for the borrower and how can the borrower manage these risks?

9.9 Your credit score is 700 (out of 1,000 possible). Credit is granted automatically if a credit score is less than 600. What are the probabilities of the borrower making an error in granting you credit (i.e., your probability of default)? The bank tightens its credit granting policy and changes the required score to 550. What is the error the banks will make for an applicant such as you with a score of 600?

9.10 The bank's clients database has indicated the following information: Clients with a score higher than the decisive credit score of 600 defaulted with a probability (frequency) of 0.05 while for a decisive score of 700, 10 percent of the credit granted defaulted. The distribution of scores for the whole population of applicants is given to you and specified by:

$$g(x) = (1+\alpha)x^\alpha, 200 \leq x \leq 1000$$

with a mean of 550. Determine the probability that an applicant with a score of 550 will default, (and the same probability for an applicant with a score of 500 to default). The current economic environment indicates a 12 percent default in similar credit contracts. How would you use this data to determine the probability that an applicant with a score of 650 will default? What is this probability?

9.11 A loan of $2,000 is made to be repaid in full next year with a surcharge of 12 percent. The probability of default of an applicant is calculated to be 5 percent while the expected recovery in case of default is based on a collateral held by the bank, the current worth or which is $1,800 and which is expected to maintain its value next year. On the basis of these expectations, should the applicant be granted the loan? What if the collateral is a risky asset whose value-price next year might be only $1,200 but could be $3,000 with equal probability? What would you do if markets were complete?

9.12 Assume that a bank has capital of $10 billion. Basel II VaR regulation requires that the risk exposure be limited to 5 percent probability of losing this money. The loans that the bank makes consist of a portfolio with expected payout in a month of $8 billion with a rate of return of 12 percent. What is the maximum amount of money that the bank can lend? If the bank can acquire insurance for the period at a rate of 8 percent (yearly) on the portfolio outstanding, how much more credit can the bank make?

9.13 A bank's loan of $200,000 is based on the home collateral currently valued at $210,000. The loan has to be repaid in full next year including an interest rate of 6 percent . House prices are believed to increase at a rate of 4 percent, but a house might decline at a rate of 6 percent. A parallel market for the house allows other persons to buy the house in the following year at a price of $220,000. The price of this option is $2,500. The risk-free rate today is 4 percent. Calculate the probability of a loan default based on these values. What is the spread that the bank is using for such a loan? How much money will the bank make? To solve this problem, calculate first the probability that the option is exercised, corresponding to the price increasing by 4 percent. In this case (by risk neutral pricing),

$$p = \frac{C(1 + R_f)}{S(1) - K} = \frac{2,500(1 + 0.04)}{210,000 * (1.06) - 220,000}$$

$$= \frac{2,500 * 1.04}{222,600 - 220,000} = \frac{2,600}{2,600} = 1$$

As a result, using the option's price, the probability of exercising the option is 1, and therefore the probability $1 - p$ of default (in which case the house would be worth less than $220,000) is null. If you want to, demonstrate how this means that there is no default according to the market. In other words, show that:

$$1 - \frac{C(1 + R_f)}{S(1) - K} = 1 - 1 = 0 = \text{Probability of default}$$

Calculate then the expected profit of the borrower in receiving the loan. Finally, calculate the spread of the bank and the profit it makes by such a transaction.

9.14 Banks may equally use the price of the house by buying a put option with a strike equal to the house or on a real estate index strongly correlated to the price of the house. Explain a price of the loan:

$$L + Put\,(L(1 + \delta),\, T) = \frac{L(1 + \delta)}{1 + R_f}$$

Assume, for example, that at the put exercise $L(1 + \delta) - P(T) < 0$. Show that the bank collects then $L(1 + \delta)$. Next assume the opposite with the borrower's defaulting but the bank recovers the house at its price $P(T)$ in which case the put is exercised, providing $L(1 + \delta) - P(T)$. As a result, show that the bank collects its money $L(1 + \delta) - P(T) + P(T) = L(1 + \delta)$.

9.15   What are the rights of the bond and equity holders if the firm is (a) alive and (b) defaulting?

9.16   What is the price of an option that gives a bondholder the right to take full control of the firm if the firm's value falls below 90 percent of its debt (and not before)?

9.17   What are the effects if a firm debt rated AAA is down-rated to A? Discuss the effect on the probability of default, the price of the firm equity, and the price of the debt held by bondholders.

9.18   Assume that a firm with a bond covenant states that if it is down-rated from A to B, the bondholders have the option to demand immediate reimbursement and renegotiation of the debt interest rate charges. What is the effect of such a covenant on the equity price of the firm currently rated A?

9.19   What are the differences between a sovereign bond rated AAA and a corporate bond rated AAA?

REFERENCES

Acharya, V., and L. Pedersen. 2005. Asset pricing with liquidity risk. *Journal of Financial Economics* 77:375–410.

Altman, E. 1989. Measuring corporate bond mortality and performance. *Journal of Finance* 44:909–922.

Altman, Ed, B. Brady, A. Resti, A. Sironi. 2003. The link between default and recovery rates: Theory and empirical evidence and implications. NYU Solomon Center, Stern School of Business, New York.

Altman, E. I., and V. Kishore. 1996. Almost everything you wanted to know about recoveries on defaulted bonds. *Financial Analyst Journal*, November/December.

Amihud, Y., and H. Mandelson. 1986. Asset pricing and the bid-ask spread. *Journal of Financial Economics* 17:223–249.

Artzner, P., and F. Delbaen. 1992. Credit risk and prepayment option. *ASTIN Bulletin* 22:81–96.

———. 1995. Default risk and incomplete insurance markets. *Mathematical Finance* 5:187–195.

Barlow, R., and F. Proschan. 1965. *Mathematical theory of reliability*. New York: John Wiley & Sons.

Belkin, B., S. Suchower, and L. Forest Jr. 1998. A one-parameter representation of credit risk and transition matrices. *CreditMetrics® Monitor*, Third Quarter. http://www.riskmetrics.com/cm/pubs/index.cgi.

Bielecki, T., and M. Rutkowski. 2002. *Credit risk: Modeling, valuation and hedging.* New York: Springer Verlag.

Black, Fischer. 1976. The pricing of commodity contracts. *Journal of Financial Economics*, January/March: 167–179.

Black, F., E. Derman, and W. Toy. 1990. A one factor model of interest rates and its application to treasury bond options. *Financial Analysts Journal*, January–February: 33–39.

Blanchet-Scalliet, C., and F. Patras. 2008. Counterparty risk valuation of a CDS. www.defaultrisk.com.

Bluhm, C., L. Overbeck, and C. Wagner. 2003. *Introduction to credit risk modeling.* London: Chapman and Hall.

Bonfim, Diana. 2009. Credit risk drivers: Evaluating the contribution of firm level information and of macroeconomic dynamics. *Journal of Banking & Finance* (Elsevier) 33 (2) (February): 281–299.

Brennan, M. J., and E. S. Schwartz. 1979. A continuous time approach to the pricing of corporate bonds. *Journal of Banking and Finance* 3:133–155.

Caouette, J. B., E. I. Altman, and P. Narayanan. 1998. *Managing credit risk: The next great financial challenge.* New York: John Wiley & Sons.

Chance, D. 1990. Default risk and the duration of zero-coupon bonds. *Journal of Finance* 45(1):265–274.

Cossin, D., and H. Pirotte. 2001. *Advanced credit risk analysis: Financial approaches and mathematical models to assess, price and manage credit risk.* Chichester, UK: John Wiley & Sons.

Cox, J. C., J. E. Ingersoll, and S. A. Ross. 1985. A theory of the term structure of interest rates. *Econometrica* 53:385–407.

Cox, J. J., and N. Tait. 1991. *Reliability, safety and risk management.* Oxford: Butterworth-Heinemann.

Das, S., and P. Tufano. 1996. Pricing credit sensitive debt when interest rates, credit ratings and credit spreads are stochastic. *Journal of Derivatives* 5 (2).

Duffie, G. R. 1998. The relation between treasury yields and corporate bond yield spreads. *Journal of Finance* 53:2225–2242.

————. 1999. Estimating the price of default risk. *Review of Financial Studies* 12:197–226.

Duffie, D., and N. Garleanu. 2001. Risk and valuation of collateralized debt valuation. *Financial Analysts Journal* 57(1):41–62.

Duffie, J. D, N. Garleanu, and L. Pedersen. 2005. Over the counter markets. *Econometrica* 73:1815–1847.

Duffie, J. D., and R. Kan. 1996. A yield-factor model of interest rates. *Mathematical Finance* 6:379–406.

Duffie, D., and D. Lando. 2001. Term structures of credit spreads with incomplete accounting information. *Econometrica* 69:633–664.

Duffie, D., and K. J. Singleton. 1997. Modeling term structures of defaultable bonds. *Review of Financial Studies* 12(4):687–720.

————. 2003. *Credit pricing, measurement and management.* Princeton, NJ: Princeton University Press.

Elandt-Johnson, R. C., and N. L. Johnson. 1980. *Survival models and data Analysis.* New York: John Wiley & Sons.

Elton, E. J., M. Gruber, D. Agrawal, and C. Mann. 2001. Explaining the rate spread on corporate bonds. *Journal of Finance*, February.

Ganguin, Blaise Paul, and John Bilardello. 2004. *Standard & Poor's fundamentals of corporate credit analysis.* New York: McGraw-Hill.

Glosten, L., and P. Milgrom. 1985. Bid, ask, and transaction prices in a specialist market with heterogeneously informed agents. *Journal of Financial Economics* 14:71–100.

Grenadier, S. 1995. Valuing lease contracts a real-options approach. *Journal of Financial Economics* 38:297–331.

———. 1996. Leasing and credit risk. *Journal of Financial Economics* 42:333–354.

Hauser, Shmuel, Eldor Rafi, and Menachem Brenner. 2001. The price of options illiquidity. *Journal of Finance* 56 (2).

Heath, D., R. Jarrow, and A. Morton. 1992. Bond pricing and the term structure of interest rates: A new methodology for contingent claims evaluation. *Econometrica* 60:77–105.

Hendel, I., and A. Lizzeri. 2002. The role of leasing under adverse selection. *Journal of Political Economics* 110:113–143.

Ho, Thomas, and Hans R. Stoll. 1981. Optimal dealer pricing under transactions and return uncertainty. *Journal of Financial Economics* 9:47–73.

Hull, J., and A. White. 1992. The price of default risk. *Risk* 5:101–103.

———. 1995. The impact of default risk on the prices of options and other derivatives securities. *Journal of Banking and Finance* 19:299–322.

Jarrow, R. A., D. Lando, and S. Turnbull. 1997. A Markov model for the term structure of credit spreads. *Review of Financial Studies* 10:481–523.

Jarrow, R., and S. Turnbull. 1995. Pricing derivatives on financial securities subject to credit risk. *Journal of Finance* 50:53–86.

Kau, J. B., D. C. Keenan, W. J. Muller, and J. F. Epperson. 1995. The valuation at origination of fixed-rate residential mortgages with default and prepayment. *Journal of Real Estate Finance and Economics* 11:5–36.

Kijima, M., and K. Komoribayashi. 1998. A Markov chain model for valuing credit risk derivatives. *Journal of Derivatives*, Fall.

Kim, J. 1999. Conditioning the transition matrix. In *Credit Risk*, a special report by Risk, October.

Lando, D. 2000. Some elements of rating-based credit risk modeling. In *Advanced fixed-income valuation tools*, ed. N. Jegadeesh and B. Tuckman. New York: John Wiley & Sons.

———. 2004. *Credit risk modeling*. Princeton, NJ: Princeton University Press.

Lewis, Craig M., and James S. Schallheim. 1992. Are debt and leases substitutes? *Journal of Financial and Quantitative Analysis* 27:497–511.

Lindskog, F., and A. McNeil. 2001. Common Poisson shock models: Applications to insurance and credit risk modeling. ETH preprint.

Litzenberger, R., and D. Modest. 2008. Crisis and non-crisis in financial markets: A unified approach to risk management. SSRN, July 15. http://ssrn.com/abstract=1160273.

Longstaff, F., and E. Schwartz. 1995. A simple approach to valuing risky fixed and floating rate debt. *Journal of Finance* 50:789–819.

Melnikov, Alexander, and Yuliya Romanyuk. 2008. Efficient hedging and pricing of equity-linked life insurance contracts on several risky assets. *International Journal of Theoretical and Applied Finance (IJTAF)* (World Scientific Publishing Co. Pte. Ltd.) 11(03):295–323.

Merton, Robert C. 1973. An intertemporal capital asset pricing model. *Econometrica* 41 (September): 867–887.

———. 1974. On the pricing of corporate debt: The risk structure of interest rates. *Journal of Finance* 29:449–470.

Moody's Special Report. 1992. Corporate bond defaults and default rates. New York: Moody's Investors Services.

Oakes, D. 1989. Bivariate survival models induced by frailties. *Journal of the American Statistical Association* 84:487–493.

———. 1994. Multivariate survival distributions. *Journal of Nonparametric Statistics* 3(3 & 4):343–354.

Pykhtin, M., ed. 2005. *Counterparty credit risk modeling.* London: Risk Books.

Pyndick, Robert S. 1982. Adjustment costs, uncertainty and the behavior of the firm. *American Economic Review* 72(June):415–427.

Reisman, A., P. Ritchken, and C. S. Tapiero. 1986. Reliability, pricing and quality control. *European Journal of Operations Research* 6.

Ritchken, P., and C. S. Tapiero. 1986. Contingent claim contracts and inventory control. *Operation Research* 34:864–870.

Schönbucher, P. 2003. *Credit derivatives pricing models, pricing, implementation.* London: Wiley-Finance.

Standard & Poor's. 1999. Rating performance 1998, stability and transition. New York: Standard & Poor's.

Tapiero, C. S. 1996. *The management of quality and its control.* London: Chapman and Hall.

———. 2000. Ex-post inventory control. *International Journal of Production Research*, April.

———. 2005. Reliability design and RVaR. *International Journal of Reliability, Quality and Safety Engineering* 12 (4) (August).

Tobin, J. C. 1958. Liquidity preference as behavior towards risk. *Review of Economic Studies* 25:65–86.

Wang, G. H. K., and Yau, J. 2000. Trading volume, bid-ask spread, and price volatility in futures markets. *Journal of Futures Markets* 20:943–970.

CHAPTER 10

Multi-Name and Structured Credit Risk Portfolios

OVERVIEW

Prices of financial instruments traded over the counter (OTC) and in financial (credit derivatives) markets may differ. While the price of an OTC financial contract is based on an exchange between specific parties, in a financial credit derivatives market, these instruments are standardized and are traded among the many buyers and sellers of these products. For these reasons, the approaches we use to price these instruments differ. For example, credit default swaps (CDSs) and interest-rate swaps, privately negotiated and unregulated, may default due to parties' intent or their inability to meet contractual obligations. In a financial market, default is mostly due to economic factors such as liquidity of the instrument, the market appetite for risk or its flight from risk, and so on. The rise of insurance firms as third-party guarantors of CDS trades has contributed immensely to the growth of a market for credit risk and credit derivatives, mitigating some of the risks inherent in these financial products. The recent credit crisis has contributed to the reassessment and the management of such products, calling for their standardization and regulation. A call for greater transparency and regulation, a greater understanding of (intra-portfolio) tranches correlation, and a better appreciation of how to price both credit and counterparty risks have raised both practical and academic challenges. This chapter attends to these issues in assessing both the modeling of credit derivatives and their price. We first consider basic CDS contracts and subsequently some basic credit portfolios and CDOs. A historical perspective for the evolution of these products with their many applications is outlined. Subsequently, the modeling of CDOs, their essential risk characteristics, and approaches to price these contracts are considered.

INTRODUCTION

Credit risk portfolios consist of risk-prone individual contracts (called *names*) such as mortgage-backed securities (MBSs), loans, bonds, credit default swaps (CDSs), and other contracts, assembled into a portfolio. These portfolios are used as collateral for other financial products and allow other investors to share in the risks and rewards that these portfolios provide. These portfolios have returns and losses with names that may be statistically independent or dependent, may be subject to contagious risks and to latent and common risks—mostly macroeconomic discrete risk events, rare and unpredictable. The statistical properties of these portfolios as well as the appetite of buyers and sellers for safety and profit-risk determine the price of these portfolios. For example, the price and the revenues (and losses) of a portfolio of mortgages may depend on interest rates, the leverage of the individual mortgage granted, and the price of houses against which mortgages are issued by banks. Thus, a fallout in the market price of houses (the collateral used in mortgages) can induce both a default contagion and fallout in the mortgage market. By the same token, latent factors such as wars, hurricanes, or weather-related disasters in a specific region may contribute to the collective default of mortgages in a given area. Similar concerns arise in portfolios consisting of sovereign bonds. When a sovereign nation assumes excessive debt beyond its ability to service it sustainably, default with systemic economic implications to the sovereign nation can set in a financial flight to safety and to a deterioration in the nation's well-being (for example, the case of Greece in 2010 and its dire effects on the strength of the euro versus the dollar).

Nonetheless, even though credit risk portfolios can be a risky business, they have been commensurably profitable to the banks marketing such products, have contributed to an expansion of financial liquidity, and are used profusely by firms seeking to leverage their equity and off-balance-sheet accounting (to reduce the funds they hold as required by regulation). Other reasons are elaborated in this chapter.

Collateralized debt obligations (CDOs), as their name implies, are debts financed and insured by their and collateral. These collaterals have a price distributed to tranche holders based on agreements drawn to manage portfolio losses (and revenues). The basic idea is both simple and efficient. It allows more debtors to participate in a fixed-income market (and thus provide more liquidity to financial markets) and at the same time contributes to a reduction in the cost of debt. A CDO consists of a portfolio of assets that produce revenues and losses. The CDO notional is the contracted debt whose collateral is the underlying portfolio. The tranches make up the CDO structure with a set of rules to manage the portfolio losses that tranche holders assume, and the fixed income they collect in exchange. In Figure 10.1, we use three tranches (but there can be more), which we have called superior, mezzanine, and equity. Each of these tranches has rights and precedence over returns and losses, as we show here by a number of examples.

CDOs have, to some extent, become the black sheep of finance due to their complexity and their systemic effects during the recent financial crisis. They have also provided to the initiated prospects of riches and to others great losses. Given their importance and the volumes traded, they will most likely continue to provide needed liquidity to firms and loans to consumers. Furthermore, the ability of such structured products allows a financial innovation that can be used in other contexts such as joint insurance, the creation of investment pools catering to a broad variety of tastes for risk and rewards. For these reasons, the prospects for CDO-like financial products remain, in this author's view, important.

Credit risk portfolios assume many forms. For example, collateralized mortgage obligations (CMOs) are based on portfolios backed by mortgages. These portfolios consist of a pool of loan mortgages, assembled, risk-engineered, and priced to

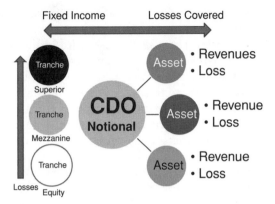

FIGURE 10.1 CDO: A Collateralized Debt Obligation

facilitate their marketability and exchange (whether between two or three parties or in a financial market). These products use credit contracts and obligations that are *assembled* (similarly to assembly lines in industrial production lines) into very large portfolios to replicate by aggregation a portfolio consisting of desirable statistical properties that enhances their collective rating and therefore their price. They are then sold and resold through intermediaries as packaged products, and become notes, papers, options of various sorts, rights, obligations, and so on, that are bought and sold worldwide in financial markets. Their securitization may reduce a costly credit risk to a less costly one, passed through to other willing parties. This mechanism has allowed banks granting mortgages to build CDOs that are then sold to prospective buyers of the risk-rewards CDO tranches provide. In this process, banks have become intermediaries while buyers of the CDO tranches have become debt holders and inherently responsible for the portfolio losses.

It is such a process that has rendered the business of credit risk and credit derivatives extremely profitable, complex, and a seemingly nontransparent business. It is an important process, however, because it allows financial institutions to provide credit at a better price and profit for their initiators. At the same time, it may also falter due to systemic and counterparty risks and excesses that are calling for greater financial regulation. The regulation of credit derivatives is difficult, however, due to their complexity and their global outreach. Further, financial technology and ingenuity can render some or all regulations relating to these products ineffective. Investment banks and intermediaries are continually planning new forays into the securitization of new products such as life insurance contracts, extremely difficult to price but promising great profits.

The availability of credit and its insurance using credit derivatives is essential to the process of liquidity creation. Risk insurance underlies the basic function and popularity of credit derivatives. It is for these reasons that insurance firms such as AIG, Fannie Mae (in the mortgage business), and others have become a vital part of the financial economy. These institutions are enablers that have grown immensely because of the risk protection they have provided to credit risk markets. Their importance arises due to their guaranteeing, mitigating, and absorbing the financial market and counterparty risks due to information and power asymmetries that are prevalent in OTC and markets' credit risks. These same reasons lead to opportunities to profit beyond the normal rate of market returns for some initiated investors willing to bear credit risk while to others, lost in credit market complexity, to lose their investments. The need for engineering valuation, pricing, risk sharing, and risk management in credit products cannot be overstated. In this chapter, we extend individual credit contracts to credit portfolios and their derivatives. We introduce and model multi-name credit portfolios, assess the risks of such portfolios, and provide some approaches to their pricing. Due to the breadth and importance of these problems, only essential concepts and models are presented. The motivated reader may then consult the many references at the end of this chapter, including, among others, Andersen, Sidenius, and Basu (2003), Bluhm and Overbeck (2004), Brigo (2005), Burtschell, Gregory, and Laurent (2005), Duffie (1999), Embrechts, Lindskog, and McNeill (2001), Gregory and Laurent (2003b), KMV (1997), Laurent and Gregory (1999), Lucas, Goodman, and Fabozzi (2006), Merton (1974), Schönbucher (2003), Stulz (2009), and Tapiero and Totouom-Tangho (2010).

The potential variety of credit risk portfolios and their profitability has led to a plethora of financial products engineered to facilitate their risk sharing and their marketing through an ever-greater number of financial entities (pension funds all over the world, hedge funds, banks, etc.). These products are priced in essentially two ways:

1. Based on parametric models assuming that financial markets are complete, with parameters selected to comply with such an assumption. To price in this way, replication is sought by fitting financial markets data to a pricing model (in Chapter 11 we consider such techniques for estimating implied risk-neutral distributions). However, when markets are beset by potential extreme events, this implies that markets are not complete. Hence, these portfolios can assume a model risk that cannot be priced simply. Such a situation did occur during the recent financial crisis.

2. The apparent similarity between insurance and credit and derivatives products led as well to alternative real and actuarial approaches to pricing such portfolios. Insurance and credit products have many similarities, although they differ in the valuation of credit. While traditional insurance is based on the risk exchange between an individual party and an insurance firm, in a credit derivative market, it is based on the trades that buyers and sellers of risk seek and are willing to pay for.

For example, while an insurer uses risk-adjusted return on capital (RAROC) valuation, portfolio optimization (based on Markowitz's model and utility-based approaches), and value at risk (VaR) (consisting of setting aside some capital to meet contingent and mostly unpredictable claims), the standard credit derivatives industry uses replication and hedging to price such products. The latter approach allows financial firms to avoid setting aside capital to meet regulated capital adequacy ratios (and thereby assume more risk), since all risks are embedded in current market prices. The VaR and Markowitz utility optimization approaches also differ and can lead to significantly different valuations when events have statistical tail risks (i.e., risks that do not have a normal probability distribution). For example, while the Markowitz approach and its many variants (see Chapters 5 and 6) will recommend investment in low-volatility and good credit quality products, such recommendations falter when risk events are rare and extreme or have an appreciable within-portfolio correlation (leading to far more risk bearing).

In contrast to the "insurance-insured" price exchange approach, financial markets for credit risks portfolio require an extensive market liquidity to calibrate the portfolio uniquely. Layering of CDOs (also called tranches as stated earlier) of notional contribute also to their liquidity as they provide a greater variety in risk/return for investors and speculators. A rich credit derivatives market is thus needed to determine a market price for credit.

Many credit products such as over-the-counter (OTC) credit default swaps are based on standardized exchanges to facilitate their buying and selling trades. These are also used as a reference notional to construct portfolios consisting of credit default swaps (CDSs), rated and insured (to reduce their apparent risks). Nevertheless, as the crisis of credit markets has demonstrated, there are no fail-safe mechanisms to remove entirely the risks of credit. In all credit risk transactions, risk is always omnipresent—both for the buyers and the sellers of risk. In the next section we define and price credit swaps and subsequently, both a historical review of CDOs, their modeling, and pricing are considered.

CREDIT DEFAULT SWAPS

Credit default swaps (CDSs) are products exchanged between two parties designed to transfer the credit risk exposure of financial entities. The swap consists of a buyer and a seller, where the buyer pays a periodic fee in return for a contingent payment by the seller if a credit event (such as a default) happens to the reference entity underlying the swap. Most CDS contracts are physically settled as follows: If a credit event occurs, then the protection seller must pay the par amount of the contract to the protection buyer, who is obliged to deliver a bond or loan of the name against which protection is being sold. Figure 10.2 summarizes the CDS transaction.

Figure 10.2 states the basic principles in a CDS in which a protection buyer, Bank A, pays a fixed amount to the protection provider, X. Conditional on default, Bank A receives payment for the default reference bond. In Figure 10.2, a partial recovery of a reference bond is implied. A CDS is therefore used as a sort of insurance policy or a hedge, while at the same time it lacks the requirement to actually hold any asset or suffer a loss. A CDS is not actually an insurance contract but an OTC exchange between the two willing parties to this contract. Some problems arose relating to OTC CDSs pointing out to both the power and information asymmetries inherent in such an exchange, and to many and derived issues met when seeking to price fairly these products. For these reasons, both the protection buyer and supplier in a CDS assume risk. Current attempts are made to rein in these important financial products by standardizing CDS contracts and their trades, hoping that these will reduce their counterparty risks.

Developments and derivatives of CDSs are numerous. In particular, a credit default swaption (or credit default option) provides an option to buy protection (a payer option) or sell protection (a receiver option) on a CDS on a specific reference

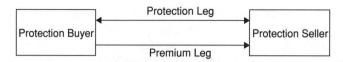

The Premium Leg: Cash Flows
Fixed rate paid on an amortizing notional as
defaults happen on the tranche e.g., tranche 3 defaults, 5 defaults

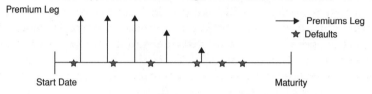

The Protection Leg: Cash Flows
Cash flow paid when defaults happen on the tranche
(e.g., Tranche 3 defaults, 5 defaults)

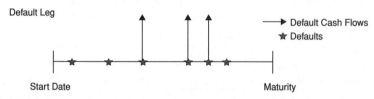

FIGURE 10.2   The Credit Default Swap Contract

credit with a specific maturity. The option is usually European (i.e., exercisable at only one date in the future). The strike price is defined as a coupon on the CDS. Credit default options on single credits are extinguished upon default without any cash flows. Therefore, buying a payer option is not a useful protection against an actual default; it merely provides protection against a rise in the credit spread. However, options on credit indexes such as iTraxx and iBox include defaulted entities in the intrinsic value of the option when exercised.

In practice, there are numerous CDS contracts, each with its own specific clauses. In order to increase their tradability and their transparency, efforts have been made to standardize their terms of trade. Further, to mitigate counterparty risks, investors may face a clearinghouse as the counterparty with payments assured within a reasonable amount of time. The clearinghouse matches opposite sides of a transaction between the many clearing member firms. If one of the members fails, then the position can be assigned to another member or closed in an open market transaction. Any loss in such a transaction is then compensated by the margin deposit held by the clearinghouse. An increase in such margins is assumed to reduce some of the contracts' risks. This system works as long as there is no systemic default. Problems arise when market liquidity is sharply curtailed and transactions become transaction-specific, which creates a counterparty risk assumed by the parties of the transaction without any recourse. For this reason, the usefulness of clearinghouses and insurance, acting as a proxy for financial markets, is theoretically and practically important as they relieve the counterparty and market risk and augment the liquidity of credit transactions.

Trades in CDSs can be made without any ownership of the reference asset. For example, if a hedge fund manager believes that the reference asset is toxic and is likely to fail, he will buy a quantity of CDSs (thus raising their price if the quantity is large) in the expectation of the reference asset defaulting. Such a trade is necessarily a speculation that may also provide a signal to financial markets of a troubled reference asset and usher in its default. Such transactions are facilitated by the creation of portfolios of CDS contracts that allow buyers and sellers to assume parts of the risk embedded in the CDS contracts. There are various types of swaps, based on the same exchange principles, we consider below total return swaps (TRSs).

EXAMPLE: TOTAL RETURN SWAPS

Total return swaps (TRSs) are bilateral financial contracts in which one party (the TR payer) pays the total positive return of an asset—a bond, a loan, or another reference asset (a financial obligation)—while the other party (the TR receiver) pays a fixed- or floating-rate payment and compensates negative total returns (losses) on the reference asset. Total return swaps allow a transfer of credit risk by the transfer (at a price) of a bond default risk in exchange for a risk-free bond. Such a transaction would mitigate the effects of default risk by the sharing of the risk between the two parties privy to the exchange. Total return and other swaps are useful because they are off-balance-sheet instruments allowing firms (banks) to reduce the amount of regulated capital they have to set aside and provide greater flexibility in tailoring investments to their specific accounting needs for a more favorable balance sheet (since in credit derivatives the reference entity is not a party of the credit derivatives transaction and therefore it need not be recorded in its books). Off-balance-sheet accounting, however, does not remove the risk but alters its accountability.

Pricing Credit Default Swaps—The Implied Market Approach

To price credit default swaps (as well as credit derivatives), there are numerous approaches, essentially based on a price implied in the spread of the CDS (or derivatives of the CDS) and the pricing of collateral underlying the credit product. The latter approach is based on Merton's model (1974). This model consists of pricing an asset default (a loan, a mortgage, a corporate debt, etc.) in terms of the contract obligations and the price of residual assets (essentially collateral obligations). In this case, default is market based, defined by the prices of the outstanding debt and its collateral. Recovery is defined as well by the difference of the loss and the collateral. In such a framework, default does not recognize future prospects of the collateral but rather its current value, priced to market. In a cyclical financial market, default is therefore predictable since once asset prices fall, default might necessarily occur (although the default time may be unknown). In other words, in an improving financial market, default will not occur while in a declining market it is doomed to occur. For these reasons, as the market for CDS grew, improved OTC models were developed.

However, as the credit derivative sector matured and the CDS market became appreciably liquid, models were less relevant as their default spreads were available directly through their financial and observed prices. In other words, prices became calibrated to a forward-looking financial model, with presumed and predictable state prices (i.e., prices implied in a complete financial market). In this sense, default prices are implied by the price spread, with one defining the other. This approach is broadly practiced in determining implied risk-neutral distributions using current options prices and requires an information-rich financial environment to compensate for the complexity and the many sources of risks that such products are subject to. The next generation (following the CDS contracts) of credit products were baskets or portfolios with underlying assets rather than a single entity as had been the case with CDS contracts. These financial products are considered subsequently.

EXAMPLE: THE CDS PRICE SPREAD

The price of a CDS equates the protection and premium legs to define an accredited default spread. Consider for example a default bond with its price at time t and a maturity at time $T > t$. Default may thus occur in the time interval $t \leq x \leq T$. Let the current price of this default bond at time x be $B_D(t, x)$. The probability of no default is thus $1 - F_D(x \mid x > t)$, $x < T$. Let $s(x)$ be the spread for a default at time x, its current price, and the conditional probability of default at x, expressed by the hazard rate of the default distribution, are thus:

$$P(s, t) = \int_t^T B_D(t, x)s(x)[1 - F_D(x \mid x > t)]dx \tag{10.1}$$

$$h_t(x) = \frac{f_D(x \mid t \leq x \leq T)}{1 - F_D(x \mid t \leq x \leq T)} \quad \text{or} \quad 1 - F_D(x \mid t \leq x \leq T) = e^{-\int_t^T h_t(z)dz} \tag{10.2}$$

Say that such a bond has a recovery rate R, the price of the protection leg is then:

$$Q(s, t) = (1 - R) \int_t^T B_D(t, x)\mathbf{1}_{x < T}dx = (1 - R) \int_t^T B_D(t, x) f_D(x \mid t) \, dx$$

$$= (1 - R) \int_t^T B_D(t, x)h_t(x) \left[1 - F_D(x \mid t \leq x \leq T)\right] dx \tag{10.3}$$

$$= (1 - R) \int_t^T B_D(t, x)h_t(x)e^{-\int_t^T h_t(z)dz} dx$$

In equilibrium, for the exchange to occur, both the protection and the premium leg are equated, namely, $P(s, t) = Q(s, t)$. Thus,

$$
\int_t^T B_D(t, x)s(x)[1 - F_D(x \,|\, x > t)]dx =
$$
$$
(1 - R) \int_t^T B_D(t, x)h_t(x) \,[1 - F_D(x \,|\, t \le x \le T)] \, dx
\tag{10.4}
$$

As a result,

$$
B_D(t, x)s(x)[1 - F_D(x \,|\, x > t)] = (1 - R) \, B_D(t, x)h_t(x) \,[1 - F_D(x \,|\, t \le x \le T)]
\tag{10.5}
$$

A solution for the CDS price spread is therefore:

$$
s(x) = (1 - R)\, h_t(x)
\tag{10.6}
$$

In this problem, the spread implies both the expected recovery and the default hazard rate of the bond. For example, if default is modeled by an (implied) exponential probability distribution with mean μ, its hazard rate is also μ (defining, in fact, the implied discount rate applied to price the default risk). The spread is then $s(x) = (1 - R)\,\mu = \bar{s}$. The implied probability distribution of no default is thus:

$$
F(t) = 1 - e^{-[\bar{s}/(1-R)]t}
$$

Explicitly, trades on the likelihood of default of an underlying asset are based on a price that traders (buyers and sellers) use to express the bets they are willing to place on the default probability. The presumption that default has an exponential probability distribution is therefore not a "real default" but merely an agreed-on single parameter used to price default in a trading model. In this case, $h(\tau \,|\, t) = \bar{h}$ or $\bar{s} = (1 - R)\bar{h}$ and $F(t) = 1 - e^{-[\bar{s}/(1-R)]t}$ are not real physical estimates but model terms reduced to assess the bets made on the asset's default. For example, assume that the following swaps are priced as basis points with trades with the following data:

Bonds	1	2	3	5	10
Bid (pbs)	4.0	12.0	25.0	40.0	55.0
Ask (bps)	8.0	20.0	31.0	55.0	70.0

If the recovery rate is assumed to be $R = 0.3$, we have:

Years	1	2	3	5	10
Spreads (pbs)	4.0	8.0	6.0	15.0	25.0
PD, $f(t)$	Implied	Implied	Implied	Implied	Implied

where the implied probability of default corresponding to each case is found by:

$$
\begin{aligned}
&F(1) = 1 - e^{-[.04/(1-R)]}, \; f(1) = [.04/(1-\delta)]\,e^{-[.04/(1-R)]} \\
&F(2) = 1 - e^{-2[.04/(1-R)]}, \; f(2) = [.04/(1-\delta)]\,e^{-2[.04/(1-R)]} \\
&F(3) = 1 - e^{-3[.04/(1-R)]}, \; f(3) = [.04/(1-\delta)]\,e^{-3[.04/(1-R)]} \\
&F(5) = 1 - e^{-5[.04/(1-R)]}, \; f(5) = [.04/(1-\delta)]\,e^{-5[.04/(1-R)]} \\
&F(10) = 1 - e^{-10[.04/(1-R)]}, \; f(10) = [.04/(1-\delta)]\,e^{-10[.04/(1-R)]}
\end{aligned}
\tag{10.7}
$$

For example, the conditional probability of default (the hazard rate) at time $t = 10$, given that there was no default at time $t = 0$ is:

$$
f(10)/(1 - F(0)) = .04/(1 - R) = .04/.7 = .0057
$$

Example: An OTC (Swap) Contract under Risk-Neutral Pricing and Collateral Prices

We extend the CDS pricing example to include a collateral underlying the CDS contract. In this case, the underlying collateral's price relative to that of the debt obligation is used to determine the risk of default. For example, assume a debt obligation is backed by the price of a house. If the price of the collateral (house) falters, it may lead the debt holder to default if the price of its collateral is smaller than its obligations. Say that an applicant comes to a bank for a mortgage whose underlying house current price is π. The applicant can finance the house with personal sources that are equal to $V < \pi$ and therefore, a loan for $\pi - V$ is needed. However, the price of houses may increase or decrease over time at a random rate, $\tilde{r}$. At time t, after the contract has been negotiated, the price of the house is modeled by the random price $\pi e^{\tilde{r}t}$. When the mortgage collateral (the house) price is smaller than the loan or, $\pi e^{\tilde{r}t} \le (\pi - V)(1 + \delta)$ where δ is an interest rate charged by the bank for the loan, the loan is assumed to default. Or

$$
e^{\tilde{r}t} \le (1 - V/\pi)(1 + \delta) = \xi
$$

Equivalently,

$$
\tilde{r} \le \ln\left((1 - V/\pi)(1 + \delta)\right)^{\frac{1}{t}}
$$

The probability of loan default is thus:

$$
P\left(\tilde{r} \le \xi^{\frac{1}{t}}\right) = \int_{-\infty}^{\xi^{\frac{1}{t}}} f_r(x)dx = F_r\left(\xi^{\frac{1}{t}}\right)
\tag{10.8}
$$

while the probability of no default is its complementary probability. The return to the bank is thus (for which it initially gave the applicant a loan of $\pi - V$):

$$
\begin{cases}
\pi\,Min\left(e^{\tilde{r}t}, \xi\right) = \pi e^{\tilde{r}t} & if\,\tilde{r} \le \ln\left(\xi^{\frac{1}{t}}\right) \\
\pi\xi & if\,\tilde{r} > \ln\left(\xi^{\frac{1}{t}}\right)
\end{cases}
\tag{10.9}
$$

If the collateral has a risk-neutral distribution, the price of the loan granted from the bank's viewpoint defines one leg of the transaction:

$$\left(1 - \frac{V}{\pi}\right) = e^{-R_f t}\left\{\xi\left(1 - F_r^Q\left(\ln\left(\xi^{\frac{1}{t}}\right)\right)\right) + \int_{-\infty}^{\ln\left(\xi^{\frac{1}{t}}\right)} e^{xt} f_r^Q(x)dx\right\} \qquad (10.10)$$

Now consider the buyer of the house. His return at time t is null if

$$\tilde{r} \leq \ln\left(\xi^{\frac{1}{t}}\right)$$

Otherwise, it is not null:

$$\frac{\tilde{V}}{\pi} = \begin{cases} 0 & if\ \tilde{r} \leq \ln\left(\xi^{\frac{1}{t}}\right) \\ e^{\tilde{r}t} - \xi & if\ \tilde{r} > \ln\left(\xi^{\frac{1}{t}}\right) \end{cases} \qquad (10.11)$$

Thus, if the house price at time t is less than the loan amount, the mortgage holder gets nothing in case of default (whether willingly or as stated in the mortgage contract). If the mortgage amount is smaller than the price of the house, the mortgage holder's return is the residual price of the house, namely its current price less the reimbursement of the loan with its additional interest and the penalties paid to the bank. Thus, under risk-neutral pricing, the mortgage holder's investment has a price given by an expectation, per equation (10.11):

$$V = \pi e^{-R_f t}\left(E_r^Q\left(e^{\tilde{r}t}\right) - \xi - \int_{-\infty}^{\ln\left(\xi^{\frac{1}{t}}\right)} \left(e^{\tilde{r}t} - \xi\right) f_r^Q(x)dx\right) \qquad (10.12)$$

In a complete market, the prices for both parties are found by the simultaneous equations (10.10) and (10.12), expressing the *swap* exchange between the bank and the borrower:

$$\begin{aligned}\left(1 - \tfrac{V}{\pi}\right) &= e^{-R_f t}\left\{\xi\left(1 - F_r^Q\left(\ln\left(\xi^{\frac{1}{t}}\right)\right)\right) + \int_{-\infty}^{\ln\left(\xi^{\frac{1}{t}}\right)} e^{xt} f_r^Q(x)dx\right\} \\ \tfrac{V}{\pi} &= e^{-R_f t}\left(E_r^Q\left(e^{\tilde{r}t}\right) - \xi - \int_{-\infty}^{\ln\left(\xi^{\frac{1}{t}}\right)} \left(e^{\tilde{r}t} - \xi\right) f_r^Q(x)dx\right)\end{aligned} \qquad (10.13)$$

Or, in terms of the loan leverage, we obtain two equations in the two parameters (λ, δ) that define the borrower leverage and the bank interest charge for the loan δ,

$$\lambda = \frac{V}{\pi}$$

$$e^{R_f t} = \left\{E_r^Q\left(e^{\tilde{r}t}\right) - \xi F_r^Q\left(\ln\left(\xi^{\frac{1}{t}}\right)\right) + \xi F_r^Q\left(\ln\left(\xi^{\frac{1}{t}}\right)\right)\right\}$$

and finally

$$1 = e^{-R_f t} E_r^Q \left(e^{\tilde{r}t} \right) \tag{10.14}$$

In other words, under risk-neutral pricing, the price of a current dollar equals the price of expected uncertain future payments at time t. In such a framework, the price of leverage for the creditor and the borrower corresponds to a risk-sharing agreement.

In an OTC contract, however, the risk-neutral distribution is not unique. Each of the parties to the contract has a different risk-bearing capacity (if this were not the case, there would be no exchange), and each possesses information the other party might not have. In such an environment, counterparty risk arises, resulting potentially in mispricing by one or the other parties privy to the financial exchange. Insurance and guarantees by a third party may then mitigate the risks that each of the parties to the contract may deem unbearable.

Of course, when such contracts are aggregated into extremely large portfolios, the statistical assumption that risks are diversified may be true or may not be true. Further, in practice it is difficult to determine the underlying risk-neutral distributions $f_r^Q(x)$. Although implied estimation techniques can be used when the underlying asset and its optional derivatives are richly traded (as will be seen in Chapter 11), it remains embedded in a model whose parameters define the current state of beliefs regarding the underlying asset When both the creditor and the borrower have an estimate of the future price of the house, one seeking an optimal loan demand and the other a granting policy (based on the loan's leverage), their personal differences will be expressed by different future price estimates of the collateral. The optimization of the expected utility of such a transaction by each of the parties will define the creditor and the borrower risk-bearing capacity based on the personal information each has. Such problems are technically more difficult, however, and require a careful assessment of the OTC contracts.

EXAMPLE: PRICING A PROJECT LAUNCH

A firm seeks to launch a new project whose rate of return is predicted to be normally distributed with a mean of 8 percent and a variance two times its mean. A loan for \$1 million is approved for 10 years by the bank at an interest rate of δ percent yearly. The project's required investment is \$1.5 million, and the firm itself can invest \$500,000. For simplicity, we shall let all payments be made only at the end of the tenth year. The risk-free rate for 10-year loans is (at the time the loan is made) equal to 0.04.

For the bank leg, repeating equation (10.10) by inserting numerical values and setting

$$\xi = \left(1 - \frac{500,00}{1,500,000} \right) (1 + \delta)$$

we have:

$$\left(1 - \frac{500,00}{1,500,000}\right) = e^{-(.04)(10)}$$

$$\times \left\{ \begin{array}{l} \left(1 - \frac{500,00}{1,500,000}\right)(1+\delta)\left(1 - F_r^Q\left(\ln\left(\left(1 - \frac{500,00}{1,500,000}\right)(1+\delta)\right)^{\frac{1}{10}}\right)\right) \\ + \int\limits_{-\infty}^{\ln\left(\left(1-\frac{500,00}{1,500,000}\right)(1+\delta)\right)^{\frac{1}{10}}} e^{10x}\, f_r^Q(x)\,dx \end{array} \right\} \quad (10.15a)$$

or

$$e^{(.04)(10)} = \left\{ (1+\delta)\left(1 - F_r^Q\left(\ln\left(\frac{2}{3}(1+\delta)\right)^{0.1}\right)\right) + \frac{3}{2} \int\limits_{-\infty}^{\ln\left(\frac{2}{3}(1+\delta)\right)^{0.1}} e^{10x}\, f_r^Q(x)\,dx \right\} \quad (10.15b)$$

Note that $f_r^Q(x)$ is a normal probability distribution with mean 0.08 and variance 0.16, and therefore the only parameter remaining unknown is the interest rate δ that the bank charges. Of course the firm may or may not accept such a rate, or may increase (or decrease) the loan it seeks from the bank.

Thus, turning to the loan demand of the firm or person, the self-investment is given by a solution for V^* in equation (10.13), or:

$$\frac{V}{1,500,000} = e^{-0.04(10)} \left(\begin{array}{l} E_r^P\left(e^{10\tilde{r}}\right) - \left(1 - \frac{V}{1,500,000}\right)(1+\delta) - \\ \int\limits_{-\infty}^{\ln\left(\left(1-\frac{V}{1,500,000}\right)(1+\delta)\right)^{0.1}} \left(e^{\tilde{r}t} - \left(1 - \frac{V}{1,500,000}\right)(1+\delta)\right) f_r^P(x)\,dx \end{array} \right) \quad (10.16)$$

where $f_r^P(x)$ is now the firm probability estimate of the asset growth rate. Combining this equation with equation (10.15a) with the loan sought and granted V, yields:

$$\left(1 - \frac{V}{1,500,000}\right) = e^{-(.04)(10)}$$

$$\times \left\{ \begin{array}{l} \left(1 - \frac{V}{1,500,000}\right)(1+\delta)\left(1 - F_r^Q\left(\ln\left(\left(1 - \frac{V}{1,500,000}\right)(1+\delta)\right)^{0.1}\right)\right) \\ + \int\limits_{-\infty}^{\ln\left(\left(1-\frac{V}{1,500,000}\right)(1+\delta)\right)^{0.1}} e^{10x}\, f_r^Q(x)\,dx \end{array} \right\} \quad (10.17)$$

A simultaneous solution of equations (10.16) and (10.17) provides a solution for both the loan demanded and granted V and its interest rate charge δ. This problem is, of course, biased by the personal information that the creditor and the firm have.

Under risk-neutral pricing, however, there is a unique price for both the loan and the interest, as equation (10.14) has indicated.

At present, say that the creditor seeks to remove entirely its loan risk. One possibility is to seek insurance by, let's say, an international insurance company, IIG. The cost of insurance is then that required by IIG (i.e., the risk premium it can extract from such a contract). Alternatively, assume that derivatives of the underlying collateral are traded. Then, to obtain for sure$(\pi - V)(1 + \delta)$, note that two cases arise. In the first case,

$$\pi e^{\tilde{r}t} \leq (\pi - V)(1 + \delta)$$

and default occurs. In this case, a put insurance

$$Max\left((\pi - V)(1 + \delta) - \pi e^{\tilde{r}t}, 0\right)$$

lets the bank take over the project since:

$$Max\left((\pi - V)(1 + \delta) - \pi e^{\tilde{r}t}, 0\right) + \pi e^{\tilde{r}t}$$
$$= (\pi - V)(1 + \delta) - \pi e^{\tilde{r}t} + \pi e^{\tilde{r}t} = (\pi - V)(1 + \delta)$$

In the second case,

$$\pi e^{\tilde{r}t} > (\pi - V)(1 + \delta)^t$$

no default occurs and therefore the put option is worthless since

$$Max\left((\pi - V)(1 + \delta)^t - \pi e^{\tilde{r}t}, 0\right) = 0$$

and the bank collects

$$(\pi - V)(1 + \delta)^t$$

Thus the put insurance price for the bank is under a risk-neutral probability distribution:

$$Put\left(t, (\pi - V)(1 + \delta)^t\right) = e^{-R_f t} E_r^Q Max\left((\pi - V)(1 + \delta)^t - \pi e^{\tilde{r}t}, 0\right)$$

$$= e^{-R_f t} \int_{-\infty}^{\ln((1-V/\pi)(1+\delta))^{\frac{1}{t}}} \left((\pi - V)(1 + \delta)^t - \pi e^{xt}\right) f_r^Q(x)\, dx \tag{10.18}$$

In other words, the bank buying a put option with a strike $(\pi - V)(1 + \delta)^t$ and maturity t has acquired the protection against its loan default. The firm (we'll call it BIG) selling the put option collects the premium and assumes the contract risk. Of course, in case of mispricing due to systemic risks, the cost to BIG of such contracts can be extremely large. Consider again the bank, which spends $(\pi - V) + Put\left(t, (\pi - V)(1 + \delta)^t\right)$ at time $t = 0$ while at time t, it collects for sure

$(\pi - V)(1 + \delta)^t$. As a result, the present value of such a transaction is:

$$(\pi - V) + Put\ \left(t, (\pi - V)(1 + \delta)^t\right) = e^{-R_f t} \left((\pi - V)(1 + \delta)^t\right) \tag{10.19}$$

and the price of the put is:

$$Put\ \left(t, (\pi - V)(1 + \delta)^t\right) = e^{-R_f t} \left((\pi - V)(1 + \delta)^t\right) - (\pi - V) \tag{10.20a}$$

For example, for a loan of \$100,000 we have

$$Put\ \left(t, 100,00(1 + \delta)^t\right) = e^{-(0.04)t} \left(1000,000(1 + \delta)^t\right) - 1000,000$$

The creditor can self-insure by buying a put option. The interest charged by the creditor is then a solution of:

$$Put\ \left(t, 100,000(1 + \delta)^t\right) = e^{-(0.04)t} \int_{-\infty}^{\ln((100.000/\pi)(1+\delta))^{\frac{1}{t}}} \left(100,000(1 + \delta)^t - \pi e^{xt}\right) f_r^Q(x)\, dx$$

$$= e^{-(0.04)t} \left(1000,000(1 + \delta)^t\right) - 1000,000 \tag{10.20b}$$

where $f_r^Q(x)$ is the implied risk-neutral distribution and π the initial investment. If the firm also invests \$100,000, then $\pi = 200,000$ (i.e., a 50 percent leverage of its investment), and:

$$Put\ \left(t, 100,000(1 + \delta)^t\right) = 100,000 e^{-(0.04)t} \int_{-\infty}^{\ln(0.5(1+\delta))^{\frac{1}{t}}} \left((1 + \delta)^t - 2e^{xt}\right) f_r^Q(x)\, dx \tag{10.21}$$

Equating these two equations, we have at last the price of the loan expressed by its interest charge:

$$e^{-(0.04)t} \int_{-\infty}^{\ln(0.5(1+\delta))^{\frac{1}{t}}} \left((1 + \delta)^t - 2e^{xt}\right) f_r^Q(x)\, dx = e^{-(0.04)t} \left((1 + \delta)^t\right) - 1 \tag{10.22}$$

Generally, in terms of the leverage

$$\ell = \left(1 - \frac{V}{\pi}\right)$$

we have:

$$\ell + \frac{Put\left(t, \pi\ell(1+\delta)^t\right)}{\pi} = e^{-R_f t}\left(\ell(1+\delta)^t\right)$$

$$Put\left(t, \pi\ell(1+\delta)^t\right) = \pi e^{-R_f t} \int_{-\infty}^{\ln((1-V/\pi)(1+\delta))^{\frac{1}{t}}} \left(\ell(1+\delta)^t - e^{xt}\right) f_r^Q(x)\,dx \tag{10.23}$$

Then,

$$1 + e^{-R_f t} \int_{-\infty}^{\ln(\ell(1+\delta))^{\frac{1}{t}}} \left((1+\delta)^t - \frac{1}{\ell}e^{xt}\right) f_r^Q(x)\,dx = e^{-R_f t}(1+\delta)^t$$

$$e^{R_f t} + \int_{-\infty}^{\ln(\ell(1+\delta))^{\frac{1}{t}}} \left((1+\delta)^t - \frac{e^{xt}}{\ell}\right) f_r^Q(x)\,dx = (1+\delta)^t \tag{10.24}$$

And finally, in terms of leverage, the interest rate to charge is a solution of:

$$1 = \frac{e^{R_f t}}{(1+\delta)^t} + \int_{-\infty}^{\ln(\ell(1+\delta))^{\frac{1}{t}}} \left(1 - \frac{e^{xt}}{\ell(1+\delta)^t}\right) f_r^Q(x)\,dx \tag{10.25}$$

A fully leveraged loan has an interest rate charge given by setting $\ell = 1$ in equation (10.25).

CREDIT DERIVATIVES: A HISTORICAL PERSPECTIVE

Credit derivatives* were the fastest-growing financial products in capital markets, assuming complex structures and forms, called by some financial weapons of mass destruction and by others the new means to create liquidity. Banks, insurance companies, hedge funds, pension funds, asset managers, and structured finance vehicles have used and are likely to continue to use credit derivatives for arbitrage, speculation, hedging, and securitization, and to pass through their credit risks. Essentially these structured products combine insurance and financial innovation to allow risks to be shared far more extensively than vanilla options and insurance. Although credit derivatives have attracted attention already at the beginning of the twenty-first century, they have expanded both quantitatively and qualitatively with a plethora of names. In 2003 a number of papers, a retrospective history, and edited books on *Credit Risk Modeling* (Gordy and Jones 2003), as well as *Credit Derivatives: The Definitive Guide* by Jon Gregory (2003), appeared, forerunners of an extensive credit derivatives literature.

---

*This section has been written with Daniel Totouom-Tangho, BNP-Paribas, New York.

Credit derivatives came to the attention of the public at large in an article in *Global Finance* in March 1993, pointing to three Wall Street firms, J.P. Morgan, Merrill Lynch, and Bankers Trust, which were marketing early forms of credit derivatives (note that only J.P. Morgan remains standing). *Global Finance* predicted then that within a few years, credit derivatives would rival the $4 trillion market for interest rate swaps. In retrospect, this turned out both to be true and to have far-reaching consequences, some of which have been revealed in the recent financial crisis.

The introduction of credit derivatives encountered some critical comments, however. In November 1993, the *Investment Dealers Digest* carried an article entitled "Derivatives Pros Snubbed on Latest Exotic Product," expressing doubt as to the completion of specific private credit derivative deals. Further, it also pointed to Standard & Poor's refusal to rate credit derivatives as these products represented bets by investors that none of the corporate issuers in the reference group would default or go bankrupt. Explicitly, a commentator was quoted as stating, "It [credit derivatives] is like Russian roulette. It doesn't make a difference if there's only one bullet: If you get it you die." The subsequent marketing of credit derivatives was unbridled, however, with hundreds of possible applications for commercial banks, changing the risk profile of their loan books by off-balance-sheet accounting and managing large bond and derivatives portfolios; for manufacturing companies overexposed to a single customer; for equity investors in project finance dealing with excessive sovereign risk; for institutional investors with excessive risk appetites; and so on. Additional uses are being marketed today such as credit derivatives with underlying life insurance contracts (Goldman Sachs). In this sense, such structured products, providing a more refined exchange and diversification of risks, have traded volumes and a popularity that is a testament to their usefulness.

Credit Derivatives: Historical Modeling

Credit derivatives have evolved, starting from credit default swaps (CDSs), increasingly liquid and allowing securitized CDS portfolios and synthetic CDOs (i.e., CDOs that do not require any of the parties to hold any assets and, therefore, appear to be at times much more of a casino rather than a real market).

The next generation consisted of baskets or portfolios with multiple underlying assets rather than a single entity as had been the case with CDS. Examples of such second-generation products include first-to-default (or more generally the nth-to-default) assets, and subsequently collateralized debt obligations (CDOs). The first CDOs were called cash CDOs, requiring the product initiator to purchase the underlying bonds, which contributed to distortions in bonds markets.

Significant milestones in the development of credit derivatives include the 1992 ISDA3 use of the term *credit derivatives* to describe a new, exotic type of OTC contract. In 1993 KMV introduced the first version of its Portfolio Manager model—an extension of the Merton model that allows the estimation of the loss distribution of a portfolio of loans based on calibrated default probabilities. The best-known representative of this type of default probabilities is the Expected Default Frequency (EDF) from Moody's KMV.

In 1994 the use of credit derivatives expanded appreciably when in September 1996 the first collateralized loan obligation (CLO) was marketed by the UK's

National Westminster Bank. A balance sheet CLO is a form of securitization in which assets (bank loans) are removed from a bank's balance sheet and packaged into marketable securities that are sold to investors. Different tranches of the CLO have different risk-return characteristics and can be targeted at specific investor classes. Their appeal to certain tranches has been their attractive yields compared to similarly rated securities. For their initiators, they allow listing some assets off balance sheet and reduce their risk exposure.

A main alternative to a balance sheet CLO is the *arbitrage* CLO. In such a CDO, an asset management firm buys credit risk before selling claims on repackaged risks. The originator of the deal then profits from the yield differential between the portfolio cost of funding the assets and the price of the securities.

A significant step in the development of a CLO market was a $5 billion Repeat Offering Securitization Entity (ROSE) Funding No. 1, issued by the National Westminster Bank in September 1996. This CLO was backed by an international portfolio of more than 200 commercial loans. A year later, Nations Bank launched a $4 billion CLO, the first significant deal in the United States. Japanese and Continental European banks soon followed. Deutsche Bank's first Core CLO was largely backed by loans to medium-size German companies.

J.P. Morgan's Broad Index Secured Trust Offering (BISTRO) deal in December 1997 is generally viewed as the first synthetic securitization. The aim of BISTRO transactions was to remove the credit risk on a portfolio of corporate credits held on J.P. Morgan's books, with no funding or balance sheet impact. In 1998 McKinsey introduced its Credit Portfolio View, which is a credit risk portfolio model, and in July 1999 credit derivative definitions were formally agreed on.

Subsequently, synthetic CDOs were created (currently criticized by many politicians and economists as contracts that contribute little to the economy and much to speculators). With synthetic CDOs, it became no longer necessary to physically acquire the underlying assets, making it possible to sell individual tranches of the CDO. Nowadays the standard CDOs (e.g., iTraxx and CDX) are based on portfolios of 125 entities or names. Such products make it possible to bet on market trends of all sorts.

Pricing CDOs has always been challenging however, due to the CDOs' portfolio assets' composition, their dependence, potential contagion risk and the distribution and apportionment of payments and risks assumed by CDO tranches. Essential issues include:

- Selecting asset classes that define the CDO's underlying collateral portfolio.
- Selecting the notional of the portfolio and that allotted to the tranches.
- Modeling the default probabilities of the individual entities (usually done via the CDS spreads if the CDS for that name is sufficiently liquid). In real terms, however, multiple sources of risks, statistical dependence, contagious processes, rare events, and macroeconomic factors are determinant factors for the portfolio default.
- Modeling the correlation (or, more accurately, the dependency structure) between the names in the portfolio.
- Defining the CDO structure, the evolution of prices of the underlying assets of the CDO, returns generated by such a portfolio, and their distribution across the tranches.
- Defining the notional residual in each of the tranches.

Modeling and pricing techniques, including the covenants (agreements) of such credit products, can lead to a CDO complexity that may seem at times to be non-transparent. For these reasons, the analysis of CDOs has evolved into complex financial models and tools that use models of basket dependence (at times modeled by copulas and in some cases modeled by intertemporal shifts in the underlying and tranches' covariations). Recently, dynamic (time varying) considerations have been made, leading to even more complex models making use of dynamic factor copulas. These models require generally a great deal of financial information, and their model analysis is based on extensive optimization and simulation results.

The modeling of CDOs, CLOs, and other structured letters were also designed to take advantage of raters' techniques that are often publicly shared, in order to obtain a quality rating (essential for its commercial marketing). The rating of such products by leading raters such as S&P, Moody's, Fitch, and so on, was and still is important, as it provides a risk definition that investors and traders use. A AAA rating (such as was given to the Goldman Sachs BISTRO CDO) is therefore essential for marketing CDO tranches by their originators. To acquire a marketable rating, however, originators of these products have essentially used raters' models to obtain high-quality ratings.

Theoretically, desirable CDOs consist of assets that are large and statistically independent (drawn from disparate regions, economic risks, environments, industries, and so forth). In addition, raters that are transparent regarding their rating methods and requirements have motivated CDO originators to comply with the rating methods used in order to obtain a desirable rate. The prices of a CDO tranches, however, are a function of the engineered rights and obligations of the CDO tranches, and the appetite for risk and returns that are necessarily a function of the common (shared) information, the private information by the managers and the originators of these products, and of course the economic and financial trends.

A CDO's risk-reward properties and the prices of its tranches are thus defined in terms of:

- The definition of the portfolio assets (such as bonds, MBSs, ABSs); their returns (whether deterministic or stochastic); their individual statistical dependence; and their aggregate dependence on rare events, contagions, macroeconomic factors, and so forth that define the portfolio losses apportioned to tranches.
- Tranches or layering the portfolio in risk classes to meet the demand for risk and rewards by prospective investors.
- Defining the rights and the obligations for each risk class (also called payment waterfall), including:
  - The sequencing and the schedule of returns allocation to tranche holders.
  - The sequencing and the schedule of losses allocated to tranches.
  - The legal rights and the recourse to each tranche holder (many of which are defined as clauses in the offering circular).
- Having the portfolio and the CDO tranches rated appropriately to secure acceptability by investors ("marketing the CDO to meet the need of investors"), managing the risks, and pricing the portfolio's and CDO tranches' risks to assure the CDO's viability.

In practice, the complexity and the statistical dependence of the CDO notional (its returns and its losses) are modeled by multivariate probability models (or multivariate stochastic processes). Due to their mathematical complexity and the lack of information required to capture their dependence and their evolution, simplifications are made. In particular, copulas are used to model the statistical dependence structure (in as few parameters as realistic) of the many random factors that contribute to the gains and losses of the CDO underlying.

Credit Derivatives and Product Innovation

Future generations are likely to tap into longer-lived credit derivatives and to a far broader set of securitized products to be traded in financial markets. In the **first-generation products**, credit derivatives were defined as arrangements that allow one party (protection buyer or originator) to transfer the credit risk of a reference asset (or assets), which it may or may not own, to one or more other parties (the protection sellers). The main first-generation credit derivatives currently being used are as stated earlier: total return swap, credit default swaps, and so on.

Standardization of CDS contracts have become extremely liquid however leading to synthetic products which did not require any of the parties to hold any assets and therefore, appear to be at times much more of a "casino" rather than a real market. Currently, the typical maturities available for CDS contracts are 3, 5, 7 and 10 years with 5 years being most liquid. Almost any maturity is possible for an over-the-counter CDS.

To price credit derivatives there are two essential approaches. One based on the price of the collateral underlying the credit product (Merton's 1974 model) and the other implied in the traded spread (providing a price for risk). The essential difference between a total return swap and a credit default swap is that the latter does not provide protection against loss in asset value but against specific credit events. In a sense, a total return swap is not a credit derivative at all, in the sense that a CDS is.

Another first-generation credit product is, for example, the credit-linked note (CLN). A CLN is a security issued by a special-purpose company or trust, designed to offer investors par value at maturity unless a referenced credit defaults. In case of default, investors may still recover part of the default asset, however. The trust may also enter into a default swap with a dealer. In case of default, the trust will pay the dealer par minus the recovery rate, in exchange for an annual fee that is passed on to investors in the form of a higher yield on their note. The purpose of the arrangement is to pass through the risk of a specific default to investors willing to bear that risk in return for the higher yield it makes available. The CLNs themselves are typically backed by very highly rated collaterals, such as U.S. Treasury securities. A CLN is thus a security with an embedded credit default swap allowing the issuer to transfer a specific credit risk to credit investors. Technically, CLNs are created through a special-purpose company (SPC) or trust, which is collateralized with AAA-rated securities. Investors buy the securities from the trust that pays a fixed or floating coupon during the life of the note. At maturity, the investors receive par unless the referenced credit defaults or declares bankruptcy, in which case they receive an amount equal to the recovery rate.

The second generation of credit derivatives arose following the development of fixed income and interest rate products. Portfolio products such as synthetic CDOs and nth-to-default baskets, with enhanced returns and customized risks, borrowed techniques from the securitization business. The number and types of products created were numerous. We consider a few as follows.

First-to-default basket: In a first-to-default basket, the risk buyer typically takes a credit position in each credit equal to the notional at stake. After the first credit event, the first-to-default note (swap) stops and the investor no longer bears the credit risk to the basket. The first-to-default credit-linked note will either be unwound immediately after the credit event—this is usually the case when the notes are issued by a special purpose vehicle (SPV), a manager of sorts of the cash flows of the portfolio, whether active or passive—or remain outstanding. This is often the case with issuers, with losses on default carried forward and settled at maturity. Losses on default are calculated as the difference between par and the final price of a reference obligation, as determined by a bid-side dealer poll for reference obligations, plus or minus, in some cases, the mark-to-market on any embedded currency/interest rate swaps transforming the cash flows of the collateral.

Collateralized debt obligation (CDO): Collateralized debt obligations discussed earlier are similar to asset-backed securities and structured finance products. In a CDO, a portfolio of bonds, loans, or other fixed income securities is gathered together, and used to create a new set of fixed income securities collateralized by the portfolio. There are many types, forms, structures, and names for CDOs. Some are securitized portfolios of bonds, real estate properties, asset-backed securities (ABS), portfolios backed by the revenues and the obligations of mortgages (MBSs) or CDSs (called, as stated earlier, synthetic CDOs), and so on. There are therefore many CDO variations with a plethora of names, and optional rights based on the underlying portfolio. Further, due to their complexity and at times nontransparency, their pricing is obviously difficult and may further bear counterparty risk.

CDOs typically issue four classes of securities designated as senior debt, mezzanine debt, subordinate debt, and equity. Specific examples will be considered in the next section. Any losses from the portfolio of investments are applied to equity first before being applied to other ones. As a result, products ranging from the risky equity debt to the relatively low-risk senior debt can be created from one basket of bonds or loans (see Figure 10.3). CDOs can be split, into two broad classes: balance sheet CDOs and arbitrage CDOs. Balance sheet CDOs are those that result in transfer of loans from the balance sheet and hence impact the balance sheet of the originator. Arbitrage CDOs are those where the originator merely repackages an assembly of assets: buying loans or bonds or ABS from the market, pooling them together, and securitizing these packaged assets. The prime objective in balance sheet CDOs is the reduction of regulatory capital, while the purpose in arbitrage CDOs is making arbitraging profits.

From a legal point of view, most CDOs are constructed via a special-purpose vehicle (SPV), currently proposed to be an important and regulating intermediary that can assure buyers and sellers in such products.

The term *CDO* is often used as a generic term that includes a broad variety of products:

- Collateralized bond obligations (CBOs)—CDOs backed primarily by bonds.
- Collateralized loan obligations (CLOs)—CDOs backed by leveraged loans.
- Structured finance CDOs (SFCDOs)—CDOs backed by asset-backed securities.

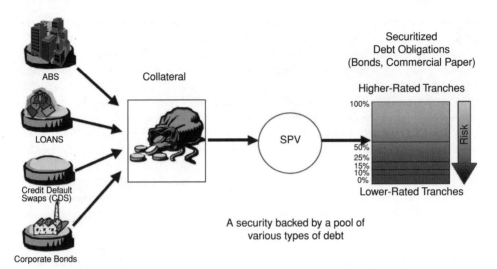

FIGURE 10.3 Securitized Debt Obligations
Source: BNP Paribas.

- Collateralized mortgage obligation (CMOs)—CDOs backed primarily by residential or commercial mortgages.
- Commercial real estate CDOs (CRE CDOs)—CDOs backed by real estate assets.
- CDO-squared—CDO backed by securities issued by other CDO vehicles.
- CDO^n—Generic term for CDO3 (CDO cubed) and higher. These are particularly difficult vehicles to model due to the possible repetition of exposures in underlying CDOs.

Finally, third-generation credit derivatives are pointing to many future developments. These result from an evolution from basket derivatives through CDO^n and other products. Market value CDO transactions such as collateralized fund obligations (CFOs) are such innovations, alongside constant proportion portfolio insurance (CPPI) and constant proportion debt obligations (CPDOs) as we outline later. The CFO methodology in particular enhances the framework of market value transactions as opposed to classical cash transactions where one disregards the market value of the asset. The net asset value and liquidity profile monitoring are key factors in the CFO methodology as well as in the following types of transactions:

- Structured investment vehicle (SIV), which can be seen as a long or long-short credit-only hedge fund strategy.
- Market value CDO.
- Equity default swap equity CDO.
- FX CDO.
- Commodities CDO.

Some of these financial products as well as others are briefly discussed below:
Forward-starting CDS: The only difference between a forward-starting contract and a regular contract is that a regular CDS starts immediately, while a forward

CDS starts at a future date. The pricing of such CDS involves therefore multiple time periods and requires the development of a dynamic model to be calibrated.

Forward-starting CDO and possibly options on CDO tranches: The availability of CDO data for multiple time horizons presents an important challenge to develop a dynamic model that fits market data and tracks the evolution of the credit risk of a portfolio. For example, options on tranches of CDOs cannot be valued in a satisfactory way without a dynamic model. Currently, some research is devoted to such problems.

Market value CDO: Market value CDOs closely resemble hedge funds. They are considered to be asset-backed securities (ABS) due to their fundamental structure. As with other ABS, a market value CDO is a debt obligation issued by a bankruptcy-remote SPV secured by some form of receivables. CDOs also often use overcollateralization and subordinated notes to achieve the desired credit quality. These products differ from a traditional ABS structure with respect to:

- The servicer's level of involvement.
- The diversity of assets.
- The number of tranches issued.

In a market value CDO, the portfolio manager does more than simply collect and service the portfolio; the manager also actively trades the asset pool (as a hedge fund manager would). Common market value CDO portfolios include cash, treasuries, bonds, loans, commercial papers, mezzanine debt, distressed debt, equity, emerging market debt, and even other CDOs. The primary impetus for issuing a CDO is either to take advantage of an arbitrage opportunity or to improve a financial institution's capital ratios. The issuance of a market value CDO provides an insurance company or investment manager with the means to rapidly expand assets under management, leading in turn to increased management fees. Demand for market value CDOs typically originates from investors who seek some exposure to the high yield market, but are constrained by minimum rating requirements. Market value CDOs also provide an investment opportunity not commonly available in traditional ABS, such as notes whose credit ratings cover a broader credit spectrum (AAA to B) and long terms to maturity (4 to 15 years).

Collateralized fund obligations (CFO): Unlike cash flow deals, underlying asset pools for CFOs are hedge fund assets' valued at each valuation date at their marked-to-market (MTM) prices. The market value CFO meets principal (if applicable) and interest liabilities by generating cash from trading assets and from interest or dividends on invested assets. Hedge fund assets do not generate predictable cash flow streams, but have significant market value, upside potential, as well as significant downside potential. Market value deal managers trade actively and aggressively and can employ leverage. Of course, not every trade results in a gain. The ratio of the market value of assets to the face value of liabilities is a key risk metric of a market value CFO. The amount of debt or note tranches that a CFO can issue as a percentage of market value is limited by a haircut to maintain a set level of theoretical overcollateralization. The CFO methodology enhances the framework of a market value transaction as opposed to a classical cash transaction where one disregards the market value of the asset. The net asset value and liquidity profile monitoring are key factors in CFO methodology, and also in other new types of transactions such the structured investment vehicle (SIV), which can be seen as long or long-short credit-only hedge fund strategy, market value CDO, equity default swap, equity CDO, FX CDO, commodities CDO, and so on.

Constant proportion portfolio insurance (CPPI): The constant proportion portfolio insurance (CPPI) is a technique for leveraging up investments while providing full or partial protection. This method has been used extensively in equities and hedge funds and is now applied to credit market. The investment is comprised of two parts: risky and risk-free assets (the latter consisting mainly of zero coupon bonds). The higher the amount of risky assets in the portfolio, the higher the potential returns over the principal amount. The fraction of risky assets in a dynamic basket is referred to as "exposure." It is adjusted from time to time to maximize potential returns and ensure principal protection. CPPI rebalances between an investment in the risky asset and a zero coupon bond to provide principal protection.

Constant proportion debt obligation (CPDO): Constant proportion debt obligations (CPDOs) respond to a growing need for rated coupons. CPDOs are essentially a variant of CPPI. The main differences are in their fixed coupon with no upside and different leverage rules. Like credit CPPI, CPDOs provide a leveraged exposure to credit portfolios, although they do not offer principal protection to investors. Constant proportion debt obligations (CPDOs) are engineered to combine attractive yields and high ratings for investors who typically take exposure to a large diversified portfolio of credits without engendering the traditional correlation risk present in single-tranche CDO (STCDO) transactions. A constant proportion debt obligation could be backed by an index of debt securities (such as CDX or Itraxx) or could be deal specific. This is periodically rolled, thus introducing market risk through the rollover. The leverage of the CPDO is periodically readjusted to match the asset and liability spread.

*   *   *

Currently, credit derivatives are reengineered following the 2008 financial crisis and to meet potential future regulation. Their usefulness fuels a continuous financial innovation to provide liquidity and at the same time provide sources of profit to financial institutions. Their pricing, however, remains challenging, although the principles applied in practice are simple, as we will see in the next section. We consider next a number of examples.

CDO EXAMPLE: COLLATERALIZED MORTGAGE OBLIGATIONS (CMOS)

CMOs or real estate investment conduits (REMICs) consist of mortgage contracts (or other real estate assets) where the assets are used as collateral, and the individual granted the mortgage is the borrower. Such contracts provide initially a loan to buy, say, a home, and in return, the individual makes a scheduled payment of the principal and the interest. There are of course many variations of such contracts, some with payment of the interest only for a certain period of time and then a payment of both the principal and the interest accrued. When the loan is substantially smaller than the price of the house, the mortgage is secured by the house collateral. For this reason, the securitization of collateralized mortgage-backed debt obligations seems to be safe in periods of increasing or stable real estate prices. Their relative safety and the regular interest and principal payments they make have desirable yields and are suited for investors seeking safe and fixed incomes. However, adverse movements in the price of collateral can lead to a substantial default risk. In such cases, a combination of highly leveraged home acquisitions combined with an unexpected decline in home prices led to a default contagion in mortgages. Given the political and social importance of home ownership, governments have contributed to mortgage marketing and safety through insurance vehicles. These vehicles, such as GNMA or Ginnie Mae, FNMA or Fannie Mae, and Freddie Mac, provide guarantees, allowing mortgage banks to lend more money. When CMOs are used as (credit risk) pass-through vehicles, these same institutions are freed from some of the risk they own and can therefore lend or secure even more mortgage contracts.

EXAMPLE: THE CDO AND SPV

In Figure 10.3, BNP Paribas provides a typical CDO with, on the left side, collateralized assets (of ABSs, loans, CDSs, and corporate bonds). Figure 10.4, however, indicates the CDO waterfall. A portfolio of assets produces revenues (interest and principal) used first to feed obligations to tranche holders (first tranche A, the superior tranche and so on to lower tranches) until the equity tranche holder (tranche C in Figure 10.4) is paid for. Excess revenues are then diverted to a reserve managed by a special-purpose vehicle (SPV) as well as used to pay for performance and administrative fees of the CDO. Finally, excess portfolio losses sustained by the portfolio may be compensated in whole or in part by the tranche holders' notional. These relationships can turn out to be extremely complex and at times nontransparent to an individual investor. For these reasons, the pricing of the CDO is necessarily difficult and at times can be questionable. Furthermore, a portfolio can be composed of one or more types of assets, such as rated and junk corporate bonds. On the right side of Figure 10.3, the CDO notional is layered into tranches (note that there can be more than three tranches). The lower the tranche, the higher the risk assumed by the tranche holder, and therefore its rates of return (indicated by the basis points allocated to a tranche) will reflect the risk it assumes (Figure 10.4). In Figure 10.3, the lower tranche assumes the first 10 percent of the notional loss, while the second tranche assumes the next 5 percent notional loss, and so on. Such a loss is incurred, however, only after the first (equity or junior) tranche has been wiped out. The senior tranche assumes 50 percent of the notional risk, which is paid for only once the first 50 percent of all other lower tranches have all been liquidated. In addition, Figure 10.3 points out a special-purpose vehicle (SPV). An SPV is essentially a passive or active intermediary manager (contracted for at the time the CDO is created). An active SPV may be called to manage the collateral portfolio, collecting and allocating portfolio returns to tranche holders, set aside funds to meet future tranches payments, and so on. The roles of an SPV, acting as a trust for the CDO, can also vary. When a CDO is assembled and delivered to an SPV, the SPV may securitize and manage the portfolio into financial papers, debt obligations, bonds, commercial papers, and so forth (acting, however, as the trust CDO manager and interacting with liquidity and swap providers). In this sense, the SPV can provide the

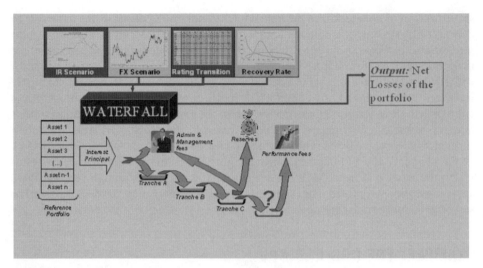

FIGURE 10.4   A Generic Market Value CDO Structure
Source: BNP Paribas.

protection for buyers and the protection for sellers, respectively, while at the same time handling the many legal, tax, and other issues associated with the CDO.

A CDO is thus just a series of structured rights and obligations that buyers and sellers of the CDO tranches assume with collateral of the underlying portfolio. Throughout, returns are distributed to the CDO according to rules defined initially and based on the tranches' notional (Figure 10.4). A common rule provides for the senior tranche to be paid first and the equity tranche paid last. In most CDOs, the portfolio collateral can be invaded by the SPV to set aside funds to meet payment obligations to the tranches as well as meet regulation capital adequacy ratios (if there is indeed a regulation of such financial products). If the portfolio does not produce sufficient returns, funds set aside by the SPV can be used or assets liquidated to meet obligations to tranche holders. At the CDO maturity, the equity tranche is paid in full only after the holder of the superior and other tranches have been fully paid. Maturity of a CDO can be defined in several ways as well. A CDO maturity with an underlying portfolio of bonds can be equated to the maturity of these bonds or at their default time—whichever comes first. Similarly, for an underlying portfolio of mortgage loans, maturity is defined when borrowers have repaid their mortgage debt in full. These payments can be complex, however, since mortgage holders may have options to liquidate at specific dates, options to refinance anytime or at specific times, and so on. Default can also be a cause for a CDO expiry (in which case expiry is a random time). For example, a mortgage holder may default for personal reasons. Default due to the home's collateral market price falling below the mortgage debt amount may also lead to a contagious risk in a portfolio of subprime mortgages and therefore to a CDO's expiry. These defaults and options have both costs and values that ought to be accounted for. Holders of the CDO portfolio obligations assume then credit (default) and interest risk as well as price, currency, and liquidity risks. The interaction of these risks in an unfavorable economic environment can therefore be important and difficult to value.

CDOs can become complex and misunderstood by buyers and sellers (and therefore it is difficult to know what their true intrinsic price is), providing a chance for the initiated to profit immensely by the arbitrage opportunity such vehicles provide (in particular when CDOs are secured either by excessive positive ratings or by third-party insurance). At the same time, these vehicles provide lenders an opportunity to intermediate between individual and financial markets and make money without (apparently) assuming any risk. For example, a bank, by selling debt obligations to a CDO originator, may shrink its balance sheet liabilities, increase its equity and its equity-to-debt ratio, and meet more easily capital adequacy requirements (CAR) and thus increase its liquidity and ability to take more risks. In this process, the bank is reduced to a financial intermediary with a locked-in population who turn to banks to obtain their needed loans. In some cases, banks are both intermediaries as well as investors-insurers to CDOs and thus assume some of the CDOs' risks. A hedge fund manager, with an appetite for risk, may lock in the high yield of the CDO and at the same time obtain options on desirable financial or real (assets) properties. Such investments are not similar to investments in bonds since bonds have well-defined maturities, payments, and principals, while in CDOs the maturity is variable and so are the interest returns and the principal payments. The presumption that investment in CDOs is as secure as Treasury bills can of course be misleading—their yield accounts for their added risks.

A structure based on the number of tranches, their rights and obligations, the sequencing of payments, and so forth reflects some of the elements that render such instruments extremely rich and diverse, attracting a broad variety of investors. These characteristics explain their extraordinary marketing success and growth prior to the credit crisis of 2007–2009. For these reasons, these instruments are most likely to remain an essential and dominant part of the financial landscape (although with different names).

Modeling Credit Derivatives

To model and price CDOs, there are numerous considerations due to the CDOs' portfolio assets compositions, their dependence, contagion risk, and apportionment of payments and risks to CDO tranches. The essential steps to follow include:

- Select the assets that define the underlying portfolio (such as bonds, MBS, ABS, etc.); their returns (whether deterministic or stochastic); their individual statistical dependence; and their aggregate dependence on rare events, contagions, macroeconomic factors, and so on.
- Model the default probabilities of the individual names to be insured by the CDO (which can be done financially via the CDS spreads if the CDS for that name is sufficiently liquid). In real terms modeling of losses and defaults involves multiple sources of risks, as stated earlier.
- Define the CDO structure (the tranches) and the distribution of returns (by basis points) and the notional of each tranche. Define the rights and the obligations for each tranche (also called payment waterfall in Figure 10.4), including:
  - The sequencing and the schedule of returns allocated to tranche holders.
  - The sequencing and the schedule of losses of notional allocated to tranches.
  - The legal rights and the recourse to each tranche holder (many of which are defined as clauses in the offering circular).

- Modeling the correlation (or more accurately, the dependency structure) of the portfolio's names and their effect of intra- and inter-tranches' correlations.
- Modeling the rules for risk and returns sharing both over time and at the CDO expiry.
- Rating and securitizing the portfolio and selling the CDO in a financial market, rating the portfolio appreciably to secure its acceptability by investors, and manage the risks and the pricing of portfolios losses.

The modeling and pricing techniques of such credit products, can be daunting. Pricing models require generally a great deal of financial information and their model analysis is based on extensive optimization and simulation results.

CDO: Quantitative Models

CDO quantitative models are varied, defined in terms of the number of assets; their statistical and probability characteristics and relationships; their gains (coupon payments, dividends, returns, etc.); their losses; their number of tranches; and their distribution of gain and losses. For simplicity we consider first a numerical example, and subsequently more general models.

We proceed by a simple numerical example, gradually building it up to describe assets and probability models for assets and notional dependence. For example, if a portfolio consists only of corporate coupon-paying and rated bonds, then of course the returns are predictable as long as the bond has not defaulted, while the bond prices (making up the portfolio of collateral bonds) are likely to be a function of interest rates and the rating of firms and institutions that have issued these bonds. The advantage of this approach is that it is instructive, stating explicitly the underlying assumptions that define the portfolio asset dependence structure.

EXAMPLE: A CDO WITH NUMBERS

Consider a portfolio of 10 bonds each with notional value of $1 million (M) and a CDO notional of $10M. We assume three tranches: a 25 percent senior tranche (with notional of $2.5M), a 35 percent mezzanine tranche (with notional of $3.5M), and a junior equity tranche with the remaining 40 percent (or a notional of $4M). The CDO contract apportions revenues to the tranches according to the following interest:

Senior tranche:	50 basis points (BP)	Equivalent to 0.50 percent of the notional
Mezzanine tranche:	100 BP	Equivalent to 1 percent of the notional
Equity tranche:	250 BP	Equivalent to 2.5 percent of the total return on the notional

In case of no portfolio default, the notional remains whole and each of the tranches receives income according to its contracted BP revenues, or:

$$\text{Senior tranche: } (2,500,000)(0.5/100) = \$12,500$$
$$\text{Mezzanine tranche: } (3,500,000)(1.0/100) = \$35,000$$
$$\text{Equity tranche: } (4,000,000)(2.5/100) = \$100,000$$

The portfolio total return on its $10M notional is therefore a total return on investment (TRI):

$$TRI = 12,500 + 35,000 + 100,000 = \$147,500$$

If there is no default, the rate of return for the equity tranche holder is thus substantial. Say that a bond default occurs, resulting in a loss of $1M, with a remaining CDO notional of $9M. Since the equity tranche is first to cover the loss of the bond, its notional at the next distribution period is $4M – $1M = $3M, and distribution of the TRI will be:

Senior tranche: (2,500,000)(0.5/100) = $12,500
Mezzanine tranche: (3,500,000)(1.0/100) = $35,000
Equity tranche: (3,000,000)(2.5/100) = $75,000

The portfolio total returns on the remaining CDO notional of $9M is now:

$$TRI = 12,500 + 35,000 + 75,000 = \$122,500$$

Note that the equity holder now has a return of $75,000 compared to the previous $100,000 while the mezzanine and the senior tranches are not affected. These tranches will not be affected, in fact, until the equity notional is liquidated. For this reason, the senior tranche is often deemed very safe while the equity tranche is not.

Assume next that four additional bonds default, resulting in a residual CDO notional of $5M. The remaining portfolio notional is then: $9M – $4M = $5M. Since the equity holder has a notional of $3M, he is wiped out with the remaining $5M – $3M = $2M absorbed by the mezzanine tranche (whose residual notional is 3.5 – 2 = 1.5). At the next period, the distribution of returns is as follows:

Senior tranche: (2,500,000)(0.5/100) = $12,500
Mezzanine tranche: (1,500,000)(1.0/100) = $15,000
Equity tranche: $0

while the total returns with a remaining CDO notional of $4M for the mezzanine and superior tranches (since the notional of the equity tranche holder has been wiped out) is:

$$TRI = (12,500) + 15,000 = \$27,500$$

This demonstrative example indicates that pricing a CDO is necessarily fueled by the losses in notional and the tranches' basis points that are compensating the tranche holders for their losses. This model indicates therefore the essential modeling elements of a CDO: losses, structure (or tranches—theirs rights and obligations) and the price of each tranche as indicated in Figure 10.5.

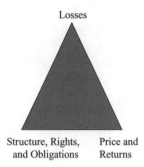

Losses

Structure, Rights,   Price and
and Obligations   Returns

FIGURE 10.5 Elements of a CDO Model (with and without Intermediate SPV)

EXAMPLE: A CDO OF ZERO COUPON BONDS

The following model is a simple one-period example, or equivalently, a payment made initially to tranches to cover notional losses at another set period, say T, with expiry of the bonds an instant before, or $T-1$. The purpose of this example is to set the stage for a more general multiperiod CDO. Say that a portfolio consists of k types of zero coupon bonds, with $(M_i(0), B_i(0))\, i = 1, 2, \dots k$ their number and the initial price at initiation. The initial price of such a portfolio is defined for simplicity by:

$$\mathbf{B}(0) = \sum_{i=1}^{k} \sum_{j=1}^{M_i(0)} B_i(0) \tag{10.26}$$

As in the previous example, we let the CDO initial notional $N(0)$ be equal to the portfolio price. This notional is thus a sort of insurance for the portfolio with notional apportioned to the three tranches: superior, mezzanine, and equity, given by $N_S(0)$, $N_M(0)$, $N_E(0)$ with $N(0) = N_S(0) + N_M(0) + N_E(0)$. Let the cumulative loss during these period be $Z(T-1)$. In this case, the residual notional for each of the tranche holders can be written as a set of three simultaneous equations:

$$0 \leq N_S(T) = Min\,(N(T-1), N_S(0))$$

$$0 \leq N_M(T) = Max\,[Min\,\{N(T-1) - N_S(T), N_M(0)\}\,;0]$$

$$0 \leq N_E(T) = N(T-1) - N_S(T) - N_M(T) \quad \text{with} \quad N(T-1) = N(0) - Z(T-1)$$

$$\tag{10.27}$$

Explicitly, the residual of the senior tranche equals the residual notional of the CDO or that of the superior tranche, whichever is smallest. This equation implies that the notional of both the mezzanine and the equity tranche holders has been liquidated. Similarly, the notional of the mezzanine tranche holder is equal to the residual notional, once the superior tranche has been paid or the initial mezzanine notional whichever is smaller. However to avoid negativity of the mezzanine tranche holder at expiry, we have added an additional $Max\{-,0\}$ operator, which is not needed in this particular case, but will be needed for a notional collateralized by securities for examples. Finally, the equity holder notional equals the residual notional once the superior and the mezzanine tranches have been paid. When the equity holder assumes the residual value of the portfolio then the equity holder collects:

$$0 \le N_E(T) = N(T-1) - N_S(T) - N_M(T)$$

where $N(T-1)$ is the portfolio (notional) residual at time T, the zero coupon bonds' expiry date. These expressions can be written as follows (all of which are a function of the initial notional and the cumulative losses):

$$0 \le N_S(T) = N(0) - Max\,(Z(T-1),\,N(0) - N_S(0))$$
$$0 \le N_M(T) = Max\,[Min\,\{Max\,(N(0) - N_S(0) - Z(T-1),\,0)\,,\,N_M(0)\}\,;0]$$
$$0 \le N_E(T) = N(T-1) - N_S(T) - N_M(T) \quad \text{with} \quad N(T-1) = N(0) - Z(T-1)$$

$$(10.28)$$

If the cumulative loss in notional up to time $T-1$ has a risk-neutral probability distribution, model say $f^Q(Z(T-1))$, then the current price of the terminal notional equals the current notional less the price (risk premium for the potential future aggregate) loss assumed by each tranche. Namely:

$$N_S(0) - \pi_S(0) = e^{-R_f(0,T-1)}E^Q\{N(0) - Max\,(Z(T-1),\,N(0) - N_S(0))\}$$
$$N_M(0) - \pi_M(0) = e^{-R_f(0,T-1)}E^Q\{Max\,[Min\,\{Max\,(N(0) - N_S(0) - Z(T-1),\,0)\,,\,N_M(0)\}\,;0]\}$$
$$N_E(0) - \pi_E(0) = e^{-R_f(0,T-1)}E^Q(N(0) - Z(T-1)) - (N_S(0) - \pi_S(0)) - (N_M(0) - \pi_M(0))$$

$$(10.29)$$

In other words, the price of the superior tranche notional (the premium received by the superior tranche holder) equals $\pi_S(0) = b_S \alpha N(0)$ where b_S is the basis point return for the senior tranche and α is the proportion of the notional held by the senior tranche holder. Similarly for the mezzanine tranche and finally for the equity tranche holder, the price $\pi_E(0) = b_E(1 - \alpha - \beta)N(0)$ is the price for the residual equity notional (with b_E the tranche basis point and $(1 - \alpha - \beta)N(0)$ the tranche notional). It equals the present expected residual price of the CDO notional. This simple case points to essential difficulties in pricing CDO tranches: namely, defining the future losses and determining the risk-neutral framework to allow a no-arbitrage price. Such problems are resolved by finding an implied risk-neutral distribution for the losses that require optional information (in particular derivatives drawn on the underlying portfolio; see Chapter 11). The previous equation indicates however a correspondence between losses and prices. For example, say that cumulative losses are assumed to have a probability distribution with parameters (μ, ς, χ) or $f^Q(Z(T-1)|\mu, \varsigma, \chi)$. In this case, the residual notional price defined earlier, using the risk-neutral (no-arbitrage) model $f^Q(Z(T-1)|\mu, \varsigma, \chi)$ for losses, provides with equations (10.28) and (10.29) a system of three equations in the three unknown parameters μ, ς, χ—the parameters of the risk-neutral distribution of losses. In other words, loss pricing in the CDO is implied in the risk premium of the CDO tranches.

A development of equation (10.29) in terms of basis points yields and setting the random proportional loss in notional to be $z(T-1) = Z(T-1)/N(0)$, yields:

$$b_S(0) = \frac{1 - \alpha e^{-R_f(0,T-1)} + e^{-R_f(0,T-1)} E^Q \{Max\,(z(T-1) - (1-\alpha)\,,0)\}}{\alpha} \qquad (10.30)$$

$$b_M(0) = 1 - \frac{e^{-R_f(0,T-1)} E^Q \{Max\,[Min\,\{Max\,(1-\alpha-z(t-1),0)\,,\beta\}\,;0]\}}{\beta} \qquad (10.31)$$

$$b_E(0) = 1 - \frac{e^{-R_f(0,T-1)} \left(1 - \alpha\,(1-b_S(0)) - \beta\,(1-b_M(0))\right)}{1-\alpha-\beta} - \frac{e^{-R_f(0,T-1)} E^Q\,(z(T-1))}{1-\alpha-\beta} \qquad (10.32)$$

Thus, given the basis points (tranche prices) $b_S(0), b_M(0), b_E(0)$, a solution of (10.30)–(10.32) provides a solution for the implied default probability parameters μ, ς, χ. This problem is thus a sort of insurance contract with a price for risk paid initially as an insurance premium to tranche holders that assume the potential losses later. This formulation has the advantage of defining a specific probability model for the proportional loss as a probability distribution to be defined between 0 and 1. The definition of these distributions is challenging as they are assumed to represent the aggregate statistical behavior of the portfolio and ought to be based on a limited number of parameters that can be estimated either statistically (if valuation of the CDO is actuarial) or implicitly (based on a no-arbitrage assumption). In our case, we can assume, for example, that proportional losses of notional are modeled by a variety of probability models we have to select to be both statistically realistic and computationally feasible. Here we list a number of such models, moving from the simple to the more general (and more complex):

- Given by a two-parameter beta probability distribution.
- Given by a multivariate beta probability distribution expressing the correlation structure of the underlying portfolio.
- Given by mixture probability distributions representing the potential mixtures probabilities of rare events (expressing rare and significant losses).
- Given by logit probability estimates of the odds of a proportional loss in terms of numerous and likely macroeconomic and other factors (or other related econometric model estimates).
- Given by a multivariate logit model expressing the covariation of assets (for example, expressing the default probabilities of codependent and rated bonds).
- Given by a copula, defining a general (and statistically appropriate) model based on the marginal probability distributions of the bonds default (and by implication the loss in notional).
- Other models designed to be both statistically reasonable and computationally tractable.

Throughout, a choice of models is based on a realistic appreciation of the information available (prices of the tranches and other relevant statistical information), the number of parameters that can be estimated with the available underlying statistical information, and of course our ability to compute these parameters under a no-arbitrage assumption (and obtain a financial estimate of the probability of a notional loss). Examples and problems are considered subsequently and in particular in the www.charlestapiero.com web site. Such problems are in general technically daunting, however.

The one-period problem example can be generalized further to two or more periods and to rated coupon-paying default bonds. Consider first the number $\tilde{M}_i(t)$ of nondefaulted bonds rated i at time t in a portfolio of coupon-paying bonds, and assume that it is represented by a discrete time stochastic process:

$$\tilde{M}_i(t+1) = M_i(t) - \tilde{n}_i(t), \ M_i(0), \ i = 1, 2, \ldots, k \text{ given} \tag{10.33}$$

where $\tilde{n}_i(t)$ are the random number of bonds rated i that have defaulted at time t (defined as a random default process). The next example provides a simplified (albeit still complex) development of such CDOs.

EXAMPLE: A CDO OF DEFAULT COUPON-PAYING BONDS

Consider a CDO whose initial notional is $N(0)$ with an underlying portfolio consisting of rated coupon-paying bonds. The CDO has three tranches, a superior, a mezzanine, and an equity tranche, each assuming initially the notional $N_S(0) = \alpha N(0)$, $N_M(0) = \beta N(0)$, and $N_E(0) = (1 - \alpha - \beta)N(0)$, respectively. At time t, the probability of a bond rated i to default is $\tilde{p}_i(t)$, a random variable. Assume first (and for simplicity) that the bonds in any rating class are statistically independent. Thus, if there are $\tilde{M}_i(t)$ live bonds at time t and if there is no migration of bonds from one rate to another, the number of bonds defaulting and the number of bonds remaining alive at time $t + 1$ are given by $\tilde{n}_i(t)$ and $\tilde{M}_i(t+1)$, given by equation (10.33):

$$\tilde{n}_i(t) \sim \binom{\tilde{M}_i(t)}{\tilde{n}_i(t)} [\tilde{p}_i(t)]^{\tilde{n}_i(t)} [1 - \tilde{p}_i(t)]^{\tilde{M}_i(t) - \tilde{n}_i(t)} \tag{10.34}$$

The number of default bonds at time t is thus a mixture binomial probability distribution since $\tilde{p}_i(t)$, the probability of default, is not known for sure. Further, any prediction on the number of future defaults of bonds will in fact be confronted with random live bonds and random default probabilities. For example, consider the initial period and let the number of defaulting bonds be $\tilde{n}_i(0)$; this results in a Lexian (binomial randomized) probability distribution, with mean and variance:

$$E(\tilde{n}_i(0) | M_i(0)) = M_i(0)E(\tilde{p}_i(0))$$

$$\text{var}(\tilde{n}_i(0) | M_i(0)) = M_i(0)E(\tilde{p}_i(0))[1 - E(\tilde{p}_i(0))] + M_i(0)(M_i(0) - 1))\text{var}(\tilde{p}_i(0))$$

$$\tag{10.35}$$

However, a prediction for future losses, say at a future time, $t + 1$, is a mixture distribution with:

$$\tilde{n}_i(t+1) \sim \binom{\tilde{M}_i(t) - \tilde{n}_i(t)}{\tilde{n}_i(t+1)} [\tilde{p}_i(t+1)]^{\tilde{n}_i(t+1)} [1 - \tilde{p}_i(t+1)]^{\tilde{M}_i(t) - \tilde{n}_i(t) - \tilde{n}_i(t+1)}$$

(10.36)

If each live bond pays a coupon c, then at any time t the total portfolio revenue available to meet obligations to the CDO tranche holders is random and given by:

$$C(t) = c\left(\tilde{M}_i(t) - \tilde{n}_i(t)\right) = c\left(M_i(0) - \sum_{j=0}^{t} \tilde{n}_i(j)\right)$$

(10.37)

A recursive development of the number of default processes over time leads, however, to:

At the first period, $t = 0$: $\tilde{n}_i(0) \sim \binom{M_i(0)}{\tilde{n}_i(0)} [\tilde{p}_i(0)]^{\tilde{n}_i(0)} [1 - \tilde{p}_i(0)]^{M_i(0) - \tilde{n}_i(0)}$

(10.38)

At period $t = 1$:

$$\tilde{n}_i(1) \binom{M_i(0) - \tilde{n}_i(0)}{\tilde{n}_i(1)} [\tilde{p}_i(1)]^{\tilde{n}_i(1)} [1 - \tilde{p}_i(1)]^{M_i(0) - \tilde{n}_i(0) - \tilde{n}_i(1)}$$

(10.39)

And therefore to a joint probability distribution:

$$f(\tilde{n}_i(0), \tilde{n}_i(1)) = \binom{M_i(0) - \tilde{n}_i(0)}{\tilde{n}_i(1)} \binom{M_i(0)}{\tilde{n}_i(0)}$$

$$\times [\tilde{p}_i(0)]^{\tilde{n}_i(0)} [\tilde{p}_i(1)]^{\tilde{n}_i(1)} [1 - \tilde{p}_i(0)]^{M_i(0) - \tilde{n}_i(0)} [1 - \tilde{p}_i(1)]^{M_i(0) - \tilde{n}_i(0) - \tilde{n}_i(1)}$$

(10.40)

And generally at times $t = 1, 2, \ldots, T$, we have the explicit joint probability distribution for the number of defaulting bonds at times $0, 1, 2, \ldots, t$:

$$f(\tilde{n}_i(0), \tilde{n}_i(1), \ldots, \tilde{n}_i(t), \tilde{p}_i(0), \tilde{p}_i(1), \ldots, \tilde{p}_i(t))$$

$$= \prod_{j=1}^{t} \binom{M_i(0) - \sum_{j=1}^{t-1} \tilde{n}_i(j)}{\tilde{n}_i(t)} \prod_{j=0}^{t} \left\{ [\tilde{p}_i(j)]^{\tilde{n}_i(j)} [1 - \tilde{p}_i(j)]^{M_i(0) - \sum_{j=1}^{t} \tilde{n}_i(j)} \right\}$$

(10.41)

Note that the default probability of a bond at time $t = 0$ applies to the period $t = 0$ and may change from period to period. Further, these probabilities can be dependent, reflecting contagious processes or their dependence on macroeconomic and other factors (such as interest rates, the stock market, and so on). In particular, bonds that are differently rated have dependent probabilities of defaults as they are both dependent on the macroeconomic factors at play at any given time. Such models are therefore necessarily complex and may be a poor representation of the physical and actuarial statistical factors that define the loss probabilities. For this reason a number of other techniques are used that emphasize an arbitrary definition of the default probabilities, expressed in terms of a select few parameters, and use observed data to calibrate the model default probability distribution. As stated in Chapter 4, a careful application of copulas can in such cases be useful. For example, for two risk sources with marginal cumulative density functions (u_i, v_j) and an algebraic structure defined by $C(u_i, v_j)$, an appropriate copula might be found and used to model the joint cumulative distribution corresponding to the covariations of the two specific risk sources defined by the copula. An explicit expression for the probability distribution of bonds rated i and j default rates can be defined in terms of the copula as follows:

$$C(u_i, v_j) = C(F_i(\eta_i), F_j(\eta_j)) = F_{ij}(\eta_i, \eta_f) \tag{10.42}$$

While the joint probability distribution is:

$$f_{ij}(\eta_i, \eta_f) = \frac{\partial^2 C(u_i, v_j)}{\partial \eta_i \partial \eta_j} = \frac{\partial^2 F_{ij}(\eta_i, \eta_f)}{\partial \eta_i \partial \eta_j} \tag{10.43}$$

This approach is broadly used in practice and at times without much care given to the selection of the appropriate copula, or using a blanket copula to cover all the cross-risks between assets. For this reason, it is important to be aware and be specific about what a copula actually implies. Nevertheless, such an approach is practically useful when Monte Carlo simulation is used to simulate the joint probability distributions of simultaneous risk events. This example is expanded further to account for the migration of rated bonds.

EXAMPLE: A CDO OF RATED BONDS

Say that a CDO consists of $M_i(0)$ rated bonds, each of which has the same par value $\bar{B}$. The initial notional is thus:

$$N(0) = \sum_{i=1}^{m-1} M_i(0)\bar{B}, \; \bar{B} = B_i(0, T)(1 + R_i(0, T))^T \tag{10.44}$$

where $B_i(0, T)$ is the market price of a bond rated i at time $t = 0$, while $R_i(0, T)$ is the interest rate of this bond at time $t = 0$ whose maturity is at time T. As a result, the market price of the portfolio is:

$$S(0) = \sum_{i=1}^{m-1} M_i(0)B_i(0, T) \tag{10.45}$$

We consider three tranches: senior, mezzanine, and equity with initial proportional $N_S(0) = \alpha N(0)$, $N_M(0) = \beta N(0)$, $N_E(0) = (1 - \alpha - \beta)N(0)$ where α, β, $1 - \alpha - \beta$ are their respective proportions. The underlying portfolio whose current price is $S(0)$ is therefore the underlying collateral to the CDO. Each bond is assumed as well to provide a coupon of c per period, paid as long as the bond is alive. The total return of the portfolio are therefore $\tilde{C}(t) = \sum_{i=1}^{m-1} c\tilde{M}_i(t)$ where $\tilde{M}_i(t)$ is the number of live bonds at time t. These returns will be used to meet obligations to the tranche holders, as we will see. Bonds may over time both migrate from one rate to another and default. The rate m is used to denote default and has an absorbing probability $p_{im}(t), i = 1, 2, ..m-1$ at time t, while the migration probabilities are $p_{ij}(t), i, j = 1, 2, ..m-1, i \neq j$. The number of live bonds at any time t are thus random variables denoted by $\tilde{M}_i(t), i = 1, 2, ..m-1$, while the number of bonds rated i defaulting at time t are $\tilde{n}_i(t), i = 1, 2, ..m-1$. Rated bonds can migrate from period to period, however. We denote by $\tilde{n}_{ij}(t), i, j = 1, 2, ..m-1$ the number of migrating bonds from i to j. In this case, the number of bonds rated i at time t is given by:

$$\tilde{M}_i(t+1) = \tilde{M}_i(t) - \tilde{n}_i(t) - \sum_{\substack{j \neq i}}^{m-1} \tilde{n}_{ij}(t) + \sum_{\substack{j \neq i}}^{m-1} \tilde{n}_{ji}(t), i, j = 1, 2, ..m-1 \qquad (10.46)$$

where $\tilde{n}_i(t)$ and $\tilde{n}_{ij}(t), i, j = 1, 2, ..m-1$ are random variables that are practically codependent and $p_{ij}(t), i, j = 1, 2, ..m-1$ are the migration probabilities at time t for rated bonds. Both are a function of a broad range of economic factors. As a result, the CDO notional and the portfolio price at time t are random processes:

$$
\begin{aligned}
N(t) &= \sum_{i=1}^{m-1} \tilde{M}_i(t)\bar{B}, \\
S(t) &= \sum_{i=1}^{m-1} \tilde{M}_i(t)B_i(t, T)
\end{aligned}
\qquad (10.47)
$$

where $B_i(t, T)$ is the market price of a bond rated i at time t, which is a function of their interest rate. The notional of each of the tranches at time t (starting from the superior tranche) are then given as follows:

$$N_S(t) = Max\{N_S(t-1) - Max[\tilde{n}(t-1) - N_M(t), 0]; 0\}, N_S(0) = \alpha N(0)$$

$$N_M(t) = Max\{N_M(t-1) - Max[\tilde{n}(t-1) - N_E(t), 0]; 0\}, N_M(0) = \beta N(0)$$

$$N_E(t) = Max\{N(t) - N_S(t) - N_M(t); 0\}, N_E(0) = N(0) - N_S(0) - N_M(0)$$

$$(10.48)$$

where $\tilde{n}(t-1)$ is the total number of bonds that has defaulted at time $t-1$ and therefore given by:

$$\tilde{n}(t) = \sum_{i=1}^{m-1} \tilde{n}_i(t) \qquad (10.49)$$

The rationality of this equation is as follows. The superior tranche notional is not affected as long as the mezzanine notional is not exhausted. As long as the mezzanine notional lives, the superior tranche equals the previous period notional.

When losses at time $t - 1$ are larger than the mezzanine notional, the superior tranche is then affected, absorbing all residual losses. Similarly, the mezzanine notional is not affected as long as the residual notional of the equity tranche remains alive. Finally, the equity residual, equals the portfolio residual notional.

The CDO expiry time arises then in two circumstances: first, at the planned time T, which is likely to occur as long as the underlying portfolio can meet obligations to tranche holders, and second, whenever the portfolio manager is no longer able to meet debt payments. In some cases, some stipulations can be made for the CDO to assume the capital of the portfolio if the residual notional is larger than the underlying price of the portfolio, or $N(t) > S(t)$ with probability:

$$P\left(N(t) > S(t)\right) = 1 - P\left(\sum_{i=1}^{m-1} \tilde{M}_i(t)\left(\bar{B} - B_i(t, T)\right) \leq 0\right) \tag{10.50}$$

If this is the case, the residual notional $\sum_{i=1}^{m-1} \tilde{M}_i(t)\left(\bar{B} - B_i(t, T)\right)$ is distributed to the tranche holders according to their notional holdings at that time with all residual notional (if any) given to the equity holder. At time T, in case of no portfolio default, we have as seen previously:

$$
\begin{aligned}
N_S(T) &= Min\left(N(T-1), N_S(0)\right) \\
N_M(T) &= Min\left[Max\left(N_M(T-1), 0\right), N_M(0)\right] \\
N_E(T) &= N(T) - N_S(T) - N_M(T)
\end{aligned}
\tag{10.51}
$$

On the revenue side, we noted earlier a random revenue distributed to tranche holders:

$$\tilde{C}(t) = \sum_{i=1}^{m-1} c\tilde{M}_i(t), \ \tilde{C}(t) = \tilde{C}_S(t) + \tilde{C}_M(t) + \tilde{C}_E(t) \tag{10.52}$$

Let the contracted revenues for each of the tranche holders be defined as follows:

$$
\begin{aligned}
\tilde{C}_S(t) &= \begin{cases} b_S \alpha N(0) & if\ t < T_2 \\ b_S N_S(t) & t \geq T_2 \end{cases} \\
\tilde{C}_M(t) &= \begin{cases} b_M \beta N(0) & if\ t < T_1 \\ b_M N_M(t) & T_1 \leq t \leq T_2 \end{cases} \\
\tilde{C}_E(t) &= \begin{cases} b_E N_E(t) & if\ t < T_1 \\ 0 & T_1 \leq t \leq T_2 \end{cases} \\
\tilde{C}(t) &= \sum_{i=1}^{m-1} c\tilde{M}_i(t), \ \tilde{C}(t) = \tilde{C}_S(t) + \tilde{C}_M(t) + \tilde{C}_E(t)
\end{aligned}
\tag{10.53}
$$

Explicitly, as long as the superior tranche notional is not lost, the senior tranche receives a return that is equal to b_S basis points, its initial notional, or the portfolio return—whichever is least. The remaining returns (once the superior tranche has been paid) are paid to the mezzanine tranche holder following the same rule as that of the senior tranche holder with payments made proportional (basis point b_M) to the mezzanine tranche holder or the residual return. Finally, the equity tranche holder receives the remaining income or nothing (if his notional is wiped out). The times $\{T_1, T_2\}$ define the first time to the equity tranche holder exhausting his notional and the time for the mezzanine tranche holder to exhaust his tranche notional, or,

$$
\begin{aligned}
\tilde{T}_1 &= Inf\,\{t > 0, N_E(t) = 0\} \\
\tilde{T}_2 &= Inf\,\{t > 0, N_M(t) = 0\}
\end{aligned}
\tag{10.54}
$$

Finally, the expiry time of the CDO occurs at its planned time T or as soon as there are no sufficient funds in the portfolio (or revenues from the sale of the portfolio capital by the SPV). In other words, expiry time is defined by $\{T' \wedge T\}$ where,

$$
T' = Inf\,\{t > 0, \tilde{C}(t) + \tilde{S}(t) \le \tilde{C}_S(t) + \tilde{C}_M(t) + \tilde{C}_E(t)\}
\tag{10.55}
$$

In this case, the portfolio and CDO distributed revenues are given instead by the following equations:

$$
\begin{aligned}
S(t) &= \sum_{i=1}^{m-1} \tilde{M}_i(t) B_i(t, T) - \sum_{k=1}^{t} \delta(k) \\
\tilde{C}(t) &= c \sum_{i=1}^{m-1} \tilde{M}_i(t) + \delta(t)
\end{aligned}
\tag{10.56}
$$

where $\delta(k)$ is the amount of capital that the SPV uses to meet obligations to tranche holders (which reduces the number of live bonds, however). This amount equals:

$$
\delta(t) = Max\left\{\tilde{C}_S(t) + \tilde{C}_M(t) + \tilde{C}_E(t) - c \sum_{i=1}^{m-1} \tilde{M}_i(t), 0\right\}
\tag{10.57}
$$

which is nothing if the portfolio revenues are sufficiently large to meet the tranche holders' contracted revenues or are equal to the residual required to meet tranche holders' payments.

The CDO model thus constructed is necessarily a complex model that can be analyzed through simulation. Nevertheless, there remain two problems in CDO modeling and pricing. The first problem consists in defining the statistical characteristics of the random variables implied in equation (10.46), $\tilde{n}_i(t)$ and $\tilde{n}_{ij}(t)$, $i, j = 1, 2, ..m - 1$. The second is how to calculate the price (the basis points) paid to each of the tranche holders. Both problems are challenging, and a broad variety of techniques can be applied. These are summarized by Figure 10.6. The first problem is defining the model bonds' default, while the second consists in pricing the resulting CDO returns and tranches—one defining the other. For example, in equations (10.30) to (10.32), we have obtained for a simple case the prices (in basis points) that each tranche holder ought to be compensated for the risk it assumes. In our case is it more difficult since we have considered a more complex structure with payments to be made to tranche

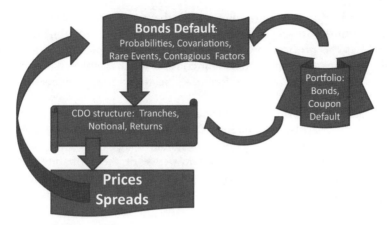

FIGURE 10.6 Default Models and Their Prices

holders on a regular basis. Nonetheless, simplifications allow the construction of treatable models. In the following, we consider a sample of default models and subsequently outline approaches to their pricing. Extensions and the development of more extensive models can be found in www.charlestapiero.com.

EXAMPLES: DEFAULT MODELS FOR BONDS

If defaults are statistically independent with known probabilities, then approximate normal distribution can be considered, as seen earlier in equations (10.34) to (10.41). In a CDO of rated bonds, however, the probabilities of default and migration are given by a Markov chain such as in equation (10.58):

$$
\mathbf{P}(t) = \begin{pmatrix}
p_{11}(t) & p_{12}(t) & \dots & \dots & p_{1m}(t) \\
p_{21}(t) & p_{22}(t) & \dots & \dots & p_{2m}(t) \\
\dots & \dots & \dots & \dots & \dots \\
p_{m-1,1}(t) & p_{m-1,2}(t) & \dots & \dots & p_{m-1,m}(t) \\
0 & 0 & \dots & \dots & 1
\end{pmatrix} \tag{10.58}
$$

In vector notation, the number of rated non-defaulting bonds at time t is thus:

$$
\mathbf{M}(t+1) = [\mathbf{P}(t)]\,\mathbf{M}(t), \quad \mathbf{M}(0) \geq 0 \tag{10.59}
$$

As a result, the number of rated bonds $i = 1, 2, \dots, m-1, m$ at time $t+1$, is given by the product vector:

$$
\mathbf{M}(t+1) = \prod_{j=0}^{t} [\mathbf{P}(j)]\mathbf{M}(0), \quad \mathbf{M}(0) \geq 0 \tag{10.60}
$$

For known Markov migration chains, the number of expected defaulting bonds at that time is therefore given by using the default probability $p_{im}(t)$ (with $p_{m,m}(t) = 1$) as the probability of default in a binomial process with parameters $(M_i(t), p_{im}(t))$. This assumption does not consider the dependence between the migration probabilities nor their randomness due to a broad number of economic factors.

Again, as stated before, if the probabilities of default are small, they can be approximated by a Poisson probability distribution with mean $\lambda_i(t) = M_i(t)p_{im}(t)$. If this (Poisson) mean has a gamma probability distribution with parameters $\mu_i(t)$ and $\xi_i(t)$ (expressing the lack of knowledge of the probability of default), then the resulting mixture probability distribution for the number of defaults has a negative binomial distribution given by:

$$\Pr(\tilde{n}_i(t) = z) = \frac{\Gamma(\mu_i(t) + z)}{z!\,\Gamma(\mu_i(t))} \frac{[\xi_i(t)]^{\mu_i(t)}}{[1 + \xi_i(t)]^{z+\mu_i(t)}} \tag{10.61}$$

with mean and variance:

$$E(\tilde{n}_i(t)) = \frac{\mu_i(t)}{\xi_i(t)}; \quad \text{var}(\tilde{n}_i(t)) = E(\tilde{n}_i(t))\left[1 + \frac{E(\tilde{n}_i(t))}{\mu_i(t)}\right] \tag{10.62}$$

Assuming that these simplifications hold for all migrating random variables from asset class i (rated bonds i) and all asset classes migrating to asset i, then a probability model for calculating the number of assets (bonds rated) in any given class at time $t + 1$, $\tilde{M}_i(t + 1)$, is well defined statistically. Namely, assuming that the vector probabilities $\{p_{ij}(t)\}, i = 1, 2 \ldots, m - 1, j = 1, \ldots, m$ have multinomial probability distributions, then:

$$M_i(t + 1) = M_i(t) - \tilde{n}_i(t) + \sum_{j=1}^{m-1} \tilde{n}_{i,j}(t)$$

$$P(\tilde{n}_i(t), \tilde{n}_{i,1}(t), \ldots, \tilde{n}_{i,i}(t), \ldots, \tilde{n}_{i,m-1}(t)) = \frac{[M_i(t)]!\,[p_{im}(t)]^{\tilde{n}_i(t)} \prod_{j=1}^{m-1} [p_{ij}(t)]^{\tilde{n}_{i,j}(t)}}{\tilde{n}_i(t)!\tilde{n}_{i,1}(t)! \ldots \tilde{n}_{i,i}(t)! \ldots \ldots, \tilde{n}_{i,m-1}(t)!} \tag{10.63}$$

with the first two moments easily calculated. These assumptions are, however, oversimplified. Rather, both default probabilities and migration probabilities are dependent across the rating matrix. Further, the number of elements to be accounted for may lead to an excessive number of parameters for these probabilities (and thus renders the model over specified).

An alternative approach consists in constructing a Bernoulli dependence model as indicated in Chapters 4 and 9. In this case, we can hypothesize that the probability of default for a rated bond is:

$$f(z_i = 1 \mid p_{im}(t)) = p_{im}(t) \text{ and } f(z_i = 0 \mid p_{im}(t)) = 1 - p_{im}(t), i = 1, 2, \ldots, m - 1 \tag{10.64}$$

However, if two rated bonds have a default probability that is covariant, we can then state that (where covariation is assumed to be a function of time only):

$$f\left(z_i = 1, z_j = 1 \,|\psi_{ij}(t)\right) = \psi_{ij}(t) = \psi(t) \tag{10.65}$$

and construct a joint probability model of bonds with default covariation:

$$E\left(z_i z_j \,|\psi(t)\right) = \psi(t) \text{ and } \mathrm{cov}\left(z_i, z_j \,|\psi(t)\right) = \psi(t) - p_{im}(t) p_{jm}(t)$$

On the basis of these observations, we can say that the joint distribution is a joint Bernoulli distribution as indicated in Chapter 4. In practice, the assumptions made regarding the default probabilities based on the multinomial distribution might be too simple, Extensions accounting for our lack of knowledge can then be considered by assuming that default probabilities are random (as stated earlier and resulting in a mixture distribution of the multinomial). For example, we can assume (as indicated earlier) that the probabilities of default and migration are estimated by a logit regression (a function of the many plausible factors that determine the probabilities of default and migration). In addition, since default migration probabilities may be statistically as well as causally dependent (i.e., contagious) or subject to random and rare events with significant consequences, it may require that we alter our model to reflect these facts. While these lead to complex statistical and computational problems, assumptions other than the ones made here may be required to approximate the probability distributions for default risks and their consequences. For example, a multivariate binomial model can be used (which accounts for the statistical dependence of the individual random variables in their multivariate setting). Approximations such as a multivariate normal model (as presumed by the KMV model to be seen and based on a multivariate normal probability distribution) can also be reached. In the past few years much use has been made of copulas, however, providing a general algebraic definition of a multivariate probability distribution based only on the marginal distributions and using calibration of these algebraic and statistical structures to fit observed prices. These examples, albeit simple, demonstrate both the variety and the numerous approaches, whether ad hoc or not, that one can apply to model and price credit derivatives.

Problem 11.1 Assume that default probabilities of rated bonds in an underlying portfolio over a period of 24 months (two years) are given. Assume further that over this period of time a number of salient factors such as interest rates, economic rate of growth, house prices, and other macroeconomic factors and financial indexes are given. How would you use the logit regression type models to obtain an econometric and statistical estimate of the probability distribution of bonds defaulting? How would you use these results to forecast future bond defaults? How would you use these results to define a model that calibrates a probability of default for a rated bond based on the assumption that prices are assumed to be no-arbitrage prices?

Problem 11.2 Say that that the average probability distribution of default in a portfolio of bonds is random, with a known mean and a known variance. Construct a model (based on a randomized binomial probability distribution of default) to estimate the risk of default expressed by the variance of the number of defaulting bonds and the size of the portfolio. Discuss the implications of the results you obtain for the prices of such a portfolio and its CDOs. In particular discuss the effects of size of the underlying portfolio's and CDO's risks and prices.

Problem 11.3: A Simple Portfolio of Loans   Let a portfolio of CDO-candidate assets consist of N loans, $L_i, i = 1, 2, \ldots, N$, paying at their maturity (the notional) $L_i(1 + R_i)$ if there is no default. Say that each loan is backed by collateral whose price at the loan maturity is random and given by $0 < \tilde{\eta}_i$. Default is then a conditional probability event. That is, loan recovery is $\tilde{\Phi}_i = Min(\tilde{\eta}_i, L_i(1 + R_i))$. For the portfolio as a whole, total recovery is $\sum_{i=1}^{N} \tilde{\Phi}_i$ with mean and variance given by $E\left(\sum_{i=1}^{N} \tilde{\Phi}_i\right)$ and var $\left(\sum_{i=1}^{N} \tilde{\Phi}_i\right)$. If these assets are statistically independent, then their mean and variance are a function of their default and collateral. If default is defined by the random price $f_i(\eta)$ of the collateral at its maturity only (as stated earlier), then in case of loan independence show that:

$$E\left(\sum_{i=1}^{N} \tilde{\Phi}_i\right) = \sum_{i=1}^{N} \left\{ L_i(1 + R_i)\left(1 - F_i^{(1)}(L_i(1 + R_i))\right) + F_i^{(1)}(L_i(1 + R_i)) \right\} \quad \text{where}$$

$$1 - F_i(L_i(1 + R_i)) = \int_{L_i(1+R_i)}^{\infty} f_i(\eta)\,d\eta, \; F_i^{(k)}(L_i(1 + R_i)) = \int_{0}^{L_i(1+R_i)} \eta^k f_i(\eta)\,d\eta, \; k = 1, 2$$

(10.66)

and:

$$\text{var}\left(\sum_{i=1}^{n} \tilde{\Phi}_i\right)$$

$$= \sum_{i=1}^{n} \left\{ \begin{array}{l} (L_i(1 + R_i))^2 \, F_i(L_i(1 + R_i))(1 - F_i(L_i(1 + R_i))) + F_i^{(2)}(L_i(1 + R_i)) \\ - \left[\left(F_i^{(1)}(L_i(1 + R_i))\right)^2 + 2L_i(1 + R_i)F_i^{(1)}(L_i(1 + R_i))(1 - F_i(L_i(1 + R_i)))\right] \end{array} \right\}$$

(10.67)

In this case justify that individual probabilities of default defined by the collateral price are:

$$P\tilde{D}_i = \begin{cases} 1 & \text{if} \quad \tilde{\eta}_i < L_i(1 + R_i) \\ 0 & \text{if} \quad \tilde{\eta}_i \geq L_i(1 + R_i) \end{cases}$$

(10.68)

And calculate their mean and variance. On the basis of these results show that for a portfolio consisting of N loans, the average probability of default and its variance are:

$$P\hat{D} = E(P\tilde{D}) = \frac{1}{N} \sum_{i=1}^{N} E(P\tilde{D}_i) = \frac{1}{N} \sum_{i=1}^{N} F_i(L_i(1 + R_i))$$

(10.69)

$$\sigma_{PD}^2 = \text{var}(P\tilde{D}) = \frac{1}{N^2} \text{var}\left(\sum_{i=1}^{N} P\tilde{D}_i\right) = \frac{1}{N^2}\left(\sum_{i=1}^{N} F_i(L_i(1 + R_i))(1 - F_i(L_i(1 + R_i)))\right)$$

(10.70)

Given these results, discuss the effects of the number of loans on the underlying portfolio on the portfolio risks (measured by the default variance) and price and how such a model can help you construct (in principle and not just technically) underlying portfolios for CDOs. Discuss also alternative approaches to extending such models to reflect the statistical dependence of the underlying assets of the portfolio. Finally, discuss how statistical dependence of assets affects the risk and the price of the CDO tranches.

Problem 11.4 Assume that the assets of a portfolio consist of two baskets, one of securities and the other of bonds. In this case, the portfolio can appreciate or depreciate over time since securities' and bonds' prices change over time. Let the CDO notional be $N(0)$ at time $t = 0$, which is greater than the initial price of the portfolio. Discuss how such a portfolio affects the prices of the CDO tranches. In particular discuss the effects of the portfolio price variations on the probability of the CDO closure (i.e., its bankruptcy or its takeover of the portfolio). Finally, construct a model CDO with three tranches with such a portfolio as its underlying.

CDO Models and Price Applications

The number of CDO models is of course extremely large. Their pricing techniques for tranches may also be subject to many sources of risk that seem at times to be non-transparent and therefore analytically intractable. However, tranches' prices provide a derivative price for estimates of the notional loss distribution—apportioned to each tranche. Recently, dynamic (time varying) variations in CDOs notional (and thus losses) variations are being modeled rendering their pricing such even more complex. These models require generally a great deal of financial information and their analysis is based on extensive implied optimization problems. Due to their complexity, their acceptability by investors have depended on their risk safety—which was provided by commercial raters such as S&P, Moody's, Fitch, etc. Although rating these products has faltered prior and during the financial crisis (misleading investors and contributing appreciably to the financial systemic risks of 2008), rating is still and will remain important as it provides a risk definition that investors and traders in these products might not by themselves be able to evaluate. Some examples are considered next to highlight some of the techniques used.

Example Consider the problem defined in equations (10.30) to (10.32) where (b_S, b_M, b_E) are prices (in basis points). These reflect the percentile return per unit of the CDO notional while $z(T - 1)$ is the proportional residual loss in the CDO notional. Assume that each bond has a par value of $1 million and therefore the number of bonds equals its notional divided by $1 million, or $m = N(0)/(1,000,000)$. If all bonds have a marginal beta probability distribution of default $B(p_i|r_i, s_i)$, $i = 1, 2, \ldots, m$ and if we set u_i to be the cumulative distribution, then a joint probability distribution of all bonds can be defined by a copula (see Chapters 3 and 4) expressing the cumulative joint probability distribution of default of all bonds $C(u_1, u_2, \ldots, u_m)$. A mathematical simulation (by Monte Carlo techniques) can then provide an estimate of the probability distribution of the number of defaulting bonds (and therefore the average notional loss). Note that this copula is overparametrized, and thus additional assumptions are required to reduce the number of parameters to account for. For example, setting the probability distribution of default to be the same for all bonds will reduce the copula to be a function of three parameters: two parameters defined by the marginal beta probability distribution and another parameter implied in the structural definition of the copula. Say that these parameters are given by r, s, and c; then inserting these results into our equations (10.30) to (10.32) provides three equations in the three basis points of each tranche. In other words, the three parameters of the copula imply the three parameters of the implied loss distribution, and vice versa; given the three (basis points) prices of each of the tranches, these imply the probability distribution of the notional loss.

EXAMPLE: THE KMV LOSS MODEL

The KMV model (KMV 1997; Li 1999 and 2000) is a popular model based on setting a normal co-dependence between a portfolio's names through a common factor to reduce the number of parameters used to calibrate and fit a model to price evidence. Explicitly, the KMV model assumes that all names' credits and collateral are binomial and independent and therefore can be approximated by a normal vector of a common mean. Thus, for each collateral, we have:

$$V_i(t) = \sqrt{\rho}\, Y + \varepsilon_i \sqrt{1-\rho}, \varepsilon_i \, N(0,1) \tag{10.71}$$

Further, if risk sources have the same distribution with a common parameter, the price of a specific individual collateral will be responding to one source of risk (although the price of the portfolio will be subject to the many sources of risks that collaterals are subjected to):

$$V_i(t) = \sqrt{\rho}\, Y + \varepsilon \sqrt{1-\rho}, \varepsilon \sim N(0,1) \tag{10.72}$$

Default is then assigned the probability that $0 \le K_i - V_i(t)$, or:

$$p(y,t) = P\left(V_i(t) \le K_i\right) = \Phi\left(\frac{K_i - y\sqrt{\rho}}{\sqrt{1-\rho}}\right) \tag{10.73}$$

where Φ is the cumulative standard normal probability distribution. In this specific case, the portfolio risk is:

$$\sum_{i=1}^{\tilde{D}} \xi_i \tag{10.74}$$

where $\tilde{D}$ is the number of defaults, assumed to be a binomial probability distribution (or a Lexian binomial mixture since the individual probabilities differ, each with its own probability distribution). Using the KMV model, we have then a probability for the number of defaults:

$$f(D|y) = \binom{N}{D} p(y,t)^D [1 - p(y,t)]^{N-D} \tag{10.75}$$

and therefore, unconditionally on the probability of default:

$$f(D) = \int_{-\infty}^{+\infty} f(D|Y=y)\phi(y)dy = \int_{-\infty}^{+\infty} \binom{N}{D} p(y,t)^D [1 - p(y,t)]^{N-D}\phi(y)dy$$

$$= \int_{-\infty}^{+\infty} \binom{N}{D} \left(\Phi\left(\tfrac{K_i - y\sqrt{\rho}}{\sqrt{1-\rho}}\right)\right)^D \left[1 - \left(\Phi\left(\tfrac{K_i - y\sqrt{\rho}}{\sqrt{1-\rho}}\right)\right)\right]^{N-D} \phi(y)dy \tag{10.76}$$

For example, if we use a credit VaR approach and let $\xi_i = Max\left(K_i - \tilde{V}_i(T), 0\right)$ be the loss in case of default (a random variable), then the total loss is

$$\sum_{i=1}^{\bar{D}} Max\left(K_i - V_i(T), 0\right) \tag{10.77}$$

while for a given risk exposure, the VaR (see Chapter 3) is a solution to:

$$P\left(\sum_{i=1}^{\bar{D}} Max\left(K_i - \tilde{V}_i(T), 0\right) \geq VaR\right) \leq P_{VaR} \tag{10.78}$$

These can be calculated either by simulation or by approximations of the random variables that define the risk exposure. Further, calculating the expected value and the variance of the number of defaults, the expected loss at a specific instant of time is calculated as well by their compound sum.

In practice, the financial engineering of basket portfolios is complex and uses both simplifying assumptions and Monte Carlo simulation techniques to determine the risk-reward properties of the CDO tranches. Furthermore, the loss distributions of the CDO are likely to be far more complex than presumed in these examples. Explicitly, the statistical dependence of the CDO notional, the temporal dependence of losses on the remaining portfolios at the CDO maturity, and so forth are rendering some of these problems computationally difficult (albeit approximations are always made).

CDOs of Baskets of Various Assets

Portfolios underlying assets can be real, consisting of real assets (such as rental apartments, car leases, investments of various sorts, etc.) or be synthetic, indexed to indexes such as exchange-traded funds (ETFs) of various interests (such as portfolios to replicate the price of water and infrastructure investments) or consisting of multiple baskets of indexes on investments in real assets (such as housing indexes). CFOs, synthetic CDOs, and other CDO-like financial products are examples of the underlying (collateral) used in credit derivatives. These products provide broad opportunities for financial innovation. The rationale of these products remains the same, however: namely, portfolios investments can be enhanced by leveraging, but leverage requires credit (debt) and parties willing to assume credit risk. These financial products are thus useful for two reasons. First, they can provide a far broader variety of risk-reward to investors in portfolios' debts and thereby contribute to far more credit in credit markets. Second, they allow many more investors to participate in such markets, contributing to market efficiency, augmenting market liquidity, and reducing the price of debt. However, the nontransparency, the complexity, and the handling of these products by financial stakeholders (providing them with extremely large profits) have also led to extremely large losses for investors unaware of their investment risks. These issues are currently the subject of debates on the regulation of credit derivatives, with results and consequences yet to be assessed. Nevertheless, these products are powerful financial weapons that are likely to be applied in different manners and for different purposes as their demands is not likely to abate.

CREDIT RISK VERSUS INSURANCE

The discourse on the regulation of CDSs and credit derivatives has attracted much public attention. It is also recognized that insurance is an important part of CDS and credit derivatives. Credit default swaps are in fact insurance-type contracts. The buyer of the insurance gets paid if the subject of the swap cannot meet its obligations. The seller of the swap gets a continuing payment from the buyer until the insurance expires (a sort of insurance premium). Treating CDSs as insurance products would mean that they would be subject to the same regulation that insurance firms are subject to, namely, capital adequacy requirements (CAR). By comparison, treating CDSs as traded financial products does not require such capital provisions in case of default. For these reasons, there is a clear distinction between insurance and CDSs (as well as CDOs). As repeatedly stated here, insurance prices are based on a specific type of exchange between two specific parties, whereas CDSs are an exchange when traded OTC with a financial entity selling a product, the other buying it. In a credit (CDS) financial market, their price is defined by the market demand and supply of such products, calibrated to some future states (using implied risk-neutral distributions) with losses priced by CDS spreads. In insurance, however, the price is actuarial, based on statistical models assumed to be predictive of future losses. We consider next a problem of insurance-reinsurance and compare it to the CDO pricing approach in order to emphasize both their similarity and their differences.

Example: Insurance and Reinsurance   Assume that CDO losses at time t are $\tilde{X}(t)$. For the CDO we noted that the loss is distributed sequentially to tranches until they each exhaust their notional. For an insurance contract, consisting of the insured, the insurer, and the reinsurer, losses are distributed among the parties to the contract with no reference to a notional. For the insured the loss is $Min\left(\tilde{X}(t), A\right)$, where A is the insured's franchise whose price is the premium paid to the insurance firm. The insurer, acting as an intermediary, collects the insured premium and assumes part of the risk or $Min\left(\tilde{X}(t) - A, B - A\right)$. In other words, the insurer reinsures the remaining risk (in excess of B) or $Min\left(\tilde{X}(t) - B, 0\right)$ by paying a premium to a reinsurer who assumes the excess (over the strike B) loss.

Such contracts correspond to stop-loss reinsurance contracts. For an insurance firm, these are OTC contracts among the three parties: the insured, the insurer, and the reinsurer. The price (insurance premium) is then defined by the willingness to pay and to bear risks by each of the parties, summarized by the amounts to be paid by the insured to the insurer and by the insurer to the reinsurer. The following cash flow payments result:

$$\begin{cases} -\prod_A & -Min\left(\tilde{X}(t), A\right) & \text{versus self insurance} \\ \prod_A - \prod_B & -Min\left(\tilde{X}(t) - A, B - A\right) & \text{versus no reinsurance} \\ \prod_B & -Min\left(\tilde{X}(t) - B, 0\right) & \text{versus no reinsurance} \end{cases} \qquad (10.79)$$

For the insured, a premium $\prod_A$ and a loss $Min\left(\tilde{X}(t), A\right)$ are incurred, compared to a loss of $\tilde{X}(t)$ if the insured chooses to self-insure. Similarly, the insurer collects a premium from the insured and passes on part of this premium to the reinsurer, or $\prod_A - \prod_B$. In exchange, the insurer assumes a loss of $Min\left(\tilde{X}(t) - A, B - A\right)$ for the reinsurer. Valuation of these streams can be compared using expected utility arguments (see Chapters 5 and 6).

In a financial credit risk context, insurance losses are marketed and sold through a financial market and the premiums are determined by financial institutions and investors interacting in a financial market. In this case, if we assume that implicitly, markets are complete, the price—the premium for each of the tranches—is given under some implied risk-neutral probability distribution by:

$$\pi_i = e^{-R_f t} E^Q \left(Min\left(\tilde{X}(t), A\right)\right) = A e^{-R_f t} - e^{-R_f t} E^Q \left(Max\left(A - \tilde{X}(t), 0\right)\right)$$

$$= A e^{-R_f t} - Put\left(A, t\right)$$

$$\pi_I = e^{-R_f t} E^Q \left(Min\left(\tilde{X}(t) - A, B - A\right)\right) = (B - A) e^{-R_f t} - e^{-R_f t} E^Q \left(Max\left(B - \tilde{X}(t), 0\right)\right)$$

$$= (B - A) e^{-R_f t} - Put\left(B, t\right)$$

$$\pi_R = e^{-R_f t} E^Q \left(Max\left(\tilde{X}(t) - B, 0\right)\right) = Call\left(B, t\right) \tag{10.80}$$

In other words, given the following optional prices: $\{Put\left(A, t\right), Put\left(B, t\right), Call\left(B, t\right)\}$ with strikes A, B, and B and with maturities at time t, we have a system of three equations in three unknowns that define the price of each of these contracts:

$$\pi_i = A e^{-R_f t} - Put\left(A, t\right); \quad \pi_I = (B - A) e^{-R_f t} - Put\left(B, t\right); \quad \pi_R = Call\left(B, t\right) \tag{10.81}$$

Note that the time t is a fixed date, which we shall call a *settlement date*, while the underlying is the total loss in the relevant interval $[0, t]$ that spans the option prices. In practice, put and call option prices used in seeking the price for each of the insurance tranches might not be traded and, therefore, unlike the insurance-actuarial approach, a financial approach seeks to determine the implied risk-neutral probability distribution that allows application of risk-neutral pricing. This is a far more difficult problem, however, as it will require much more information to allow the pricing of the optional products. In the next chapter a number of numerical techniques are introduced that highlight the various approximations we can used to estimate the implied risk-neutral distribution in the option prices previously defined.

SUMMARY

This chapter has provided an introduction to modeling and pricing a CDS and multi-name credit portfolios (CDOs). CDOs are difficult to price and require the application of computational and simulation techniques. Extensions and numerical computer-aided applications are drawn in this chapter's extension at www.charlestapiero.com. The problems outlined here have been oversimplified to provide an outline of alternative approaches to price such products. These include Monte Carlo simulation techniques, calibration to fit a copula that prices future losses (prices), presumed to be a statistical pricing model when markets are complete.

Credit derivatives have been the product of a financial innovation that has altered both the scope and the structure of financial institutions and financial markets. For these reasons, these products are the subject of an intense polemic regarding their usefulness, their market price, and their regulation as well as their future prospects. Given their usefulness, these financial products are not expected to disappear but rather be expanded further with a broad variety of names to cater to the needs of the many investors with broad tastes for risk and rewards.

TEST YOURSELF

10.1 What are fractional reserves and how have such reserves contributed to the quantity of credit that banks can lend?

10.2 Explain how credit derivatives contribute to the growth of credit and its liquidity.

10.3 You bought an apartment—congratulations! The price is $1 million but you need $500,000 to make the transaction. What are the sources of funds you can turn to and what are the risks of each? In particular, consider turning to banks and asking for a mortgage. What will the bank do once you apply for a mortgage? What are the essential criteria and risks it will confront and how can it manage these risks?

10.4 What is a counterparty risk? How can a third party relieve the counterparty risk and what are the resulting risks for the third party and the two parties involved in the credit transaction?

10.5 Define a CDS and state where and why these products are used.

10.6 What is a credit derivative? Give three examples and explain why these are called *derivatives*.

10.7 What is a CDO tranche? How do a CDO, CMO, MBS, and CDS differ? How do they differ from a synthetic CDO? How are they similar?

10.8 What are the differences between a junior (or equity) tranche, a mezzanine tranche, and a superior or senior tranche? How are the returns and the payments (losses) made, by whom and when?

10.9 How can we calculate the average life maturity of a tranche payment in a CMO?

10.10 What is the difference between a bond and part ownership of a tranche CDO?

10.11 How does the seller of assets for a CDO profit from such a sale?

10.12 What is a sequential pay CMO?

10.13 What is a synthetic CDO and who owns it?

10.14 How would you construct a CDO with sovereign debt obligations?

10.15 How does the price randomness of collateral affect the price of CDOs?

10.16 Assume that a loan of $1,000,000 is to be repaid in one year with an interest rate of 12 percent. The loan collateral is assumed to consist of a security whose current price is also $1,000,000 but whose rate of return is 9 percent with a volatility equal to twice that of the rate of return. What would in this case be the probability of default and what are the expected values and the variance of the loan recovery?

10.17 Repeat your analysis in question 10.16 by assuming that at maturity the underlying name collateral has an extreme (Weibull) probability distribution with the same mean and the same variance.

10.18 Discuss both the significance and the difficulties we encounter in practice when the collateral probability distribution has to be determined.

10.19 Consider a set of five loans, each of which is charged an interest rate for the year. The amounts are given in the following table and probability of default is specified. In addition, see the table of $S(ij)$ correlations.

Loan Number and Rate	Amount in Dollars	PD (mean)	Mean Loss (%)	Variance (% of Mean)
Loan 1: 0.12	100,000	0.06	25	80
Loan 2: 0.10	300,000	0.05	60	110
Loan 3: 0.06	500,000	0.04	40	200
Loan 4: 0.08	250,000	0.03	50	60
Loan 5: 0.04	650,000	0.02	15	50

Correlations:

1	0.2	0.1	0.05	−0.3
	1	0.2	.08	0.05
		1	0.1	0.3
			1	−0.2
				1

Calculate the mean loss and its variance as well as the portfolio average rate of return and its variance. Subsequently, assume a quadratic utility and calculate the certain equivalent of the portfolio. Finally, use the VaR approach to provide an indication of how much money must be set aside to meet a given risk exposure. To perform your calculations construct a spreadsheet program and calculate all the relevant terms needed to answer the problem's questions.

REFERENCES

Acharya, V. V., R. F. Engle, S. Figlewski, A. W. Lynch, and G. M. Subrahmanyam. 2009. Centralized clearing for credit derivatives. In *Restoring Financial Stability*, ed. V. V. Acharya and M. Richardson. Hoboken NJ: John Wiley & Sons.

Acharya, Viral V., and Timothy C. Johnson. 2007. Insider trading in credit derivatives. *Journal of Financial Economics* 77:110–141.

Altman, E. I., and H. A. Rijken. 2004. How rating agencies achieve rating stability. *Journal of Banking & Finance* 28:2679–2714.

Amato, J. D., and E. M. Remolona. 2005. The pricing of unexpected credit losses. Working paper 190, Bank for International Settlements.

Andersen, L. 2006. Portfolio losses in factor models: Term structure and intertemporal loss dependence. www.defaultrisk.com.

Andersen, L., and J. Sidenius. 2004. Extensions to the Gaussian copula: Random recovery and random factor loadings. *Journal of Credit Risk* 1 (1):29–70.

Andersen, L., J. Sidenius, and S. Basu. 2003. All your hedges in one basket. *Risk* 16:11.

Ashcraft, Adam B., and Til Schuermann. 2008. Understanding the securitization of subprime mortgage credit. *Federal Reserve Bank of New York Staff Reports* 318 (March).

Avallenada, M., and J. Zhu. 2001. Distance to default. *Risk* 14 (12):125–129.

Basel Committee on Banking Supervision. 2008. Principles of sound liquidity risk management and supervision. Basel, Switzerland: Bank for International Settlements (BIS).

Black, F., and J. Cox. 1976. Valuing corporate securities: Liabilities: Some effects of bond indenture provisions. *Journal of Finance* 31:351–367.

Bluhm, C., and L. Overbeck. 2004. Analytic approaches to collateralized debt obligation modeling. *Economic Notes*, Banca Monte Dei Paschidi Siena SpA 33 (2):233–255.

Bohn, J. R. 2000a. A survey of contingent-claims approaches to risky debt valuation. *Journal of Risk Finance* 1 (3):53–78.

Brigo, D. 2005. Market models for CDS options and callable floaters. *Risk*, January. Also in *Derivatives trading and option pricing*, ed. N. Dunbar, London: Risk Books.

_____. 2006. Constant maturity credit default swap valuation with market models. *Risk*, June.

_____, and A. Alfonsi. 2005. Credit default swaps calibration and derivatives pricing with the SSRD stochastic intensity model. *Finance and Stochastic* 9 (1).

_____, and M. Morini. 2006. Structural credit calibration. *Risk*, April.

Burtschell, X., J. Gregory, and J.-P. Laurent. 2005a. A comparative analysis of CDO pricing models. Working paper, ISFA Actuarial School, University of Lyon and BNP Paribas.

_____. 2005b. Beyond the Gaussian copula: Stochastic and local correlation. *Petit Déjeuner de la Finance*, October 12. http://laurent.jeanpaul.free.fr/Petit_dejeuner_de_la_finance_12_octobre_2005.pdf.

Cohan, William D. 2009. *House of cards*. New York: Doubleday.

Cooper, I., and M. Martin. 1996. Default risk and derivative products. *Applied Mathematical Finance* 3:53–74.

Coval, J., and E. Stafford. 2008. The economics of structured finance. Finance working paper 09-660, Harvard Business School.

Crosbie, P. 1999. Modelling default risk. KMV Corporation. www.kmv.com.

Das, S. R. 1995. Credit risk derivatives. *Journal of Derivatives* 2:7–21.

Das, S. R., and R. K. Sundaram. 2000. A discrete-time approach to arbitrage-free pricing of credit derivatives. *Management Science* 46:46–62.

Duffie, D. 1999. Credit swap valuation. *Financial Analysts Journal* 55:73–87.

Duffie, D., and N. Garleanu. 2001. Risk and valuation of collateralized debt valuation. *Financial Analyst Journal* 57 (1):41–62.

Embrechts, P., F. Lindskog, and A. McNeil. 2001. Modeling dependence with copulas and applications to risk management. Working paper, Department of Mathematics, ETHZ CH-8092, Zurich.

Giesecke, Kay. 2008. Portfolio credit risk: Top down vs. bottom up approaches, in *Frontiers in Quantitative Finance: Credit Risk and Volatility Modeling*, ed. R. Cont. Hoboken, NJ: John Wiley & Sons.

Gordy, Michael B. 2000. A comparative anatomy of credit risk models. *Journal of Banking and Finance* 24 (1–2) (January):119–149.

Gordy, Michael B. 2001. Calculation of higher moments in CreditRisk+ with applications. Working paper. http://mgordy.tripod.com.

Gordy, Michael B., and David Jones. 2003. Random tranches. *Risk*, 16 (3) (March): 78–83.

Gregory, J., and C. Donald. 2005. Structured credit related value strategy. Internal report, BNP Paribas, September.

Gregory, J., and J. Laurent. 2003a. Basket default swaps, CDOs and factor copulas. Working paper, BNP Paribas, France.

———. 2003b. I will survive. *Risk*, June: 103–107.

Grossman, S. J., and M. M. Miller. 1987. Liquidity and market structure. *Journal of Finance* 43:617–633.

Hawkes, A. G., and D. Oakes. 1974. A cluster process representation of a self-exciting process. *Journal of Applied Probability* 11:493–503.

Hull, J., and A. White. 2000. Valuing credit default swaps I: No counterparty default risk. *Journal of Derivatives* 8 (1):29–40.

———. 2001. Valuing credit default swaps II: Modeling default correlations. *Journal of Derivatives*, Spring: 12–21.

———. 2003. The valuation of credit default swap options. *Journal of Derivatives* 10 (3): 40–50.

———. 2006. Valuing credit derivatives using an implied copula approach. *Journal of Derivatives* 14 (2): 8–28.

———. 2006. Dynamic models of portfolio credit risk: A simplified approach. Working paper, University of Toronto.

———. 2004. Valuation of a CDO and an nth-to-default CDS without Monte Carlo simulation. *Journal of Derivatives* 2:8–23.

Jarrow, R. A., D. Lando, and S. Turnbull. 1997. A Markov model for the term structure of credit spreads. *Review of Financial Studies* 10:481–523.

Jarrow, R., and S. Turnbull. 1995. Pricing derivatives on financial securities subject to credit risk. *Journal of Finance* 50:53–85.

Jarrow, R. A., and Y. Yildirim. 2002. Valuing default swaps under market and credit risk correlation. *Journal of Fixed Income* 11:7–19.

Jarrow, R., and F. Yu. 2001. Counterparty risk and the pricing of defaultable securities. *Journal of Finance* 56:1765–1800.

Joe, H. 1997. Multivariate models and dependence concepts. *Monographs on statistics and applied probability*, vol. 37. London, Weinheim, New York: Chapman and Hall.

Joshi, M., and A. Stacey. 2005. Intensity gamma: A new approach to pricing portfolio credit derivatives. www.defaultrisk.com.

KMV Corporation. 1997. Modeling default risk. Technical document, Moody's KMV. http://www.kmv.com.

Laurent J.-P. and H. Pham. 1999. Dynamic programming and mean-variance hedging. *Finance and Stochastics* 3 (1):83–110.

———, and J. Gregory. 2005. Basket default swaps, CDOs and factor copula. *Journal of Risk* 7 (4): 103–122.

Li, D. 1999. The valuation of basket credit derivatives. *CreditMetrics Monitor*, April.

———. 2000. On default correlation: A copula function approach. *Journal of Fixed Income* 6 (March):43–54.

Lijuan, Cao, Zhang Jingqing, Lim Kian Guan, and Zhonghui Zhao. 2008. An empirical study of pricing and hedging collateralized debt (CDO). In *Advances in Econometrics*, vol. 22: *Econometrics and Risk Management*, 15–54.

Lindskog, F. 2000. Modeling dependence with copulas. RiskLab, ETH, Zurich.

Lipon, A., and A. Sepp. 2009. Credit value adjustment for credit default swaps via the structural default model. *Journal of Credit Risk* 5 (2):123–146.

Lo, A., C. Petrov, and M. Wierzbicki. 2003. It's 11 pm—Do you know where your liquidity is? The mean variance liquidity frontier. *Journal of Investment Management* 1:55–93.

Longstaff, Francis A., Sanjay Mithal, and Eric Neis. 2005. Corporate yield spreads: Default risk or liquidity? New evidence from the credit default swap market. *Journal of Finance* 60:2213–2253.

Longstaff, F., and E. Schwartz. 1995. Valuing credit derivatives. *Journal of Fixed Income* 5:6–12.

Lopez, J. A., and M. Saidenberg. 2000. Evaluating credit risk models. *Journal of Banking and Finance* 24:151–165.

Lucas, D., L. Goodman, and F. Fabozzi. 2006. *Collateralized debt obligations: Structures and analysis*, 2nd ed. Hoboken, NJ: John Wiley & Sons.

Mason, J. R., and J. Rosner. 2007. Where did the risk go? How misapplied bond ratings cause mortgage backed securities and collateralized debt obligation market disruptions. Working paper, Hudson Institute, Croton-on-Hudson, NY.

Markit. 2009. The CDS big bang: Understanding the changes to the global CDS contract and North American Conventions. http://www.markit.com/cds/announcements/resource/cds_big_bang.pdf.

McGinty, L., E. Bernstein, R. Ahulwalia, and M. Watts. 2004. *Introducing base correlation, Research Note, credit derivatives strategy*. New York: J.P. Morgan.

Merton, R. 1974. On the pricing of corporate debt: The risk structure of interest rates. *Journal of Finance* 29:449–470.

Minton, Bernadette, René M. Stulz, and Rohan Williamson. 2009. How much do banks use credit derivatives to hedge loans? *Journal of Financial Services Research* 35:1–31.

Moody's Investors Service. 1992. Corporate bond defaults and default rates. *Moody's Special Report*. www.moodys.com.

_____. 1997. Moody's rating migration and credit quality correlation, 1920–1996. www.moodys.com.

_____. 2008. Corporate one-to-five-year rating transition rates, special comment. www.moodys.com.

Pastor, L., and R. Stambaugh. 2003. Liquidity risk and expected stock returns. *Journal of Political Economy* 111 (3):642–685.

Pirrong, Craig. 2009. The economics of clearing in derivatives markets: Netting, asymmetric information, and the sharing of default risks through a central counterparty. Unpublished working paper, University of Houston, Houston, TX.

Pykhtin, M., ed. 2005. *Counterparty credit risk modeling*. London: Risk Books.

Schmidt, W., and I. Ward. 2002. Pricing default baskets. *Risk* 15 (1):111–114.

Schönbucher, P. 2003. Credit derivatives pricing models, pricing, implementation. London: Wiley-Finance.

Standard & Poor's. 1999. Rating performance 1998, stability and transition. New York: Standard & Poor's.

Stulz, René M. 2009. Credit default swaps and the credit crisis. SSRN, September. http://ssrn.com/abstract=1475323.

Tapiero, Charles S. 1998. *Applied stochastic models and control in finance and insurance.* Boston: Kluwer Academic Press.

_____. 1988. *Applied stochastic models and control in management.* Amsterdam and New York: North-Holland.

Tapiero, C. S., and D. Totouom-Tangho. 2010. CDO and structured financial products: A modeling perspective. Working Paper, Department of Finance and Risk Engineering, New York University Polytechnic Institute, Brooklyn. (Forthcoming, Risk and Decision Analysis).

Totouom-Tangho, D. 2007. Dynamic copulas: Applications to finance and economics. Doctoral thesis, Mines Paris/ParisTech, ed. 396 (November).

Totouom-Tangho, D., and M. Armstrong. 2005. Dynamic copula processes: A new way of modeling CDO tranches. Working paper. www.cerna.ensmp.fr/Documents/DTT-MA-DynamicCopula.pdf.

_____. 2007a. Dynamic copula processes: A new way of modeling CDO tranches. *Advances in Econometrics*, Elsevier.

_____. 2007b. Dynamic copula processes: Comparison with five 1-factor models for pricing CDOs. Working paper, Cerna, Ecole des Mines de Paris.

_____. 2007c, Dynamic copulas processes and forward starting credit derivatives. Working paper, Cerna, Ecole des Mines de Paris.

CHAPTER 11

Engineered Implied Volatility and Implied Risk-Neutral Distributions

OVERVIEW

In this chapter, we estimate parameters of model based implied probability distributions. The techniques we use include essentially the following:

Parametric approaches

A-parametric density estimation and related techniques

Entropy and Information measures

The parametric approach assumes a parametric risk-neutral distribution model with parameters estimated by best fit techniques. The a-parametric approach is distribution-free, defined by empirical risk-neutral distributions concurrent with properties of risk neutrality. Finally, entropy related techniques are explained and used to estimate the risk-neutral distribution that fits best a given data set and a prior personal probability distribution of future prices. Problems of particular importance include calculation of the implied volatility.

INTRODUCTION

Trading in derivatives (options, credit derivatives and forwards, for example) is based on beliefs regarding future prices and losses. For example, the price of a European option whose maturity is at a future date T implies a belief regarding the underlying price of the option at its maturity. By the same token, an implied volatility expresses a current belief about the volatility of the underlying asset at time T.

To determine an implied distribution (or its implied volatility), data and beliefs (formulated as models or personal probability distributions) pertaining to future

---

This chapter was written with Oren Tapiero.

underlying state prices are used with financial markets assumed to be complete. Explicitly, when markets are complete, the current price at time t is:

$$S_t = e^{-R_f(T-t)} E_t^Q \left\{ \tilde{S}_T \, | \Im_t \right\} \tag{11.1}$$

where $\tilde{S}_T$ is the future underlying price (a random variable) and E_t^Q is an expectation with respect to a risk-neutral measure.

If European call and put options with strikes $K_i, i = 1, \ldots, n$ and maturity at T are traded, and their observed call and put prices at time t are $C_t(K_i, T)$ and $P_t(K_i, T)$, we have also:

$$
\begin{aligned}
C_t(K_i, T) &= \left(\frac{1}{1 + R_f(t, T)} \right)^{T-t} E_t^Q \{ C_T(K_i, T) \, | \Im_t \}, \, T > t \\
P_t(K_i, T) &= \left(\frac{1}{1 + R_f(t, T)} \right)^{T-t} E_t^Q \{ P_T(K_i, T) \, | \Im_t \}, \, T > t
\end{aligned} \tag{11.2}
$$

with

$$E_t^Q \{ C_T(K_i, T) \, | \Im_t \} = \int C_t(K_i, T) \, f_{T|t}^Q(S_T) dS_T \tag{11.3}$$

where $f_{T|t}^Q(S_T)$ is a conditional (filtered) risk-neutral probability distribution at time t of the underlying price at time T. The implied risk-neutral problem is then an inverse problem that seeks a risk-neutral distribution using current call and put prices traded at time t for time T—the options' maturity—or:

$$\{ C_t(K_i, T), \, P_t(K_i, T) \} \Rightarrow f_{T|t}^Q(S_T) \tag{11.4}$$

Such problems are theoretically and computationally challenging. Approaches we can use are forcibly based on models and assumptions made regarding the implied risk-neutral distribution and the data available for such purposes. For these reasons, one has to use implied distributions with great care, and recognize that these are not future prices but only a fleeting belief, perhaps held one instant and changing an instant later.

For example, assume \$10 is the current price of an option whose exercise is in six weeks (the time T). An instant later, its implied risk neutral distribution may change due to a broad set of factors summarized by "new information." In this case, the implied risk-neutral distributions at times t and $t+1$ are:

$$\left\{ f_{T|t}^Q(S_T) \, | \Im_t \right\} \quad \text{and} \quad \left\{ f_{T|t+1}^Q(S_T) \, | \Im_{t+1} \right\}$$

If markets are complete and prices adhere forcibly to a risk-neutral measure, then current and observable financial data will imply a future risk neutral distribution, and vice versa. Such an inverse approach is used in numerous and important problems in financial pricing including default pricing, credit default swaps, and other situations where market exchanges reflect the preferences and assessments of traders and speculators. For example, a price spread pertaining to a future financial settlement reflects the default risk in such a settlement. In reverse, the future default risk is priced by the current spread. When data in not available or it is insufficient to derive a reliable estimate of future state probability distributions, investors and traders beliefs can be modeled by a personal estimate of future probability distribution as we shall see subsequently.

The implied distribution of a future underlying is of paramount importance in financial pricing practice. For example, the price of options (Chapters 7 and 8) and the price of credit risk and CDO's (Chapters 9 and 10) are determined by such "inverse" problems.

The techniques we use to calculate these implied risk neutral distributions are approximations, including:

- Parametric approaches and utility based approaches (embedded in kernel pricing).
- A-parametric and density estimation and related techniques.
- Entropy and information models approaches.

The parametric approach assumes a model for a risk-neutral distribution with parameters estimated by techniques of best fit between theoretical and observed prices. The a-parametric approach is a "distribution free" model, seeking an empirical risk-neutral distribution concurrent with properties of risk neutrality. When markets are complete (or are assumed to be complete), the underlying asset prices are assumed to define a unique martingale. Thus, estimation problems are reduced to a computational problem seeking to fit uniquely available option prices to the implied pricing martingale. Finally, we shall also use entropy and implied utility approaches (based on kernel pricing, see Chapters 5 and 6). These two latter approaches provide a utility-based explanation and an extension of entropy techniques when applied to calculate the implied risk neutral distribution. In the next section we consider first the estimation of implied volatility. Subsequently, the approaches stated above are considered (see also www.charlestapiero.com for extensions and examples).

THE IMPLIED VOLATILITY

Volatility is an indicator of a process risk. Focusing on only one moment of the returns distribution can be misleading however (as broadly discussed in Chapter 3 where higher-order moments such as skewness and kurtosis were introduced). Nonetheless, volatility is extensively used in practice to price options (see Chapter 7). For these reasons, any means to explicitly or implicitly reveal a process' volatility is important and useful. We distinguish between real and implied volatility. The former uses past statistical data while the latter is model based that uses the current option price to determine a future volatility. The example is below is based on a normal rates of returns model for an underlying security. Subsequently, an extension by Dupire is considered.

EXAMPLE: THE IMPLIED VOLATILITY IN A LOGNORMAL PROCESS

Assume a price process with a normal rate of return with parameters (μ, σ),

$$\frac{\Delta S}{S} = \mu dt + \sigma \Delta W(t), \ S(0) > 0 \tag{11.5}$$

To define a risk-neutral process (see Chapter 8), we use a measure transform leading to:

$$\frac{\Delta S}{S} = R_f dt + \sigma \Delta W^Q(t), \ S(0) > 0 \quad \text{and} \quad S(t) = S(0)e^{R_f t - \frac{1}{2}\sigma^2 t + \sigma W^Q(t)} \tag{11.6}$$

where $W^Q(t)$ is a standard and adapted Wiener process under the risk-neutral measure. Call and put options with maturities at time T_k and strikes K_i, with $i = 1, \ldots u; k = 1, \ldots v$ are theoretically priced at time t by $C(t : T_k, K_i)$, $P(t : T_k, K_i)$:

$$C(t : T_k, K_i) = e^{-R_f(T_k - t)} \int_{K_i}^{\infty} (\tilde{S}_{T_k} - K_i) f_{T_k|t}^Q \left\{ \tilde{S}_{T_k} \Big| \Im_t, \sigma_{T_k|t}^Q \right\} d\tilde{S}_{T_k}, \ T_k > t$$

$$P(t : T_k, K_i) = e^{-R_f(T_k - t)} \int_{-\infty}^{K_i} (K_i - \tilde{S}_{T_k}) f_{T_k|t}^Q \left\{ \tilde{S}_{T_k} \Big| \Im_t, \sigma_{T_k|t}^Q \right\} d\tilde{S}_{T_k}, \ T_k > t \tag{11.7}$$

where $\sigma_{T_k|t}^Q$ is an implied volatility at time t. Further,

$$S(T_k) = S(t)e^{\left(R_f - \frac{1}{2}\sigma_{T_k|t}^2\right)(T_k - t) + \sigma_{T_k|t} W^Q(T_k - t))} \tag{11.8}$$

For example, for call options, their prices are (see also Chapter 7):

$$C(t | K_i, T_k) = S(t)N(d_1) - K_i e^{-R_f(T_k - t)} N(d_2),$$

$$d_1 = \frac{\ln(S(t) \Big/ K_i) + (R_f + \left(\sigma_{T_k|t}^Q\right)^2 \Big/ 2)(T_k - t)}{\sigma_{T_k|t}^Q \sqrt{T_k - t}}, d_2 = d_1 - \sigma_{T_k|t}^Q \sqrt{T_k - t} \tag{11.9}$$

where $N(d_1)$ defines the normal integral. Thus, given the current price of a call, and assuming that financial prices are (implicitly) complete, we calculate by numerical inversion the implied volatility $\sigma_{T_k|t}^{Q,C}$. Assuming that markets are complete, the options price set $\{C(t : T_k, K_i), P(t : T_k, K_i)\}$ provides the implied volatility of the underlying process at time T_k (assuming that other parameters needed to calculate the option prices are known at time t). Note however that at a later time $t+1$, when new information is given, option prices change and the implied volatility at the options' maturity will also change.

If the implied volatilities calculated by call and put options for a specific maturity are equal, their equality strengthens the argument for market completeness. If they are not, it strengthens the counterargument. The implication of such inequality is that the demand and supply for the underlying at the options' exercise time are not in equilibrium. The assumption of an implied lognormal model may be too stringent however. To reconcile the disparities between a theoretical model and an unfolding set of observable prices, a richer class of models would the be needed. An important model allowing us to expand on the lognormal underlying process and calculate the implied volatility was suggested by Dupire which we consider next.

The Dupire Model

Let the underlying risk-neutral process be defined by a volatility $\Lambda(S, t)$ below:

$$\frac{\Delta S(t)}{S(t)} = R_f dt + \Lambda(S, t)\Delta W^Q(t), \, S(0) > 0 \tag{11.10}$$

The price of a call option whose exercise is at time T and strike is K, is given by:

$$C(S_t, t) = e^{-R_f(T-t)} \int_K^\infty (S(T) - K) \, f^Q(S(T)) dS(T) \tag{11.11}$$

The first derivative with respect to the strike is:

$$\frac{\partial C(S_t, t)}{\partial K} = -e^{-R_f(T-t)} \int_K^\infty f^Q(S(T)) dS(T) = -e^{-R_f(T-t)}\left(1 - F^Q(K)\right) \tag{11.12}$$

while a second derivative yields:

$$f^Q(K) = e^{R_f(T-t)} \frac{\partial^2 C(S_t)}{\partial K^2} \tag{11.13}$$

An estimate of the implied volatility due to Dupire and proved in the Appendix is then:

$$\Lambda(K, T) = \sqrt{\frac{\left(R_f K \dfrac{\partial C}{\partial K} + \dfrac{\partial C}{\partial T}\right)}{\dfrac{1}{2} K^2 \dfrac{\partial^2 C}{\partial K^2}}} \tag{11.14}$$

Equation (11.14) can of course be expressed in terms of the Greeks of the call option, yielding (see Chapter 8):

$$\Lambda(K, t) = \sqrt{\frac{-\theta_K + R_f K \Delta_K}{\frac{1}{2} K^2 \Gamma_K}} \qquad (11.15)$$

Whether volatility is precisely priced or not it has become important in practice because of its use by investors and traders. Often the price of an option is used as a measure of the price of volatility.

THE IMPLIED RISK-NEUTRAL DISTRIBUTION

Central banks, risk managers, and institutional investors use option prices to derive the implied risk-neutral densities to gain a better appreciation of financial markets' expected future returns. For example, the European central bank uses implied risk-neutral densities to reveal the market beliefs regarding future exchange rates for the dollar and the euro in order to better manage their currency. Similar uses are made by the national banks of England, Canada, and of course many other countries. The advantage of using option prices lies in their being forward looking. A written option embeds the expectation regarding the future of the option writer. The more liquid and deeper the option's market, the more reliable are such estimates.

For a deflated stock price S_t at time t (with linear and normal rates of returns) and B_t, a bond (deterministic) price at time t, let,

$$S_t^Q = \frac{S_t}{B(t)} \qquad (11.16)$$

where S_t^Q is a martingale and therefore it is mean-stationary with a conditional filtration $\Im_t$ at time t:

$$S_t = E^Q \left(\frac{S_t}{B(t)} \mid \Im_t \right) = \cdots = E^Q \left(\frac{S_T}{B(T)} \mid \Im_t \right), T \geq t \qquad (11.17)$$

By the same token, for call and put prices at time t, on the underlying stock price at time T, we have:

$$C_t = E^Q \left(\frac{C_t}{B(t)} \mid \Im_t \right) = \cdots = E^Q \left(\frac{C_T}{B(T)} \mid \Im_t \right), T \geq t$$
$$P_t = E^Q \left(\frac{P_t}{B(t)} \mid \Im_t \right) = \cdots = E^Q \left(\frac{P_T}{B(T)} \mid \Im_t \right), T \geq t \qquad (11.18)$$

where (C_t, P_t) are the observed call and put option prices with specific strikes and expiry time T. The financial engineering question is then of course how, on the basis of available information (say, given at time t), we can extract the risk-neutral probability distribution of the stock price at time T. A simple binomial example demonstrates one approach to solving such a problem.

EXAMPLE: AN IMPLIED BINOMIAL DISTRIBUTION

Consider a binomial (risk-neutral) pricing model and let (p_i^Q, h_i, ℓ_i) be the model parameters at time $t = i$. Say call and put options are traded with a maturity at time T_q with strikes (K_n, Q_n), $n = 1, 2, \ldots, N$. Initially,

$$E^Q\left(\frac{S_0}{B(0)} \,|\, \Im_0\right) = S_0 = E^Q\left(\frac{S_{T_q}}{B(T_q)} \,|\, \Im_0\right) = \left(\frac{1}{1 + R_{f,T_q}}\right)^T E^Q\left(S_{T_q} \,|\, \Im_0\right) \quad (11.19)$$

where R_{f,T_q} denotes the risk free rate of return of a bond paying \$1 at time T_q. As seen earlier for a binomial model, at time i with rates of growth and declines (h_i, ℓ_i), the underlying security price model has (under risk-neutral probabilities) the following distribution:

$$\tilde{S}_{T_q,i} = (1 + h_i)^j(1 - \ell_i)^{T_q-i-j}S_i, \quad \text{wp} \begin{pmatrix} T_q - i \\ j \end{pmatrix} \left(p_i^Q\right)^j \left(1 - p_i^Q\right)^{T_q-i-j}$$

$$S_i = E^Q\left(\frac{\tilde{S}_{T_q,i}}{B(T_q - i)}\right)$$

$$= \left(\frac{1}{1 + R_{f,i,T_q-i}}\right)^{T_q-i} \sum_{j=0}^{T_q-i} S_i \begin{pmatrix} T_q - i \\ j \end{pmatrix} \left(p_i^Q(1 + h_i)\right)^j \left(\left(1 - p_i^Q\right)(1 - \ell_i)\right)^{T_q-i-j}$$

$$i = 1, 2, \ldots, T_q - i$$

$$(11.20)$$

By the same token, for call and put option prices, we have:

$$C_i = E^Q\left(\frac{C_{T_q}}{B(T_q - i)} \,|\, \Im_i\right) = \left(\frac{1}{1 + R_{f,i,T_q-i}}\right)^{T_q-i} E^Q\left(C_{T_q} \,|\, \Im_i\right)$$

$$P_i = E^Q\left(\frac{P_{T_q}}{B(T_q - i)} \,|\, \Im_i\right) = \left(\frac{1}{1 + R_{f,i,T_q-i}}\right)^{T_q} E^Q\left(P_{T_q} \,|\, \Im_i\right)$$

$$(11.21)$$

The implied risk-neutral probability p_i^Q at time i is then defined by N current and observed call and put options prices, $\hat{C}_i^{(n)}$ and $\hat{P}_i^{(n)}$, all of which expire at time $T_q > i$ with strikes $K_n, n = 1, 2, \ldots, N$. A simple least squares approximation for the risk neutral probabilities are given by minimizing their binomial price error estimate, or:

$$\text{Min}_{p_i^Q} \sum_{n=1}^{N} \left\{ \hat{C}_i^{(n)} - E^Q \left(\frac{C_{T_q}^{(n)} | \Im_i}{B(T_q - i)} \right) \right\}^2 + \sum_{n=1}^{N} \left\{ \hat{P}_i^{(n)} - E^Q \left(\frac{P_{T_q}^{(n)} | \Im_i}{B(T_q - i)} \right) \right\}^2 \quad (11.22)$$

Note that probability estimates are specific to: the current time; the exercise time of the options; the model security's rate of return parameters (h_i, ℓ_i) assumed at that time; and, of course, the risk-free rate for a bond at time i paying \$1 at $T_q - i$ periods hence, its maturity.

For example, say that the probability of the security increasing j times over the remaining times to maturity is $p_{i,j}^Q, j = 1, 2, \ldots, T_q - i$. In this case, call and put option prices are reduced to:

$$C_i^{(n)} = \left(\frac{1}{1 + R_{f,i,T_q-i}} \right)^{T_q-i} \sum_{j=1}^{T_q-1} \text{Max} \left\{ S_i (1 + h_i)^j (1 - \ell_i)^{T_q-i-j} - K_n, 0 \right\} \left(p_{i,j}^Q \right)$$

$$P_i^{(n)} = \left(\frac{1}{1 + R_{f,i,T_q-i}} \right)^{T_q-i} \sum_{S_{T_q,i} < K_n} \text{Max} \left\{ K_n - S_i (1 + h_i)^j (1 - \ell_i)^{T_q-i-j}, 0 \right\} \left(p_{i,j}^Q \right)$$

$$(11.23)$$

An "estimate" of these probabilities, found by a quadratic best fit is:

$$\text{Min}_{p_{i,j}^Q, j=1,2,\ldots,T_q-i} \sum_{n=1}^{N} \left\{ \hat{C}_i^{(n)} - E^Q \left(\frac{C_{T_q}^{(n)} | \Im_i}{B(T_q - i)} \right) \right\}^2 + \sum_{n=1}^{N} \left\{ \hat{P}_i^{(n)} - E^Q \left(\frac{P_{T_q}^{(n)} | \Im_i}{B(T_q - i)} \right) \right\}^2$$

$$(11.24)$$

The solution of this problem provides an implied (and approximate) probability distribution $p_{i,j}^Q$ at time i based on the observed N call and put options prices with strikes $K_n, n = 1, 2, \ldots, N$. At time $i + 1$, new option prices are observed, new information updates our future estimates, and therefore new risk-neutral probabilities will be obtained. Given the number of parameters to estimate and the paucity of data, additional simplifications are needed to reduce the number of parameters to estimate.

EXAMPLE: CALCULATING THE IMPLIED RISK-NEUTRAL PROBABILITY

Say that at time $t = 0$, a stock price can either increase or decrease in any one month by 2 or 1 percent. The current price is \$10 while the risk-free rate is

8 percent. First, note that the probability distribution of the stock price in six months is:

$$\tilde{S}_6 \equiv (1+h)^j (1-\ell)^{6-j} S_0 \quad \mathrm{wp} \begin{pmatrix} 6 \\ j \end{pmatrix} \left(p_0^Q\right)^j (1-p_0^Q)^{6-j}, \; j = 0, 1, \ldots, 6 \quad (11.25)$$

Inserting our numbers and parameters, we have:

$$\tilde{S}_6 \equiv 10(1+0.02)^j (1-.01)^{6-j} \quad \mathrm{wp} \begin{pmatrix} 6 \\ j \end{pmatrix} \left(p_0^Q\right)^j (1-p_0^Q)^{6-j}, \; j = 0, 1, \ldots, 6$$

$$(11.26)$$

If markets are complete:

$$S_0 = \left(\frac{1}{1+R_{f,6}}\right)^6 E^Q (\tilde{S}_6)$$

$$= \left(\frac{1}{1+R_{f,6}}\right)^6 \sum_{j=0}^{6} S_0 \begin{pmatrix} 6 \\ j \end{pmatrix} \left[p_0^Q(1+h)\right]^j \left[(1-\ell)(1-p_0^Q)\right]^{6-j} \quad (11.27)$$

or

$$1 = \frac{1}{\left(1+\dfrac{0.08}{12}\right)^6} \sum_{j=0}^{6} \begin{pmatrix} 6 \\ j \end{pmatrix} \left[1.02 p_0^Q\right]^j \left[0.99(1-p_0^Q)\right]^{6-i} \quad (11.28)$$

where p_0^Q is a risk-neutral probability distribution (assumed to be the same over the six months) and therefore over one month we have:

$$p_0^Q = \frac{(0.08/12) + 0.01}{0.02 + 0.01} = 0.555 \quad (11.29)$$

Similarly, for a call option price:

$$C_0 = \frac{1}{\left(1+\dfrac{0.08}{12}\right)^6} \sum_{j=0}^{6} \left\{ \begin{pmatrix} 6 \\ j \end{pmatrix} \mathrm{Max}\left\{10(1.02)^j(0.99)^{6-j} - K, 0\right\} \left(p_0^Q\right)^j \left(1-p_0^Q\right)^{6-j} \right\}$$

$$(11.30)$$

In other words, if the option price is C_0, the implied risk-neutral probability can be found by solving equation (11.30). When the underlying distribution is a trinomial model, the number of parameters increases and therefore more data is needed to estimate such parameters. For example, let the underlying price at time $t = 1$ be:

$$S_1 = \begin{cases} (1+h)S_0 & \text{wp} & p_0^Q \\ S_0 & \text{wp} & 1 - p_0^Q - q_0^Q \\ (1-\ell)S_0 & \text{wp} & q_0^Q \end{cases} \tag{11.31}$$

At time i, the price of a call option whose exercise time is T is (under a risk neutral Q measure and monthly periods):

$$C_i = \left(1 + \frac{R_f}{12}\right)^{-(T-i)} E^Q(C_T) \tag{11.32}$$

For the trinomial model (11.31), the distribution of the underlying states at maturity is:

$$\tilde{S}_{T,i,j} = (1+h)^j (1+0)^{T-i-k} (1-\ell)^k S_0, \text{wp} \binom{T-i}{j,\,k} \left(p_0^Q\right)^j (q_0^Q)^k (1 - p_0^Q - q_0^Q)^{T-i-j-k}$$

$$i = 0, 1, 2, \ldots; j = 0, 1, 2, 3, \ldots \tag{11.33}$$

Thus

$$C_i = \left(1 + \frac{R_f}{12}\right)^{-(T-i)} \sum_{j=0}^{T-i} \sum_{k=0,\,j+k<T-i} \text{Max}\left(S_0(1+h)^j(1+0)^{T-i-j-k}(1-\ell)^k - K, 0\right) p_{jk}^Q \tag{11.34}$$

where

$$p_{jk}^Q = \binom{T-i}{j,\,k} \left(p_0^Q\right)^j \left(q_0^Q\right)^k \left(1 - p_0^Q - q_0^Q\right)^{T-i-j-k} \tag{11.35}$$

In this example there are two risk-neutral probabilities, therefore additional information is needed to obtain a unique solution (although two option prices would allow calibration of the two risk neutral probabilities). Practically, a best fit, least squared error solution is found by solving:

$$\min_{p_0^Q, q_0^Q} \sum_{n=1}^{N} \left[C_{i,K_n} - \left(1 + \frac{R_f}{12}\right)^{-(T-i)} \sum_{j=0}^{T-i} \sum_{k=0,\,j+k<T-i} \right.$$

$$\left. \times \text{Max}\left(S_0(1+h)^j(1+0)^{T-i-j-k}(1-\ell)^k - K_n, 0\right) p_{jk}^Q \right]^2 \tag{11.36}$$

where $K_n, n = 1, 2, \ldots, N$ are n strikes for call options with a maturity at time T. The probabilities p_0^Q, q_0^Q can also be found by solving (where the error estimate is calculated in relative terms):

$$\underset{p,q}{\text{Min}} \sum_{n=1}^{N} \left\{ \left[1 - \frac{C_{i,K_n}}{\hat{C}_{i,K_n}} \right]^2 + \left[1 - \frac{P_{i,K_n}}{\hat{P}_{i,K_n}} \right]^2 \right\} \tag{11.37}$$

with

$$C_{i,K_n} = \left\{ \begin{array}{l} p_0^Q [(1+h)S_i - K_n]^+ + \\ q_0^Q [(1-\ell)S_i - K_n]^+ \\ (1 - p_0^Q - q_0^Q)[S_i - K_n]^+ \end{array} \right\}; \quad P_{i,K_n} = \left\{ \begin{array}{l} p_0^Q [K_n - (1+h)S_i]^+ + \\ q_0^Q [K_n - (1-\ell)S_i]^+ + \\ (1 - p_0^Q - q_0^Q)[K_n - S_i]^+ \end{array} \right\} \tag{11.38}$$

where $(S_i, C_{i,n}, P_{i,n})$ is an observed financial data set at time i. Note that the strikes of the call and put options need not be the same (although we have assumed that for every call contract, there is a put contract with the same strike). Further, we have standardized the error estimate. We have done so since there is some evidence that it provides a better estimate of the risk-neutral probabilities. When we move from time i to, say, $i + 1$, new information alters the underlying security prices and the estimate of the risk-neutral probabilities.

IMPLIED DISTRIBUTIONS: PARAMETRIC MODELS

Parametric models assume a probability distribution given, and use financial prices to estimate the implied parameters of such a distribution. For example, say that the underlying is a mixture of two lognormal distributions. Each of these distributions then has rates of returns that are normally distributed, with mean and variance $(\alpha_i t, \sigma_i^2 t), i = 1, 2$ given by:

$$\alpha_1 t = \left(R_f - \frac{1}{2}\sigma_1^2 \right) t, \quad \text{and} \quad \alpha_2 t = \left(R_f - \frac{1}{2}\sigma_2^2 \right) t \tag{11.39}$$

A mixture probability distribution of the rates of return is thus a mixture of two normal probability distributions:

$$\hat{f}(V, t) \sim \theta_1 L(\alpha_1 t, \sigma_1^2 t) + \theta_2 L(\alpha_2 t, \sigma_2^2 t) \tag{11.40}$$

where the cumulative distribution of the natural logarithm price is:

$$
P\left(\tilde{V}(t) \le \ln S(t)\right) = \theta_1 N\left(\frac{\ln S(t) - \left(R_f - \frac{1}{2}\sigma_1^2\right)t}{\sigma_1\sqrt{t}}\right)
$$

$$
+ \theta_2 N\left(\frac{\ln S(t) - \left(R_f - \frac{1}{2}\sigma_2^2\right)t}{\sigma_2\sqrt{t}}\right) \tag{11.41}
$$

Elementary but tedious analysis of the moments can provide an estimate of the variance, the distribution skewness, and its kurtosis. Simple moments can be used to obtain the implied volatility estimates and the mixture parameters. More generally, mixture lognormal models can be constructed as two or more sources of risk models and their underlying risk neutral process defined theoretically. (See also www.charlestapiero.com for additional developments.)

In practice a large variety of explicit probability distributions such as the Burr, the Generalized Beta distributions and copulas are often used. Next we consider as an example the Generalized Beta of the second kind to highlight some of the technical difficulties we encounter.

EXAMPLE: THE GENERALIZED BETA OF THE SECOND KIND

The *generalized beta of the second kind* (GB2) is "a family rich" probability distribution that has been applied by Anagnou, Bedendo, Hodges, and Tompkins (ABHT 2002) and by Tunaru, Kadam, and Albota (TKA, 2005)). Its main feature is its generality with many distributions being particular cases of GB2. For example, the lognormal, the gamma, the log-t and log-Cauchy distributions are all special cases. All these distributions were used in asset return models in TKA. An additional feature is that it allows for positive and negative skewness and infinite (volatility) moments. The GB2 distribution function, given below, has four parameters:

$$
GB2(y; a, b, p, q) = \frac{|a| y^{ap-1}}{b^{ap} B(p, q) [1 + (y/b)^a]^{p+q}} \tag{11.42}
$$

for $y > 0$, where $B(p, q) = \Gamma(p)\Gamma(q)/\Gamma(p+q))$. The hth moment of the distribution is explicitly given by:

$$
E(y^h) = \frac{b^h B\left(p + \dfrac{h}{a}; q - \dfrac{h}{a}\right)}{B(p, q)} = \frac{b^h \Gamma\left(p + \dfrac{h}{a}\right)\Gamma\left(q - \dfrac{h}{a}\right)}{\Gamma(p)\Gamma(q)} \tag{11.43}
$$

The parameters of this distribution have the following meaning:

- a is the speed at which the tails of the distribution converge to the x axis. As a tends to infinity, the GB2 converges to a lognormal distribution.
- aq measures the thickness of the distribution.
- As p increases, q decreases, and vice versa.
- p and q must be larger than zero, in order for $B(p, q)$ to be defined.

Following TKA, the prices of European call and put options using the GB2 distribution are defined by:

$$C_{GB2}(K, \tau) = S I_z(q - a^{-1}, p + a^{-1}) - K I_z(q, p)$$
$$P_{GB2}(K, \tau) = K I_{1-z}(q, p) - S I_{1-z}(p + a^{-1}, q - a^{-1}) \tag{11.44}$$

where

$$z = \frac{(\lambda S/K)^a}{1 + (\lambda S/K)^a}, \lambda = \frac{B(p, q)}{B(p + a^{-1}, q - a^{-1})},$$
$$B_z(p, q) = \frac{z^p F_1^2(p, 1 - q, 1 + p; z)}{p}, I_z(p, q) = \frac{B_z(p, q)}{B(p, q)}$$

and the hypergeometric function:

$$F_q^p \left(a_1 \ldots a_p, b_1 \ldots b_q; z \right) = \sum_{i=0}^{\infty} \frac{(a_1)_i \ldots (a_p)_i}{(b_1)_i \ldots (b_q)_i} \frac{z}{i!}$$

An estimate of this distribution's parameters is then reduced to a numerical optimization problem (based on relative error estimates) which can be formulated as follows:

$$\operatorname*{Min}_{a,b,p,q} \sum_{i=1}^{n} \left[\frac{C(K_i, \tau) - \hat{C}_i}{\hat{C}_i} \right]^2 + \sum_{j=1}^{m} \left[\frac{P(K_i, \tau) - \hat{P}_i}{\hat{P}_i} \right]^2 \tag{11.45}$$

or:

$$\operatorname*{Min}_{a,b,p,q} \sum_{i=1}^{n} \left[C(K_i, \tau) - \hat{C}_i \right]^2 + \sum_{j=1}^{m} \left[P(K_i, \tau) - \hat{P}_i \right]^2 + \left[\frac{bB(p + 1/a; q - 1/a)}{B(p, q)} - F \right]^2 \tag{11.46}$$

Note that the mean of the distribution (moment for $h = 1$) ought to be equal to the forward price:

$$F = \frac{bB(p + 1/a; q - 1/a)}{B(p, q)} \tag{11.47}$$

The numerical solution of these problems is straightforward. There are nonetheless some difficulties due to the important and needed data that a multiplicity of parameters (four in our case) requires for the parameters' estimates be meaningful.

THE A-PARAMETRIC APPROACH AND THE BLACK-SCHOLES MODEL

Unlike the parametric approach where a risk-neutral distribution model is assumed a priori, the a-parametric approach derives the implied probability density function (PDF) directly from the second derivative of option prices with respect to their strike. For example, for a vanilla call option with strike K and maturity T, we have seen that:

$$C(S(0),0) = e^{-R_f T} \int_K^\infty (S(T) - K) f^Q(S(T)) dS(T) \tag{11.48}$$

where $f^Q(S(T))$ is the underlying risk-neutral distribution at its underlying maturity. Note again that:

$$\frac{\partial C(S(0),0)}{\partial K} = -e^{-R_f T} \int_K^\infty f^Q(S) dt = -e^{-R_f T}\left[1 - F^Q(K)\right]$$

$$\frac{\partial^2 C(S(0),0)}{\partial K^2} = e^{-R_f T} f^Q(S) \quad \text{and} \quad f^Q(S) = e^{R_f T}\frac{\partial^2 C(S(0),0)}{\partial K^2} \tag{11.49}$$

and therefore, a numerical discretization yields (see also Breeeden and Litzenberger, 1978):

$$-e^{-R_f T}\left[1 - F^Q(K_i)\right] = \frac{C(S(0),0\,|\,K_i, T) - C(S(0),0\,|\,K_{i-1}, T)}{K_i - K_{i-1}} \tag{11.50}$$

or

$$F^Q(K_i) = 1 - e^{R_f T}\left[\frac{C(S(0),0\,|\,K_i, T) - C(S(0),0\,|\,K_{i-1}, T)}{K_i - K_{i-1}}\right] \tag{11.51}$$

The explicit expression to the implied risk-neutral distribution is thus:

$$f^Q(K_i) = e^{R_f T}\frac{\partial^2 C(S(0),0\,|\,K_i, T)}{\partial K^2}$$

$$= e^{R_f T}\frac{C(S(0),0\,|\,K_{i+1}, T) - C(S(0),0\,|\,K_i, T) + C(S(0),0\,|\,K_{i-1}, T)}{(K_{i+1} - K_i)^2}$$

$$\tag{11.52}$$

Such a relationship is of little use if options are not traded at all possible strikes. To circumvent this difficulty, Shimko (1993) suggests an approach based on an estimate of the smile. In particular, given a volatility smile, found through an appropriate fitting technique (such as a spline fitted to available implied volatilities or nonlinear regression as will be considered below). Other techniques for densities estimation are also used in practice (see the many references to this effect at the end of this chapter as well as extensions and programs in www.charletapiero.com).

EXAMPLE: THE SHIMKO TECHNIQUE

A discretized model of equation (11.52), a function of the strike and volatility, yields:

$$f^{Q}(K_i) \approx e^{R_f(T-t)} \frac{C_t\left(\sigma_{i+1,t},\, K_{i+1}\right) + C_t\left(\sigma_{i-1,t},\, K_{i-1}\right) - 2C_t\left(\sigma_{i,t},\, K_i\right)}{(\Delta K_i)^2} \qquad (11.53)$$

where $C_t\left(\sigma_{i,t},\, K_i\right)$ is the call option price corresponding to a strike K_i and implied volatility $\sigma_{i,t}$ estimated at time t and corresponding to the option's strike. For a discrete state approximation of the call option's second-order derivative in equation (11.53) to be precise, a continuum of strikes for call option prices is needed (which is not possible since the number of options with different strikes traded is not usually large). As a result, a *smile*, expressing volatility as a function of the strikes, $\sigma_{i,t} = \sigma_t(K_i)$, is used. Using neighboring strikes, we obtain a numerical technique providing an a-parametric definition of the risk-neutral distribution which is coherent with the options smile, or:

$$f^{Q}(K_i) \approx e^{R_f(T-t)} \frac{C_t\left(\sigma_t(K_{i+1}),\, K_{i+1}\right) + C_t\left(\sigma_t(K_{i-1}),\, K_{i-1}\right) - 2C_t\left(\sigma_t(K_i),\, K_i\right)}{(\Delta K_i)^2}$$

$$(11.54)$$

where $\Delta K_i = K_{i+1} - K_i = K_i - K_{i-1}$. To obtain a set of implied and neighboring strikes, Shimko, suggests that the implied volatility corresponding to a set of traded options be fitted to a quadratic regression such as:

$$\sigma_j^{IV} = \beta_0 + \beta_1 K_j + \beta_2 K_j^2 + \varepsilon_i \qquad (11.55)$$

where ε_i is a random error, a zero mean and normally distributed random variable, while σ_j^{IV} is the implied volatility corresponding to a call option whose strike is $K_j, j = 1, 2, \ldots, n$. A regression over n data points of (11.55) provides parameter estimates (b_0, b_1, b_2) that define the smile. In other words, the implied volatility estimate of the smile is some function:

$$\sigma_{t,i} = \sigma_t(K_i) = b_0 + b_1 K_i + b_2 K_i^2 \qquad (11.56)$$

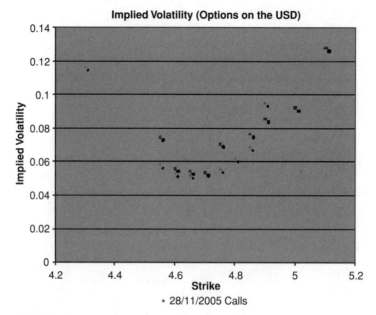

FIGURE 11.1   The Smile

Inserting the volatility estimate in, say, a Black-Scholes call option price, we have:

$$C_{t,i}^{synthetic} = C_t^{BS}(S_0, K_i, T - t, R_f, \sigma_t(K_i)) \tag{11.57}$$

Graphically, the smile and its fit to a quadratic regression may look like Figures 11.1 and 11.2, while the implied density function calculated by the synthetic

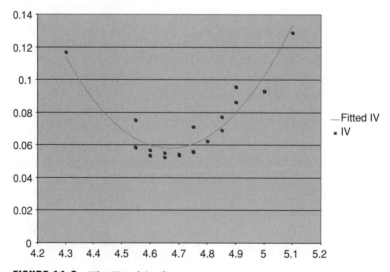

FIGURE 11.2   The Fitted Smile

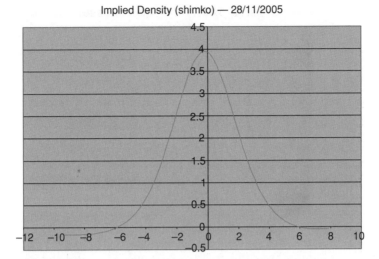

FIGURE 11.3 The Implied Risk-Neutral Distribution

call option prices, used in equation (11.54), is given in Figure 11.3 (see also the spreadsheet program in www.charlestapiero.com).

THE IMPLIED RISK-NEUTRAL DISTRIBUTION AND ENTROPY

The use of entropy functions to estimate implied risk-neutral distributions in practice was justified by both its analytical convenience and by some similarities between physics and finance (with an extensive literature on econophysics). The term entropy arose in quantum mechanics following the extraordinary and revolutionary contribution by Max Planck stating that light was not moving in a continuum but in quantas. Important contributions by Niels Bohr, Albert Einstein and by L. Boltzman in 1886 (who introduced the statistical approach to quantum mechanics). Boltzman in particular observed that entropy relates to "missing information" inasmuch as it pertains to the number of alternatives that remain possible to a physical system after all the macroscopically observable information concerning it has been recorded. In this sense, information can be interpreted as that which changes a system's state of randomness (or, equivalently, as that quantity which reduces entropy). Financial modelling based on entropy, although applied, can be misleading however if it is not properly understood. Next we consider specific and simple cases to explain the various meanings of entropy functions in a financial context. In particular we consider the "syntactic properties of entropy," the use of entropy as a logarithmic distance measure between probability distributions as well as the relationship between kernel pricing and relative entropy.

Assume an asset of m potential bid prices and let N be the volume of all bids at all prices. The probability of a specific bid price is given by the number of bids made for a particular price i given by N_i. Thus, the frequency of particular bid price is:

$$0 \le p_i = \frac{N_i}{N}, \quad \sum_{i=1}^{m} N_i = N \tag{11.58}$$

The total number of potential "bids-prices distributions" is therefore a combination of all bids made by all participating traders and investors at all prices, or:

$$W = \frac{N!}{\prod_{i=1}^{m} N_i!}, \quad \sum_{i=1}^{m} N_i = N \tag{11.59}$$

The term W thus defines the number of possible bids underlying the "broad variety of potential distributions" that bid prices can assume. These distributions have particular mathematical properties that relate to entropy functions. In particular, the more "evenly" distributed are bid prices the larger W. Instead of equation (11.59), it is convenient to consider its natural logarithmic function, $\ln(W)$, or:

$$\ln W = \sum_{j=1}^{N} \ln j - \sum_{i=1}^{m} \sum_{j=1}^{N_i} \ln j \tag{11.60}$$

Note that when N is large, (and therefore can be presumed to be more liquid and thereby more complete), a continuous integral approximation to (11.60) using the integral below leads to:

$$\sum_{j=1}^{N} \ln j \approx \int_{1}^{N} \ln(x)dx = N \ln(N) - N \tag{11.61}$$

And,

$$\ln W = N \ln(N) - N - \left(\sum_{i=1}^{m} \left(Np_i \ln(Np_i) - Np_i \right) \right) \tag{11.62}$$

The average number $(\ln W)/N$ reduces to the entropy function, expressing an index for the potential number of "bids distributions," denoted by $H(p)$, or:

$$\frac{\ln W}{N} = \sum_{i=1}^{m} \left(p_i \ln \left(\frac{1}{p_i} \right) \right) = H(p) \quad \text{or} \quad W = e^{NH(p)} \tag{11.63}$$

Entropy can be shown to be a positive function whose maximum is defined when the bid prices frequencies are equi-probable, namely that $p_i = 1/m$. A proof is a simple exercise and results from the solution of the optimization problem below:

$$\underset{\{p_i, i=1,2,\dots,m\}}{\text{Max}} \; H(p) = \sum_{i=1}^{m} \left(p_i \ln \left(\frac{1}{p_i} \right) \right) \; \text{Subject to}: \sum_{i=1}^{m} p_i = 1, \; p_i \geq 0 \quad (11.64)$$

This particular property has been used to justify the use of entropy functions as "distance measures" between a given probability and the (equi-probable) maximum entropy function. In particular, since $H^{\max} = H(1/m)$ is the maximum entropy, $H^{\max} - H(p)$ can be interpreted as a sort of "distance" between a given probability distribution $\{p_i, i = 1, 2, \dots, m\}$ and the uniform probability distribution. An explicit measure of such distance is thus an expected value under some probability measure (a P measure in our case) of the logarithmic ratio of probabilities, or:

$$H^{\max} - H(p) = \ln(m) - \sum_{i=1}^{m} \left(p_i \ln \left(\frac{1}{p_i} \right) \right) = \sum_{i=1}^{m} \left(p_i \ln \left(\frac{p_i}{1/m} \right) \right)$$

$$= E^P \left(\ln \left(\frac{\tilde{p}}{1/m} \right) \right) \quad (11.65)$$

Equation (11.65) is thus a measure of relative information to that of a state of total ignorance characterized by equi-probabilities for all prices. An extension of this relative distance to that of two probability measures, say P and Q, is then:

$$D(Q, P) = H(p) - H(q) = E^Q \left(\ln(\tilde{q}) \right) - E^P \left(\ln(\tilde{p}) \right)$$

$$= E^Q \left(\ln \left(\frac{\tilde{q}}{1/m} \right) \right) - E^P \left(\ln \left(\frac{\tilde{p}}{1/m} \right) \right) \quad (11.66)$$

If "entropy" is interpreted as a "state of knowledge," or a departure from the equi-probable price distribution then $D(Q, P)$ is a measure of "state of knowledge" of one distribution relative to the other. In our case, equation (11.66), provides a measure of "market price entropy" (measure Q) relative to the personal price entropy (measure P).

Extending an interpretation of (11.65) and (11.66) to an expectation relative to a specific (market or personal) distribution (measures Q or P), the expected logarithmic distance "relative" entropy functions (Kulllback, 1959) are given by:

$$I(Q, P) = E^P \left(\ln \left(\frac{\tilde{q}}{\tilde{p}} \right) \right) = \sum_{i=1}^{m} p_i \ln \left(\frac{q_i}{p_i} \right) \quad \text{and}$$

$$I(P, Q) = E^Q \left(\ln \left(\frac{\tilde{p}}{\tilde{q}} \right) \right) = \sum_{i=1}^{m} q_i \ln \left(\frac{p_i}{q_i} \right) \quad (11.67)$$

Then, under an investor's personal measure P, $I(Q, P)$ denotes "sort of distance" between these two measures while $I(P, Q)$ denotes the distance under a model risk neutral probability measure. Their sum is defined by Kullback as a divergence:

$$J(P, Q) = E^Q \left(\ln \left(\frac{\tilde{p}}{\tilde{q}} \right) \right) + E^P \left(\ln \left(\frac{\tilde{q}}{\tilde{p}} \right) \right) = \sum_{i=1}^{m} (q_i - p_i) \ln \left(\frac{p_i}{q_i} \right) \tag{11.68}$$

Under a P (investor's estimate) measure, implied risk neutral probabilities may be found by minimizing the expected "distance" between these probabilities subject to the probability constraints defining the information available to the investor. For example, let a model implied risk neutral probabilities for an asset priced at a future time T be defined in terms of some parameters $q_i (\mu, \xi)$. The "relative distance" (with respect to the investor's P measure) to a market price distribution subject to put and call option prices at that future time is found by solving the following problem for the risk neutral probabilities parameters:

$$\underset{\tilde{q}}{\text{Min}} \ I(P, Q) = E^P \left(\ln \left(\frac{\tilde{q}}{\tilde{p}} \right) \right) \quad \text{or} \quad \underset{(\mu, \xi)}{\text{Min}} \ I(P, Q) \sum_{i=1}^{m} p_i \ln \left(\frac{q_i (\mu, \xi)}{p_i} \right)$$

Subject to:

$$C_{0,j} = \beta^T E^Q \left(\max \left(\tilde{S} - K_j, 0 \right) \right) = \beta^T \sum_{i=1}^{m} q_i (\mu, \xi) \max \left(S_i - K_j \right)$$

$$P_{0,k} = \beta^T E^Q \left(\max \left(V_k - \tilde{S}, 0 \right) \right) = \beta^T \sum_{i=1}^{m} q_i (\mu, \xi) \max \left(V_k - S_i \right)$$

$$\beta = \left(\frac{1}{1 + R_f(0, T)} \right), q_i (\mu, \xi) \geq 0, \ \sum_{i=1}^{m} q_i (\mu, \xi) = 1,$$

$$i = 1, 2, \dots, m, \quad j = 1, 2, \dots, u; \quad k = 1, 2, \dots, v \tag{11.69}$$

This is a standard constraint optimization problem in two parameters which can be solved numerically. When the objective between the P and Q measures distances is assumed to be the divergence of these two distributions, then a solution to problem (11.69) will use the objective estimate (11.68). The choice of a "distance measure" and the information available to an investor determines the estimate of the risk neutral (Q) probabilities. Below a number of examples and extensions are considered to highlight the applications of the entropy based approaches.

EXAMPLES AND APPLICATIONS

The Maximum Entropy distribution
Consider the following entropy maximization problem:

$$\underset{q_i, i=1,2,\dots,n}{\text{Max}} \sum_{i=1}^{n} q_i \ln \left(\frac{1}{q_i} \right) \text{ Subject to}: S_{0,k} = \frac{1}{1 + R_f} \sum_{i=1}^{n} q_i S_{i,k} \tag{11.70}$$

And $\sum_{i=1}^{n} q_i = 1, 0 \le p_i \le 1, k = 1, 2, \ldots, m$. We assume here that $S_{0,k}$ are m derivative prices of some underlying distribution. A solution to this problem is given by the solution of n simultaneous non linear equations of the form:

$$q_i^* = \frac{\exp\left(-\sum_{k=1}^{m} \lambda_k S_{i,k}\right)}{\sum_{i=1}^{n} \exp\left(-\sum_{k=1}^{m} \lambda_k S_{i,k}\right)}, \quad \sum_{i=1}^{n}\left(\frac{\exp\left(-\sum_{k=1}^{m} \lambda_k S_{i,k}\right)}{\sum_{i=1}^{n} \exp\left(-\sum_{k=1}^{m} \lambda_k S_{i,k}\right)}\right) = 1 \qquad (11.71)$$

where λ_k are the Lagrange multipliers of the optimization problem. Replacing the risk neutral probability estimate (11.71) into the constraint prices in (11.70);

$$S_{0,k} = \frac{1}{1 + R_f} \sum_{i=1}^{n} q_i^* S_{i,k}$$

$$= \frac{1}{1 + R_f} \sum_{i=1}^{n} \left\{ \frac{\exp\left(-\sum_{k=1}^{m} \lambda_k S_{i,k}\right)}{\sum_{i=1}^{n} \exp\left(-\sum_{k=1}^{m} \lambda_k S_{i,k}\right)} \right\} S_{i,k}, \quad \sum_{i=1}^{n}\left(\frac{\exp\left(-\sum_{k=1}^{m} \lambda_k S_{i,k}\right)}{\sum_{i=1}^{n} \exp\left(-\sum_{k=1}^{m} \lambda_k S_{i,k}\right)}\right) = 1$$

$$(11.72)$$

we obtain a system of nonlinear equations in the m Lagrange multipliers. Their solution reinserted in (11.71) will provide a numerical estimate of the implied risk neutral probabilities.

Problem
Consider the following continuous maximum entropy problem and show that its solution is an exponential risk neutral probability distribution:

$$\underset{f^Q(.)}{\text{Max}} \int_0^\infty f^Q(x) \ln\left(\frac{1}{f^Q(x)}\right) dx \quad \text{Subject to:}$$

$$(11.73)$$

$$S_{0,k} = e^{-R_f T} \int_0^\infty f^Q(x) S_{T,k}(x) dx \quad \text{and} \quad 1 = \int_0^\infty f^Q(x)$$

Calculate as well the solution of the relative entropy problem defined below and show that it has also an exponential probability distribution:

$$\underset{f^Q(.)}{\text{Min}} \int_0^\infty f^Q(x) \ln\left(\frac{f^P(x)}{f^Q(x)}\right) dx \quad \text{Subject to:}$$

$$S_{0,k} = e^{-R_f T} \int_0^\infty f^Q(x) S_{T,k}(x) dx \quad \text{and} \quad 1 = \int_0^\infty f^Q(x) \tag{11.74}$$

Finally discuss what are the similarities and the differences between these two problems.

The Exponential Implied Risk-Neutral Distribution
In many applications an implied exponential probability distribution is determined by solving the minimum relative entropy problem subject to currently observed call and put option prices with expiry date at time T:

$$\underset{\tilde{q}}{\text{Min}}\, I(P, Q) = E^Q\left(\ln\left(\frac{\tilde{p}}{\tilde{q}}\right)\right) = \sum_{i=1}^m q_i \ln\left(\frac{p_i}{q_i}\right)$$

Subject to:

$$C_{0,j} = \beta^T E^Q\left(\max\left(\tilde{S} - K_j, 0\right)\right) = \beta^T \sum_{i=1}^m q_i \max\left(S_i - K_j\right) \tag{11.75}$$

$$P_{0,k} = \beta^T E^Q\left(\max\left(V_k - \tilde{S}, 0\right)\right) = \beta^T \sum_{i=1}^m q_i \max\left(V_k - S_i\right)$$

where $\beta = \left(\frac{1}{1 + R_f(0, T)}\right)$, $q_i \geq 0$, $\sum_{i=1}^m q_i = 1$, $i = 1, 2, \ldots, m$, $j = 1, 2, \ldots, u$; $k = 1, 2, \ldots, v$. This is a standard constraint optimization problem whose solution is given by the simultaneous solution of the following system of linear equations:

$$\frac{q_i}{p_i} e^{1 + p_i/q_i} = \exp\left\{\mu_0 + \beta^T \sum_{j=1}^u \lambda_j \max\left(S_i - K_j, 0\right) + \beta^T \sum_{j=1}^v \xi_k \max(V_k - S_i, 0)\right\}$$

$$C_{0,j} = \beta^T \sum_{i=1}^m q_i \max\left(S_i - K_j, 0\right) \tag{11.76}$$

$$P_{0,k} = \beta^T \sum_{i=1}^m q_i \max(V_k - S_i, 0)$$

$$\sum_{i=1}^m q_i = 1, \quad i = 1, 2, \ldots, m, \quad j = 1, 2, \ldots u; \quad k = 1, 2, \ldots, v$$

Namely, optimization with respect to the risk-neutral probabilities provides a system of nonlinear equations in the Lagrange multipliers λ_j and ξ_k in the implied risk-neutral probabilities. In continuous time, this is reduced to a simple implied exponential probability distribution as indicated in the previous problem.

Divergence as an index of "distance" between distributions
Let (N_A, N_B) be the total number of ask and bid prices and let the numbers for (m) ask-bid prices (x_i), $i = 1, 2, \ldots m$ be $(N_A(x_i), N_B(x_i))$. Then,

$$W_A = \frac{N_A!}{\prod\limits_{i=1}^{m} N_A(x_i)}, \ \sum_{i=1}^{m} N_A(x_i) = N_A \ \text{and} \ W_B = \frac{N_B!}{\prod\limits_{i=1}^{m} N_B(x_i)}, \ \sum_{i=1}^{m} N_B(x_i) = N_B \quad (11.77)$$

The ask and bid entropy functions are:

$$H_K(p) = \sum_{i=1}^{m} \left(p_K(x_i) \ln \left(\frac{1}{p_K(x_i)} \right) \right) = \sum_{i=1}^{m} \left(\frac{N_K(x_i)}{N_K} \ln \left(\frac{N_K}{N_K(x_i)} \right) \right), K = A, B$$

$$(11.78)$$

While their divergence is:

$$J(A, B) = \sum_{i=1}^{m} (p_A(x_i) - p_B(x_i)) \ln \left(\frac{p_B(x_i)}{p_A(x_i)} \right)$$

$$= \sum_{i=1}^{m} \left(\frac{N_A(x_i)}{N_A} - \frac{N_B(x_i)}{N_B} \right) \ln \left(\frac{N_A N_B(x_i)}{N_B N_A(x_i)} \right) \quad (11.79)$$

The larger the divergence, the more disparate these distributions and therefore the "more distant" are bid and ask prices (implying perhaps that the market is more or less liquid). Say that a given price $\pi = x_i$ is observed (or set by a market maker). The volume $V(\pi)$ transacted equals then:

$$V(\pi) = \min \left(\sum_{\forall i, x_i \geq \pi} N_A(x_i), \sum_{\forall i, x_i \leq \pi} N_B(x_i) \right) \quad (11.80)$$

And therefore if a market maker set the price at a given time to π, the liquidity (volume) will be that of equation (11.80). A market maker maximizing liquidity will then maximize (11.80) while a market maker seeking to minimize the divergence will use a price that minimizes the ex-post divergence (11.79). Explicitly if the price set is $\pi = x_i$, then for the ask side, we have a volume of transactions for the following ask prices $x > \pi$ and for bids with prices $x < \pi$.

Entropy and Time

At any time T, entropy is an index of dispersion. Thus, if $H_{T+1}^m(q) > H_T^m(q)$, this implies that entropy is growing and dispersion is increasing. In other words if we interpret entropy as a measure of disorderliness, a chaotic growth in future market prices arises if the number of states increases (i.e., m increases), the entropy increases or both. In other words:

$$D^{m_{T+1}}(Q_{T+1}, Q_T) = H_{T+1}^{m_{T+1}}(q) - H_T^{m_T}(q) = E_{T+1}^Q(\ln(\tilde{q})) - E_T^Q(\ln(\tilde{q})) > 0$$

$$(11.81)$$

A Binomial Model

Say that $p_i, i = 1, 2, 3, \ldots n$ is a known empirical distribution for prices at a future date, and let $q_i, i = 1, 2, 3, \ldots, n$ be a model risk-neutral probability distribution for prices S_i at a given future time n. Then, for a binomial risk-neutral process (with two parameters), we have:

$$q_i = \binom{n}{i} q^i (1-q)^{n-i} \quad \text{and}$$

$$\underset{0 \le p \le 1}{\text{Min}} \ I(P, Q) = \sum_{i=1}^n \left(\binom{n}{i} p^i (1-q)^{n-i} \right) \ln \frac{\binom{n}{i} p^i (1-p)^{n-i}}{\left(\binom{n}{i} q^i (1-q)^{n-i} \right)} \quad (11.82)$$

which can be minimized with respect to parameter q_i subject to a set of constraints representing the risk-neutral pricing of observable assets, such as:

$$\sum_{i=0}^n q_i = \sum_{i=0}^n \binom{n}{i} q^i (1-q)^{n-i} = 1 \text{ and } S_0 = \left(\frac{1}{1+R_f} \right)^n \sum_{i=0}^n S_i \binom{n}{i} q^i (1-q)^{n-i}$$

$$(11.83)$$

And for a call option:

$$C_0 = \left(\frac{1}{1+R_f} \right)^n \sum_{i=0}^n \binom{n}{i} q^i (1-q)^{n-i} Max(S_i - K, 0) \quad (11.84)$$

Problem: The Lognormal Model

Let models be defined by normal rates of return:

$$d \ln S(t) = \mu_i dt + \sigma_i dW_i, \quad i = 1, 2, \ldots, n. \quad (11.85)$$

Assume that a series of returns are calculated daily. Determine the risk-neutral probability distribution that best fit this model. Additional problems and development can be found in www.charlestapiero.com.

Problem: The Implied Loss in a CDO (refer to Chapter 10)
Let (π_E, π_M, π_S) be the prices of three tranches in a CDO. Use the relative entropy approach to calculate an implied risk-neutral loss distribution.

RISK ATTITUDE, IMPLIED RISK-NEUTRAL DISTRIBUTION AND ENTROPY

In Chapters 5 and 6, an implied risk-neutral distribution was found to be implied by a utility function's Arrow-Pratt index of risk aversion. The problem was stated as follows: Consider an asset whose current price is $1 and whose future price is random and given by W_T. The investor's rationale is to optimize his future expected utility based on a private (measure P) distribution subject to an investment of $1 now. The mathematical expression of this problem is:

$$\begin{cases} \underset{W}{\text{Max}}\, E^P u(W_T) = \int u(W_T) f^P(W_T) dW_T \\[2mm] \text{Subject to: } 1 = \dfrac{1}{(1+R_f)^T} E^Q(W_T) = \int W_T f^Q(W_T) dW_T \end{cases} \qquad (11.86)$$

where E^P is an expectation of the utility using the investor's personal-subjective probability distribution, while E^Q is an expectation that uses a risk-neutral probability distribution (since the price now is a risk-free discounted value of the next-period expected price). A solution is straightforward and leads, as seen in Chapter 5, to:

$$\begin{cases} f^Q(W_T) = f^P(W_T) e^{-A(W_T)} \\[2mm] A(W_T) = \displaystyle\int\limits_0^{W_T} A_r(w)\, dw = \ln \dfrac{f^P(W_T)}{f^Q(W_T)} \end{cases} \qquad (11.87)$$

where $A_r(w)$ is the Arrow-Pratt index of absolute risk aversion. In this case, the expected integral of the investor's Arrow-Pratt index of risk aversion with respect to a risk-neutral measure yields the relative entropy measure:

$$E^Q(A(W_T)) = E^Q\left(\ln \frac{f^P(W_T)}{f^Q(W_T)}\right) \qquad (11.88)$$

For example, assume that an investor has an exponential utility function whose index of risk aversion is $\mu > 0$. Then:

$$A(W_T) = \mu W_T = \ln \frac{f^P(W_T)}{f^Q(W_T)}, \quad f^Q(W_T) = f^P(W_T) e^{-\mu W_T}$$

And therefore, the implied risk neutral distribution (assuming kernel pricing) depreciates the probabilities of the investors' private future estimates as indicated above.

Problem
What is the relationship between the entropy of a risk-neutral probability distribution and a risk-averse personal investor whose utility function is of the HARA type?

Problem
Consider and solve the following divergence minimization problem:

$$\underset{f^Q(W_T)}{\text{Min}} J(Q:P) = \int_{\underline{W}_T}^{\overline{W}_T} \left(f^Q(v) - f^P(v) \right) \ln \frac{f^P(v)}{f^Q(v)} dv$$

(11.89)

$$\text{Subject to: } 1 = e^{-R_f T} \int_{\underline{W}_T}^{\overline{W}_T} v f^Q(v) \, dv \quad \text{and} \quad 1 = \int_{\underline{W}_T}^{\overline{W}_T} f^Q(v) \, dv$$

What is the implied risk neutral probability distribution? Assume also that an investor has an exponential utility function with an index of risk aversion μ. In this case, $A(w) = \mu(w - \underline{W}_T)$ and $E^Q A(w) = \mu(E^Q(w) - \underline{W}_T)$ and $E^P A(w) = \mu(E^P(w) - \underline{W}_T)$. Further, since,

$$A(v) = \mu(v - \underline{W}_T) = \ln \frac{f^P(v)}{f^Q(v)}$$

(11.90)

We have also:

$$\underset{f^Q(W_T)}{\text{Min}} J(Q:P) = \int_{\underline{W}_T}^{\overline{W}_T} \left(f^Q(v) - f^P(v) \right) \ln \frac{f^P(v)}{f^Q(v)} dv = \int_{\underline{W}_T}^{\overline{W}_T} \left(f^Q(v) - f^P(v) \right) \mu(v - \underline{W}_T) dv$$

(11.91)

And therefore, for an implied exponential utility function the divergence is,

$$J(Q:P) = \mu \left(E^Q(v) - E^P(v) \right)$$

(11.92)

Discuss the solutions you obtain to these problems and calculate the implied risk-neutral distribution that minimizes the divergence between private and the risk-neutral probability distribution of future state prices.

SUMMARY

Techniques to extract risk-neutral distributions from available prices are necessarily approximate for two reasons. First, financial markets might not be complete and therefore the artifice of risk-neutral pricing is wrong. Second, the information we have to construct the risk-neutral distribution implied by financial prices is limited (mostly *very* limited). Given the practical importance of such implied distributions to price assets, three approaches were outlined in this chapter.

A first parametric approach consists in assuming a probability distribution model and fitting observed prices to this model to recover its parameters. Such an approach depends on the choice of the distribution and an appreciation of financial markets' evolution. Mixture stochastic processes (such as a mixture of lognormal distributions) and parameter-rich distributions (such as the GB2 distribution) were used. Fitting such distributions is a numerical challenge, however, with relatively few acceptable statistical tools (i.e., providing a probability confidence for the parameters estimates) to confirm the statistical validity of these estimates.

The second, a-parametric approach we used provided a "model free" risk-neutral distribution. Numerical techniques as well as semi-modeling techniques are then used. For example, the Shimko modeling approach constructs such a distribution from the *smile* of estimated volatilities as a function of options strikes. However, these volatilities are calculated by inverting the Black-Scholes option price model (and are therefore also model-specific). Other techniques include among many others, the entropy models considered here. Such an approach relates the implied risk-neutral distribution as well to kernel pricing (as introduced in Chapters 5 and 6), through the implied Arrow-Pratt index of risk aversion of the investor and his private probability distribution of future state prices.

APPENDIX: THE IMPLIED VOLATILITY— THE DUPIRE MODEL*

Let the underlying risk-neutral process be defined by a volatility function $\Lambda(S, t)$:

$$\frac{\Delta S(t)}{S(t)} = R_f dt + \Delta(S, t) dW^Q(t), S(0) > 0 \tag{A.1}$$

Thus, the price of a call option under a Q risk-neutral process whose exercise is at time T and strike is K is given by:

$$C(S_t, t : K, T) = e^{-R_f(T-t)} \int_K^\infty (S(T) - K) f^Q(S(T) : S(t), t) dS(T) \tag{A.2}$$

while the first derivative with respect to the strike is:

$$\frac{\partial C(S_t, t : K, T)}{\partial K} = -e^{-R_f(T-t)} \int_K^\infty f^Q(S(T) : S(t), t) dS(T)$$

$$= -e^{-R_f(T-t)} \left(1 - F^Q(K : S(t), t)\right) \tag{A.3}$$

---

*Requires a slightly more advanced mathematical background; please see the Introduction.

A second derivative yields now:

$$f^Q(K : S(t), t) = e^{R_f(T-t)} \frac{\partial^2 C(S_t, t : K, T)}{\partial K^2} \tag{A.4}$$

Further, a derivative with respect to the T (and simplifying our notation) is:

$$\frac{\partial f^Q}{\partial T} = e^{R_f(T-t)} \left(R_f \frac{\partial^2 C}{\partial K^2} + \frac{\partial}{\partial T} \frac{\partial^2 C}{\partial K^2} \right) = e^{R_f(T-t)} \frac{\partial^2}{\partial K^2} \left(R_f C + \frac{\partial C}{\partial T} \right) \tag{A.5}$$

The Fokker-Planck partial differential equation (corresponding to the evolution of the risk-neutral probability distribution of the market price process) of the underlying defines the time variation of the underlying risk-probability distribution, which is given by:

$$\frac{\partial f^Q}{\partial T} = -R_f \frac{\partial \left(K f^Q \right)}{\partial K} + \frac{1}{2} \frac{\partial^2 \left(\Lambda^2(K, t) K^2 f^Q \right)}{\partial K^2}, \ f^Q(S_0, 0, K, 0) = \delta(K - S_0) \tag{A.6}$$

where δ is the Dirac delta function, which means in this case that the initial stock price is known. Note that in this case,

$$\frac{\partial f^Q}{\partial T} = -R_f \frac{\partial \left(K f^Q \right)}{\partial K} + \frac{1}{2} \frac{\partial^2 \left(\Lambda^2(K, t) K^2 f^Q \right)}{\partial K^2} = e^{R_f(T-t)} \frac{\partial^2}{\partial K^2} \left(R_f C + \frac{\partial C}{\partial T} \right) \tag{A.7}$$

or

$$-R_f \frac{\partial^2}{\partial K^2} \left(K \frac{\partial C}{\partial K} - C \right) + \frac{1}{2} \frac{\partial^2}{\partial K^2} \left(\Lambda^2(K, t) K^2 f^Q \right) = \frac{\partial^2}{\partial K^2} \left(R_f C + \frac{\partial C}{\partial T} \right) \tag{A.8}$$

$$\frac{\partial^2}{\partial K^2} \left\{ -R_f \left(K \frac{\partial C}{\partial K} - C \right) + \frac{1}{2} \left(\Lambda^2(K, t) K^2 \frac{\partial^2 C}{\partial K^2} \right) - \left(R_f C + \frac{\partial C}{\partial T} \right) \right\} = 0 \tag{A.9}$$

Integrating twice, we obtain

$$-R_f \left(K \frac{\partial C}{\partial K} - C \right) + \frac{1}{2} \left(\Lambda^2(K, t) K^2 \frac{\partial^2 C}{\partial K^2} \right) - \left(R_f C + \frac{\partial C}{\partial T} \right) = A + BK \tag{A.10}$$

where A and B are two integration constants. Since all functions vanish when K tends to infinity, these constants are necessarily equal to zero and therefore,

$$\Lambda(K, T) = \sqrt{\frac{\left(R_f K \frac{\partial C}{\partial K} + \frac{\partial C}{\partial T} \right)}{\frac{1}{2} K^2 \frac{\partial^2 C}{\partial K^2}}} \tag{A.11}$$

This information is of course available in the Greeks and therefore provides a direct way to calculate the implied volatility by:

$$\Lambda(K, t) = \frac{1}{\sqrt{2}} \sqrt{\left(-\theta_K + R_f K \Delta_K\right)/K^2 \Gamma_K} \qquad \text{(A.12)}$$

TEST YOURSELF

The self-testing questions for this chapter are technical, empirical, and extensive. For this reason, they have been placed on the companion web site (www.charlestapiero.com).

REFERENCES

Aït-Sahalia, Y., and A. Lo. 1998. Nonparametric estimation of state-price densities implicit in financial asset prices. *Journal of Finance* 53:499–547.

———. 2000. Nonparametric risk management and implied risk aversion. *Journal of Econometrics* 94:9–51.

Alonzo, Francisco, Roberto Blanco, and Gonzalo Rubio, 2005. Testing the forecasting performance of IBEX 35 option implied risk neutral densities. Working paper No. 0504, Bank of Spain.

Anagnou, I., M. Bedendo, S. Hodges, and R. Tompkins, 2002, The relation between implied and realized probability density functions, Working paper, University of Warwick.

Bates, D. S. 1991. The crash of '87: Was it expected? The evidence from options markets. *Journal of Finance* 46:1009–1044.

Bliss, R., and N. Panigirtzoglou. 2002. Testing the stability of implied probability density functions. *Journal of Banking and Finance* 26:381–422.

Boltzmann, L., 1974. The second law of thermodynamics. Populare Schriften, Essay 3, address to a formal meeting of the Imperial Academy of Science, 29 May, 1886, reprinted in Ludwig Boltzmann, Theoretical physics and philosophical problem, S. G. Brush (Trans.). Boston: Reidel. (Original work published 1886).

Brailsford, Timothy J., and W. Faff, Robert, 1996. "An evaluation of volatility forecasting techniques," *Journal of Banking & Finance*, Elsevier, vol. 20(3):419–438, April.

Breeden, D., and R. Litzenberger. 1978. Prices of State-Contingent Claims implicit in option prices. *Journal of Business* 51:621–651.

Britten-Jones, M., and A. Neuberger. 2000. Option prices, implied price processes and stochastic volatility. *Journal of Finance* 5:839–866.

Burnham, Kenneth P., and David R. Anderson. 2001. Kullback-Leibler information as a basis for strong inference in ecological studies. *Wildlife Research* 28:111–119.

———. 2002. *Model selection and multimodel inference: A practical information-theoretic approach*, 2nd ed. New York: Springer Science.

Christensen, B., and N. Prabhala. 1998. The relation between implied and realized volatility. *Journal of Financial Economics* 50:125–150.

Christoffersen P., and S. Mazzotta. 2004. The informational content of over-the-counter currency options. Working paper, European Central Bank.

Corrado, C., and T. Miller. 1996. Efficient option-implied volatility estimators. *Journal of Futures Markets* 16:247–272.

Dupire, Bruno. 1994. Pricing with a smile. *Risk*, January.

Fackler, P. L., and R. P. King. 1990. Calibration of option-based probability assessments in agricultural commodity markets. *American Journal of Agricultural Economics* 72: 73–83.

Gibbs, J. W. 1873/1931. A method of geometrical representation of thermodynamic properties of substances by means of surfaces. Reprinted in *The Collected Works of J. W. Gibbs, Volume I Thermodynamics*, ed. W. R. Longley and R. G. Van Name, footnote page 52. New York: Longmans, Green, 1931.

Jackwerth, J. C. 1999. Option implied risk neutral distributions and implied binomial trees: A literature review. *Journal of Derivatives* 7:66–82.

———. 2000. Recovering risk aversion from option prices and realized returns. *Review of Financial Studies* 13(2): 433–451.

Jaynes, E. T. 1957a. Information theory and statistical mechanics. *Physical Review* 106:620.

———. 1957b. Information theory and statistical mechanics II. *Physical Review* 108:171.

Kullback, S. 1959. *Information Theory and Statistics*. New York: John Wiley & Sons.

———. 1987. The Kullback-Leibler distance. *American Statistician* 41:340–341.

Kullback, S., and R. A. Leibler. 1951. On information and sufficiency. Annals of Mathematical Statistics 22(1): 79–86. doi:10.1214/aoms/1177729694. MR39968.

Lucas, R. 1978. Asset prices in an exchange economy. *Econometrica* 46:1429–1446.

Mammen, E. 1991. Estimating a smooth monotone regression function. *Annals of Statistics* 19:724–740.

Mayhew, S. 1995. Implied volatility. *Financial Analysts Journal* 51:8–20.

Meyers, R. J., and S. D. Hanson. 1993. Pricing commodity options when the underlying future price exhibits time-varying volatility. *American Journal of Agricultural Economics* 75:121–130.

Perignon C., and C. Villa. 2002. Extracting information from option markets: Smiles, state price densities and risk aversion. *European Financial Management*, May.

Pratt, J. W. 1964. Risk aversion in the small and in the large. *Econometrica* 32: 122–136.

Rényi, A. 1961. On measures of information and entropy. *Proceedings of the 4th Berkeley Symposium on Mathematics, Statistics and Probability 1960.* 547–561. The Regents of the University of California. *All rights reserved.*

———. 1970. *Probability Theory*, Appendix, Sec. 4. New York: Elsevier.

Rodriguez, R. N. 1977. A guide to the Burr Type XII distributions. *Biometrika* 64:129–134.

Rouge, R., and N. El Karoui. 2000. Pricing via utility maximization and entropy. *Mathematical Finance* 10:259–276.

Rubinstein, M. 1976. The valuation of uncertain income streams and the pricing of options. *Bell Journal of Economics* 7:407–425.

———. 1994. Implied binomial trees. *Journal of Finance* 64:771–818.

Sherrick, B. J., S. H. Irwin, and D. L. Forster. 1992. Option-based evidence of the nonstationarity of S&P 500 futures price distributions. *Journal of Futures Markets* 12:1–16.

Shimko D., 'Bounds of Probability,' *Risk*, Vol. 6,1993, pp. 33–37.

So, J. 1987. The sub-Gaussian distribution of currency futures: Stable paretian or nonstationary? *Review of Economics and Statistics* 69:100–107.

Tadikamalla, P. R. 1980. A look at the Burr and related distributions. *International Statistical Review* 48:337–344.

Tapiero, C. S. 2004. Risk management. In *Encyclopedia on Actuarial Science and Risk Management*, ed. J. Teugels and B. Sundt. New York and London: John Wiley & Sons.

Tribus, Myron. 1961. *Thermodynamics and Thermostatics*. New York: D. Van Nostrand.

Tribus, M., and E. C. McIrvine. 1971. Energy and information. Scientific American 224:179–186.

Tunaru Radu, Ashay Kadam and George Albota, 2005, An Investigation of Parametric Risk Neutral Density Estimation, Cass Business School, City University London, Working version June.

Acknowledgments

Numerous discussions with well-known financial academics and managers and with my students at NYU–Polytechnic Institute have contributed to this book. Among the many I have consulted are Nassim Nicholas Taleb, whose extraordinary efforts remind us all that finance is about practice, not only theories; Alain Bensoussan; Pierre Vallois; Tyrone Duncan; Elias Shiu; Lorne Switzer; Sébastien Galy; Daniel Totouom-Tangho; JeanCarlo Bonilla; Roy Freedman; Daniel, Dafna, and Oren Tapiero (each of whom is involved in the real world of finance and economic development); Konstantin Kogan; Aimé Scannavino; Bertrand Munier; Mirela Ivan; Kevin Koshy; and many others whose names would fill pages of this book. I have learned from, interpreted, and used many other authors' contributions in a manner that is coherent with the intent of the book. I apologize if I have failed to refer fully to some of their work.

My colleagues in the Department of Finance and Risk Engineering, in particular Phil Maymin and Barry Blecherman, are gratefully acknowledged for both their comments and their contributions to making the Finance and Risk Engineering program at NYU–Polytechnic Institute far more in tune and sensitive to bridge economic theory and financial practice.

Last but not least, this book could not have been written without the tolerance of my life partner, Carole Solomon, a woman of great distinction, who had to endure many moments of my escaping into isolation in order to complete this book.

About the Author

Charles S. Tapiero is the Topfer Chair Distinguished Professor of Financial Engineering and Technology Management at the New York University Polytechnic Institute. He is also chair and founder of the Department of Finance and Risk Engineering. He has a worldwide reputation as an active researcher, consultant, and board member to large firms and to academic journals. Currently he is also co-founder and co-editor in chief of *Risk and Decision Analysis* (IOS Press). His fields of interest span financial engineering, risk assessment and analysis, actuarial and insurance finance, computational finance, and networks and supply chain risks. Professor Tapiero has held numerous public positions of responsibility at the highest levels of an industrial conglomerate (Koor Industries, 1994–2000) and at quasi-government agencies (1978–1982), as well as professorial positions in the United States, Europe, and Israel.

Professor Tapiero has published 13 books and over 350 papers on a broad range of issues spanning risk analysis, actuarial and financial risk engineering, and management. His books include *Applied Stochastic Models and Control in Finance and Insurance* (Kluwer Academic Press, 1998), *Risk and Financial Management: Mathematical and Computational Methods* (John Wiley & Sons, 2004), and *Supply Chain Games* (Springer, 2007). For a complete list, refer to his web sites:

www.charlestapiero.com
www.polyrisk.org
www.poly.edu/fe

Index

Abacus, 28
ABS. *See* Asset-backed securities (ABS)
Actuarial approach, 356, 395
Actuarial risk, 330
Actuarial science, 36
Actuarial techniques, 297
Adverse selection risk, 36, 196–197, 330
Agency problems, 193–195
AICPA. *See* American Institute of Certified Public
     Accountants (AICPA)
AIG (American International Group), 24, 343,
     355
Airbus, 12
Air transport accidents, 40
Alternative market structures, 56–57
American Institute of Certified Public Accountants
     (AICPA), 13
American Law Institute, 14
Analytic variance-covariance approach, 98
Annuities and obligations (problem), 235
Antipersistent time series, 134
A-parametric approach, 420–421
APT. *See* Asset price theory (APT)
Arbitrage, 368
Arbitrage CDO, 373
Arbitrage CLO, 370
Arbitrage-free price process, 259
Arbitrage pricing theory, 45
ARCH and GARCH estimators, 80–81
     AR (1)-ARCH (1) model (example), 81–82
     A GARCH, (1,1) model (example), 83
Arrow, Kenneth, 44, 205
Arrow-Debreu framework, 45, 145, 206–218, 297
     binomial option pricing (example), 212–213
     generalization to multiple periods (example),
        215–218
     generalization to *n* states (example), 210–212
     implied risk-neutral probability (problem), 213
     options pricing (problem), 218
     the price of a call option (example), 213-214
Arrow-Pratt index of risk aversion, 157, 158
Asian crisis of 1998, 198
Asian options (example), 227–228
Asset allocation:
     asset pricing theory (APT), 188
     efficiency frontier (problem), 185–186
     Markowitz-based approach, 181, 186–187

two-securities portfolio (problem), 187–188
two-securities portfolio problem (example),
     182–184
two-stock portfolio (example), 184–185
Asset-backed securities (ABS), 373
Asset price theory (APT), 145, 188
Asset pricing:
     Arrow-Debreu fundamental approach to,
        206–218
     overview of, 2–3
Assets:
     multiple, 226
     pricing of, 259–271
     real and financial, 15–16
Asymmetry, 68
ATM. *See* At-the-money (ATM)
At-the-money (ATM) options, 237
Attitudes, 5
Auction-rated security (ARS) crisis, 22–23
Autoregressive processes, 75–77
Axiomatic rationality, 145
AYGO pension. *See* Pay-as-you-go (PAYGO)
     pension

Bankers Trust, 369
Banking-money system crisis, 23–24
Bank interest rate on a house loan (example), 333
Bankruptcy, 303–304, 343
Bankruptcy index contract, 296
Barrier and other options (example), 228–229
Basel Committee on Bank Supervision, 25
Bayesian default model (example), 322–323
Bayesian probabilities (example), 311–312
Bayes' objective, 146
Behavioral finance (BH), 7
Beta:
     calculation of, 72–77
     problem, 72–73
BH. *See* Behavioral finance (BH)
Bid-ask spreads, 55–56
Binary options, 227
Binomial approximation, 277–278
Binomial cash flow, 262
Binomial distribution, 392
Binomial market, 207
Binomial model, 249–251, 305–306
Binomial option pricing (example), 212–213

Binomial option pricing model, 45
  change of measure in a binomial model
    (example), 249–251
  implied binomial distribution (example),
    413–415
Binomial price process, 216
BISTRO. *See* Broad Index Secured Trust Offering
    (BISTRO)
Bivariate data matrix and PCA (example),
    117–119
Bivariate dependent default distribution
    (example), 314–315
Black, Fischer, 45, 205
Black Scholes model, 75, 276–281, 420–421
  binomial approximation to, 277–278
  and portfolio replication, 278–281
Black-Scholes vanilla option, 276–284
Black swans, 26
Block, 56
Blyth, William, 20
Boeing, 12
Bohr, Niels, 422
Boltzman, L., 422
Bonds, 2, 9–10, 353
  calculating the spread of a default bond
    (example), 328–329
  CDO of default-coupon-paying bonds
    (example), 385–387
  CDO of zero coupon bonds (example), 382–385
  default, 300–301
  default models for (example), 391–395
  pricing a fixed-rate bond (example), 232–234
  pricing default bonds and the hazard rate
    (example), 331–332
  pricing of default bonds (example), 330–331
  rated, in CDO's (example), 387–391
  rating, 300–301
Bonus-malus insurance contracts, 36
Book of Calculations (Fibonacci), 292
Born, Max, 127
Broad Index Secured Trust Offering (BISTRO),
    370, 371
Brownian motion, 111
Brownian-normal like process, 131
Business enterprises, scoring, 300–301
Business firm, rating score of, 302
Business risk analysis factors, 303
Butterfly spread, 226
Buying Long, 15
Buy insurance to protect the portfolio from loan
    defaults (example), 333

Calculating the spread of a default bond
    (example), 328–329
Call (long) options, 17, 18
Call (short) option, 17
Capital adequacy ratio (CAR), 295, 296

Capital adequacy requirements (CAR), 379–398
Capital asset pricing model (CAPM), 45
  moments and (example), 70–72
CAPM. *See* Sharpe's capital asset pricing model
    (CAPM); Capital asset pricing model (CAPM)
CAR. *See* Capital adequacy ratio (CAR); Capital
    adequacy requirements (CAR)
Carbon dioxide emission rights, 3
Carbon dioxide emissions trading, 20
Cash CDOs, 369
Cash-settled stock index futures, 53
Catastrophic risks, 4, 40–41
Causal dependence, 127–129
CCAPM. *See* Consumption-based capital asset
    pricing model (CCAPM)
CDD. *See* Cooling degree day (CDD)
CDOs. *See* Collateralized debt obligations (CDOs)
CDSs. *See* Credit default swaps (CDSs)
Central banking, 293
Certainty equivalent, 97, 158
Certificate of deposits (CDs), 292
CFOs. *See* Collateralized fund obligations (CFOs)
CFRM. *See* Comprehensive financial risk
    management (CFRM)
Change measures, 129–130
Change of measure in a binomial model
    (example), 249–251
Chaos theory, 127
Chicago Climate Exchange, 3
Chicago Mercantile Exchange (CME), 21, 296
Chooser options (example), 228
Clayton copula, 123
Clearinghouses, 54, 358
CLN. *See* Credit-linked note (CLN)
CLO. *See* Collateralized loan obligation (CLO)
Closing transactions, 236
CME. *See* Chicago Mercantile Exchange (CME)
CMOSs. *See* Collateralized mortgage obligations
    (CMOs)
Coase, 48
Collateral:
  credit risk and, 334–337
  price of, 323, 324
Collateralized debt obligations (CDOs), 50, 353,
    354, 355, 373–374. *See also* Collateralized
    debt obligations (CDOs) quantitative models
    of baskets of various assets, 397
  collateralized loan obligations (CLO), 369–370
  collateralized mortgage obligations (CMOs),
    354–355
  collateralized mortgage obligations (CMOs)
    (example), 376–377
  and copulas, 371, 372
  defining maturity of, 375, 378–379
  forward-starting, 375
  generic market value structure, 378
  historical perspective, 353–354

KMV loss model (example), 396–397
market value, 375
modeling and pricing considerations, 370–371
models and price applications, 395–397
risk-reward properties, 371, 397
and special purpose vehicles (SPVs) (example), 377–379
synthetic, 369, 370, 372, 397
Collateralized debt obligations (CDOs) quantitative models:
CDO of default-coupon-paying bonds (example), 385–387
CDO of rated bonds (example), 387–391
CDO of zero coupon bonds (example), 382–385
A CDO with numbers (example), 380–381
default models for bonds, 391–395
Collateralized fund obligations (CFOs), 374, 375–376
Collateralized loan obligation (CLO), 369–370
Collateralized mortgage obligations (CMOs), 354–355, 376–377
Collateral pricing and credit risk, 334–337
Collateral risk, 295
Commodities CDO, 374
Commodities trading, 21
Common options, 14
Co-monotonic copula, 121
Complete markets
defined, 225
martingales and, 222
pricing and, 222–224
risk-neutral pricing and, 224–227
uniqueness and, 226
Complex financial products and insurance finance, 26, 296
Complexity:
finance and, 25
growth of, 46
technology and, 49–53
Compound options, 226
Comprehensive financial risk management (CFRM), 49
Conditional copulas, 124–126
Conditional kernel pricing, 188–193
Condors, 226
short and long, 245
Constant proportion debt obligations (CPDOs), 374, 376
Constant proportion portfolio insurance (CPPI), 374, 376
Constant rate of return hypothesis, 73–74
Constant volatility, 81
Consumption, price and utility of, 161–164
Consumption-based capital asset pricing model (CCAPM), 145
Contagious processes, 110
Contagious risk, 354, 370, 378, 379

Contemporary risk, managing, 298–299
Contracts. *See also* Insurance contracts
bankruptcy index, 296
credit, 2, 6, 355
franchises, 39–40
long, 15
mortgage, 3
stop-loss reinsurance, 398
Cooling degree day (CDD), 21
Copulas, 111, 120–126
and CDOs, 371, 372
Clayton, 123
co-monotonic, 121
conditional, 124–126
Copulas and conditional dependence (example), 124–125
Copulas and the conditional distribution (example), 125–126
counter-monotonic, 121
Gaussian (normal), 122
Gumbel, 122, 123–124
Gumbel copula, the highs and the lows (example), 123–124
mixture, 121
Copulas and conditional dependence (example), 124–125
Copulas and the conditional distribution, 125–126
Counter-monotonic copula, 121
Counterparty financial risk management. *See* Strategic risk management
Counterparty-related risks, 5
Counterparty risk, 230, 295
Covered call, 226
Covered position, 236
Cox, John, 45
CPDOs. *See* Constant proportion debt obligations (CPDOs)
CPPI. *See* Constant proportion portfolio insurance (CPPI)
Credit. *See also* Credit risk; Credit scoring
and credit risk, 294–296
defined, 291
and money, 291–294
rating default bonds, 300–301
rating matrix, 302
risk factors in granting, 300
scoring/rating of companies, 301–302
Credit contracts, 2, 6, 355
Credit default option. *See* Credit default swaption
Credit default swaps (CDSs), 9, 50, 294, 296, 353, 398. *See also* Credit default swaps (CDSs) pricing
and clearinghouses, 358
contract, 358
credit default swaption, 357
forward-starting, 374

Credit default swaps (CDSs) (*Continued*)
  implied market approach to pricing, 359–360
  overview, 353, 357
  price spread (example), 360–364
  pricing a project launch (example), 364–368
  total return swaps (TRSs), 359
Credit default swaps (CDSs) pricing:
  The CDs price spread (example), 360–362
  implied market approach, 359–360
  OTC under risk-neutral pricing (example),
    362–364
  pricing product launch (example), 364–368
Credit default swaption, 357, 358
Credit derivatives, 355
  first generation products, 369, 372
  historical modeling, 369–372
  historical perspective, 368–369
  modeling, 379–380
  and product innovation, 372–376
  second generation, 369, 372–373
  third generation, 374–375
Credit Derivatives : The Definitive Guide
  (Gregory), 368
Credit granting, 317–319. *See also* Credit scoring
    system
  approximate solution (example), 326
  and bank profits from a loan (example),
    341–342
  Bayesian default model (example), 322–323
  and creditor's risks (example), 319–322
  financial approach (example), 323–326
  parameters of, 318
  Rate of return of loans (problem), 327
  Reduced form (financial) model, 327–334
Credit granting and creditor's risks (example),
  319–322
Credit-linked note (CLN), 372
Credit pricing, real, 297
Credit rating, 301–304, 319, 375
Credit risk, 7, 19, 294, 355
  and collateral pricing, 334–337
  default and the price of homes (example),
    339–341
  defined, 295
  diversification of, 296, 298
  pricing principles, 296–299
  tools for mitigating, 296
  2008 financial meltdown and, 296
  types of risks in, 295
Credit Risk Modeling (Gordy and Jones), 368
Credit risk portfolios, 298, 353–354, 356.
    See also Collateralized debt obligations
    (CDOs); *See also* Collateralized mortgage
    obligations (CMOs)
  historical perspective of credit derivatives,
    368–369

  overview, 353
  regulation of, 398
Credit risk *vs.* insurance, 398–399
Credit scores:
  defined, 299–300
  factors in determining, 300
  individual, 299–300
  real approaches, 304–305
Credit scoring system, 299–300
Credit Suisse First Boston, 29
Crises. *See also* Financial meltdown of 2008
  Asian crisis of 1998, 198
  Auction-rated security (ARS) crisis, 22–23
  banking-money system crisis, 23–24
  credit crisis of 2008-2009, 353
  and mortgage-backed securities, 22
  savings and loan (S & L) crisis, 22
  2008-2009 financial, 296
  Wall Street Crash of 1929, 261
Cyber risks, 52, 53

Daiwa Bank, 296
Dark pools, 53
Data transformation, 88–90
Debreu, Gerard, 44, 205
Default bonds, 300–301
  calculating the spread of a default bond
    (example), 328–329
  pricing default bonds and the hazard rate
    (example), 331–332
  pricing of default bonds (example), 330–331
Default models and their prices, 391
Default models for bonds (example), 391–396
Default probability, 297, 299
Default risk, 295, 342
Degree of absolute prudence, 158
Delta, 285
Dependence, types of, 110
Dependence modeling. *See also* Intertemporal
    models; Statistical dependence
  approaches to, 111
  Copulas, 111, 120–127
  intertemporal models, 126–132
  introduction to, 109–111
  long-run memory and fractal models, 111
  overview of, 109
  short-term memory models, 111
  statistical functional dependence, 111–120
  time, memory, and causal dependence, 127–129
Derivative exchange, 54
Derivative risks, 230–231
Derivatives, 12. *See also* Credit derivatives;
    Options
Derivatives pricing. *See* Options pricing
"Derivatives Pros Snubbed on Latest Exotic
    Product," 369

Deutsche Bank, 370
Disasters, 40–41. *See also* Catastrophic risks
Discount factor, 177–178
Distribution flatness, 68
Dupire model, 411–412, 433–435

Ebbers, Bernard, 29, 30
Economic equilibrium, 24–25
EDF. *See* Expected Default Frequency (EDF)
Efficiency curve, 183
Efficiency frontier (problem), 185–186
Efficient market hypotheses (EMH), 7, 131
Eigenvalues, 115, 116
Einsten, Albert, 422
EMH. *See* Efficient market hypotheses (EMH)
Endogenous financial valuation, 318
Endogenous model, 301
Endogenous risks, 5
Enron, 28, 29–30, 197
Entropy:
    divergence as an index of "distance" between
        distributions, 429–430
    exponential implied risk neutral distribution,
        428–429
    and kernel pricing, 432
    maximum entropy distribution, 427–428
    and time, 430
Environment, finance and ETF indexes, 37–38
Environmental risks, 3–4
Equal Credit Opportunity Act, 300
Equilibrium, 24, 110, 129, 197, 205, 206
Equity, 373
Equity default swap equity CDO, 374
Equity premium puzzle, 145
ETF indexes. *See* Exchange-traded fund (ETF)
    indexes
Ethics, finance and, 27–30
Euro-Greek crisis of 2010, 38
Event risks, 5, 297
Ex ante risk management, 47
Exchange options (example), 228
Exchange-traded fund (ETF), 397
Exchange-traded fund (ETF) indexes, 37
Exogenous model, 301
Exotic options, 12, 18–19
Expected Default Frequency (EDF), 369
Expected utility, 145–146, 157–158
    Tchebycheff bounds on, 160
    and time, 177–178
Expected value (or Bayes') objective, 146
Exponential utility function (example), 164
Ex post risk management, 47
External-hazard risks, 5
Extreme distributions, 87
Extreme measures of volatility, 84–85
Extremes statistics, 98

Fannie Mae. *See* Federal National Mortgage
    Association (FNMA)
Federal Home Loan Mortgage Corporation
    (FHLMC), 22, 377
Federal National Mortgage Association (FNMA),
    22, 29, 355, 377
FHLMC. *See* Federal Home Loan Mortgage
    Corporation (FHLMC)
Fibonacci, 292
Fidelity, 53
Filtering, 128
Filtration, 67, 220, 253
Finance:
    environment, ETF indexes and, 36–37
    and ethics, 27–30
    global, 4, 50
    pension and, 37–38
    retailing and, 51–52
Finance, real-life crises and
    Auction-rated security (ARS) crisis, 22–23
    banking-money system crisis, 23–24
    concerns raised from, 24–27
    future implications of, 25
    real assets and, 15
    savings and loan (S & L) crisis, 22
Finance and complexity, 25
Financial asset:
    real and, 15–16
    value of, 7
Financial economic theory, 6–7
Financial engineering, 1
Financial enterprises, scoring/rating, 301–304
Financial institutions:
    changing, 46
    as market makers, 55–56
    purposes of, 6
Financial instruments, 7–16. *See also* Bonds
    assets, real and financial, 15–16
    constructing (example), 11–12
    derivatives, 12–15
    financial markets, 16
    portfolios, 10–12
    securities/stocks, 7
Financial intermediation, 25–26
Financial markets, 46, 56
    financial asset trading in, 16
    intervention in, 26
Financial measurement, 26
Financial meltdown of 2008, 46
    concerns raised from, 24–27
    effect on credit markets, 296
    finance and complexity, 25
    future implications of, 25
    and information asymmetry, 195
    and mortgage-backed securities, 22
    real assets and, 15

Financial meltdown of 2008 (*Continued*)
  reengineering of credit derivatives, 376
  risk and the financial meltdown (example),
    153–154
  short-selling and, 262
Financial modeling, 73–77
Financial products, scoring/rating, 301–304
Financial risk externalities, management of, 48
Financial risk management:
  essentials of, 47–49
Financial risk pricing, 44–46
Financial technology, 4
Financial Times, 17, 23
First-generation credit products, 372
First-to-default basket, 373
Fixed-income problems, 231
  annuities and obligations (problem), 235
  pricing a fixed-rate bond (example), 232–234
  pricing a forward (example), 231–232
  the term structure of interest rates (example),
    234–235
FNMA. *See* Federal National Mortgage
    Association (FNMA)
Forward-starting CDO, 375
Forward-starting CDS, 374
Fractal models, 111
Fractional Brownian motion, 132
Franchise contracts, 39–40
Franchisee fees, 40
Freddie Mac. *See* Federal Home Loan Mortgage
    Corporation (FHLMC)
Froot, Kenneth, 45
Fundamental finance approach, 142. *See also*
    Arrow-Debreu framework
Fundamental theorem of risk neutral pricing, 225
Fundamental theory of finance, 128, 129
Future prices, 262–263
FX CDO, 374

Gamma, 285
Garman and Klass volatility estimators, 84
Gaussian (normal) couplas, 122
GEIX. *See* Global Energy Innovation Index
    (GEIX)
Generalization to multiple periods (example),
    215–218
Generalization to *n* states (example), 210–212
Generalized beta of the second kind (example),
    419–420
General Motors, 38
Ginnie Mae. *See* Government National Mortgage
    Association (GNMA)
Global Energy Innovation Index (GEIX), 37
Global finance, 4, 6, 50
Global Finance, 369
Globalization, 4, 6, 46
Globalization and finance's multipolarity, 28

Global warming, 3, 40
GNMA. *See* Government National Mortgage
    Association (GNMA)
Going risk-free rate, 9
Goldman Abacus, 28
Goldman Sachs, 28, 195–196, 369
Government National Mortgage Association
    (GNMA), 22, 377
Greeks, 219, 284–287
Green innovation, 37
Gumbel copula, the highs and the lows (example),
    123–124
Gumbel family copula, 122

Harrison-Pliska martingale no-arbitrage theorem,
    221
HDD. *See* Heating degree day (HDD)
HealthSouth, 29
Heating degree day (HDD), 21
Hedge funds, 5
  assets of, 375
  and price of quality claims, 44
  rates of return (example), 337–338
Hedging, 15, 236
Herd effect, 134
High-frequency trading software, 196
High-low estimators of volatility, 83–84
Historical VaR approach, 97–98
Homoskedasticity, 81
Hurst index, 133–134

IBM, 17
  IBM day-trades record (example), 7–9
  returns statistics (example), 69–70
ICAPM. *See* Intertemporal capital asset pricing
    model (ICAPM)
IFAC. *See* International Federation of
    Accountants (IFAC)
Implicit risks, 231
Implied binomial distribution (example),
    413–415
Implied (inverse) financial models, 76–77
Implied risk-neutral distribution, 412–413.
    See also Implied risk-neutral distribution and
    entropy; Implied risk-neutral distribution:
    parametric models
  calculating the implied risk-neutral probability
    (example), 415–418
  implied binomial distribution (example),
    413–415
Implied risk-neutral distribution: parametric
    models, 418
  a-parametric approach, 420–421
  Black-Scholes model, 420–421
  generalized beta of the second kind (example),
    419–420
  Shinko technique (example), 421–422

Implied risk-neutral distribution and entropy,
422–427, 422–433
binomial model, 430–431
divergence as an index of "distance" between
distributions, 429–430
exponential implied risk neutral distribution,
428–429
and kernel pricing, 432
maximum entropy distribution, 427–428
and time, 430
Implied risk-neutral probability calculation
(example), 415–418
Implied risk-neutral probability (problem), 213
Implied volatility, 410
Dupire model, 411–412, 433–435
in longnormal process (example), 410–411
Incentive options, 13–14
Incentive stock options (ISOs), 14
Independence, 110
Individual credit score, 299–300
Information asymmetry, 195–200
adverse selection risk, 196–197
and financial meltdown of 2008, 195–196
high-frequency trading software, 196
moral hazard risks, 197–199
signaling and screening, 199–200
Information technology, Madoff and, 52
Information technology (IT) growth, risks of, 46
Infrastructure finance, 36–37
Initial margin, 236
Insider trading, 195, 196
Insurance, 35–36. *See also* Insurance contracts
adverse selection and, 197
catastrophic risk and, 40–41
credit risk *vs.*, 398–399
defined, 167
equity-linked life insurance (example),
338–339
and kernel pricing, 169
moral hazard and, 197–199
price and demand for, 167–169
reinsurance and insurance (example), 398–399
risk finance and, 35–36
signaling and screening, 200
utility theory in, 150–151, 167–169
Insurance contracts, 2–3, 6
bonus-malus, 36
defined, 167–168
pricing, 3
Insurance finance, 26
Integrated financial risk management, 26
Interest rates:
effect on volatility, 66
term structure of interest rates (example),
234–235
Intermediaries, liquidity and, 56
Intermediation, financial, 25

Internalization through taxation (Pigouvian tax),
48
International Federation of Accountants (IFAC),
28
International Herald Tribune, 20
Intertemporal capital asset pricing model
(ICAPM), 145
Intertemporal models, 126–133
persistence and short-term memory, 130–132
quantitative time and change, 129–130
time, memory, and causal dependence,
127–129
Intervention in financial markets, 26
In-the-money (ITM) options, 237
Intraday prices, 84–87, 85, 87–88
Inventories:
market makers and, 55
Inventory pricing, 42–43, 191–193
Investment Dealers Digest, 369
Investments. *See* Asset allocation; Portfolios
Irrational exuberance, 6
ISOs. *See* Incentive stock options (ISOs)
ITM options. *See* In-the-money (ITM) options

J. P. Morgan, 369, 370
Jensen's inequality, 159–160
Joint Bernoulli distribution, 393
Joint cumulative distribution, 121
"Joseph effect," 134

Kernel pricing:
and the CAPM (example), 165–166
conditional, 188–193
and exponential utility function (example), 164
and the HARA utility function (example),
166–169
in infrastructure investments, 161–162,
188–191
in insurance, 169
in inventory pricing, 191–193
Keynes, John Maynard, 145
KMV loss model (example), 396–397
Kozlowski, Dennis, 29, 30
Kurtosis, 68–69
Kyoto Protocol, 38

Latent risk, 295
Law, John, 23
Lay, Kenneth, 29–30
Least squares estimation, 77–78
Legal risks, 295
Lehman Brothers, 24
Lending rates of return (problem), 334
Leverage:
effect on volatility, 65–66
risk management and, 342–344
Levy processes, 110

LGD. *See* Loss given default (LGD)
Limit order, 236
Linear risk-sharing rule (example), 194–195
Liquefying (or securitizing), 7
Liquidity, 53, 54, 55–56
Liquidity risk, 342
Living Omnimedia, 29
Lloyd's of London, 49
Loan underwriting standards, 298
Logit model, 305, 306–308
Long butterfly spread *vs.* calls, 244–245
Long call *vs.* put, 243
Long condor, 245
Long contracts, 15
Long put spread *vs.* call, 243–244
Long-run memory, 134
Long-run memory dependence, 110
Long-run memory models, 111
Long straddle, 241
Long straddle *vs.* call, 244
Long straddle *vs.* put, 244
Long strangle strategy, 242
Look-back options (example), 227
Lorenz, Edward, 127
Loss given default (LGD), 300
Lotteries, utility of, 147–149
    (example), 148
Lucas, Robert, 205

Macdonald, James, 23
Macroeconomic and external (latent) real risks, 295
Madoff, Bernard (Bernie), 29, 30, 40, 52
Malkiel, Burton, 224
Management's risk and moral hazard, 27
Man-made and derived disasters, 40
Market completeness, 142, 205
    defined, 225
    martingales and, 220–222
    pricing and, 222–224
    risk-neutral pricing and, 224–226
Market efficiency, 223–224
Market index and PCA (example), 119–120
Market liquidity, 3
Market maker, 53–57, 142
    NYSE as, 56–57
    role of, 54–55
Market of derivative exchange, 54
Market order, 236
Market prices, 142, 208
Markets, complete *vs.* incomplete, 205
Market value CDO, 374, 375
Markov model, 131
Markowitz, Harry, 44
Martingales, 220–222
    change of measures, 248–249
    defined, 221
    essentials of, 246–248

implied, 225
    and market completeness, 222, 225–226
    price deflator and, 220–222
    risk-neutral pricing and, 339
Maximax (minium) objective, 146
Maximum likelihood estimation, 79–81
MBSs. *See* Mortgage-backed securities (MBSs)
MC. *See* Mississippi Company (MC)
Mean reversion, 110
Mean reversion models, 75–77
Memory, 127–132
Merrill Lynch, 369
Merton, Robert, 45, 205
Merton model, 359, 369
Mezzanine debt, 373
Miller, Merton, 44
Minimax (maximin) objective, 146
Minimax regret objective, 146
Mississippi Company (MC), 23
Mixture copula, 121
Modeling rates of return, 72–73. *See also*
        statistical estimations
    analytic variance-covariance approach, 98
    autoregressive processes, 75–77
    constant rate of return hypothesis, 73–75
    gain/loss estimations, 97–98
    implied (inverse) financial models, 76–77
    mean reversion models, 75–77
    moments and CAPM (example), 70–72
    moments and measures of volatility, 67–70
    Monte Carlo simulation and VaR, 98
    price of disappointment, 66
    probability of the range (problem)
    statistical orders, volume, and prices, 85–87
    Taylor series expansion (example), 90
    value at risk (VaR) and risk exposure, 90–94
    VaR, normal rate of return, and portfolio
        design (example), 95–98
    VaR and extreme statistics, 98–99
    VaR and shortfall (example), 94–95
Modigliani, Franco, 44
Money:
    credit and, 291–294
    reengineering of, 294
    and utility theory, 144
Monte Carlo simulation, 127, 387, 397
    VaR and, 98
Montreal Stock Exchange, 16
Moral hazard risks, 36, 193–194, 197–199
Morality in management, 27
Mortgage-backed securities (MBSs), 9, 22, 294, 296, 353
Mortgage contracts, 3
Mulligan, James (Captain), 129
Multiple assets options, 226
Multiple risks longnormal model, 119
Muth, John, 222

Naked position, 236
National Westminster Bank, 370
Natural disasters, 40. *See also* Catastrophic risks
Naturally derived disasters, 40
Newton Raphson iteration techniques, 306
New York magazine, 195
New York Stock Exchange (NYSE), 16, 53, 56–57
New York Times, 28
Nontransparent risks, 231
Novikov's condition, 248
nth-to-default baskets, 372
Numératire, 210

Obligations and annuities (problem), 235
On Incentive Options and Taxes, 13
Opening transactions, 236
Operational risk (op risk), 53
Op risk. *See* Operational risk (Op risk)
Option applications:
 future prices, 262–262
 immunization strategies, 260–261
 insurance pricing, 264–269
 options implied insurance pricing (example), 266–267
 risk-free portfolios, 260–261
 self-financing trading strategy, 270–271
 short-selling, 261–262
 spread options pricing, 269–270
 trinomial random walk (example), 267–268
Option contracts, 16–17
 prices of (problem), 17–19
Options, 12. *See also* Option applications; Options pricing; Options trading strategies; Options trading
 Asian options (example), 227–228
 at-the-money (ATM), 237
 barrier and other options (example), 228–229
 binary, 227
 Chooser options (example), 228
 and commodities trading, 21
 common, 14
 as compensation, 13–14, 19–20
 compound, 226
 defined, 12
 derivatives exchange, 230–231
 exchange (example), 228
 exotic, 12, 18–19
 generalization to multiple periods, 215–218
 history of, 16
 implied risk-neutral probability (problem), 213
 incentive, 13–14
 in-the-money, 237
 and inventory pricing, 193
 (ISO incentive stock options), 14
 look-back options (example), 227
 management stock options (example), 19–20
 mortgage-backed securities (MBSs), 15, 21–22
 out-of-the-money, 237

over-the-counter, 12–13
packaged, 226, 227
Passport options (example), 230
path-dependent, 226
price of equity (example), 19
prices of (problem), 17–19
real uses of, 229–231
securitization and, 21–22
taxation of, 14–15
trading on, 53–54
types of, 17, 226–228
uses of, 12, 19, 230
Options and their prices (problem), 218
Options implied insurance pricing (example), 266–271
Options pricing. *See also* Black Scholes model; Put-call parity
 and Arrow-Debreu framework, 212–218
 binomial, 212–213
 change of measure in binomial model (example), 249–251
 fixed-income problems, 232
 formal notations, key terms, and definitions, 253–254
 and Greeks, 294–297
 options and their prices (problem), 218
 payout terms, 227
 price of a call option (example), 213–214
 proving the put-call parity (problem), 219
Options trading:
 the CO_2 index, 20–21
 on commodities (metal, gold, silver, corn, oil), 20–21
 credit derivatives, 21–22
 mortgage-backed securities, 21–22
 securitization, 21–22
 the weather and insurance, 21
Options trading strategies:
 long butterfly spread with calls, 244–245
 long call *vs.* put, 243
 long condor, 245
 long put *vs.* call, 243–244
 long straddle, 241
 long straddle *vs.* call, 244
 long straddle *vs.* put, 244
 long strangle, 242–243
 short butterfly, 245
 short call spread *vs.* put, 243
 short condor, 245
 short put spread *vs.* call, 243
 short straddle, 241
 short straddle *vs.* call, 244
 short straddle *vs.* put, 244
 short strangle, 242–243
 the spread, 241–242
 strap, 242
 strip, 242
Orders, type of, 236

OTC contracts, 6
OTM options. *See* Out-of-the-money (OTM)
    options
Out-of-the-money (OTM) options, 237
Over-the-Counter Options, 12–14
Over-the-counter (OTC) credit default swaps, 357
Oxford Energy Associates, 20

Packaged options, 226, 227
Parametric models. *See* Implied risk-neutral
    distribution: parametric models
Parkinson volatility estimators, 83–84
Passport options (example), 230
Path-dependent options, 226
Pay-as-you-go (PAYGO) pension, 38
PD. *See* Probability of default (PD)
PDF. *See* Probability density function (PDF)
Pension, finance and, 37–38
Pension firms, 39
Pensions, 38–39
Persistent, 110
Persistent random, 130
Piaget, J., 128
Pigou, 48
Planck, Max, 422
Poisson probability distribution, 392
Portfolio Manager model, 369
Portfolio of default loans (example), 315–316
Portfolio of dependent default loans (example),
    316–317
Portfolios, 10–12. *See also* Asset allocation
    constructing (example), 11–12
    risk-free, immunization and, 260–261
    self-financing, 11–12
Portfolio strategies (problem), 240–245
Power utility function (example), 151–152
Price contagion, 110
Price discovery, 230
Price of a call option (example), 213–214
Price of disappointment, 66
Prices/pricing, 63
    of assets, 259–271
    bid-ask, 55–56
    credit risk, 298–299
    of options, 19, 218
    price deflator and pricing martingale, 220–222
    risk-neutral, 224–226
    of securities, 8–9
    and value, 141–143
Pricing a fixed-rate bond (example), 232–234
Pricing a forward (example), 231–232
Pricing a multiperiod forward (problem), 264–266
Pricing default bonds and the hazard rate
    (example), 331–332
Pricing default bonds (example), 330–331
Pricing product launch (example), 364–368
Principal-agent problems, 193–195

Principal component analysis (PCA) (example),
    115, 116–120
Principle of insufficient reason, 146
Probability default models, 312–314
    Bivariate dependent default distribution
        (example), 314–315
    The Joint Bernoulli default distribution
        (problem), 317
    Portfolio of default loans (example), 315–316
    Portfolio of dependent default loans (example),
        316–317
Probability density function (PDF), 67
Probability distributions, 67–70
    parametric models, 408, 418–420
    Poisson probability distribution, 392
    synthetic, 208–210
Probability measure, 225
Probability models:
    copulas, 111, 120–126
    fractal models, 110, 111, 131–132
    intertemporal models, 126–133
    long-run memory models, 131–132, 134
    R/S index, 133–135
    short-term memory models, 130–132
    statistical models, 111, 113–120
Probability of default (PD), 300, 303
Probability of the range (problem), 87
Probit model, 308
Process default, 296
Product innovation, in derivatives, 372–376
Protective put, 226, 237, 239–240
Prudence, 158
Put-call parity, 218–220
    and dividend payments (example), 219–220
    options (problem), 220
    proving (problem), 219
Put options, 17, 18

Quadratic utility function, 149–150
Qualitative time and change, 129–130
Quality claims, price of, 43–44
Quattrone, Frank, 29, 30

Randomness, 127
Random Nikodym derivative, 251–253
    two-stage random walk and (example),
        251–253
Random volatility, 271–273
Random walk, 247, 251–253
    two-stage random walk and the random
        Nikodym derivative (example), 251–253
Range, 69–70, 83
    probability of the range (problem), 87–89
Range/scale analysis. *See* R/S index
RAROC. *See* Risk-adjusted return on capital
    (RAROC)
Rate of return. *See* Modeling rates of return

Rating matrix, 302
Rational expectations, 222
Real assets, 15–16
Real credit pricing, 297
Real estate investment conduits (REMICs), 376
Real options, 273–276
  allowing staged investments, 274
  option for new licensing, 285–276
  options based on operating conditions, 275
  options to defer an investment, 274
Recovery, defined, 359
Recovery risk, 295, 300
Reduced form (financial) model, 327–334
  bank interest rate on a house loan (example), 333
  buy insurance to protect the portfolio from loan defaults (example), 333
  calculating the spread of a default bond (example), 328–329
  lending rates of return (problem), 334
  the loan model again (example), 328–329
  pricing default bonds and the hazard rate (example), 331–332
  pricing default bonds (example), 330–331
  use the portfolio as an underlying and buy or sell derivatives on this underlying (problem), 334
Reinsurance and insurance (example), 398–399
Reliability, price of, 42–43, 178–180
REMICs. *See* Real estate investment conduits (REMICs)
Repeat Offering Securitization Entity (ROSE), 370
Retailing, and technology, 51–52
Retailing, finance and, 51–52
Rho, 285
Risk. *See also* Credit risk
  adverse selection, 36
  catastrophic, 4, 40–41
  categories of, 5–6
  contemporary, 298–299
  counterparty-related, 5
  cyber, 52, 53
  defined, 1–2
  derivative, 230–231
  event risks, 5, 297
  external-hazard, 5
  factors defining value and price of, 4–6
  history of, 5
  information technology, 46
  latent, 295
  legal, 295
  moral hazard, 36, 193–194, 197–199
  overview, 1–7
  recovery, 295, 300
  safety, reliability and, 178–180
  strategic, 5
  summary of, 30

terrorism, 52
third-party guarantee, 295
and utility of time, 177–178, 177–188
and utility theory, 143–144
Risk-adjusted return on capital (RAROC), 356
Risk behavior, 5
Risk cyber, 52, 53
Risk events, 5
Risk exposure to substantial losses of a credit portfolio, 295
Risk externalities, 6, 48
Risk externalities and regulation, management of, 47
Risk factors aggregation (example), 115–116
Risk finance, 2
  basic concepts, 4–6
  focus of, 2–3
  insurance and, 35–37
Risk-free portfolios, 260–261
Risk-free zero-coupon bond, price of, 9
Risk management, 2. *See also* Utility theory
  comprehensive, 49
  essentials of, 47–49
  ex ante, 47
  ex post, 47
  and leverage, 342–344
  robust, 47–48
  strategic, 48
  types of, 47–48
Risk measure incoherence, 90
Risk measurement, 66. *See also* Modeling rates of return
  calculating the beta of a security (problem), 72–73
  data transformation, 88–90
  extreme measures, volume, and intraday prices, 85–90
  high-low estimators of volatility, 83–84
  IBM returns statistics (example), 69–70
  intraday prices and extreme distributions, 87–88
  moments and measures of volatility, 67–70
  moments and the CAPM (example), 70–72
  overview of, 63–66
  price of disappointment, 66
  probability of the range (problem), 87
  statistical estimations, 77–83
  statistical orders, volume, and prices, 85–87
  Taylor series expansion (example), 89–90
  value at risk (VaR) and risk exposure, 90–94
Risk mitigation, 2
Risk-neutral distribution (RND), 169
Risk-neutral probabilities, 225
Risk of loss (risk exposure), 300
Risk premium, 63, 158
RND. *See* Risk-neutral distribution (RND)
Robust risk management, 47–48

Roger and Satchell volatility estimators, 83, 84
Roll, Richard, 224
ROSE. *See* Repeat Offering Securitization Entity (ROSE)
Ross, Stephen, 45
R/S index, 133–135
Rubinstein, Mark, 45
Russel, Bertrand, 128

Safety, price of, 41–42, 178–180
Samuelson, Paul, 205
Savage regret objective, 146
Savings and loan (S & L) crisis, 22
Say, J. B., 141
Scharfstein, David, 45
Scholes, Myron, 45
Scrushy, Richard, 29, 30
SDF. *See* Stochastic discount factors (SDF)
Second generation of credit derivatives, 372–373
Second Life, 53
Securitization
    defined, 3, 6, 21–22
    John Law introduction of, 23
Securitization of catastrophic insured risks, 40
Securitized debt obligations, 374
Self-financing portfolio, 11–12
Self-financing trading strategy, 270–271
Selling Short, 15
Senior debt, 373
Separatrix, 309–310
Separatrix and Bayesian probabilities (example), 311–312
Separatrix (example), 310–311
Shad-Johnson Accord, 52
Sharpe, William, 45
Sharpe's capital asset pricing model (CAPM), 44
Shiller, Robert, 6
Shinko technique (example), 421–422
Short butterfly, 245
Short call spread *vs.* put, 243
Short condor, 245
Short put spread *vs.* call, 243
Short selling, 15
Short straddle, 241
    vs. call, 244
    vs. put, 244
Short strangle strategy, 242–243
Short-term memory models, 111, 130–132
Signaling and screening, 199–200
Single price hypothesis, 224
SIV. *See* Structured investment vehicle (SIV)
Skewness, 68–69
Skilling, Jeffrey, 29
Smith, Adam, 55
Smith, Clifford, 45
Soros, George, 53
Special-purpose vehicle (SPV), 373

Special purpose vehicles (SPVs) (example), 377–379
Speculating, 236
S & P 500 index, 111
Spreads, bid-ask, 55–56
Spread strategy, 241–242
SPV. *See* Special-purpose vehicle (SPV)
State preference theory, 44, 145
Statistical dependence, 111–120
    aggregation and risk factors reduction, 114–115
    bivariate data matrix and PCA (example), 117–119
    market index and PCA (example), 119–120
    principal component analysis (PCA) (example), 116–117
    quantitative statistical probability models, 113–114
    risk factors aggregation (example), 115–116
Statistical estimation of default, 305–310
Statistical estimations:
    AR (1)-ARCH (1) model (example), 81–82
    ARCH and GARCH estimators, 80–81
    A GARCH, (1,1) model (example), 83
    least squares estimation, 77–78
    maximum likelihood, 79–80
    statistical orders, volume, and prices, 85–86
Statistical functional dependence, 111–120
    aggregation and risk factors reduction, 114–116
    bivariate data matrix and PCA (example), 117–119
    market index and PCA, 119–120
    principal component analysis (PCA) (examples), 116–120
    qualitative statistical probability models, 113–114
    risk factors aggregation (example), 115–116
Stein, Jeremy, 45
Stewart, Martha, 29, 30
Stochastic discount factors (SDF), 145
Stocks/securities, 2, 7–9
    calculating the beta of security (problem), 72–77
    IBM day-trades record (example), 7–9
    price of, volatility and, 64–65
    trading of, 53–54
Stop-limit order, 236
Stop-loss measure, 91
Stop-loss order, 236
Stop-loss reinsurance contracts, 398
Stop order, 236
Straddle, 241
Strap strategy, 242
Strategic risk, 5
Strategic risk management, 47
Strike price, 17, 358
Strip strategy, 242
Structured investment vehicle (SIV), 374, 375

Stulz, René M, 45
Subordinate debt, 373
Swiss Re, 41
Synthetic CDO, 369, 370, 372, 373, 397
Synthetic probability distributions, 208–210

TARP. *See* Troubled Asset Relief Program
    (TARP)
TASE 25, 111, 112
Taxation, of options, 14–15
Taylor series approximation, 277
Taylor series expansion, 279, 285
Taylor series expansion (example), 88–90
TBTF. *See* To become too big to fail (TBTF)
Tchebycheff bounds on expected utility, 160
Technological disasters, 40
Technology:
    and complexity, 49–53
    cyber risks, 52
    and need for regulation, 51–52
    retailing and, 51–52
    terrorism risks, 52
    virtual markets, 52
    virtual products, 52–53
Term structure of interest rates, 9
Term structure of interest rates (example),
    234–235
Terror acts, 40
Terrorism risks, 52
The Joint Bernoulli default distribution (problem),
    317
The loan model again (example), 328–329
The Notion of Time in Infants (Piaget), 128
Theta, 285
The two-stage random walk and the random
    Nikodym derivative (example), 251–253
The Wealth of Nations (Smith), 55
Third-generation credit derivatives, 374
Third-party guarantee risk, 295
Time, 127–129
    and expected utility, 177–178
    relationship to risk, 177–189
Time and experience (Russel), 128
Timing, 5
To become too big to fail (TBTF), 47
Total return swaps (TRSs), 359, 372
Tradable commodities, 21
Tranches, 353, 354, 355, 357, 358, 370, 371
Troubled Asset Relief Program (TARP), 23
TRSs. *See* Total return swaps (TRSs)
Two-securities portfolio (problem), 187–188
Two-securities portfolio problem (example),
    182–184
Two-stage random walk and the Radon Nikodym
    derivative (example), 251–253
Two-stock portfolio (example), 184–185
Tyco, 29

Uncertainty, defined, 1
U.S. policy of 2009, 3
Utility, 141
    behavioral derivates of, 156–158
    and behavioral derivatives, 156–158
    capital asset pricing model (CAPM), 144–145,
        165–166
    in credit risk pricing, 297
    essential facets of, 143
    example, 149
    expected utility, 145–146, 177–178
    exponential utility function (example), 164
    historical perspective, 144–145
    insurance and, 150–151
    in insurance exchanges, 151–152
    Jensen's inequality, 159–160
    and kernel pricing, 161–162
    kernel pricing and the CAPM (example),
        165–166
    kernel pricing and the exponential utility
        function (example), 164
    kernel pricing and the HARA utility function
        (example), 166–169
    linear risk-sharing rule (example), 194–195
    and lotteries, 147–148
    marginal utility, 158
    power utility function (example), 151–152
    prelude to, 145–146
    price and demand for insurance, 167–169
    price and utility of consumption (example),
        161–164
    principal-agent problems, 193–194
    quadratic utility function, 149–150
    rational foundations, 155–161
    risk and, 143–144
    risk and financial meltdown (example),
        153–154
    risk aversion and, 157–158, 183
    and risk premium, 155–156
    specific utility functions (example), 159–161
    utility of a lottery (example), 149–151
    valuation and the pricing of cash flows
        (example), 152–153
Utility frameworks, 142–143
Utility measurement of money, 142
Utility theory, 177–204

Valuation and cash flow pricing (example),
    152–153
Value, and price, 141–143
Value at risk (VaR) measure:
    defined, 90
    and extreme statistics, 98–99
    gain/loss estimations, 98–99
    historical VaR approach, 97–98
    normal rate of return, and portfolio design
        (example), 95–99

Value at risk (VaR) measure (*Continued*)
  pitfalls when misunderstood, 91–92
  and shortfall (example), 94–95
Value at risk (VaR) models, 24
VaR models. *See* Value at risk (VaR) models
Vega, 285
Venture capitalist (VC) investor, 199
Virtual economic universes, 53
Virtual markets, 52
  participants of, 53
Virtual products, 52
Volatility, 64
  constant, 81
  and data transformation, 88–90
  defined, 64
  effects on security price, 64–65
  expectations and, 67–70
  Garman and Klass volatility estimators, 83, 84
  high-low estimators of, 83, 84
  and interest rates, 66
  leverage and, 65–66
  models of rates of return, 73–77
  moments and measures of, 66–69, 67–77
  Parkinson volatility estimators, 83, 84
  and price of disappointment, 66
  random, 271–273
  rate of return, 95

reasons for change in, 65
Roger and Satchell volatility estimators, 83, 84
Volatility, moments and measures of:
  Beta calculation, 72–77
  expectations, 67–69
  IBM returns statistics (example), 69–70
  Kurtosis, 67–69
  models of rates of return, 73–77
  moments and the CAPM (example), 70–72
  probability distribution, 67–70
  the range, 67–69
  skewness, 67–69
Volume, 85–87

Wall Street Crash of 1929, 261
Wall Street Journal, 17, 24, 224
Warranties, price of, 42–43
Warrants, 226–227
Weather derivative contracts, 21
Wild money, 296
Williams, John Burr, 7, 144
WorldCom, 29
World Economic Forum, 3

Yahoo! Finance, 17, 18
Yang and Zhang volatility estimators, 83–84
Yield, 9

Z-score approach, 303